America's #1 Selling

Antique Trader®

ANTIQUES&
COLLECTIBLES

2010 PRICE GUIDE • 26th Edition

©2009 Krause Publications, Inc., a subsidiary of F+W Media, Inc.

Published by

krause publications

A subsidiary of F+W Media, Inc.

700 East State Street • Iola, WI 54990-0001
715-445-2214 • 888-457-2873
www.krausebooks.com

Our toll-free number to place an order or obtain
a free catalog is (800) 258-0929.

All rights reserved. No portion of this publication may be reproduced or
transmitted in any form or by any means, electronic or mechanical, including
photocopy, recording, or any information storage and retrieval system, without
permission in writing from the publisher, except by a reviewer who may quote
brief passages in a critical article or review to be printed in a magazine or
newspaper, or electronically transmitted on radio, television, or the Internet.

ISSN 1536-2884

ISBN-13: 978-1-4402-0361-9
ISBN-10: 1-4402-0361-X

Designed by Wendy Wendt
Edited by Dan Brownell

Printed in United States of America

On front cover:

Cranberry swirl pitcher, 9-3/4" h., mold blown opalescent glass, w/ruffled rim and applied clear handle, **$495**.

Newcomb College Pottery bowl-vase, w/white daffodil blossoms & pale green leaves against a dark blue ground, by Alma Mason, No. HD7, 7" d., 4 1/2" h., **$2,640**.

Grandfather clock, Christopher H. Strieby, Wooster, Ohio, Federal style, cherry & poplar, signed "C.E. Strieby, Wooster, Ohio #48," ca. 1830-1850, 102" h., **$16,100**.

Tiffany "Nasturium" lamp, shade stamped "Tiffany Studios - New York," base stamped "Tiffany Studios - New York 550," shade 21-3/4" d., overall 31-1/2" h., **$186,300**.

Parian statue, figure of girl reading, Copeland, England, modeled by P. MacDowell, issued at the Ceramic and Crystal Palace Art Union, impressed mark, ca. 1869, 13-1/4" h., **$499**.

On spine:

Roseville jardiniere, "Pine Cone" pattern, twig handles, blue ground, No. 632-4", 4" h., **$316**.

On back cover:

Rookwood vase, 10-3/4" h., standard glaze, w/bust of an Apache, Shape No. 827, 1898, decorated by Grace Young, **$25,960**.

Centaur weathervane, molded copper & cast lead, w/molded sheet copper tail, attributed to A.L. Jewell & Co., Waltham, Massachusetts, 1852-67, 39 1/4" l., 32 1/4" h., **$51,700**.

America's #1 Selling Price Guide

Antique Trader®

ANTIQUES&
COLLECTIBLES

2010 PRICE GUIDE • 26th Edition

More Great Books in the Antique Trader® Series

Antique Trader® Bottles Price Guide

Antique Trader® Book Collectors Price Guide

Antique Trader® Collectible Cookbooks Price Guide

Antique Trader® Collectible Paperback Price Guide

Antique Trader® Furniture Price Guide

Antique Trader® Guide to Fakes & Reproductions

Antique Trader® Indian Arrowheads Price Guide

Antique Trader® Jewelry Price Guide

Antique Trader® Kitchen Collectibles Price Guide

Antique Trader® Limoges Price Guide

Antique Trader® Perfume Bottles Price Guide

Antique Trader® Pottery & Porcelain Price Guide

Antique Trader® Radio & Television Price Guide

Antique Trader® Royal Doulton Price Guide

Antique Trader® Salt & Pepper Shaker Price Guide

Antique Trader® Stoneware/Blue & White Pottery Price Guide

Antique Trader® Teapots Price Guide

Antique Trader® Vintage Magazines Price Guide

Market Reports

Introduction

Listings

Welcome to Antique Trader 2010

Welcome to *Antique Trader Antiques & Collectibles 2010 Price Guide*! Last year we reached a monumental landmark, as we celebrated our 25th anniversary. Thank you for your continued support; it's been a privilege serving you all these years. We look forward to many more years offering the most comprehensive information available.

Each year, we spend thousands of hours organizing and preparing this information so you can spend less time researching and more time buying and selling. As we all know, knowledge is power, and time is money. If you use this guide to hone your skills in just a couple of categories or save even a few hours of research, your money has been well spent. If you study the book in depth, you'll find it to be one of the best investments you've ever made, so be sure to take advantage of all the photos, descriptions, prices, and new features we have assembled for you.

Changes for 2010

As we begin our next quarter century, we are introducing some changes and additions.

First, we revised the layout from a two-column to a three-column format. The three-column format permits more flexibility in design so photos can be run in one-, two-, or three-column sizes to showcase them at their optimum size. After all, a picture really is worth a thousand words! This also enables us to increase the size of many photos without sacrificing quantity of photos, a key feature of the book. In addition, the three-column format allows us to add more white space to separate listings and to stagger the photos to create a more visually interesting arrangement of text and photos.

Second, we deleted the captions and made the photos and descriptions a single unit so readers don't have to search through the listings to match them to photos. The description is directly below or to the side of each photo. Arrows have been added to clarify where necessary.

Third, we added market reports that cover the trends and issues affecting a number of popular categories. The reports are based on interviews with specialist dealers, but they aren't written for the experts in those categories; the experts already know the trends. Rather, the reports are intended for novices who want background information about a category or for those who are somewhat familiar with a category but want an update on current buying and selling trends. Each market report ends with a list of representative auction houses. Space does not permit listing every auction house in the category, so we have selected a representation with significant depth.

Fourth, we sprinkled practical advice and interesting facts throughout the pages. We believe collectors will enjoy learning (or at least being reminded of) tips that others have learned through experience.

A Note on Pricing

This book is only a guide to values, which can vary over time and are affected by many factors such as quality of design and workmanship, condition, rarity, demand, and regional tastes. Furthermore, the majority of the values in this book are the prices the items received at an auction, rather than an estimated value. An auction value can reflect wholesale or retail value depending on the desirability of the item and the amount of competition that went into the bidding.

When you are selling to dealers, they may offer you 50 percent or less of the values listed here, as they have overhead and must make enough profit to stay in business. However, the more desirable a piece, the faster a dealer will most likely be able to resell it, and, therefore, the more likely he will be willing to pay a proportionately higher percentage of its resale value.

Collectors can almost always get a better price by selling directly to an end user such as another collector, but that can take a lot more time. Dealers earn their profit by being middlemen and doing the legwork of finding customers. It takes a great deal of time and effort to build a network of contacts. The more research and networking you do yourself, the higher the price you are likely to receive.

Thank You!

A warm thank you to all auction houses, dealers, and contributors who provided photos, descriptions, and prices for this edition. Thank you also to Wendy Wendt, our graphic designer, who implemented our new layout.

Finally, we extend Kyle Husfloen a heartfelt thank you for more than 35 years of service working with *Antique Trader* magazine and 20 years as the editor of this annual and the associated Antique Trader books. Kyle has moved on to other opportunities, and we wish him well. Kyle has an incredible depth of knowledge in antiques, and we consider ourselves very fortunate to have benefitted from his experience for so many years.

Dan Brownell, Editor

Note: Although descriptions, prices, photos, and illustrations have been double-checked to ensure accuracy, the publisher, editor, and contributors cannot be responsible for typographical or other errors or losses incurred as a result of consulting this book.

Taking Advantage of the Market in a Slow Economy

Antiques collectors and dealers can find opportunities in a down economy that are unavailable during boom times. Just as shrewd investors buy stock when the market is down and sell when it is up, antiquers can make the best of the current economy by working *with* market trends rather than *against* them. It's currently a seller's market for top quality auction merchandise and a buyer's market for mid range and below in the retail venue, so now is the time to sell high-end pieces for top prices and find bargains in mid level and lower wares. When the economy recovers, these trends will change, and savvy buyers and sellers will adapt once again.

Americans do not have to look any farther than the front-page headlines of their local newspaper to be reminded of the effects of the recession. Among the news reports of unemployment figures and home foreclosures are stories about cash-strapped collectors selling their treasures. Anyone who needs cash to pay bills or to have an emergency fund for unexpected expenses may be contemplating selling antiques. While antiques are not as liquid as some forms of investment, they still have monetary value. Ernie Jarrell, manager of Heart of Ohio Antique Center in Springfield, Ohio, believes, however, that sellers must be realistic about values. "It's definitely a buyers' market out there and now is a good time for dealers to be buying."

He observes dealers being more selective and conservative in their buying habits. "Dealers you used to see on a regular basis who came in with a trailer and may have spent $10,000 to $15,000 buying 12 pieces of furniture and smalls. Now they spend $5,000 or $6,000, they want a little better deal and they look over things harder. They definitely have an idea what they want to buy and where they can sell it," said Jarrell.

One of the easiest ways to sell antiques is consigning them to a reputable auction house. There is the risk of one or more items selling for disappointing prices, but generally most things will sell for fair market value, the price paid by a willing buyer to a willing seller.

"I hear people say things are screaming at auctions, but sales on the retail side aren't doing so well. I don't understand why people always seem to get caught up in the moment at an auction, but they won't pay the prices at an antique mall or shop that they would at an auction," Jarrell said.

Jack Christy of Christys of Indiana, said his auction house in Indianapolis has seen more consignments coming through the doors and attributes it to two related factors: a generation of collectors is aging and their children are often not interested in their parents' belongings, especially collections.

Christy saw a dramatic decline in prices in the last quarter of 2008, down by as much as 70 percent. "The encouraging part, people are beginning to invest their money in antiques, something that is tangible, something besides the stock market," Christy said.

He advises against liquidating when there is such a surplus of many common items in the marketplace. "High-end art is always good, and coins in gold and silver, of course. If you can liquidate something that's doing very well in the market, that's the best thing to get the quickest amount of cash," said Christy, adding, "The key to what's going on is people are buying what they can use, what they need."

Practicality is a major concern. "Big dining room suites like those of the 1930s are not being put in small places. People are downsizing into condos and patio homes, and those big dining room suites and Colonial bedroom suites, well there's just not room for them," he said.

An advantage of consigning to an auction house is the relatively quick payoff. "We always pay within a week. If it sells at our Market Day auction on Wednesday, you're paid on Tuesday. I think that the key to auctioneers being successful is turning the money over as quickly as possible," said Christy, who cautions sellers about parting with family heirlooms.

"If they really have some things that are dear to them I don't think they have to sell them," he said.

Estate tag sales are a popular alternative to auctions in some areas of the country. Judy Campbell of Midland, Mich., has been conducting estate tag sales for nearly 20 years. As a member of the Appraisers Association of America for nearly that long, Campbell stays on top of values of antiques, collectibles, fine art and household furnishings.

She contends that tag sales, where each item is priced, are fair to both the seller and buyers. "I do a lot of research into fair market value, and by tagging the items accordingly, I think it's fair to the public and fair to the client," said Campbell, who constantly adjusts pricing to market conditions.

"I follow how I did with previous sales. I always do an inventory before I go into a sale as to what the maximum gross would be. Then at the end of the sale I see what sold at full price and what sold at half price on the second day, and that tells me how my pricing was and how to go forward with the next sale," she said.

Campbell often takes consignments, especially when an estate or household she is selling lacks a desirable category. "It's sort of a bonus to the buyers to have these consignments available. Sometimes it will be somebody who has some nice artwork and perhaps the client doesn't have any artwork and we need that draw to attract customers," said Campbell.

Superior quality sterling silver flatware by the likes of Georg Jensen, Tiffany and Gorham, especially vintage Gorham, attracts customers to Campbell's sales. "These are turnarounds that can be resold. Dealers especially know the route to go, and they have their collectors and contacts who buy specifically that," she said. "Fifties Modernism is very strong here, probably because we have the Alden B. Dow architectural influence in Midland."

Whether consigning to an auction or tag sale, always get a contract signed with the person handling your items.

For categories that are not selling well, Campbell recommends donating those items to charity and taking a tax deduction. "A lot of people like that cash in

hand. Other people are passionate about a museum or historical society and they want to donate it there. It's just a personal preference … personal and practical, said Campbell.

The IRS requires that deductions for contributions of antiques and art be supported by a written appraisal from a qualified appraiser if the deduction is more than $5,000. "Otherwise everyone would be jumping all over the moon putting down their own values," said Campbell. "Any donation that would be considered collectible or antique is a flag up to the IRS."

Individuals with the time and inclination for listing their antiques and collectibles on Internet auction sites may try the do-it-yourself method of selling, but prices realized on eBay, for example, are not as impressive as they once were.

EBay reported its fourth quarter 2008 earnings dropped 41 percent and the total amount of sales, excluding vehicles, fell 12 percent. Yet the number of active buyers and sellers grew nearly 4 percent to 86.3 million.

"It's hard to tell which has affected prices more. I think eBay and the recession both brought down prices as much as 50 percent on a lot of things," said Verlon Webb, owner of Webb's Antique Malls in Lake City, Fla., and Centerville, Ind. "Almost all collectibles, unless they're really rare are worth about half of what they were about five or 10 years ago. We sort of got blindsided there."

Webb sees people wanting to sell anything of value. "You don't want to take your dresser or your bed out of the house. Any of the things sitting around that aren't really necessary, they're trying to sell," said Webb.

"Talking to dealers who do high-end shows, the high-end merchandise is still doing phenomenal, but the middle-of-the-road everyday items seem to be the hardest to sell right now," said Jarrell, who advises holding antiques until the economy improves. "It's like a guy told me, the nice thing about antiques is they don't spoil and they don't eat hay."

Cowan's Auction in Cincinnati, has experienced a drop in consignments since the economy slipped into a recession. "Other than estates, we've been down a little in the number of consignments," said Wes Cowan. "I think some people are reluctant to sell right now."

He concurs with other experts that prices for high-quality antiques remain high. "There will never be a fallout in these items, in good economic times or bad," said Cowan, who is confident about the auction business. "I'm very optimistic. We're very conservative with our estimates and both our auctions this year have exceeded our expectations by significant amounts."

Also on a brighter note, Cowan said there has never been a better time to buy antiques priced in the mid-range. "It's a great opportunity," he said.

Tom Hoepf

Sources:

Judy Campbell, appraisals/estate sales, Midland, Mich., www.judycampbell.com, (517) 631-9263.

Jack Christy, Christys of Indiana Inc., Indianapolis, Ind., www.christys.com, (317) 784-0000.

Wes Cowan, Cowan's Auctions, Cincinnati, Ohio, www.cowanauctions.com, (513) 871-1670.

Ernie Jarrell, Heart of Ohio Antique Center, Springfield, Ohio, www.heartofohioantiques.com, (937) 324-2188.

Verlon Webb, Webb's Antique Malls, Lake City, Fla., and Centerville, Ind., e-mail: webbslc@msn.com, (386) 758-5564.

Buying and Selling Advice

General Advice

If you haven't started a collection yet, but plan to and are still deciding what to collect, choose a category that will hold your interest for the long term. Collect what you like, rather than for investment. While some categories may well appreciate over time, the demand and popularity of categories can change, leading to a decrease in value. Study your category thoroughly. Visit shops, attend shows, and join a club to learn the ins and outs of the hobby, as it's important to understand the quirks of your category before purchasing.

If you are already collecting, but are a beginner, focus your collection early on to help you make the most of your time and money. Without a plan, you may find yourself spending too much on lower quality items covering too broad a range. Buy the best quality you can afford, as it's better to focus on quality than quantity. Establishing a well-defined goal will help you be more selective. Collections that are well defined and higher quality tend to be more satisfying and more valuable than random collections of lower quality items.

Condition is everything! Better to buy one item in mint condition than five with flaws. The mint condition item will generally appreciate in value, while flawed pieces may only maintain their value or even depreciate.

Avoid buying made-for-collector items. They are produced in such large quantities that they are more likely to lose value than appreciate. If you do buy them, at least be sure that it's because you really love them and don't expect to ever sell them for a profit.

Beware of fakes and reproductions. They are the bane of collecting, and counterfeiters are getting better by the year. Fakes of lower value items are generally easier to detect, as counterfeiters usually don't consider it worth their time and effort to make high quality fakes. They are only intended to fool the careless. Fakes of higher value items, however, have gotten quite good, and extra care is needed to determine whether they are genuine. Rely on the help of trusted experts. This is one reason it is important to develop relationships with more experienced club members, dealers, etc.

Inventory your collection by taking photos of every piece and listing the description (maker, measurements, style, pattern, marks, etc.), date purchased, amount paid, date sold, and amount received. Antiques and collectibles are typically not covered by household insurance. If your collection becomes valuable enough to insure, ask your insurance agent about adding a rider to cover your collection. Expensive items like jewelry, coins, and guns may need a formal appraisal to be covered. Be sure

your inventory is kept up-to-date and your agent has a copy.

Hiring an Appraiser

Do I need to hire an appraiser? If you want an official valuation of your personal property that will hold up in court under a legal challenge, you should hire a reputable certified appraiser. Formal appraisals are expensive, and it probably won't make sense to pay for one unless you really need it. A formal appraisal should be conducted for property of significant value that needs to be appraised for legal purposes such as inheritance, divorce, charitable donation, or insurance.

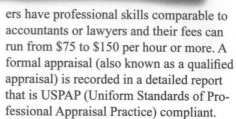

Unlike real estate appraisers, there are no federal or state licensing requirements for personal property appraisers. Good personal property appraisers, however, are highly knowledgeable and experienced professionals. Reputable appraisers are certified by appraisal organizations such as the AAA (Appraisers Association of America), the ANA (Appraiser's National Association), ASA (American Society of Appraisers, and ISA (International Society of Appraisers). Personal property appraisers have professional skills comparable to accountants or lawyers and their fees can run from $75 to $150 per hour or more. A formal appraisal (also known as a qualified appraisal) is recorded in a detailed report that is USPAP (Uniform Standards of Professional Appraisal Practice) compliant.

Before hiring an appraiser, ask your insurance agent or banker for recommendations. Also, verify his credentials to ensure he is certified. Ask about his experience. Like doctors, some appraisers are generalists, while others are specialists. If you have a specialized collection, hire an appraiser with significant experience in that area. Do not hire any appraiser who offers to be paid with antiques or collectibles or on a percentage basis. Both are highly unethical practices because they create a conflict of interest that encourages a biased appraisal favoring the appraiser. An honest appraiser will only charge on an hourly or per-job basis.

Venues for Buying and Selling

Private Sales Between Collectors

Buying or selling directly between collectors is one of the best options because you can often find the best quality pieces before they are sold to the general public via other venues.

Pros: By buying directly from collectors, you can avoid the markup of buying through an intermediary like a dealer or auction. Conversely, when selling directly to another collector, you can often charge premium prices for top quality pieces while avoiding sales commissions.

Cons: Collectors who want to buy or sell directly from other collectors usually have already established a relationship with them through a club or other collecting associated venue. Those who want to buy directly from collectors will have to compete with others who want to do the same, so those with the best network have the best chance of getting premium items. Collectors who want to sell lower quality items may have a more difficult time finding buyers, so in these cases, they may need to cast a wider net by selling via an online auction, a dealer, or an auction house.

Advice: Join a club, attend shows and auctions, get to know dealers, and establish relationships whenever possible. Building a network can help you buy and sell directly, which omits the middleman.

Clubs

Clubs often hold their own shows where collectors can buy and sell their goods.

In addition, they typically sponsor seminars conducted by their own members, which is a tremendous help in developing expertise within a category. Clubs also often plan trips together to museums, shows, antique malls, etc.

Pros: Clubs help collectors form mutually beneficial relationships for learning, buying, and selling.

Cons: Becoming an active, contributing member can require a substantial commitment of time and effort.

Advice: Serious collectors should join and contribute to a club. The time invested is well worth the effort, as clubs can provide opportunities not available anywhere else.

Online Auctions

Online auctions such as eBay provide a global marketplace, connecting collectors of even the most obscure categories. Unlike brick-and-mortar store owners, individuals with very little experience or financial investment can sell online easily. Online sellers don't have to be saddled with the overhead costs of running an ongoing business, such as rent or mortgage, insurance, inventory, advertising, utilities, employee salaries and benefits, etc. Because of the lower threshhold of professionalism needed to sell through individual online auctions, sellers often lack expertise about the items they sell and sometimes do a poor job of listing them. eBay's fees and restrictions have been steadily increasing, while quality of goods has been decreasing, causing

their policies about payment, shipping and returns. Ask questions before bidding and, after winning an item, pay promptly.

Online Stores

While online auctions sellers can sell small amounts casually and infrequently, owners of online stores run a permanent ongoing business and thus assume some of the burdens of the brick-and-mortar store owners. To stay in business, they generally have to be more professional than the casual sellers who rely on online auctions.

Pros: Online stores typically have lower overhead than brick-and-mortar stores, so they can pass on their savings to their customers.

Cons: Buyers can't personally inspect the products they want to buy. Unlike online auctions, online stores don't have a feedback system, so it can be harder to evaluate a seller's trustworthiness.

Advice: The longer a store has been in business, the more likely it has been successful because of good business practices such as fair pricing, accurate descriptions, generous return policies, and good customer service. Read chat boards, and ask fellow collectors for recommendations.

increasing dissatisfaction, but new online auction companies have been steadily growing and giving eBay significant competition.

Pros: Online auctions provide a worldwide market. Because of the vast amount of items being offered online, creating intense competition, buyers can find excellent deals. Some of the newer auction companies like Bonanzle, eBid, OnllineAuction, Webstore, and Wensy are like eBay in that they host general auctions and sell almost everything, but offer free or low-cost listings and final value fees. SeeAuctions and AntiqueSpider also offer excellent rates but specialize in antiques and collectibles.

Cons: It can be harder to make informed purchasing decisions with online auctions because many listings have poor quality photos, inaccurate or insufficient descriptions because the sellers are either dishonest or lack expertise. Buyers are unable to personally handle and inspect pieces, which encourages dishonest sellers to sell fakes and reproductions.

Advice: When selling, provide multiple good-quality photos; describe items completely and accurately, noting all marks, measurements, and flaws; answer all questions promptly and use adequate packing materials when shipping. When buying, be sure to check the seller's feedback and carefully read

Online Malls

Online malls are groups of online stores which, like stores in brick-and-mortar malls, have grouped together to pool costs, allowing them to reduce overhead, provide improved services, and attract more customers. Some well-known antiques and collectibles online malls include Ruby Lane, GoAntiqes, and TIAS.

Pros: Malls require storeowners to meet certain criteria, so malls tend to have more consistent quality than standalone stores. In some malls, management reviews items to make sure that they meet the mall's rules. Ruby Lane is especially noted for strictly controlling the merchandise that its storeowners offer. Because of the large network of retailers, malls offer a large selection of items.

Cons: Overhead is higher for online malls, which means fewer cost savings to pass on to customers.

Advice: Online malls are a good place to shop when finding bargains is less important than locating hard-to-find pieces, or when buyers want the peace of mind of buying from vetted retailers.

Brick-and-Mortar Shops and Malls

Brick-and-mortar shops and malls are physical stores that customers can visit for a personal, hands-on shopping experience. These stores usually charge higher prices because of overhead.

Pros: Brick-and-mortar shops and malls allow potential buyers the ability to personally inspect and evaluate goods before purchase. Dealers often give loyal customers special treatment like offering layaway, giving first dibs on new stock, and keeping want lists. Dealers not only sell but also buy items. Dealers who don't want to lay out the money to buy certain items will sometimes allow collectors to consign them.

Cons: Brick-and-mortar stores and malls generally charge higher prices because of their higher overhead and have less selection than what's available on the Internet. Also, customers are becoming more reluctant to travel to stores because of the time and expense compared to the ease of viewing items online at home.

Advice: It's a good idea to establish a long-term relationship with an honest, knowledgeable dealer. Good dealers are courteous and attentive to their customers and willingly share their knowledge with eager collectors. They make sure their goods are clean, neatly displayed, clearly priced and marked with an accurate description, and their stock is kept fresh. They guarantee their items to be as described and will accept returns.

Thrift Stores

Thrift stores like Goodwill, St. Vincent de Paul, and the Salvation Army offer a wide variety of used consumer items, not just antiques and collectibles, so collectors have to spend a considerable amount of time weeding through items to find what they want.

Pros: It is still possible to find overlooked antiques and collectibles at thrift stores, although it is becoming more difficult. Donating to charity provides tax deductions, so this makes an attractive way to dispose of useful, but unwanted low-value items. Plus, recycling goods rather than trashing them is always a good idea, and it provides affordable used items for people in need.

Cons: Because people are more aware of the value of antiques now than a generation ago, due in part to the antiques boom from the 1970s to 1990s and, more recently, the popularity of *The Antiques Roadshow*, fewer antiques are being donated. Plus, many thrift stores are using appraisers or dealers to sort through goods, pull out valuable items, and price them at top value, and in some cases, like Goodwill, list them on their own online

store or auction site. Thus, fewer valuable items are slipping through the cracks to be discovered by keen-eyed collectors.

Advice: If you want to have the best chance of finding undiscovered gems at a thrift store, learn when the shelves are restocked and items repriced. No doubt you will have to compete with other bargain shoppers, so arrive early and have a strategy in mind. Know which shelves you're going to visit first. If you want to dispose of items for a tax deduction, use a valuation guide such as the one on shopgoodwill.com to help you determine the allowable deduction for each item and calculate the total. On the donation form at the thrift store, list the items and total estimated value, and be sure to keep a copy of the donation form for your tax records.

Auctions

Auction houses earn a commission by selling items that the owners have consigned to them. The commission ranges from 15 to 25 percent of the hammer price. Buyers also pay a commission (called a buyer's premium) of 15 percent to 25 percent. Auctions are held at all levels—local, regional, and national. Many auction houses now offer a variety of ways to bid, including the traditional bid from the auction floor, absentee bid, telephone bid, and live online bid, in which a person can bid live via the Internet through companies such as Live Auction-

eers, Proxibid, Artfact, and icollector. Some companies are general auction houses, while others are known for particular specialties. Because of highly publicized sales of record breaking items by world renowned companies like Christies and Sotheby's, many people believe that all auction items are sold at premium prices. Actually, that's a misconception. Usually, only rare, high-end, or very desirable items in mint condition command exceptionally high prices. Dealers acquire much of their stock from auctions because they can buy at wholesale prices and resell at retail. In most auctions, sellers set reserve prices to protect themselves from unexpectedly low bids. If the bidding doesn't reach the reserve price, the item isn't sold. Some auctions, however, are absolute and no reserve prices are set.

Pros: Sellers who are disposing of high value items may fare the best in an auction venue. Competition among bidders boosts prices, and auctioneers are adept at generating exciting, fast-paced bidding wars to encourage higher and higher bids. Buyers are able to inspect and evaluate items firsthand by attending the auction preview.

Cons: Since prices are not set, sellers risk getting less than an ideal price. Commissions are high, with auction houses receiving a hefty percentage of the selling price.

Advice: If you've never bought or sold at an auction, start by attending a local auction to learn how they operate. If, after attending a few auctions, you intend to start buying, attend the auction preview first to choose and inspect the items you want to bid on. Before consigning items to an auction house for sale, read the contract carefully for details concerning commission percentage, advertising costs, photography costs (if a catalog is to be published), and be sure to ask questions to clarify anything you don't understand. Compare costs, services, reputation, and satisfaction among auction companies. If you have a specialized collection, a specialty auction house might be better choice than a general one, even if it is more expensive, because it will likely be better equipped to draw the bidders who will be willing to pay the most for your pieces.

Estate Sales

Estate sales are typically handled by estate liquidation specialists who help their clients sell off the personal property of a deceased family member. The sales are usually held on location in the home. Estate sales professionals are paid on commission. They advertise the sale, and clean, organize, and price the property, provide security during the sale, maintain sales records, and clean up afterward. Estate liquidators endeavor to sell the personal property in a quick, efficient manner for as high a price as possible and leave the home "broom clean" after the sale so a real estate agent can take over and prepare the house for sale.

Pros: Estate sales provide speedy disposal of personal property, which allows for quick listing of the home for sale. Estate sales companies are experienced and can efficiently handle the myriad of details while the family is grieving and handling the stressful complexities of administering the will and handling other legal issues.

Cons: The cost of hiring a company to conduct a sale can be high. In addition, there is a substantial risk of theft before and during the sale because some thieves have become adept at targeting estate sales. It is not uncommon for a thief to attend the first day of a sale and open a window to allow for easy reentry when the house is unattended at night.

Advice: Before signing a contract with an estate sales company, get recommendations from friends, neighbors, etc, and read the fine print carefully to ensure you understand all the policies. Don't be afraid to shop around and compare rates and services, but remember, you get what you pay for. It's best that family members, with the permission of the executor (who has legal authority to administer the will) take or purchase what they want before the sale and not attend during the sale to avoid being tempted to hold back items. Also, insensitive shoppers have been known to make rude remarks about personal property that could be highly offensive to family members who overhear them.

Shows

Local, regional, and national shows are held regularly. Many provide previews for an additional cost, allowing those customers first shot at buying the best pieces.

Pros: Shows provide buyers access to a large quantity of items. Buyers can personally inspect pieces and ask questions, and shows are also a good place to develop relationships with dealers and other enthusiasts. Dealers don't like to haul the same pieces to show after show, so they may be willing to drop prices significantly toward the end of a show, providing shoppers with bargains.

Cons: Shows usually last for only few days at most, so the window for buying or selling is relatively short. Plus, there can be a substantial cost in transportation, lodging, food, admissions, booth fees, etc.

Advice: There are varying strategies for shopping at shows, each with ardent supporters. Some believe it is best to arrive early to beat others to the best deals. Others wait until the end of the show to look for sleepers that others have overlooked or to negotiate big discounts. Of course, waiting to the end of the show means taking the risk that the piece you wanted has already been sold.

SPECIAL CONTRIBUTORS AND ADVISORS
by Subject

ABC Plates: Joan M. George

Black Americana: Leonard Davis and Caroline Torem-Craig

Character Collectibles: Dana Cain

Chase Brass & Copper Company: Donald-Brian Johnson

Cloisonné: Arlene Rabin

Compacts & Vanity Cases: Roselyn Gerson

Decals: Jim Trautman

Eyewear: Donald-Brian Johnson

Jewelry (Costume): Marion Cohen

Kitchenwares:
  Cow Creamers: LuAnn Riggs
  Egg Cups: Joan M. George
  Egg Timers: Ellen Bercovici
  Pie Birds: Ellen Bercovici
  Reamers: Bobbie Zucker Bryson
  String Holders: Ellen Bercovici

Lighting: Carl Heck

Lighting Devices:
  1930s Lighting: Donald-Brian Johnson
  Moss Lamps: Donald-Brian Johnson

Nativity Sets: Donald-Brian Johnson

Plant Waterers: Bobbie Zucker Bryson

Pop Culture Collectibles: Dana Cain and Emmett Butler

Ribbon Dolls: Bobbie Zucker Bryson

Steins: Andre Ammelounx

Vintage Clothing: Nancy Wolfe and Madeleine Kirsh

CERAMICS

Abingdon: Elaine Westover

American Painted Porcelain: Dorothy Kamm

Amphora-Teplitz: Les and Irene Cohen

Bauer Pottery: James Elliott-Bishop

Belleek (American): Peggy Sebek

Belleek (Irish): Del Domke

Blue & White Pottery: Steve Stone

Blue Ridge Dinnerwares: Marie Compton and Susan N. Cox

Brayton Laguna Pottery: Susan N. Cox

Buffalo Pottery: Phillip Sullivan

Caliente Pottery: Susan N. Cox

Catalina Island Pottery: James Elliott-Bishop

Ceramic Arts Studio of Madison: Donald-Brian Johnson

Clarice Cliff Designs: Laurie Williams

Cleminson Clay: Susan N. Cox

deLee Art: Susan N. Cox

Doulton/Royal Doulton: Reg Morris, Louise Irvine and Ed Pascoe

East Liverpool Potteries: William and Donna J. Gray

Flow Blue: K. Robert and Bonne L. Hohl

Franciscan Ware: James Elliott-Bishop

Frankoma Pottery: Susan N. Cox

Gonder Pottery: James R. and Carol S. Boshears

Hall China: Marty Kennedy

Harker: William A. and Donna J. Gray

Hull: Joan Hull

Ironstone: General - Bev Dieringer; Tea Leaf - The Tea Leaf Club International

Limoges: Debby DuBay

Majolica: Michael Strawser

McCoy: Craig Nissen

Mettlach: Andre Ammelounx

Noritake: Tim Trapani

Old Ivory: Alma Hillman

Pacific Clay Products: Susan N. Cox

Phoenix Bird & Flying Turkey: Joan Collett Oates

Pierce (Howard) Porcelains: Susan N. Cox

Quimper: Sandra Bondhus

Red Wing: Gail Peck

Royal Bayreuth: Mary McCaslin

Rozart Pottery: Susan N. Cox

R.S. Prussia: Mary McCaslin

Russel Wright Designs: Kathryn Wiese

Schoop (Hedi) Art Creations: Susan N. Cox

Shawnee: Linda Guffey

Shelley China: Mannie Banner; David Chartier; Bryand Goodlad; Edwin E. Kellogg; Gene Loveland and Curt Leiser

Stoneware and Spongeware: Bruce and Vicki Waasdorp

Vernon Kilns: Pam Green

Warwick China: John Rader, Sr.

Zeisel (Eva) Designs: Kathryn Wiese

Zsolnay: Federico Santi/ John Gacher

GLASS:

Animals: Helen and Bob Jones

Cambridge: Helen and Bob Jones

Carnival Glass: Jim and Jan Seeck

Central Glass Works: Helen and Bob Jones

Consolidated Glass: Helen and Bob Jones

Depression Glass: Linda D. Carannante

Duncan & Miller: Helen and Bob Jones

Fenton: Helen and Bob Jones

Fostoria: Helen and Bob Jones

Fry: Helen and Bob Jones

Heisey: Helen and Bob Jones

Higgins Glass: Donald-Brian Johnson

Imperial: Helen and Bob Jones

McKee: Helen and Bob Jones

Morgantown: Helen and Bob Jones

New Martinsville: Helen and Bob Jones

Opalescent Glass: James Measell

Paden City: Helen and Bob Jones

Pattern Glass: Green Valley Auctions

Phoenix Glass: Helen and Bob Jones

Wall Pocket Vases: Bobbie Zucker Bryson

Westmoreland: Helen and Bob Jones

Contributors and Advisors Contact Info.

Andre Ammelounx
P.O. Box 136
Palatine, IL 60078
(847) 991-5927

Mannie Banner
126 S.W. 15th St.
Pembroke Pines, FL 33027

Ellen Bercovici
360 -11th Ave. So.
Naples, FL 34102

Sandra Bondhus
P.O. Box 100
Unionville, CT 06085
e-mail: nbondhus@pol.net

James R. and Carol S. Boshears
375 W. Pecos Rd., #1033
Chandler, AZ 85225
(480) 899-9757

Bobbie Zucker Bryson
Bluffton, SC
Napkindoll@aol.com

Emmett Butler
Denver, CO
(303) 840-1649

Dana Cain
5061 S.Stuart Ct.
Littleton CO 80123
e-mail: dana.cain@att.net

CAS Collectors
206 Grove St.
Rockton, IL 61072
Web: www.cascollectors.com
www.ceramicartstudio.com

Linda D. Carannante
TLC Antiques
Pottstown, PA
(610) 246-5241

David Chartier
1171 Waterside
Brighton, MI 48114

Les and Irene Cohen
Pittsburgh, PA
or
Amphora Collectors International
21 Brooke Dr.

Elizabethtown, PA 17022
e-mail: tombeaz@comcast.net

Marion Cohen
14 Croyden Ct.
Albertson, NY 11507
(516) 294-0055

Neva Colbert
69565 Crescent Rd.
St. Clairsvville, OH 43950
(740) 695-2355
e-mail: georgestreet@1st.net

Marie Compton
M&M Collectibles
1770 So. Randall Rd., #236
Geneva, IL 60134-4646
eBay: brdoll

Susan N. Cox
El Cajon, CA
e-mail: antiquefever@aol.com

Caroline Torem-Craig
New York, New York

Leonard Davis
New York, New York

Bev Dieringer
P.O. Box 536
Redding Ridge, CT 06876
e-mail: dieringer1@aol.com

Janice Dodson
P.O. Box 957
Bloomfield Hills, MI 48303

Del E. Domke
16142 N.E. 15h St.
Bellevue, WA 98008-2711
(425) 746-6363
e-mail: delyicious@comcast.net

Debby DuBay
Limoges Antiques Shop
62 Merchants Row.
Rutland, VT 05701
(802) 773-6444

Joan M. George
67 Stevens Ave.
Oldbridge, NJ 08856
e-mail: drjgeorge@nac.net

Roselyn Gerson
12 Alnwick Rd.
Malverne, NY 11565
(516) 593-8746
e-mail: compactlady@aol.com

William A. and Donna J. Gray
2 Highland Colony
East Liverpool, OH 43920
e-mail: harkermate@comcast.net

Pam Green
You Must Remember This
P.O. Box 822
Hollis, NH 03049
e-mail: ymrt@aol.com
Web: www.ymrt.com

Green Valley Auctions
2259 Green Valley Lane
Mt. Crawford, VA 22841
(540) 434-4260
Web: www.greenvalleyauctions.com

Linda Guffey
2004 Fiat Court
El Cajon, CA 92019-4234
e-mail: Gufantique@aol.com

Carl Heck
Box 8516
Aspen, CO 81612
(970) 925-8011
Web: www.carlheck.com

Alma Hillman
197 Coles Corner Rd.
Winterport, ME 04496
e-mail: oldivory@adelphia.net

K. Robert and Bonne L. Hohl
47 Fawn Dr.
Reading, PA 19607

Joan Hull
1376 Nevada S.W.
Huron, SD 57350

Hull Pottery Association
11023 Tunnel Hill N.E.
New Lexington, OH 43764

Louise Irvine
England: (020) 8876-7739
e-mail: louiseirvine@blueyonder.co.uk

Helen and Bob Jones
Berkeley Springs, WV
e-mail: Bglances@ aol.com

Donald-Brian Johnson
3329 South 56th St., #611
Omaha, NE 68106
e-mail: donaldbrian@msn.com

Dorothy Kamm
10786 Grey Heron Ct.
Port St. Lucie, FL 34986
e-mail: dorothykamm@adelphia.net

Edwin E. Kellogg
4951 N.W. 65th Ave.
Lauderhill, FL 33319

Madeleine Kirsh
C. Madeleine's
13702 Biscayne Blvd.
North Miami Beach, FL 33181
(305) 945-7770

Curt Leiser
National Shelley China Club
12010 - 38th Ave. NE
Seattle, WA 98125
(206) 362-7135
e-mail: curtispleiser@cs.com

Gene Loveland
11303 S. Alley Jackson Rd.
Grain Valley, MO 64029

Mary McCaslin
6887 Black Oak Ct. E.
Avon, IN 46123
(317) 272-7776
e-mail: Maryjack@indy.rr.com

Metz Superlatives Auction
P.O. Box 18185
Roanoke, VA 24014
(540) 985-3185
Web: www.metzauction.com

Reg G. Morris
2050 Welcome Way
The Villages, FL 32162
e-mail: modexmin@comcast.net

Craig Nissen
P.O. Box 223
Grafton, WI 53024-0223

Joan C. Oates
1107 Deerfield Lane
Marshall, MI 49068
e-mail: koates120@earthlinks.net

Gail Peck
Country Crock Antiques
2121 Pearl St.
Fremont, NE 68025
(420) 721-5721

Arlene Rabin
P.O. Box 243
Fogelsville, PA 18051
e-mail: arjw9299@verizon.net

John Rader, Sr.
Vice President, National Assn. of Warwick China & Pottery Collectors
780 S. Village Dr., Apt. 203
St. Petersburg, FL 33716
(727) 570-9906
Author of "Warwick China" (Schiffer Publishing, 2000)
or
Betty June Wymer, 28 Bachmann Dr., Wheeling, WV 26003, (304) 232-3031)
Editor, "The IOGA" Club Quarterly

LuAnn Riggs
1781 Lindberg Dr.
Columbia, MO 65201
e-mail: artichokeannies@bessi.net

Tim and Jamie Saloff
P.O. Box 339
Edinboro, PA 16412
e-mail: tim.salofff@verizon.net

Federico Santi
The Drawing Room Antiques
152 Spring St.
Newport, RI 02840
(401) 841-5060
Web: www.drawrm.com

Peggy Sebek
3255 Glencairn Rd.
Shaker Heights, OH 44122
e-mail: pegsebek@earthlink.net

Jim and Jan Seeck
Seeck Auctions
P.O. Box 377
Mason City, IA 50402
(641) 424-1116
e-mail: jimjan@seeckauction.com

Laurie Stoltenberg
Reflections Antiques & Gifts
9492 1st St.
Nelsonville, WI 54458
(715) 824-2628

Steve Stone
12795 W. Alameda Pkwy.
Lakewood, CO 80225
e-mail: Sylvanlvr@aol.com

Michael G. Strawser Auctions
P.O. Box 332
Wolcottville, IN 46795
(260) 854-2859
Web: www.majolicaauctions.com

Phillip Sullivan
P.O. Box 69
South Orleans, MA 02662
(508) 255-8495

Mark and Ellen Supnick
7725 NW 78th Ct.
Tamarac, FL 33321
e-mail: saturdaycook@aol.com

Tea Leaf Club International
P.O. Box 377
Belton, MO 64012
Webb: www.tealeafclub.com

Tim Trapani
7543 Northport Dr.
Boynton Beach, FL 33437

Jim Trautman
R.R. 1
Orton, Ontario CANADA L0N 7N0
e-mail: trautman@sentex.net

Bruce and Vicki Waasdorp
P.O. Box 434
Clarence, NY 14031
(716) 759-2361
Web: www.antiques-stoneware.com

Elaine Westover
210 Knox Hwy. 5
Abingdon, IL 61410-9332

Kathryn Wiese
Retrospective Modern Design
P.O. Box 305
Manning, IA 51455
e-mail: retrodesign@earthlink.net

Laurie Williams
Rabbitt Antiques and Collectibles
(408) 248-1260
e-mail: rabbitt3339@yahoo.com

Nancy Wolfe
Galena, IL 61036

Auction Houses Providing Color Digital Images:

American Pottery Auction
Vicki and Bruce Waasdorp
P.O. Box 434
Clarence, NY 14031
(716) 759-2361
Web: www.antiques-stoneware.com
(Stoneware Pottery)

Garth's Arts & Antiques
P.O. Box 369
Delaware, OH 43015
(740) 362-4771
Web: www.garths.com
(Americana)

Green Valley Auctions
2259 Green Valley Lane
Mt. Crawford, VA 22841
(540) 434-4260
Web: www.greenvalleyauctions.com
(American Glass & Lighting)

Glass Works Auctions
Box 180
East Greenville, PA 18041
(2150 679-5849
Web: www.glswrk-auction.com

Heritage Auction Galleries
3500 Maple Avenue
Dallas, TX 75219-3941

(800) 835-3243
Web: www.HeritageAuctions.com
(Victoriana)

Morphy Auctions
2000 N. Reading Road
Denver, PA 17517
(717) 335-3435
Web: morphyauctions.com
(Advertising, Toys, Games, Disney)

Neal Auction Company
4038 Magazine St.
New Orleans, LA 70115
(504) 899-5329
Web: www.nealauctions.com
(Americana)

Seeck Auction Company
Jim and Jan Seeck
P.O. Box 377
Mason City, IA 50402
Web: www.seeckauction.com

Skinner, Inc.
357 Main St.
Bolton, MA 01740
(978) 779-6241
Web: www.skinnerinc.com
(Americana & Jewelry)

Other Auction Houses Providing Photographs:

Charlton Hall Auctioneers
912 Gervais St.
Columbia, SC 29201

Christie's New York
20 Rockefeller Plaza
New York, NY 10020

Cincinnati Art Galleries
225 East Sixth St.
Cincinnati, OH 45202

Fontaines Auction Gallery
1485 W. Housatonic St.
Pittsfield, MA 01210

Guyette & Schmidt, Inc.
P.O. Box 522
West Farmington, ME 04922

Norman Heckler & Company
79 Bradford Corner Road
Woodstock Valley, CT 06282

Jackson's International Auctioneers &
Appraisers
2229 Lincoln St.
Cedar Falls, IA 50613

James D. Julia, Inc.
P.O. Box 830
Fairfield, ME 04937

McMasters-Harris Auction Company
P.O. Box 755
Cambridge, OH 43725

New Orleans Auction Gallery
1330 St. Charles Ave.
New Orleans, LA 70130

Past Tyme Pleasures
39 California Ave., Suite 105
Pleasanton, CA 94566

Rago Art & Auction Center
333 No. Main St.
Lambertville, NJ 08530

Slater's Americana, Inc.
5335 No. Tacoma Ave., Suite 24
Indianapolis, IN 46220

Michael G. Strawser Majolica Auctions
P.O. Box 332
Wolcottville, IN 46795

Treadway Toomey Galleries
John Toomey Gallery
818 North Blvd.
Oak Park, IL 60301

Treadway Gallery, Inc.
2029 Madison Road
Cincinnati, OH 45208

Other Photographs Provided By:

Susan Eberman, Bedford, IN; Ellen R. Hill, Bennington, NH; Mary Ann Johnston, New Cumberland, WV; Vivian Kromer, Bakersfield, CA; Pat Moore, San Francisco, CA; Margaret Payne, Columbus, IN, John Petzold, and Dr. Leslie Piña.

ABC PLATES

These children's plates were popular in the late 19th and early 20th centuries. An alphabet border was incorporated with nursery rhymes, maxims, scenes or figures in an apparent attempt to "spoon feed" a bit of knowledge at mealtime. An important reference book in this field is *A Collector's Guide to ABC Plates, Mugs and Things* by Mildred L. and Joseph P. Chalala (Pridemark Press, Lancaster, Pennsylvania, 1980).

5" d., "Christmas Day," black transfer-printed scene of a young boy enjoying Christmas dinner, red vitruvian scroll border band **$400**

5" d., "Going to School," black transfer- printed scene w/two boys wearing long pants & fancy collars on the way to school, one carries a lunch pail **$225**

5" d., "Laughing," brown transfer-printed scene w/added colors showing the head of a mirthful lady **$300**

5" d., "The Happy Children," black transfer- printed scene of a seated Victorian mother w/her children within a pious verse border **$350**

5" d., "The Husband and the Stork," part of an Aesop's Fables series, green transfer- printed center scene, quality bone china w/a scalloped rim **$300**

5" d., "The Morning Walk," early black transfer scene of a mother & daughter on a morning stroll, surrounded by a verse that describes the scene **$350**

5 1/4" d., "Football," center w/ transfer-printed & colored scene of children playing football, mid-19th c. **$250**

5 1/4" d., "Girl with a Pitcher," center w/early transfer-printed scene of a girl getting a pitcher of water from a stream, first half 19th c. ... **$300**

5 1/2" d., motto-type, an oval wreath encloses a motto telling how to run a successful business, black transfer **$230**

5 3/4" d., "Shuttlecock - D E F," blue transfer-printed center scene of boys playing shuttlecock (badminton) w/three letters above the scene, 19th c. **$230**

5 3/4" d., "The Shepherd's Boy," part of an Aesop's Fables series, black transfer- printed center scene shows the boy chasing a wolf that carries off a sheep, T. & B. Godwin, New Wharf, England, ca. 1834 .... **$500**

6" d., "Princess Alexandra," transfer-printed & color-tinted bust portrait of the princess surrounded by flowers, commemorating the marriage of Edward, the Prince of Wales (later Edward VII) on March 10, 1863 .... **$375**

6" d., "Quizzing," sepia transfer-printed scene w/added colors showing an amusing head of a 18th c. matron looking through a monocle **$300**

6" d., Sign Language plate, black transfer- printed scene of early wooden dolls framed by a printed border of hands showing positions for various letters, embossed alphabet border ... **$300**

6" d., "The Blind Girl," transfer-printed & color-tinted scene of Victorian children giving alms to a seated blind girl by a gate, late 19th c. **$175**

6" d., "Snuffing," a black transfer-printed scene tinted in color, shows a bust portrait of a comical gentleman in 18th c. dress taking snuff **$300**

6 1/4" d., "Ball Game," red transfer-printed scene of three young Victorian men playing catch, mid-19th c. **$200**

6 1/4" d., Boy crossing a stile, transfer-printed sepia & color-tinted scene of a young man stepping across a stile **$175**

6 1/4" d., "David and Goliath," red transfer-printed center scene based on biblical story **$175**

6 1/4" d., "Dr. Franklin's Maxims," mulberry transfer-printed center scene showing a woman yelling at a dog, sayings by Benjamin Franklin surround the scene, bone china **$250**

6 1/4" d., girls & a dog scene in purple transfer printing, shown in a formal garden setting of the early 19th c. **$225**

6 1/2" d., "The Old Hound," part of an Aesop's Fables series, mulberry transfer- printed center scene shows a man throwing a stick to attract the attention of the old dog **$250**

6 1/2" d., "The Travelers and the Bear," part of an Aesop's Fables series, black transfer-printed center scene shows a bear attacking some men on a roadway, cheap heavy pottery **$250**

6 5/8" d., "Flowers That Never Fade - Attachment," black transfer-printed & color- tinted center scene of children standing around another seated boy reading, surrounded by a pious verse, part of a series promoting family ties **$250**

6 3/4" d., clock face, transfer-printed clock dial in black w/printed upper & lower case letters & Arabic & Roman numerals, late 19th c. **$200**

6 3/4" d., "Cricket," black transfer-printed center scene of boys playing cricket, scene found in other colors, 19th c. **$225**

6 3/4" d., hunting scene printed in brown, hunters in wide fields w/ their dogs **$175**

ABC PLATES

6 3/4" d., "I is for Isobel," green transfer- printed scene of a young girl riding a donkey w/a man standing alongside **$225**

7" d., "Abraham Lincoln," brown transfer- printed center scene showing a bust portrait of Lincoln, ca. 1865, a companion plate shows a portrait of George Washington **$500**

7" d., "Frolics of Youth - The Fall of China," a play on words w/a blue transfer-printed scene of two Victorian boys, one shooting a slingshot to knock down a stack w/a china vase & toys **$250**

7" d., "Leopard," a square brown transfer- printed center scene w/added colors showing a leopard in a tree, scattered letters around the borders, part of the Wild Animal series by Brownhills Pottery, England, late 19th c. **$350**

7" d., "The Old Grandpa," a black transfer- printed scene tinted in color, shows an elderly gentleman greeting two children **$220**

7 1/4" d., "At the Seaside," center color-tinted scene of two children at the beach, an inner alphabet band & outer Roman numeral band, one of a series produced by Brownhills Pottery, ca. 1895 .... **$300**

7 1/4" d., "Bubble Play," color-tinted scene of young children blowing bubbles, double alphabet border w/embossed & printed letters **$225**

7 1/4" d., "Chaffinch," brown transfer-printed & color-tinted design of two birds at the left side w/rows of the alphabet along the right side, part of the Brownhills Pottery series illustrating birds **$250**

7 1/4" d., "Daniel in the Lion's Den - He Trusted in God," black transfer-printed center scene based on a biblical story ... **$245**

ADVERTISING MARKET REPORT

Advertising items are very popular because they have so much category crossover interest. Virtually every category has an advertising subcategory because, in our highly commercial society, companies find sales success through marketing and advertising. In categories that focus on manufacturers (Coca-Cola for example), advertising makes up the bulk of the collectibles.

Lisa Baker of Vintage Depot Direct (www.vintagedepotdirect) in Paso Robles, California, said her labels and political items such as pinbacks are selling well. Customers are "buying spontaneously and for nostalgia rather than investment." Although they are purchasing lower end items, especially $10 and less, Baker's total number of items sold has actually increased because they want more items for the same amount of money. They're looking for great bargains, and she has found success in offering free shipping, as "they will buy significantly more to get it."

According to Larry Meeker of Antiques of a Mechanical Nature (www.patented-antiques), "the top and bottom ends of the advertising items are doing well." Porcelain signs, which typically sell for $500 to $1,000 are selling out, and $10 to $20 cans and tins are moving, but the $100 to $500 range is dead. "Those who are buying the more expensive items apparently have not been affected by the economy," he said.

Irene Davis of Creek House Antiques (www.creekhouseantiques.com) in New Church, Virginia, said "Anything that is rare and near-mint condition continues to bring high prices. The middle-of-the-road items in less than near-mint condition are off. Gas and oil items continue to be strong. Prices on the automotive and gas and oil collectibles do not seem to have slipped as in other areas. We see more younger collectors entering that field. We do not see this in other vintage advertising areas. But good-quality rare pieces still sell and still bring high prices. Buyers are looking for more graphics and are willing to pay high prices for colorful, eye-appealing advertising pieces. One-color pieces with just a company name are now run-of-the-mill. Shops, malls, and eBay are dead for advertising. Nothing shows up at those venues anymore. Specialized shows or Web sites and personal contact are the only way to find quality pieces."

Irene and her husband, Carter, recently opened icollect247.com to provide a Web site for quality dealers who guarantee their listings to offer pre-1970 vintage items.

Auction Houses
Rich Penn Auctions (www.richpennauctions.com)
Hakes (www.hakes.com)
James Julia (www.jamesdjulia.net)
William Morford (www.morfauction.com/index.htm)
Morphy Auctions (www.morphyauctions.com)
Past Tyme Pleasures (www.pasttyme1.com)
Heritage (www.ha.com)
Daniel Auctions (www.danielauctioncompany.com)

ADVERTISING ITEMS

Thousands of objects made in various materials, some intended as gifts with purchases, others used for display or given away for publicity, are now being collected. Also see various other categories and *Antique Trader Advertising Price Guide.*

Counter display cabinet, "Dr. Daniels' Veterinary Medicines," oak w/embossed tin color door panel, depicts likeness of the doctor w/"Dr. Daniels' Warranted Veterinary Medicines - Home Treatment for Horses and Cattle Dr. Daniels' Famous Dog Remedies" & illustrations of various product containers, original contents included, late 19th - early 20th c., some panel wear, 21 1/2", 28 3/4" h. **$1,150**

Counter display cabinet, "Putnam Fadeless Dyes-Tints," color-printed tin, slant-front style w/advertising on the front in red, blue & black & w/a vignette of General Putnam, Revolutionary hero, riding a horse in the lower corner, interior compartments complete, late 19th - early 20th c., 14 3/4 x 19" **$180**

Counter display, "Stanley Legend Powerlock," wood & composition, an upright open-front display cabinet on the right w/16 pigeonholes, a colorful half-figure of a workman on the left, reglued, 28" l., 19" h. **$55**

Counter display cabinet, "Sanford's Inks," upright oak frame w/a flat top & applied gild lettering, two long panels of glass down the front, glass sides, original double sliding back doors opening to four wooden shelves, some shelf rests replaced, late 19th - early 20th c., 11 1/4 x 27", 23 1/2" h. **$960**

Counter display case, long low rectangular design w/glass panels framed by German silver, wooden bottom & hinged & mirrored rear doors, minor flaws, early 20th c., 24 x 47", 11" h. **$1,668**

Counter display, "The Nut - Nuts of Quality - Deliciously Crisp," mahogany model of an open-sided house w/central chimney on roof, printed advertising for Nut House nuts in gold & black, encloses two spherical embossed clear glass jars w/metal covers & matching metal & wood scoop, late 19th - early 20th c., 8 x 18", 16" h. **$480**

Counter display, "Tootsie Rolls," printed tin, the high angled front w/two open tiers, dark blue ground w/white & gold lettering, further advertising down the sides, some surface scuffs & minor paint wear, early 20th c., 8 3/4 x 10 1/2", 13 1/2" h. **$345**

Paper and cardboard advertising items from before the 1940s are hard to find and have correspondingly high values. A vast amount of paper was collected during World War II paper drives, so a less-than-normal amount survived that era. Plus, paper items are fragile and easily damaged by mold and mildew generated in damp storage areas like basements and garages, so even fewer items that made it through the war survived long-term storage after the war.

Counter display, "Smith Brothers Cough Drops," lithographed tin, tall narrow upright case w/a black ground, a top upright tab showing two packages of the product, the narrow front printed in black & white w/a stack of four packages, includes four original cardboard boxes of the products, early 20th c., 10 1/2" h. **$546**

Counter display, "U.S. Cartridge Company," three-panel color-printed cardboard, tall rectangular center panel w/a dark blue band across the top printed in red & white "US Ammunition - You shoot the best when you use U.S.," a large scene by William Hamilton Foster of an old gentleman sitting on a rock in a snowy landscape w/his rifle across his lap, short side wings w/scenes of flying ducks & a stag w/boxes of the products, lightly faded, moderate soiling, wings reattached, upper fold in center section, early 20th c., center 26 x 41 1/2" **$3,393**

ADVERTISING ITEMS

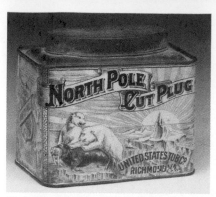

Product container, "North Pole Cut Plug Tobacco," printed tin, rectangular one- pound size w/oval pry-off lid, decorated in black & white w/a scene of polar bears attacking a walrus, some light flaking, early 20th c., 4 x 6", 5" h. **$460**

Spool cabinet, "Belding Brothers & Co.," counter display-type, upright oak case w/ seven glass-fronted narrow drawers above two narrow wooden drawers, original gilt decals, early 20th c., 18 1/2 x 20 1/4", 27 3/4" h. **$780**

Spool cabinet, "Chadwick's Spool Cotton - Six Cord - Whites - Colors - Browns - Buttons - Blacks - Needles," counter display- type, upright walnut case w/three long narrow paneled drawers w/gold lettering above an arrangement of six small drawers w/gold lettering, flat molded base, original knobs, late 19th c., 19 1/4 x 28 3/4", 22 1/2" h. **$1,035**

Spool cabinet, "George A. Clark - Clark's - O.N.T. - Sole Agent - Spool Cotton - On White Spool," counter display-type, upright walnut case w/six drawers, each w/a ruby glass insert printed in gold & w/original round brass knobs, flat molded base, late 19th c., 19 1/4 x 29", 22" h. **$690**

Store bin, "Mistletoe Coffee - Timothy Gay & Co., Boston," color-printed tin, upright rectangular form w/top lid, rolled top band above a large flat front decorated w/an oval reserve printed in color w/a scene of children pulling a harvest-laden wagon & surrounded by h.p. red & white roses & green leaves on a pale blue ground, curved bottom front w/pull-up lid w/porcelain knob, moderate scuffs, chips & pitting, top lid not original, late 19th c., 13 1/2 x 17", 20" h. **$488**

ADVERTISING ITEMS

Store box, Iten's Product - Snow White Bakery - Clinton, IA," deep rectangular pine box w/a flat hinged lid & metal bail handles on the ends, early 20th c., 13 3/4 x 22", 12 1/4" h...................... **$104**

Window display, "Lucky Strike Cigarettes," color-printed trifold cardboard, the center panel w/a large pack of Lucky Strike cigarettes above a scene of a baseball field, each wing die-cut with a figure of a baseball player, on the left "Mickey" Cochrane & on the right Jim Bottomley, each in action poses & w/their endorsement below, very bright & clean, some separation to cardboard backing & printed surface, each player the Most Valuable Player in the two leagues in 1928, 66" l., 42" h. **$34,500**

Window display, "Winchester Fishing Tackle," five-panel wooden floor screen design, double-sided w/the three sections on one side forming a scene of a man fishing flanked by fishing tackle end panels, the other side w/five tool scenes, dated 1923, wooden frame w/good replacement, each panel 20 x 47 1/2" **$4,313**

ARCHITECTURAL ITEMS

In recent years the growing interest in and support for historic preservation has spawned a greater appreciation of the fine architectural elements that were an integral part of early building, both public and private. Where, in decades past, structures might be razed and doors, fireplace mantels, windows, etc., hauled to the dump, today all interior and exterior details from unrestorable buildings are salvaged to be offered to home restorers, museums and even builders who want to include a bit of history in a new construction project.

Building corbels, carved & painted wood, one carved as a scowling man's face looking to the left, the other carved as a stern bearded man, each w/a flat molded top, from a late Victorian mansion in Binghamton, New York, ca. 1897, 6 3/4 x 10 3/4", 8 3/4" h., pr. **$9,600**

Church doors, painted & parcel-gilt wood, the pair forming a large Gothic arch, decorated w/conforming panels w/applied molding in the form of a panoply of Gothic quatrefoils, second half 19th c., each 20" w., 7' 4" h., pr. **$748**

Entrance gates, wrought iron, each w/an arched toprail w/spearhead decoration over a body of square column design decorated w/scrolling floral overlays, ending w/a rectangular panel, decorated w/highlights of gold w/mounting bars, Europe, 19th c., 12' 2" w., overall 99" h., pr. **$2,300**

Paterae are circular ornaments used in friezes. The word comes from the saucerlike vessels, or patera, that the ancient Greeks and Romans used in libations and sacrifices.

Fireplace surround, carved wood, a molded egg-and-dart valance supporting carved paterae over pairs of carved & fluted columns resting on plinth bases & flanking three concave shell carvings above a rectangular mirror above a serpentine mantelpiece, on a carved corbel bisecting a floral-carved surround, trimmed w/egg-and-dart molding, Europe, ca. 1900, molding at left side of valance broken, 12 1/2 x 60", 7' 9" h. **$1,380**

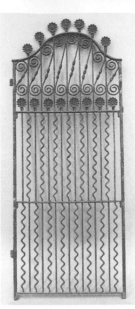

Gate, cast- and wrought-iron, Victorian Aesthetic Movement style, the arched top w/a pair of cast sunflowers on twisting wrought stems, the row of flowers repeating in the body of the gate, last quarter 19th c., American-made, 35 1/2" w., 82 1/2" h. **$1,038**

Gates, cast iron, each section composed of vertical bars separated by pairs of opposing quarter-arches filled w/scrolls beside the figure of a standing crowned lion, tight scroll panels along the bottom & side, 19th c., each pair 60" w., one pair 104" h., the other 72" h., two pairs **$7,763**

Wall panels, painted & parcel-gilt wood, tall narrow rectangular form, in the Napoleon III "Pompeian" taste w/banded narrow panels surrounding a tall central armorial panel in gold, red, black & green, France, late 19th c., 24" w., 5' 2" h., pr. **$3,680**

Library steps, mahogany, in the form of a staircase w/newels & newel posts, railings & turned spindles leading to a platform w/ gallery, on molded legs joined by stretchers w/brass casters, George III- Style, England, 23 1/2 x 39", 5' 9" h. **$1,840**

Window cornices, painted & gilt-trimmed wood, each long piece w/blocked recessed end panels filled w/gilt pineapple-filled compotes, a long narrow cross panel stenciled w/a band of flowers below the scroll-cut & arched crestrail centered by a stenciled basket of fruit, America, mid- 19th c., 42 1/4" l., 6 7/8" h., set of 3 .... **$4,183**

ART DECO

Interest in Art Deco, a name given an art movement stemming from the Paris International Exhibition of 1925, continues to grow today. This style flowered in the 1930s and actually continued into the 1940s. A mood of flippancy is found in its varied characteristics - zigzag lines resembling the lightning bolt, sometimes steps, often the use of sharply contrasting colors such as black and white and others. Look for prices for the best examples of Art Deco design to continue to rise. Also see JEWELRY, MODERN.

Bar, portable, wood & metal, a long narrow oval form in wood trimmed around each end w/ curved line-incised metal panels, raised on small metal ball feet, fitted w/square glass decanters, sets of glasses & an ice bucket, one glass missing, ca. 1950, 24" l. **$184**

Clock, gilt-bronze & onyx, half-round flat- bottomed shaped composed of arched & curved fluting centered at the top by a small onyx block above the round dial w/Arabic numerals, maquette mark of Albert Cheuret, France, ca. 1925, 14 7/8" l., 6 5/8" h. **$83,650**

Bowl, porcelain, low footring supporting the deep rounded sides w/a wide flat rim, h.p. w/a colorful design w/wide pink & white stripes around the exterior & interior, the exterior further decorated w/a colorful stylized landscape w/a church on a hill w/ small hills below & a sailing ship at sea below blue & yellow clouds, designed by Gio Ponti, executed by Richard Ginori, Italy, ca. 1925, signed, 5 3/4" d., 2 7/8" h. **$13,145**

Centerpiece bowl, glass, Macassar ebony & chrome, a wide shallow paneled pressed translucent frosted celery green glass bowl w/a Chinese Lantern plant decoration, shaped & upswept ebony side handles, resting on a ringed chrome foot, glass embossed at edge "Ezan - France," ca. 1930, 17 1/2" l., 6 1/4" h. **$345**

Jardiniere, table-top style, wrought-iron, low round cylindrical frame w/panels composed of pairs of openwork C-scrolls, small knob feet & rim balls, a frosted glass liner, designed & marked by Edgar Brandt, ca. 1925, 15" d., 5 1/4" h. **$8,963**

Lamp, table model, 11" d. domical shade in pink stained glass w/graduated rings topped by a molded stylized rose blossom, raised on a squared nickel-plated brass stem & hexagonal foot embossed w/geometric designs, shade marked "Vlieghe - France - 1137," ca. 1925, minor flakes on shade, overall 19" h. **$518**

Mirror, wall-type, wrought-iron long frame gently arched at the top & bottom & w/flat ends w/flat bars, designed & signed by Edgar Brandt, ca. 1930, 27 5/8 x 55" **$14,340**

Lamps, table, art glass, the body formed from a glass vase w/ opalescent pulled flowers on a tapered form w/a wide rim, chrome top & base, ca. 1930s, base 12" h., overall 30" h., pr. **$300**

Panels, cast & wrought iron, each tall rectangular piece composed of vertical bars accented w/angular bars & an applied wrought foliate pendant at the top & scrolling bars near the base, Europe, ca. 1920s, three panels 43 1/2 x 70 1/4", two panels 37 1/2 x 70 1/4", set of five **$2,760**

ART DECO

Tile, gilt plaster, molded in relief w/a stylized image of a nude Josephine Baker in a dancing pose, the background w/half-circles, squares & rays, possibly from one of the inner halls of the Folies Bergere in Paris, France, overall gilt finish, in a stepped walnut frame, tile 19 x 19 1/2" **$6,900**

Tureen, cover & mirrored undertray, silver, a long low round dish w/tapering cylinrical sides incised w/panels, the low domed cover w/further radiating lines centered w/a vertical pink onyx ring handle, the undertray w/a stepped edge, designed & signed by Jean E. Puiforcat, Paris, France, ca. 1926, tureen 10" d., undertray 13" d., the set **$31,070**

Vase, acid-etched & cut clear glass, the heavy slightly tapering cylindrical form cut w/two thick spiral bands down the sides against an acid-etched ground, designed by Aristide Colotte, acid-etched mark "Colotte Nancy Piece Unique," ca. 1925, 5 1/2" d., 10 1/4" h. **$15,600**

←

→

Wall sconce, patented wrought iron & glass, the iron mount w/a tiered & fluted base supporting a pair of tall flat curled arms w/a pierced leafy vine design, each fitted w/an electric socket mounted w/a trumpet-form flute & loop-etched pale yellow Daum Nancy shade, designed by Edgar Brandt, marked, France, ca. 1925, 14 1/2" w., 20 3/4" h., pr. (ILLUS. of one) **$42,000**

ART NOUVEAU

ART NOUVEAU

Art Nouveau's primary thrust was between 1890 and 1905, but commercial Art Nouveau productions continued until about World War I. This style was a rebellion against historic tradition in art. Using natural forms as inspiration, it is primarily characterized by undulating or wavelike lines and whiplashes. Many objects were made in materials ranging from glass to metals. Figural pieces with seductive maidens with long, flowing hair are especially popular in this style. Interest in Art Nouveau remains high, with the best pieces by well known designers bringing strong prices. Also see JEWELRY, ANTIQUE.

Lithograph, printed in shades of blue & green on a buff ground, reads "Tous Les Soirs - Irene Henry à l'Horlage," by H. G. Ibels, France, ca. 1900, signed in the plate, 33 x 48" **$4,200**

Tables, nesting-type, marquetry & mahogany, the graduated set each w/a rectangular top decorated w/naturalistic design, scroll-carved side aprons continuing to slender forked legs continuing to low arched feet, by Emile Gallé, France, ca. 1900, largest 14 7/8 x 22 3/4", 28 1/4" h. **$3,360**

Vase, porcelain, tapering lower body & tapering neck to a flare rim, decorated w/the bust profile of an Art Nouveau maiden wearing an ornately enameled gown & headdress as an Allegory of Germany, designed by Nikolaus Kannhauser, by Riessner, Stellmach & Kessel, stamped "Amphora 466 D" & printed factory mark, ca. 1900, 12 1/8" h. **$16,800**

Panel, carved mahogany, long rectangular board centered by a deeply carved face of an Art Nouveau maiden w/a floral headdress, flanked by panels of relief- carved oak branches w/acorns accented w/a gilt ground, Europe, early 20th c., 11 1/2 x 27 1/4" **$4,113**

Arthur Lasenby founded Liberty & Co. on Regent Street in London in 1875. Archibald Knox was one of the company's top designers and was largely responsible for the success of two of Liberty's most enduring lines: Cymric and Tudric.

Vase, sterling silver & enamel, a bullet-form body supported on three legs composed of pairs of slender bands joined by vining bands, the center of the body enameled in bluish green w/three inverted hearts, designed by Archibald Knox, retailed by Liberty & Co., England, ca. 1904, 6 1/2" h. **$19,656**

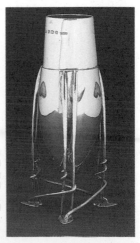

ART NOUVEAU

AUDUBON PRINTS

AUDUBON PRINTS

John James Audubon, American ornithologist and artist, is considered the finest nature artist in history. In about 1820 he conceived the idea of publishing a full color book portraying every known species of American bird in its natural habitat. He spent years in the wilderness capturing their beauty in vivid color only to have great difficulty finding a publisher. In 1826 he visited England, received immediate acclaim, and selected Robert Havell as his engraver. *Birds of America*, when completed, consisted of four volumes of 435 individual plates, double-elephant folio size, a combination of aquatint, etching and line engraving. W.H. Lizars of Edinburgh engraved the first ten plates of this four-volume series. These were later retouched by Havell, who produced the complete set between 1827 and early 1839. In the 1840s, another definitive work, *Viviparous Quadrupeds of North America*, con-

taining 150 plates, was published in America. Prices for Audubon's original double-elephant folio size prints are very high and beyond the means of the average collector. Subsequent editions of *Birds of America*, especially the chromolithographs done by Julius Bien in New York (1859-60) and the smaller octavo (7 x 10 1/2") edition of prints done by J.T. Bowen of Philadelphia in the 1840s, are those that are most frequently offered for sale.

Anyone interested in Audubon prints needs to be aware that many photographically produced copies of the prints have been issued during this century for use on calendars or as decorative accessories, so it is best to check with a print expert before spending a large sum on an Audubon purported to be from an early edition.

American Goldfinch - Plate 33, hand-colored etching, engraving & aquatint by Robert Havell, London, 1827-38, framed, scattered foxing, time staining & soiling, few small edge tears, 25 1/8 x 39" **$5,736**

American White Pelican - Plate CCCXI - hand-colored etching, engraving & aquatint by Robert Havell, Jr., London, 1827- 38, framed, only minor scuffs & stains, one tear, mounted on mat, 28 1/8 x 38 3/16" **$65,725**

Bird of Washington (The) - Plate 11, hand- colored etching, engraving & aquatint by Robert Havell, Jr., London, 1827-38, framed, few pale foxmarks, minor scuffing, some margin loss, small tears & losses in margin, 25 7/8 x 39 1/8" **$8,365**

Grey Rabbit - Plate XXII - hand-colored lithograph from "The Vivaparous Quadrupeds of North America," by Bowen of Philadelphia, 1845-48, matted & framed, 22 x 28" **$978**

Blue Crane - Plate 372, hand-colored lithography by J. Bien, New York, ca. 1859-1860, framed, 26 1/2 x 39 1/2" (foxing & small losses & tears in margins, mat & time staining, surface soiling & hanging creases) **$4,183**

Great American Hen & Young - Plate VI, hand-colored etching & aquatint by W.H. Lizars, repaired tear, light & mat stain, scattered foxing, numerous short margin tears, 26 3/8 x 39 3/4" **$32,900**

Piping Plover - Plate CCXX, hand-colored etching, engraving & aquatint by Robert Havell, London, 1827-38, framed, 21 1/4 x 27 1/2" (staining, occasional foxmark, sheet laid down on Masonite board).............................. **$2,032**

Purple Grackle - Plate VII, hand-colored, engraving & aquatint by Robert Havell, Jr., London, 1827-38, 25 5/8 x 38 5/8" (central horizontal fold, several soft creases, minor soiling, several small margin tears)......... **$2,820**

Rough-legged Falcon - Plate CCCCXXII, hand-colored etching, engraving & aquatint by Robert Havell, Jr., London, 1823-38, losses & tears along margin edges, time staining & foxing at edges, 26 x 39 1/4" **$3,107**

Texas Lynx - Plate 92 -, hand-colored lithograph by J.T. Bowen, Philadelphia, ca. 1846, framed, 19 x 25" **$2,588**

White Heron - Plate CCCLXXXVI, hand- colored etching, engraving & aquatint by Robert Havell, Jr., London, 1827-38, framed, small tears in heron's body, three repaired tears in background, several tears along margin, title text information reattached & backed, 25 5/8 x 38 1/4" **$17,925**

AUTOMOTIVE COLLECTIBLES

Clock, "Phillips 66 - Tires - Batteries," round electric back-lit wall-type w/double-bubble dome over the logo & working in black & red, white border band printed w/black Arabic numerals, black hands & red sweep seconds hand, working, ca. 1950s, 15" d. **$546**

Clock, "Quaker State Oils & Greases," round electric wall-type w/silver composition frame around the white dial w/black Arabic numerals around the green advertising panel reading "Time to Change to Quaker State Oils & Greases," black hands & sweep seconds hand, designed to be inserted into a tire store display, ca. 1930-1950, some loss to frame, missing cord, 20" d. **$650-750**

Gas pump, "Texaco Fire Chief," Wayne Pump Co. Model 80 series, patent dated 1951, w/ reproduction glass globe & Ande Rooney pump signs, fully restored, 75" h. **$863**

Oil can, "Opaline Motor Oil - Sinclair Refining Company - Chicago," one-gallon can w/top handle, screw-on cap & short spout w/ cap, printed paper labels, the front on w/a large race car above the wording in dark green & black, some light surface scuffing, early 20th c., 8" w., 11" h. **$920**

Traffic sign, "Stop - Go," four-sided sheet- metal manual-type w/two sides printed in yellow & red "Stop" & two sides printed in yellow & green "Go," on a tall slender steel shaft on a round cast-iron base, alligatored finish, early 20th c., 14" w., 78 1/2" h. **$719**

Gas pump globe, "Standard Oil," one-piece milk glass crown-shaped globe w/red trim, ca. 1940, 16" h. **$374**

MECHANICAL

BANKS

Original early mechanical and cast-iron still banks are in great demand with collectors. Their scarcity has caused numerous reproductions of both types and the novice collector is urged to exercise caution. The early mechanical banks are especially scarce and some versions are seldom offered for sale but, rather, are traded with fellow collectors attempting to upgrade an existing collection. Numbers after the bank name in mechanical banks refer to those in John Meyer's *Handbook of Old Mechanical Banks*. However, another book, *Penny Lane—A History of Antique Mechanical Toy Banks*, by Al Davidson, provides updated information and the number from this new volume is indicated in parenthesis at the end of each mechanical bank listing.

In past years, our standard reference for cast-iron still banks was Hubert B. Whiting's book *Old Iron Still Banks*, but because this work is out of print and a well illustrated book, *The Penny Lane Bank Book—Collecting Still Banks*, by Andy and Susan Moore pictures and describes numerous additional banks, we will use the Moore numbers as a reference after the name of each listing. Other newer books on still banks include *Iron Safe Banks* by Bob and Shirley Peirce (SBCCA publication), *The Bank Book* by Bill Norman (N), *Coin Banks by Banthrico* by James Redwine (R), and *Monumental Miniatures* by Madua & Weingarten (MM). We will indicate the Whiting or other book reference number, with the abbreviation noted above, in parenthesis at the end.

The still banks listed are old and in good original condition with good paint and no repair unless otherwise noted. An asterisk (*) indicates this bank has been reproduced at some time.

Mechanical

Boy Robbing Bird's Nest - 20 - a.k.a. Tree Bank, multicolored, J. & E. Stevens, ca. 1906, PL 51 .... **$9,488**

Magician Bank - 154 - magician holding top hat w/table, multicolored, J. & E. Stevens, PL 315 .... **$4,320**

Hall's Liliput Bank (with Tray) - 146 - pivoting cashier & white domed building, ca. 1877, PL 230 .... **$690**

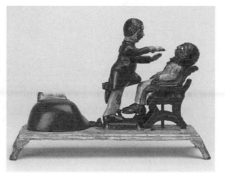

Dentist - 57 - dentist extracting tooth from seated patient, some restoration, PL 152 .... **$4,658**

POTTERY

Beware of ads in local newspapers headlined: "Antiques Wanted; Free Appraisals." It is an unethical ploy to buy antiques. Find out what your items are worth on your own before contacting potential buyers.

Professor Pug Frog's Great Bicycle Feat - 201- Mother Goose reading w/frog riding bicycle & clown holding large basket, multicolored, J. & E. Stevens, ca. 1886, small repair & paint touchup, PL 400 .... **$4,485**

Speaking Dog - 69 - seated girl w/large dog, rectangular coin trap, multicolored, J. & E. Stevens, ca. 1885, lever to activate bank not working, PL 447 .... **$500- 1,000**

Trick Dog Bank (solid base) - 72 - clown w/hoop, barrel & dog, dog jumps through the clown's hoop, modern w/ one-piece solid base, w/original paint & key, Hubley, ca. 1925-40, 8 3/4" w., PL 482 .... **$2,128**

Pottery

Bulbous-form, redware w/sgraffito decoration, wide squatty rounded shape topped by a ringed knob finial, brown & pale amber glaze, the front incised overall w/flowering leafy vines, large birds, a flowerpot & the profile bust of a man wearing a hat, a coin slot on the shoulder above the inscription "William Mountjoy is a very good boy mad (sic) the 29 May 1839," Pennsylvania, professional repair, 5 3/4" h. **$4,888**

Cat head, yellowware modeled as the head of a cat w/ detailed eyes & snout, pointed ears, mottled yellow & brown glaze, incised on the bottom "Sara Johnson Belle 1905. 25 Cents," surface chips to right ear, 3 1/4" h. **$468**

Hen on Nest, yellowware w/mottled yellow & brown glaze, ca. 1860, 3 1/2" h. **$550**

Model of a dog, seated spaniel facing viewer, overall dark green glaze, probably from Ohio & early 20th c., excellent condition, 5" h. **$358**

Pig, bulbous oblong footed animal w/pointed ears & round snout, overall light brown alkaline glaze w/lots of brown sponged bands, ca. 1890, 5 1/2" h. **$550**

Pig, fat standing animal in stoneware w/an overall sponged reddish brown & green glaze, ca. 1880, 3 1/4" l. ... **$523**

Pig, standing, creamy clay decorated w/an overall mottled sponged greenish brown decoration, early 20th c., 5 1/2" l. **$59**

STILL

Still

*Bear - Begging Bear - 715 - cast iron, A.C. Williams Co., original black paint, ca. 1910, Arcade Mfg. Co., 1910-25, 5 3/8" h. $144

*Boy Scout (Soldier Boy) - 45 - cast iron, original gold paint, A.C. Williams Co., 1910-34, 5 7/8" h. (W. 14) $150

*Elephant - Elephant with Howdah (large) - 474 - cast iron, worn original paint, A.C. Williams Co., 1910-30s, 6 3/8" l., 4 7/8" h. (W. 63).. $69

Globe - Globe Bank - 781 - cast iron, w/eagle on top, worn original red paint, Enterprise Mfg. Co., 1875, 5 3/4" h. $460

Building - State Bank - 1078 - cast iron, w/cupola dormer windows & locking door, "STATE BANK" embossed at front under eaves, Kenton Mfg. Co., ca. 1900, 5 1/2 x 7 x 8" h. $1,380

Buster Brown & Tige - 241 - figural Buster standing next to seated Tige, red & gold paint, 5" h. $127

"Crystal Bank" - 926 - clear glass cylinder w/cast iron base & domed open rib top, Arcade Mfg. Co., 1910-25, 2 11/12" d., 3 7/8" h., W. 243 .... $144

Duck - Round Duck - 619 - cast iron, original paint, large Kenton-type trap, blue & red paint, Kenton Mfg. Co., 1936-40, 4 7/8" d., 4" h., W. 325 .... $633

"Transvaal Money Box" - 78 - pipe-smoking fat man wearing green top hat & coat, "Transvaal Money Box" inscribed in gold on front of hat, original paint, John Harper, England, late 19th c., 5 3/4" h. $259

Building - "Globe Savings Fund" - 1199, cast iron w/red, gold, brown & silver paint, house w/arched door w/combination lock flanked by two arched panels on either side, the bottom two containing scroll decoration, the top two w/figures carrying vessels on their heads, the roof adorned w/ figures of mythical beasts, "Globe Savings Fund - 1888" at top, 5 1/2" w., 7" h. $1,800

Building - State Bank - 1078,- cast iron, w/cupola dormer windows & locking door, "STATE BANK" embossed at front under eaves, Kenton Mfg. Co., ca. 1900, 5 1/2 x 7 x 8" h. $1,380

Dolphin - 33, cast iron w/gold paint, boy in boat w/"Dolphin" on side, Grey Iron Casting Co.(?), 1900(?), 4 1/2" h. $460

BARBERIANA

A wide variety of antiques related to the tonsorial arts have been highly collectible for many years, especially 19th- and early-20th-century shaving mugs and barber bottles. We are now combining these closely related categories under one heading for easier reference.

Barber Bottles

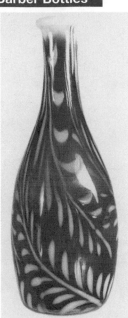

Cranberry opalescent, Fern patt., slender ovoid body tapering to a rolled lip, late 19th - early 20th c., 8 1/4" h. **$202**

Dark cobalt blue, cylindrical body tapering to a cylindrical neck w/ tooled lip, vertical optic ribbing, pontil scar, enameled in gold, orange & white w/scattered daisy flowers, late 19th - early 20th c., 8 1/4" h. **$157**

> When making offer to buy an antique, it's a good idea to have that amount ready in cash. It's more likely that your offer will be accepted without negotiation if you already have the correct amount and are willing to pay cash rather than credit.

Iridescent art glass, bulbous body tapering to a lady's leg neck w/polished lip, Loetz- style decoration w/overall random patches of golden topaz iridescence on an amethyst ground, late 19th - early 20th c., 7" h. **$246**

Iridescent art glass, bulbous body tapering to a lady's leg neck w/ polished lip, Loetz- style decoration w/overall random patches of silvery iridescence on pale yellowish green ground, late 19th - early 20th c., 7 7/8" h. **$336**

Mary Gregory, cobalt blue bulbous body tapering to a lady's leg neck, one decorated in brownish white enamel w/the figure of a running girl w/tennis racket, the other w/a figure of a boy w/a tennis racket, rolled lips, ca. 1900, 7 7/8" h., facing pair **$364**

Milk glass, ringed & gently tapering body w/a tall slender neck w/ original pewter screw-on cap, tan ground enameled w/a scene of a bird perched on a branch holding a banner w/a name & "Bay Rum," mark of the Whitall Tatum company on the bottom, late 19th - early 20th c., 9 5/8" h. **$364**

Milk glass, ringed & gently tapering body w/a tall slender neck w/ original pewter screw-on cap, the side enameled w/a scene of two swimming swans among water lilies below faded wording "E.E. Sanguine, Tonic," mark of the Whitall Tatum company on the bottom, late 19th - early 20th c., 9 5/8" h. **$224**

Milk glass, ringed & gently tapering body w/a tall slender neck w/ original pewter screw-on cap, the side enameled w/a rounded reserve decorated w/a cottage scene above the name, mark of the Whitall Tatum company on the bottom, late 19th - early 20th c., 9 3/4" h. **$336**

Milk glass, ringed & gently tapering body w/a tall slender neck w/ original pewter screw-on cap, the side enameled w/a sepia tone scene of a sailing ship below a lighthouse all above a name, mark of the Whitall Tatum company on the bottom, 9 5/8" h. **$616**

Milk glass, ringed & gently tapering body w/a tall slender neck w/ original pewter screw-on cap, the side enameled w/a scene of a lady dancer, Whitall Tatum mark on bottom, late 19th - early 20th c., 9 5/8" h. **$728**

Milk glass, slender tapering smooth cylindrical body w/a tall slender neck w/tooled lip, enameled w/a bouquet of wild roses enclosing a band printed "Bay Rum," late 19th - early 20th c., 9 1/8" h. **$235**

Occupational Mugs

Chauffeur, decorated in color w/ a scene of an early open auto w/a uniformed driver, name in gold around the top & gold band around the base, ca. 1919, 3 7/8" h. **$950**

Coal wagon driver, large h.p. color scene of a man driving a green coal wagon w/red wheels pulled by white horses, name in gold above & gold base band, ca. 1900, 3 5/8" h. **$504**

Dentist, black background decorated w/a set of dentures in color below the name in gold, French-made blank, 3 5/8" h. **$616**

Doctor, detailed color scene of a doctor attending a child in a home bedroom, name in gold below, 3 5/8" h. **$3,640**

Dump truck driver, large color scene of an early dump truck emptying a load, name of owner in black on the side of the truck & in gold at the top, German-made blank, 3 3/4" h. **$3,920**

Insurance agent, large color scene of the Rock of Gibraltar printed in white "The Prudential Has The Strength of Gibraltar," flanked by gold scrolls, name in gold above, signed by the decorator on the bottom, 3" h. **$1,680**

Liquor merchant, decorated w/a detailed scene of a shop interior w/several people, flanked by gold leaves, name in gold above, German-made blank, 4" h. **$3,080**

Metalworker, color scene of a man standing & operating a metal lathe, name in gold above, German-made blank, 3 3/4" h. **$364**

Sportsman, decorated in color w/a scene of a standing sportsman in a woodland setting aiming his rifle, his hunting dog in front of him, name in gold around the top, gold band around the base, ca. 1900, 3 5/8" h. **$101**

BARBIE DOLLS & COLLECTIBLES

At the time of her introduction in 1959, no one could have guessed that this statuesque doll would become a national phenomenon and eventually the most famous girl's plaything produced.

Over the years, Barbie and her growing range of family and friends have evolved with the times, serving as an excellent mirror of the fashion and social changes taking place in American society. Today, after more than 40 years of continuous production, Barbie's popularity remains unabated among both young girls and older collectors. Early and rare Barbies can sell for remarkable prices, and it is every Barbie collector's hope to find a mint condition "#1 Barbie."

Dolls

Barbie, "#1 Ponytail Barbie," display doll, blonde hair in braid, pale red lips, cheek blush, hoop earrings, finger & toe paint, wearing #876 Sweater Girl outfit w/orange knit shell & cardigan sweater, grey flannel sheath skirt, black #1 open-toed shoes, w/black pedestal stand & metal prongs, near mint in box, box very good condition **$9,000**

Barbie, "#3 Ponytail Barbie," straight-leg, brunette hair, red lips, earring holes, finger & toe paint, wearing "Registered Nurse" outfit, doll in good condition w/some fading, rubbing & discoloration, outfit in very good condition, water bottle end torn off, glasses missing **$550**

Barbie, "Swirl Ponytail Barbie," straight-leg, platinum blonde hair, white lips, earring holes, finger & toe paint, wearing red nylon swimsuit & white open-toed shoes, hair slightly fuzzy, ends of ponytail straight, face slightly dark, very good condition ... **$285**

Barbie, "#3 Ponytail Barbie," straight-leg, brunette hair, red lips, nostril paint, earring holes, finger & toe paint, wearing black & white striped swimsuit, hair slightly fuzzy, bottom rubber band replaced, slight fading & discoloration **$400**

Barbie, "#4 Ponytail Barbie," straight-leg, blonde hair, red lips, nostril paint, cheek blush, earring holes, finger & toe paint, wearing black & white striped swimsuit, pearl earrings, glasses, booklet, wire & pedestal stand, partial box insert w/original box, new mint doll, box very good **$550**

Barbie, "#6 Ponytail Barbie," blonde hair, orange lips, earring holes, finger & toe paint, straight-leg body, wearing red nylon swimsuit, pearl earrings, white open-toed shoes, w/black wire stand, booklet in cellophane bag, near mint in box **$375**

Barbie, "Twist 'n Turn Barbie," bent-leg, brunette hair w/plastic cover, pink lips, cheek blush, original colorful swimsuit, wrist tag, clear plastic stand & booklet, apparently never removed from box **$345**

Francie, Twist-'n-Turn model, black skin w/brunette hair w/original plastic cover, bright pink lips, original wrist tag, near mint **$1,000**

Clothing and Accessories

Automobile, Skipper's Irwin Roadster, green plastic w/orange plastic interior, white steering wheel, clear plastic windshield, grey wheel inserts, grey-painted accessories, cardboard Skipper form in seat, in box w/original cellophane cover, dated 1964, mint in box.. **$550**

Barbie & Midge case, blue vinyl w/pictures of Barbie & Midge on the front, includes accessories & two ca. 1960s Japanese Barbies & about 15 1960s & 1970s outfits, couple of splits in case, 13 1/2 x 17 1/2", the group.............. **$240**

Clothing set on hanger, round hinged goldtone metal w/"B" initial, very good condition, inner mirror scratched, indentation on bottom **$350**

BASEBALL MEMORABILIA

Baseball was reputedly invented by Abner Doubleday as he laid out a diamond-shaped field with four bases at Cooperstown, New York. A popular game from its inception, by 1869 it was able to support its first all-professional team, the Cincinnati Red Stockings. The National League was organized in 1876, and though the American League was first formed in 1900, it was not officially recognized until 1903. Today, the "national pastime" has millions of fans, and collecting baseball memorabilia has become a major hobby with enthusiastic collectors seeking out items associated with players such as Babe Ruth, Lou Gehrig, and others who became legends in their own lifetimes. Although baseball cards, issued as advertising premiums for bubble gum and other products, seem to dominate the field, there are numerous other items available.

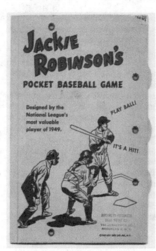

Figure of Stan Musial, plastic, Hartland, in original color-printed cardboard box w/"Major League Baseball Stars," figure near mint, box w/wear & some damage, 1950s **$438**

Game, "Jackie Robinson's Pocket Baseball Game," long fold-over cardboard printed in red & black, late 1940s, excellent condition, opens to 6 1/2 x 9" **$316**

Press guide, "Dodgers 1953 - Press - Radio - TV Guide," cover illustration by Willard Mullin, in blue, red & white, slight flaws **$63**

Pocket knife, souvenir-type, "DiMaggio's S.F. Calif.," stylized model of a baseball bat, mother-of-pearl handle, from Joe DiMaggio's restaurant, ca. 1950s, 2 1/2" l. **$193**

A mint-in-box baseball can be worth triple the amount of an unboxed ball. To receive a premium price, don't break the seal on the box.

Pinback button, "World Series - Ebbetts Field 1955 - New York Yankees - Brooklyn Dodgers," blue wording on white, near mint, 2 1/8" d. **$235**

Press pin, 1962 Yankees World Series issue, round enameled metal w/top hat logo & wording in red, white, blue & gold **$170**

Postcard, "American League Champions - Edward S. Plank - Pitcher - Athletic Base Ball Team," features large sepia tone photograph of Eddie Plank, 1905, excellent condition **$928**

BASKETS

The American Indians were the first basket weavers on this continent and, of necessity, the early Colonial settlers and their descendants pursued this artistic handicraft to provide essential containers for berries, eggs and endless other items to be carried or stored.

Rye straw, split willow and reeds are but a few of the wide variety of materials used. Nantucket baskets, plainly and sturdily constructed, along with those made by specialized groups, would seem to draw the greatest attention to this area of collecting.

Nantucket basket, woven splint, round w/wrapped rim & carved swing handle secured w/brass tacks, probably late 19th - early 20th c., losses to rim lashing, 8 7/8" d., 8 1/4" h. **$1,528**

To prevent excessive moisture loss and possible cracking of splints and cane, do not display baskets near heat sources such as fireplaces, furnace vents, or radiators.

Nantucket baskets, finely woven splint w/carved swing handles secured w/carved wooden ears, turned wooden base w/incised line decoration, some w/applied pennies on the base dated 1971 & 1972, nested set of nine, 10 3/4" d., 4 1/4" h. to 15 1/4" d., 5 1/2" h., the set **$11,750**

Nantucket purse basket, finely woven splint, flat bottom & deep round sides, the bottom faintly inscribed "Jose Formosa Reyes, Made in Nantucket," a hinged lid w/catch centered by a wooden plaque decorated w/a carved ivory spread-winged sea gull, underside of lid engraved "Margaret Alexander," bentwood swing handle, ca. 1960s, 7 x 9 1/2", overall 11" h. **$3,840**

Storage, cov., woven splint, deep rectangular shape w/fitted cover & bent splint end handles, yellow-painted vertical splints decorated w/blue & salmon-colored stamped sunburst designs, Eastern Woodland Indian, 19th c., 10 1/2 x 18", 9 1/4" h. **$940**

Utility basket, woven splint, round wrapped rim painted dark blue, hexagonal sides w/cane-style weaving painted white, American, probably late 19th c., some losses, 11" d., 4 1/4" h. **$353**

The Shakers, known for their superb baskets, learned their skills from Native American basketmakers.

BOTTLES

BOTTLES MARKET REPORT

Bottles are one of the few categories in which even novices have a reasonably good chance of finding valuable, rare specimens at little or no cost. That's because collectors have a way to obtain them besides buying them from other collectors: they can dig them out of the ground. The abundance and preservation of buried bottles can be attributed to several factors. First, bottles have been in widespread use for nearly 200 years and were produced in large quantities. Second, they were made for utilitarian rather than decorative use, which means they were eventually disposed of rather than passed from one generation to the next. Third, unlike other items made of organic material like wood or fabric, they didn't decay, so large numbers survived.

Before people hauled their trash to town dumps, they typically burned it. Many items that wouldn't burn, including bottles, were thrown into privies, where they were eventually buried and sealed when the privy was moved to another location. For many years, bottle collectors have been digging up long abandoned privies and have been finding valuable treasures. Many more are still waiting to be uncovered and will be unearthed for years to come.

Antique Trader Bottles Identification and Price Guide, 6th Edition, by Michael Polak, features an excellent chapter about digging for bottles and gives tips on locating privies, digging tools and techniques, and safety precautions. The book, available at krausebooks.com, also includes 600 color photos and 5,000 listings with current values covering more than 50 bottle categories.

At the Las Vegas Bottle Show in February 2009, Polak wasn't sure if people would be spending money, but wasn't disappointed, as he "didn't see any letdown in bottle sales." According to Polak the following bottles are hot: historical flasks, bitters, Western whiskeys, back-bar whiskeys, poisons, soda/mineral water bottles, fruit jars, and perfume bottles.

In a February 2009 e-mail press release, Jeff Wichman, owner of American Bottle Auctions, said "the overall feeling we came away with for Auction 46 was that collectors are hesitant to bring out their good stuff right now because they feel they won't get top dollar. From what we can tell, the opposite is true. Great bottles are selling for top dollar because they just aren't coming out. With so few outstanding pieces hitting the market, the collectors with the money (of which there are plenty) are willing to go the extra mile to pay whatever they need to walk away a winner. So, where is the bottle market right now? We feel it's just fine and dandy .... Checking eBay these days, there just isn't the selection there was maybe a year ago. We believe it's the lack of quality bottles versus the affect of a recession that's holding things up...."

Auction Houses
American Bottle Auctions (www.americanbottle.com)
Glass Works Auctions (www.glswrk-auction.com)
Norman Heckler (www.hecklerauction.com)
Bottle Auction (www.bottleauction.com)

BOTTLES

Castilian Bitters, cylindrical w/ swelled shoulder & ringed neck w/applied mouth, smooth base, medium amber, ca. 1865- 75, 10 1/8" h. **$672**

Clarke's Vegetable Sherry Wine Bitters Sharon Mass (below) Only 25 Cts, rectangular w/ beveled corners & applied sloping collar mouth, open pontil, bluish aqua, ca. 1840-60, 8 1/4" h. **$134**

Clarke's Vegetable Sherry Wine Bitters Sharon Mass, rectangular w/beveled corners & applied tapering mouth, smooth base, bluish aqua, ca. 1855-70, 1 gal., 14 1/4" h. **$616**

Doyle's - Hop - Bitters - 1872, semi-cabin, words around sides of sloping shoulder, square w/ paneled sides w/raised clusters of hop berries & leaves, applied sloping double collar mouth, smooth base, ca. 1872-75, yellowish olive, 9 5/8" h. ... **$392**

French Aromatique - The Finest Stomach Bitters, rectangular w/wide rounded shoulder, tooled mouth, smooth base, bluish aqua, ca. 1885-95, 7 1/4" h. ... **$90**

Greeley's Bourbon Bitters, barrel-shaped, ten rings above & below center band, applied mouth, smooth base, ca. 1860- 75, medium smoky olive topaz, 9 1/4" h. **$1,232**

Hardy's (Dr. Manly) - Genuine - Jaundice Bitters - Bangor ME, rectangular w/beveled corners, applied sloping collar mouth, open pontil, deep bluish aqua, ca. 1840-60, 6 1/2" h. **$392**

Herb (H.P.) Wild Cherry Bitters, Reading, Pa., cabin-shaped, square w/cherry tree motif & roped corners, tooled mouth, smooth base, medium yellowish amber, 10 1/4" h. **$504**

Lediard's - O.K. Plantation - Bitters 1840, semi-cabin w/ applied mouth & smooth base, yellowish amber, ca. 1865-75, very light stain, 10" h. **$2,352**

Mampe (F.J.) - Stargard I Pom - Gesertz Z. Schutzd. Warenbez V. Mai 1894 (around castle on applied seal), square w/ beveled corners, applied mouth & seal, smooth base, olive green, Germany, ca. 1880-1900, 22 3/4" h. **$952**

Mills' Bitters A.M. Gilman Sole Proprietor, cylindrical w/lady's leg neck & applied rim w/ring, smooth base, medium yellowish amber, outside stain & ground lines, recently dug, ca. 1870-80, 11 1/4" h. **$2,800**

Mishler's Herb Bitters - Table Spoon Graduation (ruler marker) - Dr. S.B. Hartman & Co., square w/ paneled sides, applied sloping double collar mouth, embossed on base "Stoeckels Grad. Pat. Feb. 6 '66W. McC.," yellow w/olive tone, ca. 1866-75, 9 3/8" h. .. **$728**

Old Sachem - Bitters - and - Wigwam Tonic, barrel-shaped, ten-rib, applied mouth, smooth base, ca. 1865-75, yellowish amber, 9 1/4" h. **$448**

Richardson's (W.L.) Bitters - South Readings - Mass, rectangular w/beveled edges & wide rounded shoulder w/short neck & applied mouth, open pontil, bluish aqua, ca. 1840-60, 7" h. **$392**

Sazerac Armotic Bitters (on base) - monogram in ring on shoulder, cylindrical w/tall lady's leg neck & applied rim ring, smooth base, ca. 1870s, milk glass, 12 1/4" h. **$336**

Sazerac Armotic Bitters (on base) - monogram in ring on shoulder, cylindrical w/tall lady's leg neck & applied rim ring, smooth base, decal showing ocean coral on the front, ca. 1870s, milk glass, 10 1/4" h. **$420**

Figurals

Clam, clear w/95% original grey & rust paint, ground lip w/original screw-on metal cap, base embossed "Pat. Apld For," ca. 1890-1910, 3 1/2" h. ... **$78**

Child sitting on chamber pot, clear, tooled mouth, smooth base, no embossing, ca. 1890-1910, 4 1/2" h. **$280**

Chinese man, clear, tooled mouth, smooth base marked "C.T.," original paper label around neck reading "For The Toilet," ca. 1890-1910, 5 1/4" h. **$112**

FIGURALS

Clam, cobalt blue, rough ground lip, original metal screw-on cap, ca. 1890-1910, 5 1/4" h. **$392**

Clam, medium amber, ground lip, original metal screw-on cap, ca. 1890-1910, 5 1/4" h. **$78**

Liberty Bell, clear, embossed "E. Hoyt & Co. - Celebrated - Perfumers - Estb. 1868 - Sesqui Centennial - 1776-1926," tooled lip w/original neck foil, smooth base, 2 1/2" h. **$96**

Log, clear, upright log embossed "Uncle Tom Log," smooth base, tooled mouth, ca. 1890-1910, 3 3/4" h. **$101**

Male Dog Sitting, tall milk glass bottle w/cylindrical neck, oval reserve on front w/original label-under-glass reading "Port," embossed under base "J. L. Dawes Patent Applied For," late 19th c., flaking on lip, minor loss to edge of label, 11 1/2" h. **$770**

Opera binoculars, clear w/original metal brackets, focusing mechanism & stopper w/screw caps, 98% original neck labels for "Bradley's Opera Bouquet Cologne - New York," ca. 1885-1910, 4 1/4" h. **$224**

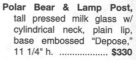

Polar Bear & Lamp Post, tall pressed milk glass w/ cylindrical neck, plain lip, base embossed "Depose," 11 1/4" h. **$330**

FLASKS

Pocket watch, clear, tooled mouth, smooth base, 100% of original paper labels of a watch face & "Extract Magnolia," metal neck band & hanger, original cork w/some advertising wrapped around it, ca. 1890-1910, 2 7/8" h. **$146**

Pot belly stove, clear, tooled mouth, smooth base, ca. 1890-1910, 4 3/4" h. **$224**

Soldier, clear, standing figure, tooled lip, pontil-scarred base, Europe, ca. 1890-1920, 9 3/4" h. **$34**

Flasks

Scottish soldier, medium olive green, standing figure wearing a kilt, pontil- scarred base, tooled mouth, probably Scottish, ca. 1890-1915, 4 7/8" h. **$280**

GI-38 - Washington bust below "The Father of His Country" - Taylor bust, "Gen. Taylor Never Surrenders, Dyottville Glass Works, Philada.," sheared mouth, smooth edges, pontil scar, medium to deep pink amethyst, small chip on Taylor side near base repaired, pt. **$1,232**

GI-39 - Washington bust below "The Father of His Country" - Taylor bust below "Gen Taylor Never Surrenders," smooth edges, sheared lip, pontil, light apple green, seed bubbles, qt...... **$235**

FLASKS

GI-39 - Washington bust below "The Father of His Country" - Taylor bust below "Gen Taylor Never Surrenders," smooth edges, sheared lip, pontil, medium emerald green, qt. **$840**

GI-48 - Washington bust below "The Father of His Country" - blank oval on reverse, sheared & tooled lip, open pontil, smooth edges, medium to light bluish green, sliver off edge of base, pt. **$336**

GI-51 - Washington bust below "The Father of His Country" - Taylor bust below "Gen Taylor Never Surrenders" smooth edges, sheared mouth, iron pontil, medium sapphire blue, qt. **$2,800**

GI-55c - Washington bust w/short queue & plain toga - Taylor bust w/collar decorations & tie, smooth edges, sheared mouth, pontil scar, medium emerald green, pt. **$1,008**

GI-72 - Taylor bust (facing left) w/"Rough and Ready" below - Ringgold bust (facing left) w/"Major" in semicircle above bust & "Ringgold" below bust, heavy vertical ribbing, sheared mouth, pontil, clear w/amethstine tint, pt. **$1,344**

GI-75 - Taylor bust facing right wearing uniform, "Zachary Taylor" above & "Rough & Ready" below - Tall corn stalk below "Corn For The World," smooth edges, sheared lip, pontil, greenish aqua, few areas of light inside stain, pt. **$1,064**

GII-40 - American eagle below rays & above olive branch & arrows, perched one oval panel lined w/ beading - same reverse, vertically ribbed sides, sheared & tooled lip, open pontil, emerald green, pt. **$4,200**

GII-47 - American eagle facing right grasping olive branch & arrow below three four-point stars - Tree w/foliage, vertically ribbed sides w/heavy medial rib, sheared & tooled lip, open pontil, aqua, qt. **$840**

GII-55 - American eagle & shield below thirteen small five-point stars - large & small bunches of grapes, fine vertical ribbing on sides, sheared & tooled lip, open pontil, dark chocolate amber, crude, qt. **$3,640**

GII-68 - American eagle in flight in downward position - large anchor w/"New London" in banner above & "Glass Works" in banner below, iron pontil on base, applied double collar mouth, smooth sides, yellow olive, pt. ... **$3,080**

GII-106 - American eagle w/shield facing left, holding banner, above oval panel w/"Pittsburgh PA" obverse - same on reverse w/plain panel, applied ring top, smooth base, smooth edges, ca. 1860, dark olive green, pt. **$476**

GII-109 - American eagle w/head to right above oval obverse & reverse, w/"Pittsburgh, PA" in oval obverse & plain oval on reverse, narrow vertical side rib, applied collared mouth w/ring, smooth base, small chip on inside of lip, yellowish amber w/olive tone, 1/2 pt. **$1,344**

GII-113 - American eagle w/head to left w/banner in beak above oval obverse & reverse, w/"Pittsburgh, PA - McC & Co" in oval obverse & plain oval on reverse, narrow vertical side rib, applied collared mouth w/ring, smooth base, light sapphire or ice blue, pt. **$532**

GII-142 - American eagle w/ pennant in beak & in talons above monument w/scroll ornament flanking a small oval at top supported by a gallery of 22 narrow ribs over a panel enclosing a six-striped flag flying to right above a narrow plain base frame - Indian standing facing right, wearing a headdress & short skirt & shooting arrow, small dog & bare stylized tree w/small bird perched on top at far left above a scrolled frame enclosing an inscription "Cunninghams & Co. - Pittsburgh, PA." surrounding four small oval petals around a pearl, smooth edges & base, applied mouth band, horizontal string of glass inside neck, weak impression, sapphire blue, qt. **$1,680**

GIV-27 - Masonic arch, pillars & pavement w/Masonic emblems & radiating triangle enclosing the letter "G" - American eagle w/"NEG Co" in oval frame below, vertically ribbed edges, sheared mouth, pontil scar, greenish aqua, some milky stain inside, very crude & bubbly, pt. ... **$448**

GIV-32 - Masonic arch, pillars & pavement enclosing farmer's arms w/sheaf of rye & implements - American eagle & shield facing right below "Zanesville" & above oval frame enclosing "Ohio" above "J. Shepard (S reversed) & Co.," sheared & tooled mouth, pontil, deep greenish aqua, crude & bubbly, pt. **$504**

Dealers exhibiting at shows normally place their best merchandise front and center. Items of lesser regard are typically placed where they get less exposure. Remember to view a display area thoroughly because the item you're looking for might be displayed under a dealer's table. If one of these items is what you want, it's likely the dealer will be more willing to consider an offer.

GIV-32 - Masonic arch, pillars & pavement enclosing farmer's arms w/sheaf of rye & implements - American eagle & shield facing right below "Zanesville" & above oval frame enclosing "Ohio" above "J. Shepard (S reversed) & Co.," sheared & tooled mouth, pontil, yellow w/amber tone, pt. ... **$2,460**

GVIII-3 - Sunburst w/twenty-four rounded rays obverse & reverse, horizontal corrugated edges, sheared & tooled lip, pontil scar, olive green, pt. **$1,008**

GVIII-9 - Sunburst w/twenty-nine triangular sectioned rays, obverse & reverse, center raised oval w/"KEEN" in reverse on obverse & w/"P & W" on reverse w/twenty-nine rays, sheared & tooled lip, pontil scar, olive amber, 1/2 pt. **$784**

GVIII-14 - Sunburst w/twenty-one triangular sectioned rays, obverse & reverse, sunburst centered by ring w/a dot in middle, sheared & tooled lip, pontil scar, medium bluish green, 1/2 pt. **$2,690**

GVIII-23 - Sunburst w/thirty-six slender rays forming a scalloped ellipse w/five small oval ornaments in center - similar but variations in size of center oval ornaments, sheared & tooled lip, open pontil, light yellowish green (citron), pt. **$1,064**

GIX-34 - Scroll w/large eight-point star above a large pearl over a large fleur-de-lis obverse & reverse, vertical medial rib on edge, sheared & tooled lip, pontil scar, yellowish amber, 1/2 pt. **$962**

GIX-34a - Scroll w/large eight-point star above a medium-sized pearl over a large fleur-de-lis obverse & reverse, vertical medial rib on edge, sheared & tooled lip, pontil scar, medium yellowish green, 1/2 pt. **$616**

FLASKS

GIX-36 - Scroll w/medium-sized eight-point star above a medium-sized pearl over a large fleur-de-lis obverse & reverse, vertical medial rib on edge, sheared & tooled lip, pontil scar, medium sapphire blue, 1/2 pt. **$1,456**

GX-19 - Summer Tree - Winter Tree, smooth sides, double collar mouth, open pontil, yellowish olive, shallow open bubble on edge of base, qt. **$2,800**

GX-30 - Trapper leaning on rifle below "The Great Western" - stag w/large antlers & head turned looking back, broad flat sides, "C" on smooth base, applied ringed mouth, aqua, pt. **$784**

GXI-23 - "For Pike's Peak" in large letters above prospector w/ tools standing on oblong frame - American eagle w/head turned right & holding a banner above an oval panel, applied ringed mouth, smooth base, yellowish amber, thin flake off side of lip, 1/2 pt. **$1,568**

GXI-27 - "For Pike's Peak" above prospector w/knapsack on shoulder & walking w/a cane above an oval - American eagle w/shield & banner above oval, applied ringed mouth, smooth base, golden yellowish amber, pt. **$4,480**

GXII-21 - Shield with clasped hands above five groups of three vertical bars & a blank oval, below an arch of 13 stars & "Union" - American eagle aop a shield & holding a long banner w/"A & Co." in its beak, a large empty oval peaked in the center top & bottom below, applied ringed lip, smooth base, medium sapphire blue, shallow flake on lip, pt. **$4,200**

GXII-33 - Clasped hands above oval all inside shield w/"Union" above shield - American eagle above shield-shaped frame, applied mouth, smooth base, amber, 1/2 pt. **$190**

GXII-40 - Clasped hands above oval w/"FA & Co.," all inside shield w/"Union" above - small cannon & large American flag, applied ringed mouth, smooth base, amber, thin flake on applied ring pt. **$532**

GXIII-11 - Soldier standing on patch of ground holding rifle & pointing to drum above bevel-edged narrow rectangular bar inscribed "BALT. MD." - Ballet dancer on patch of ground holding tambourine above bevel-edged narrow rectangular bar inscribed "Chapman," smooth edges, applied ringed mouth, smooth base, teal blue, crude & pebbly, shallow chip on lip, pt. **$532**

GXIII-11 Soldier standing on patch of ground holding rifle & pointing to drum above bevel-edged narrow rectangular bar inscribed "BALT. MD." - Ballet dancer on patch of ground holding tambourine above bevel-edged narrow rectangular bar inscribed "Chapman," smooth edges, sheared & tooled lip, open pontil, emerald green, crude & pebbly, pt. **$3,360**

Chestnut, free-blown w/outward rolled lip, open pontil, yellowish olive amber, 6 5/8" h. **$364**

Chestnut, ten-diamond patt., tooled flared out lip, pontil, bold design, amber, early 19th c., 5 1/2" h. **$5,320**

A freeblown bottle is one in which the glassblower has used only a blowpipe and has molded the final shape by hand, rather than blowing the blob of glass into a mold.

FLASKS

Pattern molded, flattened pumpkin-shaped, twenty vertical ribs, two-part mold, small applied round collared mouth, pontiled base, yellowish olive, probably Keene Marlboro Street Glass Works, Keene, New Hampshire, pt., 6 3/4" h. **$4,760**

Pattern molded, flattened rounded shape w/short neck & sheared mouth, pontil scar, ten-diamond patt., Midwest U.S.A., probably Zanesville, Ohio, 1815-30, brilliant golden amber, exterior high point wear, 4 3/4" h. **$420**

Pattern molded, plump flattened Pitkin- type, eighteen vertical ribs, Emil Larson, America, 1920-30, sheared mouth, pontil scar, bright amethyst, 6 1/4" h. **$560**

Inks

An interesting label can significantly add to the value of an antique bottle. The more color and design, the better, but condition is also important too. In an auction listing, the amount of the original label remaining is typically listed in a percentage of the total.

Cathedral, medium electric cobalt blue, master size, six Gothic arch panels embossed at the bottom "CA - RT - ER - CA - RT - ER," ABM lip, smooth base marked "Carter's," ca. 1925-35, 9 7/8" h. **$112**

Cylindrical, master size, cobalt blue, "Harrison's Columbian Ink," applied mouth, open pontil, ca. 1840-60, pinhead size flake off base edge, 9 5/8" h. **$3,360**

Cylindrical, cream-colored stoneware w/bluish grey glaze, master-size, 99% of the original colorful paper label w/"Carter's French Railroad Copying Ink - The Carter's Ink Co. Boston, New York, Chicago," w/a scene of an early train, minor discoloration to labels, ca. 1880-95, 7 3/4" h. **$840**

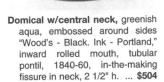

Domical w/central neck, greenish aqua, embossed around sides "Wood's - Black. Ink - Portland," inward rolled mouth, tubular pontil, 1840-60, in-the-making fissure in neck, 2 1/2" h. ... **$504**

Octagonal w/angled shoulder to short wide cylindrical neck, yellowish olive, embossed around the sides "Farleys - Ink," sheared mouth, pontil scar, probably a Stoddard glasshouse, Stoddard, New Hampshire, 1845-60, weak embossing, 1 7/8" h. **$840**

Cylindrical, medium blue green, "Hover Phila.," master size, open pontil, applied mouth w/ tooled pour spout, ca. 1840-60, 9 1/4" h. **$560**

Turtle-form, deep amber, "J & I E M," smooth base, tooled mouth, ca. 1875-85, 1 3/4" h. **$392**

Beware of fake labels attached to genuine but plain, low-value antique bottles. Modern high quality photocopiers and offset printers can produce convincing replicas.

Octagonal, aqua, short neck w/cupped applied mouth, open pontil scar, paneled embossed "Harrison's - Columbian - Ink - Patent," 98% original paper label reading "Harrison's Columbian Ink - Black...," ca. 1840-60, small chip on underside of lip (ILLUS. of front & back) **$560**

Twelve-sided cylindrical, master size, light to medium yellowish olive, heavily ribbed shoulder, cylindrical neck w/applied collared mouth w/pouring spout, open pontil scar, ca. 1830-60, 5 3/4" h. **$5,040**

Twelve-sided w/central neck, deep cobalt blue, gallon size, central neck, iron pontil, applied mouth, "Harrison's Columbian Ink" embossed on sides & shoulder, one of only five or six known to exist, ca. 1845-60, 11 1/3" h. **$30,240**

INKS

Umbrella-type (8-panel cone shape), cobalt blue, inward rolled mouth, pontil scar, 1840-60, 2 1/2" h. **$2,464**

Umbrella-type (8-panel cone shape), dark yellowish green w/ olive tone, inward rolled mouth, pontil scar, 1840-60, pinhead-sized flake on one base corner, 2 1/4" h. **$672**

Umbrella-type (8-panel cone shape), deep olive green, short neck w/rolled lip, open pontil, ca. 1840-60, slight outside dullness, tiny open bubble near base, 2 1/2" h. **$258**

Medicines

ABL Myers AM - Rock Rose - New Haven, rectangular w/paneled sides & beveled corners, applied heavy collared mouth, iron pontil scar, ca. 1845-60, brilliant bluish green, 9 1/2" h. **$5,600**

Barrell's Indian Liniment - H.C.O. Cary, rectangular w/paneled sides, rolled lip, open pontil scar, ca. 1840-60, aqua, 4 3/4" h. **$112**

Birmingham's (Dr.) - Antibillious - Blood Purifier, paneled cylinder, smooth base, applied square collar mouth, medium teal blue, ca. 1865-75, 8 5/8" h. **$1,344**

Buckhout's (E.A.) Dutch Liniment (design of standing man) - Prepared at Mechanicville Saratoga Co. N.Y., flattened rectangle w/rounded shoulders & rolled lip, open pontil scar, ca. 1840-60, bluish aqua, 4 3/4" h. **$560**

A pontil is a circular scar left on the bottom center of a handblown bottle. After the glassblower blows a bottle with a blowpipe, he attaches a pontil rod to the bottom of the bottle with a small blob of molten glass. Then he breaks the blowpipe from the neck and forms the lip of the bottle. Once the lip is finished, he snaps the pontil rod off the base of the bottle, leaving the pontil.

Carter's Extract of Smart Weed - Erie, rectangular w/paneled sides, tall neck w/applied sloping mouth, open pontil scar, ca. 1840-60, aqua, 5 1/2" h. ... **$258**

Carter's Spanish Mixture, cylindrical, applied sloping double collar mouth, ring- open pontil, 99 percent original paper label, ca. 1845-55, forest green, 8" h. **$1,456**

Cerisiaux Rheumatic Antidote or Electric Liniment - New York, rectangular w/paneled sides, applied sloping mouth, open pontil scar, ca. 1840-60, aqua, 5 1/4" h. **$269**

Clouds Cordial, rectangular form w/paneled tapering sides, smooth base, applied mouth, medium yellow olive, ca. 1870-85, 10 1/2" h. **$840**

Duffy's Tower Mint Cure, tower form embossed w/stones, windows & doors, smooth base, applied mouth, embossed w/ image of castle & "Trade Mark Est 1842," yellowish amber, ca. 1875-85, slight bruise in lip where chip has been partially polished out, 9" h. **$616**

Ellel's (Dr.) Liver Regulator - South Bend, Ind., rectangular w/arched panels & rounded shoulders, tall neck w/tooled lip, smooth base, ca. 1885-1910, cobalt blue, cleaned, 5 3/4" h. **$269**

MEDICINES

Fairchild's - Sure - Remedy, cylindrical w/alternating wide & narrow panels, rounded shoulder, applied sloping mouth, open pontil scar, ca. 1840-60, aqua, very rare, 7 7/8" h. **$1,239**

Fisher's Seaweed Extract Manx Shrub - [design of shrub] - Registered Company Ulverston - Quarrie's Patent, triangular form w/bulged neck, tooled lip, smooth base, yellow green, England, ca. 1890-1910, 5 1/4" h. **$616**

Force's Asth-Manna - Trade Mark Reg. - Asthma Bronchitis, Colds, Etc - S.B. Force M'fg. Chemist - San Francisco, Cal., square w/narrow beveled corners, tooled mouth, smooth base, medium yellowish amber, ca. 1885-1900, 8 7/8" h. **$146**

Girolamo - Pagliano, square w/ flat shoulder, inward rolled lip, open pontil, medium lime green, American, ca. 1840-60, 4 1/4" h. **$146**

Gun Wa's Chinese Remedy - Warranted Entirely Vegetable and Harmless, square w/beveled corners, tall neck w/applied sloping collar mouth, smooth base, yellow w/amber tone, lightly cleaned, 7 7/8" h. **$672**

Guysott's (Dr.) - Compound - Extract of - Yellow Dock & - Sarsaparilla, square w/beveled corners, applied double collar mouth, smooth base, ca. 1855-70, bluish aqua, tiny ding on edge of shoulder, 9 5/8" h. **$336**

Guysott's (Dr.) - Compound - Extract of - Yellow Dock & - Sarsaparilla, square w/beveled corners, applied sloping collared mouth, crude iron pontil scar, ca. 1840-60, light to medium bright bluish green, 8 7/8" h. ... **$2,016**

Guysott's (Dr.) - Compound - Extract of - Yellow Dock & - Sarsaparilla, square w/beveled corners, applied sloping collared mouth, pontil scar, ca. 1840-60, aqua w/ 90 percent original stained paper label, 9 1/8" h. **$1,232**

Harrison's (Doct.) - Tonic - Chalybeate, rectangular w/ sloping shoulder, smooth base, applied mouth, medium emerald green, ca. 1865-75, 9" h. .. **$952**

Howard's - Vegetable - Cancer and - Canker Syrup, rectangular w/beveled corners, rounded shoulders & applied square collared mouth, pontil scar, a Stoddard, New Hampshire glasshouse, ca. 1846-60, yellowish olive, interior bubble burst w/some residue, 7 3/8" h. **$14,560**

Jacob's - Cholera & - Dysentery - Cordial, square shape w/applied mouth, open pontil, number of seed bubbles, aqua, ca. 1840-60, 6 3/4" h. **$134**

Keeley's (Dr. L.E.) Double Chloride of Gold Cure For Drunkenness - A Tested and Infallible Remedy Discovered by Dr. L.E. Keeley Dwight, Ills. - K.C.C., rectangular w/sloping shoulders, tooled mouth w/pour spout, smooth base, some very light interior stains, ca. 1885-1900, 5 1/2" h. **$134**

Kidder (Mrs. E.) Dysentery Cordial Boston, cylindrical w/rounded shoulder, applied sloping collar mouth, open pontil, aqua, 7 3/4" h. **$134**

Lindsey's - Blood + Searcher - Holli-daysburg, rectangular w/beveled corners & paneled sides, applied double collared mouth, smooth base, light to medium bluish green, probably Pittsburgh, ca. 1860-70, shallow sliver on edge of base, 9" h. **$420**

Lindsey's - Blood + Searcher - Pitts-burgh, rectangular w/paneled sides, applied double collared mouth, smooth base, bluish aqua, pinhead flake at base corner, ca. 1860-70, 8 1/2" h. **$101**

Lyon's Powder - B. & P. N.Y., cylindrical w/rolled lip, pontil, deep purple amethyst, ca. 1840-60, 4 1/2" h. **$308**

Masta's Indian - Pulmonic - Balsam - Lowell, Mass., rectangular w/ applied mouth, open pontil, bluish aqua, ca. 1840-60, 5 3/4" h. **$308**

Mowe's (Dr.) Cough Balsam - Lowell, Mass., rectangular w/paneled sides, applied double collar mouth, open pontil, aqua, ca. 1840-60, 5 3/4" h. **$392**

Old Dr. - J. Townsend's - Sarsaparilla - New York, square w/beveled corners, applied sloping collar mouth, iron pontil, bluish green, ca. 1845-60, some light interior haze, 9 3/4" h. **$616**

Old Dr. - J. Townsend's - Sarsaparilla - New York, square w/beveled corners, applied sloping collar mouth, iron pontil, medium bluish green, ca. 1845-60, shallow chip on edge of base, crude, 9 5/8" h. **$392**

Quinn's Pioneer Blood Renewer - Macon Medicine Co. - Macon, Ga., rectangular w/side panels, applied double collar mouth, smooth base, some areas of milk stain, shallow flake on side of base, medium amber, ca. 1875-1885, 11" h. **$190**

Radam's (Wm.) - (design of man beating a skeleton) - Registered Trade Mark Dec. 13, 1887 (in shield below) - Germ, Bacteria or Fungus Destroyer, square w/rounded shoulder, cylindrical neck w/tooled lip, smooth base, clear, 10" h. **$448**

Vaughn's - Vegetable Lithontriptic Mixture - Buffalo, square w/ arched paneled sides, applied sloping collared mouth, smooth base, bluish aqua, ca. 1860-70, light milky inside stain, 8 1/8" h. **$246**

U.S.A. - Hosp. Dept., cylindrical w/ rounded shoulder, applied double collared mouth, smooth base, olive w/slight bit of yellow, possibly Baltimore Glass Works, Baltimore, Maryland, ca. 1860-70, small very shallow burst bubble on shoulder, 9 1/8" h. **$672**

MEDICINES

Warner's Safe Cure (motif of safe) Melbourne, Aus - London, Eng - Toronto, Can. - Rochester, N.Y., U.S.A., oval w/applied blob mouth, smooth base, yellow w/ amber tone, lightly cleaned, ca. 1885-95, 9 5/8" h. **$190**

Webber's (Dr. Jacob) Invigorating Cordial - T. Jones Agent & Proprietor - New York, rectangular w/paneled sides, applied double collar mouth, open pontil, aqua, lightly cleaned, ca. 1845-60, 10" h. **$504**

Clock face, embossed w/clock face w/Roman numerals & "Bininger's Regulator - 19 Broad St. - New York," open pontil, applied double collar mouth, amber, America, ca. 1855-70, spotty outside stains, 5 3/4" h. **$420**

Mineral Waters, Sodas & Sarsaparillas

Comstock Gove & Co., ten-pin shape w/smooth base & applied blob mouth, medium bluish green, some minor exterior wear, ca. 1855-70, 7 1/4" h. **$504**

Defender Bottling Works - 1732 2nd Ave. N.Y. - This Bottle To Be Returned, smooth base, clambroth, ca. 1885- 1900, 9 3/8" h. **$364**

Guilford Mineral - GMWS (inside circle) - Guilford - VT - Spring Water, smooth base, deep teal green, ca. 1865-75, qt. **$112**

Nash (H.) & Co - Root Beer - Cincinnati, twelve-sided w/ tapering shoulder to the applied mouth, iron pontil, cobalt blue, ca. 1845-60, professionally cleaned, 8 5/8" h. **$1,120**

Haddock & Sons, modified ten pinform soda water, outward rolled mouth, pontil scar, attributed to the Coventry Glassworks, Coventry, Connecticut, yellowish olive, ca. 1825-35, tiny bruise on lip, 1/2 pt., 6 1/2" h. **$1,680**

Middletown Mineral Spring Co. - Nature's Remedy - Middletown, Vt., cylindrical w/tall neck & applied sloping double collar mouth, smooth base, emerald green, ca. 1865-75, qt. **$280**

Oak Orchard - Acid Springs - H.W. Bostwick - Agt. No. 574 - Broadway, New York, cylindrical w/applied sloping double collar mouth, embossed on smooth base "Glass From F. Hitchins Factory - Lockport, N.Y.," deep tobacco amber, ca. 1865-75, small bruise on side of neck, qt. **$78**

Oak Orchard Acid Springs, Address G.W. Merchant, Lockport, N.Y. (around shoulder), cylindrical w/applied sloping double collar mouth, smooth base, Lockport green, ca. 1865-75, qt., 9" h. **$112**

Ogden Porter (in slug plate), cylindrical w/tall neck & applied mouth, red iron pontil mark, deep bluish aqua, some exterior scratching, ca. 1840-60, 7" h. **$246**

Pickle Jars

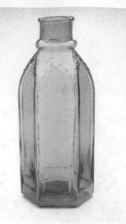

Aqua, barrel shape, six-rib, half-gallon size, iron pontil, rolled lip, ca. 1855-65, 10 5/8" h........ **$532**

Bright green, six-sided cathedral-type w/Gothic windows, outward rolled mouth, iron pontil, ca. 1845-60, 13 1/4" h. **$532**

Honey amber, six-sided cathedral-type w/simple Gothic windows, cylindrical ringed neck w/outward rolled mouth, smooth base, ca. 1860-80, rare color, 13 1/8" h. **$960**

Light to medium bright green, four-sided cathedral-type w/ Gothic windows on three sides, cylindrical ringed neck w/outward rolled mouth, pontil scar, Willington Glass Works, West Willington, Connecticut, ca. 1840-60, some very minor haze spots, 11 1/4" h. **$1,792**

Light to medium bright green, four-sided cathedral-type w/ Gothic windows, outward rolled mouth, smooth base, Willington Glass Works, West Willington, Connecticut, 1860-70, 11 3/4" h. **$2,240**

Light to medium bright green, four-sided cathedral-type w/three fancy Gothic windows, outward rolled mouth, smooth base, ca. 1860-70, shallow tiny flake on top of mouth, 11 3/4" h. **$1,120**

Light yellowish green, squared upright cloverleaf-form, outward rolled mouth, pontil scar, probably a Stoddard, New Hampshire glasshouse, ca. 1840-60, 7 3/4" h. **$1,008**

Medium green, six-sided cathedral-type w/ornate Gothic windows, cylindrical ringed neck w/outward rolled mouth, smooth base, ca. 1860-70, 13" h. **$2,464**

Olive amber, four-sided cathedral-type w/fancy Gothic arch windows on three sides, ringed cylindrical neck w/outward rolled mouth, pontil scar, severely cracked in shoulder & one panel, probably Willington Glass Works, West Willington, Connecticut, 1840-60, 8 1/8" h. **$2,464**

Rich blue green, four-sided cathedral-type w/Gothic windows, applied ring mouth, smooth base, ca. 1860-70, 14 1/8" h. **$1,120**

Yellow olive, cylindrical w/side neck & tooled mouth, smooth base, embossed w/"Skilton, Foote & Co's Bunker Hill Pickles Trade Mark" & image of monument, ca. 1880-95, light overall inside stain, 7 5/8" h. **$45**

Medium blue green, four-sided cathedral-type w/Gothic windows below rare clamshell design, applied mouth, smooth base, ca. 1860-70, 13 3/8" h. **$1,008**

Poisons

Cobalt blue, cylindrical w/overall embossed diamond lattice design, tooled lip, smooth base marked "H.B. Co.," ca. 1890-1910, 7" h. **$112**

Cobalt blue, triangular w/rounded shoulder & tooled lip, smooth base, marked "Poison - (molded one-winged owl) - The Owl Drug Co.," ca. 1890-1910, cleaned, tiny bruise on lip, 7 7/8" h. **$134**

Deep cobalt blue, lattice & diamond design full of seed bubbles, tooled mouth, "U.S.P.H.S." on smooth base, gallon size, ca. 1890-1910, 13 1/4" h. **$3,360**

Moss green, six-sided oblong form w/horizontal ribbing & four panels w/"Poison," tooled mouth, smooth base marked "C.L.G. Co. - Patent Applied For," ca. 1890-1910, 5 1/2" h. **$168**

Smoky bluish green, cylindrical w/ overall embossed diamond lattice design, tooled lip, smooth base, ca. 1890-1910, some very faint inside haze, 4 5/8" h. **$308**

Aqua, w/greenish tint, rectangular w/wide flattened shoulders, tooled mouth, smooth base, embossed "Poison" on each side, ca. 1890-1910, 5 5/8" h. **$1,064**

Whiskey & Other Spirits

Spirits, free-blown mallet-form, tall tapering neck w/applied string lip, open pontil, England, ca. 1735-45, deep olive green, several chips on string lip, 5 1/4" d., 6 3/4" h. **$784**

Spirits, free-blown onion-form, tall tapering neck w/applied string lip, open pontil, Germany, 1720-40, medium emerald green, light outside haze, 5 1/2" d., 6 1/2" h. **$157**

Spirits, free-blown bulbous onion-form, tall tapering neck w/applied string lip, open pontil, England, 1700-10, olive amber, milky inside stain, double-magnum size, 9" d., 9 5/8" h. **$2,800**

Spirits, free-blown squatty onion-form, tall tapering neck w/applied string lip, open pontil, Holland, 1720-40, yellowish olive, light outside haze, 5 1/2" d., 7 1/4" h. **$123**

BOXES

Art Nouveau box, inlaid wood, rectangular hinged top ornately inlaid w/a large center daisy-like blossom framed by numerous smaller leafy blossoms & dots, the low sides made from stained wood & trimmed w/a continuous narrow band of inlaid abalone around the bottom edge, original finish, early 20th c., unsigned, minor repair, 10" l. **$420**

Candle box, painted & decorated pine, long rectangular form w/square nail construction, a sloping hinged lid & a high arched backplate w/a hanging hole, original darkened salmon paint w/ a simple painted star & basket of flowers design in white & yellow, probably Pennsylvania, early 19th c., some wear, 5 x 12 1/4", 7 5/8" h. **$5,980**

Desk box, Arts & Crafts style, hand-hammered copper & brass, the wide copper rectangular top domed in the center & mounted w/large brass spearpoint strap hinges, the sides w/a pierced copper Gothic arch design over brass panels, brass brackets at each corner, original patina, unmarked, early 20th c., 8" l., 3" h. **$480**

Desk box, Arts & Crafts style, hand-hammered copper, the rectangular top w/a low pyramidal shape centered by a large square pointed handle, flat sides slightly flared at the bottom, original patina, attributed to Gustav Stickley, early 20th c., 10" l., 5 1/2" h. **$1,200**

Before going to an antiques market, take along a few small items you no longer wish to keep. You may be able to find a dealer willing to take them in trade toward the purchase of something of greater value. Look for dealers who carry similar types of antiques and collectibles. If one dealer is not interested in your items, he may direct you to someone who might be.

Document box, cov., painted & decorated pine, nailed construction, long rectangular form w/a hinged flat cover, the top decorated w/a large colorful basket of flowers in a framed & double pinstripe border w/ fanciful finish, the front base decorated w/a similar fanciful basket of flowers flanked by deep red scroll designs, each end w/a colorful bold large spray of flowers, the back decorated w/a series of sponged dots, the interior painted white, cover attached w/ old wire hinges, originally w/a simple leather heart attached to front now missing, couple of small splits on the front, found in Massachusetts, 19th c., 6 1/4 x 12 1/2" **$2,070**

School box, curly maple, rectangular dovetailed form w/ flat hinged cover, delicately painted designs, mainly in green, red & tan including foliage borders, agricultural tools & sheaves of wheat around the sides w/a finely done scene on the top of a dove, basket of roses, quiver of arrows & caduceus, all intertwined w/ribbons & vining flowers, brass ball feet, divided interior lined w/ pink paper w/penciled notes, alligatoring to the heavy varnish, New England, early 19th c., 6 1/4 x 10 1/4", 3 5/8" h. **$6,613**

Hanging box, painted & decorated poplar & pine, a deep rectangular dovetailed case w/a sloped hinged cover opening to a deep well w/divided interior above a narrow lower drawer w/small brass knob & divided interior, the tall narrow waisted backboard w/a heart-form lobed top around a large hanging hole, overall old dark olive green background paint w/narrow dark blue border, the center of the cover & top front panel painted w/a large red white-trimmed rose w/shaded green leaves, the drawer front w/a matching leaf sprig, old heavy varnish w/touch-ups on sides w/cover pegs broken out, some wear & damage, attributed to the Pennsylvania Amish, first-half 19th c., 7 x 10 1/2", overall 15 1/2" h. **$4,370**

Storage box, cov., painted & decorated, rectangular w/a hinged low-domed top w/scalloped ends painted on the exterior w/a red background w/ multiple colorful fleur-de-lis berries & flowers in white, blue, yellow, green & black, the wire han-dle opens top to reveal a white-painted interior decorated w/a long leafy sunflower-like blossom on a leaf stem in shades of blue, green, pink & yellow, interior lidded compartment, the exterior w/ an overall dark red painted background, the ends painted w/large rounded stylized flowerheads, the front w/an ornate leafy scroll & berry design in shades of blue, white, black, brown & green, low serpentine front & side aprons, Scandinavia, 19th c., couple of old age splits, 6 x 10 1/4", 6 1/2" h. **$805**

BOXES

Storage box, painted & decorated pine, the rectangular top w/molded edges opening to a well lined w/block-printed wallpaper in green & grey on ivory, original dark red paint stenciled in gold w/starflowers, hearts & arrows, attributed to Soap Hollow, Pennsylvania, some areas of wear, reset hinges, 9 1/2 x 14 1/2", 5" h. **$259**

Storage box, wallpaper-covered, square w/a fitted flat lid, the base wrapped in a paper w/a lattice & florette & dot design, the top paper w/ flowerheads & undulating bands, some fading, first half 19th c., 3 1/4" w., 2" h. **$259**

Storage box, painted & decorated pine, rectangular w/a hinged domed top, each side & cover w/a reddish ground bordered by pale yellow, the sides w/large stylized red & white tulips & carnations w/green leaves, the top painted w/a large lattice urn filled w/flowers, tin & wire staple hinges & hasp, penciled note on inside top reads "Made in 1802," attributed to Heinrich Bucher, Berks County, Pennsylvania, some wear, minor edge damage, 6 1/8 x 9 1/4", 4 3/4" h. **$12,938**

Storage box, rectangular w/slide-out cover, painted & decorated poplar, dovetailed sides & wooden pegged bottom, original decoration w/a dark brown stained ground decorated on the sides & flat top w/stylized large tulips & petaled blossoms w/crosshatched center in thick yellow, orange & black, molded rim band decorated w/small white bands, thin base molding, attributed to Berks County, Pennsylvania, small flaked areas, cover w/corner damage, early 19th c., 8 x 12", 4 1/2" h. **$29,900**

CANDLESTICKS & CANDLEHOLDERS

Candelabra, gilt- and patinated-bronze, six- light, Louis XVI taste bouquet-style, a lobed scroll-footed base modeled as a short column trimmed w/floral swags supporting a seated putti holding aloft a large gilt-bronze bouquet fitted w/six up-turned candlesockets, not electrified, France, third quarter 19th c., 28" h., pr. **$2,530**

Candelabra, gilt-bronze & marble, four- light, a carved grey marble plinth base on tiny gilt-bronze paw feet supporting a bulbous urn-form pedestal w/a slender leaf- trimmed shaft issuing four scroll-trimmed upturned candlearms all centered by slender shaft w/upright scrolling finial, France, late 19th c., 22 1/2" h., pr. **$518**

Candelabra, gilt-bronze, seven-light, a round foot w/a domed acanthus leaf-cast top supporting a reeded standard below a fancy disk below the spiral-reeded top socket supporting six upturned spiraling & leaf-trimmed candlearms surrounding a central upright holder w/matching leaf decoration & a removable flame cap in the socket, French Empire style, France, ca. 1860, 29" h., pr. **$1,610**

Candelabra, gilt-bronze, three-light, Oriental taste, a square foot supporting a heavy dark patinated reeded column below the figure of an Oriental man on one & an Oriental woman on the other, each of them w/leafy scrolls w/ tiny bells issuing from their heads below a leaf-cast blossom supporting three leaf-trimmed up-turned & outswept candlearms ending in bird heads topped by leaf-cast inverted bell sockets, objects missing from hand of one figure, France, late 19th c., 20 1/2" h., pr. **$1,610**

CANDLESTICKS & CANDLEHOLDERS

Candelabra, patinated bronze, four-light, in the "Pompeian" taste, a tripod base w/three paw feet on disks w/scrolled leaves surrounding the tall slender reeded shaft w/a ring-turned urn-form top supporting the three upturned candlesocket arms in the form of an Ancient Roman lamp surrounding a central taller socket, Napoleon III-style, France, third quarter 19th c., 23 1/4" h., pr. **$1,840**

Candelabra, sterling silver, five-light, a large waisted & ogee-domed base w/four scroll feet, supporting a baluster-form standard set w/a detachable set of four reeded serpentine branches around a central short column, all topped by a candlesocket, decorated overall w/ elaborate chased gadroons & acanthus leaves, America, ca. 1920, 20" h., pr. **$2,070**

Candelabra, wrought iron, an arched tripod base w/penny feet supporting a slender tall rod fitted w/a spring-adjustable cross bridge w/the top bar fitted at each end w/a small cylindrical candle socket, 20th c., 12" w., 21 3/4" h. **$360**

Candelabrum, gilt-bronze, five-light, a large fancy tapering rectangular base on scrolled paw feet supporting an elaborate figural shaft composed of large & small angels surrounding a smoking altar all supporting five arched Gothic-style arms fitted w/a candle socket, a tall slender reeded central shaft, France, late 19th c., 41" h. **$863**

Candelabrum, sterling silver, five-light, Art Deco style, a paneled domed & stepped base tapering to a paneled standard topped by leafy scrolls & petals centered by a pine cone finial & issuing five slender reeded upturned arms ending in simple paneled candlesockets, designed by Johan Rohde for Georg Jensen Silversmithy, Denmark, ca. 1930, 17" h. **$11,353**

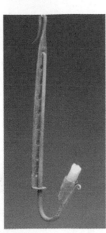

Candleholder, wrought iron trammel-type, a slender bar ending in a U-shape fitted w/a small cylindrical candle socket, the bar adjusting in a sawtooth trammel bar w/a long hooked top, some rust & pitting, early, adjusts for 14" to 22 1/2" **$173**

Candlestand, wooden, adjustable, a cricket-style Windsor base fitted w/a tall square wood shaft w/a turn-key adjustable bridge arm fitted w/four brass candle cups, early, 14 1/2" w., 44" h. **$201**

Candlestick, brass, a ring-turned socket above a turned knob & wide drip pan raised on a knob- and ring-turned shaft on a domed ringed base, hole in side of socket for candle removal, Europe, 17th c., 8 1/2" h. **$518**

• A trammel is a slotted bar that fits a corresponding holder. The slots allow the position of the holder to be adjusted by moving the holder up or down on the bar.

• The capstan style is based on a drum-shaped wheel known as a capstan, often used on ships, that is turned to raise or lower heavy weights, such as an anchor.

Candlestick, brass, capstan-style, a wide low cylindrical ring-trimmed base centered by a single short knobbed socket w/large extractor holes in the sides, minor damage, socket w/soldered repair, early, 5 1/4" d., 4 1/2" h. **$633**

Candlestick, gilt-brass, "Fonthill" style in the Gothic Revival taste, a triangular scroll-footed base composed of Gothic arch panels surrounding the ornate standard composed of Gothic designs in a knopped & stepped form topped by a pricket-type socket surrounded by a scalloped Gothic-style gallery, England, late 19th c., electrified, 44 1/2" h. **$2,070**

Candlesticks, brass-washed copper, Arts & Crafts style, hand-hammered, round base supporting a cylindrical stem below a dished drip pan & cylindrical socket, Roycrofters orb & cross mark, minor wear, early 20th c., 6 3/4" h., pr. **$489**

Candlesticks, brass, "King of Diamonds" patt., square foot w/beveled corners below the stepped base & ring-turned shaft w/a large diamond-cast center knob, tall socket w/flaring rim, bases marked, push-ups present, England, late 19th - early 20th c., 12 1/4" h. pr. **$460**

Candlesticks, brass, Federal style, a square stepped base tapering sides to the tall plain square & slightly flaring standard w/a flared, ringed top supporting a tall ringed bell-form socket w/a wide rolled rim, American, ca. 1790-1815, 10" h., pr. **$690**

Candlesticks, brass, Neoclassical taste w/a wide round raised foot w/a gadrooned rim & rayed center supporting a gently flaring shaft w/a gadrooned shoulder band below the socket, w/detachable bobeches, France, Restauration period, first quarter 19th c., 10" h., pr. **$690**

Candlesticks, brass, Queen Anne-style, an oblong octagonal base supporting a baluster- and ring-turned standard w/a cylindrical socket, side hole in socket for removing candle, probably England, 18th c., split in one stick, 8" h., pr. **$403**

Candlesticks, brass, the cylindrical stem composed of two discs & waisted sections topped by a tall cylindrical candle socket w/a flaring rim, a flaring round pedestal base on a square foot, England, ca. 1850, 8 7/8" h., pr. **$176**

Candlesticks, copper, hand-hammered Arts & Crafts style, a rectangular foot w/riveted double stems form the shaft below a bobeche & socket, Princess patt., stamped initials of Karl Kipp, good original patina, early 20th c., 8" h., pr. **$1,093**

Candlesticks, gilt-brass, slate & wood, Napoleon III style, each modeled as the figure of a seated putto holding aloft a candle socket, on black wood pedestal base wrapped w/a wide brass band embossed w/frolicking putti above the cylindrical black slate base, France, third quarter 19th c., 32" h., pr. **$1,265**

Candlesticks, gilt-bronze & enamel, pricket altar-type, the domed & scroll-pierced base raised on three outswept paw feet, the sides of the dome fitted w/round medallions w/a red enamel ground, one w/the initials "S.J.," one with building tools & the third w/flowers, each separated by a small jeweled cabochon, the tall ringed standard trimmed w/cast leaves & swags, a wide low scallop-topped bobeche around the pricket candleholder, probably from St. Joseph's Altar, France, late 19th c., 25" h., pr. **$978**

Candlesticks, sterling silver, Art Nouveau style, in the Athenic patt., a round ringed base applied w/leaves & openwork arched undulating bud supports continuing to the base of the tapering cylindrical stem chased w/swirling leaves, the vase-form sockets similarly decorated, w/removable circular nozzle, mark of Gorham Mfg. Co., Providence, Rhode Island, ca. 1905, 10 1/4" h., pr. **$10,158**

Candlesticks, wrought iron, a wide round dished base raised on three scroll feet, centering a very tall slender center shaft topped by a pricket-style candle holder fitted w/an open ring candle support, a flattened angled small candle arm about halfway down the shaft w/a small ringed candle holder, a small angled hanging hook further up the shaft, overall 23 1/2" h., pr. **$780**

Chamberstick, brass, a shallow round dished base w/a rim loop handle w/finger grip, the central cylindrical shaft w/a flattened rim, w/ejector knob on the shaft, 6" d., 4" h. **$143**

Rush light holder, iron & wood, heavy, roughly turned large wood block base supporting a tightly spiral-twisted wrought-iron upright w/a pliers-style top for gripping a rush light, the other arm of the hinged pliers also tightly twisted & angled to support a round candle pan, late 18th c., overall 10 3/4" h. **$575**

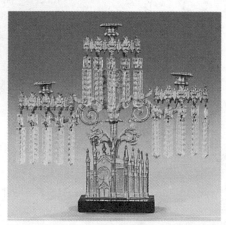

Girandole, gilt-brass & marble, three-light, Bigelow Chapel design, a rectangular black marble base supporting the silhouetted gilt model of a cathedral w/a reeded back upright mounted w/leafy scrolls & continuing up to a tall central scrolled shaft topped by a socket & a grapevine-cast ring suspending long facet-cut prisms, two scrolls arms at the sides, each ending in a matching socket & prism-hung ring, signed by W.F. Shaw, Boston, Massachusetts, ca. 1850, 17" w., 16 1/2" h. **$633**

Taperstick holders, sterling silver, a molded squared base w/chamfered shell-form corners & w/an engraved crest, a knopped- and ring-turned baluster stem supporting a ringed campana-form socket, William Grundy, London, England, 1748, 5" h., pr. **$3,910**

CANES & WALKING STICKS

Carved & painted wood cane, the arched handle realistically carved as a fox head w/an open mouth & tongue & small glass eyes h.p. w/a naturalistic painted finish, the neck continues into the varnished wood shaft w/a metal tip, late 19th c., age crack, handle 3 x 3", overall 36" l. (ILLUS. of two views of the handle) **$1,208**

Burl wood & stick walking stick, the burl knot handle carved w/a realistic head of a bearded man w/open mouth, inset glass eyes & turban-type head cover, a thin bone ferrule to the knotty stick shaft w/a nice dark patina, age cracks, late 19th - early 20th c., overall 39 1/2" l. **$201**

Carved & painted wood cane, the arched handle realistically carved w/a foxhound head w/natural painted coloring in tans, browns, black & white & inset eyes, neck continues into the mottled wood shaft w/a peeling varnish finish, iron tip, late 19th c., handle 1 1/4 x 2 1/2", overall 37 3/4" l. (ILLUS. of two views of the handle).. **$1,150**

Ebonized wood, ivory & horn cane, the ebonized wood shaft joined by a silver ferrule to the figural handle composed of a carved horn chick w/tiny glass eyes emerging from a carved elephant ivory egg, probably England, ca. 1900, overall 35 1/4" l. (ILLUS. of part)................................. **$1,008**

Carved & stained wood cane, the angled short wood handle carved as a realistic boar head w/a dark-stained head, inset glass eyes & ivory tusks, a narrow sterling silver ferrule w/English hallmarks, on a malacca shaft ending in a worn horn tip, one glass eye chips, late 19th - early 20th c., handle, 1 1/2 x 2 3/4", overall 35" l. (ILLUS. of two views)................. **$633**

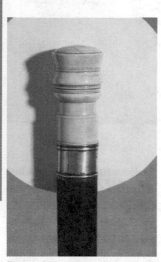

Ebony & ivory cane, the ebony shaft w/a horn ferrule joining it to the turned elephant ivory handle, the handle, when held to light to cast a shadow, showing a shadow portrait of the Emperor Napoleon I, carried by followers of the exiled emperor, France, ca. 1825, overall 36 1/4" l. (ILLUS. of handle & shadow) **$2,016**

Ebony, silver & synthetic ivory cane, the ebony shaft joined by a bronze ferrule to a figural handle w/a carved synthetic ivory head of a Victorian coachman wearing a silver cap & collar, England, second half 19th c., overall 36" l. (ILLUS. of part).................. **$952**

Enameled wood & ivory cane, the black enameled shaft w/a horn ferrule & gilt- metal collar joining it to the figural carved elephant ivory handle, the handle carved as a realistic cat head w/an articulated mouth opening to reveal a red tongue, pushing neck bow activates mouth, inset w/clear glass eyes, probably England, ca. 1890, overall 36 1/2" l. **$1,680**

Champleve is a technique in which depressions are carved into the surface of a metal and filled with enamel, then fired to melt the enamel. After cooling, the enamel is polished.

Champleve is similar to cloisonne, except that with cloisonne, the hollow areas that contain the enamel are formed by soldering strips of metal to the surface of the metal to form edges that hold the enamel.

Fruitwood & enameled silver, the fruit-wood shaft joined by a brass & iron ferrule to the round sterling quality silver handle, the handle decorated around the sides w/colorful enameled scrolls & flowers in the champleve manner, the top w/a fancy initial in the design, silver hallmarks are probably Swedish, ca. 1910, overall 34 1/4" l. (ILLUS. of part)..................... **$1,120**

Gold, quartz & tropical wood cane, the rich dark tropical wood shaft w/a white metal & iron ferrule connecting to the tau- shaped handle of gold, the presentation- type handle finely engraved overall w/leafy scrolls & inset w/double gold quartz inlays, handle at least 18k gold, America, ca. 1870, overall 36 1/4" l. **$6,160**

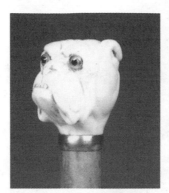

Ivory & ebony walking stick, the handle carved as the bust of a Victorian era lady w/her bosoms peeping over the front of her blouse, mounted on a silver plate ferrule on an ebony colored shaft fitted w/a horn tip, 35" l. .. **$1,438**

Ivory & malacca walking stick, the ivory handle carved as a realistic Bulldog head w/inset glass eyes, a gold-plated collar & malacca shaft, late 19th c., handle 2 x 2", overall 34 1/4" l. **$805**

Ivory & sterling silver cane, carved ivory handle mounted w/scalloped répoussé silver w/a floral design, the rosewood- type shaft fitted w/ a nickel silver tip, 36" l. **$661**

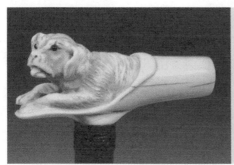

Ivory & mahogany or walnut cane, the T- shaped ivory handle carved as a Spaniel- like dog emerging from a large stylized shoe, head up w/open mouth & jet bead eyes, narrow embossed silver collar, light mahogany or walnut shaft w/a worn horn tip, late 19th c., handle 1 3/4 x 4", overall 33 3/4" l. (ILLUS. of two views of the handle).. **$920**

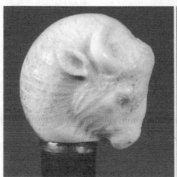

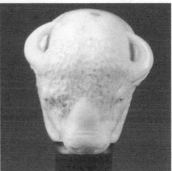

Ivory & rosewood walking stick, the ivory handle carved as a buffalo head w/open mouth, pierce-carved horns & nice patina, a thin silver collar & worn brass & iron ferrule attached to the wooden shaft, late 19th c., handle 1 3/4 x 1 3/4", overall 34 1/2" l. (ILLUS. of two views of the handle) **$920**

CANES & WALKING STICKS

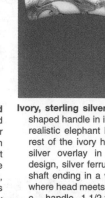

Ivory, silver & carved wood cane, folk art- style, a carved ivory handle w/sterling silver mount w/scrolling details on a long chestnut or oak shaft deeply carved w/a snake coiling down the entire length, also carved w/numerous figures, the top one probably a black man, second one a bearded Civil War soldier wearing a kepi, then two Civil War soldiers above various symbols like anvils, fighting hands w/knife, hand w/hammer, carved head, the base w/nearly full-relief carved man holding a walking stick, fine mellow varnished patina, mid-19th c., 36" l. **$4,313**

Ivory, sterling silver & bamboo cane, the T-shaped handle in ivory w/one end carved w/a realistic elephant head w/jet bead eyes, the rest of the ivory handle decorated w/sterling silver overlay in an engraved floral vine design, silver ferrule above the bamboo-type shaft ending in a white metal tip, restoration where head meets shaft, late 19th - early 20th c., handle 1 1/2 x 4 1/4", overall 34 3/4" l. **$575**

Nickel silver-tipped folk art walking stick, the silver top w/ornate scrolling details, the wooden shaft carved w/bold folk art designs including an American shield & spread-winged eagle, a carved bewhiskered Civil War soldier carrying a carved flag, the numerous deeply carved leaves & initials "US" beneath another bewhiskered Civil War soldier holding & pointing a pistol, below that deeply carved "1862 ST" over "1865 TO," further down "40 VC," remainder of shaft carved w/ various letters, honey amber patina, 34" l. **$3,738**

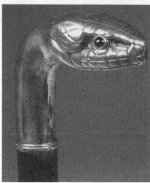

Silver & exotic wood cane, the silver figural handle in the form of a realistic cobra snake head w/detailed scales & red cabochon eyes, silver marked "900," on an exotic wood shaft w/a worn horn tip, late 19th c., handle, 2 3/4 x 3 1/4", overall 35 1/2" l. **$518**

Sterling silver & ebony cane, the ebony shaft joined by a replaced brass ferrule to the sterling silver cylindrical handle ornately cast overall w/rose blossoms, handle w/the mark of the Unger Brothers, ca. 1900, overall 36 1/4" l. **$560**

Sterling silver & exotic wood cane, the sterling silver L-shaped handle in the form of a realistic swan head w/a long bill, detailed feathers & inset glass eyes, English hallmarks & the name "Brigg," the exotic wood shaft ending in a worn white metal & iron tip, late 19th c., handle 2 1/4 x 3 1/2", overall 34 1/2" l. **$1,035**

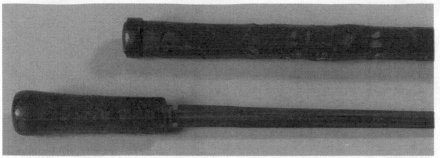

Sword cane, a wood pommel & shaft, the shaft enclosing a double-edged blade signed "Thomas Aiala," Spain, blade 16th c., overall 33 3/4" l. **$1,880**

White metal, ivory & mahogany walking stick, the handle w/ the carved ivory head of a bearded soldier wearing a ornately chased white metal helmet w/cheek guards & collar, on a tapering mahogany shaft w/a white metal tip, late 19th - early 20th c., handle 3 1/2" h., overall 34" l. (ILLUS. of two views) **$920**

Tortoiseshell veneer, gold & silver cane, the entire cylindrical shaft covered w/tortoiseshell veneer & a solid tortoiseshell ferrule, the ornate top in a Renaissance-style design in silver & gold w/four identical arched gateways each framing a gold standing armored knight or his wife, the top modeled w/a round shield w/chased floral & leaf designs centering a large faceted amethyst, Europe, early 19th c., overall 35" l. (ILLUS. of part)................................. **$3,360**

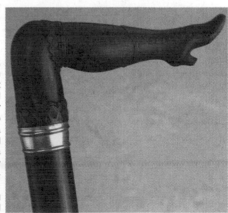

Gutta percha cane, figural, the smooth gutta percha shaft w/a white metal ferrule & silver collar joined to a figural gutta percha L-shaped handle molded as a lady's leg, finely detailed w/a high-buttoned boot, textured stocking w/garter & ruffled lace knickers, America, ca. 1890, overall 33 1/4" l. (ILLUS. of handle) **$476**

CANS & CONTAINERS

Aviation oil, "Pennzoil Safe Lubrication," cylindrical 5 qt. can, printed in yellow, black & red w/a large image of a United Airlines propeller-driven airplane over the company logo, ca. 1940s-50s, a few dents & scratches, light rust **$121**

Biscuit, "Columbia Biscuit Co.," cov., tin, rectangular, bright red ground w/yellow scroll design in upper corners & center circular panel w/color illustration of Columbia figure & "Columbia Biscuit Co." under arching blue banner reading "Columbia Biscuit Co." & over blue banner reading "Family Goods," "St. Louis" at bottom, about 8 x 10", 7" h. **$460**

Cacao, "Korff's Cacao," large upright square tin w/fitted flat cover, colorful paper labels centered by round reserves w/portraits of pretty women, Dutch, late 19th - early 20th c., 8" h. **$81**

To avoid rust, be sure to store tins in an area that is dry and check them periodically for signs of rust. Basements, attics, and garages are poor choices for storage because they are more susceptible to changes in temperature and humidity. Also, keep tins separated to prevent inadvertent scratching. If kept on display, keep them out of direct sunlight, as UV rays can cause the colors to fade over time.

Baking powder, "Calumet Double-Action Baking Powder," cylindrical can w/fitted lid & paper label, dark red background w/black & gold wording & center image of a Native American chief, early 20th c., no label on metal lid, 3" d., 5 1/2" h. **$26**

Biscuit, "Keen Robinson & Co., Ltd., London," squared form w/projecting rounded corners & curved sides, each side printed in color w/a different scene & large color florals at each corner, scenes titled "The Dog and the Shadow," "The Shepherd's Boy," "The Old Man and His Sons," & "The Dog in the Manger," early 20th c., 6 3/4" w., 6" h. **$99**

Candy, "Edward Sharp and Sons, Ltd. of Maidstone, Kent - The Toffee Specialists," rectangular low tin w/a color street scene of Canterbury, England, on the cover, coats-of-arms printed around the size, ca. 1940s, some wear, 5 3/4 x 7", 2" h. **$12**

Cigar, "Sunset Trail," oval upright tin w/flat hinged lid, dark blue background, printed on the side w/a large oval color scene of a cowboy & cowgirl riding on horseback at sunset, large orange panels w/wording at the ends, fine condition, early 20th c., 6" l., 5 1/2" h. **$575**

Cigars, "Possum Cigars - 3 for 5¢ - 'Am Good and Sweet,'" large cylindrical size w/flat fitted lid, red background w/dark gold w/brown reserves w/white & yellow wording around a color image of a white possum, slight wear, 5 1/4" d., 5 1/4" h. **$403**

Coffee, "Puritas Pure Delicious Coffee," 1/2 lb. can, short cylindrical shape w/pry-off lid, red background w/white & gold wording & gold & black image of a classical woman holding up a wreath, dated 1922, 4" d., 2 3/4" h. **$121**

Cinnamon, cov., 2-oz. container, rectangular, both sides w/ black panel on red ground w/ lithographed bust of Indian in headdress under "Mohican" in red, bottom reading "Pure Spices" in yellow, edge of lid reading "Cinnamon," 1 1/4 x 2 1/4", 3 3/4" h. **$55**

Coffee, "Bluhill Coffee," 5 lb. cylindrical lunch pail-style w/ domed shoulder, short cylindrical neck w/pry-off cover & a wire bail handle w/turned wood grip, dark blue sides w/white bands & a rectangular panel w/black wording & a black & white picture of a cup of coffee, early 20th c., 7" d., 10" h. **$330**

Coffee, "Holleb's Supreme Coffee," 1 lb. can, cylindrical w/keywind lid, black ground w/wording in white, red & gold, color image of cup & saucer w/white flowers, ca. 1930s, 5" d., 4" h. **$99**

Cookies, "Marshall Field & Company - Christmas Cookies," low round cylindrical tin w/a pry-off cover, black background printed w/red, white & black stylized Christmas trees & red & white wording, ca. 1940s, 9 3/4" d. **$15**

Engine grease, "Power-lube Lubricant," 1 lb. can, cylindrical w/ pry-off lid, yellow background w/ dark blue panel w/yellow wording & yellow & blue stalking tiger, ca. 1930s, back rough w/paint loss & fading, front w/dings, rubs & scratches, rust spots on bottom rim, no contents **$187**

Gun powder, "Hercules Powder - Black Sporting," 1 lb. can, upright rectangular shape w/small screw cap on top, paper label w/red ground w/large black & white image of Hercules against a white triangle, black & white bands w/ red & black wording, ca. 1940, 1 1/2 x 3 3/4", 6" h. **$77**

Tea, "Mazawattee Tea," rectangular three- pound tin w/a fitted cover & rounded corners, printed on the top & sides w/a colored scene of three young black boys drinking tea, England, early 20th c., good w/scattered scrapes & scratches, 5 1/2 x 8 1/2", 5 3/4" h. **$115**

With more people selling antiques and collectibles on the Internet, the perception of what is rare has changed. Some items once thought to be rare are now considered scarce after more examples have surfaced.

Syrup, "Towle's Log Cabin Syrup," 2 lb. size tin, rectangular cabin shape printed in color as a log cabin w/children playing inside & outside & woman cooking at open fireplace, 1950s, minor dings & scratches, 2 3/4 x 5", 4 1/2" h. **$55**

Motor oil, "Old Dutch Lubricant," 5 qt. can, large cylindrical shape w/ top spout neck & wire bail handle w/wooden grip, blue & black background w/black & white scene of large Dutch windmill on the upper half & white wording below, ca. 1930s, overall rust spots & wear **$231**

Peanuts, "Betteryet Whole Salted Peanuts," round 10-pound tin w/ a gold ground printed w/thin red stripes, the front w/a large black & gold oval band enclosing more advertising & facing figures of black men each holding a large peanut, Old Dominion Peanut Corp. early 20th c., overall very good, 9 1/2" d., 7 1/2" h. ... **$270**

Tea, "Ocean Blend Tea," 5-lb. container, tin litho, rectangular, bright red ground w/scene of luxury ocean liner on front & "Ocean Blend" at top over banner reading "Indian & Ceylon," "The Ocean Blend Tea Co." at the bottom & in dark blue ovals on the sides, includes partial contents, 8 1/2" h. **$92**

Tobacco, "Half and Half," vertical pocket tin w/flip-up top, dark green & black background w/a wide white diagonal band w/ black wording, a red circle in the upper left w/label of Burley and Bright Tobacco Co., ca. 1930s, 4 1/4" h. **$10**

Tobacco, "Tuxedo Tobacco" 1 lb. canister, slightly domed fitted lid, green & gold printed front panel centered by a scene of a young man wearing a tuxedo, the background in green & gold stripes, some wear, 4" d., 5 3/4" h. **$55**

Do you want to sell something to a dealer? It is always a good idea to know what amount you want, because a dealer will usually not offer a value. He will likely ask you what you want for it. Don't expect him to lock himself into an offer. It is the seller's responsibility to determine the value and set a price.

Tobacco, "Sure Shot," rectangular store bin w/a long flat lid, the long sides lithographed in yellow, black, red & green w/a scene of a Native American w/bow & arrow & marked "Sure Shot - Chewing Tobacco - It Touches The Spot," some denting to lid, overall light rust spots & wear, 10 1/4 x 15 1/2", 7" h. **$259**

If you miss out on a boxed lot at an auction, don't give up. Consider offering the winner a deal on the items you want. The winner may have bought the lot for other items in the box and may be more than willing to part with the items you want.

Tobacco, "Game Fine Cut Tobacco," rectangular store bin w/thin fitted cover, color scene of grouse in a field on both sides, 7 1/4 x 8 x 11 1/2" ... **$575**

CERAMICS MARKET REPORT

Jay Rogers, a dealer at the Atlanta Antique Gallery (atlantaantiquegallery.com) in Atlanta, Georgia, said, "We've seen a great deal of fluctuation in the market, but currently Nippon, R.S. Prussia, Newcomb College and rare Rookwood scenics and portraits are selling well. Asian porcelain, like jade, and all types of multicolored pieces with high glaze are moving, too. Imari, however, is slow. Pickard and Limoges are also slow but, in general, rare pieces at reasonable prices sell well."

Rogers sells 50 percent on the Internet, 30 percent at shows, and 20 percent to walk ins. The gallery's Web site lists 25,000 to 28,000 pieces, all over $85 each. He credits much of his success to the fact that he does so much business online, as he doesn't think he would be able to survive without the national and international market.

Most of Rogers' customers are 50s or older and affluent. Collectors account for 90 percent of his business, so he doesn't see many sales from the under 50 crowd, who buy primarily to decorate rather than collect. He has seen a dramatic drop in interest in Victorian antiques, which he attributes to the fact that they belong to grandma's generation and people today can't relate to them. In addition, the younger generation prefers the sleek look of Modernism to the fussiness of Victorian design. Yet, to illustrate that the very best of every era still draws high prices, Rogers mentioned an auction he attended recently in which a Victorian Mt. Washington toothpick holder crossed the block at $5,350.

Rogers recommends that collectors become educated by reading as much as they can and investing in various types of reference books so they can minimize costly mistakes. But inevitably collectors do make mistakes, and a big part of education is learning from them.

While economic conditions and changing demographics have greatly impacted the antiques market, Rogers believes that, ultimately, the way dealers run their business determines their success. They need to display clean, well-marked merchandise attractively in a well-lit, well-organized store, and represent merchandise honestly so customers can purchase with confidence. Building a stellar sterling reputation is essential to attract and maintain a loyal customer base and to promote business by word of mouth. Courtesy goes a long way as well. Dealers should greet customers warmly and be helpful without hovering. Building and maintaining a professional looking Web site is important, too, as visitors can tell instantly how professional a store is by the quality of its Web site.

Rogers recommends that dealers be generalists and carry a variety of times in a range of styles and price levels to appeal to as many customers as possible. "Only specialize if you're dealing with items that aren't readily available in the market," he said, citing Tiffany lamps as an example. A dealer could sell just one of those and make more than he would by selling a store full of lower end items, he added.

For Greg Myroth of JustArtPottery (www.justartpottery.com), high-end pieces like Newcomb and Teco are strong sellers. Rookwood is down a little, however. Although his mid-range pottery ($400 - $1,000) is soft, the low end is selling well and, if anything, has improved. "Mid-range customers haven't stopped buying, they're just buying more affordable pieces," he explained. For instance, middle period Roseville is harder to sell, but later Roseville floral is holding its own.

CERAMICS

Myroth attributes the strength of the high-end market to several factors. First, there are always people with money who want top quality pieces. The hard part is finding pieces to sell. Second, many people have become leery of the stock market and would rather put money in assets they can see and enjoy. They aren't buying with high expectations of making a profit, but enjoy having it and believe that it will at least do better than the stock market. Third, as people become skittish about the economy, they are less likely to try to sell their high-end pottery because they think it may go for too low a price. Consequently, with fewer pieces hitting the market, the competition increases for those that are offered, which keeps the prices up. "It's just supply and demand at work," he said.

Myroth noted that in recent years fewer people have been buying pieces to complete their collections. "In the past, some collectors wanted every Roseville wall pocket, or all pieces of a certain size, but they aren't buying that way anymore." That may be due to a move toward decorating rather than collecting. Another trend Myroth sees in the market is an increasing interest in contemporary pottery such as Ephraim Faience and Door Pottery.

Myroth advises new collectors to attend shows like the annual American Art Pottery Association Convention to gain hands-on knowledge about pottery before they start buying. "Collectors can learn a tremendous amount in two days," he commented. One of the most important thing novices need to learn is how to evaluate condition. He has found that when inexperienced buyers get a bad deal, it's usually because they purchased a piece with undisclosed damage. Sometimes the lack of disclosure is accidental because the dealer didn't know about it, but in many cases the seller deliberately withheld information, and the buyer paid mint price for a damaged piece. Pottery is easily chipped and cracked, so vintage pieces are often flawed. For example, according to Myroth, more than 50 percent of Roseville pieces are damaged in some way.

Myroth has seen a distinct drop in the quality of art pottery sold on eBay. He believes buyers are moving away from eBay because they're fed up with poorly written, inaccurate descriptions and sometimes outright deception. He has personally witnessed incidents like this, in which he has sold an item fully indicating all flaws, then later saw the piece being resold on eBay without disclosure about the damage. The dissatisfaction with eBay has driven customers to venues with better quality control.

Myroth said that some dealers don't offer an unconditional return policy, fearing that customers will take advantage of them. He said that he's never had a problem with that and rarely has returns. His return policy helps build the trust that buyers need to purchase with confidence, which has created many repeat customers. "You won't lose in the long run if you're honest and stand behind what you sell," he said.

Auction Houses
Rago (www.ragoarts.com)
Cincinnati Art Galleries (www.cincinnatiartgalleries.com)
Bonhams & Butterfields (www.bonhams.com)
Christie's (http://www.christies.com)
Jackson's International (www.jacksonsauction.com)
Treadway Toomey Galleries (www.treadwaygallery.com)

CERAMICS

Abingdon

Cookie jar, Wigwam, No. 665D, 11" h. **$750-1,000**

Figure, Scarf Dancer, No. 3902, 13" h. .... **$800 up**

> If a vase is used to hold cut flowers for an extended period, the chemicals in the water can permanently stain the inside of the vase.

Flower boat, Fern Leaf, oblong ribbed leaf shape, pink, No. 426, 1937-38, 13 x 4" (ILLUS. left) **$100**
Fruit boat, Fern Leaf, oblong ribbed leaf shape, white, No. 432, 1938-39, 6 1/2 x 15" (ILLUS. right) **$100**

Flowerpots, Nos. 149 to 152, floral decoration, 3 to 6" h., each (ILLUS. of three) **$15-30**

Vase, 8 1/4" h., Swedish, handled, white, No. 314, 1934-36 ..... **$85**

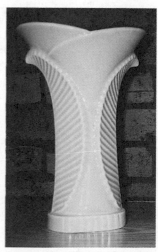

Vase, 10 1/4" h., Fern Leaf, tall ribbed leaf-shape sides taper out to top opening, blue, No. 422, 1937-39 .... **$95**

American Painted Porcelain

Bowl, 8" w., hexagonal, decorated w/ clusters of wild roses on alternating panels, mother-of-pearl lustre ground, marked "MZ - Altrolau - CM-R - Czechoslovakia," ca. 1918-39.................................... **$45**

Creamer & open sugar bowl, double-handled, yellow lustre ground, decorated w/enameled & gilded design of scrolls & flowers, burnished gold handles, marked "T&V Limoges - France," ca. 1892-1907, the set **$45**

Dish, hexagonal, decorated w/ violets, burnished gold rim, marked "MZ Altrohlau - CM-R - Czechoslovakia," signed "A. Denniston," ca. 1918-39, 5 1/4" w. **$35**

Jam jar, cov., doubled-handled, decorated w/blackberries, burnished gold handles, marked "HR" in circle & "Favorite - Hut-schenreuther, Selb, Bavaria," stamped "Wm. Macleod, Erie, PA," ca. 1905-20, 5" h.......... **$70**

Nut set: 5 x 7" footed nut bowl & six 2 7/8" d. individual footed cups; mother-of-pearl lustre interior, ivory exterior, burnished gold foot & rims, bowl marked "B & Co. Limoges, France," cups marked "Noritake, Nippon," ca. 1920-30, the set **$69**

Plate, decorated w/pink & ruby roses, burnished gold rim, marked w/a crown & crossed scepters & "R.C. Bavaria," ca. 1901-33 .... **$14**

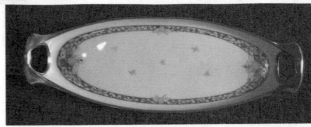

Celery tray, long oval, double-handled, decorated w/conventional floral border in enamel & burnished gold, burnished gold rim & handles, marked "Vignaud - Limoges" & signed "N. A. Ray," stamped "N.A. Ray Studio, Monesdale, PA," ca. 1911- 38, 15" l. **$95**

Demitasse cup & saucer, decorated w/conventional design, burnished gold rim & handle, signed "D.D. Portez, 1916," the set **$15**

Dessert set: 4 7/8 x 5 1/2" double-handled spoon tray & pair of cups & saucers; each decorated w/pink wild roses, signed "G.B. Shantz," tray marked "Made in Japan," cups & saucers w/a crown & wreath mark & "Epiag, Made in Czechoslovakia," ca. 1920-35, the set (ILLUS. of cup & saucer) **$70**

Dessert set: 9 1/2" d. double-handled cake plate & five cups & saucers; decorated w/a conventional border of paint, enamel & burnished gold, marked "Epiag, Aich - Czechoslovakia," ca. 1920-30, some wear, the set (ILLUS. of cake plate) ... **$80**

Fruit bowl, ribbon handle, decorated w/currants, burnished gold rim & handle, illegible signature, marked "Hutschenreuther, Selb," ca. 1880-1910, some wear, 10 1/2" l. **$105**

AMERICAN PAINTED PORCELAIN

Grape juice set: jug-form pitcher & five tumblers; decorated w/clusters of grapes, burnished gold rims, marked "T&V Limoges," ca. 1892-1907, some wear, the set **$399**

Plate, 6" d., decorated w/hawthorn, makered w/a shield & "Thomas Bavaria," ca. 1908-20 .... **$12**

Plate, 6 1/2" d., decorated w/ yellow wild roses, signed "Luken Studios," Chicago, ca. 1895-1926 .... **$15**

Spoon tray, double-handled, decorated w/yellow poppies, marked w/a wreath, "R.S. Germany" & signed "SMP," ca. 1904-38, 8 1/4" l. **$30**

Trivet, round, decorated w/a bucolic landscape, golden yellow lustre rim, marked "Japan," ca. 1915-25, 6" d. **$15**

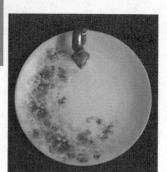

Olive dish, ring-handled, decorated w/forget-me-nots, burnished gold rim & handle, signed "Sandwich," marked "Favorite Bavaria," ca. 1908-18, some wear, 6 5/8" d. **$30**

Plate, 8 3/4" d., decorated w/pears, burnished gold rim, signed "Floyd," marked "Haviland France," ca. 1894-1915 ...... **$30**

Ring stand, decorated w/forget-me-nots, oblong shallow dished shape w/fancy central scroll handle, burnished gold rim & stem, marked "UNO-IT Favorite Bavaria," ca. 1910-20, 3 1/2" d., 3 1/2" h. **$40**

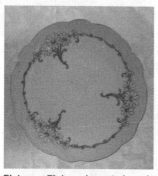

Plates, 7" d., decorated w/a conventional border design of daisies, burnished gold scalloped rim, marked w/a crown & double-headed eagle & "M.Z. Austria," ca. 1884-1909, some wear, set of 4 (ILLUS. of one).................... **$90**

Plates, 8 1/2" d., decorated w/a conventional design of grape clusters & whiplash vines, burnished gold banding, signed "C. Ludwig," marked w/a shield & "Thomas Bavaria," ca. 1908-20, set of four (ILLUS. of one).. **$120**

Ring stand, round w/central tree-form ring holder, decorated w/ forget-me-nots, burnished gold rim & handle, signed "M.L. Nobbe," marked "GDA/France," ca. 1900-41, 5 7/8" l. **$59**

Salt & pepper shakers, bulbous ovoid body w/bulbous top, decorated w/a border band of enameled flowers on a burnished gold ground, burnished gold tops, unmarked, ca. 1915-25, 3" h., pr... **$60**

Salt & pepper shakers, upright slightly flaring cylindrical shape w/an in-body twist, decorated w/a border design of conventional iris, yellow lustre ground w/scattered burnished gold leaves, burnished gold bands & tops, no mark, ca. 1912-25, 2 1/2" h., pr. **$60**

Salt & pepper shakers, upright waisted cylindrical shape w/a flaring scalloped base, decorated w/pink & yellow roses, burnished gold tops, marked w/a crown & crossed scepters & "R.C. Bavaria," ca. 1901-33, gold worn, 2 3/4" h., pr. **$30**

Stein, decorated w/currants, burnished gold rim, marked "JP/L France," ca. 1891-1932, some wear, 5" h. **$50**

Toothpick holder, short waisted cylindrical form, decorated w/pink roses & leaves on light yellow ground, w/burnished gold border & rim, ca. 1910-1920, 2 1/4" h. **$30**

Sugar shaker, cylindrical shape on foot, decorated w/conventional floral design in enamel & burnished gold outlined in black, ivory ground, w/burnished gold top, marked "H C Royal, Bavaria," ca. 1905-1920, 4 5/8" **$75**

AMPHORA - TEPLITZ

Amphora - Teplitz

The Amphora Company began in the country village of Turn, in the Teplitz region of Bohemia. The Teplitz region supported the highest concentration of ceramic production, not only in Bohemia, but throughout all of the Austro-Hungarian Empire.

Amphora's aim was always to produce richly ornamented porcelain luxury items. In addition to American exports there were sales to European dealers. Through world exhibitions and international trade shows, Amphora's collections received numerous significant awards and certificates.

By 1900 Amphora was at the pinnacle of its success. After World War I in 1918, Czechoslovakia was established. The company continued production until the end of the 1930s.

Prices vary according to rarity, design, quality and size. The variety of art produced by Amphora Company provides something for everyone. For more information on Amphora, two books serve as excellent resources: *Monsters & Maidens - Amphora Pottery of the Art Nouveau Era*, by Byron Vreeland and *Ceramics from The House of Amphora, 1890-1915* by Richard Scott - Phil and Arlene Larke.

Boudoir lamp, figural, kerosene-type, the porcelain base modeled as an owl w/amber glass eyes, brown trim on ivory ground, red rose transfer mark of Alfred Stellmacher, impressed "1003 - A," painted "27," 1876 ... **$1,500**

Candlestick, Fates Series, ivory porcelain, the tapering cylindrical shaft molded in low-relief w/ women's heads & moths, applied flower buds under the rim & two whirling women's heads form the socket opening, clear glaze w/underglaze hatching in cobalt blue & grey, soft mother-of- pearl lustre, matte yellow relief, mark of Riessner, Stellmacher & Kessel Company, Fate seal, red "RStK" transfer, impressed numbers "2006.41," inked numbers "601-1530," 1900, 11" h. **$3,600**

Candlestick, figural, porcelain, an Art Nouveau full-figure fairy resting against a column forming the base of the candlestick, at the top between her hands is a molded owl head, w/a violet lustre & matte green patina, the figure w/matte gilding & green patina, mark of Ernst Wahliss Company & "EW," a printed crown & impressed "4781" & free-hand numbers over-glaze "4781 - 298 -7," 1900, 9 1/2" h. **$4,900**

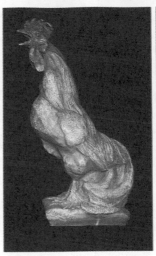

Ewer, footed bulbous ovoid body tapering to a tall pierced cylindrical neck w/a high arched & ruffled spout, a long figural curling dragon handle in green & rose trimmed w/gold, the neck & base in pink & the body h.p. w/a cobalt blue medallion among a field of red poppies, gold rose transfer mark of Alfred Stellmacher, Turn, Teplitz, printed "744" & impressed "25," 1884, 13 1/4" h. **$1,900**

Humidor, cov., figural, a massive Native American theme composed of three Indian heads w/high-glazed pink & green feathered headdresses, "jeweled" & draping beaded necklaces on two, a draping necklace of animal teeth on the third, high-glaze green & cobalt blue finial handle on a decorative mixed glazed top, basic color of Campina brown w/much contrasting high-glaze in green, pink, brown & blue, rare, impressed ovals w/"Amphora" & "Austria," a crown & "Imperial - Amphora - Turn" in a circle & "S- 1633-46," 10 1/2" h. **$5,500-6,500**

Model of a rooster, larger-than-life crowing rooster designed by Berwiel & glazed in mottled golden brown, this example found in Germany, another reported to be in a Scandinavian art museum, incised "Berwiel 08" on the side, impressed "Amphora" & "Austria" in oval, a crown, "Imperial - Amphora - Turn" in a circle & 8237/37, 26" h. **$10,500-11,000**

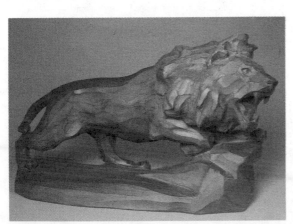

Model of a lion, terra cotta, designed to resemble carved wood w/the snarling lion posed on a rockwork base, brown glaze, impressed "Amphora" within a shield w/a crown above, ca. 1908-1912, 15" l., 8 1/2" h. **$1,600**

Figurine, the figure of a nude child holding the side of a large round basket in one hand & leaning against a square basket, all-white w/gold rim, raised on a mottled green rockwork base, impressed Amphora mark, #1421, 9" w., 8 1/2" h. **$90**

Model of a boar, seated European boar leaning to one side as though attempting to rest from a hunter's pursuit, finished in brownish gold glaze, very lifelike, rare, impressed "Amphora" & "Austria" in oval, a crown, #8236/36 & artist's mark "H" in gold, 10" h.
.... **$3,000-3,500**

Planter, figural, low flaring buttress base below the long oblong bowl w/incurved sides molded at each end w/ figural dragon handles w/their wings wrapped back over the sides, each side w/a pale blue hammered ground incised w/yellow grapes flanking an oval wreath panel enclosing a sailing ship scene, ink stamped double oval mark w/"Made in Czecho- Slovakia - Amphora," impressed "5174 - 25," inked "734 - 264 -4," ca. 1918-1939, 16" l., 16 1/4" h. **$1,800**

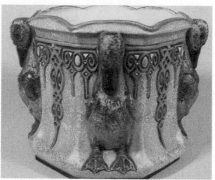

Planter, figural, the deep octagonal container w/a dark yellow speckled round & a scalloped rim trimmed in blue, the half- figure of a duck in dark blue & gold alternating on four panels w/ornate molded blue circle & scroll w/pendant bands, ink-stamped double oval mark w/"Czecho- Slovakia - Amphora," printed letter "F," ca. 1920, 8" h.
.... **$1,500**

Planter, Gres - Bijou Series, known as the "Lightning Bolt" decoration, hard earthenware, yellowish body, the mid-section double-walled w/a wide band of ornamental piercing & greyish-green marblizing, matte gilding, obliquely-grooved ringlets w/applied colored "stones" & relief web of thick threads, underglaze painting in green & cobalt blue, greenish glaze spotted w/dark green & rose frits, matted metallic gloss, marked w/ovals enclosing "Amphora - Austria," impressed crown & "3790," ca. 1918-1939, 12 1/4" d., 8 1/4" h.
.... **$21,000**

Statue, porcelain, modeled as bear attacking a large bull, animals in cream w/ tan highlights, posed on a dark brown rockwork base, signed "Jarl 1907" on the side, impressed crown & "Austria - Amphora," ca. 1907, 15 1/4" h. ... **$2,500**

An impressed mark is stamped into the clay while still wet, leaving the mark below the surface of the piece.

Vase, 5 3/4" h., wide squatty bulbous base tapering sharply to a neck w/four molded buttress handles, decorated w/a stylized scene in tans & greys of the setting sun behind a black gnarled tree, trimmed in muted gilt, base marked "Amphora - AB" & the name of a retail outlet in St. Louis, Missouri, late 19th - early 20th c. **$578**

Vase, 7 3/4" h., triangular tapering body w/bold in-body twist below the flaring three-lobed neck, colorful stylized floral decoration in shades of black, blue, yellow, brown, orange & white, bottom w/a raked finish & the impressed stylized "RStK" mark & "Austria - 8867 -6," 1900- 1904 .... **$1,200**

Vase, 8 1/2" h., conical shaper capped w/a rolled lip w/four handles depicting melting icicles & w/twelve openings around the base enclosing a circular open area, the bottom half finished w/a black glaze shading up into a rich matte gold glaze, bottom marked w/"Edda" & swastika in triangle, impressed "Austria - Amphora" in ovals & "3662 - 62," ca. 1890- 1900 .... **$2,400**

Vase, 8 1/4" h., porcelain, the oblong molded matte gold base supporting the figure of a seated white dog w/one paw raised & resting on the rim of a large bulbous handled jar w/a molded gold spider web design centered by a black faux jewel, impressed crown & conjoined double oval w/"Amphora - Austria - 8184 - 80," inked "69002" & "ES" for Eduard Stellmacher, ca. 1900-1902 .... **$1,900**

Vase, 8 1/2" h., simple ovoid body swelled slightly near the gilt-trimmed rim, a Paul Dachsel piece h.p. w/tall birch trees around the sides above stylized grass & flowers & fluffy clouds in the sky, signed on the base "Turn Teplitz PD - Made in Austria - 094 - 107," some very minor gilt wear at rim **$863**

Vase, 9" h., hard earthenware, Ibis design, footed squatty bulbous lower body below tapering long lappet panels to the wide flaring triangular rim above the molded ibis heads forming long handles, yellowish body, painting in matte gold on the rim & neck shading to a rich reddish rose at the base, impressed "Amphora- Austria" in ovals, a crown, imperial circle & "15006 - 57," 1904-1906 ... **$3,500**

Vase, 9" h., hard earthenware, pine tree design, tapering fluted good shape w/green relief tree trunks up the sides, applied pine cones branching at the neck, ochre underglaze painting, transparent matte glaze, brown frit on pine cones, patches of dark green frit on trunks, grey patina & matte gilding, Kunstkeramik Paul Dachsel Company, marked w/a black "PD" transfer, impressed "2037-12," 1908-1909 ... **$7,300**

Vase, 9" h., Marabella Series, hard earthenware, bulbous ovoid body tapering to a tiny flared neck, the greyish body decorated w/an irregular relief web of strong threads, whitish & greenish base glaze, dark green & rose frit glaze w/metallic lustre on the relief, cobalt blue & black underglaze painting of peonies on a wide middle band, matte gold sponging, red "RStK" transfer mark, impressed oval w/"Amphora - 3271," ink-printed "50," ca. 1903-04 .... **$2,900**

Vase, 9 3/4" h., carved-type, porcelain, designed as an ivory tusk deeply carved w/an Oriental figure emerging from a large pot in an Asian landscape w/a seated figure below, from the period when Alfred Stellmacher developed a technique to produced pottery that resembled ivory, on a plinth-form base, bottom marked w/"A. S." in a rose transfer, impressed "1012," 1884 .... **$1,200**

Vase, 9 7/8" h., a Paul Dachsel abstract design w/a reticulated geometric top & a reticulated handle within a reticulated handle sweeping in an arc from the top to the bottom w/abstract tendrils extending around the bottom of the body & back of the handles, several high-glazed green pods resembling teardrops of various sizes hang from the abstract handle, vines & a center funnel, the top rim & top of handle finished in gold, rare, stamped over glaze w/intertwined "PD - Turn - Teplitz" **$7,000-7,500**

Vase, 10" h., a Paul Dachsel abstract architectural style w/a geometric design consisting of a rounded bottom from which four handles begin flush & extend to the top of the rim where they flare opon, each handle suggests an abstract candelabrum w/charcoal flames rising from each, finished in iridescent gunmetal grey w/ charcoal black sheen touches, gold wash on top, modern in all respects even though produced in the 1904-10 period, rare form, stamped over glaze w/intertwined "PD - Turn - Teplitz," impressed "1049" **$8,500-9,000**

To help prevent breakage, loss or theft of items you have purchased at an antique show, don't carry more than one bag at a time. Consolidate packages into one bag. Many people carry a canvas tote bag for this reason.

Vase, 10 1/4" h., hard earthenware, Gres - Bijou Series, wide cylindrlcal body w/an angled shoulder to the short neck, yellowish body applied overall w/stone "jewels" & a relief cell design of thick threads, brown & carmine underglaze painting, glossy transparent mother-of-pearl frit dust glaze, matte & glossy gilding, mark of Riessner & Kessel Company w/impressed ovals enclosing "Austria - Amphora - 3672 - 60," 1904-1906 .... **$3,600**

Vase, 10 1/2" h., porcelain, bulbous body w/molded rim band & raised on four incurved block legs, the body h.p. w/a winter forest scene w/two jars, Asian influence on the four legs decorated w/Asian-like designs w/similar designs around the rim, marked of Ernst Wahliss Company w/red transfer "EW" in a shield topped w/a crown, impressed "9308," inked "9308/9340," ca.   1899-1909 .... **$2,800**

Vase, 11" h., bulbous ovoid body tapering to a tall slender lobed neck, four swirled loop handles around the shoulder, glossy glaze w/a tall floral plant & blue accents at the top, raked bottom surface w/a stylized "RStK" mark, impressed "Austria - Amphora" in ovals, numbered "175 G F 8852," 1900-1904 .... **$1,500**

Vase, 11" h., Russian Folk Art Series, a dark colored clay similar to terra cotta molded as a stylized rooster w/the head on one side & the long curled blue & brown tail on the other side, brightly colored green, white & tan enamel trim, impressed crown & ovals w/"Amphora - Austria - 15004 - 55 - S," the imperial circle & inked "K," ca. 1899-1900 .... **$1,500**

Vase, 11" h., tall tapering cylindrical body w/a mottled greyish blue ground applied up & around the sides w/three-dimensional stems & leaves in greens & red & numerous yellow rose blossoms, signed on the bottom "Amphora - Austria (crown) - 8000 - 5 8," few very minor chips to leaves, late 19th - early 20th c. **$633**

Vase, 11 1/2" h., Art Deco-style, a round foot ring in black, pink & white supporting the baluster-form body w/a finely speckled brown ground bolded enameled w/stylized pink, gold, white & blue blossoms on slender stems w/large green leaves, marked "Amphora - Made in Czechoslovakia" .. **$173**

Vase, 11 3/4" h., tall gently tapering body w/a reticulated rim flanked by long slender leaf handles, molded overall w/stylized flowers & leaves in shades of green & tan, marked w/the Wahliss logo & numbers 5698-2710 .... **$748**

Vase, 12" h., a wonderful & colorful dragon hugs the circumference of the top w/its huge, detailed wings draping along the sides, detailed claw-like feet decorated in two glazes, one predominately blue, the other predominately tan, a Czechoslovakian creation w/no Austrian counterpart, stamped over the glaze "Amphora - Made in Czech-slovakia" in an oval **$6,000**

Vase, 12 3/4" h., hard earthenware, figural, crudely molded leafy trees with seated Brittany grain farmer holding his scythe on one side, decorated in earthtones, impressed crown & ovals w/"Amphora - Austria - 4889 - 98 - G," ca. 1909-1910 .... **$1,000**

Vase, 12" h., figural, three standing cockatoos, fully feathered, extend around the body of the vase, their plumes rising over the rim, very detailed w/glossy glaze, subtle color mix of blues, greens & tans w/brown streaks, semi-rare, impressed "Amphora" & "Austria" in ovals, a crown & Imperial circle & "11986 - 56" **$4,500- 5,000**

Vase, 13" h., stoneware, Campina Series, bulbous ovoid body w/a wide rounded shoulder centered by a small neck flanked by low angled handles, the sides incised & painted w/a large wood ground, a yellowish body w/impressed contours, the colorful wood grouse posed on a pine bough, repeating wave-like band in dark yellow & cobalt blue around the base, bright cloisonne enamels, stylized plant designs on the back, designed by Max Von Jungwirth, impressed crown & ovals w/"Amphora - Austria, Campina rectangle, imperial circle & "11611,"ca. 1909- 1910 **$1,500**

Vase, 13" h., wide-shouldered tapering cylindrical body, a fantasy design by Paul Dachsel worthy of the description "enchanted forest," the design consists of slender molded abstract trees extending from the narrow base to the bulbous top, lovely heart-shaped leaves extend in clusters from the various branches, trees in muted green, the leaves in pearlized off-white w/gold framing, the symbolic sky in rich red extending between the trees from the bottom to the top, rare, intertwined "PD" mark rubbed off **$9,500-10,000**

Vase, 14" h., figural, a fantasy dragon featuring two flaring wings, one extending practically from the top to the bottom of the body, the other well above & beyond the rim, creature w/a convoluted tail, spine & teeth, the head w/open mouth positioned at top of the vase, bluish green gold iridescence, glazes vary from a flat tan to a variety of very iridescent colors, made in 14" & 17" size, impressed "Amphora" in oval, illegible numbers, large size w/better glazes, $6,500, 14" size w/drab glazes **$9,500-10,000**

Vases, 10 1/2" h., footed bulbous ovoid body tapering to a slender cylindrical neck w/a flattened disk rim, painted in shades of purple, pink, green, blue, black & gilt w/the bust of a young maiden wearing a voluminous hood surmounted by a Byzantine crown surrounded by a gilt aura, a lower border of roses, the crown & roses w/applied bosses, one printed w/mark "Turn - Teplitz - Bohemia - R.St. - Made in Austria," the other impressed "Amphora," each impressed "2014 -28," pr. **$14,000**

Vase, 14 1/4" h., unusual multi-spouted design, a small round dark blue base w/yellow blossoms supporting four curved tubes meeting at the base & at the top below the ringed neck in dark blue w/small yellow blossoms, each tube topped by a small cylindrical spout, the mottled yellow & blue ground on the tubes centered by a long almond-shaped dark blue reserve enclosing yellow Macintosh roses & green leaves, possibly inspired by Paul Dachsel, impressed crown & ovals w/"Amphora - Austria," number obscured by glaze, ca. 1906-1907 .... **$1,000**

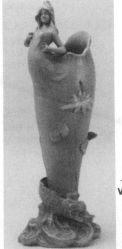

Vase, 14 5/8" h., tall gently tapering ovoid form w/a closed rim, the upper half w/a cream background decorated w/tall stems of stylized gold flowers, the lower half in dark green decorated w/a repeating band of tight scrolls in light green, marked "Turn Teplitz Bohemia - R St & K - Made in Austria - Amphora - 630" **$1,840**

Vase, 18 1/4" h., figural, a massive Art Nouveau form featuring an elegant woman wearing a diaphanous gown & standing in front of the body of the vase, her extended hand holding a 'jewel' like those adorning the sides of the piece, reticulated top finished in rich gold, impressed "Amphora - Austria" in a lozenge, 8171 .... **$45,000-50,000**

Vase, 16 1/2" h., figural, tall ovoid body w/the wave-molded base wrapped by a figural sea serpent, the tall lily-form vase molded at the rim w/an Art Nouveau maiden extending above the rim, impressed mark "BB 374..." some crazing .... **$1,0...**

Vase, 16 3/4" h., hard earthenware, slender gently tapering cylindrical body w/bulbed top w/staggered flat handles, yellowish crackle matte white & soft yellowish glaze, matte greyish green painting & grey patina, Riessner, Stellmacher & Kessel Company, impressed "3597 - 22," signed on side w/imitials "ES" in a triangle, bottom w/raised triangle w/a swastika & the letters "Edda," 1890-1903 .... **$11,000**

Vase, 19" h., hard earthenware, simple swelled cylindrical body w/flat mouth, yellowish body molded w/ overblown dandelions stamped in a layer of frit dust, applied leaves, underglaze painting in cobalt blue & light green, transparent glaze, flowers in grey & brown dotted w/whitish frits, painting in shiny gold & gold sponging, Riessner, Stellmacher & Kessel Company, impressed w/con- joined double oval w/"Amphora - Austria (crown) - 03645 23," 1899-1903 .. **$12,000**

Vase, 21" h., 18" w., figural, a wide squatty bulbous base centered by a tall neck, Art Nouveau style w/a mermaid clinging to the top rim, her well-defined body extends down along the side, applied berries, vines & leaves complete the decoration, finished in a matte tan w/gold wash & highlights, bluish berries, red stems, greenish red leaves & a high-glazed gold rim, important & very rare, would be rare even without the applied foliage, impressed "Amphora" in oval & "07 - 7 - 3" **$22,500-23,000**

Vase, 24 3/4" h., figural, porcelain, standing maiden w/calla lily, the neck applied w/lily leaves against which the maiden stands, lily-shaped mouth, vivid blue & green underglaze painting, figure w/matte gilding & gold accents throughout, Ernst Wahliss Company, impressed "Made in Austria - 4695-5," 1890-1900 .... **$9,900**

Water jug, spherical double-spouted form w/large arched & bead-trimmed gold handles from the cylindrical neck to the shoulder w/tiny arched handles above them, decorated w/a large teardrop-form reserve decorated w/long-stemmed white roses on leafy gold stems on a dark green ground, a wide center body band w/matching roses, textured background in mottled light green & gold w/tiny dotted florals, marked "Turn Teplitz - Made in Austria - PD (Paul Dachsel) - 1165," 8 1/8" h. **$1,955**

Beatrix Potter Figurines

The John Beswick factory in Longton, Stoke-on-Trent, celebrated its 100th anniversary in 1994. Originally, it produced earthenware household items and decorative ornaments. With the passage of time, the product line became more diverse and the decorations more ornate and attractive. Moreover, small domestic, farmyard and wild animal figurines were added to the product lines. Beswick was a family-owned and family-run pottery. As the owners neared retirement, they realized there were no next of kin to carry on the business. They sold the company to Royal Doulton in 1969 but Doulton later sold off the line.

Beatrix Potter is known the world over. Generations of children since the early 1900s have been fascinated by the antics of her coterie of small animals in her series of illustrated children's *Tales of Peter Rabbit and Friends*. These storybook characters have been produced as small china figurines since the 1920s, but it was not until 1947 that Beswick gained copyright approval from the Frederick Warne Co., the Peter Rabbit book publisher, to manufacture and market them. Upon acquisition of the manufacturing rights, Royal Doulton continued to promote and sell the Beatrix Potter figures using the Beswick trademark until 1989, when it switched to a "Royal Albert" under print. Royal Albert was another of its famous product lines and had greater brand recognition in the United States. The backstamp change was not well received by the global collector community. Within a decade, the Beswick backstamp was reintroduced and used on the Beatrix Potter figurines until the end of 2002, when the Warne license expired. The old Beswick factory was closed.

All the Beatrix Potter figurines were assigned a "P" or production model number. Although these "P" numbers do not appear on the figures themselves, they are used extensively by collectors to uniquely identify a particular figure.

Many varieties of backstamp exist. They indicate a period of manufacture and influence secondary market values. The basic types of backstamp are shown. If collectible subtypes exist, a range of market values is given for the basic type. Many special backstamps were used in the 1990s to promote sales. These details are outside the scope of this compendium.

Aunt Pettitoes, P2276, gold circle/oval backstamp, 1970-93 ... **$650**

Aunt Pettitoes, P2276, crown backstamp, 1970-93............. **$75**

Benjamin Bunny, P1105, ears in, shoes in, Beswick Ware backstamp, 1980-2000......... **$35**

Benjamin Bunny, P1105, ears in, shoes in, crown backstamp, 1980-2000........................... **$35**

Benjamin Bunny, P1105, ears in, shoes in, John Beswick script backstamp, 1980- 2000...... **$175**

Cousin Ribby, P2284, brown line backstamp, 1970-93............. **$65**

Benjamin Bunny, P1105, ears in, shoes in, gold circle/oval backstamp, 1980-2000 .... **$80**

Cousin Ribby, P2284, crown backstamp, 1970-93............. **$75**

Fierce Bad Rabbit, P2586, feet in, light brown rabbit, brown line backstamp, 1980-97........... **$100**

Goody & Timmy Tiptoes, P2957, crown backstamp, 1986-96 .... **$100**

Goody Tiptoes, P1675, brown line backstamp, 1961-67............. **$75**

Goody Tiptoes, P1675, crown backstamp, 1961-67............. **$45**

Christmas Stocking, P3257, crown backstamp, 1991-94 .... **$250**

Hunca Munca Sweeping, P2584, brown dustpan, Beswick Made in England backstamp, 1977-2002 .... **$35**

Hunca Munca Sweeping, P2584, brown dustpan, brown line backstamp, 1977- 2002....... **$90**

Hunca Munca Sweeping, P2584, brown dustpan, John Beswick script backstamp, 1977-2002 .... **$150**

Jemima Puddle-Duck Made a Feather Nest, P2823, crown backstamp, 1983-97............. **$40**

BEATRIX POTTER FIGURINES

Cousin Ribby, P2284, gold circle/oval backstamp, 1970-93... **$625**

Goody & Timmy Tiptoes, P2957, brown line backstamp, 1986-96 .... **$300**

Hunca Munca Spills the Beads, P3288, crown backstamp, 1992-96 .... **$70**

Goody Tiptoes, P1675, gold circle/oval backstamp, 1961-67 ... **$300**

Hunca Munca Sweeping, P2584, brown dustpan, crown backstamp, 1977-2002 .... **$35**

Jemima Puddle-Duck Made a Feather Nest, P2823, brown line backstamp, 1983-97 .... **$60**

Jemima Puddle-Duck Made a Feather Nest, P2823, John Beswick script backstamp, 1983-97 .... **$150**

Jemima Puddle-Duck with Foxy Whiskered Gentleman, P3193, Beswick Made in England backstamp, 1990-99............. **$80**

Mrs. Rabbit & Bunnies, P2543, crown backstamp, 1976-97 .... **$60**

Mrs. Rabbit & Bunnies, P2543, John Beswick script backstamp, 1976-97 .... **$145**

Mrs. Rabbit Cooking, P3278, crown backstamp, 1992-99 .... **$35**

Mrs. Rabbit, P1200, umbrella in, John Beswick script backstamp, 1975-2002 .... **$100**

Mrs. Tiggy-Winkle, P1107, plaid dress, Beswick Made in England, backstamp, 1972-2000 .... **$35**

Mrs. Tiggy-Winkle, P1107, plaid dress, brown line backstamp, 1972-2000 .... **$100**

Mrs. Tiggy-Winkle, P1107, plaid dress, gold circle/oval backstamp, 1972-2000 .... **$225**

Mrs. Tiggy-Winkle, P1107, plaid dress, John Beswick script backstamp, 1972- 2000...... **$140**

Old Woman Who Lived in a Shoe Knitting (The), P2804, brown line backstamp, 1983-2002....... **$225**

Old Woman Who Lived in a Shoe Knitting (The), P2804, crown backstamp, 1983- 2002....... **$40**

Peter Rabbit, P1098, brown line backstamp, 1948-80.......... **$110**

Peter Rabbit, P1098, light blue jacket, Beswick Made in England backstamp, 1980-2002....... **$35**

Peter Rabbit, P1098, light blue jacket, crown backstamp, 1980-2002 .... **$35**

Peter Rabbit, P1098, light blue jacket, John Beswick script backstamp, 1980-2002....... **$135**

Peter with Postbag, P3591, Beswick Made in England backstamp, 1996-2002......... **$45**

Poorly Peter Rabbit, P2560, crown backstamp, 1976-97............. **$55**

Poorly Peter Rabbit, P2560, John Beswick script backstamp, 1976-97 .... **$145**

Squirrel Nutkin, P1102, red-brown squirrel, gold circle/oval backstamp, 1983-89.... **$250-300**

Tabitha Twitchit & Miss Moppet, P2544, brown line backstamp, 1976-93.............................. **$235**

Mrs. Rabbit & Bunnies, P2543, brown line backstamp, 1976-97 .... **$100**

Mrs. Rabbit Cooking, P3278, Beswick Made in England backstamp, 1992-99 .... **$45**

Mrs. Rabbit, P1200, umbrella in, crown backstamp, 1975-2002 .... **$45**

Mrs. Tiggy-Winkle, P1107, plaid dress, crown backstamp, 1972-2000 .... **$35**

No More Twist, P3325, crown backstamp, 1992-97 .... **$65**

Old Woman Who Lived in a Shoe Knitting (The), P2804, Beswick Made in England backstamp, 1983-2002 .... **$35**

Peter Rabbit, P1098, gold circle/ oval backstamp, 1948-80 . **$300**

Peter Rabbit, P1098, light blue jacket, brown line backstamp, 1980-2002 .... **$70**

Poorly Peter Rabbit, P2560, brown line backstamp, 1976-97 .. **$120**

BELLEEK

Belleek

Belleek china has been made in Ireland's County Fermanagh for many years. It is exceedingly thin porcelain. Several marks were used, including a hound and harp (1865-1880), and a hound, harp and castle (1863-1891). A printed hound, harp and castle with the words "Co. Fermanagh Ireland" constitutes the mark from 1891. Belleek-type china also was made in the United States last century by several firms, including Ceramic Art Company, Colombian Art Pottery, Lenox Inc., Ott & Brewer and Willets Manufacturing Co.

American Belleek

Marks:

American Art China Works - R&E, 1891-95

AAC (superimposed), 1891-95

American Belleek Company - Company name, banner & globe

Ceramic Art Company - CAC palette, 1889- 1906

Colombian Art Pottery - CAP, 1893-1902

Cook Pottery - Three feathers w/"CHC," 1894- 1904

Coxon Belleek Pottery - "Coxon Belleek" in a shield, 1926-1930

Gordon Belleek - "Gordon Belleek," 1920-28

Knowles, Taylor & Knowles - "Lotusware" in a circle w/a crown, 1891-96

Lenox China - Palette mark, 1906-1924

Ott & Brewer - crown & shield, 1883-1893

Perlee - "P" in a wreath, 1925-1930

Willets Manufacturing Company - Serpent mark, 1880-1909

Cook Pottery - Three feathers w/"CHC"

Plates and Platters

Ceramic Art Company, plate, 10 1/2" d., finely h.p. in the center w/a bust portrait of a young maiden holding a closed book & a stylus, wearing a white wrap on her head, a white gown & red shawl, wide claret border band decorated w/an ornate gilt swag band w/foliate scrolls & flower garlands, gilt rim band, artist- signed, ca. 1905 .... **$2,880**

Cups and Saucers

Irish Belleek

Comports & Centerpieces

Comport, Trihorse Comport, impressed "Belleek Co. Fermanagh," D37-I **$3,400**

Lenox, demitasse cup & saucer, cov., sterling silver overlay of Art Deco design w/orange & green enameling, silver overlay around rim of cup & octagonal saucer, palette mark, 4 1/2" w. saucer **$75**

Figurines

Boy and Shell, 9" h., D9-II **$3,000**

Tea Ware - Museum Display Patterns (Artichoke, Chinese, Finner, Five O'Clock, Lace, Ring Handle Ivory, Set #36 & Victoria)

Muffin dish, cov., Artichoke Tea Ware, gilt trim, D720-I **$2,000**

Plate, Ring Handle Ivory Ware plate, h.p. Irish scene, unsigned but from the School of Eugene Sheerin, 7 1/2" d., D823-II **$1,800**

Tea Ware - Rare Patterns (Aberdeen, Blarney, Celtic (low & tall), Cone, Erne, Fan, Institute, Ivy, Lily (high & low), Scroll, Sydney, Thistle & Thorn)

Celtic Candlestick, Low, painted & gilt, 4 3/4" h., D1511-VI **$340**

Celtic Design bread plate, Celtic Design tea ware, multicolored & gilt, D1425-III **$600**

Celtic Design creamer, Celtic Design tea ware, tall shape, multicolored, ('mystery' mark, 1st Period over Celtic Scroll, probably a transition from 1st to 2nd period), 4 1/2" h., D1442-II **$400**

BELLEEK

Tea Wares - Miscellaneous

Celtic bowl of roses, h.p. colors of dark pink, yellow & green, D1510-VII **$2,600**

Plate, pottery, Scenic Celtic commemorative plate, painted & gilded, D1553-V **$800**

Plate, scenic center of Irish peasant homes w/ornate gilt scroll border, h.p. by former pottery manager Cyril Arnold, artist- signed & w/what appears to be "15 PA" following the signature, 8 1/2" d., D1527- IV **$1,200**

Wedding cup, three-handled, Shamrock patt., h.p. trim, D2105-II **$640**

• Before driving a long distance to an auction, call or e-mail the auctioneer to discuss an advertised item that interests you. Even with the help of a catalog, descriptions of some lots may not be sufficient to satisfy all your questions.

• If you haven't seen an item of interest that is about to be auctioned, ask a ring man to allow you to inspect it immediately. The auctioneer will note your interest and hold the bidding momentarily while you decide. Inspections are better made during the preview, however.

Berlin (KPM)

The mark KPM was used at Meissen from 1724 to 1725, and was later adopted by the Royal Factory, Konigliche Porzellan Manufaktur, in Berlin. At various periods it has been incorporated with the Brandenburg scepter, the Prussian eagle or the crowned globe. The same letters were also adopted by other factories in Germany in the late 19th and early 20th centuries.

With the end of the German monarchy in 1918, the name of the firm was changed to Staatliche Porzellan Manufaktur and though production was halted during World War II, the factory was rebuilt and is still in business. The exquisite paintings on porcelain were produced at the close of the 19th century and are eagerly sought by collectors today.

Centerpiece, in the Vienna style, a deep oval bowl w/serpentine sides pierced at the rim & flanked by large gold scrolling loop handles, the front finely painted w/a Classical view representing the Arts in a garden setting & the reverse depicting Neptune as a child riding a dolphin w/other putti, a gold bead band around the base of the bowl & raised on a deep maroon pedestal w/gilt scroll decoration & an oblong gold foot w/block feet alternating w/dolphin mask feet between gold knobs, titled in German on the bottom, blue sceptre mark, late 19th c., 15" l. **$4,183**

Charger, pate-sur-pate, round w/a wide dished rim band in white decorated w/ornate gold Art Nouveau floral looping panels w/small forget-me-nots & roses, the wide center w/a celadon green ground painted & hand-tooled in white slip w/a scene of a diaphanously clad Bacchante pouring a vessel of wine into Pan's lips as he kneels beside a tree stump, blue sceptre & iron-red orb marks, ca. 1895, 13 3/4" d. **$5,378**

Pate-sur-pate is French for clay on clay. It is a technique in which liquid clay or slip is painted in layers on unglazed porcelain to create a raised (relief) decoration. The technique was discovered by accident at the Sevres porcelain factory in the 1850s. Marc-Louis Solon became its most famous practitiioner and later trained English potter Frederick Alfred Rhead.

Charger, round, the wide border band w/a cobalt blue ground very ornately painted in gold w/ alternating panels of a wreath & crown & scrolls in pointed arcs, the center painted in color w/a bust portrait of a w/a fancy headdress by Wagner, in a deep giltwood shadowbox fra in red velvet, late 19th c
....

Model of a squirrel, seated animal in dark brick red holding a brown acorn, on a green & brown stump molded w/acorns & oak leaves, some gold wear, second half 19th c., 10" h. **$1,150**

Plaque, oval, a colorful scene of a Middle Eastern family showing a mother, father, son & daughter sitting on an upholstered sofa, within an ornately scrolling gilt gesso oval frame, plaque impressed on the back "KPM - T," 7 1/2 x 9 1/4" **$960**

Plaque, oval, decorated w/a color copy of "The Sistine Madonna" after Raphael, mounted in an elaborate rectangular giltwood pierce-carved frame composed of scrolling acanthus leaves w/a red velvet liner, fitted in a glazed rectangular shadowbox frame, impressed sceptre & KPM marks, late 19th c., plaque 13 1/2 x 17" **$4,025**

Plaque, rectangular, a three-quarters length standing portrait of a semi-nude young woman w/long brown hair & a red robe around her waist, artist-signed, unframed, flake to one corner, 6 3/8 x 9 3/8" **$4,025**

Plaque, rectangular, finely painted w/the portrait of an exotic raven-haired beauty playing a lyre carved as the head of an Egyptian pharaoh, a brazier at her feet, impressed monogram & sceptre mark, titled on the back, late 19th - early 20th c., mounted in giltwood frame, 6 1/4 x 9 3/8" **$4,183**

Plaque, rectangular, painted w/ a winter scene of an elderly grandfather just outside a cottage door & standing holding a small baby w/his little granddaughter nearby, titled "The First Snowfall," impressed sceptre & KPM marks, artist- signed, in a fancy acanthus leaf-carved wooden frame, late 19th c., plaque 7 1/2 x 10" **$4,370**

Plaque, rectangular, scene of two young women w/long flowing hair & wearing diaphanous gowns holding floral garland above their heads, reverse impressed "KPM" w/scepter, in very ornate gilt wood frame of pierced scroll decoration, 19th c., 7 1/2 x 10" **$4,830**

Urn, octagonal stepped base below ringed pedestal supporting baluster-form body w/trumpet neck, two gilt coiled snake- form handles, front w/h.p. decoration of winged cherub among floral bouquet, reverse w/butterflies & florals, marked w/red orb & blue underglaze circle, late 19th c., 18 3/4" h. **$3,680**

Plaque, rectangular, a long classical scene depicting the goddess Aurora & her attendants, after a painting by Guido Reni, inscribed & titled on the back along w/a label reading "Painted for Mermood and Jaccurd Jewelry Co., St. Louis," impressed KPM & other marks, artist- signed, mounted in an elaborate reticulated giltwood framed plaque, 8 x 13" **$10,638**

In Roman mythology, Aurora is the goddess of the dawn. Each morning she crosses the sky to precede and announce the arrival of the sun. Her four children are the Anemoi, or the Winds; her sister is Luna, the moon; and her brother is Sol, the sun. In Greek mythology, Aurora is known as Eos.

According to legend, Aurora fell in love with the human Tithonus, who, as a mortal, would someday face death, unlike the immortal Aurora. Aurora asked Zeus to grant Tithonus eternal life, and the wish was granted, but while he was given eternal life, he was not granted eternal youth.

Betty Lou Nichols Ceramics

Although Betty Lou Nichols (1922-1995) created a wide variety of ceramic figurines, she's best known for her distinctive line of "lady head vases." From the 1940s well into the 1960s, such vases, many sporting oversized hats with openings in the crown to accommodate small bouquets, were popular with florist shops and consumers. Today "Betty Lou's" are among the most sought-after head vases. They're immediately recognizable by their darkly-fringed, three- dimensional eyelashes, oversized hair bows and coiled ceramic curls.

A California native, Nichols immersed herself in art from an early age, later studying at Fullerton Junior College under noted ceramist Mary Hodgedon. After marriage and initial employment as a photographer, Nichols opened her first ceramics studio in 1945, in the backyard of her parents' La Habra home. As with many mid-1940s ceramics firms, the timing was right since overseas imports of decorative objects had been cut off during World War II.

Nichols' initial acclaim came with a series of "Gay 90s" figurines created for Bullock's of Los Angeles. The idea for her lady head vases is credited to noted sales representative Ruth Sloan (who also represented Kay Finch). With the introduction of head vases, success came quickly; in 1949, Betty Lou Nichols Ceramics relocated to a larger La Habra factory, eventually employing over 30 workers.

Betty Lou Nichols Ceramics remained in operation until 1962. In addition to head vases, planters and figurines, production items included decanters, plates, mugs and other decorative ware. The firm also took on special contracted projects such as ceramic figures based on characters from the Walt Disney movie *Fantasia*, and containers for products from California's Knott's Berry Farm. After her retirement from ceramic work, Nichols embarked on a successful second career as a painter, specializing in portraits and landscapes.

Abundant ruffles and flourishes contribute to the appeal and value of Betty Lou Nichols ceramics, but also contribute to their fragility. It's rare today to find a Betty Lou in pristine condition, with all eyelashes, curls and bodice trim intact. Fortunately, Betty Lou repair has become a booming cottage industry and restoration experts are readily available to bring back the bloom to these glamour girls.

Advisor/photographer for this category is Donald-Brian Johnson, an author and lecturer specializing in Mid-Twentieth Century design. Reference material courtesy of Maddy Gordon, author of *Head Vases, Etc.: The Artistry of Betty Lou Nichols* (Schiffer Publishing, Ltd., 2002).

"Anna," figurine, 9" h. (ILLUS. right) **$75-100**
"Fritz," planter, 9 1/2" h. (ILLUS. left) **$75-100**

"Dick," planter, 5" h. (ILLUS. right).................................... **$50-75**
"Holly," figurine, 7" h. (ILLUS. center) **$50-75**
"Tom," planter, 6" h. (ILLUS. left)...................................... **$50-75**

onna," planter, 8" h.
.... **$75-100**

"Olga the Flower Vendor & Tina," planter, 11" l. **$450-475**

Bisque

Bisque is biscuit china, fired a single time but not glazed. Some bisque is decorated with colors. Most abundant from the Victorian era are figures and groups, but other pieces, from busts to vases, were made by numerous potteries in the United States and abroad. Reproductions have been produced for many years, so care must be taken when seeking antique originals.

Figure of a nude woman, reclining on her stomach w/her head raised, painted hair & facial features, marked on the bottom "1627 Germany," early 20th c., 6" l. **$1,035**

Bust of Napoleon, wearing his military uniform & cockade hat, on a square black marble plinth w/applied gilt-bronze wreath & initial, France, late 19th c., overall 27" h. **$3,000**

Figure group, a family group all wearing 18th c. costume, a young man standing close behind & a pretty young woman looking down, a young boy in front reaching up to them, finely painted ornate costumes in shades of blue, pink & gold & fine facial features, on a rounded rockwork base, printed anchor mark, late 19th c., some very minor professional repairs, 26" h. **$1,955**

Figure of a nude woman, seated w/her legs extended & her hands clasped under her chin, h.p. facial features w/smiling mouth, brown mohair wig & scarf, base marked "406R," Germany, early 20th c., 3 1/4" l., 3" h. **$805**

With few exceptions, collectors should not attempt to repair antiques. In many cases, any repairs, even professional, will lower value. In some cases, repairs can increase value, but should be done by an expert. Research carefully before having any work performed.

Figure of a Victorian girl, the young blonde-haired girl walking down rocky steps & leaning on a low wall w/a lion head fountain issuing blue water, wearing a short ruffled blue dress, large blue bonnet & blue shoes, carrying a brown basket on her arm, nice coloring, "R" in diamond mark, perhaps Royal Rudolstadt, Germany, ca. 1900, 10" h. **$80-100**

BISQUE

Figure of a woman & goat, the woman standing wearing an 18th c. peasant costume in white, blue & pink w/overall tiny painted flowers, holding a sheaf of grain & looking down at a small goat jumping up to nibble on the flowers gathered in her skirt, on a round socle base decorated w/ blue & gold bands & delicate blue & yellow ribbon band, late 19th c., minor repair, 18" h. **$374**

Figure of baby in highchair, delicate baby wearing a blue-tinted bonnet, pink lace collar & white gown, in a tan-colored wicker highchair, marked w/ sunburst trademark of Gebruder Heubach, Germany, late 19th - early 20th c., 8" h. **$275-325**

Figure of gentleman, young man in gold- trimmed pastel-colored outfit w/white ruffled shirt, holding rose in one hand, on round base modeled to resemble stones or bricks of a courtyard, marked w/blue diamond "R," 20 1/2" h. **$104**

Figures of boy & girl, the girl wearing yellow skirt w/red bows & white ruffled hem, white blouse, pale blue bodice & overskirt w/white lacy trim, orange shoes, tam-like hat, holding white & orange fan in one hand, the boy in short yellow pants w/white ruffled cuffs, matching yellow jacket, pale blue stockings & shirt, yellow & orange boots, & white hat w/orange trim, standing w/one hand on hip, the other at hat, unmarked, Germany, ca. 1900, 14" h., pr. **$201**

Figures of children blowing bubbles, girl wearing a cream dress w/pink floral decoration & gold trim at collar & hem, boy w/pink flower-decorated knee breeches & cream shirt w/ dotted ruffled neck & cuffs, each holding a bubble pipe to mouth & each sitting on bench that also holds bowl for soapy water, h.p. features, unmarked, Heubach, Germany, ca. 1900, 13" h., pr. **$978**

Figures of man & woman, each dressed in pale green outfit w/peach-colored bows & decorations, the man w/knee breeches & jacket, holding flowers in one hand, a staff in the other, the woman in dress w/laced bodice & elbow-length sleeves, each standing on ornate scroll base that holds trellis-like backdrop w/molded flowers, h.p. features, unmarked, late 19th c., Germany, 16" h., pr. **$288**

Figures of man & woman, wearing buff- colored outfits & draping cloaks, h.p. features, each on molded cylindrical base, unmarked, 20 1/2" h., pr. .. **$978**

Figures of tennis players, the girl wearing aqua pleated skirt & cream colored blouse w/gold sash belt, white hat w/short aqua brim, holding racket in one hand & ball in the other, the boy wearing aqua knee breeches & matching shirt w/cream colored neckerchief, white hat w/short aqua brim, also holding racket & ball, each on base formed to resemble green grass of playing field, h.p. features, unmarked, Heubach, Germany, 15" h., pr. **$748**

Figures of young woman & man, each dressed in Renaissance-style costumes in pale pink & cream shades trimmed in white & decorated w/darker peach flowers, each wearing brimmed hat, the woman holding one hand to forehead, the other holding skirt, h.p. features & florals on tinted ground, unmarked, Germany, ca. 1900, 16 1/2" h., pr. **$316**

Figures of young woman & man, the woman wearing rose-colored dress w/gold bodice trimmed in white lace & pale aqua short sleeves, the narrow skirt w/pale aqua bows down front & matching wide sash at waist, white long gloves, pink shoes, elaborately styled powdered hair, the fair-haired man w/long curls, wearing rose-colored short lace-trimmed pants & matching jacket w/gold trim & pale aqua cloak, rose boots, h.p. features, gilt accents, unmarked, Germany, ca. 1900, 16" h., pr. **$173**

Figures of man & woman, wearing buff-colored outfits & draping cloaks, h.p. features, each on molded cylindrical base, unmarked, 20 1/2" h., pr..... **$978**

Figures of tennis players, the girl wearing aqua pleated skirt & cream colored blouse w/gold sash belt, white hat w/short aqua brim, holding racket in one hand & ball in the other, the boy wearing aqua knee breeches & matching shirt w/cream colored neckerchief, white hat w/short aqua brim, also holding racket & ball, each on base formed to resemble green grass of playin field, h.p. features, unmarke Heubach, Germany, 15" h., ... $

BLUE & WHITE POTTERY

Blue & White Pottery

The category of blue and white or blue and grey pottery includes a wide variety of pottery, earthenware and stoneware items widely produced in this country in the late 19th century right through the 1930s. Originally marketed as inexpensive wares, most pieces featured a white or grey body molded with a fruit, flower or geometric design and then trimmed with bands or splashes of blue to highlight the molded pattern. Pitchers, butter crocks and salt boxes are among the numerous items produced, but other kitchenwares and chamber sets are also found. Values vary depending on the rarity of the embossed pattern and the depth of color of the blue trim; the darker the blue, the better. Some entries refer to several different books on Blue and White Pottery. These books are: *Blue & White Stoneware, Pottery & Crockery* by Edith Harbin (1977, Collector Books, Paducah, KY); *Stoneware in the Blue and White* by M.H. Alexander (1993 reprint, Image Graphics, Inc., Paducah, KY); and *Blue & White Stoneware* by Kathryn McNerney (1995, Collector Books, Paducah, KY).

Coffeepot, cov., embossed Bull's-Eye patt., w/ bottom plate **$3,250**

Ewer & basin set, embossed Beaded Rose patt., A.E. Hull Pottery Co., the set **$750**

Pitcher, 10" h., 7" d., embossed American Beauty Rose patt., Burley-Winter Pottery Co. .. **$475**

Teapot, cov., Swirl patt., spherical body w/row of relief-molded knobs around the shoulder, inset cover w/knob finial, swan's-neck spout, shoulder loop brackets for wire bail handle w/turned wood grip, metal bottom plate, 6" d., 6" h. **$800**

Pitcher, 6 3/4" h., stenciled Wildflower patt., hall boy-type w/ cylindrical body & five stencils per side, Brush-McCoy Pottery Co. (ILLUS. right) **$550**

Pitcher, 6" h., stenciled Wildflower patt., hall boy-type w/waisted body & five stencils per side, Brush-McCoy Pottery Co. (ILLUS. left) **$750**

Vase, 11" h., Diffused Blue, wide ovoid body w/ short flared neck & pointed shoulder handles **$325**

Umbrella stand, embossed Two Stags patt., tall trees & large oak leaves & acorns, solid blue, Logan Pottery Co., 21" h. **$2,250**

Wall pocket, long pointed shape, h. p. blue iris decoration & blue rim bands, 11" l. **$250**

Water cooler, cov., stencile Wildflower patt., domed cover button knob atop a tall cylindr section above the wider lindrical base section w/a a circle above the metal sp gal. ....

BLUE RIDGE DINNERWARES

Blue Ridge Dinnerwares

The small town of Erwin, Tennessee, was the home of the Southern Potteries, Inc., originally founded by E.J. Owen in 1917 and first called the Clinchfield Pottery.

In the early 1920s Charles W. Foreman purchased the plant and revolutionized the company's output, developing the popular line of handpainted wares sold as "Blue Ridge" dinnerwares. Freehand painted by women from the surrounding hills, these colorful dishes in many patterns continued in production until the plant's closing in 1957.

*Blue Ridge
Hand Painted
Underglaze
Southern Potteries Inc.
MADE IN U.S.A.*

Ashtray, individual, Fall Colors patt. **$25**

Coaster/butter pat, Astor shape, Mariner patt., 4" d. **$150**

...er, 6 1/2" h., china, Swirl
..be, Anniversary Song patt.
.... **$175**

Cake plate, handled, Fruit Fantasy patt., 9 x 10 1/2" **$75**

Bowl, 5 1/4" d., cereal, Candlewick shape, Quaker Apple patt. **$5**

Bowl, 7" l., tab-handled, Colonial shape, Wild Strawberry patt. **$25**

Cake lifter, Berry Delicious patt., 9" l. **$25**

Cake plate, 11" d., Candlewick shape, Bleeding Heart patt... **$35**

Celery dish, leaf-shaped, Easter Parade patt., 11" l. **$22**

Chocolate pot, cov., china, Chintz patt., 9 1/2" h. **$165**

Cigarette box, cov., square, Butterfly patt., 4 1/4" w. **$110**

Creamer & sugar bowl, pedestal-based, Rose of Sharon patt., the set **$95**

Creamer & sugar bowl, regular size, Colonial shape, Garden Lane patt., the set **$35**

Cup & saucer, demitasse size, Colonial shape, Peony patt., saucer 5" d., the set **$55**

Cup & saucer, jumbo size, Colonial shape, Red Apple patt., saucer 7 1/2" d., the set **$100**

Cup & saucer, regular size, Candlewick shape, Bluebell Bouquet patt., saucer 6" d., the set **$17**

Gravy boat, Colonial shape, Wrinkled Rose patt., 7 1/2" l. **$25**

Mug, child's, Yellow Bunny patt., 2 3/4" h. **$225- 250**

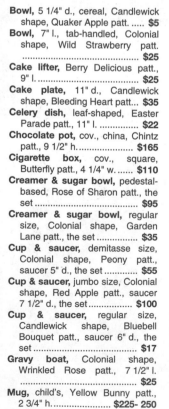

When stacking plates, place acid-free paper or cloth separators between to cushion shocks and prevent chips and cracks. Don't stack more than six high. Do not hang cups by their handles.

Pitcher, 4" h., miniature, Virginia shape, Sheree patt. **$300**

Pitcher, 5 1/2" h., china, Chick shape, Flora patt. **$110**

Pitcher, 6" h., china, Martha shape, Sea Green patt. **$85**

Pitcher, 6" h., earthenware, Abby shape, yellow **$40**

Pitcher, 6 1/2" h., earthenware, Martha shape, Blue Beauty patt. **$65**

Plate, 6" d., bread & butter, Colonial shape, Paper Roses patt........ **$8**

Plate, 7" d., dessert, Piecrust shape, Magnolia patt........................ **$15**

Plate, 7" w., square, Poinsettia patt. **$25**

Plate, 8" d., salad, Colonial shape, Orchard Glory patt................ **$13**

Plate, 8" d., salad, Skyline shape, Windmill patt........................ **$60**

Plate, 9" d., luncheon, Colonial shape, Big Apple patt. **$12**

Plate, 9" d., luncheon, Skyline shape, Red Barn patt. **$35**

Plate, 10" d., dinner, Colonial shape, Christmas Tree with Mistletoe patt. **$75**

Plate, 10" d., dinner, Colonial shape, Iris Anne patt. **$28**

Platter, 11 1/2" l., Colonial shape, Polka Dot patt....................... **$25**

Platter, 13" l., Colonial shape, Apple Trio patt................................ **$30**

Platter, 15" l., Skyline shape, Loretta patt. **$18**

Relish dish, deep shell shape, Ridge Rose patt., 9 x 9" **$95**

Relish dish, four-part w/center handle, Ridge Daisy patt., 8 1/2" w. **$45**

Salt & pepper shakers, china, Chintz patt., 5 3/4" h., pr. **$74**

Salt & pepper shakers, range-size, Mardi Gras patt., 4 3/8" h., pr......... $25

Vase, 8" h., china, ornate loop shoulder handles, Stephanie patt. $65

Salt & pepper shakers, short, Skyline shape, Cheerio patt., 2 1/2" h., pr.......................... $15

Snack plate w/cup well, Skyline shape, Spiderweb Blue patt. $15

Soup plate, flanged rim, Colonial shape, Mardi Gras patt., 8" d. $15

Spoon rest, Apple patt., 6 1/2" l. $18

Teapot, cov., china, Mini Ball shape, Dogtooth Violet patt., 5 1/2" h. $225

Teapot, cov., Colonial shape, Becky patt., 8"h. $110

Toast dish, cov., Jonquil patt. $110

Vegetable bowl, oval, Colonial shape, Poinsettia patt., 7 x 9" $26

Vegetable bowl, round, Colonial shape, Fruit Punch patt., 9" d. $35

Creamer & sugar, Colonial shape, Garden Lane patt., the set $45

Cake lifter, Pomona patt., 9" l. $32

Bowl, 9" d., Belvedere patt., deep shell shape, in shades of blue & red... $75

BRAYTON LAGUNA POTTERY

Brayton Laguna Pottery

In the 1940s California saw an influx of pottery companies; however, it was Durlin Brayton who earlier, about 1927, began his enterprise. During these previous years Brayton created an assortment of products along with many beautiful glazes, honing his skills before other artists arrived. He married his second wife, an artist, Ellen Webster Grieve, in 1936 and together they became very successful. Durlin Brayton's talent caught the eye of Walt Disney, who bestowed on him the honor of being the first pottery licensed to create ceramic copies of some of Disney's most famous characters. Brayton did this from 1938 until 1940. Ellen Grieve Brayton died in 1948 and Durlin Brayton followed shortly after in 1951. The pottery continued to operate until 1968.

Brayton collectors need to familiarize themselves with the marks, lines and glazes produced by this firm. There are as many as a dozen marks; however, not all Brayton is marked. Hand-turned pieces were the first used and many were marked with Durlin Brayton's handwriting with "Brayton Laguna" or "Brayton Tile." These items have become scarce. Assorted lines include: African-American figures, animals, Art Deco designs, Blackamoors, Calasia (a design of circles and feathers), Children's Series, Circus Series, Disney Characters, Gay Nineties, Hillbilly Shotgun Wedding, kitchen items, sculptures, tiles, Webtonware and the Wedding Series, plus a few others.

Figure of a baby, standing w/hands on hips, wearing swimming trunks, Hillbilly Shotgun Wedding series designed by Andy Anderson, ca. 1938, three pots & dog walker stamp mark, scarce, 4 1/4" h. **$325**

Figure of a boy, "Eugene," Children's Series, standing w/hat on head, handkerchief pinned at his chest, arms behind his back holding a flower, stamped mark "Eugene" above the line & "Brayton Pottery" below the line, 7" h. (ILLUS. right) **$105**

Figure of a girl, "Ellen," Children's Series, standing w/pigtails & hat, tied at the neck w/a large polka dot bow, arms bent at elbows & palms forward, one leg slightly twisted w/right toes on top of left foot, stamped mark "Ellen" above the line & "Brayton Pottery" below the line, 7 1/2" h. (ILLUS. left) **$115**

Figure of a Dutch boy, standing wearing dark blue pants, light blue jacket, red cap & yellow wooden shoes, designed by Frances Robinson, ca. early 1940s, 8" h. (ILLUS. right) **$110**

Figure of a Dutch girl, standing wearing a white apron w/blue trim, light blue blouse, white cap & yellow wood shoes, holding a flower in one hand, designed by Frances Robinson, ca. early 1940s, 7" h. (ILLUS. left).... **$115**

Figure of a clown, sitting w/feet crossed, hands behind back, white clothing w/red dots, blue, red, green & yellow ruffles on neck collar, wrists & ankles, black shoes, ink stamped w/three pots on left & dog-walker on right, 5 1/4" l., 6" h. **$165**

Model of bear, turquoise, sitting w/front legs outstretched, incised underglaze mark "Brayton's Laguna, Cal.," 3" h. **$120**

→

Buffalo Pottery

Incorporated in 1901 as a wholly owned subsidiary of the Larkin Soap Company, founded by John D. Larkin of Buffalo, New York, in 1875, the Buffalo Pottery was a manufactory built to produce premium wares to be included with purchases of Larkin's chief product, soap.

In October 1903, the first kiln was fired and Buffalo Pottery became the only pottery in the world run entirely by electricity. In 1904 Larkin offered its first premium produced by the pottery. This concept of using premiums caused sales to skyrocket and, in 1905, the first Blue Willow pattern pottery made in the United States was introduced as a premium.

The Buffalo Pottery administrative building, built in 1904 to house 1,800 clerical workers, was the creation of a 32-year-old architect, Frank Lloyd Wright. The building was demolished in 1953, but many critics considered it to be Wright's masterpiece.

By 1910 annual soap production peaked and the number of premiums offered in the catalogs exceeded 600. By 1915 this number had grown to 1,500. The first catalog of premiums was issued in 1893 and continued to appear through the late 1930s.

John D. Larkin died in 1926, and during the Great Depression the firm suffered severe losses, going into bankruptcy in 1940. After World War II the pottery resumed production under new management, but its vitreous wares were generally limited to mass-produced china for the institutional market.

Among the pottery lines produced during Buffalo's heyday were Gaudy Willow, Deldare, Abino Ware, historical and commemorative plates, and unique handpainted jugs and pitchers. In the 1920s and 1930s the firm concentrated on personalized wares for commercial clients including hotels, clubs, railroads, and restaurants.

In 1983 Oneida Silversmiths bought the pottery, an ironic twist since, years before, Oneida silver had been featured in Larkin catalogs. The pottery has now ceased all domestic production of ceramics. - Phillip M. Sullivan.

Abino Ware (1911-1913)

Author's Note: Today this is a seller's market with prices escalating rapidly.

Candlestick, Nautical design, 9" h.
.... $1,200
Matchbox holder w/ashtray
.... $2,000
Pitcher, 7" h., octagonal jug-type, Portland Head Light scene
.... $2,800+
Pitcher, 10 1/2" h., tankard-type
.... $2,100
Saucer, windmill decoration ... $200
Teacup, windmill decoration
.... $400
Vase, 8" h., seascape decoration
.... $2,200+

Blue Willow Pattern (1905-1916)

Author's Note: Pieces dated 1905 and marked "First Old Willow Ware Manufactured in America" are worth double the prices shown here.

Chop plate, scalloped edge, 11" d.
.... $275
Match safe, 2 3/4 x 6" $250
Oyster tureen, notched cover
.... $600
Pitcher, jug-type, "Hall Boy," 6 1/2 oz., 3 pts............................. $325
Pitcher, cov., jug-type, 3 1/2 pts.
.... $450
Pitcher, jug-type, "Chicago," 4 1/2 pts. $450

Mug, tankard-type, windmill scene, 1912, marked w/number 264, signed by R. Stuart, white interior, not in the Altman book, 7" h.
.... $2,000

Pitcher, 9" h., octagonal jug-type, windmill decoration, 1912, bears number 220 & signed by C. Harris, not in Altman book
.... $3,250

Cuspidor, full Willow decoration, dated 1911, not in Altman book, 7 1/4" d. top, 5" h. $500

Pitcher, wash-type ....

BUFFALO POTTERY

Deldare Ware (1908-1909, 1923-1925)

Author's Note: "Fallowfield Hunt" and "Ye Olden Days" scenes are similarly priced for the equivalent pieces in this line.

Calendar plate, 1910, 9 1/2" d. .... **$2,800+**
Calling card tray, round w/tab handles, "Ye Olden Days" scene, 7 3/4" d. .... **$450+**
Candleholder, shield-back style, "Ye Olden Days" scene, 7" h. .... **$2,000+**
Candlestick, "Ye Olden Days" scene, 9 1/2" h. **$750**
Dresser tray, rectangular, "Dancing Ye Minuet" scene, 9 x 12" **$900**
Fruit bowl, 9" d., 3 3/4" h.,"Ye Village Tavern" scene, 1909 .... **$600**
Humidor, cov., octagonal, 7" h. **$1,400**
Pitcher, 8" h., octagonal, "Ye Olden Days" scene **$850**

Pitcher, 12 1/2" h. tankard-type, double- decorated w/"The Great Controversy" scene on one side & "All You Have To Do To Teach a Dutchman English" scene on the other side, artist-signed, 1908 .... **$1,250+**
Plate, 6 1/4" d., salesman's sample .... **$2,400+**
Punch bowl, footed, 14 3/4" d., 9 1/4" h. .... **$7,000+**
Relish dish, oblong, 6 1/2 x 12" **$500**
Salad bowl, 12" d., 5" h. **$600**
Vase, 8 1/2" h., 6" d., footed tapering ovoid body w/a flaring rim, "Ye Olden Days" scene, black ink mark .... **$1,300+**
Vase, 9" h., tall waisted cylindrical form, "Ye Olden Days" scene, 1909 .... **$1,400**
Wall plaque, 12" d. **$1,000**

Jardiniere & garden seat pedestal base, "Ye Lion Inn" scenes on jardiniere, two "Ye Olden Days" scenes on base, 1908, jardiniere 9" h., base 13 1/2" h., the set **$12,000**

Plates, 9 1/4" d., "The Fallow Field Hunt - The Start," artist-signed, set of 4, each $300

Emerald Deldare (1911)

Candlestick, Bayberry decoration, 9" h. **$1,000**
Plaque, round, "Friday," scene of monks at a long table eating fish on Friday, 12" d. .... **$2,000+**
Plaque, round, "Lost," scene of herd of sheep in blizzard, 13 1/2" d. .... **$2,200+**
Plate, 8 1/4" d., stylized floral & geometric decoration.......... **$750**
Vase, 8" h., 6 1/2" d., ovoid w/a wide shoulder tapering to a short flaring neck, olive green ground decorated in shades of green & white w/a kingfisher & iris, signed by J. Gerhardt, 1911 .... **$1,800**

Saucer, round, "Dr. Syntax and the Bookseller," 1911 (ILLUS. with teacup) **$350**
Teacup, tapering body w/angled handle, "Dr. Syntax at Liverpool," 1911 (ILLUS. with saucer).. **$400**

Pitcher, 9" h., octagonal, angled handle, color scene of "Dr. Syntax Setting Out to the Lake,s (sic)," signed by R. Stuart, dated 1911 .... **$1,900**

Gaudy Willow (1905-1916)

Author's Note: Pieces dated 1905 and marked "First Old Willow Ware Manufactured in America" are worth double the prices shown here. This line is generally priced five times higher than the Blue Willow line.

Bone dish, 3 1/4 x 7 1/4" **$225**
Boston egg cup, 7 oz............ **$350**
Butter dish, cover & insert, the set, 7 1/4" d............................. **$750**
Cake plate, double-handled, 10 1/4" d........................... **$600**
Creamer, round, 1 pt., 2 oz. ... **$500**
Gravy/sauceboat, 14 1/2 oz. **$450**
Pickle dish, square, 4 1/2 x 8 1/4" **$350**
Plate, dinner, 10 1/2" d.......... **$275**
Platter, 18" l., oval............. **$1,000+**
Saucer, 6 1/2" d...................... **$50**
Sugar bowl, cov., round, 24 1/4 oz. **$500**
Teacup, 10 oz. **$200**

Jugs and Pitchers (1906-1909)

Jug, "George Washington," blue & white, 1907, 7 1/2" h. **$700**
Jug, "Mason," brown/beige colors, 1907, 8 1/2" h................ **$1,100+**
Pitcher, 8 3/4" h., bone china, melon- shaped, white, 1909 .... **$1,200**
Pitcher, "Art Nouveau," gold & blue, 1908, 9 1/2" h................ **$1,200+**
Pitcher, "Buffalo Hunt," jug-form, Indian on horseback hunting buffalo, dark bluish green ground, 6" h...................................... **$350**
Pitcher, "Chrysanthemum," dark green, 1908, 7 1/2" h.......... **$500**
Pitcher, "Cinderella," jug-type, ca. 1907, marked w/Buffalo transfer logo & date, "Cinderella" & "1328," 6" h.................................. **$700+**
Pitcher, "John Paul Jones," blue & white, 1908, 8 3/4" h. .... **$1,250+**

Pitcher, "Marine Pitcher, Lighthouse," blue & white, 1907, 9 1/4" h.......................... **$1,250+**
Pitcher, "New Bedford Whaler - The Niger," bluish green, 1907, 6" h. **$900**
Pitcher, "Pilgrim," brightly colored, 1908, 9" h........................ **$1,100**
Pitcher, "Robin Hood," multicolored, 1906, 8 1/4" h..................... **$700**
Pitcher, "Roosevelt Bears," beige, 1906, 8 1/4" h................. **$3,400**
Pitcher, "Sailor" patt., waisted-tankard form, decorated in blues w/the heads of two seamen above scenes of sailing ships, opposite side w/a lighthouse & rocky coastline, 1906, 9 1/4" h. .... **$1,250+**
Pitcher, "Whirl of the Town," brightly colored, 1906, 7" h. **$700**

Pitcher, "Gloriana," blue on white, ca. 1908, 9" h. (ILLUS. right) **$900**
Pitcher, "Holland," decorated w/three colorful h.p. scenes of Dutch children on the body w/band near the rim decorated w/a rural landscape, ca. 1906, marked w/Buffalo transfer logo & date, "Holland" & "9," overall consistent staining, 5 3/4" h. (ILLUS. left) **$750**

• An item's provenance is its pedigree or record of who owned it in the past. Sometimes an antique inadvertently acquires an embellished provenance over several generations. Because oral histories can be so unreliable, verifiable information, such as written documents, are needed to establish the authenticity of a provenance. A provenance that includes a famous historical figure, a celebrity or a major museum, can dramatically increase the value of an antique.

• Before selling or discarding a family heirloom, no matter how insignificant it may seem, ask other members of the family it they want it. Adult grandchildren who have fond memories of time spent at their grandparents' house might enjoy having a keepsake.

• Bidders at estate auctions are sometimes perplexed and irritated when items are bid higher than their fair market value. The reason may be that a family member is bidding to retain a family heirloom. If this happens repeatedly, especially to high value items, it can be detrimental to an auction because bidders are likely to become frustrated and leave.

BUFFALO POTTERY

Plates - Commemorative (1906-1912)

B. & M. Smelter, and the largest smokestack in the world. Great Falls, Montana, deep green, ca. 1909, 7 1/2" d. **$150**

Gen. A.P. Stewart Chapter, United Daughters of the Confederacy, No. 81, Richmond, Virginia, blue & white, 1907, 10 1/2" d. **$350**
George Washington & Martha Washington, deep bluish green, 7 1/2" d., each **$275**

Hadley's 40th Anniversary Sale, Pioneer, Ohio - 1868-1908, deep bluish green w/three vignettes, not in Altman book, 7 1/2" d. **$200**

Improved Order of the Redman, green border w/multicolored design, 7 1/2" d. **$200**
Locks (The), Lockport, New York, deep bluish green, 7 1/2" d.... **$150**
New Bedford, Massachusetts, blue & white, 1908, 10 1/2" d. **$200**

World's & National Woman's Christian Temperance Union, center view of a house & vignettes around the border, blue & white, ca. 1908, 9" d. **$400**

Richest Hill in the World, Butte, Montana, deep bluish green, 7 1/2" d.............................. **$175**
State Capitol, Helena, Montana, deep bluish green, 7 1/2" d. **$175**

Plates - Historical - Blue or Green (1905-1910)

Capitol Building, Washington, D.C., 10" d............................ **$95**
Faneuil Hall, Boston, 10" d. **$95**

Independence Hall, Philadelphia, 10" d...................................... **$95**
Mount Vernon, 10" d. **$95**

Niagara Falls, 10" d................ **$95**
White House, Washington, 10" d. **$95**

Miscellaneous Pieces

Cup, demitasse size, white w/red band & logo of the Marine Corps, Ye Olde Ivory, bottom marked "Buffalo China - Made in U.S.A. C-10," not in Altman book, 2 1/2" h. **$75**

Christmas Plate, 1950, first of a series of annual plates ending in 1962, 9 1/2" d. **$75**

Boston egg cup, white w/Blue Lune liner, a small blue picture of the ship Mayflower on the side, inside base reads "Made Expressly for The Mayflower - Washington, D.C. - Buffalo China," undated, not in Altman book, 3 1/2" d., 3 3/4" h. **$100**

Cup & saucer, Bluebird patt, china mark, set **$75**
Gravy boat, Seneca patt., 8 1/2" l. **$45**

→ **Feeding dish,** child's, alphabet border, Dutch children at play in center, ca. 1916, 7 3/4" d. **$125**

Mugs, decorated w/various color transfer scenes of friars in a shaded brown to white ground, white interior, gold-rimmed tops, originally part of a mug & pitcher set, 5 1/2" h., each (ILLUS. of two) **$150**

Pitcher, York patt., white body w/ blue & red flowers, 1910, rare, 7 1/2" h. **$650**

Pitchor, Geranium patt., blue & white, small size (ILLUS. front row, right) **$275**
Pitcher, Geranium patt., pale green & brown on white, small size, 1906-1909 (ILLUS. front row, left) **$175**
Pitchers, Geranium patt., large sizes, multicolored design or dark blue & white, 1906-1909, each (ILLUS. in back row) **$400**

Pitcher, 9" h., flattened ovoid body tapering to a wide arched spout, printed in red w/the Larkin Company logo, possibly used in the Larkin Company cafeteria in Buffalo, printed on the base "Vitreous (above a buffalo) Buffalo Pottery," undated, ca. 1908, 10 cup size, not in Altman book **$1,000**

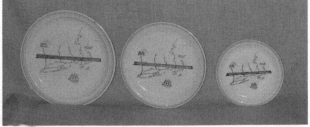

Plate, 6 3/8" d., bread & butter, made for the New York, New Haven & Hartford Railroad, ca. 1935 (ILLUS. right) **$95**
Plate, 8 3/8" d., luncheon, made for the New York, New Haven & Hartford Railroad, ca. 1935 (ILLUS. center) **$150**
Plate, 9 3/4" d., dinner, made for the New York, New Haven & Hartford Railroad, ca. 1935 (ILLUS. left) **$175**

Plate, 10 1/4" d., dinner, Bangor patt., eagle backstamp, 1906 .... **$600**
Plate, 10 1/4" d., dinner, Japan patt., multicolored, 1906 ..... **$250**
Plate, 10 1/2" d., Stuyvesant Hotel service, green & gold **$250**
Plate, 10 3/4" d., Jack Dempsey photograph, Buffalo China **$500**
Plate, 10 3/4" d., Pere Marquette Hotel service, Ye Olde Ivory **$300**
Plate, 11" d., Breakfast at the Three Pigeons, Fallowfield Hunt line, on Colorido Ware **$750**
Plate, 11" d., George Washington portrait, gold-embossed border band, made for the Chesapeake & Ohio Railroad, 1932 .... **$750**
Portland vase, reproduced in 1946, 8" h. **$1,000**

Plate, 6 1/2" d., Bluebird patt., china mark **$75**
Plate, 9" d., dinner, Hotel Robert Fulton service, Buffalo China **$250**
Plate, 9" d., Multifleur patt., Buffalo China **$300**

Plate, 9 1/2" d., Bing Crosby portrait, Buffalo China **$600**
Plate, 9 1/2" d., dinner, Roycroft Inn service **$400**
Plate, 10" d., New York World's Fair, 1939 .... **$550**

BUFFALO POTTERY

Platter, 13 1/4 x 18 1/2", Turkey patt., large colorful turkey in landscape in center, fall landscape border scenes, Colorido Ware, 1937, Buffalo China .... **$3,200+**

Salt & pepper shakers, from the Roycroft Inn, pr................... **$800**

Teapot, cov., tea ball-type w/built-in tea ball, Argyle patt., blue & white, 1914 .... **$300**

Tom & Jerry set: punch bowl & 12 cups; Colorido Ware, the set .... **$1,000+**

Do not store antiques and collectibles wrapped in newspaper, as it has a high-acid content and the ink can rub off, causing permanent stains. Also, don't store antiques and collectibles in rental storage units for long periods because the temperature and humidity can vary greatly.

Vase, 6 3/4" h., 3 3/8" d., cylindrical waisted shape, h.p. scene similar to a village scene of bygone days as used on Deldare, marked "Buffalo China Rouge Ware," not in the Altman book **$1,500**

Vase, 10 1/2" h., 2 3/4" d. base, tall ovoid body tapering to a widely flaring trumpet neck w/gently fluted rim, long angular shoulder handles, a wide white body band decorated w/large blossoming branches w/green & brown leaves, shoulder & base bands w/stylized natural design in brown & white, brown neck & handles, from the 1906 Premium catalog, dated 1906, not in the Altman book **$600**

Capo-di-Monte

Production of porcelain and faience began in 1736 at the Capo-di-Monte factory in Naples. In 1743 King Charles of Naples established a factory there that made wares with relief decoration. In 1759 the factory was moved to Buen Retiro near Madrid, operating until 1808. Another Naples pottery was opened in 1771 and operated until 1806 when its molds were acquired by the Doccia factory of Florence, which has since made reproductions of original Capo-di-Monte pieces with the "N" mark beneath a crown. Some very early pieces are valued in the thousands of dollars but the subsequent productions are considerably lower.

Box, box., rectangular waisted shaped w/ beveled corners, conforming gilt-metal hinged fittings w/matching low domed cover, the sides molded & colored w/scenes of putti & nudes in landscapes, molded scene of female nudes in a landscape on the cover, signed on the bottom w/the blue "N" & crown mark, slight flake at rim, late 19th - early 20th c., 8 x 10 3/4", 5" h. **$360**

Ewer, Baroque-style, the pedestal base composed of brightly colored molded scrolls & mounted with two figures of child mermaids blowing horns & w/a dolphin, the tall cylindrical body ornately molded w/ nude figures w/leafy trim & oval blue reserves all in bold colors, the wide shoulder w/fancy molded details including a seated bearded merman w/his arms wrapped around the arched spout & grasping the horns of a grostesque sea creature, the ornate S-scroll handle down his back, blue mark on base, late 19th - early 20th c., 16 3/4" h. **$920**

Teapot, cov., three gold paw feet supporting the spherical body decorated w/two large round reserves w/colorful landscapes w/naked frolicking figures, a cobalt blue background & inset cover w/ball finial, pink ribbed serpentine spout & ornate pink-trimmed C-scroll handle, late 19th - early 20th c., 9 1/2" w., 6 1/4" h. **$374**

Urns, cov., a tripartite plinth base supporting three incurved legs & a rounded dish all in white w/gold trim, the base supporting a large bulbous urn-form body molded in bold relief w/a continuous scene of knights in battle & decorated w/polychrome, the incurved shoulder w/reticulated panels below the gilt rim supporting a high domed matching reticulated cover topped w/a crown-form finial in gold & dark blue, late 19th - early 20th c., crown finials restored, 12" h., pr. **$489**

Urns, campana-form, a gilded square foot supporting a bell-shaped base w/a red & white band below a green & yellow leaf band, the large urn w/large green & yellow leaves around the swelled base w/double mask head gold handles below the tall cylindrical sides & wide rolled rim w/red trim, the sides molded in bold relief w/ semi-nude classical figures decorated in bright colors, blue mark on base, late 19th - early 20th c., 6" w., 8" h., pr. **$489**

Ceramic Arts Studio of Madison

During its 15 years of operation, Ceramic Arts Studio of Madison, Wisconsin, was one of the nation's most prolific producers of figurines, shakers, and other decorative ceramics. The Studio began in 1940 as the joint venture of potter Lawrence Rabbitt and entrepreneur Reuben Sand. Early products included hand-thrown bowls, pots, and vases, exploring the potential of Wisconsin clay. However, the arrival of Betty Harrington in 1941 took CAS in a new direction, leading to the type of work it is best known for. Under Mrs. Harrington's artistic leadership, the focus was changed to the production of finely sculpted decorative figurines. Among the many subjects covered were adults in varied costumes and poses, charming depictions of children, fantasy and theatrical figures, and animals. The inventory soon expanded to include figural wall plaques, head vases, salt-and-pepper shakers, shelf-sitters, and "snuggle pairs."

Metal display accessories complementing the ceramics were produced by another Reuben Sand firm, Jon-San Creations, under the direction of Zona Liberace (stepmother of the famed pianist). Mrs. Liberace also served as the Studio's decorating director.

During World War II, Ceramic Arts Studio flourished, since the import of decorative items from overseas was suspended. In its prime during the late 1940s, CAS produced over 500,000 pieces annually, and employed nearly 100 workers.

As primary designer, the talented Betty Harrington is credited with creating the vast majority of the 800-plus designs in the Studio inventory--a remarkable achievement for a self-taught artist. The only other CAS designer of note was Ulle Cohen ("Rebus"), who contributed a series of modernistic animal figurines in the early 1950s.

The popularity of Ceramic Arts Studio pieces eventually resulted in many imitations of lesser quality. After World War II, lower-priced imports began to flood the market, forcing the Studio to close its doors in 1955. An attempt to continue the enterprise in Japan, using some of the Madison master molds as well as new designs, did not prove successful. An additional number of molds and copyrights were sold to Mahana Imports, which released a series of figures based on the CAS originals.

Both the Ceramic Arts Studio- Japan and Mahana pieces utilized a clay both whiter and more lightweight than that of Madison pieces. Additionally, their markings differ from the "Ceramic Arts Studio, Madison Wis." logo, which appears in black on the base of many Studio pieces. However, not all authentic Studio pieces were marked (particularly in pairs); a more reliable indicator of authenticity is the "decorator tick mark." This series of colored dots, which appears at the drain hole on the bottom of every Ceramic Arts Studio piece, served as an in-house identifier for the decorator who worked on a specific piece. The tick mark is a sure sign that a figurine is the work of the Studio.

Ceramic Arts Studio is one of the few figural ceramics firms of the 1940s and '50s that operated successfully outside of the West Coast. Today, CAS pieces remain in high demand, thanks to their skillful design and decoration, warm use of color, distinctively glossy glaze, and highly imaginative and exquisitely realized themes.

Many pieces in the Ceramic Arts Studio inventory were released both as figurines and as salt- and-pepper shakers. For items not specifically noted as shakers in this listing, add 50 percent for the shaker price estimate.

Complete reference information on the Studio can be found in *Ceramic Arts Studio: The Legacy of Betty Harrington* by Donald-Brian Johnson, Timothy J. Holthaus, and James E. Petzold (Schiffer Publishing Ltd., 2003). The official Ceramic Arts Studio collectors group, "CAS Collectors," publishes a quarterly newsletter, hosts an annual convention, and can be contacted at www.cascollectors.com The Studio also has an official historical site, www.ceramicartsstudio. org. Photos for this category are by John Petzold.

Accordion Lady, 8 1/2" h. $500-600

Bali-Kris, carrying dagger, 8 1/4" h. $120-140

Balinese Woman lamp, Moss Mfg., scarce........................ $350- 375

Balky Colt, 3 3/4" h......... $100-125

Bamboo bowl, 2 1/2" h....... $25-30

Cockatoo plaques, A & B, 8" & 8 1/4" h., pr................. $180- 220

Diana pitcher, Wedgwood-style, 3 1/2" h. $60-75

Frisky Colt, 3 3/4" h. $100-125

Harmonica Boy, shelf-sitter, 4" h. $120-140

Kitten with Ball, 2" h. $50-60

Modern Fox, 6 1/2" l....... $120-150

Musical Score metal shelf, Jon-San Creations, 12 x 14" $85-100

One-Piece Scotties, 2 3/4" h. $100-125

Our Lady of Fatima, 9" h. $260-285

Petrov & Petrushka, Russian boy & girl, 5" & 5 1/2" h., pr ... $120-150

Pixie Riding Snail, 2 3/4" h. $40-50

Smi-Pi, chubby man carrying basket, scarce, 6 1/4" h. $350-450

Adam & Eve (one-piece), extremely rare, 12" h. .... $10,000+

Baby Chick & Nest snuggle pair, 1 1/4" h. & 1 3/4" h., pr. $160-200

Ballerina Quartet, left to right: 5" h. Rose, 6" h. Daisy, 3 1/2" h. Violet & 6" h. Pansy, the set **$1,040-1,120**

Bride & Groom, 4 3/4" h. & 5" h., pr. **$250-300**

Harlequin Boy & Girl with Masks, 8 1/2" & 8 3/4" h., pr. **$1,800-1,900**

Robins on Tree Trunk planter, Ceramic Arts Studio (Japan), 8" l. **$35-45**

Wee Piggy Boy & Girl salt & pepper shakers, 3 1/4" h. & 3 1/2" h., pr. **$50-70**

Wing-Sang & Lu-Tang on Bamboo Vases, scarce, 6 1/4" h., pr. **$90-100**

Young Love Boy & Girl, shelf-sitters, 4 1/2" h., pr. **$90-100**

CHINESE EXPORT

Chinese Export

Large quantities of porcelain have been made in China for export to America from the 1780s, much of it shipped from the ports of Canton and Nanking. A major source of this porcelain was Ching-te-Chen in the Kiangsi province, but the wares were also made elsewhere. The largest quantities were blue and white. Prices fluctuate considerably depending on age, condition, decoration, etc.

ROSE MEDALLION and CANTON export wares are listed separately.

Creamer, helmet-shaped, armorial-type, blue band decoration & h.p. blue, red & gold crest below the spout, ca. 1790, 6 3/4" l., 5 1/2" h. **$500**

Cups, cov., footed ovoid body w/a twined strap handle, low domed cover w/gold figural nut finial, decorated around the sides & cover w/a colorful flowering tree design w/an orange top rim band, 19th c., overall 3 1/2" h., set of 7 .... **$977**

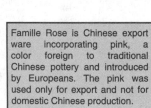

Pitcher, 6 1/2" h., Famille Rose palette, slightly swelled cylindrical shape w/a deeply scalloped rim & pointed rim spout, jagged arched handle, the sides decorated w/ large colorful panels of flowers, minor rim chips, 19th c. **$863**

Famille Rose is Chinese export ware incorporating pink, a color foreign to traditional Chinese pottery and introduced by Europeans. The pink was used only for export and not for domestic Chinese production.

Dishes, round, armorial-type, decorated w/two dark blue overglazed bands centering the colorful arms of Oliphant impaling Browne, minor decoration wear, ca. 1790, 6 1/8" d., 1 1/4" h., pr. (ILLUS. of one) **$920**

Plates, 10" d., green Fitzhugh patt., ca. 1800, pr. (ILLUS. of one) **$1,150**

Punch bowl, a deep footring & deep rounded sides, made for the American market & decorated on the sides w/the Arms of New York State in red, white, blue & gold on each side, narrow wavy blue line rim band, a pink peony sprig in the interior bottom, ca. 1795, 11 1/2" d. . **$3,840**

Punch bowl, a deep footring & deep rounded sides, made for the American market & decorated on the sides w/a spread-winged eagle w/shield on the front & back, a gilt carnation on each side & repeated in the interior beneath a border matching the exterior grisaille & gilt lines, ca. 1800, 11 1/2" d. **$2,640**

Sauce tureen, cov., Rose Mandarin design, a deep flaring foot supporting the squatty bulbous oblong body w/double loop end handles, the high domed & stepped cover w/a large gold flower finial, 19th c., 8" l., 6" h. **$1,265**

Teapot, a round foot below a low flaring base below a wide slightly concave body band below a wide slightly rounded shoulder centering a short gold neck, a serpentine spout & C-scroll handle, the high domed cover w/a gold ball finial above a scene of a woman & a cartouche of a man above a band of flowers & birds, the wide shoulder painted overall w/colorful birds, flowers & butterflies, the body band decorated w/ continuous scenes of Chinese ladies, ca. 1840, restoration to rim & spout, chip at pot mouth, wear to cover gilt, 9" h. **$690**

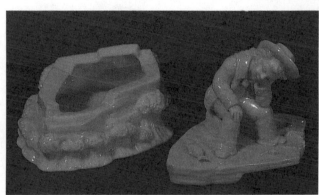

Teapot, a footed spherical double-walled style w/the outer layer pierced overall w/a delicate green vine w/orange blossoms, a light blue shoulder band & the matched domed & pierced cover w/a button finial, a C-form handle & a straight angled silver spout, unmarked, late 18th - early 19th c., chips & repairs on cover, small chip on base rim, 6" h. **$230**

Tea set: cov. teapot, cov. tea caddy, helmet-shaped creamer, cov. cream pot & handleless cup; the oval teapot w/upright sides & a tapering shoulder to the inset cover w/berry finial, the bulbous tapering cream pot w/domed cover, upright flat- sided rectangular tea caddy w/arched shoulder, short neck & domed cap, each piece h.p. on the side in sepia, orange & gold w/a spread-winged American eagle w/shield, made for the American market, late 18th c., teapot 8 1/2" l., the set **$5,175**

CHINESE EXPORT

Teapot, cov., Rose Medallion patt., a round flaring foot supporting a wide urn-form body w/a serpentine spout & C-scroll handle, the high domed cover w/a gold ball finial, the cover, shoulder & body all decorated w/h.p. cartouches featuring birds, flowers & butterflies or Chinese figures, gold trim, ca. 1860, 11" l., 10 1/2" h. **$920**

Tureen, cov., armorial-type, famille rose palette, footed squatty bulbous oval body w/gilt twisted branch end handles, domed cover w/gilt artichoke finial, decorated w/continuous scenes of Chinese figures in a landscape on the cover, the base painted w/the arms of Grant w/family mottoes, a rim band decorated w/ flowers, butterflies & birds, the sides w/a continuous scene of Chinese figures on balconies & in gardens, portions of interior cover rim restored, gilt wear, glaze flaws, ca. 1810, 13 1/2" l., 9" h. **$4,140**

Umbrella stand, Famille Rose palette in a Mandarin design, the tall cylindrical ribbed body decorated up the sides w/three bands containing alternating figural & floral panels, 19th c., 24 3/4" h. **$4,025**

Urn, cov., wide baluster-form body w/foo dog head & ring shoulder handles, domed cover w/figural foo lion finial, famille rose palette, the sides painted w/large reserves w/festival scenes & crowds of Chinese figures, floral background & wide geometric base band, cover finial w/broken tail, second half 19th c., 21" h. **$403**

Vase, 9 1/2" h., moon flask-form, short cylindrical neck flanked by figural red dragon handles above the flattened round sides w/a blue ground ornately decorated w/ white floral scrolls, one side w/a large round reserve painted w/a color scene of mounted warriors, the other sides w/a reserve of birds among flowering branches, upright base w/a pink & green geometric design, worn gilt on mouth rim, ca. 1880 .... **$374**

Chintz China

There are over fifty flower patterns and myriad colors from which Chintz collectors can choose. That is not surprising considering companies in England began producing these showy, yet sometimes muted, patterns in the early part of this century. Public reception was so great that this production trend continued until the 1960s.

Tea set: breakfast set: cov. teapot, cup, creamer, open sugar bowl, toast rack & oblong paneled tray w/end handles; Majestic patt., Countess shape, Royal Winton, the set **$1,750-2,000**

Tea set: stacking-type, cov. creamer, sugar & teapot; Florence patt., Delamere shape, Royal Winton, the set **$1,750- 2,000**

Teapot, cov., Summertime patt., Ajax shape, Royal Winton **$950**

Teapot, cov., DuBarry patt., Diamond shape, James Kent, Ltd. **$950-1,000**

Teapot, cov., Joyce-Lynn patt., Ascot shape, Royal Winton **$1,300-1,500**

Royal Winton was founded in 1885 in Stoke-on-Trent, England, by Leonard Lumsden Grimwade and was originally known as Grimwade Brothers. By 1906, the company was running four factories. In 1928, the firm released "Marguerite," its first Chintz pattern, and in 1929, it adopted its present name, Royal Winton. Over the years, the company produced more than 60 Chintz designs.

In 1995, the company was sold and began releasing reissues of its most popular patterns. New releases have been marked with "1995" to avoid confusion with original pieces.

Clarice Cliff Designs

Clarice Cliff was a designer for A.J. Wilkinson, Ltd., Royal Staffordshire Pottery, Burslem, England when it acquired the adjoining Newport Pottery Company, whose warehouses were filled with undecorated bowls and vases. In about 1925, her flair with the Art Deco style was incorporated into designs appropriately named "Bizarre" and "Fantasque" and the warehouse stockpile was decorated in vivid colors. These hand-painted earthenwares, all bearing the printed signature of designer Clarice Cliff, were produced until World War II and are now finding enormous favor with collectors.

Note: Reproductions of the Clarice Cliff "Bizarre" marking have been appearing on the market recently.

Bowl, 16 3/8" d., a wide flat bottom & wide flaring sides, Latona patt., decorated around the exterior w/a polychrome scene of stylized trees in shades of red, orange, green, blue, black & cream, printed Bizarre Ware backstamp, surface wear to interior center, ca. 1930 .... **$1,645**

Charger, large round dished form, Crest patt., three large Japanese-style crests in gold, blue, rust red, black & green on a mottled green ground **$12,000**

Pitcher, 11 5/8" h., jug-form, the ovoid ribbed body tapering to a flat rim, decorated in the Fantasque Blue Chintz patt. in shades of blue, rose red, greens & cream, cream-colored handle, printed Bizarre Ware backstamp, ca. 1930 .... **$1,880**

Pitcher, 12" h., "Bizarre" ware, Lotus shape, ringed ovoid body tapering to a wide cylindrical neck, heavy loop handle, Delicia Citrus patt., large stylized red, yellow & orange fruits around the top w/green leaves & streaky green on a cream ground **$2,200**

Cleminson Clay

Betty Cleminson, a hobbyist, began working in her Monterey Park, California, garage in 1941. She called the business Cleminson Clay. However, the business proved so successful that two years later Betty was forced to make several key decisions: She moved to El Monte, California, built a large factory, hired over fifty employees, including many artists, and changed the name to "The California Cleminsons." Later, another major decision was made to encourage her husband, George, to join the company. He had taught school but was also proficient at handling the financial affairs. He also oversaw the construction of the new building. At one point during the later years, the Cleminsons had about 150 employees. Due to the competition from imports, Betty, like so many American potters, was forced to close her operation in 1963. She died on September 30, 1996 at the age of 86.

The Cleminsons created a variety of gift wares including butter dishes, canisters, cookie jars, salt and pepper shakers and string holders. An assortment of hand painted plates, wall plaques and other items with novelty sayings were a big hit with collectors.

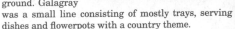

Distlefink was a highly successful dinnerware line when it was introduced. However, today the light brown ground is not nearly as popular as the white ground. Galagray was a small line consisting of mostly trays, serving dishes and flowerpots with a country theme.

The incised, stylized "BC" mark signifies Betty Cleminson. It was the first mark used. Another mark was a facsimile of a plate with a ribbon at the top and the words "The California" over "Cleminsons" with the initials "bc" in the center, along with a boy and girl, one on each side of the plate. The words "hand painted" appear below the plate. This mark is the most familiar to collectors and can be found with or without the boy and girl. - Susan Cox

Bowl, 3" d., 2 3/4" h., straight 1/4" base rising to a lightly flared rim, Galagray line, grey ground w/red gloss inside & red abstract leaves around the outside center .. **$36**

Egg cup, boy's face on front, "For A Good Egg" on reverse, no mark, 3 3/4" h. **$55-60**

Cleanser shaker, figure of a woman standing, yellow hair, pink scarf over head, pink & white dress w/ grey trim, five holes in top of head, originally included a card around her neck w/a poem explaining that she was a cleanser shaker, marked w/copyright symbol & the plate w/a girl & boy on each side, 6 1/2" h. **$55**

Pie bird, figural, model of a bird, white body decorated in pink, blue & green, early mark, 1941, 4 1/2" h. **$90**

Creamer, figural, model of rooster, white w/green & pink accents, stamped mark, 5 1/2" h. **$59**

CLEMINSON CLAY

Ring holder, figural, model of a hand, palm facing forward, large flower covers the wrist, 3" h. **$58**

Salt & pepper shakers, figural, a man & woman artist, each holding a palette in one hand, the woman's palette w/"Salt" & the man's with "Pepper," each w/black ties, 6" h., pr. **$70**

Salt box w/hinged wooden cover, cylindrical w/high arched back crest w/hanging hole decorated w/an apple on a branch, the sides w/scrolls & small leaves below "Salt," maroon & green, 7 1/2" h. **$75**

Serving dish, Galagray line, grey ground w/muted red country motif, scalloped rim on one edge, stamped mark w/boy & girl & the words "Galagray Ware" underneath along w/copyright symbol, 8 1/4" l. **$15**

String holder-wall pocket, figural, a model of a house w/a red base & chimney & yellow trim around the door & brown roof, wording reads "Friends From Afar and Nearabout Will Find Our Latchstring Always Out" **$95**

Tea bag holder, model of a teapot w/"Let Me Hold The Bag" in center, stamped mark, 4 1/4" w. **$25**

Vase, model of a watering can **$33**

Wall plaque, figural, model of a key printed w/"Welcome Guest" on a white ground w/the edge trimmed in yellow, yellow ground w/a green & rust stripe, 7" h. **$38**

Sock darner, white ground w/h.p. woman's face & brown hair, blue & maroon accents, words "Darn It" on front near bottom, feet on bottom unseen from standing position, 5" h. **$79**

Wall plaque, oval w/scalloped rim trimmed in brown on inside edge, applied pansy- like flowers & leaves in center, one in pinks, one yellow & blue, h.p. background flowers, green gloss leaves, two factory holes for hanging, 6 3/4" h. **$51**

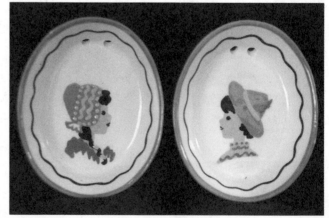

Wall plaques, oval, white ground, blue rims, scalloped brown line inside rims, centers w/bust profiles of boy in blue Alpine-type hat & girl in blue & pink bonnet, both w/brown hair & eyes, each plaque w/two holes for hanging, bc mark, 4 1/4" h., pr **$38**

Wall pocket, model of a scoop, white body w/ blue & red flowers & green leaves, second mark without boy & girl on each side, marked "hand painted" & copyright symbol, 9" l. **$52**

Clewell Wares

Although Charles W. Clewell of Canton, Ohio, didn't operate a pottery, he is responsible for a category of fine art pottery through his development of a unique metal coating placed on pottery blanks obtained from Owens, Weller and others. By encasing objects in a thin metal shell, he produced copper- and bronze-finished ceramics. Later experiments led him to chemically treat the metal coating to attain the bluish green patinated effect associated with copper and bronze. Although he produced metal-coated pottery from 1902 until the mid-1950s, Clewell's production was quite limited, for he felt no one else could competently recreate his artwork, therefore he operated a small shop with little help.

Lamp, table-type, a hammered brass ringed foot supporting to tall baluster-form body w/a fine crusty bluish green finish, hammered- copper cap & eletrical fittings at the top, bottom signed "Clewell 277-6" & w/old paper label under the cap reads "$45.00," lamp body 15 3/4" h. **$978**

Mug, footed paneled ovoid form w/faux rivets along panels, presentation-type, panels on front read "APA - 1908," marked on base "Clewell Canton, O," 4 1/4" h. **$150**

Vase, 4 1/2" h., footed wide bulbous ovoid body w/a short wide flaring rim, original shaded & mottled dark brown to green patina, marked, No. 417-206 .... **$570**

Vase, 8" h., cylindrical slightly flaring form molded in high relief w/vertical vines topped by leaves & berries, good original patina, minor lines **$374**

Vase, 9 7/8" h., squatty bulbous base tapering to a tall cylindrical neck, nicely patinated, incised "Clewell 266-2," few minor breaks in copper **$805**

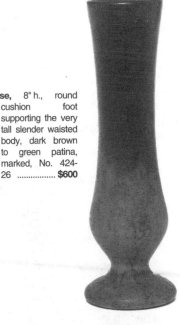

Vase, 8" h., round cushion foot supporting the very tall slender waisted body, dark brown to green patina, marked, No. 424-26 .... **$600**

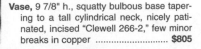

CLIFTON POTTERY

Clifton Pottery

William A. Long, founder of the Lonhuda Pottery, joined Fred Tschirner, a chemist, to found the Clifton Art Pottery in Newark, New Jersey, in 1905. Crystal Patina was its first art pottery line and featured a subdued pale green crystalline glaze later also made in shades of yellow and tan. In 1906 its Indian Ware line, based on the pottery made by American Indians, was introduced. Other lines the Pottery produced include Tirrube and Robin's-egg Blue. Floor and wall tiles became the focus of production after 1911, and by 1914 the firm's name had changed to Clifton Porcelain Tile Company, which better reflected its production.

Teapot, cov., a tall tapering cylindrical base below the squatty bulbous pot w/a short, wide angled spout & large ring handle, a low domed cover w/ a button finial, overall medium green crystalline glaze, 6 1/2" h. **$150**

Vase, 3 1/2" h., 3 1/2" d., miniature, spherical body tapering to a tiny neck, deeply molded overall w/ stylized swirling fish, dark green mottled glaze, signed & dated 1906, No. 180 .... **$300**

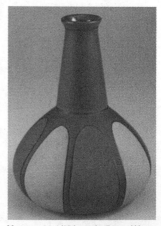

Vase, 6 1/8" h., Crystal Patina line, footed squatty bulbous lower body tapering to a wide cylindrical neck w/a flaring rim, shaped light brown to pale green glaze w/long dark green streaks, incised company logo, dated 1906 ...... **$288**

Vase, 8 1/2" h., 5 1/4" d., Tirruba Line, footed bottle-form w/a wide squatty lower body tapering sharply to a flaring neck, matte red ground h.p. w/a white nasturtium blossom & pale green leaves up the side, stamped "Clifton - 140" **$374**

Vase, 11 1/2" h., Indian Ware, bulbous gourd-form body w/a tall tapering cylindrical neck, dark brown ground decorated around the bottom w/alternating ovals of tan & medium brown, marked "Middle Mississippi Valley - 231" **$690**

Copeland & Spode

W.T. Copeland & Sons, Ltd., has operated the Spode Works at Stoke, England, from 1847 to the present. The name Spode was used on some of its productions. Its predecessor, Spode, was founded by Josiah Spode about 1784 and became Copeland & Garrett in 1843, continuing under that name until 1847. Listings dated prior to 1843 should be attributed to Spode.

COPELAND
SPODE
ENGLAND
New Stone

Compotes, open, 9 1/4" d., Imari patt., the shallow round bowls w/three floral panels alternating w/cobalt blue & gold bands, pedestal base w/decorated panels on the round foot, one w/pinhead size flake, Copeland, 19th c., pr. **$440**

Ewers, large inverted pear-shaped body on a ringed stem & domed foot, tall reeded gilt scroll handle w/paired snakes & a Bacchic mask at the base & paired snakes at the top at the wide arched spout over the ringed cylindrical neck, overall cobalt blue ground, decorated overall in the Persian taste w/gold strapwork, pendent rosettes & trailing flowers all extensively trimmed w/enameled beads & jewels in white, ruby, blue & turquoise, Copeland, probably decorated by William Henry Goss, green printed marks, ca. 1855, 15 1/8" h., pr. **$20,315**

Salt dip, triple, three deep rounded dishes joined across the top w/an arched three- part handle in white w/gold wrapped ribbon decor, each bowl decorated on the exterior in color w/a shell surrounded by entwined rose & cornflower garlands, each interior w/a berried laurel wreath, dated 1895, printed gold crowned Copeland mark, mark of retailer T. Goode & Son, London, 4" w. **$1,673**

Tea set: cov. teapot & seven handled cups & saucers; the oval pot w/upright sides & a flat shoulder centered by a domed cover w/oval knob finial, serpentine spout & C-form handle, each piece decorated w/a wide orange-painted band trimmed w/stylized white flowerheads & bands of gilt leaves, Spode, Pattern No. 878, England, ca. 1820, some gilt wear, two saucers w/hairlines, the set (ILLUS. of part) **$405**

Tea set: cov. teapot, cov. sugar bowl, creamer, eight 9" d. plates & eight cups & saucers; Classical Revival style, serving pieces of squatty bulbous oblong boat shape w/angled collars & inset domed covers w/button finials, pointed C-scroll handles, each piece decorated w/a dark cinnamon brown band painted w/gilt roses, marked "Spode - Copelands China - England - Tiffany & Co. - New York," ca. 1890s, one plate w/small flake, gilt wear to rims, teapot 5" h., the set **$715**

Teacup & saucer, footed deep rounded teacup decorated in the Sevres-style w/a cobalt blue ground centering a large oval reserve of colorful fruits framed by fancy gilt scrolling, matching saucer, printed green Copeland monogram marks, ca. 1870, saucer 5 1/2" d., set **$538**

Dinner service: eleven dinner plates, eight each luncheon plates, salad/dessert plates, bread & butter plates, cream soup bowls, saucers & teacups, sauce dishes, cereal bowls, six coffee cups & saucers, seven square dessert plates, two graduated platters, one each oval open vegetable dish, relish dish, butter cover, cov. teapot, milk pitcher, cov. sugar bowl, creamer & gravy boat w/undertray; Tower patt., pink, early 20th c., 112 pcs. (one dinner plate chipped, gravy boat stained) **$1,100**

Dinner service: twelve each dinner plates, luncheon plates, teacups & saucers, fourteen square dessert plates, ten each bread & butter plates, soup/cereal bowls, sauce dishes, cream soup bowls & saucers, six egg cups, two each round meat platters & square open vegetable dishes, one each teapot, cov. sugar bowl, creamer, gravy boat w/undertray, round cov. vegetable bowl, cov. soup tureen w/ ladle, scalloped round vegetable bowl, rectangular cov. vegetable dish, triple divided relish server & relish dish; Tower patt., blue, early 20th c., 134 pcs. **$1,900**

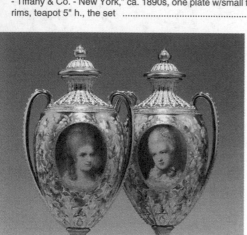

Vases, cov., 11" h., a square foot & tapering pedestal in white w/heavy gold trim, the large ovoid body tapering to a short flaring neck w/domed cover & pointed knob finial, long low C-scroll handles from the shoulder to the vase, each painted on the front w/a large oval reserve portrait of an 18th c. beauty surrounded by a gold background painted overall w/meandering pink & green rose vines, neck & cover w/gold decoration matching the foot, printed green Copeland marks, ca. 1900, artist-signed, pr. **$1,793**

Pitcher, 9" h., ironstone, underglaze-blue transfer-printed floral design w/polychrome enamel, impressed "Greek 12," Spode (minor wear & crazing, tip of spout is broken off at hinge & needs to be reattached) **$110**

Plates, dinner, 9 3/4" d., h.p. in iron-red underglaze-blue & gilt w/a central urn brimming w/flowers within a border of dense floral scrolls, fans & arched panels within a shaped brown-edged rim, ca. 1815-30, "2283" pattern number in iron-red, set of 12 (one w/minor hairline to center, small rim chips & surface wear) **$1,150**

Plates, 9 3/4" d., gilt rim & turquoise border, center cartouche w/painted landscape, marked "Copeland and Garret," ca. 1845, pr. **$252**

Dinner service, 14 soup plates, 23 luncheon plates, a large 15" l. cov. tureen & undertray, a small tureen w/mismatched cover, two small trays, four graduated oval platters, largest 21" l., & ten 10 1/4" d. dinner plates; all in an Imari-style colorful transfer-printed decoration of black florals in center & around borders decorated w/underglaze-blue & red enamels, the set (chips, stains) **$990**

Dinner service: thirteen 9 3/4" d. dinner plates, three rimmed soup plates, six dessert plates; each round w/a central botanical specimen on a white ground, continuing to a wide rim w/molded scrolling leafage & dolphin decoration ending in a gilt edge, Spode, ca. 1813-15, some w/iron-red factory mark, the set **$920**

Dinner service, sixteen 10" d. plates, eight 7" d. plates, ten 6" plates, ten 5" d. bowls, sixteen cups & saucers & one extra saucer, 13" l. platter, 10" l. oval vegetable dish (hairline); "India Tree" patt., each piece marked "Copeland Spode England India Tree," 20th c., the set **$690**

Cowan

R. Guy Cowan opened his first pottery studio in 1912 in Lakewood, Ohio. The pottery operated almost continuously, with the exception of a break during the First World War, at various locations in the Cleveland area until it was forced to close in 1931 due to financial difficulties.

Many of this century's finest artists began with Cowan and its associate, the Cleveland School of Art. This fine art pottery, particularly the designer pieces, are highly sought after by collectors.

Many people are unaware that it was due to R. Guy Cowan's perseverance and tireless work that art pottery is today considered an art form and found in many art museums.

Ashtray/nut dish, figural clown Periot, blue or ivory glaze, designed by Elizabeth Anderson, Shape No. 788, 2 1/2 x 3", each (ILLUS. lower center) **$125**

Vase, 4 3/4" h., bulbous body w/horizontal ribbing, wide cylindrical neck, green glaze, Shape No. V-30 (ILLUS. lower left) **$60**

Vase, 7 1/2" h., footed, tapering cylindrical body, green drip over yellow glaze, Shape No. 591, 8" h. (ILLUS. far right) **$275**

Vase, 8" h., bulbous body tapering to cylindrical neck w/flaring rim, black drip over Feu Rouge (red) glaze Shape No. V-932 (ILLUS. top) **$350**

Ashtray, model of a ram, green, designed by Edris Eckhardt, 5 1/4" l., 3 1/2" h. (ILLUS. lower left) **$275**

Ashtray/nut dish, model of a chick, green glaze, Shape No. 768, 3 1/2" h. (ILLUS. bottom center) **$75**

Flower frog, figural, Pan sitting on large toadstool, ivory glaze, designed by W. Gregory, Shape No. F-9, 9" h. (ILLUS. top) **$675**

Vase, 7 1/2" h., tall slender ovoid body w/short cylindrical neck, orange lustre, Shape No. 552 (ILLUS. lower right) **$100**

Bookends, figural, "Monk"/ Readers, pine green glaze, 6 3/8" h., pr. (ILLUS. of one, left with mustard yellow Monk bookend) **$900**

Bookends, figural, "Monk"/ Readers, pine green glaze, 6 3/8" h., pr. (ILLUS. of one, left with mustard yellow Monk bookend) **$900**

Watch for bargains. A dealer who specializes in a particular category may inadvertently underprice an item in a different category.

COWAN

Ashtray, three-section base w/figural leaping gazelle & foliage on edge, Oriental Red glaze, designed by Waylande Gregory, 5 3/4" h. (ILLUS. lower right) **$350**

Bookends, model of a stylized horse, back legs raised in kicking position, black, designed by Waylande Gregory, Shape No. E-1, 9" h., pr. (ILLUS. center rear) **$2,400**

Bookends, figural, a nude kneeling boy & nude kneeling girl, each on oblong bases, white glaze, designed by Frank N. Wilcox, Shape No. 519, Marks 8 & 9, ca. 1925, 6 1/2" h., pr. (ILLUS. left front & right rear) **$400**

Bookends, figural, model of a unicorn, front legs raised on relief-molded foliage base, orange glaze, designed by Waylande Gregory, Shape No. 961, mark No. 8, 7" h., pr. (ILLUS. left) **$850**

Flower frog, model of a deer, designed by Waylande Gregory, ivory glaze, Shape No. F-905, 8 1/4" h. (ILLUS. right).... **$425**

Flower frog, model of a reindeer, designed by Waylande Gregory, polychrome finish, Shape No. 903, 11" h. (ILLUS. center) **$1,250**

Bookends, figural, model of a seated polar bear, front paws near face, ivory glaze, designed by Margaret Postgate, 6" h., pr. (ILLUS. left) **$1,250**

Model of horse, standing animal on an oblong base, Egyptian blue glaze, designed by Viktor Schreckengost, 7 3/4" h. (ILLUS. right) **$4,500**

Bookends, figural, modeled as large rounded stylized elephants w/trunk curved under, standing on a stepped rectangular base, overall Oriental Red glaze, designed by Margaret Postgate, Shape No. E-2, 7 1/4" h., pr. (ILLUS. top center & lower left)... **$1,800**

Paperweight, figural, modeled as a large rounded stylized elephant w/trunk curved under, standing on a stepped rectangular base, ivory glaze, designed by Margaret Postgate, Shape No. D-3, 4 3/4" h. (ILLUS. lower center)..................... **$250**

Paperweight, figural, modeled as a large rounded stylized elephant w/trunk curved under, standing on a stepped rectangular base, blue glaze, designed by Margaret Postgate, Shape No. D-3, 4 3/4" h. (ILLUS. lower right) **$300**

Paperweight, figural, modeled as a large rounded stylized elephant w/trunk curved under, standing on a stepped rectangular base, overall Oriental Red glaze, designed by Margaret Postgate, Shape No. D-3, 4 3/4" h. (ILLUS. top right)............. **$350**

COWAN

Bookends, "Kicking Horse," modeled as a wild horse w/rear legs raised, on a rectangular base, gunmetal black glaze, No. #E-1, designed by Waylande Gregory, 9 1/4" h., pr. **$2,400**

Bowl, 5 1/4" d., individual, green & black, designed by Arthur E. Baggs (ILLUS. right)........................ **$2,500**

Vase, 6 1/2" h., spherical body w/flaring cylindrical neck flanked by scroll handles, Egyptian blue, designed by Viktor Schreckengost, Shape No. V-99 (ILLUS. center) **$450**

Vase, 8" h., cylindrical body, black w/overall turquoise blue decoration, triple-signed (ILLUS. left) **$650**

Bust of a woman, close-cut hair in ringlets, original sculpture by Jose Martin, terra cotta, 13 1/2" h. **$7,000**

Bust, "Antinea," stylized human head w/a long neck raised atop a fluted block, gunmetal black glaze, designed by A.D. Jacobson, limited edition of 100, 14" h. (ILLUS. left).............................**$7,200**

Bust, "Guilia," stylized female head tilted above her shoulder, on a low square base, gunmetal black glaze, designed by A.D. Jacobson, limited edition of 500, 10" h. (ILLUS. center)................... **$4,800**

Bust, "La Reveuse" (The Dreamer) stylized female head sleeping w/head resting on one hand, gunmetal black glaze, designed by A.D. Jacobson, limited edition of 25, 12" h. (ILLUS. right) **$11,500**

Bust, "Head of a Young Girl," stylized long head w/ straight hair atop a long neck & tall block base, gunmetal black glaze, designed by Waylande Gregory, 16" h. (ILLUS. left) **$3,500**

Bust, "Head of a Young Girl," stylized long head w/ straight hair atop a long neck & tall block base, ivory glaze, designed by Waylande Gregory, 16" h. (ILLUS. right) **$3,000**

COWAN

Candlestick, figural, Byzantine figure flanked by angels, salmon glaze, designed by R.G. Cowan, 9 1/4" h. (ILLUS. right) **$400**

Candlestick, figural, Byzantine figure flanked by angels, golden yellow glaze, designed by R.G. Cowan, 9 1/4" h. (ILLUS. left) **$300**

Candlestick, flared base below twisted column, blossom-form cup, green & orange drip glaze, Shape No. 625-A, 7 3/4" h. (ILLUS. far right) **$125**

Vase, 4" h., waisted cylindrical body w/bulbous top & wide flaring rim, mottled orange glaze, Shape No. 630 (ILLUS. second from left) **$85**

Vase, 4 3/4" h., wide tapering cylindrical body, mottled orange, brown & rust, Shape No. V-34 (ILLUS. second from right) **$55**

Vase, 8" h., bulbous body tapering to cylindrical neck w/flaring rim, gold, Shape No. V-932 (ILLUS. far left w/No. 625-A candlestick) **$150**

Vase, 8" h., footed bulbous body w/trumpet-form neck, yellow shading to green drip glaze, Shape No. 627 (ILLUS. top center) **$275**

Candlestick, two-light, large figural nude standing w/head tilted & holding a swirling drapery, flanked by blossom-form candle sockets supported by scrolled leaves at the base, matte ivory glaze, designed by R.G. Cowan, Shape No. 745, 7 1/2" w., 9 3/4" h. **$850**

Candlesticks, model of a marlin on wave-form base, verde green, designed by Waylande Gregory, 8" h., pr. (ILLUS. right) **$1,500**

Vase, 13 1/2" h., baluster-form body w/flaring rim, light blue glaze, Shape No. 563 (ILLUS. left) **$350**

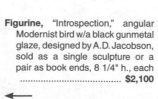

Figurine, "Introspection," angular Modernist bird w/a black gunmetal glaze, designed by A.D. Jacobson, sold as a single sculpture or a pair as book ends, 8 1/4" h., each **$2,100**

Candlestick, figural, seminude female standing before figural branches on round base w/flared foot, one arm across her body & the other raised overhead, shaded tan & green glaze, designed by R.G. Cowan, Shape No. 744-R, 12 1/2" h. **$1,000**

Decanter w/stopper, figural King of Clubs, a seated robed & bearded man w/a large crown on his head & holding a scepter, black glaze w/gold, designed by Waylande Gregory, Shape E-4, 10" h. (ILLUS. left) **$650**

Decanter w/stopper, figural Queen of Hearts, seated figure holding scepter & wearing crown, Oriental Red glaze, designed by Waylande Gregory, Shape No. E-5, 10 1/2" h. (ILLUS. right)............. **$625**

Wine cups, Oriental Red glaze, Shape No. X-17, 2 1/2" h., each (ILLUS. of two) **$40**

Figurine, "Chinese Horse," standing on a rectangular base, Egyptian blue glaze, designed by Ralph Cowan w/instruction from Waylande Gregory, 9" h. (ILLUS. left) **$1,500**

Figurine, "Jockey/Fox Hunter," standing man in riding gear, Shadow White glaze (white w/black highlights), designed by Waylande Gregory, 8 1/2" h. (ILLUS. right)............. **$330**

Figurine, "Mary," a kneeling female holding the end of a long pleated robe, on a stepped rectangular base, terra cotta glaze, sculpture limited to an edition of 50, designed by Margaret Postgate, 14 1/2" l., 10 1/4" h. **$6,000**

Figurine, "Spanish Dancer," female wearing a long dress in an angled pose, in a special ivory glaze, designed by Elizabeth Anderson, 8 1/2" h. (ILLUS. left) **$575**

Figurine, "Spanish Dancer," female wearing a long dress in an angled pose, polychrome hand-decorated glazes, designed by Elizabeth Anderson, 8 1/2" h. (ILLUS. right) **$850**

Figurine, "Nautch Dancer," female dancer w/long swirling dress, Shadow White glaze (white w/ black highlights), designed by Waylande Gregory, 17 1/2" h. (ILLUS. right) **$5,500**

Figurine, "Nautch Dancer," female dancer w/long swirling dress, special silver (metallic silver) glaze, designed by Waylande Gregory, from the artist's own family w/Cleveland show provenance, 17 1/2" h. (ILLUS. left) **$6,500**

Figurine, "Pelican," stylized head of a bird in gunmetal black, bronze & silver glazes, sold as a single piece or as pairs for book ends, designed by A.D. Jacobson, limited edition, each (ILLUS. of two) **$3,800**

Do not overload glass display shelves, especially top shelves, as a collapsing top shelf can create a domino effect on lower shelves.

COWAN

Figurine, "Spanish Dancer," female, white, designed by Elizabeth Anderson, Shape No. 793, 8 1/2" h. (ILLUS. right)........ **$575**

Figurine, "Spanish Dancer," male, white, designed by Elizabeth Anderson, Shape No. 793, 8 3/4" h. (ILLUS. left) **$575**

Flower frog, fluted flower-form base centered by relief-molded stalk & leaves supporting the figure of a female nude standing w/one leg bent, knee raised, leaning backward w/one arm raised overhead & the other resting on a curved leaf, ivory glaze, designed by R.G. Cowan, Shape No. F-812-X, 10 1/2" h. (ILLUS. center) **$775**

Figurine, "Woodland Nymph," nude young female seated on a tree stump, special ivory glaze, designed by Waylande Gregory, 14" h. **$3,000**

Figurine, "Torso," female figure w/a terra cotta crackle glaze, designed by Waylande Gregory, 17" h. **$3,000**

Figurine, Russian peasant, "Tambourine Player," white crackle glaze, designed by Alexander Blazys, Shape No. 757-760, 9" h. **$650**

Figurine/candleholder, "Rowfant," a seated animal w/front paws resting atop a closed book, pine green glaze, limited edition of 156 pieces commissioned by the Cleveland Rowfant Club in 1925, designed by Frank N. Wilcox **$1,550**

Flower frog, "Debutante," figural, an Art Deco nude female dancer leaning backward w/one arm extended up, long leafy foliage below, special ivory glaze, designed by R.G. Cowan, 14 1/2" h. **$1,850**

Flower frog, figural, Art Deco-style nude dancing woman in a curved pose, standing on one leg & trailing a long scarf, ivory glaze, designed by Walter Sinz, Shape No. 698, 6 1/2" h. (ILLUS. left) **$175**

Flower frog, figural, "Awakening," an Art Deco woman draped in a flowing scarf standing & leaning backward w/her arms bent & her hands touching her shoulders, on a flower-form pedestal base, ivory glaze, designed by R.G. Cowan, Shape No. F-8, impressed mark, 1930s, 9" h. (ILLUS. right) .. **$325**

Flower frog, figural, "Diver," waveform base w/tall wave supporting nude female figure, back arched & arms raised over head, ivory glaze, designed by R.G. Cowan, Shape No. 683, 8" h. (ILLUS. right) **$700**

Flower frog, figural, "Wreath Girl," figure of a woman standing on a blossom-form base & holding up the long tails of her flowing skirt, ivory glaze, designed by R.G. Cowan, Shape No. 721, 10" h. (ILLUS. center) **$475**

Flower frog, figural, nude female, one leg kneeling on thick round base, head bent to one side & looking upward, one arm resting on knee of bent leg w/the other hand near her foot, ivory glaze, designed by Walter Sinz, 6" h. (ILLUS. left) **$375**

Flower frog, figural, Art Deco style, two nude females partially draped in flowing scarves, each bending backward away from the other w/ one hand holding the scarf behind each figure & their other hand joined, on an oval base w/flower holes, ivory glaze, designed by R.G. Cowan, Shape No. 685, 7 1/2" h. (ILLUS. lower right) **$575**

Flower frog, figural, "Marching Girl," Art Deco style, a nude female partially draped w/a flowing scarf standing & leaning backward w/ one hand on her hip & the other raising the scarf above her head, on an oblong serpentine-molded wave base w/flower holes, ivory glaze, designed by R.G. Cowan, Shape No. 680, 8" h. (ILLUS. lower left) **$275**

Flower frog, figural, "Repose," Art Deco style, a seminude sinewy woman standing & slightly curved backward, her arms away from her sides holding trailing drapery, in a cupped blossom-form base, ivory glaze, designed by R.G. Cowan, Shape No. 712, 6 1/2" h. (ILLUS. lower center) **$375**

Flower frog, figural, "Scarf Dancer," Art Deco-style nude dancing woman in a curved pose standing on one leg & holding the ends of a long scarf in her outstretched hands, ivory glaze, designed by R.G. Cowan, Shape No. 686, 7" h. (ILLUS. top) **$275**

Flower frog, figural, "Swirl Dancer," Art Deco nude female dancer standing & leaning to the side, w/one hand on hip & the other holding a scarf which swirls about her, on a round lobed base w/flower holes, ivory glaze, designed by R.G. Cowan, Shape No. 720, 10" h. **$1,150**

Flower frog, figural, nude woman w/ long flowing scarf, ivory, designed by R.G. Cowan, Shape No. 687, 11 3/4" h. **$675**

When you're bidding on a lot, and your competition is a couple who confer before each bid, bid quickly and decisively. Their delays may make them uncomfortable enough to drop out of the race.

COWAN

Lamp base, round domed base below Modernist teardrop-shaped body decorated w/nude female figure, ivory & brown glaze, designed by Waylande Gregory, 11" h. **$1,500**

Lamp, "Aztec," table model, figural, a stylized standing man in an angular Art Deco form, special ivory glaze, designed by Waylande Gregory, 13" h. **$1,800**

Lamp, "Cat," table model, figural, designed as a seated angular Art Deco style cat, special ivory glaze, designed by Waylande Gregory, 9 3/4" h. **$480**

Urn, Lakeware, blue, Shape V-102, 5 1/2" h. (ILLUS. left) **$85**
Vase, 4" h., bulbous ovoid tapering to cylindrical neck, Jet Black glaze, Shape No. V-5 (ILLUS. center) **$275**
Vase, 6 1/2" h., footed, squatty bulbous base w/trumpet-form neck, flattened sides w/notched corners, green glaze, Shape No. V-649-A (ILLUS. right) **$85**

Model of bird on wave, Egyptian blue, designed by Alexander Blazys, Shape No. 749-A, 12" h. **$1,400**

Vase, 9 3/4" h., "Amazon," nearly spherical body w/a cylindrical neck, incised w/a continuous band of stylized dancing nude Amazon women, in charcoal grey & Shadow White glazes, designed by Thelma Frazier **$2,100**

←   →

Vase, 6 1/2" h., bulbous body w/short molded rim, black w/Egyptian blue bands & center decoration, designed by Whitney Atchley, Shape No. V-38 .... **$1,750**

Delft

In the early 17th century, Italian potters settled in Holland and began producing tin-glazed earthenwares, often decorated with pseudo-Oriental designs based on Chinese porcelain wares. The city of Delft became the center of this pottery production and several firms produced the wares throughout the 17th and early 18th century. A majority of the pieces featured blue on white designs, but polychrome wares were also made. The Dutch Delftwares were also shipped to England, where eventually the English copied them at potteries in such cities as Bristol, Lambeth and Liverpool. Although still produced today, Delft peaked in popularity by the mid-18th century.

Bleeding bowl, round w/scalloped flange edge handles, white ground h.p. in dark blue w/a border of stylized small leaves & scrolls & a central large floral bouquet, possibly Bristol, England, ca. 1740, 9 1/4" l. **$588**

Bottle, wide cylindrical body tapering to a tall stick neck, h.p. overall w/vining flowers & leaf sprigs against a mottled green ground, England, 18th c., 8 1/2" h. **$764**

Bowl w/attached cover, 8 1/2" d., small footring supporting the deep rounded sides w/a flared rim & attached low, domed cover pierced w/a large center hole surrounded by a band of small holes, decorated in blue w/ stylized flowers & vines, England, ca. 1740 .... **$1,763**

Bowl, 8 7/8" d., thick footring & deep gently flaring sides, white ground h.p. overall w/dark blue leafy floral vines & scattered leaf sprigs, England, ca. 1740 .... **$588**

Tobacco jar w/brass cover, bulbous ovoid body, white ground h.p. w/a scene of a Native American seated by a covered jar marked "Havana" atop a plinth base, monogram of the Dutch East Indies Company within a small box at one side, mark on bottom for the Blum factory, Holland, mid-18th c., 10 3/8" h............................ **$3,290**

DERBY & ROYAL CROWN DERBY

Derby & Royal Crown Derby

William Duesbury, in partnership with John and Christopher Heath, established the Derby Porcelain Works in Derby, England, about 1750. Duesbury soon bought out his partners and in 1770 purchased the Chelsea factory and six years later, the Bow works. Duesbury was succeeded by his son and grandson. Robert Bloor purchased the business about 1814 and managed successfully until illness in 1828 left him unable to exercise control. The "Bloor" Period, however, extends from 1814 until 1848, when the factory closed. Former Derby workmen then resumed porcelain manufacture in another factory and this nucleus eventually united with a new and distinct venture in

1878 which, after 1890, was known as Royal Crown Derby.

A variety of anchor and crown marks have been used since the 18th century.

Candlesticks, decorated in the Imari taste, squared foot w/incurved sides & a dolphin head at each corner, tapering to a tall baluster stem supporting a squatty socket w/a widely flaring dished bobeche, in shades of white, brick red, cobalt blue & gold, Royal Crown Derby mark, 10 1/2" h., pr. **$1,093**

Figure group, bisque, modeled as two Classical maidens by a flowering tree pointing down at the sleeping figure of Cupid, his head resting on his quiver, his bow on the ground at his side, rockwork base w/scattered blossoms, incised Derby crown mark, crossed batons & "D" mark w/triangle, incised Model No. 195, attributed to J.J. Spengler, ca. 1775, 12 1/4" h. **$3,824**

Dinner service: 12 dinner plates, six luncheon plates, five bread & butter plates, three large soup bowls, two small soup bowls, five cups & saucers, five oval vegetable bowls, four crescent-shaped bone dishes, two oval platters, one oval open vegetable dish, a cov. cigarette box & an English saucer in a similar design; composed of several very similar Imari patterns w/different factory marks, in shades of brick red, cobalt blue, white & gold, Royal Crown Derby, second quarter 20th c., the set **$2,300**

Service plates, round, cobalt blue ground, the broad rim richly gilded w/elaborate radiating foliate cartouches alternating w/beaded lozenges below a beaded white band, interrupted at intervals corresponding to the shaped rim, iron-red printed crowned monogram marks, date cypher for 1906, 10" d., set of 12 .... **$3,600**

Teapot, cov., Old Avesbury (gold Avesbury) patt., oblong cylindrical body w/narrow angled shoulder, domed cover w/flower finial, straight spout, angled scrolled handle, modern, part of Royal Doulton Tableware, Ltd., England **$1,350**

Vase, cov., 6 1/2" h., a wide squatty bulbous body w/a wide shoulder centered by a small ringed cylindrical neck fitted w/a ball stopper & flanked by gold scroll handles, the pink ground ornately decorated w/floral swags & fruiting vines w/lattice panels around the shoulder, printed mark, 1891 .... **$646**

Vase, 15 1/2" h., ringed pedestal foot supporting a tall ovoid body w/a slender trumpet neck w/rolled scalloped rim, long delicate double C-scroll gold handles from base of neck down the sides, cobalt blue ground w/scattered delicate gilt scrolls, the front & back each w/a large colorful floral bouquet within an ornate raised gilt acanthus leaf & bellflower scrolling cartouche, embossed roses above the round foot, Royal Crown Derby red crowned monogram mark, Shape No. 1492, artist-signed & dated 1920 ... **$3,107**

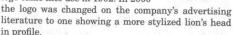

Doulton & Royal Doulton

Doulton & Co., Ltd., was founded in Lambeth, London, in about 1858. It was operated there until 1956 and often incorporated the words "Doulton" and "Lambeth" in its marks. Pinder, Bourne & Co., Burslem was purchased by the Doultons in 1878 and in 1882 became Doulton & Co., Ltd. It added porcelain to its earthenware production in 1884. The "Royal Doulton" mark has been used since 1902 by this factory, which is still in operation. Character jugs and figurines are commanding great attention from collectors at the present time.

John Doulton, the founder, was born in 1793. He became an apprentice at the age of 12 to a potter in south London. Five years later he was employed in another small pottery near Lambeth. His two sons, John and Henry, subsequently joined their father in 1830 in a partnership he had formed with the name of Doulton & Watts. Watts retired in 1864 and the partnership was dissolved. Henry formed a new company that traded as Doulton & Co.

In the early 1870s the proprietor of the Pinder Bourne Co., located in Burslem, Staffordshire, offered Henry a partnership. The Pinder Bourne Co. was purchased by Henry in 1878 and became part of Doulton & Co. in 1882.

With the passage of time, the demand for the Lambeth industrial and decorative stoneware declined, whereas demand for the Burslem manufactured and decorated bone china wares increased.

Doulton & Co. was incorporated as a limited liability company in 1899. In 1901 the company was allowed to use the word "Royal" on its trademarks by Royal Charter. The well known "lion on crown" logo came into use in 1902. In 2000 the logo was changed on the company's advertising literature to one showing a more stylized lion's head in profile.

Today Royal Doulton is one of the world's leading manufacturers and distributors of premium grade ceramic tabletop wares and collectibles. The Doulton Group comprises Minton, Royal Albert, Caithness Glass, Holland Studio Craft and Royal Doulton. Royal Crown Derby was part of the group from 1971 until 2000 when it became an independent company. These companies market collectibles using their own brand names.

Animals & Birds

Dog, Scottish Terrier, Ch. "Albourne Arthur," black, HN 1015, 1931-60, 5" **$315**

Kitten, licking hind paw, brown & white, HN 2580, 2 1/4" **$75**

Dog, Springer Spaniel, "Dry Toast," white coat w/brown markings, HN 2517, 1938- 55, 3 3/4"......... **$175**

Dogs, Cocker Spaniels sleeping, white dog w/brown markings & golden brown dog, HN 2590, 1941-69, 1 3/4" h. **$105**

Duck, Drake, standing, white, HN 806, 1923-68, 2 1/2" h........ **$105**

Horses, Chestnut Mare and Foal, chestnut mare w/white stockings, fawn-colored foal w/white stockings, HN 2522, 1938- 60, 6 1/2" h............................... **$695**

Monkey, Langur Monkey, long-haired brown & white coat, HN 2657, 1960-69, 4 1/2" h....... **$255**

Tiger, crouching, brown w/dark brown stripes, HN 225, 1920-36, 2 x 9 1/2" **$575**

Just because a bidder keeps competing for an item does not necessarily mean he knows something you don't. He may have caught auction fever or is misinformed about the value of the item being sold. Bid your limit and keep your emotions in check.

Always keep the original boxes and tags that collectibles came with. They add significant value to the resale value of the collectibles. Collectibles retain their greatest value when unopened. The great debate, however, is whether collectibles should be displayed and enjoyed, or packed away to retain maximum value. This, of course, is for the collector to decide.

Pony, Shetland Pony (woolly Shetland mare), glossy brown, DA 47, 1989 to present, 5 3/4" **$45**

Bunnykins Figurines

Bride, DB 101, cream dress, grey, blue & white train, 1991 to 2001 .... **$45**

Footballer, DB 119, red, 1991, limited edition of 250 .... **$650**

Airman, DB 199, limited edition of 5000, 1999 .... **$75**

Astro, Music Box, DB 35, white, red, blue, 1984-89 .... **$300**

Aussie Surfer, DB 133, gold & green outfit, white & blue base, 1994 .... **$115**

Banjo Player, DB 182, white & red striped blazer, black trousers, yellow straw hat, 1999, limited edition of 2,500................... **$150**

Be Prepared, DB 56, dark green & grey, 1987-96 .... **$60**

Mystic, DB 197, green, yellow & mauve, 1999 .... **$55**

Bedtime, DB 63, second variation, red & white striped pajamas, 1987, limited edition **$425**

Bogey, DB 32, green, brown & yellow, 1984-92 .... **$150**

Boy Skater, DB 152, blue coat, brown pants, yellow hat, green boots & black skates, 1995-98 .... **$45**

Busy Needles, DB 10, white, green & maroon, 1973-88............... **$75**

Cavalier, DB 179, red tunic, white collar, black trousers & hat, yellow cape, light brown boots, 1998, limited edition of 2,500.......... **$265**

Choir Singer, DB 223, white cassock, red robe, 2001, RDICC exclusive.................................... **$45**

Clown, DB 129, white costume w/ red stars & black pompons, black ruff around neck, 1992, limited edition of 250.................... **$1,500**

Cowboy, DB 201, 1999, limited edition of 2,500................... **$125**

Cymbals, DB 25, red, blue & yellow, from the Oompah Band series, 1984-90 .... **$115**

Dodgem Car Bunnykins, DB 249, red car, 2001, limited edition of 2,500................................... **$175**

Dollie Bunnykins Playtime, DB 80, white & yellow, 1988, by Holmes, limited edition of 250 .... **$225**

Drum-Major, DB 109, dark green, red & yellow, Oompah Band series, 1991, limited edition of 200 .... **$525**

Drummer, DB 89, blue trousers & sleeves, yellow vest, cream & red drum, Royal Doulton Collectors Band series, 1990, limited edition of 250 .... **$525**

Eskimo, DB 275, yellow coat & boots, orange trim, Figure of the Year, 2003 .... **$65**

Federation, DB 224, blue, Australian flag, limited edition of 2,500 .... **$165**

Fisherman, DB 170, blue hat & trousers, light yellow sweater, black wellingtons, 1997-2000 .... **$45**

Gardener, DB 156, brown jacket, white shirt, grey trousers, light green wheelbarrow, 1996-98 .... **$50**

Goalkeeper, DB 120, yellow & black, 1991, limited edition of 250 .... **$650**

Halloween, DB 132, orange & yellow pumpkin, 1993-97...... **$80**

Harry the Herald, DB 115, yellow & dark green, 1991, Royal Family series, limited edition of 300 .... **$1,000**

Jogging, Music Box, DB 37, yellow & blue, 1987-89 .... **$275**

King John, DB 91, purple, yellow & white, Royal Family series, 1990, limited edition of 250 .... **$550**

Little John, DB 243, brown cloak, 2001 .... **$60**

Master Potter, DB 131, blue, white, green & brown, 1992-93, RDICC Special **$250**

Minstrel, DB 211, 1999, limited edition of 2,500................... **$105**

Mr. Bunnykins at the Easter Parade, DB 18, red, yellow & brown, 1982-93 .... **$85**

Mrs. Bunnykins at the Easter Parade, DB 19, pale blue & maroon, 1982-96............... **$75**

Oompah Band, DB 105, 106, 107, 108, 109, green, 1991, limited edition of 250, the set...... **$2,750**

Piper, DB 191, green, brown & black, 1999, limited edition of 3,000 .... **$150**

Prince Frederick, DB 48, green, white & red, Royal Family series, 1986-90 .... **$125**

Ringmaster, DB 165, black hat & trousers, red jacket, white waistcoat & shirt, black bow tie, 1996, limited edition of 1,500..................... **$500**

Saxophone Player, DB 186, navy & white striped shirt, blue vest, black trousers, 1999, limited edition of 2,500................... **$150**

Scotsman (The), DB 180, dark blue jacket & hat, red & yellow kilt, white shirt, sporran & socks, black shoes, 1998, limited edition of 2,500 .... **$185**

Sweetheart, DB 174, white & blue, pink heart, 1997, limited edition of 2,500 .... **$205**

Sousaphone, DB 86, blue uniform & yellow sousaphone, Oompha Band series, 1990, limited edition of 250 .... **$500**

Susan, DB 70, white, blue & yellow, 1988- 93 .... **$125**

Tally Ho!, DB 12, burgundy, yellow, blue, white & green, 1973-88 .... **$105**

Touchdown, DB 29B (Boston College), maroon & gold, 1985, limited edition of 50 .... **$2,000**

Touchdown, DB 99 (Notre Dame), green & yellow, 1990, limited edition of 200...................... **$625**

Tyrolean Dancer, DB 246, black & white, 2001 .... **$60**

Will Scarlet, DB 264, green & orange, 2002 .... **$60**

Wizard, DB 168, brown rabbit, purple robes & hat, 1997, limited edition of 2,000................... **$400**

In addition to collector clubs devoted to a single type of antique or collectible, another type of club is the study group. These local groups usually meet monthly for members to share and explore their interests. Meetings often feature a guest speaker. Some groups sponsor annual antique shows.

Burslem Wares

Bowl, 16" d., 9" h., a wide round pedestal base in brown & green supporting a wide, deep curved bowl decorated w/a continuous band of large bright yellow tulips on dark green leaves & stems, ca. 1910 .... **$3,600**

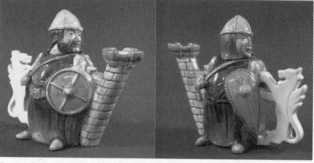

Teapot, cov., figural Norman and Saxon model, designed by Anthony Cartlidge, limited edition of 1,500, introduced in 2003 (ILLUS. of both sides)... **$300**

Teapot, cov., figural Pirate and Captain model, designed by Anthony Cartlidge, limited edition of 1,500, introduced in 2003 (ILLUS. of both sides) **$300**

Teapot, cov., Polar Bear Series, footed very wide squatty low body tapering to a flat rim & conical cover w/disk finial, short angled spout & loop handle, overall crackled background w/a center band of walking polar bears, ca. 1920s **$90**

Tyg (three-handled mug), Vellum Ware, ornately scroll- molded cylindrical body decorated w/a large panel of Spanish Ware floral decoration, three figural cherub handles, ca. 1895 .... **$800**

Vase, 4 1/2" h., flask-shape, Titanian Ware, flattened rounded form w/a tiny cylindrical neck, h.p. w/a scene of a blue & white heron perched on a branch w/a full moon & pale blue sky in the background, designed by Harry Allen, ca. 1920 .... **$1,000**

Vase, 3 1/2" h., miniature, bone china, cylindrical w/small brown twig-type handles on the lower sides, the body printed w/a stylized dark blue Art Nouveau floral design on a grey ground, ca. 1910 .... **$200**

Vase, bone china, footed tapering ovoid body w/a small trumpet-form neck, dark blue ground h.p. w/ white swans & trimmed w/raised paste gold, designed by Fred Hodkinson, ca. 1910 .... **$1,000**

There are three types of porcelain: hard paste, soft paste, and bone. Bone china is the strongest of the three because of the addition of bone ash derived from cattle bones. While it is the hardest of the three, it is still relatively fragile and should be handled with care.

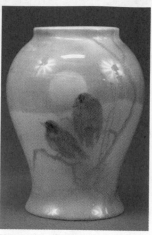

Vase, 5 7/8" h., Natural Foliage Ware, tapering gourd-form body, decorated w/scattered brown leaves on a mottled green & yellow ground, impressed mark, Shape No. 7669 .... **$173**

Vase, 6" h., bone china, footed ovoid body w/a short trumpet neck, dark yellow ground h.p. w/a large bird perched on a blossoming branch, designed by Arthur Eaton, ca. 1920 .... **$400**

Vase, 7" h., Titanian Ware, bulbous ovoid body w/flared foot & wide flat mouth, h.p. scene of two large perched birds, designed by Edward Raby, ca. 1920 .... **$1,000**

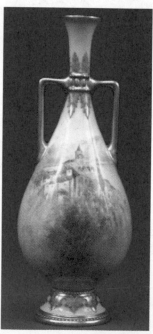

Vase, 8 1/4" h., bone china, footed ovoid body tapering to a green flared neck flanked by angled gold shoulder handles, the sides h.p. w/a cottage & garden scene, designed by John Hugh Plant, ca. 1910 .... **$1,000**

Vase, 9 1/4" h., Holbein Ware, cylindrical w/a silver rim band, decorated w/a scene of a lady wearing a shawl in a landscape, deep rose red sky above the trees & figure in shades of dark green, brown & pink, Burslem, ca. 1900 .... **$800**

Vase, 10 1/4" h., bone china, gold domed foot below the sharply tapering ovoid body w/a tall slender trumpet neck, angular gold handles from neck to shoulders, h.p. w/an Italian lake scene, titled "La Madonna del Sasso Locarno," designed by Percy Curnock, ca. 1910 . **$1,500**

Flambé Glazes

Animals & Birds

Fox, seated looking up, Rouge Flambé glaze color variation, Model 14, ca. 1912- 96, 4 1/2" h. **$300**

Geese, two flying together, "Going Home," Rouge Flambé glaze, designed by Adrian Hughes, test market only, 1982, 6 1/4" h. **$1,200**

Kittens, two kittens curled up together, Rouge Flambé, 2 1/2" **$600**

Owl with owlet, Rouge Flambé, Model 71, ca. 1912, 4 3/4" h. **$3,000**

Pig, Rouge Flambé, fat squatty animal, Model 72, ca. 1912, 2" h. **$850**

Rabbit, Rouge Flambé, seated animal w/one long ear to side, Model 1165, 1913-96, 2 1/2" h. ... **$250**

Flambé in French means singed by flame. Flambé glaze gets its appearance from certain effects produced inside the kiln. These effects were likely accidental at first, caused by unpredictable conditions inside the kilns. Over time, however, this popular glaze was purposely produced through more consistent and carefully regulated processes.

Tortoise, Rouge Flambé, 1920-46, 2" h. ... **$2,000**

Miscellaneous Pieces

Vase, Mottled Flambé, tall slightly tapering cylindrical body w/a rounded shoulder & small trumpet neck, ca. 1955 .... **$1,500**

Vase, Sung Ware glaze, footed sharply tapering ovoid body w/a tiny flared mouth, decorated w/ stylized red gnomes & toadstools on a black ground **$4,000**

Vase, 4" h., miniature, Rouge Flambé, squatty bulbous nearly spherical body tapering to a tiny trumpet neck, ca. 1915 ..... **$300**

Vase, 6" h., Sung Ware glaze, very bulbous ovoid body tapering to a short cylindrical neck, bold streaky glaze, designed by Charles Noke, ca. 1925 .... **$800**

Vase, 6 3/8" h., Sung Ware glaze, footed bulbous ovoid body tapering to a small flared neck, decorated w/a soaring peacock above a colorful background dotted w/stylized flowers, shades of red, purple & black, imprinted & painted marks **$2,530**

Vase, 8" h., Rouge Flambé, footed bulbous lower body tapering to cylindrical sides & a flaring rim, decorated w/a woodland landscape, ca. 1945 .... **$500**

Vase, 9" h., Rouge Flambé glaze, nearly spherical body w/a short cylindrical neck, red w/black swirls & gold flecks, marked on the bottom "Royal Doulton Flambé - Veined - 1618," early 20th c. $200-300

Vase, 8 5/8" h., Sung Ware, simple swelled cylindrical body tapering to a flat mouth, decorated by Charles Noke w/an elaborate scene of an Arab potter at his wheel, working under a grape arbor loaded w/ grapes, background mottled Flambé glaze in shades of deep purple, deep red, gold & blue, Flambé logo on the base w/"Sung Noke No. 915," crazing w/several long craze lines, early 20th c. **$2,990**

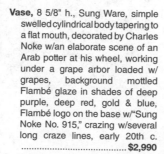

Lambeth Art Wares

Jug w/stopper, stoneware, miniature, footed squatty bulbous body w/a slender cylindrical neck w/a disk stopper & angled brown handle, buff ground applied around the body & shoulder w/ bands of blue flowerheads, ca. 1880, 3 1/2" h. **$500**

Jug, Copper Ware, footed tapering cylindrical body w/a pointed angled handle, glossy copper glaze molded w/riveted seams & simulated dents, ca. 1895, 6" h. **$650**

Jug, stoneware, footed bulbous ovoid body tapering to a tall slender cylindrical neck w/a long handle from the rim to the shoulder, the body divided into wide bands, the bottom band decorated w/swirled ribs below molded narrow blue bands flanking a wide body band decorated w/incised tightly scrolling leafy branches dotted w/small applied florettes, a ribbed shoulder band applied w/a narrow flowering vine & the upper neck incised w/ another band of swirled ribs, silver rim band, designed by Arthur Barlow, 1874, 10 1/2" h. **$800**

Liquor spigot measure, stoneware, two-section cylindrical shape w/a rounded bottom w/a button finial, a short cylindrical spigot on the lower front & a threaded projection at the top back, metal fitting & handle at the top, decorated in pale mottled green applied w/a spade-shaped brown Art Nouveau leaf, ca. 1910, 6" l. **$500**

Match holder, cov., stoneware, Silicon Ware, flaring base & cylindrical sides w/a domed cover, light brown ground deco-rated around the sides w/a wide band composed of light blue small leaves flanking a band composed of pairs of white scrolls w/blue dots, white dot bands around the cover & base, ca. 1880, 3 1/4" h. **$350**

Match holder & striker, stoneware, domed wide foot supporting a slightly tapering cylindrical ribbed striker w/open top for holding matches, the base decorated w/a blue band decorated w/an Art Nouveau design of a band of spade-shaped brown leaves, ca. 1910 .... **$500**

Model of a sea lion, stoneware, the animal perched on a rocky outcrop, overall tan lustre glaze, designed by Richard Garbe, 1931, 8" h. **$1,250**

Mustard pot w/silver rim & hinged cover, stoneware, footed squatty spherical brown body w/loop handle decorated w/a band of white-dotted rings enclosing a large molded blue florette, cobalt blue neck band, ca. 1885 .... **$500**

Pitcher, 7 1/2" h., stoneware, jug-form, the ovoid body w/a short flaring neck w/a rim spout & a high arched handle, the buff body decorated w/large bold-relief sun-flower-shaped medallions each enclosing a different classical portrait, each medallion ringed by a motto written in black, ca. 1885 .... **$500**

Pitcher, 11" h., Hannah Barlow Doulton Lambethware, design of hounds chasing fox, 1875, vertical hairline crack **$1,250**

Potpourri jar, cov., stoneware, a bulbous ovoid body tapering to a wide cylindrical neck, the mottled bluish black ground applied around the shoulder w/pierced blue flower blossoms below an upper band of pierced trefoils, the domed cover w/a knob finial pieced w/small holes separated w/a thin molded scroll band, ca. 1900 .... **$1,500**

• Remove rings before handling valuable ceramics to prevent scratching.
• Display pieces in glass cabinets to reduce dust, but make sure the cabinet is not placed on a shaky floor.

Salt dip, stoneware, footed wide squatty shape w/a wide flat rim, overall gilt circle decoration, ca. 1884 .... **$400**

Remove loose lids from pieces before picking them up and don't pick up them up only by their handles or tops. Pick up only one item at a time and use both hands.

Trinket dish (bibelot), stoneware, figural, shallow rounded dish w/a green exterior & cobalt blue interior, mounted on the rim w/the seated figure of a pixie in shades of brown, designed by Harry Simeon, ca. 1925, 4 1/4" d. **$2,000**

Salt shaker w/silver plate rim & top, stoneware, tall urn-form, banded decorated w/a wide center band molded w/florette diamonds in dark blue, shoulder & base bands w/light & dark blue diamonds, buff bands trimmed w/ tiny white dots, ca. 1880 ..... **$300**

Tumbler, stoneware, tall slightly tapering cylindrical form, the tan sides applied w/white relief golfing scenes, a dark brown top band below the silver rim, ca. 1900 .... **$500**

Umbrella stand, Chine Ware, cylindrical body w/a short waisted neck below the wide rolled rim, the main body decorated overall w/large pale blue florals on a darker blue ground, ca. 1890, 14" h. **$1,000**

Vase, faience, footed ovoid body tapering to a short trumpet neck, the tan foot below the dark cobalt blue body decorated w/large yellow irises & long green leaves, the neck decorated w/brick red blossoms on a tan ground, ca. 1880 .... **$1,200**

Stoneware is a type of pottery between earthenware and porcelain. It is heavier than porcelain, opaque, and darker in color because it is made from a less pure clay. Because it is durable and impervious to liquids, it is commonly used for vases, pitchers, etc.

Tumbler, stoneware, tall slightly tapering cylindrical form, incised w/long stylized leaves & indigo blue foliage w/dark green trim, impressed marks & dated 1877, 4 5/8" h. **$115**

DOULTON & ROYAL DOULTON

Vase, Marqueterie Ware, footed ribbed ovoid body tapering to a cylindrical neck w/a molded blue band flanked by small gold scroll handles, blue & white body band & gold & blue ground, Lambeth factory, ca. 1895 .... **$800**

Vase, stoneware, bulbous ovoid body tapering to a short rolled neck, mottled dark blue ground decorated w/a scene of a blue bird perched on a leafy branch besides its neck, a white full moon in the background, ca. 1925 . **$850**

Vase, stoneware, gently swelled cylindrical body w/a wide flat rim, a narrow brown base band below a dark blue band, the upper body w/a white ground tube-lined w/a decoration of a large blue birds among blue & yellow stylized flowers & leaves, designed by Harry Simeon, ca. 1925 .... **$700**

Series Wares

Dickens Ware Series

Loving cup, three-handled waisted cylindrical shape, color scene of Bill Sykes, Charles Noke, 1912 .... **$400**

Oatmeal dish, round, color scene of Tony Weller, Charles Noke, darker colors variation, 1931 .... **$100**

Pitcher, jug-type, cylindrical body w/ rim spout & brown angled handle w/White Hart sign, relief-molded w/a scene of Poor Jo & Fat Boy, No. D5864, Charles Noke, 1937 .... **$600**

Plate, round w/flanged rim, color scene of Mr. Micawber, Charles Noke, pale colors variation, 1912 .... **$200-250**

Plate, round w/flanged rim, color scene of Sairey Gamp, Charles Noke, 1912 .... **$200**

Porridge bowl, round w/lightly scalloped rim, color scene of the Artful Dodger, Charles Noke, 1912 .... **$300**

Tea caddy, cov., tapering cylindrical body w/an angled green shoulder & small cylindrical neck, color scene of Barnaby Rudge, Charles Noke, 1912 .... **$350**

Vase, footed tapering waisted cylindrical body w/long loop handles up from the base, color scene of Sairy Gamp, Charles Noke, 1912 .... **$500**

Pitcher, Friar shape jug-type, footed swelled square body w/an arched rim spout & pointed angled handle, color scene of Trotty Veck, Charles Noke, 1912 .... **$300**

Tray, long rectangular form w/low serpentine sides & flaring incurved ends w/notched corners, low-relief scene of Captain Cuttle & Mr. Toots, No. D5833, Charles Noke, 1937 .... **$350**

Barlow Family Doulton Wares

Vase, stoneware, footed ovoid body tapering to a trumpet neck, the wide body band incised w/a scene of sheep, decorative base & neck bands, decorated by Hannah Barlow, ca. 1880 .... **$1,800**

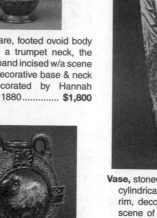

Vase, 9 3/4" h., stoneware, moon flask- shaped, oblong pedestal foot supporting a large flattened disk-form body, the outer cross-and-ring border molded w/scrolls, the center circle molded in high-relief w/the figure of a standing sheep, the short neck flanked by curling handles resembling horns, decorated by Hannah Barlow, ca. 1880 .... **$4,000**

Hannah Barlow was one of nine children born to Iram and Hannah Barlow in Hertfordshire, England, in the mid-1800s. Hannah and two siblings, Florence and Albert, gained recognition as superb Doulton studio artists.

Vase, stoneware, tall gently tapering cylindrical body w/a low rolled rim, decorated w/a pate-sur-pate scene of wild turkeys, decorated by Florence Barlow, ca. 1885 .... **$3,000**

Vase, 13" h., stoneware, footed tall ovoid body w/a swelled shoulder ring below the tall trumpet neck, the body incised w/oval panels decorated w/birds against an incised blue & white ground, decorated by Hannah & Florence Barlow, ca. 1905 .... **$2,000**

Vase, 7 3/4" h., stoneware, moon flask- shaped, brown scroll feet support the upright flattened round body w/a small short cylindrical neck, the body incised w/a detailed scene of deer, decorated by Hannah, Florence & Lucy Barlow, 1883 .... **$3,000**

Vase, 18" h., stoneware, tall swelled cylindrical body w/a wide trumpet neck, the band band, shoulder & neck decorated w/stylized green leafy vines & spearpoints on dark brown, the wide body band incised w/a scene of bears, decorated by Hannah Barlow, ca. 1880 .... **$1,500**

Dresden

Dresden-type porcelain evolved from wares made at the nearby Meissen Porcelain Works early in the 18th century. "Dresden" and "Meissen" are often used interchangeably for later wares. "Dresden" has become a generic name for the kind of porcelains produced in Dresden and certain other areas of Germany, but perhaps should be confined to the wares made in the city of Dresden.

Compote, large reticulated basket raised on tree-form stem w/ applied cherubs, footed base, all-over floral decoration, w/pastel flower colors on white, made by Carl Thieme Factory, ca. 1901, 19" h. **$728**

Figure group, modeled as standing man & lady flower sellers in 18th c. costume w/a young boy seated in front, all centered by a tall flower-applied covered urn, on a molded oblong base, Thieme factory mark, late 19th c., 9" h. **$650-750**

Plates, 10 7/8" d., each divided into four panels divided by gilt & floral bands & border, alternating designs of colorful flowers & romantic figures in 18th costume, marked "Dresden, Germany," early 20th c., set of 12......................... **$550-650**

Vase, cov., 24 3/8" h., a ringed pedestal base supporting a large bulbous ovoid body tapering to a short flared neck w/a domed cover w/pointed gold finial, cobalt blue ground w/ornate delicate gold trim, the front centered by a large oval reserve h.p. w/two scantily clad putti seated on a classical plinth within a rocky garden landscape, the back decorated w/a loose floral bouquet, jeweled gilt trellis border, blue crowned "RK" & Dresden mark of Richard Klemm **$6,000**

Vase, 10 5/8" h., flat-bottomed ovoid body tapering to a slender neck w/upright rounded rim flanked by high ornate pierced scroll gold handles, the body painted w/a realistic landscape showing a tiger descending a rocky ledge among tall grasses within a pale yelllow border, the reverse decorated w/a gilt butterfly & foliage flanked by ducks in flight, cobalt blue neck w/gold trim, gilt castle mark, Germany, early 20th c. .. **$1,680**

From the 19th century through the first quarter of the 20th century, Dresden was a center of art and culture. It lost its dominance as a result of the upheaval caused by World War II and post war occupation, but is making great strides in recovery since German reunification.

Teapot, cov., wide tapering bulbous ribbed lower body tapering to a tall swirled & gently flaring neck w/arched rim, ornate conforming cover w/fancy gold scroll finial, tall molded serpentine spout, very ornate C-scroll handle, decorated w/bands of green trimmed in gold around the top & base, a large cluster of green & white lily- of-the-valley on the sides, Dresden, Germany, ca. 1900 .... **$125**

Fiesta (Homer Laughlin China Co. -HLC)

Fiesta dinnerware was made by the Homer Laughlin China Company of Newell, West Virginia, from the 1930s until the early 1970s. The brilliant colors of this inexpensive pottery have attracted numerous collectors. On February 28, 1986, Laughlin reintroduced the popular Fiesta line with minor changes in the shapes of a few pieces and a contemporary color range. The effect of this new production on the Fiesta collecting market is yet to be determined.

For additional information on Fiesta Ware see *Warman's Fiesta Ware Identification & Price Guide* by Mark F. Moran (Krause Publications, 2004).

Ashtray grey........................ $80-90
Ashtray medium green $200-230
Ashtray yellow..................... $35-45
Bowl, cream soup cobalt blue $50-70
Bowl, cream soup forest green $50-70
Bowl, cream soup ivory $50-70
Bowl, cream soup red........ $50-70
Bowl, dessert, 6" d. chartreuse $35-50
Bowl, dessert, 6" d. light green $35-50
Bowl, dessert, 6" d. rose $35-50
Bowl, dessert, 6" d. turquoise $35-50
Bowl, fruit, 11 3/4" d. cobalt blue $300-350
Bowl, fruit, 11 3/4" d. ivory $300-350
Bowl, fruit, 11 3/4" d. light green $300-350
Bowl, fruit, 11 3/4" d. yellow $300-350
Bowl, individual fruit, 4 3/4" d. chartreuse $25-35
Bowl, individual fruit, 4 3/4" d. forest green $25-35
Bowl, individual fruit, 4 3/4" d. grey $25-35
Bowl, individual fruit, 4 3/4" d. red $25-35
Bowl, individual fruit, 4 3/4" d., medium green $650-700
Bowl, individual fruit, 5 1/2" d. turquoise $25-40
Bowl, individual fruit, 5 1/2" d. grey $25-40
Bowl, individual fruit, 5 1/2" d. light green............................. $25-40
Bowl, individual fruit, 5 1/2" d. red $25-40
Bowl, individual salad, 7 1/2" d. medium green $100-150
Bowl, individual salad, 7 1/2" d. turquoise $100- 150
Bowl, individual salad, 7 1/2" d. yellow $100-150
Bowl, nappy, 8 1/2" d. chartreuse $40-65

Bowl, nappy, 8 1/2" d. cobalt blue $40-65
Bowl, nappy, 8 1/2" d. forest green $40-65
Bowl, nappy, 8 1/2" d. grey $40-65
Bowl, nappy, 8 1/2" d. medium green $150-175
Bowl, nappy, 9 1/2" d. cobalt blue $55-70
Bowl, nappy, 9 1/2" d. forest green $55-70
Bowl, nappy, 9 1/2" d. grey $55-70
Bowl, nappy, 9 1/2" d. ivory $55-70
Bowl, nappy, 9 1/2" d. light green $55-70
Bowl, nappy, 9 1/2" d. turquoise $55-70
Bowl, nappy, 9 1/2" d. yellow $55-70
Bowl, salad, large, footed, 11 3/8" d., light green $550-625
Bowl, salad, large, footed, 11 3/8" d., red............ $550- 625
Bowl, salad, large, footed, 11 3/8" d., turquoise ... $550-625
Bowl, salad, large, footed, 11 3/8" d., yellow $550-625
Bowl, salad, large, footed, 11 3/8" d., cobalt blue $550-625
Cake plate, 10 3/8" d. cobalt blue $950-1,050
Cake plate, 10" d. ivory $850-900
Cake plate, 10" d. light green $900-950
Cake plate, 10" d. red ...... $1,500+
Calendar plate, 10" d., 1954 ivory $40-50
Calendar plate, 10" d., 1955 ivory $40-50
Calendar plate, 10" d., 1955 light green $40-50
Calendar plate, 10" d., 1955 yellow $40-50
Candleholders, bulb-type, pr. cobalt blue......................... $120
Candleholders, bulb-type, pr. ivory.................................. $120

Ashtray cobalt blue $50-60

Bowl, dessert, 6" d. medium green $700-800

Bowl, individual fruit, 5 1/2" d. rose $25-40

Candleholders, bulb-type, pr. red
.... $120

Candleholders, bulb-type, pr. yellow $90-125

Candleholders, tripod-type, pr. cobalt blue................... $650-700

Candleholders, tripod-type, pr. ivory............................ $600-650

Candleholders, tripod-type, pr. light green $475- 525

Candleholders, tripod-type, pr. red............................... $675-725

Candleholders, tripod-type, pr. turquoise $675- 725

Candleholders, tripod-type, pr. yellow $400-425

Carafe, cov. cobalt blue
.... $225-325

Carafe, cov. ivory............ $225-325

Carafe, cov. red.............. $225-325

Carafe, cov. turquoise $250

Carafe, cov. yellow $250

Casserole, cov., two-handled, 9 3/4" d. forest green.. $300-325

Casserole, cov., two-handled, 9 3/4" d. medium green
.... $1,600-1,700

Casserole, cov., two-handled, 9 3/4" d. yellow $150

Casserole, cov., two-handled, 9 3/4" d. chartreuse,... $300-325

Casserole, cov., two-handled, 9 3/4" d. cobalt blue.... $250-275

Casserole, cov., two-handled, 9 3/4" d. grey $300-325

Casserole, cov., two-handled, 9 3/4" d. ivory $250-300

Casserole, cov., two-handled, 9 3/4" d. light green $150-175

Casserole, cov., two-handled, 9 3/4" d. red................ $250-300

Casserole, cov., two-handled, 9 3/4" d. rose.............. $300-325

Casserole, cov., two-handled, 9 3/4" d. turquoise $160-180

Coffeepot, cov. chartreuse
.... $325-350

Coffeepot, cov. cobalt blue
.... $250-300

Coffeepot, cov. forest green
.... $325-350

Coffeepot, cov. grey....... $675-725

Coffeepot, cov. ivory $230

Coffeepot, cov. light green
.... $225-250

Coffeepot, cov. red........ $275-325

Coffeepot, cov. rose....... $275-425

Coffeepot, cov. turquoise...... $180

Coffeepot, cov. yellow.... $200-250

Coffeepot, cov., demitasse, stick handle cobalt blue $600-625

Coffeepot, cov., demitasse, stick handle ivory $625-650

Coffeepot, cov., demitasse, stick handle light green....... $675-725

Coffeepot, cov., demitasse, stick handle turquoise........ $700-725

Candleholders, bulb-type, pr. turquoise
.... $90-125

Carafe, cov. light green
.... $225-325

Coffeepot, cov., demitasse, stick handle yellow..................... $400

Compote, 12" d., low, footed cobalt blue................ $200- 225

Compote, 12" d., low, footed ivory
.... $200-225

Compote, 12" d., low, footed light green $150- 175

Compote, 12" d., low, footed red
.... $700-725

Compote, 12" d., low, footed turquoise $700-725

Compote, 12" d., low, footed yellow $400-425

Compote, sweetmeat, high stand cobalt blue..................... $75-100

Compote, sweetmeat, high stand light green $75-110

Compote, sweetmeat, high stand turquoise $95

Creamer forest green......... $25-40

Creamer red............................ $25

Creamer yellow.................. $25-40

Creamer & cov. sugar bowl, individual size, on figure-8 tray, yellow on cobalt tray, the set
.... $700-750

Coffeepot, cov., demitasse, stick handle red $700-725

Creamer, ring-handled, chartreuse
.... $25-40

Creamer, ring-handled, cobalt blue $25

Creamer, ring-handled, grey
.... $25-40

Creamer, ring-handled, light green
.... $25-40

Creamer, ring-handled, medium green $125-150

Creamer, stick handle cobalt blue
.... $60-65

Creamer, stick handle light green
.... $35-45

Creamer, stick handle turquoise
.... $100-125

Creamer, stick handle yellow
.... $35-45

Cup & saucer, demitasse, stick handle chartreuse...... $500-550

Cup & saucer, demitasse, stick handle forest green.... $400-450

Cup & saucer, demitasse, stick handle ivory $95

Cup & saucer, demitasse, stick handle red $100-125

Cup & saucer, demitasse, stick handle rose................. $400-450

FIESTA

Cup & saucer, ring handle chartreuse $30-45

Cup & saucer, ring handle grey $30-45

Cup & saucer, ring handle light green $30-45

Cup & saucer, ring handle medium green $70

Cup & saucer, ring handle rose $30-45

Egg cup chartreuse $125-175

Egg cup forest green...... $125-175

Egg cup grey.................. $500-550

Egg cup light green............. $70-80

Egg cup rose.................. $400-450

Fork (Kitchen Kraft) cobalt blue $150

Fork (Kitchen Kraft) red........ $150

Fork (Kitchen Kraft) yellow ... $150

French casserole, cov., stick handle cobalt blue $3,550-3,650

French casserole, cov., stick handle ivory $525- 575

French casserole, cov., stick handle light green....... $575-625

French casserole, cov., stick handle yellow............. $275-325

Gravy boat chartreuse........ $70-80

Gravy boat grey.................. $70-80

Gravy boat light green $45-65

Gravy boat rose.................. $70-80

Marmalade jar, cov. cobalt blue $365

Marmalade jar, cov. ivory...... $365

Marmalade jar, cov. light green $300-400

Mixing bowl, nest-type, size No. 1, 5" d. cobalt blue $275

Mixing bowl, nest-type, size No. 1, 5" d. light green........... $250-325

Mixing bowl, nest-type, size No. 1, 5" d. turquoise............. $250-325

Mixing bowl, nest-type, size No. 2, 6" d. cobalt blue $125

Mixing bowl, nest-type, size No. 2, 6" d. light green.......... $110-160

Mixing bowl, nest-type, size No. 2, 6" d. yellow $110-160

Mixing bowl, nest-type, size No. 3, 7" d. cobalt blue.......... $135-170

Mixing bowl, nest-type, size No. 3, 7" d. light green........... $135-170

Mixing bowl, nest-type, size No. 4, 8" d. cobalt blue.......... $200-225

Mixing bowl, nest-type, size No. 4, 8" d. light green........... $100-120

Mixing bowl, nest-type, size No. 4, 8" d. turquoise............ $150-175

Mixing bowl, nest-type, size No. 5, 9" d. cobalt blue.......... $225-270

Mixing bowl, nest-type, size No. 5, 9" d. light green.......... $225-270

Mixing bowl, nest-type, size No. 5, 9" d. turquoise............. $225-270

Mixing bowl, nest-type, size No. 5, 9" d. yellow $225-270

Gravy boat yellow $45-65

Plate, 9" d. medium green $70-80

Mixing bowl, nest-type, size No. 6, 10" d. ivory................. $300-375

Mixing bowl, nest-type, size No. 6, 10" d. light green......... $300-375

Mixing bowl, nest-type, size No. 7, 11 1/2" d. cobalt blue.. $550-650

Mixing bowl, nest-type, size No. 7, 11 1/2" d. light green .. $550-650

Mixing bowl, nest-type, size No. 7, 11 1/2" d. turquoise $550-650

Mug red............................ $70-80

Mug, chartreuse................. $80-90

Mug, cobalt blue................. $80-90

Mug, forest green $75-85

Mug, grey $70-80

Mug, ivory $65-75

Mug, light green $55-65

Mug, medium green $115-125

Mug, rose $75-85

Mug, turquoise $40-50

Mug, yellow $40-50

Mustard jar, cov. ivory.... $300-375

Mustard jar, cov. red $300-375

Mustard jar, cov. yellow . $300-375

Onion soup bowl, cov. cobalt blue $700-750

Onion soup bowl, cov. ivory $700-750

Onion soup bowl, cov. light green $700-750

Onion soup bowl, cov. medium green $700-750

Onion soup bowl, cov. red $700-750

Onion soup bowl, cov. yellow $700-750

Pie server (Kitchen Kraft) cobalt blue $150

Onion soup bowl, cov. turquoise $8,000

Pitcher, jug-type, 2 pt. chartreuse $125- 150

Pie server (Kitchen Kraft) light green.................................. $150

Pie server (Kitchen Kraft) yellow $150

Pitcher, jug-type, 2 pt. cobalt blue $100-125

Pitcher, jug-type, 2 pt. grey $125-150

Pitcher, jug-type, 2 pt. ivory $100-125

Pitcher, jug-type, 2 pt. light green $75-85

Pitcher, jug-type, 2 pt. rose $125-150

Pitcher, jug-type, 2 pt. turquoise $75-85

Pitcher, jug-type, 2 pt. yellow $75-85

Pitcher, juice, disc-type, 30 oz. grey .... $3,000+

Pitcher, juice, disc-type, 30 oz. red $600-700

Pitcher, juice, disc-type, 30 oz. turquoise .... $10,000+

Pitcher, juice, disc-type, 30 oz. yellow $40-50

Pitcher, w/ice lip, globular, 2 qt. ivory........................... $125-150

Pitcher, w/ice lip, globular, 2 qt. red $125-150

Pitcher, water, disc-type chartreuse $250-300

Pitcher, water, disc-type forest green $250-300

Pitcher, water, disc-type light green $100-125

Pitcher, water, disc-type rose $275-375

FIESTA

Pitcher, water, disc-type yellow $110-140

Plate, 10" d. chartreuse...... $40-50

Plate, 10" d. forest green $40-50

Plate, 10" d. grey $40-50

Plate, 10" d. medium green $150-200

Plate, 10" d. rose $40-50

Plate, 10" d. turquoise $40-50

Plate, 10" d., cobalt blue..... $40-50

Plate, 10" d., forest green ... $40-50

Plate, 10" d., light green $40-50

Plate, 10" d., medium green $150-200

Plate, 10" d., red............... $40-50

Plate, 10" d., turquoise $40-50

Plate, 6" d. chartreuse.......... $5-10

Plate, 6" d. forest green $5-10

Plate, 6" d. grey $5-10

Plate, 6" d. medium green .. $25-35

Plate, 6" d. rose $5-10

Plate, 7" d. chartreuse.......... $8-12

Plate, 7" d. forest green $8-12

Plate, 7" d. grey $8-12

Plate, 7" d. medium green .. $50-60

Plate, 7" d. rose $8-12

Plate, 9" d. chartreuse....... $15-25

Plate, 9" d. forest green $15-25

Plate, 9" d. light green $15-25

Plate, 9" d. red.......................... $15

Plate, 9" d. rose $15-25

Plate, 9" d. yellow $15-25

Plate, chop, 13" d. chartreuse $80-100

Plate, chop, 13" d. cobalt blue $45

Plate, chop, 13" d. forest green $80-100

Plate, chop, 13" d. grey.... $80-100

Plate, chop, 13" d. light green $40-60

Plate, chop, 13" d. medium green $600-700

Plate, chop, 13" d. rose ... $80-100

Plate, chop, 13" d. yellow... $40-60

Plate, chop, 15" d. cobalt blue $90

Plate, chop, 15" d. forest green $150-175

Plate, chop, 15" d. grey $150-175

Plate, chop, 15" d. light green $150-175

Plate, chop, 15" d. red $80-110

Plate, chop, 15" d. rose . $150-175

Plate, grill, 10 1/2" d. chartreuse $70-80

Plate, grill, 10 1/2" d. cobalt blue $40

Plate, grill, 10 1/2" d. forest green $70-80

Plate, grill, 10 1/2" d. light green $35-50

Plate, grill, 10 1/2" d. turquoise $35

Plate, grill, 10 1/2" d. yellow ... $35

Plate, grill, 12" d. cobalt blue $50-70

Plate, grill, 12" d. ivory $50-70

Plate, grill, 12" d. red $50-70

Plate, grill, 12" d. yellow.... $50-70

Platter, 12" oval chartreuse $45-65

Platter, 12" oval grey.......... $45-65

Platter, 12" oval light green $45-65

Platter, 12" oval medium green $200-225

Platter, 12" oval red........... $50

Platter, 12" oval yellow........ $45-65

Relish tray w/five inserts cobalt blue $355

Relish tray w/five inserts light green $300-375

Relish tray w/five inserts multicolored................. $300-375

Salt & pepper shakers, pr. chartreuse $25-45

Salt & pepper shakers, pr. forest green $25-45

Salt & pepper shakers, pr. grey $25-45

Salt & pepper shakers, pr. light green $25-45

Salt & pepper shakers, pr. medium green $225- 250

Salt & pepper shakers, pr. red $25

Salt & pepper shakers, pr. rose $25-45

Salt & pepper shakers, pr. yellow $25-45

Soup plate, rimmed, 8 3/8" d. cobalt blue.................... $40-65

Soup plate, rimmed, 8 3/8" d. forest green, ... $40-65

Soup plate, rimmed, 8 3/8" d. medium green $125-150

Soup plate, rimmed, 8 3/8" d. red $50

Soup plate, rimmed, 8 3/8" d. rose $40-65

Soup plate, rimmed, 8 3/8" d. yellow $40-65

Soup plate, rimmed, 8 3/8" d., chartreuse $40-65

Spoon (Kitchen Kraft) light green $125-140

Spoon (Kitchen Kraft) red $140-150

Sugar bowl, cov. chartreuse $60-70

Sugar bowl, cov. forest green $60-70

Sugar bowl, cov. grey $60-70

Sugar bowl, cov. light green $45-60

Sugar bowl, cov. red $60-70

Sugar bowl, cov. rose $60-70

Syrup pitcher w/original lid, cobalt blue $350-450

Syrup pitcher w/original lid, ivory $350-450

Syrup pitcher w/original lid, light green $350-450

Syrup pitcher w/original lid, red $350-450

Syrup pitcher w/original lid, yellow $350-450

Teapot, cov., large size (8 cup), cobalt blue.................. $300-400

Teapot, cov., large size (8 cup), light green $300- 400

Teapot, cov., large size (8 cup), red.... $300-400

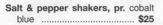

Salt & pepper shakers, pr. cobalt blue $25

Teapot, cov., medium size (6 cup), medium green ... $1,600-1,700

FLORENCE CERAMICS

Florence Ceramics

Some of the finest figurines and artwares were produced between 1940 and 1962 by the Florence Ceramics Company of Pasadena, California. Florence Ward began working with ceramics following the death of her son, Jack, in 1939.

Mrs. Ward had not worked with clay before her involvement with classes at the Pasadena Hobby School. After study and firsthand experience, she began production in her garage, using a kiln located outside the garage to conform with city regulations. The years 1942-44 were considered her "garage" period.

In 1944 Florence Ceramics moved to a small plant in Pasadena, employing fifty-four employees and receiving orders of $250,000 per year. In 1948 it was again necessary to move to a larger facility in the area with the most up-to-date equipment. The number of employees increased to more than 100. Within five years Florence Ceramics was considered one of the finest producers of semi-porcelain figurines and artwares.

Florence created a wide range of items including figurines, lamps, picture frames, planters and models of animals and birds. It was her extensive line of women in beautiful gowns and gentlemen in fine clothes that gave her the most pleasure and was the

foundation of her business. Two of her most popular lines of figurines were inspired by the famous 1860 Godey's Ladies' Book and by famous artists from the Old Master group. In the mid-1950s two bird lines were produced for several years. One of the bird lines was designed by Don Winton and the other was a line of contemporary sculpted bird and animal figures designed by the well-known sculptor Betty Davenport Ford.

There were several unsuccessful contemporary artware lines produced for a short time. The Driftware line consisted of modern freeform bowls and accessories. The Floraline is a rococo line with overglazed decoration. The Gourmet Pottery, a division of Florence Ceramics Company, produced accessory serving pieces under the name of Scandia and Sierra.

Florence products were manufactured in the traditional porcelain process with a second firing at a higher temperature after the glaze had been applied. Many pieces had overglaze paint decoration and clay ruffles, roses and lace dipped in slip prior to the third firing.

Figures

"Christening (The)," woman w/ dress trimmed in lace at neck, sleeves & front of dress, holding an infant in a long white christening dress, articulated fingers, 10" h. **$2,000-2,500**

"Dora Lee," woman wearing a long widely flaring & swirling royal red gown, a small round hat on her head w/a ribbon, arms away from the body, 9 1/2" h. **$750-900**

"Fair Lady," woman in Gay Nineties gown standing on scrolled base decorated w/a small basket of strewn flowers across the front, royal red dress w/ornate white lace collar, upswept brown hair w/roses, arms away from body w/articulated fingers, 11 1/2" h. **$1,750-2,000**

"Georgia," woman standing wearing a long wide real brocade fabric gown, her hands lifting sides of gown at the front, 12" h. **$1,500-2,000**

"Lady Diana," woman stepping forward w/her arms away from her body, wearing flowers in her piled hair & a low-cut narrow lilac gown w/a flaring lacy collar, tight waist & over gown pulled into a bustle, the half-length sleeves w/ plain cuffs, 10" h. **$500-575**

"Little Princess," girl standing in a long- sleeved very wide 17th c. farthingale gown, her hair in long curls, arms outstretched to edges of gown, 8 1/2" h. . **$1,000-1,250**

"Karen," woman in late Victorian costume, wearing a narrow-waisted fur-trimmed half-length coat over a widely flaring gown, small fur-trimmed hat, w/arms away from body, articulated fingers, 8 1/2" h. .. **$1,250-1,500**

"Jeannette," Godey lady, rose colored full- skirted dress w/ peplum, white collar, flower at neck, left hand holding hat w/ bow, right hand holding parasol, 7 3/4" h. **$125-150**

"Joyce," woman wearing full off-the-shoulder gown w/shoulder ruffles, a wide- brimmed picture hat, arms away at the front, 8 1/2" h. **$325-350**

"Linda Lou," girl standing wearing a long full green dress w/peplum & long sleeves, holding a bouquet of flowers to her cheek, a high-fronted bonnet on her head, 7 3/4" h. **$100-125**

"Love Letter," woman standing reading a small letter, her hair piled on her head, wearing an off-the-shoulder long gown w/lace bands, 12" h. **$1,500-,750**

"Marc Antony," Roman warrior wearing helmet, breastplate, white short garment & long flowing cape, one sandaled leg resting on a rectangular block on a square base, 13" h. **$750-1,000**

FLOW BLUE

Flow Blue

Flow Blue ironstone and semi-porcelain was manufactured mainly in England during the second half of the 19th century. The early ironstone was produced by many of the well known English potters and was either transfer-printed or hand-painted (brush stroke). The bulk of the ware was exported to the United States or Canada.

The "flow" or running quality of the cobalt blue designs was the result of introducing certain chemicals into the kiln during the final firing. Some patterns are so "flown" that it is difficult to ascertain the design. The transfers were of several types: Asian, Scenic, Marble or Floral.

The earliest Flow Blue ironstone patterns were produced during the period between about 1840 and 1860. After the Civil War, Flow Blue went out of style for some years but was again manufactured and exported to the United States beginning about the 1880s and continuing through the turn of the century. These later Flow Blue designs are on a semi-porcelain body rather than heavier ironstone and the designs are mainly florals. Also see *Antique Trader Pottery & Porcelain Ceramics Price Guide*, 5th Edition.

ATHENS
(Charles Meigh, ca. 1840)

Waste bowl $225

CASHMERE
(Francis Morley, ca. 1850)

Waste bowl $450

DELHI
(Unknown maker, ca. 1860)

Pitcher & bowl set, child's, the set
.... $850

DELHI (Unknown, pattern looks exactly like "Lahore" by Corn)

Pitcher & bowl set, child's size, 2 pcs.
.... $850

FLORAL - ROSES
(Unknown maker, ca. 1860)

Master waste jar, cov., bulbous ovoid body w/a molded & scalloped flaring rim, ornate C-scroll handles & low domed cover w/C-scroll handle, long swags of roses down the sides
.... $450

FLORAL
(Davenport, ca. 1840)

Knife rest $550

• Cobalt oxide was used to produce Flow Blue because it could survive the intense heat needed to glaze the pieces. Adding lime or ammonia chloride enhanced the blur, which conveniently hid defects in the blanks.
• Closely related to Flow Blue is Mulberry ware, which was also produced with the same blurred effect but with a blackish or brownish purple color.

FLORAL
(Unknown maker, ca. 1860)

Teapot, cov., flaring foot, bulbous tapering body w/flaring rim, domed cover w/floral finial, serpentine spout & C-scroll handle, bands of flowers around the base, rim & cover $395

FLORAL
(Unknown maker, ca. 1890)

Vase, bulbous ovoid base tapering sharply to a tri-lobed flaring rim, large roses $125

FORGET ME NOT
(Unknown maker, ca. 1860)

Sauce tureen, cover, ladle & undertray, child's size, 4 pcs.
.... **$350**

HADDON (W. H. Grindley &
Co., ca. 1891)

Pitcher **$350**

HONG KONG (Charles
Meigh, ca. 1845)

**Sauce tureen, cover, ladle &
undertray,** 4 pcs. **$950**

Soup tureen, cover & ladle, the
set **$975**

LA BELLE (Wheeling
Pottery Co., American, ca.
1893-1900)

Bowl, serving, fancy rounded shell-
shape w/fluted & scroll-molded
sides trimmed in gold **$195**

Celery dish, long narrow oval shape w/scroll-molded ends, trimmed in gold
.... **$195**

LINTON (Thomas Godwin, ca. 1848)

Teapot, cov., footed squatty round shape w/scroll-molded spout & C-scroll
handle **$350**

One can never overemphasize the importance of condition in collecting.
Serious collectors learn to accept nothing but the best condition. Items
in top condition always hold their value better and are easier to sell than
pieces with damage. Consideration may be given to pieces with damage
if they are scarce or rare.

FLOW BLUE

MANILLA (Podmore, Walker & Co., ca. 1834- 1859)

Gravy boat $225

Relish dish, mitten-shaped $250

MELBOURNE (W.H. Grindley & Co., ca. 1891)

Saucer tureen, cover, ladle & undertray, 4 pcs. $450

ORIENTAL (Unknown maker, ca. 1860)

Mug, cylindrical w/angled handle, gold & polychrome trim $325

OXFORD (Johnson Bros., ca. 1900)

Gravy boat & undertray, 2 pcs. $145

> When is it acceptable to ignore the rule about avoiding antiques in damaged condition? If you really love a piece and can overlook the flaws, go ahead and buy it. But don't overpay. Be sure the price reflects the damage, and don't expect to sell it at a profit later.

OREGON (T. J. and J. Mayer, ca. 1845)

Relish dish, oblong fluted shape $195

Vegetable dish, cov., footed oblong shape w/ruffled rim & loop end handles, rose bud finial $650

PINWHEEL (Unknown maker, ca. 1840)

Cup & saucer, handleless cup, gaudy decoration, the set . **$125**

SHANGHAI (W.H. Grindley & Co., ca. 1898)

Sauce tureen, cover, ladle & underplate, 4 pcs. **$450**

Soup tureen, cover & undertray, 3 pcs. **$1,525**

SCINDE (J. & G. Alcock, ca. 1840)

Pitcher, footed, octagonal, angled handle **$295**

Potato bowl, round **$395**

Sugar bowl, cov., Full Panel Gothic style **$450**

Platter, 18" l. **$450**

SHAPOO (Thomas Hughes, ca. 1860)

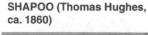

Sugar bowl, cov., footed octagonal shape **$350**

FRANKOMA

Frankoma

John Frank started his pottery company in 1933 in Norman, Oklahoma. However, when he moved the business to Sapulpa, Oklahoma, in 1938 he felt he was home. Still, Mr. Frank could not know the horrendous trials that would follow him.

Just after his move, on November 11, 1938, a fire destroyed the entire operation, which included the pot and leopard mark he had created in 1935. Then, in 1942, the war effort needed men and materials, so Frankoma could not survive. However, in 1943, John and Grace Lee Frank bought the plant as junk salvage and began again. The time in Norman had produced some of the finest art ware that John would ever create and most of the items were marked either "Frank Potteries," "Frank Pottery," or to a lesser degree, the "pot and leopard" mark. Today these marks are avidly and enthusiastically sought by collectors.

Another elusive mark wanted by collectors shows "Firsts Kiln Sapulpa 6-7-38." The mark was used for one day only and denotes the first firing in Sapulpa. It has been estimated that perhaps 50 to 75 pieces were fired on that day.

The clay Frankoma used is helpful to collectors in determining when an item was made. Creamy beige clay know as "Ada" clay was in use until 1953. Then a red brick shale was found in Sapulpa and used until about 1985 when, by the addition of an additive, the clay became a reddish pink. Rutile glazes were used early in Frankoma's history. Glazes with rutile have caused more confusion among collectors than any other glazes. For example, a Prairie Green piece shows a lot of green and it also has some brown. The same is true for the Desert Gold glaze; the piece shows a

sandy-beige glaze with some amount of brown. Generally speaking, Prairie Green, Desert Gold, White Sand and Woodland Moss will be the most puzzling to collectors. In 1970 the government closed the rutile mines in America and Frankoma had to buy rutile from Australia. It was not the same, so the results were different. Values are higher for the glazes with rutile. Also, the pre-Australian Woodland Moss glaze is more desirable than that created after 1970.

After John Frank died in 1973, his daughter Joniece Frank, a ceramic designer at the pottery, became president of the company. In 1983 another fire destroyed everything Frankoma had worked so hard to create. They rebuilt, but in 1990, after the IRS shut the doors for nonpayment, Joniece, true to the Frank legacy, filed for Chapter 11 (instead of bankruptcy) so she could reopen and continue the work she loved. In 1991 Richard Bernstein purchased the pottery and the name was changed to Frankoma Industries.

The company was sold again in 2006. The new owners are concentrating mostly on dinnerware, none of which is like the old Frankoma. The have a "Collectors Series," "Souvenir & State Items," and "Heartwarming Trivets." None of these is anything like what Frankoma originally created. The company is doing some Frankoma miniatures such as a dolphin on a wave, a fish, a wolf, a bear, etc. These, too, do not resemble Frankoma miniatures, and all their glazes are new.

Flower holder, model of a miniature hobby horse, Ada clay, 1942, Prairie Green, marked "Frankoma," rare, 3 1/2" h. **$340**

Do not display fragile items too close together, as one falling piece could knock over and damage others.

Figure of Indian Chief, No. 142, Desert Gold glaze, Ada clay, 7" h. **$190**

Model of a Pekinese dog, standing on hind legs, designed by Joseph Taylor, 1934- 38, glossy black glaze, marked "Frankoma," 7 1/2" h. **$590**

Salt & pepper shakers, figural, in the form of a bull head, Ada clay, matte yellow glaze, 1 3/4" h., pr. **$165**

When storing antiques or collectibles in boxes, place them on planks to keep them off the floor to allow air flow and prevent soaking in case the floor becomes wet. Do not place near exterior walls or windows, where they are more suseptible to changes in temperature and humidity. Also, keep stacks low and with the lightest boxes on top to keep them from falling over or crushing lower boxes. If possible, place boxes on shelves so they can be individually removed and replaced.

Stein, footed, advertising-type, for John Frank Memorial Charity Gold Tournament, Blue, 150 created, 1973 .... **$30**

Flower holder, figural, model of a miniature duck, Ada clay, 1942, Prairie Green, marked "Frankoma," rare, 3 1/2" h......................... **$325**

Model of fish, miniature, Turquoise, Ada clay, marked "Frankoma," 2 1/2"................................. **$380**

Mug, 1970, (Republican) elephant **$70**

Mug, 1973, (Republican) elephant **$42**

Pin, in the form of an Indian pot, Prairie Green, 1" h................ **$40**

Pin, model of a bowling pin, red circle w/applied white bowling pin & applied black bowling ball, 1 1/4" d................................ **$45**

Pitcher, Mayan-Aztec patt., Model No. 7d, Desert Gold, 2 qt...... **$55**

Pitcher, Wagon Wheel patt., Model No. 94d, Prairie Green glaze, Ada clay, 2 qt. **$85**

Plate, 7" d., Wildlife Series, Limited Edition No. 1, Bobwhite quail, Prairie Green glaze, 1,000 produced **$170**

Political mug, Nixon-Ford, 1974, Coffee glaze, fewer than 500 made, very rare **$285**

Postcard, color photograph of Joniece Frank sitting w/various Frankoma products used to show the current Frankoma glazes, 5 1/2 x 6 1/2" **$20**

Salt & pepper shakers, model of a Dutch shoe, Desert Gold glaze, Model No. 915h, ca. 1957-60, 4" l., pr. **$75**

Teapot, cov., Wagon Wheel patt., Model No. 94j, Desert Gold glaze, Ada clay, 2 cup **$69**

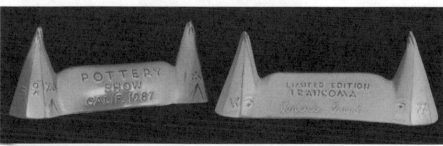

Sign, advertising "Pottery Show Calif. 1987" Prairie Green, 9" l. **$115**

Theft is a serious problem in antique stores and malls. To reduce theft, some stores do not allow shoppers to carry purses or bags, but provide lockers for customers. While some shoppers consider this insulting, there are benefits. Shoppers can shop with their hands free, and prices can be kept lower because of fewer losses.

Fulper Pottery

The Fulper Pottery was founded in Flemington, New Jersey, in 1805 and operated until 1935, although operations were curtailed in 1929 when its main plant was destroyed by fire. The name was changed in 1929 to Stangl Pottery, which continued in operation until July of 1978, when Pfaltzgraff, a division of Susquehanna Broadcasting Company of York, Pennsylvania, purchased the assets of the Stangl Pottery, including the name.

```
FULPER
```

Lemonade set: a tall tapering cylindrical tankard pitcher & four tapering cylindrical 3 1/2" h. mugs; all covered in a multi- toned glossy grey & blue drip glaze, all marked, pitcher 10" h., the set **$330**

Center bowl, Effigy-type, a wide flat-bottomed shallow bowl w/ incurved sides raised on three crouching figures resting on a molded thick disc base, multi-toned brown & blue crystalline glaze, stamped mark, 10 1/2" d., 7" h. **$360**

Vase, 9" h., small round foot supporting a very wide ovoid body w/a wide shoulder centered by a short tapering neck flanked by low loop handles, Chinese Blue Flambé glaze, raised vertical mark **$805**

Vase, 8 1/4" h., ovoid body w/a wide rounded shoulder centered by a small closed mouth, covered in a blue, brown & tan glossy streaky glaze w/green crystalline highlights, marked "Prang" **$480**

Vases often have been drilled through their bottom to create lamps. While this perhaps makes them more useful, it permanently lowers the value of the piece. The hole can be filled by an expert restorer, but it will never have the value of an undrilled piece.

Vase, 9" h., tall ovoid body w/a wide cylindrical neck w/a closed rim flanked by angled loop handles, Ashes of Roses glaze, vertical racetrack mark, very minor grinding chips at base, Shape 659 .... **$345**

Vase, 11 3/4" h., large ovoid body w/a cylindrical neck w/widely flaring mouth, matte rose glaze dripped over brown matte, raised vertical mark, drilled through center of bottom **$230**

Vase, 12 1/8" h., footed bulbous ovoid body w/a short neck w/rolled rim, low loop shoulder handles, heavy drippy green glaze over a famile rose glaze, impressed vertical mark, some burned green glaze on rim **$575**

Vase, 12" h., ringed baluster-form body w/small serpentine shoulder handles, shaded & streaky tan to dark blue & brown crystalline glaze, paper label, marked **$570**

Geisha Girl Wares

Geisha Girl Porcelain features scenes of Japanese women in colorful kimonos along with the flora and architecture of turn-of-the-century Japan. Although bearing an Oriental motif, the wares were produced for Western use in dinnerware and household accessory forms favored during the late 1800s through the early 1940s. There was minimal production during the Occupied Japan period. Less ornate wares were distributed through gift shops and catalogs during the 1960s- 70s; some of these are believed to have been manufactured in Hong Kong. Beware overly ornate items with fake Nippon marks that are in current production today, imported from China. More than a hundred porcelain manufacturers and decorating houses were involved with production of these wares during their heyday.

Prices cited here are for excellent to mint condition items. Enamel wear, flaking, hairlines or missing parts all serve to lower the value of an item. Prices in your area may vary.

More than 275 Geisha Girl Porcelain patterns and pattern variations have been catalogued; others are still coming to light.

The most common patterns include:

Bamboo Tree

Battledore

Child Reaching for Butterfly

Fan series

Garden Bench series

Geisha in Sampan series

Meeting series

Parasol series

Pointing series

The rarest patterns include:

... And They're Off

Bellflower

Bicycle Race

Capricious

Elegance in Motion

Fishing series

Foreign Garden

In Flight

Steamboat

The most popular patterns include:

Boat Festival

Butterfly Dancers

By Land and By Sea

Cloud series

Courtesan Processional

Dragonboat

Small Sounds of Summer

So Big

Temple A

A complete listing of patterns and their descriptions can be found in *The Collector's Encyclopedia of Geisha Girl Porcelain*. Additional patterns discovered since publication of the book are documented in "The Geisha Girl Porcelain Newsletter."

References: Litts, E., *Collector's Encyclopedia of Geisha Girl Porcelain*, Collector Books, 1988; "Geisha Girl Porcelain Newsletter," P.O. Box 3394, Morris Plains, NJ 07950.

Bowl, 7 1/2" d., 2" h., Torii patt., round w/gently scalloped rim, three border vignettes & central temple by lake scene, unusual combination of stenciled central design w/blue lustre frame & h.p. sides, gilded leaves on border stenciled, red & black highlights, marked in gold w/word "Sphinx" **$42**

Dish, Temple A patt., shallow oblong shape w/looped & forked brown twig handle on rim, multicolored center scene, brown border band, signed "Kutani," 4 3/4 x 5 7/8", 2 1/2" h. **$24**

Perfume bottle & stopper, Temple A patt., bulbous body tapering to a short flared neck, large ball stopper, multi-colored design w/ black trim, marked "Royal Kaga - Nippon," 4 1/2" h. **$125**

Chocolate pot, cov., Writing A patt., tall tapering lobed body w/rim spout & domed cover w/loop finial, unusual long double- loop handle, red background, decorated w/two reserves, one scenic, the other Meeting F patt., colorful stylized butterfly & flowers border, heavy gilt trim, 9 1/2" h. **$95**

Cracker jar, cov., Small Sounds of Summer patt., barrel-shaped body on three tiny feet, short, wide neck & low domed cover w/pointed disk finial, red w/ornate gold & colored background, 8" h. **$85**

Demitasse pot, cov., Ikebana in Rickshaw patt., ovoid lightly ribbed body w/serpentine pink w/gold spout & C-scroll handle, ribbed domed cover w/knob finial, rare border color combination of teal blue w/gold, 6" h. **$95**

Plate, 9 3/4" d., a green sponged background decorated in color w/five squared panels, each w/a different pattern, deep center, marked w/Japanese characters & "Nippon" **$75**

Salt dish, round w/pedestal base, Temple B patt., multi-colored decoration w/heavy gilt trim, marked "Royal Kaga Nippon," 3" d., 1 1/2" h........................ **$45**

Serving tray, Geisha in Sampan J patt., round w/scalloped edges & small open handles, three border bands in cobalt blue, red & multi-colored flowers, Double "T" in Oval mark, 10 1/4" d. **$65**

Shaving mug, Lesson/Parasol A patt., molded base w/cylindrical sides & gently flared rim, ring handle, cobalt blue & gold borders, red trim, 3 1/2" h. **$45**

Teapot, cov., individual size, Garden Bench C patt., spherical lobed body w/domed lobed cover, cobalt blue borders & trim & red spout, Japan mark, 4 1/2" h. **$25**

Syrup jug, cov., Rivers Edge patt., cylindrical w/large rim spout & long angled handle, slightly domed cover w/loop handle, red & pine green trim & black accents, marked "TN - Nippon," 4 1/2" h. **$45**

GONDER

Gonder

Lawton Gonder founded Gonder Ceramic Arts in Zanesville, Ohio, in 1941 and it continued in operation until 1957.

The firm produced a higher priced and better quality of commercial art potteries than many firms of the time and employed Jamie Matchet and Chester Kirk, both of whom were outstanding ceramic designers. Several special glazes were developed during the company's history and Gonder even duplicated some museum pieces of Chinese ceramic. In 1955 the firm converted to the production of tile due to increased foreign competition. By 1957 its years of finest production were over.

Increase price ranges as indicated for the following glaze colors: red flambé - 50 percent, antique gold crackle - 70 percent, turquoise Chinese crackle - 40 percent, white Chinese crackle - 30 percent.

Ashtray set: ashtray, cigarette holder; Mold No. 406, 3 7/8" sq. **$65-80**

Ashtray, square, w/inside concentric ridges, Mold No. 815, 10" sq. **$25-50**

Ashtray, "S" swirl design, Mold No. a 408, 2 1/2 x 10" **$25-35**

Base for bottle vase, Mold #527-B **$25-50**

Book ends, model of Trojan horse head, mottled green glaze, Mold No. 220, 7 1/2" h., pr. **$125-150**

Bowl, 8 1/2" w., 5 1/8" h., hexagonal, w/Chinese figures, Mold No. 742 .... **$15-25**

Bowl, low, scalloped tulip shape, Mold No. 523 .... **$40-60**

Candleholder, Mold No. 517, Double Cornucopia, 3 3/4" w. x 6 7/8" l., 4" h. **$35-45**

Candleholder, single shell, Mold No. 506, 2 3/4" w., 4 5/8" h. **$10-20**

Candleholders, starfish, Mold No. 501, 7 7/8" w., each **$60-80**

Casserole, cov., tab handled lid, La Gonda, Mold No. 955, 6 3/4 x 11", 5 3/8" h. **$75-100**

Cigarette cup, Sovereign, Mold No. 804, 2 5/8" h. **$40-60**

Console bowl, w/dolphins, Mold No. 556, 11 1/4" d., 4 5/8" h. **$55-70**

Console bowl, seashell shape, Mold No. 521, 7 x 12" **$30-45**

Cookie jar, cov., Mold No. P-24, 8 1/2" h. **$15-30**

Cornucopia-vase, w/round handles, Mold No. 380, 7" h. **$15-30**

Cornucopia-vase, ribbed, curled handles, Mold No. 419, 8" h. **$30-45**

Cornucopia-vase, w/leaf design, Mold No. J-61, 9" h. **$40-55**

Cornucopia-vase, double loop handle, Mold J-69, 11" h. **$30-45**

Ewer, "Z" handle, Mold No. E-65, 6 1/4" h. **$10-20**

Ewer, Mold H-33, 9" h. **$40-55**

Ewer, shell-shaped, Mold No. 508, 14" h. (no starfish) **$75-100**

Figure of Chinese peasant, kneeling & reaching forward, Mold No. 546, 4 1/2 x 6 1/2" **$25-40**

Figure of Fatima, w/rosary, Mold No. 772, 9 1/2" h. **$75-100**

Figure of Oriental man, Mold No. 551, 7" h. **$40-60**

Figure of Oriental woman, w/hands together, Mold No. 570, 6 1/4" h. **$40-60**

Jar, cov., in the form of an Oriental plum, Mold No. 529, 9 3/16" h. **$125-150**

Lamp, Double Swirl, Mold No. 2020, 30" h. **$40-60**

Lamp, figural, elephant, Mold No. 207, 10 3/4" l., 9 1/4" h. **$125-150**

Lamp, Hollywood Headboard Unit Books, Mold No. 5087, 11 1/2" w., 6 3/8" h. **$125-150**

Lamp, Mold No. H-77, double handle w/vine leaves, metal base, 7 3/4" w., 8 1/2" h. **$50-75**

Lamp base, Figure Eight Swirl, no mark, Gunmetal Black glaze, 15 5/8" h. **$75-100**

Lamp base, Rectangular Flower Center, no mark, Wine Brown glaze, 4 1/8 x 6 1/8", 11" h. **$25-40**

Lamp base, Frappe, Catalog #2067, no mark, Rutile Green w/Green Overlay glaze, 15 3/4" h. ... **$75-90**

Gonder
E-1
GONDER
U.S.A.

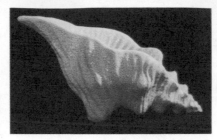

Planter, model of large conch shell, no mark, Chinese White Crackle glaze, Mold No. 793, very hard to find, 5 3/4 x 17 1/4", 8" h. **$200-250**

Lamp base, Rose Lady Head, no mark, Light Blue glaze, Mold #588, can be used as figurine, 12 1/4" h. **$150-175**

Lamp, model of Trojan horse head, Mold No. 540, 10" h. **$60-80**

Lamp, Oriental dual figures on side, 16" h. **$150- 200**

Lazy Susan, medium, Mold No. 8, 11 1/2" d. **$80-110**

Model of elephant, Mold No. 207, 11 1/2" l., 8 7/8" h. **$75-100**

Model of elephant, Mold No. 209, 8" l, 6 1/8" h. **$40-50**

Model of elephant, stylized standing animal w/greenish brown glaze & ivory trim, Mold 108 ... **$300-400**

Model of gamecock, w/flowers, Mold No. 525, hard to find, 7 1/8" w., 10 3/4" h. **$150-175**

Model of gamecock, w/plain tail feathers, Mold No. 525, hard to find, 7 1/8" w., 10 3/4" h. **$150-175**

Model of head of racing horse, Mold 874, 9 1/4" h. **$165-185**

Model of hen w/worms, Mold No. 525, very hard to find, 9" l., 6 3/4" h. **$150-175**

Model of panther, large, reclining, marked "Gonder Original 210" in script, Royal Purple glaze, 6 1/2 x 18 1/2" **$200-250**

Model of panther, recumbent, Mold No. 217, 12" l **$30-50**

Model of panther, standing, Mold No. 205, 12" h. **$40-60**

Model of racing horse head, Mold No. 576, 13 1/2" l., 5 3/4" h. ... **$150-175**

Model of rooster, Mold No. 212, scarce, 4" w., 10 1/2" h. **$150-175**

Models of geese, one looking down & one w/neck stretched upward,

Mold Nos. B- 14 & B-15, 3 1/2 & 5 1/2" h., pr. **$25-40**

Pedestal base, Mold No. 533-B, 6" d. **$25-50**

Pitcher, pistol grip, Mold No. 102, 9 1/8" h. **$125- 150**

Pitcher, twisted twig handle, Mold No. 301, 7 1/2" l., 7 7/8" h. **$100-125**

Pitcher, 7" h., ruffled lip, Mold No. 1206 .... **$25-50**

Pitcher, 5 x 8", ridged woodtone glaze, Mold No. 901 .... **$50-75**

Pitcher, 9" h., plain lip, Mold 1205 .... **$50-75**

Pitcher, 9 1/4" h., Classical style, "606 Gonder USA" mark in script, Coral Lustre glaze, Mold No. 606 .... **$75-100**

Planter bottom, Mold No. 724, for African Violet planter No. 738, 4 x 5" **$5-10**

Planter top, No. 1000, for African Violet planter No. 738, 4 x 4", 5 1/4" h. **$25-40**

Planter, African Violet two-piece w/ flared top, Mold No. 792, 5 1/4" sq., 5 1/8" h. **$20-40**

Planter, bulbous body w/tab handles, decorated w/relief-molded flowers, Mold No. H-83, 5 1/2" h. **$50-60**

Planter, double-footed, Mold No. 711, 5 x 8 5/8", 2 7/8" h. **$15-25**

Planter, "End of Day," flared square shape, four feet, Mold No. 749/20, 6 1/4" sq., 6" h. **$40-50**

Planter, figure of Bali woman w/ gourds, no bikini top, Mold No. 763, RARE, 9 1/8" w., 12 3/8" h. **$250-350**

Planter, figure of Gay 90s man w/basket, no mold number, 13 1/4" h. **$150-175**

Planter, figure of Madonna, Mold E-303 & R 003, 4 x 6" **$10-20**

Planter, figure of nude w/deer, Mold No. 593, hard to find, 9 1/2 x 14" **$250-300**

Planter, figures of Basque dancers, Mold No. 766, 12" h. **$125-150**

Planter, footed, square w/hole in base, Mold No. 706, 5" h. **$10-20**

Planter, four-footed flared square pedestal, Mold No. 753, 7 x 7 1/4", 7 1/4" h. **$25-40**

Planter, gondola or lamp, no mold number, 5 3/4" h., 14" l. **$60-80**

Planter, large rectangle w/ round corners, Mold No. 752, 4 1/2 x 9 1/4", 3 1/8" h. **$10-20**

Planter, model of Chinese sampan (junk), Mold No. 550, 10" l. **$10-20**

Planter, model of large Chinese sampan (junk), Mold No. 520, 15" l. **$25-40**

Planter, model of swan, Mold No. E-44, 5 1/2" h. **$5-15**

Planter, model of wishing well, hard to find, 6 1/2 x 9 1/4" **$100-125**

Planter, Mold No. 510, single hooked square, 3 1/4" w. x 5 3/4" l., 2 3/4" h. **$15-25**

Planter, reclining panther, Mold No. 237, 5 1/2" h., 14 7/8" l. **$125-150**

Planter, rectangular, Mold No. 701, 5 3/4 x 7 1/2" **$15-30**

Planter, shell cornucopia, Mold No. 692, 5 1/4 x 9", 4 3/4" h. **$50-75**

Planter, square flared form, Mold No. 733, 2 1/2 x 6 1/2" **$15-30**

Planter, square w/ridge & leaves, Mold No. 1002, 5 1/4 x 5 1/2", 5 3/16" h. **$15-25**

Planter, w/hole, Mold No. 738, 2 3/4 x 4 1/4" (top to Mold No. 724) **$5-25**

Planters, figures of Bali man & Bali woman w/buckets, 14" h., pr. **$60-80**

Planters, for doe or rooster figurine, Mold No. 218, 3 3/4 x 3, 2 3/4" h., pr. **$25-50**

Plaque, African mask, Mold No. 232, 5 x 7 3/4" **$75-100**

Plaque, African mask, no number **$75-100**

Relish dish, shallow, divided, six lobe-form sections, mottled yellow glaze, Mold No. 871, 11 x 18" **$90-120**

Saucer, La Gonda, Mold No. 904, 5 3/8" d. **$8-10**

GONDER

Server, La Gonda, Mold No. 916, 5 7/8 x 9 5/8" **$20-30**

Sugar bowl, Mold No. P-33, 4 5/8" h. **$15-25**

Tea cup, La Gonda, Mold No. 903, 2 1/2 x 3 1/4" **$8-10**

TV lamp, model of masted ship, 14" h. **$40-60**

Vase, 5 x 5" sq., flared, leaf decoration, Mold No. 384 .... **$25-35**

Vase, 6" h., bulbous base w/flared top, leaf decoration, Mold E-66 .... **$10-20**

Vase, 6" h., footed, squatty bulbous base, cylindrical neck w/flared rim, applied leaf decoration, Mold E-68 .... **$15-30**

Vase, 6 1/8" h., small V horn, Mold No. E-5 .... **$30-50**

Vase, 6 1/2" h., bulbous base w/ scalloped trumpet-form neck, Mold E-49 .... **$10-25**

Vase, 6 1/2" h., Mold No. 216, double horn, 11 1/2" w................ **$50-75**

Vase, 6 1/2" h., seashell shape, Mold No. 216 .... **$70-90**

Vase, 6 5/8" h., shell & seaweed, Mold No. 402, H-401...... **$75-100**

Vase, 7" h., bottle form, Mold No. 1203 .... **$30-50**

Vase, 6 1/2 x 7 1/4", scroll footed, Mold No. E-4, 304............. **$30-40**

Vase, 7 1/2" h., basketweave w/ knothole design, Mold No. 867 .... **$30-50**

Vase, 7 x 7 1/2", two-handled, bulbous base w/wide flaring neck, Mold H-42.................... **$25-35**

Vase, 7 1/4 x 8", cuspidor top, Mold No. 559, scarce **$200-250**

Vase, 8" h., flat, Lotus design, Mold No. 402 .... **$25-40**

Vase, 8" h., rectangular footed maze, Mold No. 401 .... **$35-50**

Vase, 8 1/16" h., berries & leaves, Mold No. H-55 .... **$65-85**

Vase, 5 x 8 1/2, rectangular, Mold No. H-74 .... **$15-25**

Vase, 8 1/2" h., 6 3/4" d., Leaf with Berries, Mold #H-86 or H-486, marked "H-86 Gonder U.S.A.," Mother-of-Pearl glaze **$20-35**

Vase, 8 1/2" h., footed bulbous body w/flaring rim, triple loop handles, Mold No. H- 75 .... **$15-25**

Vase, 8 1/2" h., relief-molded double leaf form w/berries, Mold J-70 .... **$35-50**

Vase, 8 1/2" h., triple leaf form, Mold No. H- 67 .... **$15-25**

Vase, 4 1/4 x 8 3/4", fluted handle, Mold H- 34....................... **$15-30**

Vase, 6 x 9", flame shape, Mold No. H-69 .... **$25-40**

Vase, 9" h., 10 1/4" w., Scarla Sunfish, marked "Gonder 522," Sea Swirl glaze **$100-125**

Vase, 9" h., footed, two-handled, bulbous base, squared top, Mold No. H-7 .... **$20-30**

Vase, 9" h., shell form, three dolphins at base, Mold No. H-85 .... **$45-60**

Vase, 9" h., two-handled fan vase, Mold No. H-10.................. **$15-30**

Vase, 9 1/4" h., large square, footed, Mold No. 704 .... **$25-40**

Vase, 9 1/2" h., two-handled, twisted baluster-form body, Mold No. H-62 .... **$15-30**

Vase, 9 3/4" h., Art Deco cactus, Mold No. 686 .... **$60-80**

Vase, 10" h., feather form, Mold No. 539 .... **$30-50**

Vase, 10" h., square form w/ impressed flower design, Mold No. 688........................... **$50-75**

Vase, 7 x 10", model of a butterfly, Mold No. 523 .... **$100-150**

Vase, 6 x 10", model of swan, Mold No. 802........................... **$25-50**

Vase, 10 1/4" h., swirled "S" handle, w/four lips, Mold No. 872 .... **$50-75**

Vase, 4 1/2 x 10 1/2, square form w/round top, Mold No. 534 .... **$50-75**

Vase, 10 7/8" h., off-center double handle, Mold No. J-35 ..... **$60-75**

Vase, 11" h., Mold No. 869, J-69, ewer type, double curved handle **$50-65**

Vase, 11 1/8" h., Mold No. 513, 813, footed double leaf, 5 5/16" w. x 9 1/2" l. **$40-60**

Vase, 11 1/2" h., orchid design, Mold No. 513 .... **$30-50**

Vase, 11 3/4" h., peacock fan, Mold No. K- 15 .... **$60-75**

Vase, 12" h., raised flowers & leaves, Mold No. M-8, hard to find **$75-100**

Vase, 6 x 12", Chinese Imperial dragon handle, w/base, Mold No. 535, 2 pcs.................. **$200-250**

Vase, 6 3/4 x 12 1/2", model of cactus, Mold No. K-26 or 826 .... **$50-75**

Vase, 6 1/2 H., double, bottle, leaf applied, Mold No. 368 or E 368 .... **$20-25**

Vase, 18 3/8" h., large bottle form, Mold No. 531, very hard to find **$175-200**

Teapot, cov., upright rectangular form, La Gonda patt., creamy yellow glaze, Mold 914 .. **$50-75**

Vase, 13 3/8" h., Seashell Ewer with Starfish, marked "508 Gonder U.S.A." in script, Chinese Turquoise Crackle glaze **$95-120**

Vase, 6 1/2 x 13" h., double, tall slender cylindrical forms joined at triangular-form base, slanted rim, mottled green glaze, Mold No. 868 .... **$150-200**

Depending on the venue, prices on antiques are seldom firm. Most dealers will not be offended if you ask, "Can you give me a better price on this?" The key is being tactful. Don't expect a dealer to be receptive to an offer of one-quarter of the marked price.

Grueby

Some fine art pottery was produced by the Grueby Faience and Tile Company, established in Boston in 1891. Choice pieces were created with molded designs on a semi-porcelain body. The ware is marked and often bears the initials of the decorators. The pottery closed in 1907.

Bowl, 3" d., 4 1/4" h., a small footring supporting the deep vertical & slightly uneven sides, wide flat rim, dappled green matte glaze, impressed mark, two pinhead-sized glaze pops **$805**

Candlestick, a wide flat dished base w/low vertical sides, centered by a tapering ringed shaft w/an ovoid socket w/a flattened flared rim, mottled yellow & brown matte glaze, circular tulip-style insignia, No. 227, glazed-over chip at top rim, 5 3/8" h. **$460**

Tile, square, a large white rabbit crouched behind a small stylized leafy shrub in white, both outlined in dark blue against a pale blue ground, impressed tulip-style mark, burst glaze bubbles, some small edge nicks, 3 7/8" w. **$690**

Tile, square, decorated in cuenca w/a large oak tree against a blue sky w/puffy white clouds, numbered 28 on the back, 6" sq. **$12,650**

Tile frieze, a landscape frieze composed of 25 six inch tiles, restoration to three corners, stamped mark, ca. 1910, 17 x 54" **$102,000**

Vase, 6 1/4" h., squatty bulbous form w/a wide flat mouth, molded around the shoulder w/seven flower buds alternating w/seven wide leaves down the sides, mottled matte yellow glaze, unmarked, restoration to center of base, ca. 1908 .... **$5,288**

Vase, 6 1/4" h., 6 3/4" d., wide squatly bulbous shape tapering to a short rolled neck, crisply decorated w/a band of long, wide pointed leaves around the sides alternating w/yellow buds below the neck, fine leathery matte green glaze, circular pottery mark & "MS" **$13,800**

Vase, 5 1/2" d., wide squatty bulbous body molded w/a repeating design of wide rounded overlapping leaves, a wide shoulder to the wide, short rolled neck, dark green matte glaze, signed "W.P.," restored rim chips **$960**

GRUEBY

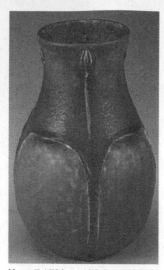

Vase, 5 1/2" h., 3 3/4" d., ovoid body swelling to a six-lobed rim, full-length tooled & applied leaves alternating w/narrow green buds against an overall fine oatmealed blue glaze, circular pottery mark **$17,250**

Vase, 7 1/2" h., 4 1/2" d., ovoid body tapering to a wide gently flaring neck, tooled & applied w/rounded leaves around the lower half w/ four buds up the sides, medium matte green glaze, small nick to one leaf edge, mark obscured by glaze **$2,875**

Vase, 9" h., tall slender gently tapering cylindrical body molded w/full-length pointed leaves alternating w/flower buds around the slightly flaring & scalloped rim, thick suspended green matte glaze, by Annie Lingley, impressed mark, minor grinding to foot chip, minor chip repair at rim **$2,880**

Vase, 5 1/2" h., 4 1/2" d., bulbous ovoid body w/a wide rolled rim, crisply tooled w/broad leaves up the sides, covered in a leathery dark green glaze, some highpoint nicks, circular mark **$2,875**

Vase, 12" h., 7 3/4" d., footed large ovoid body w/a wide flat mouth, crisply tooled & applied w/clusters of yellow daffodils & green leaves, overall fine pulled leathery matte green glaze, restoration to drilled holes in base, small kiln kiss near base, signed by Wilhelmina Post and dated 5/27/06 .... **$26,450**

Vase, 12 1/2" h., 8 1/4" d., rare large form w/bulbous body centered by a flaring cylindrical neck, tooled & applied w/large wide pointed overlapping leaves, fine organic matte green glaze, couple of very minor edge nicks, by Marie Seaman, stamped round mark **$11,500**

> A ceramic pieced signed by a well-known artist can greatly increase its value over an unsigned piece, but be sure it is guaranteed to be authentic before purchasing.

Hall China

Founded in 1903 in East Liverpool, Ohio, this still-operating company at first produced mostly utilitarian wares. It was in 1911 that Robert T. Hall, son of the company founder, developed a special single-fire, lead-free glaze that proved to be strong, hard and nonporous. In the 1920s the firm became well known for its extensive line of teapots (still a major product), and in 1932 it introduced kitchenwares, followed by dinnerwares in 1936 and refrigerator wares in 1938.

The imaginative designs and wide range of glaze colors and decal decorations have led to the growing appeal of Hall wares with collectors, especially people who like Art Deco and Art Moderne design. One of the firm's most famous patterns was the "Autumn Leaf" line, produced as premiums for the Jewel Tea Company. For listings of this ware see "Jewel Tea Autumn Leaf."

Helpful books on Hall include *The Collector's Guide to Hall China* by Margaret & Kenn Whitmyer, and *Superior Quality Hall China - A Guide for Collectors* by Harvey Duke (An ELO Book, 1977).

Baker, French Fluted shape, Silhouette patt...................... **$30**

Bean pot, cov., New England #4 shape, Fantasy patt............ **$200**

Bean pot, cov., New England shape, No. 488 patt. **$275**

Bean pot, cov., tab-handled, Sani-Grid (Pert) shape, Rose Parade patt. **$115**

Bowl, 6" d., Medallion shape, Silhouette patt...................... **$23**

Bowls, Radiance shape, Red Poppy patt., set of 3 .... **$75**

Casserole, cov., Five Band shape, Flamingo patt..................... **$75**

Coffeepot, cov., Drip-O-Lator, Waverly shape...................... **$35**

Coffeepot, cov., Medallion shape, Crocus patt...................... **$95**

Coffeepot, cov., Tomorrow's Classic patt., white **$150**

Coffeepot, cov., Tricolator, Coffee Queen, Chinese Red............ **$55**

Cookie jar, cov., Owl, brown glaze **$120**

Cookie jar, cov., Saf-Handle (Sundial) shape, Chinese Red **$200**

Custard cup, straight-sided, Rose White patt. **$25**

Mug, beverage, Silhouette patt. **$60**

Mug, flagon shape, Monk patt.. **$45**

Pitcher, ball shape, Royal Rose patt. **$95**

Pitcher, cov., jug-type, Radiance shape, No. 4, No. 488 patt. **$195**

Salt & pepper shakers, Medallion line, lettuce green, pr............ **$65**

Teapot, cov., Baltimore shape, Ivory Gold Label line **$100**

Teapot, cov., Basket shape, Warm Yellow **$150**

Teapot, cov., Basketball shape, Cobalt Blue......................... **$600**

Teapot, cov., Boston shape, Cobalt Blue w/gold Trailing Aster design, 6-cup **$150**

Teapot, cov., Casual Living Zeisel design.............................. **$120**

Batter bowl, Five Band shape, Chinese Red **$95**

Casserole, cov., Art Deco w/chrome reticulated handled base **$55**

Leftover, cov., Zephyr shape, Fantasy patt. **$225**

Cookie jar, cov., Five Band shape, Meadow Flower patt. **$325**

Coffeepot, cov., Tricolator, Ansel shape, yellow art glaze **$75**

Pitcher, jug-type, large, Doughnut shape, Chinese Red **$125**

Teapot, cov., Adele shape, Art Deco style, Olive Green **$200**

Teapot, cov., Automobile shape, Chinese Red **$650**

Teapot, cov., Birdcage shape, Jewel Tea Autumn Leaf patt., specially produced for the Autumn Leaf Club in 1995 .... **$150**

Teapot, cov., Centennial shape, Forest Green w/gold decoration **$125**

Teapot, cov., Donut shape, Orange Poppy patt. **$450**

Teapot, cov., Football shape, commemorative, "Hall 2000 Haul, East Liverpool, Ohio" Ivory **$125**

Teapot, cov., E-Shape Dinnerware, Cameo Rose patt. **$75**

Teapot, cov., Los Angeles shape, Cobalt Blue w/Standard Gold trim **$75**

Teapot, cov., Globe No-Drip patt., dark pink w/standard gold decoration **$90**

Hampshire Pottery

Hampshire Pottery was made in Keene, New Hampshire, where several potteries operated as far back as the late 18th century. The pottery now known as Hampshire Pottery was established by J.S. Taft shortly after 1870. Various types of wares, including Art Pottery, were produced through the years. Taft's brother-in-law, Cadmon Robertson, joined the firm in 1904 and was responsible for developing more than 900 glaze formulas while in charge of all manufacturing. His death in 1914 created problems for the firm, and Taft sold out to George Morton in 1916. Closed during part of World War I, the pottery was later reopened by Morton for a short time and manufactured white hotel china. From 1919 to 1921, mosaic floor tiles became the main production. All production ceased in 1923.

HAMPSHIRE POTTERY

Bowl, 2 1/4" h., wide flattened cushion-form body w/slightly raised flat mouth, molded around the top w/alternating knobs & swastikas under a mottled dark green glaze, short, tight rim line, impressed mark **$207**

Bowl, 2 3/4" h., bulbous form molded overall w/overlapping leaves w/a blue & green semi-matte glaze, marked, Shape No. 24 .... **$683**

Pitcher, 8" h., bulbous ovoid melon shaped w/large leaves forming the neck & pointed spout, vine handle, overall green matte glaze, unmarked **$288**

Vase, 4" h., 5" d., wide bulbous shape w/a wide short flat-rimmed neck, overall fine bluish green feathered glaze, marked ... **$558**

Vase, 4 1/4" h., wide ovoid body w/a wide round shoulder centered by a short molded neck, large lightly molded arched panels around the sides, crystalline matte green glaze, marked "Hampshire Pottery 640 - 110" & impressed M in a circle **$432**

When attending an antique market in the early morning, where dealers are set up both indoors and outdoors, consider covering the indoor areas first. The light is likely better, the temperature is more comfortable, and there is no dew to soak your shoes. Do outdoor dealers on paved or gravel areas next, saving those dealers set up on grassy areas for later.

Vase, 5 1/4" h., squatty bulbous body w/a wide shoulder centered by a wide gently flaring short cylindrical neck, mottled blue & green matte glaze, designed by Cadmon Robertson & marked w/his monogram, Shape No. 118 .... **$690**

Vase, 6 1/4" h., bulbous ovoid body w/a wide tapering neck, overall brownish grey matte glaze, marked **$441**

Vase, 7 1/4" h., very slightly swelling cylindrical body w/a low wide ringed neck, overall mottled & streaky dark blue & pink matte drip glaze, designed by Cadmon Robertson, company logo, Shape No. 106, some grinding chips around the base **$690**

Vase, 7 1/2" h., gently swelled cylindrical body w/an inward-rolled flat mouth, green crystalline matte glaze, marked **$460**

Vase, 7 1/2" h., very slightly swelling cylindrical body w/a lightly molded wave-like band just below the low wide ringed neck, overall two-tone "peacock" glaze, designed by Cadmon Robertson, company logo, Shape No. 105 .... **$690**

Repairing valuable ceramics should be left to professionals who can do the job expertly and minimize loss of value to the piece. Of course, the cost of the repair should be weighed against the value of the piece. But keep in mind that poorly done, do-it-yourself repairs can generally not be undone and will permanently lower a piece's value.

Vase, 8 3/4" h., 9 3/4" d., very wide squatty bulbous shaped w/a rounded shoulder centering a short wide neck w/flat rim, fine leathery green & blue matte glaze, incised mark **$2,703**

Vase, 14" h., very tall slender ovoid body tapering to a tall slender neck w/a widely flaring ruffled rim, overall nice green matte glaze, impressed mark **$1,320**

Haviland

Haviland porcelain was originated by Americans in Limoges, France, shortly before the mid- 19th century and continues in production. Some Haviland was made by Theodore Haviland in the United States during the last World War. Numerous other factories also made china in Limoges. Also see LIMOGES.

Dish, shell-shaped, incurved rim opposite pointed rim, h.p. scene of artist's waterside studio, decorated by Theodore Davis, front initialed "D," back w/presidential seal & artist's signature, part of Hayes presidential service, 8 x 9 1/2" **$2,250**

Mayonnaise bowl w/attached underplate, decorated w/pink wild roses touched w/yellow, Schleiger 141D, 5" d. **$145**

Dresser tray, h.p. floral decoration, 1892 mark **$125**

Egg cup, footed, No. 69 patt. on blank No. 1 .... **$65**

Egg cups, footed, No. 72 patt., Blank No. 22, pr. **$150**

Gravy boat w/attached underplate, Schleiger 46, Ranson blank, decorated w/pink & blue flowers **$125**

Gravy boat, No. 761 .... **$95**

Honey dish, 4" d., bowl-form, Schleiger 33, decorated w/white flowers, pink shading **$25**

Jam jar w/underplate, cov., Christmas Rose patt. **$795**

Match box, gold trim, 1882 & decorator's marks **$175**

Mayonnaise bowl w/underplate, leaf- shaped, Blank No. 271A **$225**

Muffin server, No. 31 patt., Blank No. 24 .... **$275**

Mustache cup & saucer, No. 270A patt., Blank No. 16 .... **$225**

Mustard pot w/attached underplate, cov., CFH/GDM, copper color w/gold floral design overall, cov. w/spoon slot, 2 1/2 x 4" **$225**

Olive dish, No. 257 patt. **$85**

Oyster plates, four-well, all white w/relief- molded scrolled design, 7 1/2" d., pr. **$195**

Oyster plate, six clam-shaped sections w/round center section for sauce, white, 8" d. **$225**

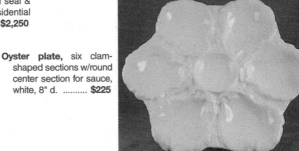

Oyster scoop, oyster-shaped, CFH/GDM, h.p., 1 3/4 x 2 1/5" **$65**

Pancake server, decorated w/yellow flowers w/pale green stems, smooth blank, 1892 & decorator marks **$195**

Pin box, cov., oblong, ornate scrolled base & rim, loop finial on h.p. floral decorated lid, marked "H & Co. L. France," 4" l **$175**

Pitcher, syrup-type, Schleiger 144, decorated w/pink roses & green scrolls **$145**

Pitcher, 8 5/8" h., Art Deco stylized figural "Farewell" cat in yellow & white, base inscribed "Theodore Haviland Limoges/France Copyright Depose" & "E.M. Sandoz sc" **$1,500**

Pitcher, 9" h., tankard-shaped lemonade- type, Ranson blank, delicate floral band around the upper body trimmed in gold, gold handle & trim bands, factory-decorated, Haviland & Co. mark **$250**

Hull

In 1905 Addis E. Hull purchased the Acme Pottery Company in Crooksville, Ohio. In 1917 the A.E. Hull Pottery Company began to make a line of art pottery for florists and gift shops. The company also made novelties, kitchenware and stoneware.

Hull's Little Red Riding Hood kitchenware was manufactured between 1943 and 1957 and is a favorite of collectors, as are the beautiful matte glaze vases it produced.

In 1950 the factory was destroyed by a flood and fire, but by 1952 it was back in production. Hull added its newer glossy glazed pottery plus pieces sold in flower shops under the names Regal and Floraline. Hull's brown dinnerware lines achieved great popularity and were the main lines being produced prior to the plant's closing in 1986.

References on Hull Pottery include: *Hull, The Heavenly Pottery*, 7th Edition, 2001 and *Hull, The Heavenly Pottery Shirt Pocket Price Guide*, 4th Edition, 1999, by Joan Hull. Also *The Dinnerwares Lines* by Barbara Loveless Click-Burke (Collector Books 1993) and *Robert's Ultimate Encyclopedia of Hull Pottery* by Brenda Roberts (Walsworth Publishing Co., 1992). -- Joan Hull, Advisor.

Baby feeding dish, divided, Little Red Riding Hood patt. ... **$1,400**

Basket, Tulip (Sueno) patt., No. 102-33-6", 6" h............................ **$350**
Basket, Orchid patt., No. 305, 7" h. **$600**
Basket, Bow -Knot patt., No. B-29, 12" h. **$2,000**
Basket, Open Rose (Camellia) patt., No.140-10 1/2", 10 1/2" h. **$1,300**
Basket, Water Lily patt., tan & brown, No. L- 14-10 1/2" **$350**
Batter pitcher, Little Red Riding Hood patt., 6 1/2" h............. **$500**
Candleholders, Open Rose (Camelia) patt., models of doves, No. 117-6 1/2", 6 1/2" h., pr. **$325**
Candleholders, Magnolia Matte patt., upright ovoid socket on an oval base w/small open legs from the bottom to the base, No. 27-4", 4" h., pr. **$100**
Candleholders, Water Lily patt., No. L-22- 4", 4" h., pr................. **$125**
Console bowl, Bow-Knot patt., pink & blue, No. B-16-13 1/2", 13 1/2" l. **$325**
Console bowl, Iris (Narcissus) patt., No. 409-12", 12" l............... **$250**
Console bowl, Orchid patt., No. 314-13", 13" l. **$375**

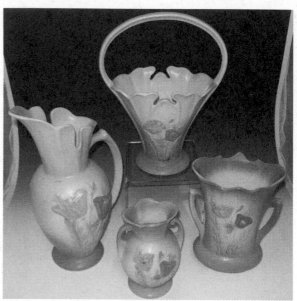

Basket, Poppy patt., No. 601, 12" h. (ILLUS. back) **$1,300**
Ewer, Poppy patt., No. 610, 13" h. (ILLUS. front row, left) **$850**
Vase, 6 1/2" h., Poppy patt., No. 612 (ILLUS. front) **$75-100**
Vase, 8 1/2" h., No. 605 (ILLUS. front row, right) **$100-125**

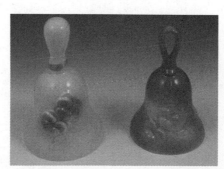

Bell, Sun-Glow patt., No. 87, closed or open handle, dark yellow or dark pink ground, 6 1/2" h., each (ILLUS. of two) **$100-200**

Lamp, Tulip (Suena), patt., No. 107-33-61/2", 6 1/2" h. **$400-600**

HULL

Cookie jar, cov., figural Ginger Bread Man, No. 123, grey Flint Ridge line, 1980s, 12" h. (ILLUS. right) **$150**
Cookie jar, cov., figural Ginger Bread Man, No. 223, sand Flint Ridge line, 1980s, 12" h. (ILLUS. left) **$500**

Vase, 8 1/2" h., Bow-Knot patt., No. B-8- 8 1/2" (ILLUS. front row, left) **$250-350**
Vase, 10 1/2" h., Bow-Knot patt., No. B-10 (ILLUS. back row) **$500-600**
Wall pocket, Bow-Knot patt., model of a whisk broom, No. B27-8", 8" h. (ILLUS. front row, center) **$250-300**

Console bowl, Wildflower patt., No. W-21 - 12", 12" l **$175**
Console bowl, 13 1/2" h., Bow-Knot patt., No. 15-13 1/2" **$1,300**
Ewer, Woodland patt., No. W6-6 1/2", 6 1/2" h. **$125**
Ewer, Magnolia patt., No. 14-4 3/4", 4 3/4" h. **$75**
Jardiniere, Open Rose (Camellia) patt., molded rams' head handles, No. 114, 8 1/2" d. **$175**
Jardiniere, Bow-Knot patt., blue or pink trim, No. B-18-5 3/4", 5 3/4" h. **$350**
Jardiniere, Orchid patt., No. 310, 9 1/2" d., 6" h. **$450**
Jardiniere, Calla Lily patt., No. 591, 7" h. **$300**
Pitcher, 5" h., Iris (Narcissus) patt., No. 401-5" **$100**
Pitcher, 8 1/4" h., Ebb Tide patt., No. E-4- 8 1/4" **$150**
Salt box, hanging-type, Utility ware, all- white semi-porcelain, upright rectangular shape, No. 111, 6" h. **$150**
Tea set: cov. teapot No. 23, open sugar bowl No.25 & creamer No. 24, teapot 0 1/2" h., Magnolia patt., the set **$400**
Tea set: cov. teapot No.110, open sugar bowl No.112 & creamer No. 111; Open Rose (Camellia) patt., teapot 8 1/2" h. the set **$550**
Tea set: cov. teapot No. S-11, cov. sugar bowl No. S-13 & creamer No. S-12; Parchment and Pine patt., teapot 6" h., 3 pcs...... **$250**

Vase, 7 1/2" h., Pagoda patt., No. P3 (ILLUS. front row, left) **$30-50**
Vase, 10" h., Pagoda patt., No. P4 (ILLUS. front row, right) ... **$40-50**
Vase, 12" h., Pagoda patt., No. P5 (ILLUS. back row, left) **$45-55**
Vase, 15" h., Pagoda patt., No. P6 (ILLUS. back row, right) ... **$50-60**

Vase, 8 1/2" h., Water Lily patt., No. L-8 (ILLUS. front row, left) **$175-225**
Vase, 8 1/2" h., Water Lily patt., No. L-A (ILLUS. back row) **$200-225**
Vase, 12 1/2" h., Water Lily patt., No. L-16 (ILLUS. front row, right) **$395**

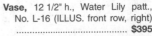

Vase, 11" h., Ebb Tide patt., upright spiral shell w/figural fish foot, No. E-7, brown ground **$125-175**

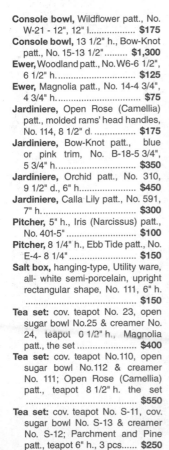

Ironstone

The first successful ironstone was patented in 1813 by C.J. Mason in England. The body contains iron slag incorporated with the clay. Other potters imitated Mason's ware, and today much hard, thick ware is lumped under the term ironstone. Earlier it was called by various names, including graniteware. Both plain white and decorated wares were made throughout the 19th century. Tea Leaf Lustre ironstone was made by several firms.

General

Cup & saucer, handleless cup, Laurel shape, all-white, Wedgwood & Co............. **$50-60**

Gravy boat, Bordered Hyacinth shape, all- white, W. Baker & Co. **$65**

Mug, child's, Sydenham shape, all-white, rare........................... **$120**

Mug, Dolphin shape, all-white, John Edwards **$75**

Pitcher, 11" h., Fig/Union shape, all-white, Davenport **$240-260**

Pitcher, 12" h., Corn & Oats shape, all-white, J. Wedgwood....... **$190-210**

Plate, 10" d., Mississippi shape, all-white, E. Pierson................... **$40**

Platter, 12" l., oval, Niagara shape, all- white, E. Walley **$35-45**

Punch-toddy bowl, cov., Hyacinth shape, all-white, H. Burgess, 12" d. **$225-245**

Soap box, cover & insert, Grape Octagon shape, all-white, Livesley & Powell, ca. 1850 .... **$170-190**

Tea set: child's, cov. teapot, cov. sugar bowl, creamer & six cups & saucers; Paneled Grape shape, all-white, the set **$750-800**

Gravy boat, Eagle shape, all-white, Davenport, ca. 1850s **$110**

Mug, Chinese shape, all-white, Anthony Shaw, ca. 1858 .... **$90**

Master waste jar, cov., Classic Gothic Octagon shape, all-white, Jacob Furnival **$950-1,050**

Syrup pitcher w/hinged pewter lid, Gothic Octagon shape w/Greybeard under spout, all-white, T. J. & J. Mayer, 5" h. **$225-300**

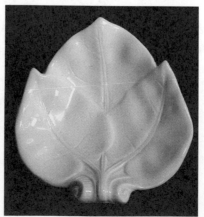

Relish dish, Pond Lily Pad shape, all-white, James Edwards **$115-130**

Tea Leaf Ironstone

Sauce tureen, cover, undertray & ladle, Delphi patt., T. Elsmore & Son, 4 pcs. **$450**

Shaving mug, Cable shape, large size, Anthony Shaw **$275**
Shaving mug, Favorite shape, Grindley **$1,050**
Shaving mug, plain rounded shape, Anthony Shaw **$170**
Slab soap, rectangular w/notched corners, Wilkinson **$140**
Sugar bowl, cov., Sunburst shape, Wilkinson **$80**

Sugar bowl, cov., Maidenhair Fern patt., T. Wilkinson, slight crazing **$80**

Sugar bowl, cov., Fig Cousin patt., pink lustre, Davenport **$395**

• Traditional tea leaf ironstone consists of a tea leaf motif with three leaves and a bud in a copper or gold lustre created by adding copper or gold oxide to the glaze. Current collectors, however, tend to consider any lustre on ironstone to be tea leaf ironstone regardless of the actual motif used.
• The tea leaf decoration probably orginated from a superstition that finding a complete open tea leaf at the bottom of a tea cup would bring good luck.
• Early ironstone was heavily decorated, but eventually the plain white pattern with lustre designs became the favorite. Ironstone shapes were originally more complex but became more simplified by the 1870s and 1880, probably to allow faster and greater production to meet demand.
• Ironstone can darken with age, but it should never be cleaned with chlorine bleach, as it will destroy the glaze.

Teapot, cov., Favorite patt., Grindley **$120**

Limoges

Limoges is the generic name for hard paste porcelain that was produced in one of the Limoges factories in the Limoges region of France during the 19th and 20th centuries. There are more than 400 different factory identification marks, the Haviland factory marks being some of the most familiar. Dinnerware was commonly decorated by the transfer method and then exported to the United States.

Decorative pieces were hand painted by a factory artist or were imported to the United States as blank pieces of porcelain. At the turn of the 20th century, thousands of undecorated Limoges blanks poured into the United States, where any of the more than 25,000 American porcelain painters decorated them. Today hand-painted decorative pieces are considered fine art. Limoges is not to be confused with American Limoges. (The series on collecting Limoges by Debby DeBay, *Living With Limoges*, *Antique Limoges at Home and Collecting Limoges Boxes to Vases* and *Antique Trader Limoges Price Guide 2007* are excellent reference books.)

Box, cov., figural, a standing white poodle wearing red caps & red sweater, on an oval box base w/ metal hinge & bands, marked "Peint Main - Limoges France," ca. 1970 .... **$300**

Bust of a young boy, all-white, mounted on a grey socle base, after a model by C. Houdon, green mark for Porcelain de Paris, France, ca. 1920s, 15" h. **$1,500**

Bust of a young girl, all-white, mounted on a grey socle base, after a model by C. Houdon, green mark for Porcelain de Paris, France, ca. 1920s, 15" h. **$1,500**

Bust of Marie Antoinette, bisque, on a cobalt blue & gilt-banded socle, red printed mark of De Pierre Fiche, ca. 1875, 24" h. **$2,875**

Game set: a 17 3/4" l. oval platter decorated w/a pair of ducks & twelve 9 1/8" d. plates, each w/a different pair of game birds, cobalt blue borders w/ornate gilt scrolls, artist-signed, early 20th c., the set **$2,115**

Plaque, pate-sur-pate, rectangular, dark blue ground finely decorated w/h.p. & hand-tooled white slip w/a scene of a scantily clad maiden in a flower-filled glen attended by birds in flight, one perched on her extended hand, impressed monogram & Grand Feu, Limoges mark, artist- signed, ca. 1900, 6 1/2 x 9 1/2" **$4,800**

Plaque, pate-sur-pate, rectangular, white slip decoration of a reclining Grecian maiden being serenaded by two putti on a dark blue ground, artist-signed, in a giltwood frame, early 20th c., 6 1/8 x 8 1/2" **$5,017**

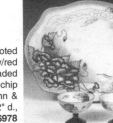

Punch set: footed punch bowl, 7 footed cups & an undertray; each h.p. w/red poppies & green leaves on a shaded ground, dark rust bases, small chip on one cup, mark of Tressemann & Vogt, (T.V. Limoges), bowl 13 1/2" d., the set **$978**

Plaque, pierced for hanging, round w/scalloped & scroll-molded gold rim, h.p. scene of brawling men, artist-signed "Messonier," George Borgfeldt (Coronet) factory Mark 1, 11" d. **$1,500**

• Consider arriving at an antique market before it opens and get in line. Do a quick walk-through, looking for items that are highest on your want list. After viewing the market quickly the first time, go through again at a deliberate pace. Rather than beginning again from the start, do an about face and view the show back to front. From a different vantage point, you might view something you didn't see the first time.

• For the cost of about one new place setting of fine china, it is possible to buy an entire set at an estate auction. Sets that are missing cups, saucers, and other pieces can be made complete by buying them from matching services.

Liverpool

Liverpool is most often used as a generic term for fine earthenware products, usually of creamware or pearlware, produced at numerous potteries in this English city during the late 18th and early 19th centuries. Many examples, especially pitchers, were decorated with transfer-printed patriotic designs aimed specifically at the American buying public.

Pitcher, 6 1/4" h., pearlware, bulbous ovoid body w/a wide short cylindrical neck w/rim spout, applied strap handle, black transfer-printed designs, the front w/an American eagle w/a ribbon in its beak inscribed "E. Pluribus Unum," w/fifteen stars above its head; the reverse w/a vignette of an embracing couple, beneath the spout is a fleet of sailing ships, the rim decorated w/blossoms, black enamel striping on the rim, shoulder & handle edges, early 19th c. (minor imperfections) **$999**

Pitcher, 8 1/8" h., jug-form, black transfer-printed design, the front w/the inscription "O Liberty thou Goddess!," a poem in an oval, bordered by a wreath of olive leaves surrounded by an entwined ribbon containing the names of fifteen states, the back w/a stern view of a sailing ship, a spread-winged American eagle below the spout, imperfections **$999**

Pitcher, 8 1/2" h., jug-type, decorated w/black transfer-printed scenes w/some hand-tinting & gilt trim, one side w/a sailing ship under full sail & flying an American flag, the other side w/a circular medallion enclosing a Latin inscription, all surrounded by circles w/the names of the first 13 states, tight crow's-foot in the base, early 19th c. **$1,725**

Pitcher, 9 1/2" h., jug-type, decorated w/black transfer-printed scenes w/some hand-tinting & gilt trim, the front w/a large oval wreath medallion topped by Masonic devices & enclosing a full-length portrait of an officer in full uniform & holding the Massachusetts state flag, the border band inscribed "Aut Vincere Aut Mori - Success to the Independent Boston Fusiliers, Incorporated July 4th, 1787 - America Fore Ever...," the reverse w/an oval design w/the allegorical figures of Liberty, Justice & Peace above the inscription "United We Stand - Divided We Fall," a wreath above the figures includes 16 stars surmounted by an American flag, a floral design below the spout, base chip, very minor discoloration & enamel loss, rare design **$11,163**

Pitcher, 10 1/4" h., jug-type, decorated w/black transfer-printed scenes, the front w/a large oval memorial scene w/weeping willows flanking a monument to George Washington w/a mourning figure below, a ribbon across the top inscribed "Washington In Glory" & a bottom ribbon w/"America In Tears," the back w/a scene of an American ship under full sail, a spread-winged American eagle below the spout, imperfections, early 19th c. **$1,293**

Pitcher, 10 1/8" h., jug-form, creamware, black transfer-printed designs trimmed in polychrome, one side printed "Success to America - Whole Militia is Better Than Standing Armies...," the back depicting a large oval memorial reserve titled "The Memory of Washington and the Proscribed Patriots of America," in addition a spread-winged American eagle w/shield below the spout w/ the full Jefferson quote "Peace, Commerce, and honest Friendship with all Nations - Entangling Alliances with none - Jefferson Anno Domini 1802," a winged figure blowing a trumpet under the handle, ca. 1802, repaired **$3,055**

Longwy

This faience factory was established in 1798 in the town of Longwy, France, and is noted for its enameled pottery, which resembles cloisonné. Utilitarian wares were the first production here, but by the 1870s an Oriental-style art pottery that imitated cloisonné was created through the use of heavy enamels in relief. By 1912, a modern Art Deco style became part of Longwy's production; these wares, together with the Oriental-style pieces, have made this art pottery popular with collectors today. As interest in Art Deco has soared in recent years, values of Longwy's modern-style wares have risen sharply.

Bowl, 10" w., 4" h., widely flaring deep bowl w/a 12-paneled rim, raised on three gold peg feet, the interior decorated w/a design of stylized pink & white blossoms alternating w/large dark turquoise blue & gold leaves against a cream ground, dark turquoise blue exterior, stamped mark **$600**

Charger, round, a black border band surrounding a stylized Art Deco landscape w/three nudes in black or white among fruiting exotic trees in shades of dark blue, grey & brown, marked, minor line & glaze flakes, minor crazing, 15" d. **$900**

Vase, 4 3/4" h., Primavera, footed wide cylindrical form w/a flat rim, decorated w/a wide body band in blue highlighted by dark blue stylized birds, plants & scattered dots, stamped & impressed marks **$300**

Console set: a pair of 4 1/2" h. vases & 9 1/2" d. center bowl;each squatty bulbous vase tapering sharply to a trumpet neck, decorated w/long white panels centered by a black stylized flowerhead w/small black panels up the neck, the center bowl w/a wide cylindrical pedestal base in white decorated w/a band of black repeating scrolls supporting the wide cupped white bowl decorated w/a repeating design of black lines, scrolls & half-round rings, all w/stamped mark, the set **$1,440**

LONGWY

Vase, 5" h., footed wide ovoid octagonal shape w/a wide flat rim, decorated w/a repeating design of full-length stripes of graduated dark pink & green blossoms & stems on an ivory crackled ground, dark pink rim & foot trim, stamped mark **$300**

Vase, 9" h., bottle-form, a round foot supporting the spherical body below a tall gently tapering ringed neck w/a flaring rim, dark turquoise ground decorated overall w/stylized pink & white blossoms & scrolling dark green leaves, a band of white & dark blue trefoils arund the rim, impressed mark **$1,020**

Vase, 9 1/2" h., slightly tapering cylindrical body w/a curved shoulder to the short molded neck, decorated around the shoulder w/a repeating design of large pointed dark yellow panels outlined in brick red & accented w/clusters of stylized light & dark blue blossoms, slender brick red stems down the sides alternating w/ creamy panels, elaborate stamped mark **$960**

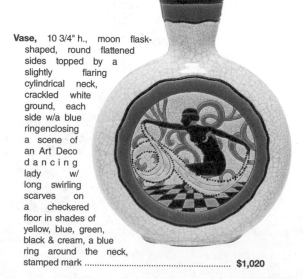

Vase, 10 3/4" h., moon flask-shaped, round flattened sides topped by a slightly flaring cylindrical neck, crackled white ground, each side w/a blue ringenclosing a scene of an Art Deco dancing lady w/ long swirling scarves on a checkered floor in shades of yellow, blue, green, black & cream, a blue ring around the neck, stamped mark **$1,020**

Majolica

Majolica, a tin-enameled glazed pottery, has been produced for centuries. It originally took its name from the island of Majorca, a source of figurine (potter's clay). Subsequently it was widely produced in England, Europe and the United States. Etruscan majolica, now avidly sought, was made by Griffen, Smith & Hill, Phoenixville, Pa., in the last quarter of the 19th century. Most majolica advertised today is 19th or 20th century. Once scorned by most collectors, interest in this colorful ware so popular during the Victorian era has now revived and prices have risen dramatically in the past few years. ALSO SEE OYSTER PLATES

Etruscan

General

Basket, Begonia Leaf patt., wicker-form forked overhead handle, wicker strap border band, 11 1/2" l. **$1,120**

Teapot, cov., Shell & Seaweed patt., spherical body molded as large shells trimmed w/seaweed, mottled green coral-form handle & spout, mottled pink, brown & green cover w/shell finial, Griffin, Smith & Hill, Phoenixville, Pennsylvania, late 19th c., 10" l., 6 1/2" h. **$525-575**

Cheese keeper, cov., Beehive & Blackberry patt., modeled as a large straw beehive w/a vine loop top handle & blackberry vines wrapping around the sides, the base a square platform w/cut-corners raised on vine legs, Minton, England, ca. 1880s, hairline In base, very rare, 13" h. **$35,200**

Compote, open, 9 1/4" h., 10 1/2" d., the wide shallow dished top composed of large overlapping green leaves raised on a tall green stem framed by three standing storks w/their heads bent down touching their breasts & glazed in mottled yellow to dark brown, on a mottled brown & bluish green tripartite base, unmarked . **$518**

Creambowls, figural, a large naturalistic nautilus shell bowl supported on a pedestal composed of entwined dolphins & green seaweed, on a round disk-form gadrooned green oval foot, Minton, England, Model No. 902, date code for 1862, overall 9" h., pr. **$3,824**

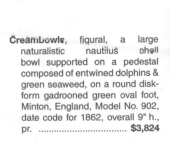

MAJOLICA

Dish, trompe l'oeil style, round, the top molded & applied w/three realistic frogs, two lizards & a snake on a bed of mossy frit, Portugal, ca. 1880, 13" d. **$1,320**

Garden seat, cylindrical, molded as a realistic tree stump in brown w/ivy climbing around the sides, an applied woodpecker & two smaller birds on the sides, draped from the top w/a turquoise blue cloth w/dark blue border bands & large blue tassels, probably Thomas Forester, England, ca. 1880, 21 5/8" h. **$2,640**

Jardiniere & pedestal, the spherical footed jardiniere w/a wide flat mouth sits atop a tall columnar pedestal w/a domed flaring foot w/a paneled bottom rim, each piece relief-decorated w/ spiny leaves & thorny branches of flowering thistles & floating dandelion seeds, each piece w/painted mark of Delphin Massier, Vallauris, France, late 19th c., jardiniere 15" h., pedestal 39" h., the set **$8,225**

Garden seat, figural, Blackamoor patt., three mottled green & brown bun feet supporting a base w/a cobalt blue border band supporting a brown mound issuing the figural pedestal composed of a full- figure Blackamoor youth seated among green & brown cattails, the top composed of a flattened cobalt blue cushion-form seat w/yellow ropetwist border, professional restoration to the seat, Holdcroft, England, late 19th c., overall 17 1/2" h. **$6,050**

Garden seat, hexagonal shape w/ short cut- out feet, modeled in the Chinese taste, each panel edged by key & stave faux bois patterns, molded in relief w/ flowering bamboo flanked by bamboo canes, probably by Joseph Holdcroft, England, ca. 1880, 18 7/8" h. **$3,360**

When seeking an auctioneer to conduct your sale, consider hiring a full-time, full-service professional. Read all the fine print and compare terms, as terms vary widely. Ask questions to clarify any points of uncertainty. Before deciding, ask for references and check on their satisfaction.

Jardiniere, deep oval form w/gently flaring paneled & scalloped sides, cobalt blue ground decorated on the sides w/oblong green scroll-framed panels enclosing colorful scenes of Classical figures & Cupids, Shape No. 1087, Minton, England, ca. 1880s, professional rim repair, 17 1/2" l., 7 3/4" h. **$3,300**

Pedestals, figural, a full-figure standing ostrich w/brown & white plumage in front of a tall flared top naturalistic pedestal w/green, blue & pink glazing, impressed numbers on base but no company name, late 19th c., top 13" d., 32 1/2" h., pr. **$2,400**

Sardine box, cov., the oblong boat-shaped base w/ alternating black & blue stripes around the sides & titled "Sardinia," a large rectangular brown plank cover w/rope & anchor finial, clusters of fish at the top of each end, impressed mark of Josiah Wedgwood, ca. 1878, slight glaze chip to rim, 9 3/4" l. **$881**

Teapot, cov., Lemon patt., model of a large yellow lemon w/molded green leaves around the sides Mintons, England, date code for 1873, Shape No. 643, 7" l., 4 1/2" h. **$8,800**

Tea set: Drum patt., cov. teapot, cov. sugar bowl & creamer; each piece w/a spherical body designed as a round drum w/wide cobalt blue bands separated by narrow brown bands joined by interwoven rope bands w/buckles, strap & buckle handles & a drum stick spout, very rare design, George Jones, England, late 19th c., teapot 6" h., the set **$12,320**

MAJOLICA

Teapot, cov., Monkey & Coconut patt., the body modeled as a large mustard yellow coconut w/the figure of a seated brown monkey at one end grasping the nut, wearing a black jacket w/dark red blossoms & green leaves, the grey head w/pale green knob finial forming the cover, molded green leaves below the curved brown bamboo-form spout, the tail of the monkey forming the handle, Mintons, England, third quarter 19th c., minor hairline in spout, 8 1/2" l., 6" h. **$6,440**

Teapot, cov., Rooster patt., model of a large, colorful, realistic rooster in shades of brown, yellow & green, red comb & wattle, oval base, George Jones, England, third quarter 19th c., 11" l. **$7,700**

Teapot, cov., Vulture & Snake patt., an elaborately modeled design w/a large standing vulture w/a yellow & black body & pink neck & head grasping the head & body of a large writhing green snake, both on a rockwork base, Model No. 1851, designed by H.H. Crealock, Mintons, England, dated ca. 1872, 8 3/8" h. **$89,625**

Umbrella stand, Banana Plant design, tall upright triangular form, the front sides molded in bold relief w/a cluster of tall wide green & yellow leaves & leafy branches w/molded bulbous brown fruit, turquoise blue background & a bark-textured pale greenish brown band at the rim & base, Joseph Holdcroft, England, ca. 1880, overall 21 1/4" h. .. **$3,346**

Teapot, cov., Tortoise patt., produced by Minton, limited edition of 2,500, introduced in 1999 .... **$750**

Marblehead

Bowl, 6" d., wide curved sides w/a wide flat rim, dark green matte glaze, impressed mark & original paper label
.... **$540**

Tile, square tile w/an incised stylized landscape of poplar trees reflected in a pond, marked & w/paper label, small chips in corners, 6" sq. **$114,000**

Pitcher, 8 3/4" h., 5 1/2" d., tankard-type, tall corseted body w/a flat mouth & small rim spout, angled side handle, incised panels down the sides incorporating stylized flower blossoms in brown, green & indigo on a speckled matte green ground, stamped ship mark & initials of artist Hannah Tutt **$5,750**

While museum employees may be able to help identify and date items that are difficult to research, they are not allowed to estimate values.

Vase, miniature, 3 1/2" h., 3" d., bulbous squatty ovoid body w/a wide flat mouth, decorated around the rim w/dark blue grapes & leaves against a speckled grey ground, impressed ship mark **$2,300**

Vase, 4 1/8" h., small tapering ovoid body w/a wide flat mouth, decorated w/six stylized flowers in green & rust up around the sides against an oatmeal yellow ground, by Hannah Tutt, impressed logo **$2,415**

Vase, 5" h., flaring ovoid body w/a wide flat mouth, blue matte glaze, company logo mark **$345**

Vase, 5 1/8" h., flaring ovoid body w/a wide flat mouth, green crystalline matte glaze, hand-thrown, company logo mark **$375**

Vase, 5 1/8" h., flaring ovoid body w/a wide flat mouth, lavender matte glaze, company logo mark .. **$432**

Vase, 7 1/4" h., swelled cylindrical body tapering to a wide flat mouth, the sides w/tall narrow vertical panels divided by narrow black stripes, each panel topped by a stylized brown flowerhead w/yellow center, against a matte green ground, decorated by Hanna Tutt, ca. 1908 .... **$50,190**

Vase, 6" h., 5 1/2" d., wide squatty gourd-form tapering to a wide flat mouth, carved in relief around the top w/a continuous band of stylized flying geese in black against a dark green matte ground, unmarked **$2,875**

Vase, 7 1/4" h., tall slightly waisted cylindrical shape, overall purple matte glaze, impressed mark **$360**

When storing antiques and collectibles, wrap them in acid-free paper instead of newspaper, add dessicant to the storage box or container to absorb excess moisture, and place in a humidity and temperature controlled area.

Martin Brothers

Martinware, the term used for this pottery, dates from 1873 and is the product of the Martin brothers—Robert, Wallace, Edwin, Walter and Charles—often considered the first British studio potters. From first to final stages, their hand-thrown pottery was completely the work of the team. The early wares may be simple and conventional, but the Martin brothers built up their reputation by producing ornately engraved, incised or carved designs as well as rather bizarre figural wares. The amusing face-jugs are considered some of their finest work. After 1910, the work of the pottery declined and can be considered finished by 1915, though some attempts were made to fire pottery as late as the 1920s.

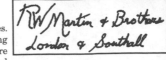

Model of grotesque creature, the reclining creature w/a smiling face w/large ears & an arched & finned body, two front legs & curling tail, body, head & legs in a mottled brown glaze, fins in a blue & cream glaze, signed "Martin Bros. 1894," 4 1/2" l. **$3,788**

Plaque, abstract grotesque undersea figure w/a stylized shell-form centered by a grinning face w/side-glancing eyes flanked by stubby hands, dark greenish brown & tan matte glaze, incised "R.W. Martin & Bros. - London & Southall - 1898," 7 1/4" h. **$13,200**

Tobacco jar, cov., figural, designed as a large stylized bird w/a stern expression, semi-gloss glaze in shades of beige, brown & ochre w/touches of blue in the wings & feathers, on orignial ebonized wood base, rim of head marked "R.W. Martin & Bros. London & Southall 3-1887," base foot rim marked "R.W. Martin & Bros. London & Southall," small firing line inside collar, tight harline from mid-back into the wing, 11" l. **$34,500**

Spoon warmer, figural, a squatty rounded grotesque creature w/front paws below the gaping grinning mouth & bulging eyes, tall curved ears meet at the top, carved fur & scale details, mottled brown glaze, incised "11-1898 - Martin Bros. - London & Southall," 5 1/2" h. **$8,400**

Plaque, abstract grotesque undersea figure w/pointed edges around a smiling face over stubby hands, worn tan matte glaze, incised "R.W. Martin & Bros. - London & Southall - 1-1898," 6 3/4" h. **$9,600**

Replacement value and fair market value are not the same thing. Replacement value is the cost required to purchase the same item at retail value. According to the IRS definition, fair market value is "the price that property would sell for on the open market. It is the price that would be agreed on between a willing buyer and a willing seller, with neither being required to act, and both having reasonable knowledge of the relevant facts."

MEISSEN

Meissen

The secret of true hard paste porcelain, known long before to the Chinese, was "discovered" accidentally in Meissen, Germany by J.F. Bottger, an alchemist working with E.W. Tschirnhausen. The first European true porcelain was made in the Meissen Porcelain Works, organized about 1709. Meissen marks have been widely copied by other factories. Some pieces listed here are recent.

Centerpiece, a domed round gadrooned base tapering to a knopped stem supporting a two-tiered top w/each dished section w/reticulated edges & h.p. in blue w/three cartouches w/blue highlights & flowers, the top center mounted w/a figure of a standing woman holding up her apron full of flowers, overall blue trim, blue crossed swords mark on base, probably late 19th c., base dish 9" d., overall 16" h. **$450**

Centerpiece, allegorical, the flaring reticulated oblong top base w/open end handles decorated overall w/encrusted colorful flowers & green leaves among gilt- trimmed scrolls, raised on an ornate flower-encrusted pedestal w/a flower-painted scrolled cartouche above a group of children representing the Four Seasons around the scrolled base, blue crossed- swords mark, modeled by Leuteritz, ca. 1880, overall 17 3/8" h. **$7,768**

Dinner service: ten 10" d. dinner plates, nine cups & saucers, eight cream soup bowls & eight underplates; Blue Onion patt., all marked w/the blue crossed swords, 19th c., the set (ILLUS. of part) **$1,725**

Figure group, a young mother in 18th c. costume seated holding her bare-bottomed toddler across her lap w/a switch to spank it in her other hand, her young daughter pulling at her arm to dissuade her, on a round molded & gilt-trimmed base, blue crossed-swords mark, late 19th c., 10 1/4" h. **$3,585**

Figure group, depicting an elegant lady in 18th c. dress standing over a cherub reading an open book, they surrounded below by ladies in waiting & two little girls, ovoid naturalistic base, late 19th - early 20th c., 12" h. **$6,463**

A putto (from the Latin "putus," meaning little man) is protrayed as a chubby human baby, often having wings. The plural of putto is "putti." The putto comes from Greek and Roman mythology and are, therefore, considered secular, whereas cherubs come from the Bible and are considered sacred figures.

Figure group, Zephyr & Flora, the standing Flora half nude wearing a pale blue drapery trimmed w/a floral garland standing beside winged Zephyr draped only in a golden brown wrap, square gilt-trimmed base, blue Crossed Swords mark, late 19th c., 11 1/2" h. **$2,400**

Figure of a putto, allegorial, the chubby child w/a staff & flowers wrapped in a long swirled pink drape, probably representing Spring, applied sunflower to the sides, on a domed gold base, underglaze-blue Crossed Swords mark, minor flaws, late 20th c., 14 1/2" h. **$2,233**

Figures of child, blond boy wearing white nightgown, blue socks & tan slippers, holding blue & white bowl or cup to lips, a horse toy on its back behind him, underglaze blue crossed-sword mark, 20th c., 7 1/2" h. **$1,035**

Figurine, Baron Munchhaussen, in a satirical pose dressed as a cavalry office riding on the full moon, on a stepped ebonized wood base, blue crossed-swords mark, signed by Alexander Struck, ca. 1941, 13 1/4" h. **$5,975**

Figure of Despina, a partially nude standing classical woman leaning back to check the sandal on her foot resting on a large rock, raised on an oval waisted plinth base incised w/a thin wave band over a band w/cattails, tridents & small dolphins, underglaze-blue Crossed Swords mark, late 19th c., 18" h. **$5,170**

Scent bottle w/stoppers, figural, modeled as the figure of a standing bearded man in a long brown hooded robe holding the neck of a white goose in one hand & a basket of colored fruit over his other arm, a long basket holding a small child, the heads of the child & the man form stoppers, blue Crossed-Swords mark & impressed "2472," late 19th c., 3" h. **$1,323**

Figures, one a seated female cherub wearing a mob cap & apron, seated on a brickwork platform using a coffee grinder w/a tall coffeepot beside her, an oblong scroll-molded base, the second a seated male cherub seated w/a bowl preparing porridge, seated on a brickwork base w/an oblong scroll-molded base, overall gilt trim on both, underglaze-blue Crossed Swords mark, late 19th c., 5 1/4" h., pr. **$2,115**

Plates, 9 1/2" d., three oblong rim reserves h.p. in dark blue w/a stylized blossom connected by reticulated basketweave section around the center w/a large blue floral decoration, blue Crossed-Swords mark, 19th c., set of 6 .... **$805**

Teapot, cov., nearly spherical slightly tapering body decorated w/a robin's-egg blue ground, the flat cover w/a gold knob finial, short curved shoulder spout & pointed arch handle, each side centered by a h.p. color scene of merchants haggling at quayside within a gold border, the cover w/two smaller views, "indianische Blumen" design under spout & on handle, blue crossed-swords mark, 1735-40, overall 4 1/4" l., 4 1/4" h. **$4,780**

Urn, a flaring gadrooned foot joined by a white-beaded disk to the large ovoid urn- form body w/ gold gadrooning around the lower portion below the wide white central band h.p. w/a large bouquet of colorful flowers, the tapering neck in deep pink below the heavy gold rolled & gadrooned rim, white & gold entwined serpent handles at each side, blue crossed-swords mark, late 19th c., 11" h. ... **$518**

Vase, 6 5/8" h., footed bottle-form body tapering to a ringed neck w/a widely flaring rim, cobalt blue ground enameled in white in the Limoges style w/a pair of amorous putti sitting on a leafy branch, one extending a floral wreath to a third in flight releasing a dove, gold banding at the foot, neck ring & rim, blue crossed- swords mark, probably designed by E.A. Leuteritz, ca. 1880 .... **$2,868**

Vases, cov., 29 7/8" h., potpourri-type, ornate Rococo style, each domed & pierced cover surmounted by a large bouquet of realistic flowers, the bulbous inverted pear-shaped body w/front & back panels finely decorated w/colorful floral bouquets, the sides very ornately encrusted w/a wide variety of large, colorful flowers & fruits, the flaring pedestal base trimmed in gold & green & mounted on one side w/the figure of a small putto or nymph, after a model by J.J. Kandler, blue crossed-swords mark, ca. 1900, pr. **$10,755**

MINTON

Minton

The Minton factory in England was established by Thomas Minton in 1793. The factory made earthenware, especially the blue-printed variety, and Thomas Minton is sometimes credited with the invention of the blue "Willow" pattern. For a time majolica and tiles were also important parts of production, but bone china soon became the principal ware. Mintons, Ltd., continues in operation today. Also see OYSTER PLATES.

Plaque, rectangular, titled "Le Panier Misterieux," finely h.p. w/a scene after Boucher showing a young shepherd secretly leaving a basket of flowers at the foot of a young sleeping maiden as her spaniel looks on, large stone monuments in a wooden garden in the background, paper label of retailer Thomas Goode & Co., London, mid-19th c., in a giltwood frame, 12 3/4 x 15 3/4" **$6,000**

Plates, dessert & soup, 9 1/2" & 10 1/4" d., each center decorated w/a floral wreath, the turquoise border band enameled in white w/arabesques, edged by gilt bands, together w/six similarly enameled soup plates w/inner gold band, Pattern No. G 5748 & H309, gilt crowned globe mark & impressed mark, retailed by Tiffany & Co., New York, New York, date cyphers for 1902, group of 12 .... **$6,573**

Plates, dessert, 8 7/8" d., a fine radiating gold-striped border band interrupted by three pate-sur-pate cameo portrait medallions of classical men & women within beaded borders & suspended from gold ribbons, the inner border & cavetto w/further flowerheads & gilt beadwork, gilt crowned globe mark & impressed marks, No. PA 9390, retailed by Tiffany & Co., New York, New York, date cyphers for 1919, set of 12 .... **$11,950**

Potpourri vases, cov., Neo-Rococo design, the short pedestal base w/heavy gold scroll feet, the tall trumpet-form body fitted w/a domed cover mounted by a figural putto, cobalt ground, the body painted front & back w/panels showing 18th c. views representing the seasons, framed by heavy gold scrolls & flanked by long ornate gold scroll handles down the sides, the flaring gold-scroll rim supporting the quatrefoil domed cover w/four reticulated rocaille-molded cartouches centering panels painted w/roses, pansies or fruit, ca. 1838, 17 1/2" h., pr. (ILLUS. of one) **$6,000**

Tray, pate-sur-pate, rectangular w/ arched & scroll-molded ends trimmed in gold, chocolate brown ground decorated in color-tinted white slip w/the figure of a Grecian maiden resting her hand above a lion-head wall fountain filling a colored jug, a balustrade w/bell-shaped krater vase behind her, a floral landscape beyond, trace of gilt crowned globe mark, signed by Louis Solon, dated 1874, 13 1/8" l. **$17,925**

Vase, 7 1/4" h., footed ovoid body tapering to a slightly flared neck w/gold rim band, the body w/a bright blue ground enameled in white w/scattered birds, insects & a leaf oak branch w/acorns, printed mark of retailers T. Good & Co., England, ca. 1875 .. **$705**

Vase, 7 7/8" h., pilgrim flask-shaped, gold foot below the flattened turquoise blue rounded body tapering to a small cylindrical neck w/gold rim flanked by gold handles, enameled in color on the front & back w/large roses & fuschia on leafy berried stems, Model No. 1348, ca. 1880 .... **$2,271**

Louis Marc Emmanuel Solon, born in France in 1835, first joined Sevres pottery, where he worked with the pate-sur-pate technique (painting clay slip in mutiple layers with a brush on a pot to create a relief design). In 1870, he moved to Minton's in England and continued his pioneering work with pate-sur-pate, training apprentices and creating masterpieces until his retirement in 1904.

Pate-sur-pate remained popular until World War I, then began to decline. After Solon's apprentices passed away in the following years, the skill was essentially lost for decades. In 1992, however, Mintons attempted to resurrect it with some success. The art is so labor intensive, however, that it is unlikely that any modern firm will invest the time and money to reach the level it achieved a century ago.

Vase, 10" h., Astra Ware, tall ovoid body w/a short trumpet neck & C-scroll shoulder handles, streaky overall metallic glaze, impressed round Astra Ware seal mark **$345**

Vase, 21 1/2" h., classical amphora form w/a small square foot, wide ovoid body & tall trumpet neck flanked by gilt handles to the top of the shoulder, painted overall w/large cascading pink & blush fully blown roses, the neck & foot gilt w/faux fluting, the handles w/acanthus leaves, printed & impressed marks, ca. 1900 .... **$2,88◦**

MOCHA

Mocha

Mocha decoration is found on basically utilitarian creamware or yellowware articles and is achieved by a simple chemical reaction. A color pigment of brown, blue, green or black is given an acid nature by infusion of tobacco or hops. When this acid nature colorant is applied in blobs to an alkaline ground color, it reacts by spreading in feathery seaweed designs. This type of decoration is usually accompanied by horizontal bands of light color slip. Produced in numerous Staffordshire potteries from the late 18th until the late 19th centuries, its name is derived from the similar markings found on mocha quartz. In addition to the seaweed decoration, mocha wares are also seen with Earthworm and Cat's Eye patterns or a marbleized effect.

Chamber pot, pearlware, footed squatty bulbous form w/a flared flattened rim, C- form handle, dark brown upper & lower bands decorated in the Cat's-eye patt., the wider central grey band decorated w/Earthworm patt. in blue, ochre & white, one rim chip, faint spider crack in base, ca. 1830, 11 3/8" d., 5 3/4" h. **$1,410**

Jar, cov., yellowware, cylindrical w/ thin incised rings around the lower body, a white & brown central band decorated w/black seaweed decoration, domed cover w/button finial decorated w/another brown seaweed-decorated band, ca. 1850, tight hairline, minor flake under cover, 4 1/2" h. **$242**

Mug, child's, yellow-glazed earthenware, cylindrical w/C-scroll handle, green ground decorated w/a bold black & white Earthworm patt., thin white & black rim & base bands, partial impressed mark on base, chips to base edge, glaze wear on rim, early 19th c., 2 5/8" h. **$2,938**

When shopping for antiques, bring the tools necessary to spot repairs and fakes. Use a blacklight to detect fluorescing modern glues that have been used to repair cracks. Bring a tape measure and antique references to verify that measurements match those of authentic pieces. Use a magnet to discern between ferrous and non-ferrous metals. A magnifying glass will help you see the dot matrix of a modern print and the brush strokes of a painting.

Earthenware is pottery made of baked clay too porous to hold liquid in its biscuit (bisque) form. The firing temperature is too low to vitrify the clay (to melt it and turn it to glass, making it impervious to liquids). To make it impervious, earthenware must be glazed and refired.

Mustard jar, cov., pearlware, footed bulbous ovoid body tapering to a flat rim, domed cover w/spoon notch & knob finial, C-form handle, dark brown body & cover bands each decorated in the black seaweed decoration, finial repair, small rim & base chips, early 19th ~., 3 1/2" h. **$1,645**

Salt dip, pearlware, footed wide squatty bulbous form w/a slightly flared rim, dark brown body band decorated in the black seaweed decoration, white foot, thin black & green rim bands, cracked, rim chip, early 19th c., 2 3/4" d. **$558**

Moorcroft

William Moorcroft became a designer for James Macintyre & Co. in 1897 and was put in charge of the art pottery production there. Moorcroft developed a number of popular designs, including Florian Ware, while with Macintyre and continued with that firm until 1913, when it discontinued the production of art pottery.

After leaving Macintyre in 1913, Moorcroft set up his own pottery in Burslem, where he contin-ued producing the art wares he had designed earlier, introducing new patterns as well. After William's death in 1945, the pottery was operated by his son, Walter.

Bowl, 5" d., Pomegranate patt., a wide round bulbous bowl raised on a small foot, in shades of dark red, purple, brown & green, signed, impressed mark, minor hairline **$840**

Bowl, 5 1/8" h., a flaring pedestal base supporting a wide flaring cylindrical bowl flanked by tall arched looped gilt handles, decorated w/h.p. sprays of roses, tulips & forget-me-nots, printed mark & signed, ca. 1907.. **$1,410**

Bowl, 7 1/2" d., Blackberry & Leaf patt., footed deep rounded form w/a wide flat rim, in shades of red, brown, blue & green, signed, impressed mark **$720**

Bowl, 12" d., Freesia patt., wide shallow shape, washed blue ground, impressed mark & signed, ca. 1935 .... **$764**

Candlesticks, Poppy patt., flaring round foot tapering to a ringed columnar standard & cupped socket, decorated on the standard & foot w/large orangish poppies against a dark blue ground, impressed mark & signed, ca. 1925, 7 7/8" h., pr. **$1,175**

Cracker jar w/silver plate rim, cover & swing bail handle, footed spherical body, white ground h.p. w/a garland of red roses & green leaves, printed mark & signed, ca. 1910, 6 3/8" h. **$588**

Pitcher, 5 1/2"h., jug-form, footed bulbous ovoid body w/a wide short cylindrical neck & pinched spout, applied strap handle, cream ground w/a central hand h.p. w/ stylized deep red florets within an entwined green ribbon design, signed & dated 1912 .... **$235**

Lamp base, Orchid patt., a gently swelled cylindrical body in shades of red, white, yellow & green on a dark blue ground, mounted on a footed bronzed metal base & w/metal top fittings, 15 1/2" h. **$540**

Vase, 8 3/4" h., baluster-form body w/a short cylindrical neck, white ground decorated around the shoulder w/clusters of lilacs alternating w/single leaves against a dark blue & gold band, scalloped blue & gold bands around the base & neck, printed mark & signed, early 20th c. **$1,050**

Tea & coffee set: tall cov. coffeepot, footed spherical cov. teapot & two footed ovoid creamers; all decorated in the Spring Flowers patt. in purple, dark pink, white, & green on a pale blue shaded to cobalt blue ground, all signed w/impressed mark, one creamer w/paper label, repaired chips to rim of one creamer, coffeepot 8 1/4" h., the set **$660**

Vase, 7 1/4" h., Claremont Toadstool patt., baluster-form body w/a short rolled neck, decorated w/large red & yellow toadstools against a mottled green & yellow shaded to dark blue ground, impressed mark & signed, ca. 1915 .... **$3,055**

Vase, 8 1/4" h., Leaf & Grape patt., slightly tapering cylindrical body w/a short rolled neck, the upper half h.p. w/large greenish yellow leaves & dark purple & pink grapes against a dark yellow shading to dark blue ground, satin glaze, impressed mark & signed, ca. 1930 .... **$588**

Vase, 9 1/2" h., Pansy patt., baluster-form w/a short rolled neck, decorated around the top half w/a wide band of large deep rose purple pansy blossoms aga[i] yellowish green leaves & st[e] dark blue background, sign[ed] impressed mark, ca. 1930

Mulberry

Mulberry or Flow Mulberry ironstone wares were produced in the Staffordshire district of England in the period between 1840 and 1870 at many of the same factories that produced its close "cousin," Flow Blue china. In fact, some of the early Flow Blue patterns were also decorated with the dark blackish or brownish purple mulberry coloration and feature the same heavy smearing or "flown" effect. Produced on sturdy ironstone bodies, the designs were either transfer-printed or hand-painted (Brushstroke) with an Asian, Scenic, Floral or Marble design. Some patterns were also decorated with additional colors over or under the glaze; these are designated in the following listings as "w/polychrome."

Quite a bit of this ware is still to be found and is becoming increasingly sought-after by collectors, although presently its values lag somewhat behind similar Flow Blue pieces. The standard references to Mulberry wares is Petra Williams' book, *Flow Blue China and Mulberry Ware, Similarity and Value Guide* and *Mulberry Ironstone - Flow Blue's Best Kept Little Secret*, by Ellen R. Hill.

ACADIA (maker unknown, ca. 1850)
Creamer, 6" h., Classic Gothic shape $150

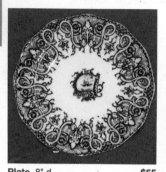

Plate, 8" d. $55

AMERILLIA (Podmore, Walker & Co., ca. 1850)
Egg cup $200

Vegetable dish, cov. $250

ATHENS (Charles Meigh, ca. 1845)
Creamer, 6", vertical-paneled Gothic shape $150
Cup plate $75
Punch cup $95
Sugar, cov., vertical-paneled Gothic shape $200

Pitcher, 6-paneled, 10" h. $350

ATHENS (Wm. Adams & Son, ca. 1849)
Cup plate $95
Plate, 8 1/2" d. $55
Soup Plate, w/flanged rim, 9" d.
.... $75
Sugar, cov., full-paneled Gothic shape $200
Teapot, cov., full-paneled Gothic shape $275

AVA (T.J. & J. Mayer, ca. 1850)
Cup & saucer, handleless, w/polychrome $95
Plate, 9 1/2" d., w/polychrome
.... $85
Plate, 10 1/2" d., w/polychrome
.... $95
Platter, 16" l., w/polychrome... $250

Sauce tureen, cover & undertray, w/polychrome, 3 pcs. $350

Joining a collector's club is an excellent way to further your experience and meet other collectors in your field. For nominal dues, collectors with similar interests meet and trade at annual conventions. Often a club sponsors an antique show that is open to the public. Many clubs publish newsletters and membership directories. Some major clubs have regional chapters, which also sponsor shows.

MULBERRY

BEAUTIES OF CHINA (Mellor Venables & Co., ca. 1845)

Cup plate $95
Plate, 7 1/2" d., w/polychrome.. $65
Platter, 14" l., w/polychrome... $225
Sauce tureen, cover, ladle & undertray, long octagon, 4 pcs. $500

BOCHARA (James Edwards, ca. 1850)

Creamer, full-paneled Gothic shape, 6" h.................................... $150
Pitcher, 7 1/2" h., full-paneled Gothic shape..................... $195
Plate, 10 1/2" d......................... $75

Teapot, cov., Pedestaled Gothic shape $350

BRUNSWICK (Mellor Venables & Co., ca. 1845)

Plate, 7 1/2" d., w/polychrome $65
Platter, 16" l., w/polychrome... $275
Relish dish, stubby mitten-shaped, w/polychrome $150
Sugar, cov., Classic Gothic shape, w/polychrome $225

BRYONIA (Paul Utzchneider & Co., ca. 1880)

Cup & saucer, handled............ $50
Gravy boat $100
Plate, 7 1/2" d......................... $35

Plate, 9 1/2" d. $40

CEYLON (Charles Meigh, ca. 1840)

Plate, 9 1/2" d........................... $65
Plate, 10 1/2" d., w/polychrome $85
Platter, 14" l., w/polychrome... $175
Vegetable bowl, open, small $125

CHUSAN (P. Holdcroft, ca. 1850)

Plate, 9 1/2" d........................... $80

Potato bowl, 11" d. $175

CLEOPATRA (F. Morley & Co., ca. 1850)

Basin & ewer, w/polychrome . $600
Soap box, cover & drainer, 3 pcs. $300
Soup plate, w/flanged rim, 9" d. $75

COREA (Joseph Clementson, ca. 1850)

Cup & saucer, handleless........ $65
Sugar, cov., long hexagon $250
Teapot, cov., long hexagon $350

COREAN (Podmore, Walker & Co., ca. 1850)

Cup & saucer, handled, large.. $85
Cup plate $100
Relish, mitten-shaped $135
Sauce tureen, cover & undertray, 3 pcs. $400

Sugar, cov., oval bulbous style $275

COTTON PLANT (J. Furnival, ca. 1850)

Creamer, paneled grape shape, w/ polychrome, 6 5/8" h........... $200

Teapot, cov., cockscomb handle, trimmed in polychrome $650

CYPRUS (Wm. Davenport, ca. 1845)

Cup plate $95
Pitcher, 11" h., 6-sided........... $250

Gravy boat, unusual handle .. $175

DORA (E. Challinor, ca. 1850)

Plate, 9 1/2" d........................... $75

Teapot, cov., Baltic shape $450

MULBERRY

FERN & VINE (maker unknown, ca. 1850)

Plate, 7 1/2" d............................ $55

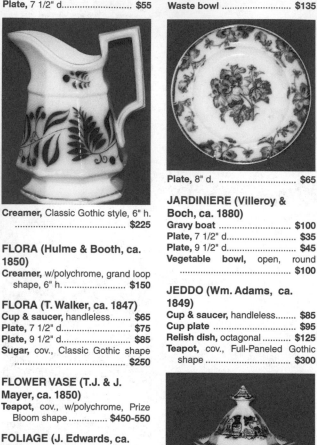

Creamer, Classic Gothic style, 6" h.
.... $225

FLORA (Hulme & Booth, ca. 1850)

Creamer, w/polychrome, grand loop shape, 6" h. $150

FLORA (T. Walker, ca. 1847)

Cup & saucer, handleless........ $65
Plate, 7 1/2" d........................... $75
Plate, 9 1/2" d........................... $85
Sugar, cov., Classic Gothic shape
.... $250

FLOWER VASE (T.J. & J. Mayer, ca. 1850)

Teapot, cov., w/polychrome, Prize Bloom shape $450-550

FOLIAGE (J. Edwards, ca. 1850)

Gravy boat............................. $150

Plate, 8" d. $75

GERANIUM (Podmore, Walker & Co., ca. 1850)

Waste bowl $135

Plate, 8" d. $65

JARDINIERE (Villeroy & Boch, ca. 1880)

Gravy boat $100
Plate, 7 1/2" d......................... $35
Plate, 9 1/2" d......................... $45
Vegetable bowl, open, round
.... $100

JEDDO (Wm. Adams, ca. 1849)

Cup & saucer, handleless........ $85
Cup plate $95
Relish dish, octagonal $125
Teapot, cov., Full-Paneled Gothic shape $300

Sugar, cov., full-paneled Gothic shape $195

KAN-SU (Thomas Walker, ca. 1847)

Cup & saucer, handleless........ $65
Plate, 7 1/2" d........................... $50
Platter, 14" l........................... $200

Vegetable dish, cov., octagonal
.... $300

MARBLE (A. Shaw, ca. 1850)

Invalid feeder, large.............. $500
Waste bowl $150

Creamer, 10 panel Gothic shape, 6" h. $250

MARBLE (Mellor Venables, ca. 1845)

Plate, 9 1/2" d........................... $50
Teapot, cov., child's, Vertical Paneled Gothic shape........ $350

Teapot, cov., Vertical Paneled Gothic shape $450

MULBERRY

MEDINA (J. Furnival, ca. 1850)

Cup & saucer, handleless........ $55
Gravy boat $135
Sugar, cov., cockscomb handle
.... $300

NANKIN (Davenport, ca. 1845)

Plate, 8 1/2" d., w/polychrome.. $75

Pitcher, 8" h., mask spout jug w/
polychrome $350

NING PO (R. Hall, ca. 1840)

Cup & saucer, handleless........ $85
Plate, 10 1/2" d......................... $95
Soup plate, w/flanged rim, 10" d.
.... $95

PARISIAN GROUPS (J. Clementson, ca. 1850)

Plate, 7 1/2" d., w/polychrome.. $60
Plate, 8 1/2" d., w/polychrome.. $70
Sauce dish, w/polychrome....... $65

Sauce tureen, cover & undertray,
w/polychrome, 3 pcs. $400

PELEW (Edward Challinor, ca. 1850)

Cup & saucer, handleless,
pedestaled........................... $75
Plate, 7 1/2" d......................... $50
Plate, 10 1/2" d........................ $70
Punch cup, ring handle $100

Teapot, cov., pumpkin shape
.... $450

PERUVIAN (John Wedge Wood, ca. 1850)

Gravy boat $145
Teapot, cov., 16-Paneled shape
.... $400
Waste bowl, "double bulge" ... $150

Cup & saucer, handleless, "double
bulge" $65

Collectors who know they can
be caught up in auction fever
and pay too much sometimes
hire an agent, usually a dealer,
to bid for them. The collector
either sets a limit beforehand
or gives the proxy the authority
to bid using his experience and
judgment. In either case, the
emotional element is removed
from the bidding.

PHANTASIA (J. Furnival, ca. 1850)

Cup plate, w/polychrome $95
Plate, 9 1/2" d., w/polychrome.. $85
Sugar, cov., w/polychrome,
cockscomb handle $350
Teapot, cov., w/polychrome,
cockscomb handle $550

Creamer, w/polychrome, cockscomb
handle, 6" h. $350

RHONE SCENERY (T.J. & J. Mayer, ca. 1850)

Gravy boat $150
Plate, 7 1/2" d......................... $35
Plate, 10 1/2" d........................ $55
Sauce tureen, cover & undertray,
3 pcs.................................... $300
Sugar, cov., full-paneled Gothic
shape $175

SCINDE (T. Walker, ca. 1847)

Creamer, Classic Gothic shape,
6" h. $100
Plate, 9 1/2" d......................... $70
Soup plate, w/flanged rim, 9" d.
.... $80
Teapot, cov., Classic Gothic shape
.... $300

SHAPOO (T. & R. Boote, ca. 1850)

Plate, 8 1/2" d.......................... $75
Sugar, cov., Primary shape $250
Teapot, cov., Primary shape... $450
Vegetable dish, cov., flame finial
.... $300

TEMPLE (Podmore, Walker & Co., ca. 1850)

Cup plate $75
Plate, 8 1/2" d... $55
Sugar, cov., Classic Gothic shape $200
Teapot, cov., Classic Gothic shape $300

Cup & saucer, handled $75

VINCENNES (J. & G. Alcock, ca. 1845)

Compote, Gothic Cameo shape $550

> A ewer is a pitcher typically with an oval body, flaring spout, and a handle whose top is level with or above the rim of the the pitcher. The ewer shape dates back to ancient times and can be found in classical Greek and Roman pieces and paintings.

VINCENNES (J. Alcock, ca. 1840)

Cup & saucer, handleless, thumbprint $95
Plate, 7 1/2" d... $60
Plate, 10 1/2" d... $80
Soup tureen, cover & undertray, 10-sided, 3 pcs. $850

Punch cup $125

WASHINGTON VASE (Podmore, Walker & Co., ca. 1850)

Creamer, Classic Gothic shape, 6" h. $225
Cup & saucer, handleless........................... $95
Plate, 10 1/2" d... $85
Soup plate, w/flanged rim, 9" d. $85
Vegetable bowl, cov.................................. $300

WHAMPOA (Mellor Venables & Co., ca. 1845)

Gravy boat $125
Plate, 10 1/2" d... $75
Sauce tureen, cov., long octagon shape, 2 pcs. $250

WREATH (Thomas Furnival, ca. 1850)

Plate, 9 1/2" d.. $75

Ewer $300

Newcomb College Pottery

This pottery was established in the art department of Newcomb College, New Orleans, Louisiana, in 1897. Each piece was hand-thrown and bore the potter's mark & decorator's monogram on the base. It was always a studio business and never operated as a factory. Its pieces are, therefore, scarce, with the early wares being eagerly sought. The pottery closed in 1940.

Bowl-vase, deep squatty bulbous shaped w/a wide flat mouth & tapering to a flat base, carved & painted around the shoulder w/white daffodil blossoms & pale green leaves against a dark blue ground, by Alma Mason, No. HD7, 7" d., 4 1/2" h. **$2,640**

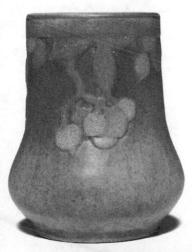

Vase, 3 1/2" h., 2 1/4" d., miniature, a swelled base tapering to cylindrical sides w/a flat rim, carved & painted w/a band of leaves & berries suspended from the rim, shades of blue & pink, by Sadie Irvine, Model #64/1 .... **$1,140**

Vase, 4 1/4" h., gently tapering cylindrical body w/a wide flat mouth, carved & decorated w/a landscape of oak trees w/Spanish moss, in shades of blue, green & cream, Sadie Irvine, No. JR9 .... **$2,880**

Bowl, 8 3/4" d., footed wide low rounded form w/a flat rim, carved & painted w/a band of jonquil blossoms & leave against a dark blue ground, by Anna Francis Simpson, marked, No. MJ73 .... **$3,2**

Vase, 5" h., a wide bulbous squatty body tapering sharply to a small base & to a short tapering neck, carved & painted around the shoulder w/white floral clusters on pale green leaves against a dark blue ground, by Alma Mason, No. HC93 .... **$3,240**

Vase, 6" h., simple ovoid body w/a wide flat rim, molded around the bottom w/a short band of overlapping wide leaves, tall wide ribbed leaves up the sides, mottled dark blue & purple matte glaze, marked, executed by MBG, No. TF75h **$2,520**

Vase, 8" h., 8" d., a wide flat mouth on bulbous rounded shoulders tapering down to a wide flat base, overall dark green crystalline glaze, by Jules Gabry, impressed marks **$1,320**

Vase, 6" h., gently swelled cylindrical body w/a flat rim, carved & molded w/ long- stemmed crocus & tall leaves around the body in pale purple & dark blue on an ivory ground, by Anna Francis Simpson, marked "RO75" **$4,200**

Vase, 12" h., bulbous ovoid body tapering to a wide flat mouth, glossy glaze over an incised scene of stylized trees in rich shades of blues & green, by Leona Nicholson, potted by Joseph Meyer, 1902 .... **$29,500**

Nippon

"Nippon" is a term used to describe a wide range of porcelain wares produced in Japan from the late 19th century until about 1921. It was in 1891 that the United States implemented the McKinley Tariff Act, which required that all wares exported to the United States carry a marking indicating their country of origin. The Japanese chose to use "Nippon," their name for Japan. In 1921 the import laws were revised and the words "Made in" had to be added to the markings. Japan was also required to replace the "Nippon" with the English name "Japan" on all wares sent to the United States.

Many Japanese factories produced Nippon porcelain, much of it hand-painted with ornate floral or landscape decoration and heavy gold decoration, applied beading and slip-trailed designs referred to as "moriage." We indicate the specific marking used on a piece, when known, at the end of each listing. Be aware that a number of Nippon markings have been reproduced and used on new porcelain wares.

Important reference books on Nippon include: *The Collector's Encyclopedia of Nippon Porcelain, Series One through Three,* by Joan F. Van Patten (Collector Books, Paducah, Kentucky) and *The Wonderful World of Nippon Porcelain, 1891-1921* by Kathy Wojciechowski (Schiffer Publishing, Ltd., Atglen, Pennsylvania).

Humidor, cov., cylindrical form, moriage decorated w/h.p. scene of white owl on branch, distant mountains in background, in browns & buffs, blue maple leaf mark, 6" h. **$3,565**

Humidor, cov., cylindrical body w/a flared rim, wide domed cover w/large knob finial, decorated w/a large relief-molded owl in brown, black & white perched on a leafy oak tree branch, on shaded yellow to orange & brown ground, tiny flakes inside rim & cover, green "M" in Wreath mark, 7" h. **$748**

Humidor, cov., hexagonal barrel-shaped body & conforming domed cover w/a large squared knob finial, the sides h.p. w/a continuous rural landscape w/large trees in the foreground, a paneled geometric rim band, the cover w/a similar landscape, green "M" in Wreath Nippon mark, 6 1/2" h. **$230**

NIPPON

Humidor, cov., three square block feet supporting the wide slightly tapering cylindrical body w/a slightly tapering cover w/large mushroom finial, the body decorated w/a landscape of a man in a canoe w/a stag in green bushes on the shore, dark yellow to pale cream ground, the feet & top rim decorated w/geometric decorative bands w/stylized symbols, matching band around the cover, 7" h. **$575**

Vase, 8" h., footed wide cylindrical body w/a wide shoulder tapering to a short neck w/rolled rim, pointed scroll shoulder handles, dark brown ground decorated on the front w/a stylized landscape showing a castle above a forest of trees in shades of brown, green, pale yellow & blue, a brown & white slip Greek key band near the base & around the base of the decorated neck, blue "Maple Leaf" mark **$127**

Urn, bolted-construction, a square foot & slender pedestal supporting the very large ovoid body tapering to a trumpet neck, angular pierced gold shoulder handles, decorated on the side w/the scene of a Native American hunter carrying a goose on his back w/a flock of geese in the distant sunset sky, elaborate gilt & geometric designs around the neck, pedestal & base, green "M" in Wreath mark, ca. 1900, 21" h. **$20,563**

Vase, 9 1/2" h., tapestry-type, tall gently tapering cylindrical body w/a flat rim, the upper body decorated w/a wide band of stylized geometric designs in shades of green, blue, rose red & gold & faux jewels, delicate gold beaded swags suspended down the sides, blue Maple Leaf mark **$1,150**

Vase, 5 3/4" h., bulbous ovoid body tapering to a short flaring neck trimmed in gold & flanked by arched gold shoulder handles, the body centered by a large gold oval reserve painted w/a full-length portrait of an exotic young woman standing in front of a peacock, surrounded by an overall gold lattice & pink rose decoration on the white ground, green Maple Leaf mark, minor gold wear **$432**

Vase, 9 3/4" h., raised disk foot below the wide gently tapering cylindrical body topped by a deep rounded cupped neck flanked by angled gold handles, a medium blue ground decorated on the body w/a pair of gold leafy bands also enclosing a large oval reserve, the reserve & space between the bands h.p. w/a continuous lakeside landscape featuring large red roses in the foreground, a white band just below the neck trimmed w/gilt florals & further gilt florals on the blue neck, green "M" in Wreath mark **$230**

Vase, 10" h., a tall ovoid body tapering to a small trumpet neck flanked by arched gold shoulder handles, the shaded grey to white ground h.p. around the base & shoulder w/large clusters of yellow & pink roses & pale green leaves w/gold highlights, blue "Maple Leaf" mark **$316**

Vase, 10 1/4" h., 5" d., baluster-form body raised on a scalloped flaring foot & tapering to a flaring pointed lobed rim, long slender S-scroll handles up the sides, decorated overall w/heavy gold stylized leaves & berries on vines, blue maple leaf mark **$175**

Vase, 10 3/4" h., a low four-lobed gold foot below the tall cylindrical body w/a swelled shoulder ring & low rounded shoulder centering a short ringed neck, four up-right scroll handles around the top of the shoulder, the sides w/a white ground decorated w/ delicate gold pendants, jewels & swags surrounding a large shield-shaped reserve bordered in gold & salmon pink & enclosing a cluster of salmon pink peony blossoms & green leaves, green "M" in Wreath mark **$196**

Wall plaque, pierced to hang, round, molded in relief w/a lion & lioness in a rocky landscape, natural coloration, 10 1/2" d. **$575**

Wine jug, cov., bulbous base tapering to short neck & flared rim, decorated w/h.p. scene of owl on branch against blue sky w/white clouds, this decoration extending to lid, applied moriage decorated C-form handle, in asymmetrical woven split bamboo basket frame, green "M" in wreath mark, 8" h. **$1,150**

Noritake

Noritake china, still in production in Japan, has been exported in large quantities to this country since early in the last century. Although the Noritake Company first registered in 1904, it did not use "Noritake" as part of its backstamp until 1918. Interest in Noritake has escalated as collectors now seek out pieces made between the "Nippon" era and World War II (1921-41). The Azalea pattern is also popular with collectors.

Ashtray, decorated w/a horse head design, 3 7/8" w., 4 1/4" h..... **$60**

Ashtray, modeled as a figural black cat, 5" d., 2 3/4" h............. **$160**

Bowl, 6" h., loop handles w/ flamingos............................. **$95**

Bowl, 4 7/8" h., decorated w/two figural owls **$475**

Bowl, 6 1/2" w., geometric shape w/ many sharp corners, decorated in green, yellow & silver.......... **$100**

Bowl, 7 3/8" w., 3" h., footed, molded on the interior w/nuts & leaves **$110**

Bowl, cov., 5 1/4 x 7 3/4", 3 1/2" h., figural ducks on the cover .. **$700**

Bowl, 9 3/8" w., 3 1/2" h., hexagonal w/two rim handles, decorated w/ birds in trees....................... **$150**

Bowl, 6 1/8" h., Gemini patt., a rounded orange bowl w/floral rim band, molded at each side w/an arched lady figure wearing a long flowered gown **$3,050**

Box, cov., slender cylindrical base w/a figural cover designed as an Art Deco lady wearing a flowered dress, legs on the base, 5" h. **$670**

Bowl, 4 1/2" h., leaf-shaped w/ orange iridescent interior, figural blue bird handle at one end **$250**

owl, 8 1/2" d., wide shallow bowl decorated on the interior w/bold stylized Art Deco flowers & leaves n deep red, orange, blue & brown, yellow border and, dark blue loop side handles **$170**

Box, cov., square geometric Art Deco design, side panels in tan decorated in black w/stylized flowers & leaves, mottled black & brown corner panels, flat inset square cover w/ upright flat rectangular finial, 4 1/2" w., 4 1/2" h. **$250**

Celery tray, narrow oblong shape w/figural rams' head handles, decorated w/a stylized floral design, 5 1/2 x 12 3/8", 2 1/2" h. **$60**

Chocolate set: cov. pot & six cups & saucers; stylized bird decoration, the set **$400**

Cigarette box, cov., the cover decorated w/a sailing ship, 2 3/4 x 3 1/2", 1 1/2" h.......... **$75**

Cigarette holder, Art Deco decoration, 2 2/3" w., 3" h. ... **$90**

Cigarette jar, cov., decorated w/a man in a cape, 3 3/4" d., 4 1/4" h. **$270**

Cigarette jar, cov., designed as a lady holding a fan & cigarette, 2 3/4" w., 5 1/2" h. **$575**

Compote, open, 7" d., 5" h., decorated w/stylized florals .. **$90**

Creamer & cov. sugar bowl, Azalea patt., pr. **$75**

Creamer, Tree in Meadow patt. **$20**

Cup & saucer, Tree in Meadow patt. **$20**

Desk set: heart-shaped tray w/pen rack at front & two cov. jars w/ floral finials; decal & h.p. florals, 6 1/2" w. **$385**

Dinner bell, figural Chinaman, 3 1/2" h.............................. **$250**

Cigarette jar, cov., cylindrical base in orange w/black, red & white spearpoint base band, figural cover w/the head of a clown wearing a pointed hat & ruffled collar, 6 1/4" h. **$1,150**

Cracker jar, cov., footed spherical body decorated w/a black band w/white swords & shields design & center oval yellow medallion w/ scene of white sailboat on lake, white clouds in distance & blue stylized tree in foreground, black & white geometric design bands around rim & cover edge, orange lustre ground, 7" h. **$210**

Condiment set: cov. mustard jar & pr. salt & pepper shakers on handled tray; bulbous blue lustre mustard jar w/red rosebud finial, green leaves, ovoid shakers w/clown head tops, red, blue, orange & white lustre, blue lustre tray, 7" l., the set **$630**

Creamer & open sugar bowl, Art Deco- style checked decoration in black, blue, brown & white, orange lustre interior basket-shaped sugar bowl w/overhead handle, creamer 3" h., sugar bowl 4 1/2" h., pr. **$125**

Condiment set: salt & pepper shakers & mustard holder; designed as a figural walking elephant carrying a three-part metal rack on its back, egg-shaped salt & pepper shakers at the sides & the mustard holder missing the cover at the center top, on an oval metal base, 4 1/4 x 5 1/4", 5 1/2" h., the set **$760**

NORITAKE

Dresser box, cov., figural Art Deco lady w/the cover & box forming her wide gown, her upper body forming the handle, decorated w/a stylized floral design in black, white, orange, red, yellow & purple, largest size, 6 1/4" d., 6 1/2" h. **$2,450**

Jar, cov., figural, designed as clown w/the wide cylindrical body in iridescent orange & purple, the wide green ruffled collar cover centered by the upturned head, rare design, hairline crack, 5 1/2" h. **$1,250**

Hair receiver, cov., Art Deco style, geometric design on gold lustre ground, 3 1/2" d. **$190**

Dresser box, cov., figural woman on lid, lustre finish, 5" h. **$770**

Figurine, advertising Geisha figurine w/"Noritake China" printed on her fan, professional repair to fan, 7 7/8" h. **$950**

Figurine, maiden carrying a bundle of sticks on her head **$55**

Flower holder, model of bird on stump, base pierced w/four flower holes, 4 1/2" h. **$95**

Hair receiver, cov., decorated w/ an Art Deco design, 3 1/2" d., 3 1/4" h. **$85**

Honey jar, cov., designed as a figural house w/figural bees on the cover, 2 1/2 x 2 3/4", 3 7/8" h. **$195**

Humidor, cov., cylindrical w/an owl molded in relief, 4 1/4" d., 6 3/4" h. **$650**

Humidor, cov., model of an owl w/ head as cover, lustre finish, 7" h. **$770**

Inkwell, model of an owl, Art Deco style, 3 1/2" h. **$260**

Figure of a lady, tall slender stylized Art Deco lady wearing a long-sleeved blue gown, overall light blue glaze, resting on original round metal base, 10 3/4" h. **$650**

Jam jar, cover & underplate, melon-shaped, pink ground w/ grey leaves, handle & leaf-shaped underplate, 5 3/4" l., 4 1/4" h., the set **$115**

Lemon dish, loop center handle, decorated w/a geometric Art Deco design, 5 1/4" d., 2 1/2" h. $80

Lemon plate, Azalea patt......... $35

Mayonnaise set, Azalea patt., 3 pcs.. $70

Napkin ring, decorated w/an Art Deco man, 2 1/4" w., 3 1/8" h. $55

Night light, figural woman, 9 1/4" h., 2 pc. $4,400

Nut set: 6" d. bowl shaped like open chestnut & six 2" d. nut dishes; earthtone ground w/h.p. nuts & leaves, the set $135

Oil & vinegar bottles w/stoppers, one- piece construction, 5 7/8" w., 3 1/2" h. $150

Plate, dinner, Azalea patt. $40

Platter, 10" l., Tree in Meadow patt. $50

Punch bowl, decorated w/a swan on a lake landscape, 12" w., 7" h. $250

Relish dish, divided, stylized floral decoration, 7 7/8 x 10 3/8", 3" h. $50

Salad set: plate, bowl, spoon & fork; Asparagus patt., the set $175

Muffineer set: shaker & creamer; each w/a flaring hexagonal foot & angular hexagonal body w/a tapering neck, the shaker w/a domed cover w/holes, the creamer w/an angular handle, each decorated w/long alternating stripes of iridescent orange & bands of red & yellow flowers on white, the set $105

Perfume bottle & stopper, footed tall ovoid body tapering to a slender neck flanked by gold handles, gold pointed stopper, the creamer body decorated w/an exotic bird on a flowering branch, 1 1/2" d., 6" h. $125

Perfume lamp, figural, designed as the figure of a lady standing wearing a long red dress decorated w/black branches & white blossoms, bottom dress hem forms the base, 5" d., 9 3/4" h. $3,550

Plate, 6 1/4" d., "Daisy," head portrait of Art Deco lady $1,920

Pin dish, figural, modeled as a reclining cl[...] colorful costume, 2 2/3 x 4 1/2", 2 1/8" h[...]

NORITAKE

Powder puff box, round, decorated w/an Art Deco lady carrying large hat boxes, iridescent purple ground, 4" d. ... **$660**

Sandwich plate, Art Deco design w/a bird- form center handle, 8" d., 5" h............................ **$195**

Smoke set: cov. cigarette jar & match holder on an oval tray; decorated w/stylized flowers, tray 7" l., jar 2 1/4" h., the set.... **$140**

Spoon holder, plain lustre decoration, 8 2/3" l., 2 3/4" h. **$45**

Sweetmeat set, Art Deco lady decoration on the set & the lacquer box, box 11 1/2" w. **$875**

Syrup & jam set, decorated w/an Art Deco design, 5 3/4" w., 5" h, three pcs. **$110**

Tea set, child's: cov. teapot, cov. sugar bowl, creamer, eight dessert plates & eight cups & saucers; Nursery Rhymes patt., the set **$750**

Salt & pepper shakers, flattened upright round shape, decorated as Flapper ladies' heads w/red tops, 1 3/4" h., pr. **$205**

Tea set: cov. teapot & six cov. cups; each in a low cylindrical shape in white w/vertical red & black hooked scrolls, low covers in red w/white scrolls & a black handle, teapot w/overhead swing bamboo handle, teapot 5" h., the set (ILLUS. of part).................. **$300**

Salt & pepper shakers, stylized Art Deco figures, tall slener ovoid shape body wearing a green shawl & long blue & white striped cape, small rounded head forms the top, 4 1/2" h., pr. **$210**

& pepper shakers, stylized figure of a taxi ...ver in yellow, blue, black, white & brown, 3 ..." h., pr. **$165**

Tea tile, round, dark iridescent blue ground centered by a white diamond enclosing the bust portrait of an exotic Art Deco lady, 5" d. **$260**

Trinket dish, oblong shape w/the figure of a seated young woman at the back rim, 5" l., 4" h. .. **$1,950**

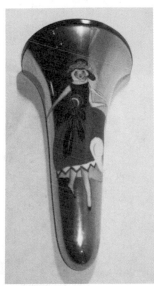

Urn, cov., Radio City patt. w/ alternating red & black & gold stripes, low cover w/scalloped rim & a small figural handle of a man holding an umbrella, 8 3/4" h. **$925**

Tea strainer & underplate, stylized floral decoration, the set **$60**
Tea tile, round, decorated w/a woman smelling a flower, 6 1/2" d., 5" h **$240**

Vase, 5" h., tall slender trumpet-form vase in light orange decorated w/a trees & cottage scene, standing on a rounded yellow rockwork base w/a white cockatoo beside it **$125**

Toast rack, figural bird, 5 1/2" w., 3 3/8" h **$70**
Trinket dish, oblong w/small figural owls on the rim, 5 1/4 x 5 3/4", 4" h **$475**

Wall pocket, trumpet-shaped, gold ground decorated w/an Art Deco lady wearing an orange & black dress, 4 1/4" w., 8" h. **$650**

Vase, 7" h., 5 1/2" w., double-tube, figural parrot **$200**
Wall pocket, designed as a figural lady molded in relief, 4 1/4" w., 8" h **$860**

The 1891 McKinley Tariff Act required that goods imported to the United States be labeled with the country of origin. After 1891, Japanese goods, for instance, were labeled Nippon, the Japanese name for Japan. In 1921 the law was updated to require that the country of origin be identified with its English name and that the words "made in" be added. Thus, beginning that year, Japanese items had to be marked "Made in Japan." However, after World War II, from 1945 to 1952, Japanese imports were marked "Made in Occupied Japan."

Ohr (George) Pottery

George Ohr, the eccentric potter of Biloxi, Mississippi, worked from about 1883 to 1906. Some think him to be one of the most expert throwers the craft will ever see. The majority of his works were hand-thrown, exceedingly thin-walled items, some of which have a crushed or folded appearance. He considered himself the foremost potter in the world and declined to sell much of his production, instead accumulating a great horde to leave as a legacy to his children. In 1972 this collection was purchased for resale by an antiques dealer.

GEO. E. OHR
BILOXI, MISS.

Bowl-vase, footed squatty bulbous body w/a thin ring around the upright neck w/a roughly scalloped rim, multi-toned pinkish brown glaze, impressed marks, cracked & glued, 3 1/2" h. **$360**

Bowl-vase, wide cylindrical shape sharply tapering at the base, an upright ruffled rim w/thin incised bands, multi-toned brown glaze, impressed mark, 2" h. **$1,080**

Puzzle mug, waisted cylindrical form w/a large hole on the outside of the rim above two rows of small holes below on each side, angled molded ropetwist handle, multi-toned glossy brown glaze, signed, 3 1/2" h. **$1,920**

Vase, 3 1/4" h., miniature, wide low flaring round foot below the wide bulbous body tapering to a wide gently flaring rim, volcanic multi-toned brown, red & green matte glaze, impressed mark **$1,320**

Some bidders like to have a seat in the front row at an auction to get a better view of what is being sold. Others prefer to be at the back to see who is bidding against them, without their own bid paddles or gestures being seen. Knowing who the competition is can have a bearing on bidding strategy. Dealers can sometimes be spotted by their dress and demeanor, so keeping a low profile is to their advantage.

Old Ivory

Old Ivory china was produced in Silesia, Germany, in the late 1800s and takes its name from the soft white background coloring. A wide range of table pieces was made with the various patterns, usually identified by a number rather than a name.

The following prices are averages for Old Ivory at this time. Rare patterns will command higher prices, and there is some variance in prices geographically. These prices are also based on the item being perfect. Cups are measured across the top opening.

Choosing an auctioneer simply because he charges less than others can be a costly mistake. An auctioneer's product knowledge, professional business practices, marketing, and experience combine to earn more dollars at the end of the day. As a veteran auctioneer once said, "It doesn't matter how good of a bid caller you are. If you don't have the buyers there, you're in trouble."

Teapot, cov., Rivoli blank, hexagonal body on short foot, angled handle, long curved spout, slightly domed lid w/cutout pointed finial, clear glaze, hand-painted decoration of purple violets & green leaves, gold highlights, Hermann Ohme, Germany, 7 1/2" h. **$475**

Toothpick holder, No. U2, Quadrille blank, 2 1/4" h. **$375**

Teapot, cov., Worcester blank, waisted lobed body w/ruffled scalloped base & rim, inset domed lid w/cutout shell finial, C-scroll handle, serpentine spout, clear glaze, the body & lid decorated w/ delicate flowers in shades of pale pink & orchid, heavy gold decoration highlighting base, handle, spout & rim, Hermann Ohme, Germany, 7 1/2" h. **$245**

Creamer & cov. sugar bowl, No. U15 Florette blank, 4" h., pr.
.... **$250**

Cup & saucer, chocolate, No. 4 Elysee bl...
2 1/2" d. ....

OYSTER PLATES

Oyster Plates

These special plates were very stylish during the second half of the 19th century. Used to serve fresh oysters on the half-shell, they are most often found made of porcelain or majolica, although other materials were sometimes used. In recent years fine individual pieces and sets have become extremely sought after.

Majolica, five-well, scalloped rim, each dark blue well molded w/colorful clusters of various small shells, yellow border band, Josiah Wedgwood, 9 1/4" d. **$4,675**

Majolica, five-well, grouping of five white shells on dark green leaves against a blue ground, Stangl Pottery, 9 1/4" d. (ILLUS. top right) **$440**

Majolica, five-well, grouping of five white shells on dark green leaves against a green ground, Stangl Pottery, 9 1/4" d. (ILLUS. bottom right) **$523**

Majolica, five-well, grouping of five white shells on dark green leaves against a pink ground, Stangl Pottery, 9 1/4" d. (ILLUS. top left)................. **$413**

Majolica, five-well, grouping of five white shells on dark green leaves against a yellow ground, Stangl Pottery, 9 1/4" d. (ILLUS. bottom left)........... **$550**

Majolica, five-well, three yellow & white wells w/seaweed sprigs & two rose red & mottled green wells, all on a molded dark green wave ground, Josiah Wedgwood, repair to one foot, 9 1/4" d. **$1,980**

Majolica, four-well, four fanned shells centered by a round well for sauce & a straight seaweed handle, mark for J.W. Boteler patent, very rare, minor professional rim nick repair, 10 1/2" w. **$4,950**

Majolica, four-well, fanned white wells centered by a pink sauce dish, on a turquoise blue ground w/green & brown handle, George Jones, England, Boteler patent mark, 9" w. **$3,300**

Majolica, four-well, light blue cockleshell wells centered by an oval pink sauce well, accent w/blossom sprigs, Holdcroft, England, minor professional repair on the back, 7 1/2 x 9" **$3,025**

Majolica, four-well, rounded rectangular shape w/pale blue wells on a yellow basketweave ground, brown central sauce dish, Minton, England, 7 1/2 x 9" **$4,180**

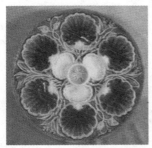

Majolica, six-well, brown cockleshell wells alternating w/green seaweed sprigs, three small inner shell wells centered by a round sauce dish, Rostrand, Sweden, 19th c., 11" d. **$3,025**

Majolica, six-well, hexagonal, dark grey shell-shaped wells on a turquoise blue ground w/ central sauce dish, Longchamp, France, 8 3/4" w. (ILLUS. bottom).......................... **$285**

Majolica, six-well, shaded green to white shell-shaped wells centered by a white sauce dish, on an emerald green ground, France, late 19th c., 9 1/4" d. (ILLUS. top left) **$121**

Majolica, six-well, tan shell-shaped wells centered on a shaded brown sauce dish, on a green ground, Sarreguemines, France, 9 1/2" d. (ILLUS. top right)....................................... **$110**

Majolica, six-well, molded shaded grey fish wells on a brown ground, centered by a round blue sauce dish, Minton, 11" d. **$3,300**

Oyster plates became popular in Victorian times, when increasing oyster consumption paralled a rising level in the standard of living. Oysters were no longer a delicacy reserved for the wealthy. Even the middle class could afford them, creating a sizable demand for oyster plates.

Parian

Parian is unglazed porcelain in the biscuit stage, and takes its name from its resemblance to Parian marble used for statuary. Parian wares were made in this country and abroad through much of the last century and continue to be made.

Bust of Alexandra, Princess of Wales, shown wearing an off-the-shoulder gown, raised on a waisted socle base, printed mark of Royal Worcester, ca. 1864, 12 1/2" h. **$470**

Figure of a girl reading, standing wearing an off-the-shoulder gown, rounded base, Copeland, England, modeled by P. Mac-Dowell, issued at the Ceramic and Crystal Palace Art Union, impressed mark, ca. 1869, shallow chip along base rim, 13 1/4" h. **$499**

Figure of Comus, the classical youth leaning on a rocky base & holding up a goblet in one hand, impressed mark of Copeland, ca. 1860, nicks along footrim, repaired chips on footrim, firing line in base & goblet rim, 12 1/2" h. **$881**

ust of Derby, older gentleman raised on a waisted circular socle, modeled by E.W. Wyon & published by John Stark, Etruria, impressed title & mark of Adams & Company, England, ca. 1867, 13 1/4" h. (ILLUS. second from left) **$470**

of John Milton, the poet w/long hair, raised on a circular socle, modeled by Matthew Noble, impressed title & ...k of Copeland, ca. 1874, 13 3/4" h. (ILLUS. second from right) **$353**

Summer, allegorical portrait of a young woman representing Summer, raised on a waisted socle base, ...ed by L.A. Malempre, impressed mark of Copeland, ca. 1870, 13" h. (ILLUS. far right) **$558**

...att, the scientist wearing a classical robe, Carrara line by Josiah Wedgwood, raised atop a waisted circular ...se, sculpted by E.W. Wyon, impressed title & factory mark, ca. 1859, 14 3/4" h. (ILLUS. far left) **$529**

Paul Revere Pottery

This pottery was established in Boston, Massachusetts, in 1906, by a group of philanthropists seeking to establish better conditions for underprivileged young girls of the area. Edith Brown served as supervisor of the small "Saturday Evening Girls Club" pottery operation, which was moved, in 1912, to a house close to the Old North Church where Paul Revere's signal lanterns had been placed. The wares were mostly hand decorated in mineral colors, and both sgraffito and molded decorations were employed. Although it became popular, it was never a profitable operation and always depended on financial contributions to operate. After the death of Edith Brown in 1932, the pottery foundered and finally closed in 1942.

Bowl, 6" d., squatty bulbous wide form w/a wide closed rim, decorated around the rim w/a band of repeating stylized white lilies against a dark blue ground, SEG mark & initialed by artist, dated "11-14," hairline, unchipped chip at rim **$780**

Bowl, 6" d., 3" h., deep rounded sides w/a wide flat rim, brown semi-matte ground decorated around the rim w/a cuerda seca band of Greek key in taupe & ivory on white, signed "SEG - 10.12 - FL" **$1,116**

Breakfast set: child's, 7 1/2" d. plate & 3 5/8" h. mug; each h.p. w/a circle enclosing a picture of a white rabbit lying on a green grassy mound, white & blue outer bands, initialed by the artist, early 20th c., the set **$1,116**

Inkwell, a rectangular box form w/a squared fitted cover on the top opening to an inkwell insert, dark blue ground decorated around the base w/a repeating design of sailing ships in light blue, green & yellow, signed & dated w/the SEG mark, 4" l. **$2,400**

Jardiniere, wide bulbous squatty body w/a closed rim, yellow ground w/a wide rim band in cuerda seca w/black-outlined white lotus blossoms trimmed w/yellow, stamped mark, firing lines around rim & base, two restored rim chips, 9" d., 7" h. **$1,495**

PEWABIC

Pewabic

Mary Chase Perry (Stratton) and Horace J. Caulkins were partners in this Detroit, Michigan, pottery. Established in 1903, Pewabic Pottery evolved from their Revelation Pottery, "Pewabic" meaning "clay with copper color" in the language of Michigan's Chippewa Indians. Caulkins attended to the clay formulas and Mary Perry Stratton was artistic creator of forms & glaze formulas, eventually developing a wide range of colors for her finely textured glazes. The pottery's reputation for fine wares and architectural tiles enabled it to survive the Depression years of the 1930s. After Caulkins died in 1923, Mrs. Stratton continued to be active in the pottery until her death, at age 94, in 1961. Her contributions to the art pottery field are numerous.

Bowl, 3" d., small round foot supporting the deep wide bell-formed bowl, a medium blue glaze applied over an iridescent yellowish green glossy glaze, round logo, some areas of thin glaze near the rim **$374**

Plate, dinner, 9 1/4" d., a crackle ivory ground decorated in squeezebag w/a border band w/ pairs of facing white rabbits alternating w/a green tree or shrub, outlined in black, stamped company name, few minor glaze nicks .. **$2,875**

Paperweight, square tile-form, incised w/a large light brown fish against a mottled blue & green ground, circular seal mark, 2 3/4" w. **$58**

Vase, experimental-type, a crimped uneven foot below the wide squatty disk-form body tapering sharply to a wide short cylindrical neck, a mottled white neck band above the dark rusty brown drippy glaze covering the sides, oak leaf mark & round paper label, some burst air bubbles & a base chip **$431**

Paperweight, round disk-type, presentation-type, the center carved w/a city skyline along a lake incised "Detroit" in shades of dark iridescent bluish green & brown, the outer brown border band incised "GFWC - 1935," 3" d. **$173**

Vase, miniature, 2 3/4" h., baluster-form body w/a widely flaring trumpet neck, a drippy white & brown glaze around the neck & shoulder above a very dark blue mottled glaze on the lower body, round company sticker, very minor base grinding **$633**

Vase, miniature, 3 1/8" h., simple ovoid body w/a short wide neck, a drippy black glaze covering most of the lustrous grey base glaze, impressed round mark, flat chip on base **$460**

Vase, miniature, 3 1/8" h., wide ovoid body w/a wide shoulder to the short, wide flat mouth, experimental type w/a drippy dark brown glaze down from the top over a moss green ground, incised mark & round paper label **$1,380**

Vase, 4 7/8" h., a wide flat base below wide gently flaring short cylindrical sides w/a wide tapering shoulder to a short flat neck, glossy glaze w/ mottled cream, brick red & shades of green, unmarked, two chips at the base **$374**

Vase, 6 3/4" h., footed wide ovoid body w/a wide shoulder to the short flaring neck, mottled & swirled iridescent glaze in shades of dark & lighter blue, impressed logo **$1,035**

Vase, 10 5/8" h., footed bulbous ovoid body w/a wide short cylindrical neck w/a flaring rim, copper red drippy glaze above a matte mauve lower body, impressed mark, very tight, faint line at rim **$3,240**

Vase, 7" h., wide cylindrical body w/a tapering rounded shoulder to the wide short cylindrical mouth, glossy glaze h.p. w/a repeating design of clusters of round brick-red stylized flowers on slender leafy stems against a mustard yellow ground, dark bands at the neck & base, round company sticker **$1,150**

Vase, 7 1/8" h., footed spherical body w/a short flaring neck, overall dark blue matte glaze w/ silvery iridescent patches, impressed twice w/logo **$690**

Phoenix Bird & Flying Turkey Porcelain

The phoenix bird, a symbol of immortality and spiritual rebirth, has been handed down through Egyptian mythology as a bird that consumed itself by fire after 500 years and then rose again, renewed, from its ashes.

The phoenix, known in Japan as the HO-O, has been used to decorate Japanese porcelain for over 100 years. However, there are a variety of phoenix designs, at least five to seven, used on Japanese blue and white porcelain. Each variety has a style of its own but all are included in the category known as "Blue Phoenix." Today, the best known and most collectible of these designs is referred to as "Phoenix Bird." Even within this pattern there are variations in the shades of blue used, the size of the design and other features. In addition to "Phoenix Bird," there are several phoenix pattern variations known as "Flying Turkey," Noritake's "Howo," "Twin Phoenix" and "Flying Dragon."

Each of these pattern variations were widely produced over a long period of time. The earliest marks found on pieces with these designs date from the Nippon Era (1891-1921). Following that period you will find many examples marked "Japan," "Made in Japan," and even "Made in Occupied Japan." In all, over 125 different marks have been cataloged for the "Phoenix Bird" pattern.

During the 1970s and 1980s a few pieces of china featuring the Phoenix Bird were produced, however, not using the early body styles and shapes. These later pieces usually have a brighter white ground with a bolder blue design. Most examples are not marked. Also, during this same period, The Takahaski firm of California began to produce a darker blue and more modern looking bird and they call their design PHYNX. Their Phoenix Bird pieces have a harsher blue with no border design at the rims of pieces and the bird is not always placed right-side up. For quick reference, collectors call this modern design "T- Bird."

After 30 years of research, most of the pieces featuring Phoenix Bird and related designs have been cataloged. Because of the wide variety in shapes and quality of the pieces made over the years, today you will find a wide range of values often based on the quality of the printed design, the shade of blue used and the uniqueness of the piece.

The standard reference for this category is *Phoenix Bird Chinaware* by Joan Collett Oates.

Bath salts jar & stopper, cylindrical w/short neck & bulbous stopper, 2 5/8" d. base, 4 3/4" h. **$110**

Bouillon cup & saucer, 3 3/4" d., 2" h., the set **$15**
Bowl, fruit or sauce, 4", 5" or 6" d., each **$5-10**
Bowl, rice, 5" d., 4 3/4" h., No. 1 .... **$12**
Bowl, 6" d., cereal **$8**
Bowl, soup, 6 1/4" d., No. B **$20**
Cake plate, round, handled, 10" d. **$35**
Candy/nut tub, 2" d., 1" h. **$18**
Chocolate cup & saucer, 2 3/4" d., 2 3/4" h., the set **$15**
Cream soup bowl, 4 3/4" d., 1 3/4" h. **$20**
Custard/noodle cup, handleless, 3" d., 2 3/4" h. **$12**

Butter dish, cover & drainer, No. 1, kidney-shaped cutouts in handles, 8 1/2" d., 3" h., 3 pcs. **$145**

Butter tub & drainer, handled, no cover, No. B, 5" d., 2 3/4" h. **$65**

Appraisers cannot ethically buy from clients. To do so is a conflict of interest, as this gives them an incentive to give a low appraisal.

Candy dish, round, on three ball feet, unusual w/a single Phoenix Bird inside, 5" d., 2" h. **$75**

Casserole, cov., angled handles & pointed handle on the cover, Flying Turkey patt., 8 1/2" w., 4 3/4" h. **$275**

Casserole, cov., cylindrical w/cupped rim, No. 2, 5 1/8" w., 3 1/2" h. **$325**

Castor set: boat-shaped base w/a mustard jar, pepper shaker & vinegar & oil bottles w/ stoppers, base 8 1/4" l., 8 pcs. **$450**

Celery tray, oblong, small cut-outs at ends, 6 x 13 1/2", 2" h. **$135**

Centerpiece bowl, marked "Japanese Porcelain Ware - Decorated in Hong Kong - ACF," ca. 1960, 10" d., 4 1/2" h.............................. **$350**

Chamberstick, No. 2, 5 1/4" d., 2 1/2" h. (ILLUS. right).. **$95**
Chamberstick, scalloped handle, No. 1, 5" d., 2" h. (ILLUS. left) **$85**

Chocolate pot, cov., scalloped base, deep collar on cover w/a cut-out for pouring cocoa, 5" d., 9" h. **$145**

Coffee biggin, cover & dripolator, this cover also fits on a teapot, making it the 43rd style cataloged in the Phoenix Bird patt., 8 1/4" h. **$500**

Coffeepot, cov., No. 4, tall ovoid body, holds nearly three measuring cups of coffee, 7 3/4" d., 7" h. **$65**

Coffeepot, cov., No. 6, tall cylindrical body w/long loop handle, 6" w., 6 5/8" h. **$125**

Coffeepot, cov., No. 7, tapering cylindrical body w/side stick handle, for right-handers only, 3 1/8" d., 5 1/2" h. **$125**

Coffeepot, cov., No. 9, octagonal body & cover, 7 5/8" h. **$150**

Coffeepot, cov., No. 15, unusual Turkish- Russian-style, 7" w., 8" h. **$95**

Condensed milk can holder, No. 2, hole in the bottom for pushing out the can, 3 3/4" d., 5 1/4" h. **$135**

Condiment set: three 6" d., 3 1/2" h. dishes in a shallow round 7 1/2" d., 1 7/8" h. covered box, the set **$200**

Espresso coffeepot, cov., No. 5, marked "Maruta - Made in Occupied Japan," 8" d., 7 1/4" h. **$85**

Gravy tureen, cover & attached underplate, Noritake's "Howo" patt., 6" l., 9" h., the set **$125**

Gravy tureen, cover & underplate, No. 2, underplate 7 1/8" d., tureen 7" l., ladle not included in this value, the set **$135**

Invalid feeder, Flying Turkey patt., 3 1/4 x 4 3/4", 1 3/4" h. (ILLUS. right) **$55**
Invalid feeder, Flying Turkey patt., 3 3/4 x 5 1/2", 2" h. (ILLUS. left) **$45**

Irish coffee cup, footed, 2 1/2" d., 3 5/8" h. **$35**

Lemonade set: 9 1/2" h. pitcher & one 3 3/4" h. tumbler, the set **$185**

Marmalade jar, cov., 5 1/4" d., 4 1/8" h. **$55**

Matchbox holder, sides w/openings for striking a match, 3 1/4 x 4", 2 5/8" h. **$145**

Rice tureen, open, No. 1, handled, on four feet, 10" w., 6 1/2" h. **$350**

PICKARD CHINA

Pickard China

Pickard, Inc., making fine decorated china today in Antioch, Illinois, was founded in Chicago in 1894 by Wilder A. Pickard. The company now makes its own blanks but once only decorated those bought from other potteries, primarily from the Havilands and others in Limoges, France.

Bowl, 10" d., h.p. blackberries, raspberries, grapes & blossoms, artist-signed **$495**

Chocolate cup & saucer, Haviland blank, "Raised Gold Daisy," artist-signed, ca. 1905 .... **$60**

Coffeepot, cov., tankard-type, tall tapering cylindrical body w/a long gold swan's-neck spout & long gold C-scroll handle, small domed cover w/gold knob finial, the cream body decorated around the top w/two wide gold bands overlapped by long looping green tendrils & small purple blossoms, pearlized finish, signed under spout, ca. 1903-05, 8 3/4" h. **$330**

Dish, leaf-shaped, overall gold w/ etched gold design, 3 1/2 x 5 1/2" **$125**

Lemonade set: pitcher & eight tumblers; the wide waisted cylindrical tankard pitcher w/a rim spout & C-scroll handle, plain cylindrical tumblers, all decorated overall w/the gold Encrusted Honeysuckle patt., unsigned, the set **$1,650**

Pitcher, 9" w., cider-type, a very wide squatty body tapering to a golden scalloped rim w/wide spout, wide ruffled gold handle, the sides h.p. w/large pink & red roses & pale green leaves on a dark green shaded to yellow ground, Limoges blank, artist-signed **$575**

Pitcher, 13" h., tankard-type, a sharply tapering cylindrical body w/a high & wide arched rim spout bordered in gold, long C-form gold handle, the sides h.p. w/purple & green grape clusters among green & yellow & orange leaves against a ground shaded from orange to yellow to dark green, artist-signed **$1,495**

Pitcher, lemonade, 6 1/4" h., bulbous ovoid body tapering to a flat rim, gilt interior band & gold angled handled, h.p. Classic Ruins by Moonlight patt., artist-signed, 1912-18 mark **$550**

Pitcher, lemonade, 6 1/4" h., bulbous ovoid body tapering to a flat ring, gold angled handle, large pink carnations on golden stems around the sides on a white ground w/gold bands at the rim & bottom, artist-signed, 1905-10 mark **$450**

Tea set: cov. teapot, cov. sugar bowl, creamer & footed compote; serving pieces w/a wide low squatty bulbous body w/looped gold handles & a gold teapot spout, a creamy lower body below a wide middle band decorated w/ colorful stylized flowering vines on a white ground, turquoise blue border bands, marked, early 20th c., the set **$460**

Tea set: cov. teapot, cov. sugar bowl, creamer & six 6" d. plates; each piece decorated overall w/a textured gold glaze, the scalloped plates w/stamped floral borders, each marked, ca. 1930, the set **$201**

Pitcher, lemonade, 6 1/2" h., squatty, bulbous, ovoid body tapering to a scalloped rim w/wide arched spout, C-form gold handle, wide gold scrolls & red gooseberries w/ green leaves on a white ground, Gooseberries Conventional patt., artist-signed, 1903-05 mark **$700**

Pitcher, 13" h., tankard-type, a sharply tapering cylindrical body w/a high & wide arched rim spout bordered in gold, long C-form gold handle, the sides h.p. w/purple & green grape clusters among green & yellow & orange leaves against a ground shaded from orange to yellow to dark green, artist-signed **$1,495**

Sugar Bowl, cov., Art Deco design w/gold panels & silver lines w/ stylized silver flowers on an off-white ground, artist-signed **$150**

Vase, 7 1/2" h., floral-decorated in the Art Nouveau style w/enamels & gilt trim, printed mark, ca. 1900 .... **$288**

Quimper

This French earthenware pottery has been made in France since the end of the 17th century and is still in production today. Because the colorful decoration on this ware, predominantly of Breton peasant figures, is all hand-painted and each piece is unique, it has become increasingly popular with collectors in recent years. Most pieces offered today date from about the mid-19th century to the present. Modern potteries continue to operate today, with contemporary examples available in gift shops.

The standard reference in this field is Quimper Pottery A French Folk Art Faience by Sandra V. Bondhus (privately printed, 1981).

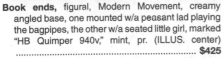

Book ends, figural, Modern Movement, creamy angled base, one mounted w/a peasant lad playing the bagpipes, the other w/a seated little girl, marked "HB Quimper 940v," mint, pr. (ILLUS. center) **$425**

Knife rests, Modern Movement, figural, one designed as a reclining peasant man, the other w/a peasant woman reclining on her stomach w/her head in her hands, by the artist C. Maillard, marked by the artist & by Henriot Quimper, mint, pr. (ILLUS. left & right)... **$200**

Bowl, 7 1/2" w., 3" h., deep w/incurved sides & angled corners, decorated w/a peasant lady, leafy sprigs on each interior side, mark of HR Quimper, mint (ILLUS. right)... **$75**

Wall pocket, figural, modeled as a bagpipe decorated w/a peasant lady, molded blue bows at the top & bottom, mark of HB Quimper, 9" h. (ILLUS. left).................... **$85**

Charger, round w/gently scalloped rim, the center decorated w/a dancing peasant couple, four flower nosegays around the rim, marked "HB Quimper . o.o," mint, 14" d. **$225**

Cake plate, round w/open loop handles, decorated in the center w/a man in the costume of Aurillac, mark of HB Quimper, mint, 12" d. **$85**

Butter dish, cov., oval shape w/ an attached undertray, yellow background glaze, marked "HenRiot Quimper 71 France," mint, 6" l. **$100**

Butter tub, cov., decorated w/a traditional peasant lady & flower garland, flat cover w/blue round button knob, marked "HB Quimper 25/485," near mint w/tiny glaze wear on inside rim, 6" w. **$35**

Chamberstick, round dished back w/center socket & ring handle, decorated w/twin daisy flowers, marked "Henriot Quimper 66," mint, 6 1/2" d. **$75**

QUIMPER

Charger, round, "Broderie Breton" patt., the center w/a sea shore scene w/a Breton fisherman holding his net, a little boy w/his toy sailboat standing beside him, marked "HB Quimper ...x," mint, 12 1/2" d. **$425**

Compote, 8 3/4" h., open, short pedestal base, deep round bowl decorated w/a traditional peasant lady flanked by floral sprigs, mark of Adolphe Porquier, 19th c., near mint w/glaze flecks **$150**

Charger, round, Modern Movement style decorated w/a fully-rigged sailing ship, titled "Thonniers" (Tuna Fishermen) below the ship among waves & fish, marked "HB Quimper France l...x," small rim chip, 12 1/2" d. **$90**

Creamer, tall bulbous shape, decorated w/traditional peasant man & geometric panels on each side of the handle, mark of HR Quimper, mint, 3" h. **$45**

Dish, doll-sized, overall geometric design, marked "Henriot Quimper France 117," mint, 3" d.......... **$30**

Egg cups, decorated in the traditional design w/yellow & blue concentric bands & a peasant figure on each w/flowers, marked "Henriot Quimper France 93" & "Henriot Quimper France 124," 3" h., pr.................................. **$50**

Figure group, Modern Movement style, a man & lady from the "Village Breton" series by artist J.E. Sevellec, facial features not painted in, marked "HenRiot Quimper JES," near mint w/tiny glaze flecks on the lady's coif, 3" h. **$150**

Figure of a peasant lady, standing w/ one hand on her hip, the other in her apron pocket, Modern Movement colors w/her name "NAIK" on the base, marked "Henriot Quimper 85," mint, 5 1/2" h................... **$85**

Compote, open, 7 x 11 1/2", oblong flaring bowl w/serpentine sides & molded open mistletoe branch handles, decorated on the inside in the "demi-fantasie" style w/a peasant man & woman w/gorse & pink bellflower sprigs, marked "Henriot Quimper 142," mint (ILLUS. of inside top) **$400**

Egg cup server, figural, the base in the shape of a large swan w/an overall dotted blue & brown design, the back molded w/six oval indentations for the small swan-shaped egg cups, mark of Henriot Quimper, near mint w/ slight glaze flecks on egg cups, swan 12" l., the set **$750**

Figure of an elderly peasant woman, Modern Movement, shown standing & leaning on her cane, by artist L. Nicot, titled "Vielle Femme à la Quenouille," marked "Henriot Quimper 30," mint, 12" h. **$450**

Figure of peasant man & peasant woman, "terre vernissée," Porquier-Beau style, each standing on a square base w/a zigzag design, mark of HR Quimper, near mint w/ slight glaze wear, 9" h., pr. ... **$1,100**

Hors d'oeuvre server, three-section, rounded serpentine sides w/a molded shell at the edge of each section, one section decorated w/a peasant lady, the other wild flowers & the third w/ the Crest of Brittany, mark of HB Quimper, 13" w. **$425**

Inkstand, "décor riche" style, the half-round footed base molded w/crests at each corner & centered by a sea shell, fitted w/two covered inkwells centered by a seated peasant man, the high arched & scroll-molded back w/a small shell finial above a letter slot decorated w/the raised crest of Quimper, mint, marked "Henriot Quimper 141," 8 1/2" l., 6 1/2" h. **$550**

Holy water fount, molded & pointed base & molded Gothic arch crest above the raised figure of Archangel Michael slaying the dragon, mark of HB Quimper, near mint w/tiny glaze flecks on rim of the bowl, 13" h. **$450**

Holy water fount, painted base below the half-round fount trimmed in dark blue, the tall pointed & scroll-bordered back molded in relief w/the figures of the Virgin & Child, unsigned but attributable to Quimper, mid-19th c., excellent condition, 7" h. **$200**

Inkstand, half-round base w/serpentine borders, the top fitted w/two covered inkwells below the arched & scalloped back w/stamp tray, decorated w/a peasant couple between the wells w/a fleur-de-lis & black ermine tails on the back, flower sprays & blue sponged trim on the lower border, mark of HB Quimper, complete w/inkwells & covers, mint, 8 1/2" l., 3 3/4" h. **$500**

Jardiniere, squatty bulbous oval form raised on lion paw feet, a molded figural satyr head at each end, the lower body decorated w/a scene of a peasant couple seated on the ground, "décor riche" blue acanthus trim above, marked "HB Quimper - 20," mint, 12" l., 8" h. **$400**

Plate, 9" d., round w/gently scalloped rim, First Period Porquier-Beau w/"scene bretonne" titled "Joyeux compagnons de Faouet," marked "Le Faouet" & blue intersecting PB mark, 19th c. **$850**

Pipe rack, modeled as a bagpipe, the half- round bottom molded at the front w/the top of the bagpipe w/a blue ribbon & pierced w/a row of four pipe holes, the upright arched & scalloped back topped by a crown above a scroll reserve forming the crest of Brittany above a peasant man & woman, marked "Henriot Quimper France 75," professional restoration to tiny glaze flecks on back of crown, 10" l., 7 1/2" h. **$350**

Planter, model of a cradle, rectangular w/gently canted sides & corner posts, serpentine top edges, decorated w/peasant figures on the front & a flower spray on the back, mark of HR Quimper, mint, 7 1/4" l., 4" h. **$325**

Inkwell, cov., round, on an attached round, ruffled underdish, decorated w/a seated peasant lady in the "demi-fantasie" style w/a flower garland, blue sponged rim, complete w/inset & cover, mark of Henriot Quimper, mint, 5" d., 4" h. **$200**

Pitcher, 6" h., figural, Modern Movement, modeled as the bust of an elderly peasant man lighting his pipe, by artist Andre Galland, the hat ribbons form the handle, marked "HenRiot Quimper 140 ag," mint............. **$200**

Planter, figural, modeled as a tall swan, decorated w/a peasant lady in a medallion on the breast of the swan, mark of HenRiot Quimper, mint, 4" h. **$85**

Platter, 10 x 13", rectangular w/cut corners, decorated w/the "panier aux fleur" (flower basket) patt., mark of HR Quimper mark, mint **$150**

Plate, 9" d., round w/scalloped rim, Second Period Porquier-Beau w/"scene bretonne" of a Breton lady & man entitled "Devideuse de Penhars," intersecting PB Quimper mark, mint **$450**

Platter, 10 x 13" oval, the center decorated w/a scene of a traditional peasant couple, flower garland border, mark of HB Qulmper, mint, 19th c. **$200**

Snuff bottle, heart-shaped, decorated w/a peasant man, the back w/a two-tone yellow fleur-de-lis, blue sponged outer rim, mark of HB Quimper, mlnt, 3" h. (ILLUS. left) **$150**

Snuff bottle, heart-shaped, decorated w/a rooster, the back w/a large flower blossom, unsigned, mint, 19th c., 3" h. (ILLUS. right).......................... **$300**

Snuff bottle, oval w/a lattice geometric design surrounded by a yellow border on both sides, Porquier, unsigned, near mint w/tiny glaze wear on lip, 19th c., 3" h. (ILLUS. center) **$325**

Tea set: footed spherical cov. teapot, spherical footed cov. sugar bowl w/scroll loop handles & footed ovoid double-spouted creamer, all in the "croisille" patt., w/"demi-fantasie" peasant figures & intricate latticework & flower sprigs, marked "Henriot Quimper France," mint, the set **$350**

Salt & pepper server, figural, open, modeled as a long pair of shoes joined w/a center ring handle, mark of HB Quimper France, mint, 3" l. **$35**

Spoon rest, figural, long shallow fish-shaped dish decorated w/a traditional peasant lady, marked "HenRiot Quimper France 238," mint, 4 1/2" l. **$30**

Toby pitcher, figural, modeled as a peasant lady decorated in Modern Movement colors, mark of HenRiot France, mint, 3 1/2" h. **$65**

Trivet, squared shape w/serpentine sides, raised on four peg feet, the top decorated w/a naively painted peasant man, flower sprigs in each corner, marked "HB" only, hairline, 6" w. **$100**

Vase, 8" h., 10 1/2" w., fan-shaped body raised on molded dolphin feet, in the "Ivoire Corbeille" patt. w/a bust portrait of a Breton lady, the reverse w/flowers & Celtic swirls, marked "Henriot Quimper 72," mint **$225**

Never hire an appraiser who offers to exchange his services for an antique or who charges based on a percentage of the appraisal. This is unethical because it gives an incentive for the appraiser to inflate values. Appraisers should only charge by the hour or by a predetermined fee for the job.

R.S. Prussia & Related Wares

R.S. Prussia & Related Wares

Ornately decorated china marked "R.S. Prussia" and "R.S. Germany" continues to grow in popularity. According to the Third Series of Mary Frank Gaston's *Encyclopedia of R.S. Prussia* (Collector Books, Paducah, Kentucky), these marks were used by the Reinhold Schlegelmilch porcelain factories located in Suhl in the Germanic regions known as "Prussia" prior to World War I, and in Tillowitz, Silesia, which became part of Poland after World War II. Other marks sought by collectors include "R.S. Suhl," "R.S." steeple or church marks, and "R.S. Poland."

The Suhl factory was founded by Reinhold Schlegelmilch in 1869 and closed in 1917. The Tillowitz factory was established in 1895 by Erhard Schlegelmilch, Reinhold's son. This china customarily bears the phrase "R.S. Germany" and "R.S. Tillowitz." The Tillowitz factory closed in 1945, but it was reopened for a few years under Polish administration.

Prices are high and collectors should beware of the forgeries that sometimes find their way onto the market. Mold names and numbers are taken from Mary Frank Gaston's books on R.S. Prussia.

The "Prussia" and "R.S. Suhl" marks have been reproduced, so buy with care. Later copies of these marks are well done, but quality of porcelain is inferior to the production in the 1890-1920 era.

Collectors are also interested in the porcelain products made by the Erdmann Schlegelmilch factory. This factory was founded by three brothers in Suhl in 1861. They named the factory in honor of their father, Erdmann Schlegelmilch. A variety of marks incorporating the "E.S." initials were used. The factory closed circa 1935. The Erdmann Schlegelmilch factory was an earlier and entirely separate business from the Reinhold Schlegelmilch factory. The two were not related to each other.

R.S. Prussia

Cracker jar, cov., Mold 704, grape leaf decoration, 7" h. ... **$450-500**

Cracker jar, cov., decorated w/ hanging basket of flowers, satin finish, 6 x 9 1/2"......... **$325- 375**

Cracker jar, cov., Hidden Image mold, image on both sides, green mum decoration **$900-1,000**

Cracker jar, cov., Lebrun portrait decoration, no hat, satin finish **$1,500-2,000**

Creamer & cov. sugar bowl, floral decoration, green highlights, pr. **$100-250**

Creamer & cov. sugar bowl, Mold 505, pink & yellow roses, pr. **$125-175**

Creamer & cov. sugar bowl, satin finish, Tiffany trim, pr. .. **$175-200**

Cup & saucer, decorated w/pink roses, peg feet & scalloped rim, cup 1 3/4" h., saucer 4 1/4" d., pr. **$125-175**

Dessert set: 9 1/2" d. cake plate & six 7" d. individual plates; Carnation mold, decorated w/ carnations, pink & white roses, iridescent Tiffany finish on pale green, the set **$1,200-1,400**

Dessert set: pedestal cup & saucer, oversized creamer & sugar bowl, two 9 3/4" d., handled plates, eleven 7 1/4" d. plates, nine cups & saucers; plain mold, decoration w/pink poppies w/tints of aqua, yellow & purple, all pieces are matching, the set... **$2,200-2,500**

Creamer & cov. sugar bowl, Ribbon & Jewel mold, single Melon Eaters decoration, pr. **$1,500-1,800**

Dresser tray, decorated w/mill scene, shaded green ground, 7 x 11" **$400-500**

Dresser tray, Icicle mold, scenic decoration, Man in the Mountain, 7 x 11 1/2" **$400-500**

Ferner, six vertical ribs, scalloped, decorated w/lilies-of-the-valley on shaded pastel ground, artist-signed, 3 7/8 x 8 1/4" .. **$300-400**

Hair receiver, cov., Mold 814, Surreal Dogwood decoration **$150-175**

Match holder w/striker, floral decoration **$100-125**

Model of a lady's slipper, embossed scrolling on instep & heel & embossed feather on one side of slipper, a dotted medallion w/roses & lily-of-the-valley on the other, shaded turquoise blue w/ fancy rim trimmed w/gold, 8" l. **$250-300**

Mug, Lily mold, Lebrun portrait decoration (no hat)...... **$200-250**

Mug, rose decoration on pink satin finish........................... **$125-175**

Mustache cup, Mold 502 .... **$250-300**

Mustard pot, cov., Mold 509a, decorated w/white flowers, glossy light green ground **$150-175**

Mustard pot, cov., Mold 521, pink rose decoration, satin finish **$200-300**

Nut bowl, footed, Point & Clover mold, decorated w/ten roses in shades of salmon, yellow & rose against a pink, green & gold lustre-finished ground, 6 1/2" d. **$150-200**

Redware

Red earthenware pottery was made in the American colonies from the late 1600s. Bowls, crocks and all types of utilitarian wares were turned out in great abundance to supplement the pewter and handmade treenware. The ready availability of the clay, the same used in making bricks and roof tiles, accounted for the vast production. The lead-glazed redware retained its reddish color, although a variety of colors could be obtained by adding various metals to the glaze. Interesting effects occurred accidentally through unsuspected impurities in the clay or uneven temperatures in the firing kiln, which sometimes resulted in streaks or mottled splotches.

Redware pottery was seldom marked by the maker.

Butter churn, ovoid form w/two sides handles, partial brown glaze, incised decoration of star punch, swag & waves in eight horizontal rows, possibly Maine, 19th c., chips, cracks & missing pieces, overall 14 1/2" h. **$2,588**

Crock, wide ovoid body w/a wide flat rim, interior brown glaze, exterior w/incised line at shoulder above stamped mark of Benjamin Dodge, Portland, Maine, 19th c., one small rim chip, 7 1/4" d., 8 1/4" h. **$1,898**

Jar, cov., ovoid body tapering to a dish rim supporting the flat cover w/knob finial, orange & green splotchy glaze, probably John Safford, Maine, 19th c., incised on base "203," 5 1/2" h. **$240**

Milk bowl, deep flat angled sides w/molded flat rim, dark brown sponged bands up the exterior & around the rim, lead- glazed, 19th c., 11" d. **$288**

Dish, deep round shape, tan-glazed & incised impressed w/tight scrolls, leaf sprigs & the monogram "BC" at the top & "1764" at the bottom, England, 10 7/8" d. **$2,115**

Salt dip, round foot & short wide stem supporting a deep rounded bowl w/flat rim, mottled brown alkaline glaze, ca. 1850, excellent condition, 2 1/4" h. **$66**

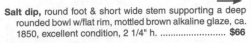

Robj Decorative Ceramics

Introduced in the early 1920s, Robj decorative ceramics, from perfume lamps and inkwells to night lights, humidors and book ends, are among today's most sought-after (and most expensive) Art Deco collectibles. Combining colorful European themes with a bright sense of whimsy, they continue to fascinate, decades after their introduction.

Unlike many recognizable names of the Art Deco era, Robj was a retailer, not a manufacturer. Founded in the early 1900s, the Parisian firm achieved its greatest acclaim in the 1920s, contracting with ceramics manufacturers in the Limoges region of France to turn out its line.

To ensure that the best designers were creating for Robj, the company held design competitions in the late 1920s; winning ceramics entered the Robj inventory. Since it was the Robj name that was being promoted, most pieces lack the name of the original designer or manufacturer. Additionally, a common Robj practice was to order ceramics in a semi-finished state. Coloring and decoration were then completed by the firm's own uncredited decorators.

Among the most recognizable Robj products are figural decanters, flasks and liqueur bottles. Since the company was only in business until 1931, this facet of its output remained largely unknown in the United States until 1933 when Prohibition ended.

Robj figural decanters feature all types of characters including French villagers, jolly monks, gendarmes and French historical figures such as Napoleon. There are also figures from other lands such as the bagpipe-toting Scotsmen (which originally held Scotch whiskey), a Robj favorite, as well as sportsmen like golfers, boxers and jockeys. Even briefcase-toting businessmen and camp followers made it into the lineup.

Collectors today love to search out these scarce items that exhibit a playfulness often missing in Art Deco Design.

Additional information on Robj is included in *Deco Décor*, a new book by Donald-Brian Johnson and Leslie Piña (Schiffer Publishing Ltd, 2009). Text for this category is by Mr. Johnson, with photos by Dr. Piña.

Decanters

Benedictine Monk, 10 1/4" h. (ILLUS. right) **$650-850**
Friar, 10 1/2" h. (ILLUS. left) **$650-850**

Boxer, long-neck decanter, 10 1/2" h. (ILLUS. left) **$500-600**
Jockey, long-neck decanter, 10 1/2" h. (ILLUS. right) **$500-600**

Attending an antique show or market is often more fun when done with friends. Save on gas by carpooling, but take a large vehicle so everyone'e purchases will fit. It's fine to split up at the market, just meet at agreed places and times. Allow time to shop at antique shops on the way home.

Caddy, 6 3/4" h. (ILLUS. right)..................... $800- 1,000
Golfer, three-piece decanter, 10 1/2" h. (ILLUS. left)
.... $1,400-1,600

Guard with Scimitar, 10 3/4" h. (ILLUS. right)
.... $1,250-1,500
Napoleon, 10 1/4" h. (ILLUS. left) $650-850

Village Lady in Apron, 10 3/4" h.
(ILLUS. right) $1,000-1,250
Village Lady in Fringed Shawl,
10 3/4" h. (ILLUS. left)
.... $1,000-1,250

Always preview items you're
interested in buying. Do not
bid on an item unless you have
inspected it, even if it's about to
be sold at what seems to be a
bargain price.

The Tamer, music box flask,
12 1/2" h. $1,750-2,000

Three Sailors ("Tres Matlelots"),
11" h. $2,000-2,250

Rogers (John) Groups

Cast plaster and terra cotta figure groups made by John Rogers of New York City in the mid- to late 19th century were highly popular in their day. Many offer charming vignettes of Victorian domestic life or events of historic or literary importance and those in good condition are prized today.

"Parting Promise," the figure of a young man about to start on a journey standing & placing an engagement ring on a young woman's finger, molded title on the front of the oval base "Provenance,"some surface chipping around base, 22" h. .. **$633**

Terra cotta is an unglazed fired pottery. It is often used for making bricks and roof tiles and for sculpting figurines. It is typically a brown to orangish color because of its iron content. Among the most well-known terra cotta figurines are the more than 8,000 Chinese terra cotta warriors made in approximately 200 B.C., which were discovered in 1974.

"Wounded to the Rear (One More Shot)," shows a standing wounded Union soldier w/his arm in a sling & a kneeling wounded soldier wrapping his leg in front, round base, uneven old finish, 23 1/2" h. **$690**

"The Council of War," President Lincoln seated reading a document & flanked by General Grant & Secretary of State Stanton, version w/Stanton wiping his glasses over Lincoln's shoulder, patent-dated 1868, some minor chips, 24" h. **$2,645**

"The Traveling Magician," an old man & a small boy seated below a raised stand w/the magician pulling a rabbit out of a top hat, a young tambourine girl asleep beside the platform, titled on the front, base marked "Patented Nov 27, 1877," some restoration w/new patina, 23" h. **$3,565**

"The Wounded Scout," a standing black man in ragged clothes supporting a wounded Union soldier, round base, some chippping & restoration, 8 1/2" d., 22 3/4" h. **$690**

Rookwood Pottery

Considered America's foremost art pottery, the Rookwood Pottery Company was established in Cincinnati, Ohio, in 1880 by Mrs. Maria Nichols Longworth Storer. To accurately record its development, each piece carried the Rookwood insignia or mark, was dated, and, if individually decorated, was usually signed by the artist. The pottery remained in Cincinnati until 1959, when it was sold to Herschede Hall Clock Company and moved to Starkville, Mississippi, where it continued in operation until 1967.

A private company is now producing a limited variety of pieces using original Rookwood molds.

Bowl-vase, footed wide squatty bulbous shape w/a short, wide neck, Standard glaze, finely painted w/creamy flying swans against a shaded brown ground, ornate pierced & scrolling silver-overlay designs w/hunting equipment up two sides & around the neck, 1892, Kataro Shirayamadani, 12" w. **$10,200**

Jug w/original stopper, wide squatty bulbous body tapering to a small neck & molded rim, small arched shoulder handle, pointed & paneled stopper, the body incised w/a repeating design of chevrons in a red, green & purple matte glaze, Shape #274Z, 1901, A.M. Valentien, 8" h. **$1,440**

Tile, advertising-type, molded w/a stylized design of rooks in a forest setting w/"Rookwood" in large letters near the bottom, glazed in rust, grey, tan, gold & cream w/black edging, Shape No. 1359, 1915, Sallie Toohey, two professionally repaired chips, 7 1/2 x 14 1/8" **$41,300**

Vase, 4 1/2" h., wide bulbous ovoid body w/a wide flat rim, Hi-glaze, decorated around the lower half w/ stylized pink & white flowers w/green leaves on brown stems, upper body in white w/a narrow streaky brown rim band, No. 931, 1931, Lorinda Epply **$520**

ROOKWOOD POTTERY

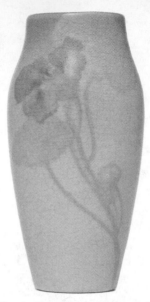

Tile, advertising-type, molded w/a stylized design of rooks in a forest setting w/"Rookwood" in large letters near the bottom, glazed in shades of dark & light blue, green & brown, Shape No. 1359, 1905, Sallie Toohey, 7 7/8 x 14 3/4" **$97,750**

Vase, 6 1/4" h., simple swelled cylindrical body, Vellum glaze, decorated w/orange nasturium blossoms on long leafy stems against a dark yellow ground, Shape 3F, 1904, Lenore Asbury, ground "X" **$600**

Vase, 7" h., bulbous ovoid shape w/a wide flat rim, incised overall w/an organic design under a mottled dark brown & green matte glaze, Shape 915D, 1919, L.N. Lincoln **$720**

Vase, 7" h., simple ovoid body tapering to a small, short cylindrical neck, Vellum glaze, decorated w/a scene of a storm at sea w/boats in shades of dark blue, grey & cream, No. 900D, 1910, Fred Rothenbusch **$1,440**

Vase, 7" h., slightly waisted cylindrical shape, Vellum glaze, a medium blue ground decorated around the base w/a band of pink & white flower clusters & stems on a dark blue ground, No. 1358E, 1925, Lenore Asbury **$1,560**

Vase, 9 1/4" h., simple ovoid body tapering to a flat rim, Black Iris glaze, a black background decorated around the upper body w/delicate maple leaves in fall colors, Shape No. 925 C, 1906, Sara Sax **$42,480**

Rose Medallion & Rose Canton

The lovely Chinese ware known as Rose Medallion was made through the past century and into the present one. It features alternating panels of people and flowers or insects, with most pieces having four medallions with a central rose or peony medallion. The ware is called Rose Canton if florals and birds or insects fill all the panels. Unless otherwise noted, our listing is for Rose Medallion ware.

Punch bowl, deep rounded sides w/colorful alternating panels of flowers & Oriental figures, late 19th c., 15" d., 6" h. **$1,668**

Punch bowl, deep rounded sides, decorated around the exterior & interior w/alternating panels featuring domestic scenes or birds in gardens, border band of alternating floral panels, w/a carved wood stand, ca. 1800, 15 1/4" d., 6 1/4" h. **$1,265**

Punch bowl, rounded deep & flaring shape, decorated inside & out w/large alternating panels of flowers & Oriental figures, second half 19th c., 11 1/2" d., 4 3/4" h. **$1,150**

Teapot, cov., small round raised foot supporting the deep rounded lower body w/a sharply angled gently angled shoulder centering the low flat mouth fitted w/a high domed cover, ornate C-scroll handle & serpentine spout, the sides & cover decorated w/ alternating panels of colorful flowers or Chinese figures, mid-19th c., 8 1/4" h. **$1,093**

Vegetable dish, cov., rectangular notched corners, the domed cover w/a large figural fruit finial & alternating panels of Chinese figures on parquet floors & bird, butterflies & flowers, small chips to interior & base rim, ca. 1880, 10 x 10 3/4", 6 3/4" h. **$920**

Vase, 25" h., traditional form w/ swelled cylindrical body tapering to a tall cylindrical neck w/a wide flattened rim, gilt figural Foo dogs & salamanders at the shoulder, decorated w/large alternating figural & flower & butterfly panels, chip on bottom of base, late 19th c. **$920**

Vase, palace-style, 35 1/2" h., 13 1/2" d., wide cylindrical body w/the rounded shoulder tapering to a large waisted neck w/a widely flaring flattened rim, the neck w/large figural Foo dog & ball handles, each side of the body & neck decorated w/large panels w/scenes of numerous people in buildings, detailed floral background & gold trim, one under rim chip, 19th c. **$2,300**

The best long-term collecting strategy is to buy an item only if you really like it, not because it is trendy. It is important to be happy with your purchase regardless of how its value fluctuates.

ROSEVILLE

Roseville

Roseville Pottery Company operated in Zanesville, Ohio, from 1898 to 1954, having been in business for six years prior to that in Muskingum County, Ohio. Art wares similar to those of Owens and Weller Potteries were produced. Items listed here are by patterns or lines.

Apple Blossom (1948)

White apple blossoms in relief on blue, green or pink ground; brown tree branch handles.

Basket, flattened fan-shaped body w/widely flaring arched rim, high round overhead branch handle, blue ground, No. 309-8", 8" h. **$175-275**

Candlesticks, footed, spherical form w/small branch handles, green ground, No. 351-2", 2" h., pr. **$92**

Wall pocket, conical w/overhead branch handle, stepped rim, green ground, No. 366-8", 8" h. **$230**

Baneda (1933)

Band of embossed pods, blossoms and leaves on green or raspberry pink ground.

Vase, 4" h., footed bulbous body w/incurved flat rim, flat shoulder handles, raspberry pink ground, No. 587-4" **$288**

Vase, 5" h., footed, pear-shaped w/small loop handles near rim, green ground, No. 601-5" (ILLUS. left) **$345**

Vase, 9" h., cylindrical w/short collared neck, handles rising from shoulder to beneath rim, green ground, No. 594-9" (ILLUS. right) **$1,150**

Vase, 12" h., expanding cylinder w/ small rim handles, green ground, No. 599-12" **$575**

Vase, 7" h., footed wide cylindrical body tapering to short wide cylindrical neck, small loop handles, raspberry pink ground, No. 592-7" **$575**

Vase, 7 1/4" h., footed, swelled cylindrical body tapering to a short, wide, cylindrical neck flanked by small down-curved loop handles, raspberry pink ground, minor glaze skips, No. 590-7" **$350-450**

Bittersweet (1940)

Orange bittersweet pods and green leaves on a grey blending to rose, yellow with terra cotta, rose with green or solid green bark-textured ground; brown branch handles.

Basket w/pointed overhead handle, asymmetrical scalloped rim, grey ground, No. 808-6", 6" h. **$115**

Bookends, handles, grey ground, No. 859, 5 1/2" h., pr......... **$144**

Coffeepot, cov., tapering bulbous base & tall body w/a flat cover w/ twig handle, long spout & long angled handle, 9 3/4" h. **$220**

Ewer, grey ground, No. 816-8", 8" h. **$173**

Planter, curved shaped sides, grey ground, No. 828-10", 10 1/2" l. $110

Tea set: cov. teapot, cov. sugar bowl & creamer, green ground, No. 871-P, S & C, 3 pcs..............$185

Wall pocket, curving conical form w/overhead handle continuing to one side, yellow ground, No. 866-7", 7 1/2" h. **$288**

ROSEVILLE

Blackberry (1933)

Band of relief clusters of blackberries with vines and ivory leaves accented in green and terra cotta on a green textured ground.

Candleholders, tapering domed base below a tall socket flanked by small open handles, No. 1086, 4 1/2" h., pr. (ILLUS. bottom left) **$748**

Console bowl, rectangular w/small handles, No. 228-10", 3 1/2 x 13" (ILLUS. top with candleholders) **$460**

Vase, 5" h., loop handles at midsection, bulbous base tapering to wide cylindrical neck, No. 570-5" (ILLUS. bottom right) **$748**

Vase, 4" h., bulbous body w/a low wide flared neck flanked by small loop handles, No. 567-4" **$400-500**

Vase, 6" h., globular w/wide low neck flanked by tiny handles, No. 574-6" **$518**

Vase, 6" h., wide flaring lower body w/a wide slightly tapering upper body flanked by small loop handles at the rim, No. 572- 6" **$431**

Vase, 8" h., handles at mid-section, slightly globular base & wide neck, No. 575-8" (bruise on one handle) **$500**

Vase, 8 1/4" h., ovoid body tapering to a short wide cylindrical neck flanked by small loop handles, No. 576-8" **$863**

Bleeding Heart (1938)

Pink blossoms and green leaves on shaded blue, green or pink ground.

Jardiniere, green ground, No. 651-6", 6" h...................... **$150- 250**

Vase, 5" h., footed trumpet-form w/ angled side handles, pink ground, No. 962-5" **$144**

Vase, 9" h., pillow-type, blue ground, No. 970-9"........................... **$300**

Bushberry (1948)

Berries and leaves on blue, green or russet bark-textured ground; brown or green branch handles.

Basket w/asymmetrical overhead handle, blue ground, No. 370-8", 8 1/2" h............................. **$259**

Ewer, cut-out rim, green ground, No. 3-15", 15" h....................... **$690**

Vase, 14 1/2" h., tall ovoid body w/ an upward pointed handle at one

side & a small downward pointed handle on the other side, blue ground, No. 39-14" **$460**

Vases, bud, 7 1/2" h., cylindrical body, asymmetrical base handles, russet ground, No. 152-7" pr. **$374**

Vase, 6" h., angular side handles, low foot, globular w/wide neck, russet ground, No. 150-0"... **$165**

Wall pocket, high-low handles, blue ground, No. 1291-8", 8" h. **$431**

ROSEVILLE

Carnelian I (1915-27)

Matte smooth glaze with a combination of two colors or two shades of the same color with the darker dripping over the lighter tone. Generally in colors of blue, pink and green.

Bowl, 9" d., 3" h., two-handled, canted sides, pink & grey, No. 164-7".................................. **$104**
Bowl, 9 1/2" d., wide squatty bulbous sides tapering sharply to a wide molded rim, deep green & light green..................................... **$69**
Candleholders, simple disk base w/incised rings at base of candle nozzle, deep green & light green, No. 1063-3", 2 1/2" h., pr...... **$110**
Ewer, footed bulbous ovoid body w/a short neck & wide arched spout, long loop handle, pink & grey, No. 1312-10", 10" h. **$259**
Plate, footed wide flattened round shape, green, 158-12", 12 1/2" d. **$300-400**
Vase, double bud, 5" h., gate-form, olive green & blue-green, No. 56-5"................................. **$115**

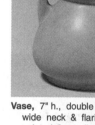

Vase, 7" h., double gourd-form w/ wide neck & flaring rim, ornate pointed & scrolled handles from mid-section of base to below rim, dark drippy moss green over pale green, ink stamp mark, No. 310-7" **$125-150**

Carnelian II (1915-31)

Intermingled colors, some with a drip effect, giving a textured surface appearance. Colors similar to Carnelian I.

Bowl, footed, six-sided, w/drip glaze in shades of rose, grey, green & tan, small separation at the rim, 4 x 15" **$330**
Candleholders, angular pyramidal base flanked by low open handles, rectangular socket, mottled pink & purple, No. 1064-3", 3 1/2" h., pr. **$173**
Urn, ornate handles, compressed globular form, intermingled shades of blue, 8" h............ **$200**
Vase, 5" h., fan-shaped body on round disk foot, scrolled handles from base to mid-section, intermingled green & pink glaze **$138**
Wall pocket, widely flaring peaked rim above a ringed neck & bullet-form base, straight handles from bottom of rim to the sides, mottled pink & purple, No. 1253-8", 8" l. **$374**

Cherry Blossom (1933)

Sprigs of cherry blossoms, green leaves and twigs with pink fence against a combed blue- green ground or creamy ivory fence against a terra cotta ground shading to dark brown.

Flowerpot, footed wide slightly flaring cylindrical shape w/small loop handles at the rim, terra cotta ground, No. 239-5", 5" h. **$288**
Jardiniere, shoulder handles, blue-green ground, No. 627-6", 6" h. **$295**
Jardiniere, two-handled, terra cotta ground, No. 627-9", 9" h...... **$750**
Jardiniere, shoulder handles, terra cotta ground, No. 627-10", 10" h. **$300**

Lamp, footed spherical vase body w/a short neck flanked by small loop handles, a low domed cap at the top for wiring, shaded yellowish green, experimental, repaired chip on base, No. 625-8", 9" h. **$863**
Urn vase, two-handled, globular w/ short collared neck, blue-green ground, 4" h........................ **$120**

Vase, 5" h., wide ovoid body tapering to a wide, slightly rolled mouth flanked by small loop handles, pink & blue ground, No. 619-5" **$375-400**
Vase, 15" h., floor-type, bulbous ovoid w/wide molded mouth, small loop shoulder handles, terra cotta to brown ground, No. 628-15" (bruise to base rim) **$1,495**

ROSEVILLE

Clemana (1934)

Stylized blossoms with embossed latticework and basketweave on blue, green or tan ground.

Vase, 6" h., footed spherical body w/a wide flat mouth flanked by small angled tab handles, blue ground, small flakes on handles, No. 280-6" (ILLUS. center) **$201**

Vase, 8 1/2" h., trumpet foot below the wide gently flaring cylindrical body flanked by small pointed handles near the base, blue ground, No. 753-8" (ILLUS. left) **$230**

Vase, 10" h., footed slightly swelled cylindrical body w/a short wide neck, small pointed shoulder handles, blue ground, No. 757-10" (ILLUS. right) **$259**

Vase, 6" h., swelled cylindrical body w/a small flat mouth, small angled handles at the shoulders, tan ground, No. 749-6" **$230**

Vase, 6 1/2" h., footed gently flaring cylindrical body w/a wide flat rim, small angled shoulder handles, green ground, No. 750-6" ... **$374**

Vase, 7 1/2" h., ovoid body tapering to a short cylindrical neck, small pointed shoulder handles, tan ground, No. 752-7" **$173**

Vase, 7" h., baluster-form body w/ wide cylindrical neck, angled shoulder handles, green ground, No. 751-7" (fleck to bottom ring) **$330**

Vase, 6 1/2" h., footed gently flaring cylindrical body w/a wide flat rim, small angled shoulder handles, green ground, No. 750-6" ... **$374**

Clematis (1944)

Clematis blossoms and heart-shaped green leaves against a vertically textured ground, white blossoms on blue, rose-pink blossoms on green and ivory blossoms on golden brown.

Basket w/high overhead handle, pedestal base, blue ground, No. 389-10", 10" h. **$150-200**

Basket, waisted cylindrical body w/a high rounded arch overhead handle w/forked ends at each side, green ground, No. 387-7" **$125**

Vase, 15" h., footed tall waisted cylindrical form w/flaring rim flanked by long pierced pointed handles, blue ground, No. 114-15" (minor base chip) **$250-350**

Vase, 12 1/2" h., tall gently swelled cylindrical body w/a flat mouth, open angled handles near the rim, blue ground, No. 112-12" **$150-200**

Vase, bud, 7" h., angular handles rising from flared base to slender neck, green ground, No. 187-7" **$150**

Vase, 6" h., two-handled, green ground, No. 102-6" ....

Columbine (1940s)

Columbine blossoms and foliage on shaded ground, yellow blossoms on blue, pink blossoms on pink shaded to green, and blue blossoms on tan shaded to green.

Basket, elaborate handle rising from midsection, tan ground, No. 365-7", 7" h. **$115**

Basket, asymmetrical overhead handle, blue ground, No. 367-10", 10" h. **$288**

Basket, pointed handle rising from flat base, ovoid w/boat-shaped top w/shaped rim, pink ground, No. 368-12", 12" h. **$335**

Console bowl, pink shading to green ground, No. 404-10", 10" l. **$150**

Jardiniere, squatty body w/small handles at shoulder, tan ground, No. 655-4", 4" h. **$115**

Rose bowl, bulbous body flanked by angled handles, wide slightly flared & shaped rim, pink ground, No. 399-4", 4" h. **$150**

Vase, 7" h., footed tall waisted form w/fanned rim, pointed angled handles at the lower body, tan ground, No. 16-7" **$115**

Vase, 4" h., ovoid body w/wide flared & shaped rim flanked by small angled handles, pink ground, No. 12-4" **$135**

Wall pocket, squared flaring mouth, conical body w/curled tip, blue ground, No. 1290-8" **$625**

ROSEVILLE

Dahlrose (1924-28)

Band of ivory daisy-like blossoms and green leaves against a mottled tan ground.

Candleholders, angular handles rising from low slightly domed base, No. 1069-3", 3" h., pr. **$150-250**

Vase, triple bud, 6" h., a domed round base w/a swelled cylindrical central shaft joined by floral panels to outcurved squared side holders, No. 76-6" **$250-300**

Vase, 6" h., cylindrical form w/small pointed handles at the shoulder, No. 363-6" **$104**

Vase, 12" h., footed wide ovoid body w/wide flaring rim, angled handles from shoulder to rim, No. 370-12" **$690**

Center bowl, 11" l., footed oval squatty bulbous body tapering to a wide flared rim, angular end handles from rim to shoulder, No. 180-8" (ILLUS. center) **$288**

Chamberstick, domed oval base w/an off- center swelled cylindrical stem flanked by asymmetrical loop handles, No. 77-7", 7 1/2" h. (ILLUS. right) **$316**

Jardiniere, bulbous slightly squatty body w/a molded rim & tiny rim handles, No. 614-7", 7" d., 4" h. (ILLUS. left) **$230**

Vase, 6" h., 8" l., flattened pillow-type, tall upright rectangular form w/small angled handles at the top ends, black paper label, No. 358-8" **$489**

Vase, 8" h., footed, bulbous lower body w/a slightly tapering upper half below the molded incurved mouth, angled handles from the rim to the shoulder, No. 367-8" **$150-200**

Dawn (1937)

Incised spidery flowers on green ground with blue-violet tinted blossoms, pink or yellow ground with blue-green blossoms, all with yellow centers.

Rose bowl, squatty spherical body w/tab handles at sides, square base, yellow ground, No. 316-6", 6" d................................. **$230**

Vase, 6" h., semi-ovoid form, tab handles at rim, square foot, pink ground, No. 827-6" **$230**

Vase, 8" h., slender cylinder w/tab handles below rim, square foot, pink ground, No. 828-8".... **$230**

ROSEVILLE

Dogwood I - Smooth (1916-19)

White dogwood blossoms & black branches against a smooth green ground.

Planter tub, oval w/upright sides, small branch handles at rim ends, 4 x 7" **$259**

Basket, wide bulbous body w/a heavy arched branch handle across the top w/forked ends, 6" h. **$288**

Basket, low widely flaring body w/ incurved rim, a high arched & pointed handle from rim to rim, w/ flower frog, 7" h. **$230**

Basket, ovoid body w/an arched & forked handle across the top, 9" h. **$316**

Vase, 8" h., ovoid body tapering to wide cylindrical neck, No. 135-8" **$230**

Dogwood II - Textured (1926)

White dogwood blossoms and brown branches against a textured green ground.

Bowl, 9" d., wide flattened squatty form w/heavy molded rim, No. 150-9" **$115**

Vase, 7 1/4" h., footed bulbous ovoid body tapering to a low wide rolled mouth, No. 301-7" **$200-275**

Falline (1933)

Curving panels topped by a semi-scallop separated by vertical pea pod decorations; blended backgrounds of tan shading to green and blue or tan shading to darker brown.

Vase, 6" h., footed, cylindrical, w/large loop handles from midsection to rim, tan shading to brown, No. 642-6" (ILLUS. right) **$633**

Vase, 6" h., globular body w/a narrow swelled shoulder below the wide short cylindrical neck, C-scroll handles from the neck to the top of the body, green - pods+ on a light shaded to dark brown ground, No. 644-6" (ILLUS. center) **$690**

Vase, 9" h., two large handles rising from midsection to neck, horizontally ribbed lower section, tan shading to blue & green, No. 652-9" (ILLUS. left) **$1,840**

Vase, 15" h., floor-type, tall ovoid body w/stepped cylindrical neck flanked by curved handles, No. 655-15" **$4,025**

Vase, 14" h., tall cylindrical body w/a flat mouth flanked by small loop handles, tan shading to green & blue, No. 654-13 1/2" **$2,990**

Careless handling at auction previews can quickly degrade the condition of many antiques and collectibles. When items are placed on tables where anyone, even children, can pick things up, damage can easily happen. Use great care when examining items and be sure to re-examine your purchases after winning them to make sure no damage took place during inspection.

ROSEVILLE

Ferella (1931)

Impressed shell design alternating with small cut-outs at top and base; mottled brown or turquoise and red glaze.

Bowl, 8" d., sharply canted sides, low foot, turquoise & red glaze, No. 211-8" (ILLUS. center) **$1,035**

Vase, 4" h., angular handles, short narrow neck, mottled brown glaze, No. 497-4" (ILLUS. left) **$500**

Vase, 4" h., angular handles, short narrow neck, turquoise & red glaze, No. 497-4" (ILLUS. right) **$546**

Vase, 6" h., handles rising from shoulder of compressed globular base to beneath the rim of the long tapering neck, mottled brown glaze, No. 502-6" (ILLUS. left)............................ **$550-750**

Vase, 6" h., bulbous base w/canted shoulder flanked by small angular handles, wide cylindrical neck, mottled brown glaze, No. 505-6" (ILLUS. right)... **$550-750**

Vase, 9" h., flaring lower body w/an angled mid-shoulder tapering to the tall flared neck, long handles from the upper neck to the shoulders, mottled brown glaze, No. 510-9" (ILLUS. center) **$1,250-1,500**

Compote, 5" d., 4" h., dome foot, turquoise & red glaze, No. 210-4" **$325**

Flower frog, turquoise & red glaze, No. 15-3 1/2", 3 1/2" h. **$125**

Urn-vase, compressed globular form w/tiny handles at midsection, reticulated foot & rim, turquoise & red glaze, No. 505-6", 6" h...**$468**

Foxglove (1940s)

Sprays of pink and white blossoms embossed against a shaded dark blue, green or pink matte- finish ground.

Ewer, wide squatty base w/a very tall tapering body w/a split neck & high arched spout, long handle from rim to top of base, pink ground, No. 6-15", 15" h...... **$500**

Vase, 7" h., semi-ovoid w/long slender angled side handles, pink ground, No. 45-7" **$230**

Basket w/circular overhead handle, footed conical body w/ widely flaring rim, pink ground, No. 374-10", 10" h. **$230**

Ewer, wide squatty body w/a wide shoulder centered by a short split neck w/long angled spout & pointed loop handle, pink ground, No. 4-6 1/2", 6 1/2" h. **$200-250**

Vase, 9" h., footed spherical body tapering to wide cylindrical neck w/flaring rim, small angled shoulder handles, green & pink ground No. 50-9" **$225-275**

Vase, 8 1/2" h., fan-shaped, handles rising from disk base to midsection, green & pink ground, No. 47-8" **$200-250**

Freesia (1945)

Trumpet-shaped blossoms and long slender green leaves against wavy impressed lines, white and lavender blossoms on blended green, white and yellow blossoms on shaded blue, or terra cotta and brown.

Ewer, footed, squatty body w/a wide shoulder tapering to a short split neck w/high arched spout, loop handle from rim to shoulder, terra cotta ground, No. 19-6", 6" h. **$104**

Vase, experimental, swelled cylindrical body w/a wide flat mouth, curved loop handles at the upper sides, pastel shaded blue to yellow ground w/pink blossoms **$4,600**

Tea set: cov. teapot No. T, creamer No.6-C & open sugar bowl No.6-C; bulbous tapering shapes, green ground, No. 6, 3 pcs. **$250-300**

Lamps, pierced brass base supporting the tall ovoid body tapering to a trumpet neck, angled loop shoulder handles, blue ground, No. 127-12", 12" h., pr. (ILLUS. of one) **$546**

Fuchsia (1939)

Coral pink fuchsia blossoms and green leaves against a background of blue shading to yellow, green shading to terra cotta, or terra cotta shading to gold.

Basket w/flower frog, a short pedestal foot supporting a wide squatty half-round body w/small half-round tabs on two sides of the incurved rim, a high round handle joining the two other edges, green ground, No. 350-8", 8" h. **$325-350**

Basket, footed inverted bell-form body w/overhead handle, terra cotta ground, No. 351-10", 10" h. **$374**

Console bowl, footed low oblong boat- shaped form w/under-rim end loop handles, blue ground, No. 353-14", 15 1/2" l. .... **$200 - 225**

Ewer, footed rounded lower body w/a wide shoulder tapering to a tall neck w/a high upright spout & long handle from rim to shoulder, terra cotta ground, No. 902-10", 10" h. **$316**

Ewer, footed rounded lower body w/a wide shoulder tapering to a tall neck w/a high upright spout & long handle from rim to shoulder, blue ground, No. 902-10", 10" h. **$345**

Jardiniere, footed spherical body w/short wide neck flanked by small angled handles, terra cotta ground, No. 645-3", 3" h. **$81**

Vase, 7" h., bulbous base tapering to flaring rim, large loop handles from shoulder to below rim, terra cotta ground, No. 895-7".... **$230**

Vase, 9" h., footed cylindrical form w/wide flaring rim & large C-form handles, green ground, No. 900-9"..................................... **$288**

Vase, 9" h., footed cylindrical form w/wide flaring rim & large C-form handles, terra cotta ground, No. 900-9"..................................... **$259**

Wall pocket, two-handled bullet shape w/fanned rim, terra cotta ground, No. 1282-8", 8 1/2" h. **$345**

Futura (1928)

Varied line with shapes ranging from Art Deco geometrics to futuristic. Matte glaze is typical although an occasional piece may be high gloss.

Vase, 7" h., nicknamed -The Bamboo Ball,+ spherical top w/large pointed dark blue & green leaves curving up the sides, resting on a gently sloped rectangular foot, shaded blue & green blue ground, No. 387-7" **$750-1,000**

Vase, 6" h., 3 1/2" d., cylindrical body swelling to wider bands at the top & base, long pierced angled handles down the sides, apricot w/green bands & handles, No. 381-6" **$403**

Vase, 14" h., 5 1/2" d., two large handles at lower half, squat stacked base & faceted squared neck, matte glaze in three shades of brown, No. 411-14" **$4,312**

Bowl, 4" h., square inverted pyramidal bowl supported between four open buttress legs on a square base, yellow speckled w/green matte glaze, No. 189-4-6"...................... **$1,265**

Candleholders, shaped square base rising to square candle nozzle, relief-molded stylized green vine & foliage on sandy beige ground, No. 1073-4", 4" h., pr. **$460**

Console bowl, cut-out base, sharply canted sides w/embossed stylized floral design, No. 196-5-6 1/2", 12" l., 5" h. **$748**

Jardiniere, flaring flat sides below the narrow angled shoulder molded w/stylized leaves & a short cylindrical neck, small squared shoulder handles, pink & lavender leaves on the grey ground, 9" d., 6" h.............. **$418**

Vase, 6" h., upright squared buttressed form, terra cotta & gold, No. 423-6", paper label **$500-600**

Vase, 8" h., upright rectangular form on rectangular foot, stepped neck, long square handles, grey & pink ground, No. 386-8" **$748**

Vase, 7" h., spherical top w/large pointed dark blue & green leaves curving up the sides, resting on a gently sloped rectangular foot, shaded blue & green blue ground, No. 387-7" (ILLUS. center) **$1,093**

Vase, 10" h., footed compressed globular base supporting long flaring squared neck w/closed rim, elongated triangular design on each side, blue & green, No. 392-10" (ILLUS. left) **$800-1,000**

Vase, 10" h., footed tall tapering ringed body w/a short flaring neck, shaded bluish green glossy glaze, No. 434-10" (ILLUS. right) **$2,760**

Wall pocket, sharply tapering sides to pointed base, wide flat mouth flanked by angular rim handles, geometric design in blue, yellow, green & lavender on brown ground, black Roseville sticker, No. 1261-8", 6" w., 8 1/4" h. **$300-400**

Gardenia (1940s)

Large white gardenia blossoms and green leaves over a textured impressed band on a shaded green, grey or tan ground.

Basket, widely flaring fan-shaped body w/high circular arched handle enclosing the body, green ground, No. 609-10", 10" h. **$175**

Bookends, green ground, No. 659, 5 1/2" h., pr. **$200-250**

Ewer, footed ovoid body tapering to a tall slender neck w/upright arched spout, loop handle from neck to shoulder, grey ground, No. 617-10", 10" h. **$175-200**

Jardiniere & pedestal base, grey ground, No. 605-8", 24 1/2" h., 2 pcs. **$920**

Jonquil (1931)

White jonquil blossoms and green leaves in relief against textured tan ground, green lining.

Strawberry jar & underplate, the body w/flat rim pierced around the top w/four projecting openings alternating w/clusters of flowers, No. 97-6", 2 pcs. **$3,105**

Jardiniere & pedestal, jardiniere No. 621- 10" & pedestal No. 621-18-10", overall 29" h........ **$1,725**

Jardiniere, bulbous form w/wide flat mouth flanked by tiny loop handles, No. 621-7", 7" d. .. **$316**

Strawberry jar, flaring cylindrical form w/wide central vase flanked on opposing sides by small tapering vases, opposing pair of handles down the other two sides, on a saucer base, No. 96-7", 7 1/4" h......................... **$633**

Vase, 6 1/2" h., wide bulbous body tapering to flat rim, C-form handles, No. 543- 6 1/2".... **$403**

Vase, 4" h., bulbous spherical form, down- turned loop handles from rim to shoulder, No. 524-4" (ILLUS. center)... **$230**

Vase, 5 1/2" h., spherical w/a wide flat rim flanked by small pointed loop handles, No. 542-5 1/2" (ILLUS. left) **$300-400**

Vase, 9 1/2" h., bulbous base tapering slightly to wide cylindrical neck, loop handles at midsection, No. 544-9" (ILLUS. right) **$805**

ROSEVILLE

Laurel (1934)

Laurel branch and berries in low relief with reeded panels at the sides. Glazed in deep yellow, green shading to cream or terra cotta.

Vase, 6" h., cylindrical w/stepped rounded shoulder flanked by low curved shoulder handles, terra cotta ground, No. 668-6" ... **$230**

Bowl, 6" d., squatty bulbous body w/incurved rim & angled shoulder handles, terra cotta ground, No. 250-6 1/4"........................... **$345**

Vase, 6" h., tapering cylinder w/wide mouth, closed angular handles at shoulder, green ground, No. 667-6".. **$259**

Vase, 7 1/4" h., tapering cylinder w/pierced angular handles at midsection, green ground, No. 671-7 1/4" **$316**

Luffa (1934)

Relief-molded ivy leaves and blossoms on shaded brown or green wavy horizontal ridges.

Jardiniere, large squatty bulbous body w/a wide flat rim flanked by tiny squared shoulder handles, brown ground, No. 631-7", 7"
.... **$288**

Vase, 6" h., tapering cylindrical body w/angled handles from shoulder to rim, green ground, No. 683-6"
.... **$230**

Vase, 6" h., tapering cylindrical body w/angled handles from shoulder to rim, brown ground, No. 683-6"
.... **$230**

Vase, 7" h., ovoid body w/small angled handles from shoulder to rim, brown ground, No. 685-7"
.... **$258**

Wall pocket, long ovoid form w/ arched & flaring rim flanked by tiny angled handles, brown ground, No. 1272-8", 8" h.
.... **$575**

Vase, 8" h., footed widely swelling ovoid body w/a wide shoulder to the short cylindrical neck flanked by low angled handles, brown ground, No. 689-8" **$345**

Vase, 8 1/2" h., ovoid body tapering slightly to a low cylindrical neck flanked by small angled handles, green ground, No. 687-8"... **$258**

Magnolia (1943)

Large white blossoms with rose centers and black stems in relief against a blue, green or tan textured ground.

Basket w/ornate overhead handle, blue ground, No. 383-7" **$230**

Ashtray, two-handled, low bowl form, tan ground, No. 28, 7" d., 2" h...................................... **$46**

Bookends, green ground, No. 13, 5 1/2" h., pr.......................... **$195**

Bowl, 10" l., two-handled, green ground, No. 450-10"............. **$145**

Candlesticks, angular handles rising from flat base to midsection of stem, blue ground, No. 1157-4 1/2", 5" h., pr...................... **$162**

Vase, experimental, bulbous nearly spherical body w/small loop handles on shoulder, shaded light blue ground w/white blossoms & brown branches **$4,025**

Vase, double bud, 4 1/2" h., gate-form, green ground, No. 186-4"
.... **$55**

Vase, 14" h., footed tall ovoid body w/angled shoulder handles, tan ground, No. 97-14" **$374**

Ming Tree (1949)

High gloss glaze in mint green, turquoise, or white is decorated with Ming branch; handles are formed from gnarled branches.

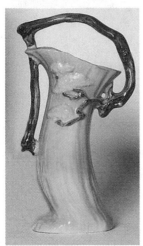

Morning Glory (1935)

Delicately colored blossoms and twining vines in white or green with blue.

Vase, 7" h., footed flattened fanned shape w/angular handles at the bottom, white ground, No. 120-7" (ILLUS. right) **$374**
Vase, 8 1/2" h., trumpet-shaped handles at base, white ground, No. 726-8" (ILLUS. left) **$600-800**
Vase, 10 1/2" h., two handles, ivory, repaired (ILLUS. center) **$700-900**

Basket w/overhead branch handle, curved body w/ asymmetrical rim, green ground, No. 510-14", 14 1/2" ... **$200-225**

Basket w/overhead branch handle, ruffled rim, white ground, No. 509-12", 13" h. **$201**
Bowl, 4 x 11 1/2", shaped sides, blue ground, No. 526-9" **$75**
Bowl, 4 x 11 1/2", shaped sides, green ground, No. 526-9" **$75**
Candleholders, squat melon-ribbed body w/angular branch handles at shoulder, blue ground, No. 551, pr. **$98**
Console set: oblong boat-form 14" l. bowl w/branch end handles, No. 528-10" & pair of candleholders, No. 551; blue ground, 3 pcs. **$180**
Ewer, white ground, No. 516-10", 10" h. **$100-150**
Planter, blue ground, No. 568-8", 4 x 8 1/2" **$125**
Vase, 8" h., asymmetrical branch handles, green ground, No. 582-8" **$110**
Vase, 6 1/2" h., single branch handle, white ground, No. 572-6" **$50-100**
Wall pocket, overhead branch handle, green ground, No. 566-8", 8 1/2" h. **$240**
Wall pocket, overhead branch handle, blue ground, No. 566-8", 8 1/2" h. **$173**

← **Vase,** 10 1/2" h., bulbous base tapering to wide molded rim, two-handled, white ground, No. 730-10" **$1,495**

Vase, 8 1/2" h., trumpet-shaped handles at base, green ground, No. 726-8" **$633**
Vase, 9" h., squatty bulbous ovoid body w/angled handles from mid-section to rim, green ground, No. 728-9" (small glaze chip to rim) **$660**
Vase, 6" h., two-handled, waisted cylinder, white ground, No. 6-6" **$375**
Vase, 7" h., tapering sides, base handles, green ground, No. 725-7" (small chips to base) **$303**

Vase, bulbous nearly spherical body tapering to a wide flat mouth, squared shoulder handles, green ground, No. 269-6, 6" h. **$575**

ROSEVILLE

Moss (1930s)

Green moss hanging over brown branch with green leaves; backgrounds are pink, ivory or tan shading to blue.

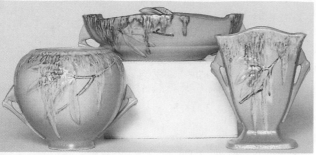

Bowl-vase, spherical body w/a wide flat mouth, small angular handles rising from base to mid-section, ivory, No. 290-6", 6" h. (ILLUS. left) **$345**

Console bowl, oval w/shaped rim & angled end handles, pink shading to green ground, No. 293-10", 10 1/2" l., 3" h. (ILLUS. center) **$259**

Vase, 7" h., flattened fan shape w/angular handles down the side, blue ground, partial foil label, No. 778-7" (ILLUS. right) **$200-250**

Vase, 6" h., footed flaring lower body below cylindrical sides, large open angular handles, pink & green ground, No. 774-6"... **$201**

Jardiniere & pedestal base, tan to blue ground, No. 635-10", 29" h., 2 pcs. **$3,738**

Panel (Rosecraft Panel 1920)

Background colors are dark green or dark brown; decorations embossed within the recessed panels are of natural or stylized floral arrangements or female nudes.

Bowl, 9" d., wide flat bottom w/ low incurved sides, pink & light green floral panels on a dark green ground, marked **$125-200**

Vase, 6" h., fan-shaped body w/wide disk foot, female nudes in panels, orange on dark brown ground **$431**

Window box, long narrow deep rectangular shape w/three panels on each long side, swirling flower & leaf design, light green on dark green ground, smal firing line on the interior, 6 x 12" **$316**

Lamp base, ovoid body on low foot, collared neck w/small squared handles, female nudes, butterscotch ground, No. X1F8, 10" h. **$1,000**

Vase, 8" h., flattened fan-shaped bowl on a short knob pedestal on flaring round foot, nudes in panels, orange on a dark brown ground **$700-800**

Vase, 8" h., two small rim handles, expanding cylinder, stylized florals, dark brown ground, No. 292-8 .... **$374**

Wall pocket, wide conical shape w/rounded end, leaves in panel, brown ground, 9" h. **$431**

Wall pocket, cylindrical w/rounded end, curved asymmetrical rim, long tan trailing leaves & berries down the front on a dark brown ground, 9" h. **$260**

Peony (1942)

Floral arrangement of white or dark yellow blossoms with green leaves on textured, shaded backgrounds in yellow with mixed green and brown, pink with blue, and solid green.

Model of a conch shell, pale yellow blossom on pink shaded to blue ground, No. 436, 9 1/2" w. **$173**

Basket, hanging-type, bulbous wide body w/a wide flat molded rim flanked by small loop handles, yellow blossoms on mixed green & brown ground, No. 467-5" **$150-250**
Wall pocket, bullet-shaped w/ widely flaring deeply ruffled rim, two side handles, white blossoms on green ground, No. 1293-8", 8" **$230**

Vase, 7 1/2" h., footed wide cylinder w/flat rim & small asymmetrical twig handles, silver foil label, minor glaze inconsistencies, brown ground, No. 704-7" **$288**

Pine Cone (1935 & 1953)

Realistic embossed brown pine cones and green pine needles on shaded blue, brown or green ground. (Pink is extremely rare.)

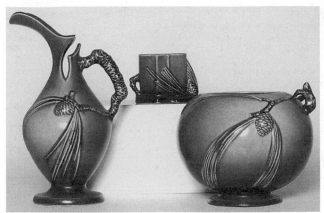

Ewer, footed ovoid body tapering to a split neck w/a high arched spout, branch handle, brown ground, No. 909-10", 10" h. (ILLUS. left)......... **$805**
Match holder, upright oval form, brown ground, No. 498, 3" h. (ILLUS. center) **$288**
Vase, 6" h., 6 1/2" d., footed spherical body w/closed rim, small branch handle at one side of rim, brown ground, No. 261-6", 6" d. (ILLUS. right) **$300-325**

Pitcher, 10 1/2" h., upright curved & fanned body w/long branch & sprig handle from rim to base, green ground, No. 485-10" **$460**
Pitcher, 9 1/2" h., ovoid body tapering to a small neck w/ pinched rim, small branch handle, blue ground, No. 708-9"... **$1,870**

Vase, bud, footed slender body w/curved sprig side handle, 7 1/2" h., green ground, No. 112-7" **$150-200**

Jardiniere, blue ground, 632-10", 10" h. **$900-1,200**

ROSEVILLE

Ashtray, blue ground, No. 25 .... **$201**

Basket, w/overhead branch handle, asymmetrical fanned & pleated body, blue ground, No. 408-6", 6 1/2" h. **$374**

Basket, long boat-shaped body w/ long arched overhead branch handle, raised on short peg feet, 12" l. **$201**

Flowerpot & saucer, brown ground, No. 633-5", 5" h. **$316**

Pitcher w/ice lip, 8" h., footed wide spherical body w/curved rim & squared spout, brown ground, No. 1321 .... **$460**

Vase, 8 1/2" h., pillow-type, wide flattened bulbous body w/ asymmetrical branch handles, green ground, No. 114-8" (ground flake on base) **$374**

Vase, 10 1/2" h., footed expanding cylinder w/wide flat mouth flanked by small twig handles, brown ground, No. 709-10".... **$400-500**

Vase, 12 1/2" h., tall tapering corseted form w/asymmetric branch handles, brown ground, No. 712-12" **$431**

Wall pocket, bucket-shaped, green ground, No. 1283-9", 9" h. **$850-950**

Wall shelf, brown ground, No. 1-5 x 8", 5" w., 8" h............. **$374**

Vase, 12 1/2" h., tall tapering corseted form w/asymmetric branch handles, green ground, w/ original gold foil sticker, No. 712-12" **$374**

Poppy (1930s)

Shaded backgrounds of blue or pink with decoration of poppy flower and green leaves.

Ewer, footed gently flaring cylindrical body w/a cut-out lip w/arched spout, C-form handle, pink ground, No. 876-10", 10" h. **$450- 550**

Vase, 10" h., two-handled, semi-ovoid, cut- out rim, pink ground, No. 875-10" **$300-400**

Vase, 15" h., footed squatty lower body tapering to tall cylindrical sides w/a flared rim, small C-scroll lower shoulder handles, grey ground, No. 878-15" **$450- 550**

Silhouette (1950)

Recessed area silhouettes nature study or female nudes. Colors are rose, orange, turquoise, tan and white with turquoise.

Basket, curved rim & asymmetrical handle, florals, orange ground, No. 710-10", 10" h. **$259**

Console set: long, narrow, footed, rectangular console bowl & a pair of short tapering candleholders; orange ground, florals, candleholders No. 751-3", bowl No. 730-10", bowl 10" l., the set **$115**

Basket, flaring cylinder w/pointed overhead handle, florals, turquoise blue, No. 708- 6", 6" h. **$173**

Vase, 7" h., fan-shaped, nude woman, orangeb ground, No. 783-7"................................ **$230**

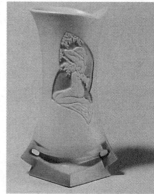

Vase, 10" h., small open handles between square base & waisted cylindrical body, shaped rim, female nudes, turquoise ground, No. 787-10" **$750-850**

ROSEVILLE

Sunflower (1930)

Tall stems support yellow sunflowers whose blooms form a repetitive band. Textured background shades from tan to dark green at base.

Bowl, 7 1/2" d., wide squatty form w/wide flat rim, No. 208-5" (ILLUS. right) **$805**
Urn-vase, nearly spherical w/closed rim flanked by tiny rim handles, 4" h. (ILLUS. left) **$575**
Vase, 9" h., bulbous base w/wide cylindrical neck, small loop handles, No. 493-9" (ILLUS. center) **$1,495**

Vase, 5" h., swelled cylindrical body w/long side handles & flat rim. No. 512-5" **$575**

Wall pocket, bucket-form w/pierced double-arch top handle, No. 1265-7", 7" h. **$1,380**

Tuscany (1928)

Marble-like finish most often found in a shiny pink, sometimes in matte grey, more rarely in a dull turquoise. Suggestion of leaves and berries, usually at the base of handles, are the only decorations.

Vase, 7" h., upright flat three-sided shape, two-handled, pink, No. 343-7" **$173**

Flower arranger vase, flaring oval foot w/ringed stem supporting a flattened urn- form body w/loop handles on the shoulder pierced w/holes, mottled pink ground, No. 69-5", 5 1/2" h...................... **$81**
Lamp, table model, upright flat three-sided vase No. 343-7" fitted on a squared gilt- metal base, pink, overall 9" h. **$150-200**

Wall pocket, conical w/wide flaring half- round ringed rim, loop handles at sides molded w/small purple grape clusters & pale green leaves, pink, No. 1254-7", 7" h. **$288**

Vase, 4" h., 6 1/2" w., bowl-form, footed widely flaring trumpet-form w/open handles from under rim to the foot, grey, No. 67-4"........ **$92**

Wall pocket, long open handles, rounded rim, mottled pink glaze, paper label, short hairline from mounting hole to rim, No. 1255-8", 8" h. **$173**

Vase, 5" h., footed wide squatty bulbous body tapering sharply to a flat mouth, loop handles from rim to shoulder, grey, No. 341-5" **$144**

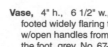

ROSEVILLE

Water Lily (1943)

Water lily and pad in various color combinations: tan to brown with yellow lily, blue with white lily, pink to green with pink lily.

Basket, trumpet-shaped w/widely flaring rim, high arched & pointed handle across the top & under the rims, pink to green ground, No. 380-8", 8" h................ **$150-200**
Basket, conch shell-shaped w/high arched handle, tan shaded to brown ground, No. 381-10", 10" h. **$288**
Console set: 14" l. bowl w/large pointed end handles, shaped sides, & pr. of 2" h. candleholders, pink shading to green ground, bowl No. 444-14", 14" l., candle- holders No. 1154-2", the set **$288**
Cookie jar, cov., angular handles, pink shading to green ground, No. 1-8", 8" h. **$403**

Ewer, squatty, flared bottom tapering to a tall split neck w/high arched spout & high pointed loop handle, tan to brown ground, No. 10-6", 6" h. **$100-125**

Wisteria (1933)

Lavender wisteria blossoms and green vines against a roughly textured brown shading to deep blue ground or brown shading to yellow and green; rarely found in only brown.

Bowl & flower frog, 6 1/2" d., 3" h., sharply flaring low rounded sides w/a closed rim, brown ground (ILLUS. center) **$374**
Bowl-vase, bulbous spherical form tapering to a small flat mouth flanked by tiny shoulder handles, brown shading to yellow & green ground, No. 632-5". 5" h. (ILLUS. right) **$450-500**
Vase, 8" h., pear-shaped body w/short cylindrical neck & tiny angled shoulder handles, brown shading to yellow & green ground, No. 636-8" (ILLUS. left) **$633**

Bowl, 6 1/2" d., 2 1/2" h., wide, low, flaring, squatty form w/a wide, closed rim, brown shaded to yellow & green ground, unmarked **$150-200**

Wincraft (1948)

Revived shapes from older lines such as Pine Cone, Bushberry, Cremona, Primrose and others. Vases with animal motifs, contemporary shapes in high gloss of blue, tan, lime and green.

Vase, 10" h., ovoid base & long cylindrical neck w/wedge-shaped closed handle on one side & long closed column-form handle on the other, shaded tan ground, No. 284-10" **$150-200**

Wall pocket, rectangular box-like holder w/horizontal ribbing & ivy leaves as rim handle, glossy light green to brown ground, No. 266- 4", 8 1/2" h. **$173**

Tea set: cov. teapot, creamer & sugar bowl; white floral decoration in relief on glossy tan ground, No. 271, 3 pcs........................... **$201**
Vase, 7" h., square, paneled sides w/swirled Art Deco style design in relief on glossy yellow and tan ground, No. 274-7"...... **$100-200**

Wisteria (1933) *(continued)*

Vase, 4" h., squatty lower body w/ small angular handles on the sharply canted upper body, brown shaded to green & yellow ground, No. 629-4" **$316**

Vase, 6 1/2" h., globular w/small flat mouth & tiny angular shoulder handles, brown to blue ground, No. 637-6 1/2" **$1,035**

Vase, 8" h., 6 1/2" d., wide, tapering, cylindrical body w/small angled handles flanking the flat rim, brown shaded to yellow & green ground, small gold sticker, No. 633-8" **$633**

Vase, 10" h., cylindrical body w/ closed rim, angled shoulder handles, brown to blue ground, silver foil Roseville label, No. 639-10" **$1,495**

Vase, 15" h., bottle-shaped w/ angular handles at shoulder, blue ground, No. 641-15" **$2,500**

Zephyr Lily (1946)

Tall lilies and slender leaves adorn swirl-textured backgrounds of Bermuda Blue, Evergreen and Sienna Tan.

Basket, footed flaring rectangular body w/upcurved rim & long asymmetrical handle, green ground, No. 394-8", 8" h. .. **$173**

Vase, 10" h., bulbous base tapering to a tall trumpet neck, low curved handles at center of the sides, terra cotta ground, No. 137-10" **$150-200**

Basket, footed cylindrical body flaring slightly to an ornate cut rim w/low wide overhead handle, blue ground, No. 395- 10", 10" h. **$230**

Tray, leaf-shaped, terra cotta ground, No. 477-12", 14 1/2" l. **$115**

Royal Bayreuth

Good china in numerous patterns and designs has been made at the Royal Bayreuth factory in Tettau, Germany, since 1794. Listings below are by the company's lines, plus miscellaneous pieces. Interest in this china remains at a peak and prices continue to rise. Pieces listed carry the company's blue mark except where noted otherwise.

Among the important reference books in this field are *Royal Bayreuth - A Collectors' Guide* and *Royal Bayreuth - A Collectors' Guide - Book II* by Mary McCaslin (see Special Contributors list).

Miscellaneous

Box, cov., shell-shaped, Little Jack Horner decoration, 5 1/2" d. **$200-250**

Candleholder, penguin decoration **$250-300**

Candlestick, decorated w/scene of cows, 4" h. **$75-100**

Candlestick, elks scene, 4" h. **$125-150**

Candlestick, figural clown, red, 4 1/2 x 6 1/2" **$500-600**

Candlestick, oblong dished base w/a standard at one edge flanked by downswept open handles, tulip-form socket w/flattened rim, interior of dished base decorated w/scene of hunter & dogs **$250-300**

Candy dish w/turned over edge, nursery rhyme scene w/Little Miss Muffet **$100-150**

Chamberstick, wide, deeply dished, round pinched sides, central cylindrical socket w/flattened rim, S-scroll handle from side of dish to socket, dark brick red ground, decorated w/"Dancing Frogs" & flying insects, rare **$1,200-1,500**

Cracker jar, cov., figural poppy, 6" h. **$600-900**

Creamer, Brittany Girl decoration **$75**

Creamer, decorated w/man in fishing boat scene **$125-175**

Creamer, figural apple **$125-150**

Creamer, figural Bird of Paradise, 3 3/4" h. **$350- 500**

Creamer, figural bull head, 4" h. **$150-200**

Creamer, figural bull, brown **$250-300**

Creamer, figural bull, grey **$250-300**

Creamer, figural butterfly, open wings **$300-400**

Creamer, figural cat handle, 4" h. **$300-400**

Creamer, figural chimpanzee, 4" h. **$250-450**

Creamer, figural clown, green, 3 1/2" h. **$300-400**

Creamer, figural clown, orange outfit, 3 5/8" h. **$350-400**

Chocolate pot, cov., tall tapering cylindrical body w/a rim spout, long gold leaf-scroll handle, inset domed cover w/knob finial, color scene of a boy w/three donkeys, 8 1/2" h. **$230**

Creamer, figural clown, red suit **$350-400**

Creamer, figural coachman, 4 1/4" h. **$250-300**

Creamer, figural cockatoo, 4" h. **$350-450**

Creamer, figural crow, black & white **$100-200**

Creamer, figural crow, black, 4 1/2" h. **$250-300**

Creamer, figural crow, black, 4 3/4" h. **$150-250**

Creamer, figural crow, brown beak **$100-150**

Creamer, figural dachshund **$200-300**

Creamer, figural eagle, grey **$250-350**

Creamer, figural elk head, shades of brown & cream, 3 1/2" d., 4 1/4" h. **$150-200**

Creamer, figural frog **$100-150**

Creamer, figural geranium, 4" h. **$400-500**

Creamer, figural girl w/pitcher, red **$600-800**

Creamer, figural grape cluster, lilac **$75-100**

Creamer, figural grape cluster, yellow, unmarked **$75-150**

Creamer, figural ibex head w/trumpet-form bowl, stirrup-type, 4 1/4" h. **$600-800**

Creamer, figural lemon ... **$150-250**

Creamer, figural leopard **$5,000-6,000**

Creamer, figural lobster **$100-150**

Creamer, figural Man of the Mountain, 3 1/2" h. **$100-150**

Creamer, figural maple leaf, 4" h. **$200-300**

Creamer, figural milk maid, red dress, 4 3/4" h. **$500-700**

Creamer, figural monk, brown, 4 1/2" h. **$500-700**

Creamer, figural monkey, brown **$350-450**

Creamer, figural monkey, green **$350-400**

Creamer, figural mountain goat **$250-300**

Creamer, figural Murex shell, colored glaze, 3 3/4" h. **$150-250**

Creamer, figural oak leaf **$150-250**

Creamer, figural oak leaf, white w/orchid highlights **$200-300**

Creamer, figural orange **$100-150**

Creamer, figural parakeet **$250-300**

Creamer, figural parakeet, green **$250-300**

Creamer, figural pig, grey **$500-600**

Creamer, figural pig, red, 4 1/4" h. **$500-600**

Creamer, figural poodle, black & white **$150-200**

Creamer, figural poppy, peach iridescent **$350-450**

Creamer, figural rooster **$300-450**

Creamer, figural Santa Claus, attached handle, red, 4 1/4" h. **$2,800-3,000**

Creamer, figural seashell, boot-shaped, 3 3/4" h. **$100-200**

Creamer, figural shell w/coral handle **$150-200**

Creamer, figural Spiky Shell, white satin finish, 4 1/4" h. **$75-125**

Creamer, figural strawberry, 3 3/4" h. **$200-250**

Pitcher, 3 1/2" h., nursery rhyme scene w/Little Boy Blue **$150-250**

Pitcher, 2" h., miniature advertising piece w/ scene of "sanatorium grounds" on front, angled handle (ILLUS. left)............. **$150-250**

Pitcher, 2" h., miniature, w/picture of Hupo bird on front, angled handle (ILLUS. right) **$250-350**

Creamer, figural trout, standing on tail, shaded brown to white w/ reddish dots **$500-700**

If interested in an item at a show of antique shop, ask the dealer about what he knows about it: its age, identifying marks, condition and if it has undergone any restoration. His response will be an indication how well he knows his subject.

Pitcher, 3 1/4" h., 2" d., decorated w/Cavalier scene, two Cavaliers drinking at a table, grey & cream ground, unmarked **$50-75**

Pitcher, 3 1/2" h., 2 1/4" d., scene of musicians, one playing bass & one w/mandolin, unmarked **$50-75**

& a long pinched spout, "tapestry" finish w/a color landscape "Don Quixote" scene **$450-600**

Pitcher, lemonade, 7 1/2 " h., figural apple **$900- 1,100**

Pitcher, milk, Cavaller musicians decoration **$100-200**

Pitcher, milk, figural lobster **$200-300**

Pitcher, milk, figural red & white parrot handle **$500-600**

Pitcher, milk, 3" h., figural shell w/ lobster handle.............. **$100-150**

Pitcher, milk, 4" h., figural St. Bernard **$400-500**

Pitcher, milk, 4 1/4" h., figural rose **$500-600**

Pitcher, milk, 4 1/2" h., figural poppy **$300-400**

Pitcher, milk, 4 1/2" h., nursery rhyme scene w/Jack & the Beanstalk **$200-300**

Pitcher, milk, 4 3/4" h., figural clown, yellow **$800- 1,000**

Pitcher, milk, 4 3/4" h., figural coachman.................... **$300-450**

Pitcher, milk, 4 3/4" h., figural cockatoo **$500-600**

Pitcher, milk, 4 3/4" h., figural eagle **$500-700**

Pitcher, milk, 4 3/4" h., figural shell w/sea horse handle **$200-350**

Pitcher, milk, 5" h., figural fish head **$400-500**

Pitcher, 5 1/4" h., figural, Santa Claus, pack on back serves as handle **$3,500-4,500**

Pitcher, 3 1/2" h., scenic decoration of Arab on horse............ **$50-100**

Pitcher, 3 3/4" h., corset-shaped, Colonial Curtsey scene w/a couple.......................... **$125-165**

Pitcher, 4 1/2" h., scene of a skiff w/ sail................................ **$75-150**

Pitcher, 5" h., double handles, scene of fisherman in boat w/sails **$100-150**

Pitcher, 5" h., figural crow **$150-200**

Pitcher, 5" h., 5" d., squatty, decorated w/hunting scene **$75-125**

Pitcher, 5 1/4" h., pinched spout, "tapestry," scene of train on bridge over raging river **$450- 550**

Pitcher, 6 3/4" h., wide ovoid body w/a flaring, lightly scalloped base

ROYAL COPLEY

Royal Copley

Royal Copley was a trade name used by the Spaulding China Company of Sebring, Ohio, during the 1940s and 1950s for a variety of ceramic figurines, planters and other decorative pieces. Similar Spaulding pieces were also produced under the trade name "Royal Windsor," or carried the Spaulding China mark.

Dime stores generally featured the Royal Copley line, with Spaulding's other lines available in more upscale outlets.

The Spaulding China Company ended production in 1957, but for the next two years other potteries finished production of its outstanding orders. Today these originally inexpensive wares are developing a dedicated collector following thanks to their whimsically appealing designs.

Advisor for this category is Donald-Brian Johnson, an author and lecturer specializing in Mid-Twentieth Century design.

Figurines

Airedale, seated, brown & white, 6 1/2" h. **$40-45**

Black Cat, 8" h. **$75-100**
Cockatoo, rose or green, 8 1/4" h., each **$45-50**
Cockatoos, 7 1/4" h. **$50-60**
Cocker Spaniel, 6 1/4" h. ... **$35-40**
Deer & Fawn, 8 1/2" h. **$60-70**
Dog pulling wagon, sitting dog, brown w/black & white spots, wagon imprinted "FLYER" on side, unmarked, 5 1/4" h. **$35-50**
Dog, 6 1/2" h. **$30-35**
Dog, 8" h. **$40-45**
Hen & Rooster, large, Royal Copley mark, 7" & 8" h., pr. **$100-130**
Hen & Rooster, Royal Windsor mark, 6 1/2" & 7" h., pr. **$120-140**
Hen & Rooster, small, Royal Copley mark, 6" & 6 1/2" h., pr. **$90-100**

Dancing lady, wearing hat & long full-skirted dress, one hand holding her hat in place while wind blows at her dress, four colorations, unmarked, 8" h., each **$135-150**

Gadwells drake & duck, Game Bird series, signed "A.D. Priollo" on base, Royal Windsor mark, series consists of Gadwells, Teals & Mallards, Gadwells & Teals are hardest to find, sizes vary, pr. (ILLUS. of drake) **$150-250**

Blackamoor Man & Blackamoor Woman, kneeling, 8 1/2" h., pr. **$100-120**

ROYAL COPLEY

Hen & rooster, black & white w/ red trim, green base, (rooster is harder to find), 5 1/2" h. & 6" h., pr. **$350-400**

Hen & rooster, black & white w/red trim, white base, 7" h. & 8" h., pr. (rooster is harder to find) **$225**

Hen & rooster, brown breast, Royal Windsor mark, 10" h. & 10 1/2" h., pr. (hens are harder to find) **$300-350**

Hen & rooster, teal breast, Royal Windsor mark, 10" h. & 10 1/4" h., pr. (hens are harder to find) **$350-400**

Hunt's Swallow, female flying toward ground, male flying upward, four colorations, some are hand-decorated, cobalt pair & females hardest to find, 8" h., pr. **$150-250**

Kitten, brown to brown grey, 8" h., each (colors hard to match) **$100-125**

Mallard Duck, 7" h............. **$40-45**
Parrots, 8" h........................ **$35-45**
Rooster, all-white, 10" h. **$129**
Sea Gulls, 8" h. **$35-55**
Swallow w/extended wings, cobalt, rose or yellow, blue is hardest, choicest & priciest coloration, 7" h., each.................. **$110-130**

Swallows on Double Stump, 7 1/2" h., pr................. **$120- 140**

Teddy bear, eyes closed & playing concertina, brown, unmarked, 7 1/2" h. (hard to find in mint condition)........................ **$90-100**

Thrushes, 6 1/2" h. **$20-25**
Titmouse, 8" h. **$25-35**
Wrens, 6 1/4" h. **$20-25**

Hen & rooster, black & white w/red trim, green base, 7" h. & 8" h., pr. **$200-225**

Kittens, black & white w/red bow at neck, sitting, one looking up & one looking down, one shown on left is harder to find, 8" h., each **$75-85**

Kingfishers, one on leaf base w/wings extended, the other flying downward, blue, rose or yellow, blue is hardest to find, rose pairs are hard to match, 5" h., pr., each **$100-150**

Dealers who set up at antiques shows sometimes remind their regular customers of an upcoming show by sending them a postcard provided by the show promoter. The card may specify that it be used for discount admission to the show. The dealer may add a personal note indicating he will be bringing a certain item that will be of interest to the customer.

One strategy at an auction is to not start the bidding or come in as the first opposing bidder. Instead wait until the initial bidding has stopped, then bid. This will surprise and discourage the previous high bidder who anticipated succeeding. The strategy changes, however, if a second person does not enter into the bidding. You must jump into the fray before the auctioneer knocks the item down to the opening bidder.

Oriental Boy & Oriental Girl, standing, 7 1/2" h., pr. **$35-55**

Spaniel Pup with Collar, 6" h. **$40-45**

Planters

Angel on Star, white relief figure on creamy yellow ground, 6 3/4" h.
.... **$30-40**

Angel, large, kneeling, blue robe, 8" h. **$70-85**

Doe & Fawn Head, rectangular log-form planter, 5 1/4" h. **$50-60**

Dog with Raised Paw, 7 1/2" h.
.... **$70-80**

Dog in Picnic Basket, 7 3/4" h.
.... **$80-90**

Clown, 8 1/4" h. **$120-145**

Apple and Finch, 6 1/2" h... **$50-60**
Balinese Girl, 8 1/2" h......... **$50-60**
Bare Shoulder Lady head vase, 6" h. **$70-80**
Big Hat Chinese Boy & Girl, 7 1/2" h., pr..................... **$50-60**
Birdhouse with Bird, 8" h. **$150-175**
Cat & Cello, rare, 7 1/2" h. **$150-175**
Dog with String Bass, rare, 7" h. **$175-200**
Gazelle, 9" h....................... **$60-70**
Gloved Lady, 6" h. **$80-90**
Indian Boy & Drum, 6 1/2" h. **$50-60**

Elf and Shoe, 6" h. **$60-70**

Fancy Finch on Tree Stump, red, white & black bird perched on brown leafy branch beside white planter, 7 1/2" h. **$90-100**

Girl on Wheelbarrow, 7" h. →
.... **$50-55**

Horse Head with Flying Mane, 8" h. $35-55

Hummingbird on flower, blue or red & white bird, red flower, green leaves form base, blue bird brings higher price, 5 1/4" h. (ILLUS. left) **$50-75**

Wall pocket, figural, "Pigtail Girl," bust of girl w/ruffled collar & bonnet, grey, deep red, turquoise, pink & deep blue, marked "Royal Copley," deep red & blue are the most desired & therefore harder to find & costlier, 7" h., each (ILLUS. right) **$75-125**

Kitten and Book, 6 1/2" h. $45-55

Palomino Horse Head, 6 1/4" h. $50-60

Ribbed Star, all-white, "Royal Windsor" sticker, 4 3/4" h. $35-40

Kitten on Cowboy Boot, 7 1/2" h. $65-70

Pigtail Girl, 7" h................... $50-55

Ram's Head, also used as book ends, planter $55

Running Horse, design on one side, 6" h.................................. $35-55

Poodle, reclining, white w/black nose & eyes, 8" l. $80-90

Rooster on wheelbarrow, 8" h. $100-125

In cataloged auctions, bidding increments are often stated in the conditions of the sale. Otherwise, auctioneers set bidding increments as they sell each item. When there is keen interest in a lot, the auctioneer may choose to increase the increment as the bidding progresses, e.g. upping the bid by $100 instead of raising it $50 each time.

ROYAL COPLEY

Siamese cats, two, one sitting & one recumbent, white w/black trim, blue eyes, green or rust woven basket, green is more desirable, 8" h., each **$175-200**

Tanagers, 6 1/4" h.............. **$30-40**
Teddy Bear in Picnic Basket, 8" h. **$80-100**
Teddy bear w/basket on back, brown w/blue, pink or yellow basket, runners on bottom, unmarked, 6 1/4" h., each **$65-75**
Teddy Bear with Mandolin, 6 3/4" h........................... **$60-85**
Wide Brim Hat Boy & Wide Brim Hat Girl, 7 1/4" h., pr... **$100-110**
Woodpeckers, 6 1/4" h....... **$30-40**
Wren on Tree Stump, 6 1/4" h. **$40-50**

Smart buying at auctions takes self-control. Establish a maximum amount you are willing to pay for a particular lot in advance and do not exceed it.

Stuffed Animal Dog, white & brown, 5 1/2" h. **$70-80**

Stuffed Animal Rooster, pale green & white, 6" h. **$80-90**

Tony Head, man wearing large blue hat, 8 1/4" h. **$60-85**

Stuffed Animal Elephant, pale green & white, 6 1/2" h. **$90-100**

Teddy Bear with Concertina, rare, 7 1/4" h. **$120-145**

Regular customers of antique malls know when dealers restock their showcases and displays with fresh merchandise. Some dealers restock every Monday following weekend auctions. Others wait until the end of the month to restock because that is when they come in to pick up their checks for items sold. To get first pick on fresh antiques, try to be at the mall when the best dealers restock their inventory.

Bank, Teddy bear, white w/black & gold trim, red bow at neck, two small holes in bottom, bank must be broken to retrieve money, 7 1/4" h. (ILLUS. left) **$175-200**
Teddy bear, white w/black trim & red bow at neck, 6 1/4" h. (ILLUS. right).............................. **$45-55**
Teddy bear, white w/black trim & red bow at neck, 8" h. (ILLUS. of two center) **$75-85**

Miscellaneous

Ashtray, heart-shaped w/two love birds sitting at top of heart, signed "Royal Copley," rose w/blue or yellow w/blue, 5 1/2", each **$35-50**

Ashtray, Leaf, 5" l **$15-20**

Bank, Teddy bear, brown, two small holes in bottom, bank must be broken to retrieve money, 7 1/2" h. **$150-160**

Coasters, Antique Autos, 4 5/8" d., set of 4 .... **$140- 160**

Creamer & sugar bowl, w/leaf handles, yellow & brown, grey & pink or tricolored, marked "Royal Copley" on bottom, tricolored & grey & pink are equally hard to find, 3" h., pr., each set ... **$50-75**

Lamp base, Birds in the Bower, 8" h. **$60-75**

Lamp base, Pig, decorated w/pink or blue stripes, factory-drilled on top & bottom, unmarked, extremely hard to find, pink is easier to locate, 6 1/2" h., each **$200-225**

Ashtray, Leaping Salmon, oblong boat- shaped bowl w/figural salmon on rim, 5 x 6 1/4" **$35-45**

Bank, Pig, standing & smiling, two small holes in bottom, printing on the front, bank must be broken to retrieve money, 4 1/2" h. ... **$35-50**

Bank, Bow Tie Pig, standing, wearing green bow tie & blue outfit, 6 1/4" h. **$85-95**

Bank, Pig, "Farmer Pig," standing & wearing neck scarf, brown w/tan scarf, pink w/blue scarf, blue w/ green scarf & brown & green w/ brown scarf, two small holes in bottom, bank must be broken to retrieve money, brown w/green scarf is hardest to find, pink is most desirable color, 5 1/2" h., each **$75-125**

Blade bank, Barber Pole in red & white w/"Blades" on the side, 6 1/4" h. **$80-90**

Bank, Rooster, one, two, three or four small holes in bottom, bank must be broken to retrieve money, three colorations available, 7 1/2" h., each (ILLUS. of two) **$75-85**

When a bidder does not wish to increase the bid by a full increment, he may signal his intentions to the auctioneer to increase the bid by a half increment. This is done by the bidder placing the fingertips of one hand to the palm of the other hand, similar to the "time-out" signal in basketball, or by moving one hand horizontally across his throat. If the auctioneer recognizes and accepts the bid, the competing bidder or bidders will be afforded the same consideration.

ROYAL COPLEY

Collectors are conscious of the idea of antiques as investments, but it should never be the driving force. The greatest benefit of collecting should be enjoyment, from the thrill of the hunt to learning more about their history. Acquire the highest quality pieces you can afford, learn as much as you can, stay focused, and someday your diligence may be rewarded.

Lamp base, Dog, Cocker Spaniel, sitting in begging position, brown or black, black is more rare than brown, 10" h. **$125-150**

Vase, 6" h., upright rectangular form w/flaring serpentine rim, dark blue centered by a large white panel decorated w/wedding bells & bluebirds & "Happy Anniversary" in gold **$60-70**

Wall pocket, Island Man, black head wearing white turban, 8" h. **$150-170**

Pitcher, Floral Beauty, 8" h. **$80-95**
Pitcher, 8" h., Pome Fruit patt., stamped or incised "Royal Copley" on bottom, five colorations, each (blue is most popular & priciest) **$80-95**
Smoking set, Ducks, 3" & 4" h., 3 pcs. **$70-85**
Vase, bud, Warbler, 5" h. **$25-30**
Vase, cylindrical, "Baby Congratulations" decal, 8" h. **$60-70**
Vase, footed, Dragon, 5 1/2" h. **$25-30**
Vase, 5 3/4" h., Fish, open center **$55-70**
Vase, 6 1/4" h., footed pillow-shape, ivy decoration **$25-30**
Vase, 7" h., Carol's Corsage **$30-40**
Vase, 7 1/4" h., Deer, open center **$40-45**
Vase, 7 1/4" h., Flying Bird, open center **$55-60**

Vase, 8 1/4" h., Dogwood.... **$35-45**
Vase, 8 1/2" h., figural, model of mare nuzzling her foal, signed "Royal Copley," medium rusty brown **$35-50**
Vase, 10" h., pink & green floral decal decoration on butterscotch or white ground, three distinct classic styles, marked "Spaulding" in gold on underside, each (collectors prefer butterscotch finish)............................ **$75-100**
Vases, 8 1/4" h., cornucopia-shaped w/decal decoration, pr. **$60-70**
Wall plaque-planters, Hen & Rooster, 6 3/4" h., pr.... **$140-170**
Wall plaque/planter, Fruit Plate, 6 3/4" d. **$60-75**
Wall plaque/planter, Straw Hat with Flowers, 7" d. **$50-60**
Wall pocket, Dancing Lady, 8" h. **$175-200**
Wall pocket, Pirate, 8" h. **$70-80**

Wall pocket, Salt Box, 5 1/2" h. **$70-80**
Wall pocket, Spice Box, 5 1/2" h. **$90-100**
Wall pocket, Straw Hat, large, 7" h. **$85-95**
Wall pocket, model of rooster, full figure walking bird, black & white w/green background or brown w/green background, signed "Royal Copley," 5 1/2" h., each (black & white version is more prized by collectors) **$45-60**
Wall pocket, figural, full face pirate head w/ruddy complexion, grey or red bandanna, signed "Royal Copley," 8" h., each........ **$45-60**
Wall pockets, figural, head of old man & old woman w/grey hair & old-style hat, deep rose & miscellaneous other colors, signed "Royal Copley," 8" h., each pr. **$80-100**

Much like a preemptive bid, jumping the bid by more than the increment is a way of gaining the upper hand and discouraging competitors. When two bidders are competing by increments of $25, one may say, "three-hundred," when the auctioneer was calling for $225. The sudden jump may discourage the competitor from continuing and anyone else from joining the bidding.

Royal Dux

This factory in Bohemia was noted for the figural porcelain wares in the Art Nouveau style it exported around the turn of the 20th century. Other notable figural pieces were produced through the 1930s. The factory was nationalized after World War II.

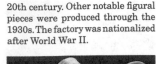

Center bowl, figural, the wave-molded foot supporting two figural maidens in gold dresses clinging to the edge of the large shell-shaped bowl w/a gold exterior, another maiden in gold seated on the edge of the bowl holding a musical instrument, 12" w., 15" h. **$1,495**

Figure group, two shepherds, the man sitting on rock w/legs crossed & about to blow into primitive pipe, the woman standing next to him holding crook, polychrome decoration in shades of buff, applied pink triangle mark, early 20th c., 21 1/2" h. **$1,035**

Figure group, young hunter wearing primitive tunic & sandals, carrying quiver & laden w/dead fowl embraces young barefoot woman, polychrome decoration in olive greens & buffs, applied pink triangle mark, first half 20th c., 22" h. **$1,150**

Figure of woman, w/h.p. features, wearing turban-style headdress & olive green tunic w/sleeves rolled up above elbows, holding water jar in each hand, a mug hanging from her sash belt, on base decorated w/leaves, applied pink triangle mark, first half 20th c., 23" h. **$920**

Figure of woman, sitting on rock-form base & reading book, wearing off-the-shoulder reddish brown top & draping long olive green skirt, applied pink triangle mark, first half 20th c., 19" h. **$1,093**

Figure of boy on donkey, the boy wearing apricot trousers & matching brimmed hat & pale olive shirt, bare feet, sitting astride saddled white donkey, both looking to side, applied pink triangle mark, first half 20th c., 14 1/4" h. **$518**

ROYAL DUX

Figures of shepherds, the young woman standing w/lamb, the young man w/goat, each w/h.p. features & wearing apricot & pale olive green clothes, each on paneled base, applied pink triangle mark, first half 20th c., 20 1/2" h., pr. **$1,725**

Figures of shepherds, w/h.p. features, the young woman wearing apricot dress & pale olive turban-style headdress, holding kid in her arms, w/two other kids at her feet, the young man wearing short apricot tunic w/sheepskin & green hat, holding panpipe as if about to play, two lambs at his feet, each on oval base, applied pink triangle mark, mid-20th c., 17" h., pr. **$1,955**

Figures of water carriers, the young man wearing apricot turban-style headdress & pale olive tunic belted w/apricot sash, holding large handled earthenware jar in both hands as if pouring contents out, the young woman wearing a pale pink veil-type headdress & pale olive gown w/apricot sash, holding handle of earthenware jar on ground at her feet, each on oval base w/pale pink floral trim, applied pink triangle mark, early 20th c., 20" h., pr. **$1,265**

Figures of woman & man, the woman wearing mid-calf-length apricot dress & pale olive short-sleeved blouse, the man wearing apricot trousers & matching brimmed hat & pale olive long-sleeved shirt, each w/one hand on hip, the other steadying a large empty basket on shoulder, each on oval base, applied pink triangle marks, first half 20th c., 16" h., pr. **$805**

Figures of women, wearing classical dress in shades of olive green & pale pink & peach, one posed as if playing cymbals, the other arching back as if dancing, holding hem of gown out in dramatic pose, each on oval bases trimmed w/scroll design, applied pink triangle mark, early 20th c., some minor professional repair, 22" h., pr. **$1,610**

Vases, 19" h., Art Nouveau style, tall ovoid body on a squared foot, molded in bold relief w/undulating foliage & fruit, the ivory ground highlighted w/dark gold, pink triangle mark, early 20th c., bases drilled for lamp adaptation, pr. **$1,380**

Royal Vienna

The second factory in Europe to make hard paste porcelain was established in Vienna in 1719 by Claud Innocentius de Paquier. The factory underwent various changes of administration through the years and finally closed in 1865. Since then, however, the porcelain has been reproduced by various factories in Austria and Germany, many of which have also reproduced the early beehive mark. Early pieces, naturally, bring far higher prices than the later ones or the reproductions.

Plate, 9 5/8" d., portrait-type, Art Nouveau taste, the center painted w/a bust profile of a lovely young brunette maiden wearing an off-the-shoulder robe, the wide gently scalloped border in pale green accented with deep maroon reserves decorated overall w/ornate gold scrolls, flowers & spider webs, artist-signed, titled in German on the back, impressed crowned "PF" mark, late 19th - early 20th c. ... **$1,800**

Ewer & undertray, the ewer w/ a domed foot & ringed stem supporting the tall ovoid body tapering to a divided mouth w/a high arched & pointed spout, a high arched gold handle from rim to center of side, ruby & gold ground, h.,p. w/a continuous scene of Roman & Renaissance figures gathered before a pyre worshipping, discussing & destroying art, reserved on a gilt ground decorated w/raised gilt grasses, titled under the base in German, within borders of fruiting vine & scrolling leaves, the ruby ground matching round undertray decorated w/ornate acanthus leaf scrolls within blue & gilt borders, blue Beehive mark, artist-signed, late 19th c., overall 17 3/4" h., 2 pr. (ILLUS. center with pair of covered vases) **$2,880**

Plate, 9 1/2" d., cabinet-type, a central color bust portrait of Marie Antoinette, signed by Wagner, the cobalt blue border band ornately decorated w/gold panels, scrolls & florals **$1,150**

Plate, 9 1/2" d., cabinet-type, the center w/a finely painted bust portrait of a Renaissance era noblewoman w/a feathered headdress, the cobalt blue border band ornately decorated w/undulating panels of fancy florals, mounted in a deep gilt-wood shadowbox frame lined in deep red velvet, overall 16" sq. **$1,725**

Tray, oval, the center h.p. w/a large rectangular panel showing a classical view allegorical of the Triumph of the Arts & Science, depicted as a gathering of classical figures supporting emblems of knowledge, attended by putti among clouds, supporting white classical portrait roundels, the outer dark green ground ornately decorated w/leafy scrolls & trellis, artist-signed, blue Beehive mark, late 19th c., 16 1/2" l. **$3,120**

ROYAL VIENNA

Urn, cover & stand, the domed stand on shaped gold tab feet & a gold border, the cobalt blue ground ornately decorated w/overall bands of delicate floral vines centering a round reserve h.p. in color w/a scene of a Greek god & goddess, the urn w/a tapering pedestal below the wide urn-form body, cobalt blue ground decorated overall w/gold bands & ornate delicate leafy vines, a large central oval reserve h.p. in color w/a group of Greek gods & goddesses, long angled gold handles flanking the shoulder & the tapering domed cover w/a pointed gold finial & h.p. w/another color reserve, late 19th - early 20th c., overall 21 1/4" h., the set **$5,581**

Vase, 5" h., ovoid body tapering to a slender neck w/a flaring rim, gilt openwork vine- like gold handles from the center neck to shoulder, a large gold oval enclosing a color portrait of a young maiden w/brown hair, background in pale shaded green w/ornate gilt decoration, artist-signed, marked on the base "Germany - Sincerity - 3666," tiny flat nick on the rim **$575**

Vase, 7" h., footed bulbous base tapering to a tall slender cylindrical body w/a bulbed forked mouth, gold ruffled loop handles on center of the blue neck trimmed w/gilt florals & a Greek key band, the main body decorated w/a color scene of a young maiden seated looking at a pair of doves w/a cherub by her side, artist- signed, blue Beehive mark on the base **$863**

Vase, 10" h., tapering cylindrical body w/an angled shoulder to the small flaring neck, iridescent lavender ground w/a tall oval reserve decorated w/ an allegorical scene of Love, a winged Cupid arranging roses in the dark hair of a standing classical young woman in a garden setting, the sides & shoulder ornately decorated w/delicate beaded gold trellis & leafy scroll designs, blue Beehive mark, artist-signed, titled on the bottom, late 19th - early 20th c. **$2,640**

Vases, 7 5/8" h., tall slightly tapering squared body w/a rounded shoulder & short cylindrical neck w/rolled rim, short gold scroll handles from rim to shoulder, ruby ground, each centered by an oval reserve h.p. w/a color bust portrait of Napoleon or Josephine, each within a raised gold border below a trellis & diaper cartouche, the back decorated w/an octagonal turquoise 'jeweled' panel of scrolling leaves above ribbon-tied floral garlands, red Beehive mark, early 20th c., pr. **$3,360**

Royal Worcester

This porcelain has been made by the Royal Worcester Porcelain Co. at Worcester, England, from 1862 to the present. Royal Worcester is distinguished from wares made at Worcester between 1751 and 1862, which are referred to only as Worcester by collectors.

Ewer, a small rounded pedestal base supporting the large ovoid body tapering to a tall slender neck w/a long upright & arched spout, ornate scroll & leaf handle, ivory ground decorated around the sides w/a fancy gold floral swag design w/further gold on the neck, handle & base, ca. 1899, 13 1/4" h. **$382**

Figures, modeled as Kate Greenaway-style young man & maiden each holding a basket, a tree trunk base behind each, decorated in shades of green, blue, brown & gold, Shape No. 880, printed mark, ca. 1890, 9 3/4" h., pr. **$588**

Figures, a male & female Middle Eastern water carrier, she standing w/a jar on her shoulder pouring into a large bowl below, he standing while holding a jar in one hand & pouring into a large bowl below, each decorated in green, tan & gold on an ivory ground, modeled by James Hadley, Shape No. 594, ca. 1891, artist-signed & printed marks, each w/gilt wear, one liner w/rim chip, 17" & 17 3/4" h., pr. .. **$881**

Vase, 6 5/8" h., footed spherical reticulated body tapering to a slender, ringed reticulated neck w/gold trim & a flaring top, long scrolled serpent handles trimmed in gold from the neck to the shoulders, glazed in pale blue & buff & trimmed w/raised gilt dots, Shape No. 871, attributed to George Owen, ca. 1900, printed mark **$31,725**

Figures, a standing male & female in peasant costume, she holding a small keg & he holding a scythe, a tree trunk vase behind each, the old ivory ground decorated in shades of gold, tan, green & red, modeled by James Hadley, ca. 1888, printed & impressed marks, 13 3/4" & 14" h., pr. **$999**

Plate, 7 7/8" d., the wide reticulated sides w/a honeycomb design in blue trimmed w/gold dots, a narrow outer & inner solid band in pink w/white & turquoise jeweling, the solid center w/a lightly embossed gilt landscape, printed mark, attributed to George Owen, dated 1882 .... **$16,450**

George Owen (1845 - 1917) was an expert at piercing, the art of hand-cutting tiny holes in damp clay to form an intricate design.

Tea set: cov. teapot, open sugar bowl, creamer & cup & saucer; each w/ a gilt rim & raised gilt dots to a blue glazed honeycomb pierced body, white & turquoise jeweled borders over pink bands, printed & raised marks, attributed to George Owen, dated 1878, teapot 4 1/2" h., the set **$28,200**

Vase, 9" h., a low round reticulated foot supporting the large spherical reticulated body tapering to an ornately pierced tall slender trumpet neck, ornate red-stained male mask head handles on the shoulder, gilt decoration w/large pierced medallions on a wide pale blue center band, Shape No. 1552, attributed to George Owen, dated 1894, printed mark **$30,500**

Vases, 4 1/4" h., spherical finely reticulated body w/blue glazed honeycomb bands flanking a buff-stained band, raised on a lobed flaring foot w/gold trim, the solid shoulder molded w/four lug handles w/gold trim, flaring & ringed cylindrical neck w/gold trim, attributed by George Owen, Shape No. 1257, printed marks, ca. 1891, pr. **$15,250**

Vases, 6 3/4" h., gently swelled cylindrical reticulated body tapering to a short cylindrical gold neck, a pierced central unique band w/a unique pierced design flanked by finer honeycomb bands in pale blue w/gilt jeweling, upper & lower border bands enameled & jeweled w/a zig-zag design, attributed to George Owen, dated 1892, printed mark, pr. **$21,150**

Vase, 10 3/8" h., a small pedestal foot supporting the large spherical body w/a tall slender waisted neck, ivory ground w/polychrome enamel floral bouquet on the side, bordered in translucent bluish grey, printed mark, ca. 1900, missing cover, gilt rim wear **$147**

Russel Wright Designs

The innovative dinnerware designed by Russel Wright and produced by various companies beginning in the late 1930s was an immediate success with a society that was turning to a more casual and informal lifestyle. His designs, with their flowing lines and unconventional shapes, were produced in many different colors, which allowed a hostess to arrange creative tables.

Although not antique, these designs, which we list here by line and manufacturer, are highly collectible. In addition to dinnerwares, Wright was also known as a trendsetter in the design of furniture, glassware, lamps, fabric and a multitude of other household goods.

American Modern (Steubenville Pottery Co.)

Coffeepot, cov., after dinner, black chutney w/chartreuse cover $100-135

Coffeepot, cov., chartreuse .... $225+

Teapot, cov., white $110-135

Modern Hostess plate & cup, white, pr............................. $150

Casual China (Iroquois China Co.)

Teapot, cov., redesigned, mustard gold, mid-1950s $250-350

Pitcher, redesigned, mustard gold $400- 500

Coffeepot, cov., oyster grey (ILLUS. right).... $225
Creamer, family-style, oyster grey (ILLUS. left) $55
Pitcher, redesigned, ripe apricot (ILLUS. center) $200

SATSUMA

Satsuma

These decorated wares have been produced in Japan since the end of the 18th century. The early pieces are scarce and high-priced. Later Satsuma wares are plentiful and, with prices rising, are also becoming highly collectible.

Jar, cov., bulbous ovoid body w/ the shoulder tapering to a short rolled neck & domed cover w/a gold pointed button finial, the sides h.p. w/a wide continuous band showing scenes of children involved in various activities, pink shoulder & cover decorated w/ornate cloud designs w/gold trim, late 19th - early 20th c., unmarked, 6" h. **$403**

Teapot, cov., footed squatty spherical body w/a wide shoulder centered by a tall cylindrical neck fitted w/a small domed cover, a long gold dragon wrapped around the base of the neck w/the neck & head forming the spout & the arched tail forming the handle, the creamy background h.p. w/exotic birds among colorful flowering plants in shades of red, blue, white & purple w/heavy gold trim, black & gold chop mark on the base, late 19th - early 20th c., 6 3/4" h. **$1,006**

Vase, 9 1/4" h., a flared round foot w/gold geometric bands below the large bulbous ovoid body w/a flat closed rim flanked by gold lion head & ring shoulder handles, the sides h.p. w/large oval panels filled w/Geisha wearing gold-trimmed robes in a landscape w/a lake & trees in the distance, the other side w/an oval panel decorated w/Rakans, signed, raised on an ornate high squared & footed bronze stand, late 19th c. (ILLUS. of vase & stand) **$588**

Vase, 24" h., 12" d., tall baluster shape /a flat upright neck rim in gold, the ornately decorated w/a Japanese figure, the back w/a group of three Japanese samurai, heavily trimmed w/gold, late 19th - early 20th c. **$510**

Vase, 16 1/4" h., a large ovoid body tapering to a wide trumpet neck, a decorative gold base band, the sides h.p. w/wide deep orange ground decorated w/large h.p. flowering peony trees & butterflies in white, gold, brown & light blue, the shoulders w/a gold molded drapery design, the neck decorated w/a band of large gold Mon emblems below a narrow paneled rim band, ca. 1900 .... **$441**

Schoop (Hedi) Art Creations

Hedi Schoop (1906-1996) was one of the most popular (and most imitated) California ceramic artists of the 1940s and '50s. Born in Switzerland, Schoop spent her early years studying sculpture, fashion design and acting. With her husband, famed movie composer, Frederick Hollander, she fled Nazi Germany in the early 1930s, settling in Hollywood, where his career flourished.

In her new environment, Schoop amused herself by creating plaster dolls, which she then painted and dressed in fashions of the day. A successful showing of the dolls at a Los Angeles department store prompted her to adapt these ideas to a more permanent medium: ceramics. Early slip-cast figures sold well from Schoop's small workshop, and a larger, North Hollywood facility, "Hedi Schoop Art Creations," opened in 1940.

Schoop designed and modeled most of the figurines released by her company, and many came equipped for secondary uses -- from flower holders and wall pockets to candlesticks and soap dishes. She was perhaps the most commercially successful California ceramics designer of the postwar period, and certainly the most ubiquitous. If a Schoop figure proved popular with consumers, an entire line of accompanying decor objects, such as planters, bowls, ashtrays and candy dishes, would be built around it. At its busiest in the late 1940s, the studio produced over 30,000 giftware items per year and employed over fifty workers.

Hedi Schoop figurines are largely representational and achieve their visual impact through overall shape and size rather than through minute detailing. The figures are often caught in motion - arms extended, skirts aflutter, heads bowed - but that motion is fluid and unhurried. Rough and incised textures combine with smooth ones; colorful glossy glazes contrast with bisque. Her subjects - ethnic dancers, musicians, peasant boys and girls - are captured at a specific moment in time. A figurine by Hedi Schoop is a captivating still photo.

The broadly drawn features, soft colors, and rippling garments of Schoop's oversize figurines and planters unfortunately made them easy to copy. During the height of her career similar designs were turned out by a variety of other California ceramics firms, usually run by former Schoop employees. The most persistent was one-time Schoop decorator Katherine Schueftan (Kay McHugh). These ceramics, marked "Kaye Figurines," and later "Kim Ward," resulted in a 1942 court injunction prohibiting copying of the Schoop line. Schueftan resurfaced in 1945 with a new line, Kaye of Hollywood," featuring less Schoop-like figures. No further court action is reported.

Due to look-alike stylings by the numerous Schoop competitors, signature identification is an important means of object verification. While some pieces carried paper labels, most featured stamped or incised signatures, often with the additional words "Hollywood, Cal." or "California."

The Schoop factory was destroyed by fire in 1958. After collaborating for a time with The California Cleminsons, popular creators of decorative kitchenwares, Schoop retired from ceramic design, focusing instead on painting - but her glamorous legacy lives on.

Advisor for this category is Donald-Brian Johnson, an author and lecturer specializing in Mid-Twentieth century design. Photos are by his frequent collaborator, Leslie Piña.

Flowerpot, floral decoration, 7 3/4" d., 7 1/2" h.............. **$25-50**

Model of cat lying down, head up, tail wrapped around side, paws tucked under body, brown collar around neck w/two yellow bells & two small brown pots attached, white rough textured body, inkstamp under glaze, "Hedi Schoop Hollywood, Cal.," 6 3/4" l., 6 1/2" h. **$157**

Planter, figure of a girl reading, green glaze, 9" h. **$75-100**

Planter, figure of a windswept lady squatting & holding a basket, 11" h. **$175- 200**

Planter, "Marguerita," figure of a girl in a black dress w/white planter basket on her head, 12 1/2" h. **$75-100**

Planter, model of a fan shell, 11 1/2" l. **$50-75**

Planter, model of a horse, brown & white glaze, 7 3/8" h.... **$125-150**

Planter, model of a horse, rough textured mane & tail, white glossy glazed body w/mint green face accents, saddle, bows in assorted areas & scalloped edging at the base, inkstamp mark "Hedi Schoop," 7 1/2" h. **$126**

Flower holder, figure of woman w/brown hair dressed in pale blue dress w/white textured hem & short puff sleeves, pink rose applied at waist, one hand holds basket on head, other hand holds skirt out to side, creating opening for flowers, inkstamp underglaze "Hedi Schoop, Hollywood, Cal.," 12 3/4" h. **$227**

Jardiniere, cylindrical, incised stylized design of a kneeling Chinese woman w/Ming trees & animals, base & design in gold glaze on a light green body, 7" h. **$148**

Planter, "Tyrolean Girl," 11 1/2" h. **$75-100**

Planters, "My Sister & I," figure of a Dutch boy & Dutch girl carrying baskets, 11" h., pr. **$200-225**

Plaque, African woman, 7 1/2 x 11" **$100-125**

Plate, grey cat w/blue eyes, 7 1/2" sq. **$75-100**

Plate, white cat in a garden, 7 1/2" sq. **$75-100**

Sèvres & Sèvres-Style

Some of the most desirable porcelain ever produced was made at the Sèvres factory, originally established at Vincennes, France, and transferred, through permission of Madame de Pompadour, to Sèvres as the Royal Manufactory about the middle of the 18th century. King Louis XV took sole responsibility for the works in 1759, when production of hard paste wares began. Between 1850 and 1900, many biscuit and soft-paste pieces were made again. Fine early pieces are scarce and high-priced. Many of those available today are late productions. The various Sèvres marks have been copied, and pieces listed as "Sèvres-Style" are similar to actual Sèvres wares but not necessarily from that factory. Three of the many Sèvres marks are illustrated here.

Box, cov., casket-form, the low rectangular serpentine sides supported on ornate gold scrolled corner legs, the dark blue sides h.p. w/ oval reserves w/colorful florals framed by ornate gilt scrolls, the hinged & low domed cover also in dark blue w/a large white reserve w/floral clusters & vines framing a central panel decorated w/a couple in 18th c. costume, pseudo-Sèvres marks, late 19th c., 6 1/2" h. **$3,220**

Cup & saucer, a footed round dished saucer holding a footed bulbous ovoid cup w/a flaring rim & a gold scroll handle, each piece w/a dark blue ground w/ornate leafy gold bands, the cup decorated on the front w/a gold round reserve h.p. in color w/a half-length portrait of Napolean in uniform, Sèvres-style cypher & letter A, 19th c., overall 3 1/2" h., the set **$441**

Coffee service: cov. coffiepot, cov. sugar bowl, cov. hot milk jug, six 9 3/8" d. plates, twelve teacups & saucers & a large 19 3/4" d. round tray; Sèvres-style, the serving pieces w/slightly tapering cylindrical bodies, each piece h.p. w/a different scene showing the campaigns of Napoleon I, each titled & artist-signed, wide cobalt blue borders w/gilt lotus & leaftip trim, 2nd half 19th c., the set **$12,925**

Jardiniere, Sèvres-style, gilt bronze-mounted, a wide low squatty bowl decorated w/upper & lower dark blue bands w/gilt stripes & floral clusters, a white central band h.p. w/playful putti alternating w/lion face masks, metal rim band joining arched scroll handles continuing down to the ornate scrolled metal platform raised on claw feet, ca. 1870, 11 1/2 x 26 1/2", 13 1/2" h. **$1,725**

Cup & saucer, each piece finely h.p. w/a wide band of colorful garden flowers edged by gilt bands & ivory formed as vitruvian scrolls, cup handle molded as a lotus blossom, blue-stencilled interlaced "C"s & incised & w/gilt marks for the years 1821-29, saucer 6" d., the set **$2,868**

Jardinieres, Sèvres-style, gilt bronze- mounted, a footed wide cylindrical body w/a dark blue ground, one side h.p. w/a large rectangular reserve of 18th c. figures in a woodland, the other side w/a large floral reserve, gold borders & lacy scrolls, metal rim band joined to lion mask & ring side handles continuing to the round base on ornate scrolled feet, blue interlaced "L"s mark, late 19th c., 10 1/2" d., 10 1/2" h., pr. **$5,060**

Teapot, cov., cylindrical body w/flat shoulder centering a short neck & low domed cover w/pointed knob finial, curved rim spout & C-scroll handle, turquoise blue ground decorated on one side w/a vignette in color of a barefoot boy playing the flute w/a dog at his feet, the other side w/a colorful bouquet of flowers within a gilt scroll border, teapot 18th c., the decoration added later, spurious blue Sevres interlaced "L"s mark, 5" h. **$598**

Plates, 9 1/2" d., each a cobalt blue border decorated w/ornate gilt leaf sprigs & ribbons & an "N" for Napoleon at the upper rim, each h.p. in the center w/a different scene of various military campaigns of Napoleon, each titled & signed on the back, set of six w/one similar Napoleonic plate, the set **$2,013**

Urn, cov., Sèvres-style, gilt bronze-mounted, the main body h.p. w/a continuous color scene of a semi-nude maiden frolicking w/putti in a garden setting, the shoulder cast w/a narrow metal band w/one side featuring frolicking putti, the other side w/a putto drawing a sword, the tapering cobalt blue neck & domed cover w/ornate gilt scrolling, upright gilt-bronze scroll shoulder handles & a gilt-bronze flame finial on the cover, late 19th c., overall 25 1/4" h. **$3,346**

Tea set: cov. teapot, cov. sugar bowl, creamer & one cup & saucer; dark Bleu Nouveau ground, the serving pieces w/bulbous ovoid bodies, each piece decorated w/gilt leaf band around the base & a band of stylized blossoms & leaves around the shoulder, further leaf band & gilt line decoration on each piece, various decorator & potter marks, France, mid- 19th c., teapot 6 1/4" h., the set $2,271

Vases, 7 1/4" h., footed bulbous ovoid body tapering to a tall gently flaring stick neck, bright blue ground decorated w/an over-all small gold flowerheads, the dark blue rim & foot band trimmed w/gold half-flowerheads within an egg-and-dart band, Second Republic era, iron-red stenciled mark & green stenciled oval, 1868-84, pr. $2,629

Vase on stand, 7 1/8" h., Sèvres-style, the vase modeled after a Sèvres "Vase Hollandais," a paneled flaring cylindrical shape decorated on the front w/an oval reserve w/a color scene of putti as musicians in a bower of clouds, the reverse w/a reserve of fruit & flowers, the conforming pierced stand w/matching flower reserves, all on a turquoise blue ground, the vase from the 18th century, the stand of later date, both decorated around 1835, probably in England (ILLUS. center).. $1,195

Vases, 11 5/8" h., Sévres-style, footed square wreath-molded base in gold supporting a slender twisted turquoise blue pedestal holding the tall urn-form turquoise blue body w/a tall tapering fluted cover w/a gold pineapple finial, high slender angled gilt-bronze handles down the sides, the body w/a gilt gadrooned rim band above a rectangular h.p. reserve decorated w/a scene of a shepherdess & putto in a landscape in the style of F. Boucher, the reverse w/another reserve showing a river landscape, a molded wreath band below the reserve & overall trimmed in ornate gold & jeweled highlights, various incised marks, 19th c., pr. (ILLUS. right and left with Sévres- style vase on stand) $3,585

Vases, cov., gilt-bronze mounted bisque, Sèvres-style, Louis XVI-Style, each of large urn form, the wide body molded w/a continuous scene of classical figures, gilt-bronze shoulder band w/Minerva head handles, gilt-bronze border on low domed cover fitted w/a gilt-bronze pineapple finial, all raised on a flaring fluted trumpet pedestal resting on a gilt-bronze square base w/patera toes, late 19th c., 16 3/4" h., pr. $4,406

Vases, 8 1/2" h., vase "Delhy" style, bottle- form w/a footed squatty bulbous body tapering to a tall cylindrical neck centered by a large ring, white ground h.p. w/brightly colored garlands of flowers & paler ferns suspended from a band of gilt lappets flanking the neck ring & around the lower body & foot, printed marks, 1865-67, pr. $4,800

SHAWNEE

Shawnee

The Shawnee Pottery Company of Zanesville, Ohio, opened its doors for operation in 1936 and, sadly, closed in 1961. The pottery was inexpensive for its quality and was readily purchased at dime stores as well as department stores. Sears, Roebuck and Co., Butler Bros., Woolworth's and S. Kresge were just a few of the companies that were longtime retailers of this fine pottery.

Shawnee Pottery Company had a wide array of merchandise to offer, from knickknacks to dinnerware, although Shawnee is quite often associated with colorful pig cookie jars and the dazzling "Corn King" line of dinnerware. Planters, miniatures, cookie jars

and Corn King pieces are much in demand by today's avid collectors. Factory seconds were purchased by outside decorators and trimmed with gold, decals and unusual hand painting, which makes those pieces extremely desirable in today's market and enhances the value considerably.

Shawnee Pottery has become the most sought- after pottery in today's collectible market.

Reference books available are Mark E. Supnick's book *Collecting Shawnee Pottery, The Collector's Guide to Shawnee Pottery* by Duane and Janice Vanderbilt and *Shawnee Pottery - An Identification & Value Guide* by Jim and Bev Mangus.

Ashtray, figural Indian Arrowhead, marked, 4 1/2"h. **$250-375**

Bank, figural bulldog, unmarked, 4 1/2" h. **$150- 175**

Bank, figural tumbling bear, unmarked, 4 3/4" h. **$150-175**

Book ends, figural, full figure of a man at potter's wheel, dark green, embossed on the front "Zanesville, Ohio," embossed on the back "Crafted by Shawnee Potteries Zanesville, Ohio 1960," 9" h., pr. **$675-775**

Cookie jar, cov., figural Drum Major, gold trim, marked "U.S.A. 10," 10" h. **$500-550**

Cookie jar, cov., figural Drum Major, marked "U.S.A. 10," 10" h. **$150-200**

Cookie jar, cov., figural Puss 'n Boots, long tail, gold trim & decals, marked "Patented Puss N Boots U.S.A.," 10 1/2" h. **$325-375**

Ashtray, figural kingfisher, parrot, bird, fish, terrier or owl, marked "U.S.A.," dusty rose, turquoise, old ivory, white or burgundy, 3" h., each (ILLUS. of fish, kingfisher & bird).. **$55-65**

Canister, cov., squared shape w/rounded corners, pale blue w/colorful fruit decal, marked "U.S.A.," 7" h. **$35-45**

Cigarette box, cov., embossed Indian arrowhead on lid, rusty brown, marked "Shawnee," 3 1/4 x 4 1/2" **$475-525**

Bank, figural Howdy Doody riding a pig, marked "Bob Smith U.S.A.," 6 3/4" h. **$500-576**

Cookie jar, cov., figural Muggsy dog, blue bow, gold trim & decals, marked "Patented Muggsy U.S.A.," 11 3/4" h. **$465- 550**

Clock, Pyramid shape, copper-clad Medallion finish, w/pink or copper face, marked "951 Kenwood U.S.A.," 7 1/2" h. **$95-125**

SHAWNEE

Cookie jar, cov., figural Smiley Pig, shamrock decoration, marked "U.S.A.," 11 1/4" h. **$150-200**

Cookie jar, cov., figural Winnie Pig, w/green collar, marked "Patented Winnie U.S.A.," 11 3/4" h. **$175-200**

Creamer, figural Smiley Pig, decorated w/embossed peach flower, marked "Patented Smiley U.S.A.," 4 1/2" h. **$55-75**

Creamer, Lobster Ware, satin charcoal grey or Van Dyke brown, figural lobster handle, marked "U.S.A.," 4 1/2" h. **$75-85**

Figurine, miniature, model of a 2 3/8" h. bear cub, 2 1/4" h. standing lamb, 2 1/4" h. standing pig, 2 1/8" h. rooster, 1 3/4" h. baby bird or 2 1/2" h. bunny w/ears down, bright white or old ivory, unmarked, each (ILLUS. left to right) **$15-25**

Figurine, miniature, model of 2 3/8" h. tropical fish, 3" h. bunny on haunches, 2 3/4" h. circus horse, 2 1/2" h. seated terrier or 2" h. fish, bright white or old ivory, unmarked, each (ILLUS. left to right) **$15-25**

Cookie jar, cov., figural Sailor Boy, decorated w/decals & gold trim, marked "U.S.A.," 11 1/2" h. **$525-575**

Creamer, ball-shaped, non-figural Red Feather circled by blue dots, marked "U.S.A.," 4" h. **$175-250**

Flower frog, figural Dolphin, swan or seahorse w/low base, colors of old ivory, turquoise or flax blue, unmarked, 3 3/4" h., each **$30-45**

Lamp base, figural Clown on drum, cold- painted, unmarked, 7 3/4" h. **$35-50**

Lamp base, figural Deer, unmarked, 7 1/2" h. **$20-35**

Lamp base, figural Elephant on ball, cold- painted, unmarked, 7 1/2" h. **$35-50**

Lamp base, figural Mother Goose, unmarked, 6 1/2" h. **$45-75**

Lamp base, figural Rabbit eating ear of corn, unmarked, 6 1/2" h. **$45-75**

Lamp base, figural Puppy, brown on cream base, unmarked, 4 3/4" h. **$65-75**

Mug, cylindrical w/figural parrot handle, marked "U.S.A.," found in old ivory, dusty rose & flax blue, 6 1/2" h. **$25-35**

Mug, Lobsterware, white w/figural red lobster handle, marked "U.S.A.," 3 1/4" h. (ILLUS. front with Lobsterware divided plate) **$55-75**

Plate, Lobsterware, stylized lobster claw shape, charcoal glaze, marked "Kenwood 912 U.S.A.," 11 1/2" l. (ILLUS. back with Lobsterware mug) **$95-125**

Pitcher, ball-type, 7 1/4" h., Fernware patt., yellow w/gold trim & flower decals, marked "U.S.A." **$95-125**

Pitcher, 7 3/4" h., figural Smiley Pig, pink & blue flower decoration, marked "Patented Smiley U.S.A." **$75-85**

Planter, model of an angel fish, marked "U.S.A.," found in yellow, flax blue, old ivory & pink, 8 1/2" h. **$55-65**

Range set: tall flattened & tapering salt & pepper shakers & flattened, domed sugar bowl/grease jar; Sahara line, Medallion copper-clad finish w/blue or pink base on sugar bowl, sugar marked "Kenwood U.S.A. 997," sugar 3 1/2" h., shakers 5 1/2" h., the set **$65-75**

Salt & pepper shakers, figural Smiley Pig, green bandana, range size, unmarked, 5" h., pr. **$65-75**
→

Salt & pepper shakers, figural Cottage, 4 or 5 holes, marked "U.S.A. 9," 3 3/4" h., pr. **$250-275**

Salt & pepper shakers, figural Smiley Pig & Winnie Pig, Winnie w/heart decoration & gold trim, Smiley w/floral decals, range size, unmarked, 5" h., pr. **$325-385**

Salt & pepper shakers, figural Smiley Pig, floral decals & gold trim, range size, unmarked, 5" h., pr., ... **$185-250**

Sugar bowl-grease jar, cov., Fruit & Basket patt., w/gold trim, marked "Shawnee U.S.A. 81," 5 1/2" h. **$125-175**
→

Teapot, cov., figural Elephant patt., green, bright blue or yellow glaze, marked "U.S.A.," 6 1/2" h., each **$165-225**

Teapot, cov., figural Tom the Piper's Son, white body w/h.p. trim or airbrushed in blues & reds, marked "Tom the Piper's Son patented U.S.A. 44," 7" h., each (ILLUS. of both designs).. **$65-75**

Teapot, cov., figural Granny Ann, lavender apron w/gold trim & floral decals or peach apron w/blue & red trim w/gold trim & floral decals, marked "Patented Granny Ann U.S.A.," each (ILLUS. of both designs) **$250-275**

Teapot, cov., figural Elephant w/ burgundy, green & brown h.p. on white ground, marked "U.S.A.," 6 1/2" h. **$225-275**

Vase, miniature, 3 1/2" h., embossed flower, marked "U.S.A." .. **$45-55**

Sugar shaker, White Corn line, single hole, airbrushed & gold trim, marked "U.S.A.," 5 1/4" h. **$275-375**

Sugar shaker, White Corn line, single hole, marked "U.S.A.," 5 1/4" h........................... **$65-95**

Teapot, cov., figural Granny Ann, in peach w/blue trim or purple w/blue trim, marked "Patented Granny Ann U.S.A.," either **$65-75**

Teapot, cov., figural Tom the Piper's Son, white body w/h.p. trim w/patches & gold trim, marked "Tom the Piper's Son patented U.S.A. 44," 7" h. **$225-250**

Vase, miniature, 2 1/2" h., embossed spinning wheel, found in burgundy, green & cobalt blue, marked "U.S.A." **$125-150**

Vase, miniature, 2 1/2" h., embossed stagecoach scene, found in burgundy, green & cobalt blue, marked "U.S.A." **$125-150**

Whatever you collect will be more enjoyable if it is used or at least displayed. Before starting a collection, consider the space you have available. You may not enjoy your collection as much if it is stored in boxes.

Shelley China

Members of the Shelley family were in the pottery business in England as early as the 18th century. In 1872 Joseph Shelley formed a partnership with James Wileman of Wileman & Co. who operated the Foley China Works. The Wileman & Co. name was used for the firm for the next fifty years, and between 1890 and 1910 the words "The Foley" appeared above conjoined "WC" initials.

Beginning in 1910 the Shelley family name in a shield appeared on wares, although the firm's official name was still Wileman & Co. The company's name was finally changed to Shelley in 1925 and then Shelley China Ltd. after 1965. The firm changed hands in the 1960s and became part of the Doulton Group in 1971.

At first only average quality earthenwares were produced, but in the late 1890s new shapes and better quality decorations were used.

Bone china was introduced at Shelley before World War I, and these fine dinnerwares became very popular in the United States and are increasingly popular today with collectors. Thin "eggshell china" teawares, miniatures and souvenir items were widely marketed during the 1920s and 1930s and are sought-after today.

Teapot, cov., Imperial Shape, Wileman & Co., first introduced w/an Intarsio patt. in the 1890s, this example w/a Shelley backstamp, patt. No. 7000, ca. 1910 .... **$1,500-2,000**

Teapot, cov., Mode Shape, Art Deco design, Blocks patt., 1929-1934 .... **$600-900**

Teapot, cov., New York Shape, Plain style, white w/green trim on rim, handle, finial & spout, from the Best Ware group, 1940, teapot only (ILLUS. w/stand - add at least $100 for stand) **$50-150**

Teapot, cov., Mayfair Shape, Chintz Blue Daisy patt. No. 14268, from the Best Ware group, 1964 (ILLUS. w/stand & sugar & creamer - add at least $100 for stand & about $150 for sugar & creamer).................... **$150-250**

Teapot, cov., New York Shape, Saltcoats Crested design, 1890-1905, overall 5 3/4" l., 4" h. **$70-100**

STAFFORDSHIRE FIGURES

Staffordshire Figures

Small figures and groups made of pottery were produced by the majority of the Staffordshire, England, potters in the 19th century and were used as mantel decorations or "chimney ornaments," as they were sometimes called. Pairs of dogs were favorites and were turned out by the carload, and 19th-century pieces are still available. Well-painted reproductions also abound, and collectors are urged to exercise caution before investing.

Dog, recumbent pug dog on a thick rectangular base, cream ground w/overall spotty dark brown translucent glaze, 18th c., 3 1/2" l. **$1,525**

Dogs, lead-glaze pearlware seated Pug-like dogs each sitted on a square pillow, dogs decorated w/yellow, tan & dark brown spots on a cream ground, the pillows w/green & brown trim, ca. 1800, 3 3/8" h., pr. **$2,350**

Figure group, modeled as the English Royal Coat of Arms decorated in polychrome overglaze enamels, impressed mark "Walton" within a raised scroll on the back, ca. 1820, 6" h. **$4,406**

Hound, standing slender animal w/ head down, white w/large black spots, on an oblong green grass & tree stump base, early 19th c., 6 3/4" l. **$1,410**

Quality trumps quantity. Novice collectors who start by buying indiscriminately will spend years and much more money upgrading their collections than those who buy only the best examples from the start.

Equestrian figures, each overglaze enamel decorated & modeled as military officers in parade garb, mounted atop stepped oval bases, each on a prancing brown steed, early 19th c., one w/restoration to one of the horse's feet, reins, stirrup straps, both ears, the other restored to all of the horse's feet, an ear, part of the reins & stirrup straps, chip to base & plume on hat, parts of stirrups missing on each, 9 3/4" h., pr. **$5,875**

Dogs, Spaniels, seated position looking at viewer, white w/large rust red spots, yellow chain collars & black face details, hairlines & minor flaking, 7 5/8" h., pr. (ILLUS. left & right) **$316**

Equestrian group, a sportsman wearing a brown jacket & black boots mounted on a tan horse, green & brown mounted background base, hairlines, 7" h. (ILLUS. center) **$345**

Staffordshire Transfer Wares

The process of transfer-printing designs on earthenwares developed in England in the late 18th century, and by the mid-19th century most common ceramic wares were decorated in this manner, most often with romantic European or Oriental landscape scenes, animals or flowers. The earliest such wares were printed in dark blue, but a little later light blue, pink, purple, red, black, green and brown were used.

A majority of these wares were produced at various English potteries right up until the turn of the 20th century, but French and other European firms also made similar pieces and all are quite collectible. The best reference on this area is Petra Williams' book *Staffordshire Romantic Transfer Patterns - Cup Plates and Early Victorian China* (Fountain House East, 1978).

Teapot, cov., footed deep oblong body w/a rim band & flaring collar & wide arched spout, serpentine spout & fancy scroll handle, highd domed cover w/pointed knob finial, decorated w/a rural landscape w/a boat on a lake w/a cottage in the distance, dark blue, minor spout chip, ca. 1830, 8 1/2" h. **$588**

Platter, 17" l., oval w/gently scalloped rim, the center w/a large urn of flowers in the foreground & an exotic garden in the background, four small scenic panels around the rim alternating w/long scroll & floral panels, deep rose on white, Japan Flowers patt., Ridgway, Morley, Wear & Company, ca. 1836-42 (ILLUS. left) **$259**
Platter, 15 3/4" l., long octagonal shape, the center w/a romantic European landscape, the border design of flowering vines, dark mulberry grey, Rhone patt., Thomas, John & Joseph Mayer, ca. 1843-55 (ILLUS. right) **$259**

Steins

Faience, cylindrical, h.p. around the sides w/oblong deep rose panels each w/a colorful flower, a background of small blue stars & small colored blossoms, Erfurt, domed pewter cover w/ball thumbrest, cover hinge a replacement, ca. 1870, 1 L, 11" h. **$817**

Meissen porcelain, cylindrical w/a hinged porcelain cover, the front w/a large four-lobed reserve painted in full color w/an elaborate battle scene w/men on horseback, the cobalt blue background completely covered w/ornate gold leafy scrolls, blue Crossed Swords mark, 19th c., .25 L, 5 1/4" h. **$4,649**

Mettlach, No. 2284, tall cylindrical body w/flaring foot, molded bands decorated in creamy relief, the wide center band w/three arched scenes showing figures drinking & playing cards against a green ground, an upper brown band molded w/a repeating design of a monkey & a cat flanking a crest, a bottom brown band printed w/ black German inscriptions, inlaid lid, 3.9 liter **$575**

Mettlach, No. 51o2, faience, footed tall baluster-form body w/a flaring neck, domed hinged pewter cover w/ball thumbrest, h.p. w/shades of dark blue w/a portrait of a man in Renaissance dress holding a goblet, blue scalloped band trim, .5 L **$1,265**

Mettlach, No. 2183-953, large baluster-form pitcher-style w/ rim spout, PUG color decoration of scenes of dwarfs, pale green ground & brown trim, domed inlaid lid, 3 1/4 liter **$483**

Mettlach, No. 2206, tall waisted & banded cylindrical body, wide etched center Gasthaus tavern scene, inlaid lid, 3 liter **$1,208**

Stoneware

Stoneware is essentially a vitreous pottery, impervious to water even in its unglazed state, that has been produced by potteries all over the world for centuries. Utilitarian wares such as crocks, jugs, churns and the like were the most common productions in the numerous potteries that sprang into existence in the United States during the 19th century. These items were often enhanced by the application of a cobalt blue oxide decoration. In addition to the coarse, primarily salt-glazed stonewares, there are other categories of stoneware known by such special names as basalt, jasper and others.

Crock, wide ovoid body w/a molded rim & eared handles, cobalt blue brushed inscription "J.S. Wadsworth - Governor Of NY State," probably from his campaign in 1862, minor chipping & hairlines, 1 1/2 gal., ca. 1862, 8 1/2" h. **$2,750**

Crock, wide ovoid body w/a wide flat rim, eared handles, incised design of a bird perched on a leaf accented in cobalt blue, impressed mark of S. Fayette & Co., Utica, New York, chip at rim, minor surface wear, ca. 1835, 9" h. **$2,860**

Crock, cylindrical w/a molded rim & eared handles, cobalt blue slip-quilled decoration of a large handled basket filled w/a very large bouquet of flowers, impressed mark of Whites, Utica (New York), tight hairlines, few flake spots in glaze, minor interior wear & staining, ca. 1865, 4 gal., 11" h. **$935**

Crock, cylindrical w/molded rim & eared handles, cobalt blue slip-quilled design of a large chicken w/wings up, unsigned, professional restoration to tight hairline on front & to rim chips, ca. 1870, 4 gal., 11 1/2" h. **$523**

TECO POTTERY

Teco Pottery

Teco Pottery was actually the line of art pottery introduced by the American Terra Cotta and Ceramic Company of Terra Cotta (Crystal Lake), Illinois, in 1902. Founded by William D. Gates in 1881, American Terra Cotta originally produced only bricks and drain tile. Because of superior facilities for experimentation, including a chemical laboratory, the company was able to develop an art pottery line, favoring a matte green glaze in the earlier years but eventually achieving a wide range of colors including a metallic lustre glaze and a crystalline glaze. Although some hand-thrown pottery was made, Gates favored a molded ware because it was less expensive to produce. By 1923, Teco Pottery was no longer being made, and in 1930 American Terra Cotta and Ceramic Company was sold. A book on the topic is *Teco: Art Pottery of the Prairie School*, by Sharon S. Darling (Erie Art Museum, 1990).

Vase, 10" h., a tall slender bullet-shaped body w/a low widely flaring neck & four full-length buttress handles, each handle decorated in silver overlay w/leafy vines & fruit, green matte glaze, impressed marks, silver marked "Shreve & Co." **$6,600**

Vase, 11 1/2" h., tall slender cylindrical shaped w/small square buttress handles down the sides, unusual matte mauve glaze, impressed mark, No. 438 designed by W.D. Gates **$2,400**

Vase, 13 1/4" h., bulbous double-gourd shape w/four open buttresses extending from the lower body to the mid body, tall slender flaring neck, good matte green glaze, impressed marks, designed by W.B. Mundie **$14,800**

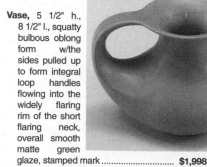

Vase, 5 1/2" h., 8 1/2" l., squatty bulbous oblong form w/the sides pulled up to form integral loop handles flowing into the widely flaring rim of the short flaring neck, overall smooth matte green glaze, stamped mark **$1,998**

Wall pocket, paneled bullet shape tapering w/a spearpoint base, overall dark green matte glaze, designed by Fritz Albert, impressed mark, repaired, 15" l. **$480**

Tiles

Batchelder Ceramics, Pasadena, California, rectangular, large shape w/a low-relief castle scene in tan, impressed mark, in a rectangular flat oak Arts & Crafts frame, 8 x 12 1/2" **$480**

German art pottery, square, incised & glazed w/a stylized Arts & Crafts yellow rose above green leaves all against a brown ground, in a square flat oak Arts & Crafts frame, early 20th c., 6" sq. **$420**

Rookwood Pottery, Cincinnati, Ohio, narrow rectangular shape molded w/a stylized tree in yellow, green & brown on a blue ground, Shape 3011 Y, in a wide flat Arts & Crafts oak frame, tile 3 x 6" **$900**

Grueby Pottery, Boston, Massachusetts, square, an incised & painted landscape w/two large fir trees in the foreground, in shades of dark & light green, blue & yellow, No. 39, 6" w. **$3,600**

Longwy Pottery, Longwy, France, square, a colorful scroll-bordered oblong central scene of bluebirds perched on bamboo stalks above a pond & peonies, narrow scrolled yellow border, outer ground in dark blue decorated w/pink, blue & purple flowers & green leaves, marked, minor chip on back, few flakes to corners, 8" w. **$270**

Van Briggle

The Van Briggle Pottery was established by Artus Van Briggle, who formerly worked for Rookwood Pottery, in Colorado Springs, Colorado, at the turn of the century. He died in 1904, but the pottery was carried on by his widow and others. From 1900 until 1920, the pieces were dated. It remains in production today, specializing in Art Pottery.

Vase, 3" h, miniature, a bulbous ovoid shape w/a tiny mouth, molded organic designs under a matte green glaze, ca. 1907-12, incised marks **$390**

Vase, 4 1/2" h., short squatty ovoid shaped w/molded stylized blossoms around the flat mouth, matte bluish green glaze, incised marks, ca. 1907-12 .... **$780**

If you plan to use a moving company to move your household possessions to another home, consider letting the movers handle the bulk of your possessions but moving your antiques and collectibles yourself, as the mover may not carry adequate insurance. Even if the mover does fully cover the damage, your valuables may be irreplaceable. Regardless of how you move, make sure all your valuables are covered by your insurance company.

Vase, 11" h., 4 1/2" d., tall tapering cylindrical body in olive green feathered glaze mounted around the rim w/a band of bronze stylized mistletoe, 1904 .... **$90,000**

Bust of Native American Chief, finely detailed, wearing a large feathered headdress, dark turquoise blue matte glaze, company logo on base w/"Van Briggle Colo. Springs Co. - Chief Two Moons - Cheyenne - Limited Edition No. 186 - 1979," 11 1/2" h........................... **$196**

Vernon Kilns

The story of Vernon Kilns Pottery begins with the purchase by Mr. Faye Bennison of the Poxon China Company (Vernon Potteries) in July 1931. The Poxon family had run the pottery for a number of years in Vernon, California, but with the founding of Vernon Kilns, the product lines were greatly expanded.

Many innovative dinnerware lines and patterns were introduced during the 1930s, including designs by such noted American artists as Rockwell Kent

and Don Blanding. In the early 1940s items were designed to tie in with Walt Disney's animated features "Fantasia" and "Dumbo." Various commemorative plates, including the popular "Bits" series, were also produced over a long period of time. Vernon Kilns was taken over by Metlox Potteries in 1958 and completely ceased production in 1960.

"Bits" Series

Plate, 8 1/2" d., Bits of Old New England Series, The Whaler **$20-30**

Plate, 8 1/2" d., Bits of Old New England, Haying **$20-30**

Plate, 8 1/2" d., Bits of Old New England, Old Dobin **$20-30**

Plate, 8 1/2" d., Bits of Old South, Cypress Swamp **$30-45**

Plate, 8 1/2" d., Bits of the California Missions Series, San Rafael Archangel **$40**

Plate, 8 1/2" d., Bits of the Old South Series, Cotton Patch **$40**

Plate, 8 1/2" d., Bits of the Old West Series, The Fleecing **$40**

Plate, 8 1/2" d., California Missions, San Rafael Archangel **$30-45**

Plate, chop, 14" d., Bits of the Old Southwest Series, Pueblo.... **$75**

Dinnerwares

Bowl, chowder, tab handle, Desert Bloom patt. **$12-15**

Bowl, chowder, tab handle, Native California patt. **$12-15**

Bowl, fruit, Calico patt. **$10-15**

Bowl, fruit, Coastline series, Turnbull design.............................. **$50-60**

Bowl, soup, Early California patt. **$12-15**

Bowl, salad, 13" d., Organdie patt. **$90-100**

Butter dish, cov., Arcadia patt. **$60-75**

Butter dish, cov., Heavenly Days patt. **$25-40**

Butter dish, cov., R.F.D.patt. **$50-60**

Butter dish, cov., Tam O'Shanter patt. **$45-50**

Candleholders, teacup form w/ metal fittings, Tam O'Shanter patt., pr. **$100-125**

Casserole, cov., individual, Gingham patt., 4" d. **$35-45**

Casserole, cov., individual, Organdie patt., 4" d. **$30-35**

Casserole, cov., Organdie patt. **$50-65**

Casserole, cov., Tam O'Shanter patt. **$50-70**

Casserole, cov., Tweed patt. **$80-100**

Casserole, cov., Vernon's 1860s patt. **$75-85**

Coaster, Gingham patt........ **$25-30**

Coffee server w/stopper, carafe form, Early California patt. **$45-60**

Coffee server w/stopper, carafe form, Tam O'Shanter patt. **$60-70**

Coffeepot, cov., 1860s patt. **$75-95**

Creamer, Native patt. **$15-20**

Cup & saucer, after-dinner size, Native patt. **$20-30**

Cup & saucer, after-dinner size, Organdie patt. **$25-30**

Cup & saucer, colossal size, Raffia patt. **$175-225**

Cup & saucer, jumbo size, Organdie patt. **$40-50**

Egg cup, Brown Eyed Susan patt. **$40-50**

Egg cup, Early California patt. **$20-25**

Egg cup, Early California patt., turquoise **$20-25**

Egg cup, Gingham patt....... **$25-30**

Egg cup, Mayflower patt. **$25-30**

Flowerpot & saucer, Gingham patt., 5" h., the set **$45-55**

Gravy boat, Gingham patt. . **$20-25**

Gravy boat, Native California patt. **$35**

Lapel pin, plate-shaped, Bel Air patt., 2 1/2" w. **$25-35**

Mixing bowls, nesting set, Gingham patt., 5" to 9" d., five pcs. **$175-200**

Mixing bowls, nesting set, Raffia patt., 5" to 9" d., five pcs. **$150-175**

Coffee server, spherical w/cylindrical neck & rim spout, attached plastic handle, Constellation patt. **$250-300**

Creamer, Modern California patt., orchid color (ILLUS. right with matching sugar bowl) **$15-20**

Sugar bowl, cov., Modern California patt., orchi color (ILLUS. right with matching creamer) **$15-20**

Flowerpot & saucer, Organdie patt., 4" h., the set **$50-60**

VERNON KILNS

Muffin cover, Early California patt., red, cover only............ **$125-150**

Mug, Barkwood patt., 9 oz. **$25**

Mug, Homespun patt., 9 oz. **$40-50**

Pepper mill, Homespun patt. **$150-175**

Pitcher w/ice lip, Early California pat., 2 qt. **$85-95**

Pitcher, Streamline shape, Tam O'Shanter patt., 1/4 pt. **$40-50**

Pitcher, jug-form, bulb bottom, Tam O'Shanter patt., 1 pt. **$25-35**

Pitcher, Modern California patt., jug-type, 1 pt. **$25-40**

Pitcher, Streamline shape, Organdie patt., 1 qt. **$45-65**

Pitcher, Streamline shape, Gingham patt., 2 qt. **$50-75**

Plate, 7" d., Calico patt........ **$10-15**

Plate, 7" d., Coastline patt. **$40-50**

Plate, 7" d., Native patt. **$8-10**

Plate, 7 1/2" d., salad, Tweed patt. **$10-12**

Plate, 9 1/2" d., luncheon, Organdie patt. **$10-12**

Plate, 9 1/2" d., Native American series, Going to Town patt., Turnbull design................ **$35-45**

Plate, 9 1/2" d., Trader Vic patt. **$100-125**

Plate, 10 1/2" d., Casa California Hermosa patt., Turnbull design **$25-30**

Plate, 10 1/2" d., dinner, Calico patt. **$25**

Plate, 10 1/2" d., dinner, Winchester '73 (Frontier Days) patt. .. **$75-85**

Plate, 10 1/2" d., Floral series, Desert Poppy patt., Harry Bird design............................ **$50-75**

Plate, 10 1/2" d., Floral series, Iris patt., Harry Bird design ... **$50-60**

Plate, 10 1/2" d., Floral series, Petunia patt., Harry Bird design **$50-75**

Plate, chop, 12" d., Brown Eyed Susan patt. **$25-35**

Plate, chop, 12" d., Cottage Window patt., Turnbull design....... **$75-95**

Plate, chop, 12" d., Frontier Days patt. **$150-175**

Plate, chop, 12" d., Monterey patt. **$25-35**

Plate, chop, 12" d., Organdie patt. **$25-30**

Plate, chop, 14" d., Gingham patt. **$35-40**

Plate, chop, 14" d., Rio Vista patt. **$40-50**

Plate, chop, 17" d., Early California patt. **$30-50**

Platter, 12" d., round, Organdie patt. **$20-25**

Platter, 12" l., oval, Tam O'Shanter patt. **$15-25**

Flowerpot, Barkwood patt., 4" h. **$30-40**

Mug, Ultra patt., maroon **$50-65**

Platter, 14" l., oval, Native California patt. **$30-35**

Platter, 14" l., oval, Organdie patt. **$25-35**

Relish dish, leaf-shaped, four-part, Native California patt....... **$50-75**

Relish dish, single leaf shape, Monterey patt., 12" l. **$35-45**

Salt & pepper shakers, Gingham patt., regular size, pr. **$20**

Salt & pepper shakers, Native California patt., pr................. **$20**

Salt & pepper shakers, Organdie patt., regular size, pr. **$10-15**

Salt & pepper shakers, Tam O'Shanter patt., large size, pr. **$45-65**

Spoon rest, Homespun patt. **$95-110**

Spoon rest, Organdie patt. ..**$75-85**

Sugar bowl, cov., Barkwood patt. **$10-15**

Teacup & saucer, colossal size, Homespun patt., 15" d. saucer, 4 qt. **$250-275**

Teacup & saucer, jumbo size, Homespun patt............... **$45-55**

Teacup & saucer, R.F.D. patt. **$10-15**

Teacup & saucer, Ultra patt. **$10-12**

Teacup & saucer, Winchester '73 (Frontier Days) patt. **$45-50**

Pitcher, Streamline shape, Hawaiian Coral patt., 1 qt. **$45-55**

Plate, 9 1/2" d., Coastline series, Florida patt., Turnbull design **$100-125**

Plate, 9 1/2" d., Garden Plate series, Celery patt., Turnbull design **$50-75**

Plate, 10 1/2" d., dinner, T631 patt., Turnbull design **$25-30**

Salt & pepper shakers, Gingham patt., large size, pr. **$50-60**

Sugar bowl, cov., Tweed patt. **$30-35**

Saucer, Trumpet Flower patt., Harry Bird design **$10-15**

Teapot, cov., Santa Barbara patt. **$75-95**

Syrup jug w/metal top & plastic handle, Raffia patt. **$50-75**

Teapot, cov., Chinling patt. **$50-75**

Tumbler, Gingham patt. **$20-25**

Teapot, cov., Linda patt....... **$40-50**
Teapot, cov., Tam O'Shanter patt. **$45-55**
Tidbit, two-tier w/wooden handle, Homespun patt............... **$30-35**
Tumbler, Bel Air patt. **$20-25**
Tumbler, Homespun patt......... **$35**
Tumbler, Tickled Pink patt........ **$20**
Vegetable bowl, open, divided, Gingham patt................... **$25-35**
Vegetable bowl, open, Ultra patt., 9" d................................ **$20-25**
Vegetable bowl, open, Tam O'Shanter patt., 9" d........ **$15-20**

Teapot, cov., Organdie patt. **$40-50**

If you want a discount greater than the typical 10 percent at an antique mall, ask the manager to call the owner of the merchandise so you can make an offer directly. Make a reasonable offer. Do not make an offer so low that the dealer is insulted and believes you are wasting his time.

VERNON KILNS

Disney "Fantasia" & Other Items

Bowl, 6" d., chowder, Nutcracker patt. **$50**
Bowl, 8" d., soup, Flower Ballet patt. **$50**
Bowl, 8" l., No. 134, decorated figural bird **$75-85**
Decanter, Penquin patt **$100-125**

Figure of Baby Weems, No. 37, 6" h. **$150-175**
Figure of Sari, May & Veive Hamilton design, 14 1/2" h. .... **$2,600+**
Plate, 17" d., chop, Fantasia patt. .... **$600+**
Salt & pepper shakers, Hop Low patt., pr. **$50-75**

Tray, hors d'oeuvre, May & Vieve Hamilton design, 16" d. **$400-600**
Vase, 4 1/2" h., Pine Cone patt., No. 5, ivory......................... **$95- 125**
Vase, 5" h., Pine Cone patt., No. 2, Turquoise **$225-275**
Vase, 12" h., carved handles, May & Vieve Hamilton design .. **$1,500+**

Don Blanding Dinnerwares

Creamer, after-dinner size, Hawaiian Flowers patt., blue **$40-50**
Creamer, Lei Lani patt., regular size................................... **$35-45**
Cup & saucer, after-dinner size, Hawaiian Flowers patt..... **$75-95**
Cup & saucer, after-dinner size, Hilo patt. **$50-75**
Cup & saucer, Coral Reef patt., blue **$40-50**
Cup & saucer, Lei Lani patt. **$40-50**
Plate, 7" d., Honolulu patt. .. **$40-50**
Plate, chop, 14" d., Hilo patt. **$150-200**
Plate, chop, 14" d., Honolulu patt. **$150-200**

Platter, 16 1/2", Lei Lani patt. **$200-250**
Salt & pepper shakers, Hawaiian Flowers patt., maroon, pr. **$25-40**
Salt & pepper shakers, Lei Lani patt., pr. **$25-40**
Sugar bowl, cov., Coral Reef patt., blue **$85-95**
Sugar bowl, cov., Hawaiian Flowers patt., blue **$75-85**
Teapot, cov., Hawaiian Flowers patt. **$275-300**
Tumbler, Hilo patt., #4, 5 1/2" h. **$125-150**

Music Masters

Plates, 8 1/2" d., brown transfer-printed, the complete set of 8 .... **$100-150**

> Rockwell Kent (1882-1971) was a prolific American commerical artist famous for his murals, paintings, and illustrations for literary classics, including a 1930 edition of *Moby Dick*.

Rockwell Kent Designs

Bowl, chowder, "Our America" series, coconut tree, blue **$60-70**
Creamer, regular, "Our America" series, houseboaters, brown **$75-90**
Cup & saucer, Moby Dick patt., maroon............................ **$45-50**
Cup & saucer, Salamina patt. **$50-60**
Plate, 6 1/2" d., "Our America" series, steamship, blue ... **$45-50**
Plate, 6 1/2" d., Salamina patt.. **$40**
Plate, 9 1/2" d., Moby Dick patt., blue **$110-145**
Plate, 10 1/2" d., Salamina patt. **$50-75**
Plate, 17" d., chop, Salamina patt. **$400-500**
Sugar bowl, cov., Moby Dick patt. **$35-50**
Sugar bowl, cov., Moby Dick patt., blue **$85-105**

Bowl, 11" d., salad, Moby Dick patt., red **$325-375**

Cup & saucer, Our America patt., blue **$50-65**

Dinner service: four 9 1/2" d. luncheon plates, four 6 3/4" w. chowder bowls, four 6 1/4" d. bread & butter plates, four cups & saucers, an 8" d. bowl & a 9" d. bowl; Salamina patt., ca. 1935, one chowder bowl repaired, the set (ILLUS. of part)...................................... **$920**

States Map Series - 10 1/2" d.

Plate, Virginia, blue **$20-25**

Plate, Connecticut.................... **$20**
Plate, Delaware, blue.......... **$20-25**
Plate, Georgia, blue **$20-25**
Plate, Texas, blue **$40-50**

States Picture Series - 10 1/2" d.

Plate, Wisconsin, blue **$15-25**

Plate, Alaska, blue **$25**
Plate, Hawaii, multicolored **$40-50**
Plate, New Jersey, multicolored **$40-50**

Plate, Rhode Island, blue ... **$15-25**

Plate, North Dakota, multicolored **$25**
Plate, Vermont, blue **$18-20**
Plate, Virginia, maroon........ **$18-20**
Plate, Wyoming, multicolored **$40-50**

Miscellaneous Commemoratives

Ashtray, Connecticut, round, red **$15-20**

Plate, 10 1/2" d., Christmas Tree patt. (ILLUS. w/Christmas Tree teacup & saucer) **$65-75**
Teacup & saucer, Christmas Tree (ILLUS. with Christmas Tree plate) **$30-35**

Cup & saucer, after-dinner size, Oklahoma A&M **$20-30**

Plate, 10 1/2" d., The Presidents, maroon **$20-30**

Ashtray, Vermont **$15-20**
Cup & saucer, after-dinner size, Niagara Falls **$25**
Cup & saucer, after-dinner size, Yosemite National Park... **$20-30**
Plate, 8 1/2" d., Memento Plate of factory **$75**
Plate, 10 1/2" d., Alaskan Husky, multicolored..................... **$30-45**
Plate, 10 1/2" d., Beaumont, Texas, Spindletop **$70-85**
Plate, 10 1/2" d., Caracas, Venezuela **$25-35**
Plate, 10 1/2" d., General MacArthur, brown **$20**
Plate, 10 1/2" d., Hollywood Stars, blue **$70-80**
Plate, 10 1/2" d., Knott's Berry Farm, California................... **$35**
Plate, 10 1/2" d., Notre Dame University, brown............. **$20-25**
Plate, 10 1/2" d., Old Man of the Mountain, New Hampshire **$20-25**
Plate, Statue of Liberty, multi-colored **$50-75**
Plates, 8 1/2" d., Cocktail Hour series, brown transfer, complete set of 8 .... **$400-600**

Plate, Postmasters Convention, showing buildings in Boston, border reading "Souvenir of the 48th National Convention of the National Association of Postmasters of the United States - Boston, Massachu-setts, October 12-16, 1952," multicolor **$30-35**

WARWICK

Warwick

More and more pottery and china collectors have turned their attention to the products of the Warwick China Company that operated in Wheeling, West Virginia, from 1887 to 1951. Prime interest seems to be in items manufactured prior to 1911, especially the items marked "IOGA," which were produced from 1903 to December 1910. Many collectors have speculated over the years the exact meaning of the word "IOGA." After much research it has been discovered that this is a Native American word meaning "Beautiful." The innovator of the "IOGA" ware was company president, Thomas Carr.

Products produced from 1887 until 1911 were made of a semi-porcelain clay, including fine china and earthenware items, IOGA ware as well as Flow Blue china that was made during the mid-1890s. In 1911 Warwick China switched to a vitrified clay and produced heavier restaurant (commercial) ware as well as fine china.

From its founding through 1911, the firm decorated its wares with colorful decals of beautiful women, monks, Native Americans, fraternal order symbols, flowers, birds, pine cones, fishermen, champion bulldogs as well as portraits of notable men or nationally recognized buildings. There were also some other miscellaneous designs. Warwick China Company was the first company to use photographic transfers as decorations on the IOGA pieces beginning in 1905. These transfers were used on the grey vases and depicted the "Wheeling Girls of the Evening." Many of the decals were based on paintings by artists such as H. Richard Boehm, Richard Beck and Arthur Stambra. Some of the pieces were also individually hand painted.

As noted, in 1911 the Warwick China Company began production of restaurant ware, banquet ware and fine dinner ware. This change of products was brought about by the new company president, Charles Jackson. Warwick continued making these wares until the company closed in 1951.

For more infomation about Warwick China, contact The National Association of Warwick China & Pottery Collectors.

Cuspidor, squatty low round body w/ a widely flaring rim, white ground decorated w/colorful flower bouquets, ca. 1930s, 7 1/2" d., 5"h. **$55**

Pitcher, 10" h., 6 1/4" d., tankard-style, style "VP," long handle from rim to base, dark brown shaded to yellow ground printed w/a color Native American portrait, IOGA mark, ca. 1908 .... **$300**

Vase, 8" h.,"Chicago" style, footed cylindrical shape w/arched & scalloped rim, semi-porcelain, IOGA mark, dark brown shaded to tan ground w/a color portrait of a pretty young woman, rare matte finish 8 .... **$250**

Vase, 11 1/2" h., 6" d., "Hyacinth" style, tall ovoid body w/a short flaring neck, dark blue shaded ground w/decals of large pink, yellow & red roses, IOGA mark, ca. 1906 .... **$275**

The cuspidor, also known as as a spittoon, derives its name from the verb "cuspir," which means "to spit." Cuspidors are used for spitting chewing tobacco juice into. They are typically squatty shaped to help prevent them from tipping over and have wide lips to prevent spilling in case they do tip.

Vase, 11 3/4" h., "Verona" style, tall slightly tapering lobed & ribbed design w/small loop handles near the top, dark brown shaded to yellow decorated w/full-length rear view of a nude young lady, a "Wheeling Girl of the Evening," semi-porcelain, IOGA mark, ca. 1906, very rare **$1,500**

←

Vase, 11 3/4" h., "Verona" style, tall slightly tapering lobed & ribbed design w/small loop handles near the top, dark grey shaded to white decorated w/three-quarters length view of a half-nude young lady w/arms above her head, a "Wheeling Girl of the Evening," semi-porcelain, IOGA mark, ca. 1906, very rare **$1,500**

→

Commercial China

Ashtray with matchbox holder, saucer base, white ground printed w/the advertising logo for Red Raven Splits, 5 1/2" d., 2" h. **$20-30**

Mug, white ground printed in black w/a seated puppy & black borders, 3 1/4" d., 3 1/4" h. **$15-22**

Mustard jar, cov., cylindrical w/ flared rim & inset cover w/spoon notch, classical- style black & brown border bands, ca. 1940s, 3 1/2" d., 3 1/2" h. **$18**

Ashtray-candleholder-matchbox holder combination, saucer base, white w/a printed gold logo & dark blue bands, 6 1/2" d., 2" h. **$27-35**

Mug, white ground printed w/logo of the "Ararat Temple, Kansas City, MO," ca. 1940, 3 1/4" d., 3 1/4" h. **$10-20**

In ceramics, the term "ground" is short for background, the area behind a design or pattern.

Watt Pottery

Founded in 1922, in Crooksville, Ohio, this pottery continued in operation until the factory was destroyed by fire in 1965. Although stoneware crocks and jugs were the first wares produced, by 1935 sturdy kitchen items in yellowware were the mainstay of production. Attractive lines like Kitch-N-Queen (banded) wares and the hand-painted Apple, Cherry and Pennsylvania Dutch (tulip) patterns were popular throughout the country. Today these hand- painted utilitarian wares are "hot" with collectors.

A good reference book for collectors is *Watt Pottery, An Identification and Value Guide*, by Sue and Dave Morris (Collector Books, 1933).

Baker, cov., Apple (two-leaf) patt., No. 70...................................... **$95**

Baker, cov., Apple patt., No. 96, w/advertising, 8 1/2" d., 5 3/4" h. **$50**

Baker, open, Apple patt., No. 95 .... **$65**

Baker, Apple patt., rectangular, No. 85, 5 1/4 x 10", 2 1/4" h. (tight hairline down side) **$700**

Baker, cover & warming stand, Apple patt., No. 601, ribbed, 8" d. **$105**

Bean cup, Apple patt., No. 75, 3 1/2" d......................... **$235**

Bean pot, cov., Apple patt., No. 93, only one known **$3,500**

Bean pot, cov., Apple patt., oversized, No. 502 (minor chip on bottom edge) **$900**

Bowl, Apple patt., No. 95 .... **$55**

Bowl, Apple patt., oversized spaghetti, No. 25 .... **$265**

Bowl, canoe-shaped, Brown Drip Glaze, No. 88 .... **$90**

Bowl, canoe-shaped, Brown Drip Glaze, No. 89 .... **$85**

Bowl, 4" d., Kolor Kraft line, No. 04, w/lip & shoulder, green....... **$145**

Bowl, 4" d, 2" h., Cherry patt., No. 04 .... **$55**

Bowl, 4 3/4" d., 1 3/4" d., Apple patt., No. 602, ribbed, South Dakota advertising **$50**

Bowl, 5 3/4" d., Apple patt., No. 23 .... **$85**

Bowl, 6" d., Kolor Kraft line, No. 06, w/lip & shoulder, blue........... **$20**

Bowl, 6" d., 1 3/4" h., cereal or salad, Apple patt., No. 94..... **$25**

Bowl, cov., 7 3/4" d., 3" h., Apple patt., No. 600, ribbed, advertising **$60**

Bowl, 8" d., 1 1/2" h., individual sphaghetti, Apple patt., #44 RF, green band on outside **$205**

Bowl, 8" d., 1 1/2" h., individual sphaghetti, Apple patt., #44, green band on inside.......... **$110**

Bowl, cov., 8" d., 3 3/4" h., Apple patt., No. 110....................... **$75**

Bowl, cov., 8 1/2" d., Apple patt., No. 67................................. **$70**

Bowl, 9" d., Kolor Kraft line, No. 09, w/lip & shoulder, yellow........ **$35**

Bowl, 9 1/2" d., 4" h., salad, Apple patt., No. 73, w/South Dakota advertising............................ **$45**

Bowl, 10 1/2" d., Apple patt., No. 58, rare............................... **$600**

Bowl, 13" d., Apple patt., spaghetti, No. 39................................. **$145**

Bowl, Apple patt., small sized spaghetti, No. 24 .... **$75**

Bowl, cov., 7 1/2" d., Apple patt., No. 66................................. **$125**

Bowl, cov., 7 1/2"d., Apple patt., w/ advertising, No. 66 .... **$205**

Canister, cov., "Coffee," Apple patt., No. 82 (minor nick)............ **$425**

Canister, cov., "Flour," Apple patt., No. 81 (minor hairline in cover) **$425**

Canister, cov., "Sugar," Apple patt., No. 81 (minor hairline in cover) **$425**

Canister, cov., Apple patt., No. 72, 9 1/2" h............................. **$425**

Canister, cov., Apple patt., No. 82, three leaves on cover, 7" h., 5" d. **$950**

Casserole warmer, electric, Apple patt., cut-away base rim, No. 133, 7" d., 2" h........................ **$1,400**

Casserole warmer, electric, round w/flat base, Apple patt., No. 133, rare.................................. **$2,800**

Casserole, cov., Apple (two-leaf) patt., individual, French handled, No.18, 8" l. **$80**

Casserole, cov., Apple patt., individual, tab handled, No.18, 8" l. **$195**

Casserole, cov., Apple patt., No. 52, 6 1/2" d. (small repaired chip on cover) **$115**

Casserole, cov., Apple patt., No. 53, w/advertising, 7 1/2" d.. **$135**

Casserole, cov., Apple patt., No. 54, 8 1/2" d. **$225**

Casserole, cov., Apple patt., square, No. 84, rare (minor hairline in base, lid does not fit snugly) **$300**

Casserole, cov., oval, Applie patt., No. 86, glued chip on cover edge, rare, 8" l. **$600**

Casserole, cov., Silhouette, patt., individual, tab handled, No.18, 8" l. **$75**

Casserole, cov., Apple patt., No. 2/48 .... **$255**

Casserole, cover & metal warming stand, Apple (two leaf) patt., No. 3/19, casserole 8 1/2" d., 5 1/4" h................................... **$75**

Bowl, 13" d., Apple (two-leaf) patt., spaghetti, No. 39 .... **$95**

Coffee server, cov., Apple patt., No. 115, rare **$4,000**

Casserole, cover & metal warming stand, Apple patt., No. 3/19, casserole 8 1/2" d., 5 1/4" h. **$195**

Cheese crock, cov., Apple patt., No. 80, two-leaf cover **$725**

Chip-n-dip set, Apple patt., No. 119 & 120 bowls, the set.......... **$185**

Cookie jar, cone-top, Apple patt., No. 91, 10 3/4" h. (minor crow's-foot in cover) **$750**

Cookie jar, cov., Apple patt., eared handles, No. 503, 8 1/4" h., 8 1/4" d............................... **$450**

Cookie jar, cov., Apple patt., No. 21, 7 1/2" h. (minor hairline in cover) **$175**

WATT POTTERY

Cookie jar, cov., Cross-Hatch Pansy (Old Pansy) patt., No. 21, 7 1/2" h. **$375**

Creamer, Open Apple patt., No. 62, hairline in handle, 4 1/4" h. **$825**

Creamer, Autumn Foliage patt., No. 62, 4 1/4" h. (ILLUS. right)........... **$235**
Pitcher, 5 1/2" h., Autumn Foliage patt., No. 15 (ILLUS. center) ....**$**
Pitcher, 6 1/2" h., Autumn Foliage patt., No. 16 (ILLUS. left) **$65**

Grease jar, cov., Apple patt., No. 47, w/advertising, 5" h. **$700**

Advertisements for "antiques wanted" that offer free house calls should be ignored. Do not let any stranger into your home. The fewer people who know what you have in your home, the more secure you are.

Creamer cinnamon drip glaze over brown, No. 62, 4 1/4" h., 4 1/2" d. **$350**
Creamer, Apple (two leaf) patt., No. 62, 4 1/4" h. **$135**
Creamer, Apple patt., No. 35, very rare, 5" l., 2 3/4" h. **$1,700**
Creamer, Apple patt., No. 62, w/ advertising........................... **$155**
Creamer, Brown Banded, No. 62, 4 1/4" h. **$525**
Creamer, Brownstone line, No. 62, brown body, green neck, 4 1/4" h. **$265**
Creamer, Dutch Tulip patt., No. 62, 4 1/4" h. **$175**
Creamer, Rooster patt., No. 62, 4 1/4" h. **$200**
Creamer, Starflower (five-petal) patt., No. 62, w/advertising, 4 1/4" h. **$305**
Creamer, Tear Drop patt., No. 62, 4 1/4" h. **$300**
Cruet set, cov., oil & vinegar bottles, Apple patt., No. 126, 7" h., the set **$2,000**
Cup & saucer, Cut-Leaf Pansy (Rio Rose) patt., No. 40, the set **$105**
Cup, Tropicana patt., rare **$800**

Fondue pot, cov., handled, Apple patt., No. 506, hairline in cover, chip inside rim, 9" l., 3" h. **$275**
Grease jar, cov., Apple patt., w/ Wisconsin advertising, No. 01, 5 1/2" h.............................. **$375**
Ice bucket, cov., Apple patt., No. 59 .... **$185**
Ice bucket, cov., Butterfly patt., No. 59 (repaired spot on cover) **$475**
Mixing bowl, Apple (two leaf) patt., No. 05, ribbed, 5" d., 2 3/4" h. **$45**
Mixing bowl, Apple (two-leaf) patt., No. 04, ribbed, 4 1/4" d., 2" h. **$75**
Mixing bowl, Apple (two-leaf) patt., No. 05, ribbed, 5" d., 2 3/4" h. **$75**
Mixing bowl, Apple (two-leaf) patt., No. 64, 7 1/2" d., 5" h. **$30**
Mixing bowl, Apple (two-leaf) patt., No. 65, 8 1/2" d., 5 3/4" h. **$50**
Mixing bowl, Apple (w/only stem) patt., No. 09, ribbed, w/South Dakota advertising, rare, 9" d., 5" h. **$350**
Mixing bowl, Apple patt., 7 1/2" d., 5" h., No. 64 .... **$55**
Mixing bowl, Apple patt., No. 06, rimmed, w/advertising, 6" d. **$70**
Mixing bowl, Apple patt., No. 65, 8 1/2" d., 5 3/4" h................. **$45**
Mixing bowl, Butterfly patt., No. 05, 5" d., 2 3/4" h................. **$775**
Mixing bowl, Cherry patt., No. 04, ribbed, 4 1/4" d., 2" h.......... **$105**
Mixing bowl, Double Apple patt., No. 05, ribbed, 5" d., 2 3/4" h. **$75**
Mixing bowl, Double Apple patt., No. 06, ribbed, 6" d., 3 1/2" h. **$105**
Mixing bowl, Double Apple patt., No. 07, ribbed, 7" d., 4" h... **$115**
Mixing bowl, Dutch Tulip patt., No. 05, ribbed, w/advertising, 5" d., 2 3/4" h.............................. **$185**
Mixing bowl, Dutch Tulip patt., No. 05, rimmed, 5" d., 2 3/4" h. **$115**
Mixing bowl, Old Pansy patt., No. 05, ribbed, banded, 5" d., 2 3/4" h. **$60**
Mixing bowl, Open Apple patt., No. 05, ribbed, 5" d., 2 3/4" h. **$165**
Mixing bowl, Raised Pansy patt., No. 05, ribbed, 5" d., 2 3/4" h. **$85**
Mixing bowl, Reduced Decoration Apple patt., No. 63, deep sides, 6 1/2" d., 4" h...................... **$70**

WATT POTTERY

Mixing bowl, Reduced Decoration Apple patt., No. 64, deep sides, 7 1/2" d., 5" h.............. **$75**

Mixing bowl, Rooster patt., No. 05, rimmed, 5" d............... **$55**

Mixing bowl, Starflower patt., No. 05, rimmed, 5" d................. **$35**

Mixing bowl, Tear Drop patt., No. 05, ribbed, 5" d., 2 3/4" h...... **$40**

Mixing bowl, White Daisy patt., No. 05, ribbed, 5" d., 2 3/4" h.... **$165**

Mixing bowl, Apple patt., No. 04, ribbed, 4 1/4" d., 2" h........... **$40**

Mixing bowl, Cross-Hatch Pansy (Old Pansy) patt., No. 05, ribbed, 5" d., 2 3/4" h...................... **$145**

Mixing bowl, Apple patt., ribbed, No. 06, w/Minnesota advertising, 6" d., 3 1/2" h...................... **$30**

Mixing bowl, Cross-Hatch Pansy (Old Pansy) patt., No. 6, ribbed, 6" d., 3 1/2" h...................... **$100**

Mixing bowl, Cross-Hatch Pansy (Old Pansy) patt., No. 07, ribbed, 7" d., 4" h...................... **$90**

Mixing bowl, Apple (two-leaf) patt., No. 08, ribbed, 8" d., 4 1/2" h. **$75**

Mixing bowl, Cross-Hatch Pansy (Old Pansy) patt., No. 08, ribbed, 8" d., 4 1/2" h...................... **$75**

Mixing bowl, Apple patt., No. 09, ribbed, w/North Dakota advertising, 9" d., 5" h. **$45**

Mixing bowl, Cross-Hatch Pansy (Old Pansy) patt., No. 09, ribbed, 9" d., 5" h.............. **$85**

Mixing bowls, Apple (two-leaf) patt., No. 63, 6 1/2" d., 4" h.. **$25**

Mug, Apple patt., cylindrical, No. 61, rare, 3 3/4" d., 3" h. **$1,700**

Mug, Apple patt., No. 701, cylindrical, 3 3/4" h. **$650**

Mug, Apple patt., No.501, barrel-shaped, 4 1/2" h. **$300**

Mug, Apple patt., waisted cylindrical form, No. 121, 3 3/4" h. **$115**

Pie plate, 1993 WCA Commemorative................. **$450**

Pitcher, 4 1/2" h., olive green over brown drip glaze, No. 62 .... **$225**

Pitcher, 5 1/2" h., Apple (two leaf) patt., No. 15........................ **$140**

Pitcher, 5 1/2" h., Apple patt., No. 15 .... **$50**

Pitcher, 5 1/2" h., Apple patt., No. 15, sample-type w/wording "This is a sample imprint for this size space," rare **$375**

Pitcher, 5 1/2" h., Apple patt., No. 15, w/advertising in black print (hairline in handle)............. **$100**

Pitcher, 5 1/2" h., Apple patt., No. 15, w/advertising in red print **$115**

Pitcher, 5 1/2" h., Cherry patt., No. 15 .... **$175**

Mug, Starflower (five-petal) patt., cylindrical, No. 61, 3 3/4" d., 3" h. **$225**

Pitcher, 5 1/2" h., Starflower (four-petal) patt., No. 15 .... **$85**

Pitcher, 5 1/2" h., Tulip patt., No. 15 (ILLUS. center)............................. **$475**
Pitcher, 6 1/2" h., Tulip patt., No. 16 (ILLUS. left)................................. **$115**

Pitcher, 5 1/2" h., Cherry patt., No. 15., w/advertising **$155**

Pitcher, 5 1/2" h., Double Apple patt., No. 15........................ **$305**

Pitcher, 5 1/2" h., Dutch Tulip patt., reduced design w/some leaves omitted, rare, No. 15 .... **$425**

Pitcher, 5 1/2" h., Old Pansy patt., No. 15................................... **$195**

Pitcher, 5 1/2" h., olive green over brown drip glaze, No. 15 ...... **$85**

Pitcher, 5 1/2" h., Rooster patt., No. 15 .... **$175**

Pitcher, 5 1/2" h., Starflower (four-petal) patt., No. 15, w/Minnesota advertising............................ **$50**

Pitcher, 5 1/2" h., Tear Drop patt., No. 15................................... **$40**

Pitcher, 5 1/2" h., Yellow Swirl patt., No. 15................................... **$60**

Pitcher, 6 1/2" h., Tear Drop patt., No. 16................................... **$105**

Pitcher, 6 1/2" h., Apple (two leaf) patt., No. 16........................ **$140**

Pitcher, 6 1/2" h., Apple patt., No. 16 .... **$155**

Pitcher, 6 1/2" h., Apple patt., No. 16, w/ Ohio advertising....... **$125**

Pitcher, 6 1/2" h., Brownstone line, No. 16, brown body, green neck **$105**

Pitcher, 6 1/2" h., Butterfly patt., No. 16, very rare (repair to top edge)................................. **$375**

Pitcher, 6 1/2" h., Cherry patt., No. 16 .... **$85**

Pitcher, 6 1/2" h., Dutch Tulip patt., No. 16................................. **$235**

Pitcher, 6 1/2" h., Rooster patt., No. 16 .... **$195**

Pitcher, 6 1/2" h., Starflower (five-petal) patt., No. 16............ **$70**

Pitcher, 8" h., 8 1/2" d., Apple patt., w/ice lip, bulbous body, No. 17 .... **$170**

Pitcher, 8" h., Quilted Morning Glory patt., w/ice lip, No. 17 (repair by spout) **$235**

Pitcher, 8" h., 8 1/2" d., refrigerator-type, square-shaped, Apple (two-leaf) patt., No. 69 (minor rough spot on lip).......................... **$205**

Pitcher, 8" h., Apple patt., No. 17 .... **$350**

Plate, dinner, Apple patt., No. 29 .... **$300**

Plate, dinner, Apple patt., No. 29, w/advertising **$350**

Platter, 12" d., Apple patt., No. 49 .... **$205**

Platter, 15" d., Apple patt., No. 31 .... **$95**

Wedgwood

Reference here is to the famous pottery established by Josiah Wedgwood in 1759 in England. Numerous types of wares have been produced through the years to the present.

Basalt

Bust of the Duke of Edinburgh, mounted on a waisted round socle, impressed title & mark, dated 1953, 9" h.................. **$353**

Candlesticks, each w/a very tall slender fluted columnar standard w/the socket having a pierced rim, raised on a square plinth base w/foliate trim, impressed mark, early 19th c., 12 1/2" h., pr. (one socket rim restored, footrim chips).................................... **$646**

Figure of Cupid, shown seated on a rock atop w raised round base, impressed mark & title, late 19th c., 8" h. **$411**

Incense burner, a squatty bulbous round bowl molded w/foliate festoons, raised on three figural dolphin legs atop w/ molded round base, pierced insert & flat cover, 19th c., 4 1/8" h. (restoration to dolphin tails, shallow flakes on cover).................................... **$823**

Potpourri, cov., wide gently flaring cylindrical base w/upturned loop rim handles, low domed cover pierced w/overall holes centered by a knop handle, impressed mark, 19th c., 9" d. **$940**

Tea set: cov. teapot, cov. sugar bowl & creamer; footed squatty bulbous bodies w/angular handles & low domed covers, each piece decorated in color w/ floral sprays on the black ground, covers w/figural sybil finials, early 20th c., impressed marks, teapot 5 1/4" h., the set **$353**

Bust of Venus, posed w/her head tilted down, mounted atop a waisted round socle, impressed mark, 19th c., 9 1/4" h. **$705**

Candlesticks, a wide round foot w/an arabesque floral border tapering to a cylindrical columnar shaft molded in relief w/classical figures, round cupped socket, first half 20th c., 9 3/4" h. .. **$235**

Vase, 14" h., footed tali ovoid body tapering to a tall slender cylindrical ringed neck w/a flattened rim, upright arched lion head & mask shoulder handles, molded w/a central relief frieze depicting Hercules in the Garden of the Hesperides within foliate borders, impressed mark, dated 1868 (haldes w/chips & restored terminals) **$1,293**

Urn, a wide round low foot supporting the wide campana-form crater bowl w/a flaring rim flanked by high upright looped handles, the sides decorated w/polychrome floral sprays, top fitted w/a pierced grid, impressed mark, mid-19th c., 10 1/4" w. **$1,998**

Caneware

Honey pot, cov., designed as a beehive dish w/cover set on a four-legged bench, impressed mark, early 19th c., 6 3/4" h. (cover restored).............. **$1,293**

Pie dish, cov., a low shallow oval pie crust form base w/a low slightly domed latticework cover w/a grape leaf handle, ca. 1800, impressed mark, 7 3/4" l. (slight rim chip) **$588**

Teapot, cov., spherical bamboo-molded body w/a bamboo-molded spout & loop handle, domed cover w/bamboo twig handle, trimmed w/dark blue banding & dots, impressed lower case mark, 19th c., 4 1/4" h. (chips on spout) **$2,760**

Teapot, cov., footed wide squatty body w/a low domed cover w/ button finial, short gently arched spout & arched C-scroll handle, smear-glazed & applied around the middle w/a wide band of tight scrolls & leaftips in green, radiating spearpoints applied around cover, impressed mark of Josiah Wedgwood, England, 19th c., 4" h. (faint spider crack in base)............................. **$2,432**

Vase, 7" h., trumpet-form w/flared foot & ringed & widely flaring mouth, applied black classical figures in relief between floral & leaf w/berry bands, impressed mark, early 19th c. (disk lid missing).............................. **$690**

Josiah Wedgwood spelled his last name with only one "e." Ceramics marked with the name Wedgewood with two "e's" were not produced by Josiah Wedgwood or his firm.

WEDGWOOD

Jasper Ware

Bowl, cov., 6" h., tall cylindrical base sharply tapered at the bottom, flat rim fitted w/a high domed cover w/a knop finial, the base sides applied w/white relief classical scenes within foliate frames, radiating acathus leaves on the cover, dark blue ground, late 18th - early 19th c. (ILLUS. front row, second from left) **$1,116**

Custard cup, cov., cylindrical solid white cup w/a twisted handle & latticework surface, pierced lattice cover, impressed mark, late 18th c., 2 1/2" h. (ILLUS. front row, second from right) **$1,175**

Dish, deep, round, white relief engine- turned striping surrounding a central cameo depicting "The Infant Academy," acanthus & stiff leaf border, lilac ground, impressed mark, late 18th c., firing lines in the relief, 8 1/4" d. (ILLUS. front row, far left) **1,293**

Tea bowl & saucer, footed deep rounded bowl w/white relief engine-turned striping & applied relief of putti, lapidary-polished interior, matching saucer w/white relief engine turning w/an acanthus & stiff leaf border, on a green ground, impressed marks, late 18th c., saucer 5 1/8" d., the set (ILLUS. front row, third from left) **$1,410**

Tea tray, oval, applied white narrow acanthus & stiff leaf border band & central sunflower within an oval band, blue ground, impressed mark, late 18th c., 17 1/2" l. (ILLUS. top row) **$1,528**

Cracker jar, cov., cylindrical dark yellow body w/applied black fruiting grapevine festoons around the sides between lion masks & rings, silver plate rim, cover & bail swing handle, impressed mark, ca. 1930, worn plating, 5 1/4" h. (ILLUS. center) **$764**

Pitcher, 5 1/2" h., jug-form, the ovoid body decorated w/applied white relief classical figures between vertical bands & foliate borders, crimson ground, impressed mark, ca. 1920, relief loss (ILLUS. left) **$646**

Pitcher, 8" h., footed bulbous body tapering to a tall cylindrical neck w/a flat rim w/pinched rim spout, applied strap handle, applied white relief band of classical figures between floret banded borders, impressed mark, ca. 1900, slight firing flaw below spout (ILLUS. right) **$1,528**

Cheese dish & cover, round base w/flanged rim trimmed w/applied white relief running oak leaf border, the wide domed cover w/ a continuous band of white relief classical figures, white relief oak leaf band on the top centered by a low loop handle, black ground, impressed mark, ca. 1900, 11" d. **$1,116**

Earrings, teardrop-shaped, each w/applied white relief classical figures centering borders of stiff leaves & beaded festoons, dark blue ground, late 18th - early 19th c., 1 1/4" l, pr. (very slight nick to relief) **$1,175**

Medallion, oval, applied white classical relief two classical women standing under a swag, on a solid blue ground, mounted in a cut-steel beaded frame attributed to Matthew Boulton, impressed mark, late 18th c., overall size 1 3/4 x 2 5/8" **$1,410**

Medallion, pyrometer-type, oval, white jasper ground decorated w/a blue wash on the impressed bead border surrounding "By J. Wedgwood F.R.S.," No. 79 on the back, late 18th c., 1 1/2 x 2" (back edge chips)..................... **$1,116**

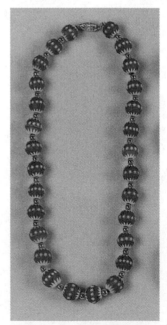

Necklace, consisting of 28 round beads, each w/applied white relief stiff leaf borders & banded star centers, dark blue ground, 19th c., restrung, 18" l. ... **$1,998**

Plaque, long narrow rectangular shape, applied white relief scene of the Judgment of Hercules against a light blue ground, impressed mark, 19th c., mounted in an ebonized wood frame, some surface wear, 5 3/4 x 16" **$1,763**

Teapot, cov., a squatty bulbous body w/a short angled spout & C-form handle, domed cover w/button finial, crimson ground applied w/white classical figures, ca. 1920, restoration to a figure & to rim chips on cover, 5 1/4" h. **$940**

Portrait medallion of Francisco Albani, oval, applied white relief almost full face bust on a solid blue ground, impressed mark of Wedgwood & Bentley, ca. 1779, 1 3/4 x 2 1/8" **$323**

Portrait medallion, double-type, oval, applied white relief bust portraits of Phthias facing Sappho, on a solid blue ground, Wedgwood & Bentley impressed mark, ca. 1779, 2 x 2 3/4" (rim chip) **$441**

Portrait medallion, oval, double, applied white relief bust portraits of two facing

Portrait medallion, oval, a raised white relief portrait of the young Queen Charlotte, on a solid blue ground, impressed mark of Wedgwood & Bentley, ca. 1779, mounted in a turned walnut frame, 2 1/2 x 3 1/4" **$1,410**

Vase, cov., 10" h., thick square base supporting the classical urn-form body w/a tapering shoulder & domed cover w/acorn finial, engine-turned white striping on the pedestal, lower body, shoulder & cover, the upper body w/a wide panel of white relief classical figures depicting the Dancing Hours, applied leaf sprigs around the square base, on a black ground, impressed mark, dated 1954 .... **$499**

Vase, cov., 12 1/4" h., small round pedestal base support the large urn-form body w/the wide shoulder centered by a rolled rim & fitted w/a low domed cover w/pointed finial, long C-scroll white handles from the shoulder to the base of the body, the body decorated in applied white relief w/a band of zodiac signs at the top above applied floral swags joining oval classical medallions, white lappet designs on the rim & cover, black ground, impressed marks, mid-19th c. (rim chip under edge of cover) **$2,350**

classical heads, one identified as Chrysippus, on a solid blue ground, impressed mark, ca. 1779, mounted in a brass frame, 2 3/4" (surface flake, back edge chips)........................ **$823**

Tobacco jar, cov., wide tapering cylindrical body w/ a fitted low domed cover w/button finial, the sides decorated in applied white relief w/Egyptian figures & designs, star & zig-zag borders, black ground, retailed by W.T. Lamb & Sons, 20th c., 6 1/4" h. (cover restored, slight nicks to jar rim) **$764**

Rosso Antico

Wine cooler, barrel shaped w/scrolled male mask head handles, incised vertical lines to a black slip surface, horizontal engine-turned bands, impressed mark, ca. 1800, shallow chips to handles, 9" h. **$2,585**

Biggin, cov., a squatty bulbous teapot-form base w/long spout & O-scroll handle, molded overall w/floral scrolls & arabesques, the upper slightly flaring cylindrical section molded w/a band of palmette, the slightly domed cover w/a figural spaniel finial, impressed mark, ca. 1840, 5 3/4" h. (insert strainer w/rim chip) **$518**

WEDGWOOD

Miscellaneous

Bowl, 9 1/4" d., 4" h., Fairyland Lustre, footed wide deep rounded shape, Willow patt., the exterior decorated w/lots of coral enamel against a midnight lustre background, the trees decorated w/brightly colored Japanese lanterns, the interior decorated w/flame lustre background shading to pink lustre at the bottom, interior center decorated w/a medallion of the Willow patt., inside rim covered w/tree leaves & lanterns, base w/Portland vase mark & "Wedgwood - Made in England - Z5407" **$2,760**

Bowl, 10 1/2" d., 4 3/4" h., Fairyland Lustre, Imperial type, footed deep round sides brightly decorated on the exterior against a rich midnight blue background w/colors of orange, yellow, blue & green, the interior decorated w/three large elephants, one large horse & rider, one large camel & flying birds, decoration done in black lustre against a cream & yellow ground, Portland Vase mark & "Wedgwood - England - Z5266" **$4,888**

Bowl, 11" d., 5 3/4" h., Fairyland Lustre, pedestal-footed wide deep rounded shape, Poplar Tree patt., the exterior decorated w/framed views of an Italianate park w/cypress, statues & a fountain, also a bridge over a river & an architectural figure that appears to be a viaduct or bridge, the interior decorated in the Woodland Bridge patt., a slender tree in the foreground extends upward from an elaborate root system supporting a bird nest in gilt, entire design w/numerous hidden elves & trolls, birds & fairies flying across the sky, bottom center w/a medallion w/a mermaid gazing into a mirror, base w/Portland vase mark & "Wedgwood - Made in England - Z4968" **$10,350**

Crocus pot & undertray, majolica, a tall domed top w/a molded basketweave design & pierced w/ numerous holes, dark green glaze, impressed mark on undertray, ca. 1870, 6 1/2" h. (slight glaze nicks along pierced holes, chip under foot of the undertray).......... **$499**

Egg basket & stand, Queen's Ware, each of oval shape & w/ wide ribbed panels & enamel decorated bellflowers & stiff leaf borders, impressed mark, ca. 1800, 11 7/8" l. (surface wear to dish center) **$881**

Malfrey pot, cov., Fairyland Lustre, Pattern Z5257, bulbous ovoid body tapering to a domed cover, decorated in the Bubbles II in the moonlight patt. on a dark blue ground, printed marks, ca. 1920, 7" h. **$39,950**

Malfrey pot, cov., Fairyland Lustre, Shape 2312, ovoid body tapering to a domed cover, Ghostly Woods patt., the cover in the Owls of Wisdom, base & cover trimmed in dragon bead decoration, the inside of rim of both decorated in the Pan-Fei border, inside of cover w/light blue lustre background & two elves on a branch, base w/Portland vase mark & "Wedgwood - England - Z4968," 14" h. **$40,250**

WELLER

Weller

This pottery was made from 1872 to 1945 at a pottery originally established by Samuel A. Weller at Fultonham, Ohio, and moved in 1882 to Zanesville. Numerous lines were produced, and listings below are by pattern or line.

Reference books on Weller include *The Collectors Encyclopedia of Weller Pottery* by Sharon & Bob Huxford (Collector Books, 1979) and *All About Weller* by Ann Gilbert McDonald (Antique Publications, 1989).

Coppertone (late 1920s)

Vase, 7" h., spherical shape w/ closed rim & small arched side handles, unmarked **$480**

Hudson (1917-34)

Underglaze slip-painted decoration, "parchment-vellum" transparent glaze.

Vase, 6 1/2" h., spherical double-gourd shape w/a flat rim, arched handles from upper body to shoulder, decorated w/large white & blue dogwood flowers & leaves on a pale green to dark blue ground, artist-signed, impressed mark **$345**

Vase, 9 3/8" h., gently swelled cylindrical form tapering slightly to a wide flat mouth, decorated w/a continuous landscape w/two white peacocks displaying their plumage, trees & hills in the background, signed by Hester Pillsbury, average crazing, minor glaze nicks on base, tight hairline at rim **$4,715**

Vase, 6 3/4" h., gently swelled cylindrical body w/a wide flat mouth, decorated w/pale yellow wild roses on leafy stems against a dark blue shaded to pale yellow ground, artist-signed, Weller script mark **$374**

Vase, 15 1/4" h., tall swelled cylindrical body tapering to a short trumpet neck, decorated w/light blue & white irises on pale green leafy stems against a dark blue shaded to pale lavender ground, artist-signed, repair to rim **$1,035**

Manhattan (early 1930s-'34)

Simple modern shapes embossed with stylized leaves or leaves and blossoms and glazed in shades of green or brown.

Vase, 6" h., cylindrical body w/flaring rim, w/iridescent metallic glaze, Weller script mark & "D 977 - TK" in blue slip **$805**

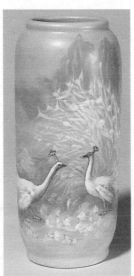

WELLER

Marbleized (Bo Marblo, 1915)

Simple shapes with swirled "marbleized" clays, usually in browns and blues.

Vase, 9" h., tall slightly tapering cylindrical form, overall swirled black, grey & rose glaze, impressed Weller mark **$288**

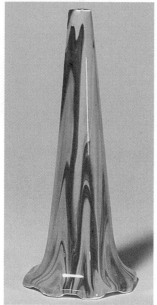

Vase, 10" h., a flaring ruffled foot tapering to a very tall slender body w/a tiny mouth, overall long streaks in shades of brown, orange & green, impressed Weller mark, crazing **$173**

Matt Green (ca. 1904)

Various shapes with slightly shaded dark green matte glaze and molded with leaves and other natural forms.

Vase, 13 1/2" h., tall simple ovoid body w/a short cylindrical neck, molded overall w/thistles on leafy stems, unmarked **$720**

Souevo (1907-10)

Unglazed redware bodies with glossy black interiors. The exterior decorated with black & white American Indian geometric designs.

Vase, 7" h., bulbous ovoid body w/ short cylindrical neck, decorated w/Native American designs in black & white of stepped cross devices centered by a small diamond-shaped checkerboard , dark brown neck & base band, unmarked, minor rim flakes **$220**

Minerva (about 1915)

A little known early line that was glazed in dark brown over brick red; the designs were then etched through the brown to expose the red. Design themes included landscapes, animals and mythical scenes.

Jardiniere & pedestal, the large deep square jardiniere w/a wide molded rim, each side etched w/a scene of satyrs dancing in a woodland, the matching square pedestal decorated on each side w/a tall figure of Pan playing his pipes, Weller block letter mark, jardiniere 12 1/2 x 16", pedestal 24" h., 2 pcs. **$5,546**

> Keep an inventory of your antiques and collectibles. It will be easier to maintain using a computer and a program like Excel, but if necessary, use index cards or a notebook. List the name of the item and description, including size, markings, date acquired, and price paid. When selling, update the listing with date sold and price. Also, take a photo of every item you own. This will document the information you need to file a police report or insurance claim if they are stolen or lost in a fire, flood, earthquake, or other natural disaster. Keep a copy of the inventory in a safe deposit box or other safe place.

WILLOW WARES

Willow Wares

This pseudo-Chinese pattern has been used by numerous firms throughout the years. The original design is attributed to Thomas Minton about 1780, and Thomas Turner is believed to have first produced the ware during his tenure at the Caughley works. The blue underglaze transfer print pattern has never been out of production since that time. An Oriental landscape incorporating a bridge, pagoda, trees, figures and birds supposedly tells the story of lovers fleeing a cruel father who wished to prevent their marriage. The gods, having pity on them, changed them into birds, enabling them to fly away and seek their happiness together.

Blue

Baby feeder, flat boat-shaped w/top opening, unmarked, early 19th c. **$600-700**

Bowl, flat-bottomed "rose bowl," Royal Doulton, England **$150-175**

Bowl, round, serving-type w/fluted rim, in fitted silver plate stand w/swing handle & wooden grip, Spode, England **$200- 225**

Bowl, 6 5/8" d., round w/scalloped rim, stenciled pattern **$75-85**

Box, cov., tin, upright w/slanted hinged cover, rectangular w/ bowed front, 6" h. **$75-100**

Candles, sealed in original box, Kameyama, mid-20th c., pr. of boxes **$20-25**

Chamberstick, dished base w/S-scroll rim handle, shaped center socket, Cardew Blue, modern **$25-30**

Ashtray, round, unmarked, American **$12-15**
Batter jug, frosted glass, Hazel Atlas Glass, 9" h. **$100-125**
Bell, modern, Enesco, Japan **$20-25**
Bone dish, ca. 1890, unmarked, England **$40-45**
Bowl, berry, Allertons, England **$12-15**
Bowl, berry, Japan **$6-8**
Bowl, berry, milk glass, Hazel Atlas Glass Company **$12-15**
Box, cov., model of a miniature piano, modern **$5-10**
Butter dish, cov., round domed cover, Allerton, England, 8" d. **$100-125**
Butter dish, cov., rectangular, for stick, Japan, 7" l. **$40-50**
Butter dish, drain & cover, cov., square, Ridgways, England **$100-125**
Butter pat, Buffalo Pottery .. **$30-35**
Butter pat, Carlton/Grindley Hotel, 3" **$20-25**
Butter warmer, server & candleholder, black stand, Japan **$50-60**
Cake plate, Green & Co., 8" sq. **$40-45**
Candle & napkin set, in box, Alladin, Denmark, the set **$25-30**
Charger, Moriyama, Made in Japan, 11 3/4" d. **$75-85**

Cheese dish, cov., rectangular w/slanted rectangular cover, Minton, England **$125-150**

Cheese stand, J. Meir & Sons, England, 8 1/2" d. **$150-175**

WILLOW WARES

Cigarette dish, "Who Burnt Our Tablecloth?," Japan......... **$35-40**

Condiment cruet set: cov. oil & vinegar & mustard cruet, salt & pepper; carousel- type base w/ wooden handle, Japan, 7 1/2" h., the set **$150-175**

Creamer, Allerton, England. **$35-40**

Creamer, cow-shaped, unmarked, England, mid-19th c. ... **$400-500**

Cruets w/original stoppers, oil & vinegar, Japan, 6" h., the set **$45-50**

Cup & saucer, Booths, England **$35-40**

Cup & saucer, demitasse, Copeland, England **$35-40**

Cup & saucer, Japan **$7-10**

Cup & saucer, oversized, "For Auld Lang Syne," W. Adams, England **$75-100**

Cup, farmer's mug, Japan, 4" h. **$12-15**

Drainer, butter, ca. 1890, England, 6" sq. **$50**

Dresser box, cov., Gibson, 3 1/2" h. **$100-125**

Egg cup, Allertons, England, 4 1/2" h. **$45-50**

Fish set, fork & knife blue Willow handles, in original box, the set **$175-200**

Ginger jar, cov., Japan, 5" h. **$30-35**

Gravy boat, Buffalo Pottery **$75-85**

Hot pot, electric, w/cord, Japan, 6" h. **$60-75**

Juice reamer, modern, China **$12-15**

Knife rest, ca. 1860, unmarked, England **$75-85**

Lamp, w/ceramic shade, Japan, 8" h. **$50-60**

Lamp, w/reflector plate, Japan, 8" h. **$60-70**

Lamp, Wedgwood, England, 10" h. **$200-225**

Lighter, teacup-shaped, Japan **$35-40**

Coffeepot, cov., unmarked, England, ca. 1890, 8 3/4" h. **$150-175**

Cup & saucer, cov., oatmeal/ bouillon, double-handled, Gibson, the set **$50-60**

Gravy boat w/attached underplate, round, double-spouted, Allertons, England **$125-150**

Compote, open, low octagonal foot & matching octagonal bowl, gold rim bands, Minton, England **$200-225**

Creamer, cow-shaped, W. Kent, England, 1950s **$250-300**

Drainer, platter, oval, impressed Davenport mark, England, 9 3/4 x 13 3/4" **$200- 250**

Gravy boat, ca. 1890, unmarked, England, 7" l. **$45-50**

Mug, Maling, England, 4 1/2" h. **$50**

Condiment set, figural "Snack Hound," five sections shaped like a dachshund, Japan **$40-45**

WILLOW WARES

Mustard pot, cov., ca. 1870, unmarked, England, 3" h. **$90-100**

Nut dish, scalloped shape, ca. 1900, 7" l. **$75-85**

Mustache cup & saucer, Hammersley & Co. **$90-100**
Napkin holder, Japan **$45-50**
Pie bird, modern **$20-25**
Pie server, Moriyama, Japan **$50-60**
Pitcher w/ice lip, 10" h., Japan **$100**
Pitcher, 6" h., scalloped rim, Allerton, England................ **$100**
Place mat, cloth, 12 x 16"... **$15-20**
Plate, bread & butter, Allertons, England............................ **$10-12**
Plate, bread & butter, Japan ... **$5-7**
Plate, "Child's Day 1971," Sandman w/willow umbrella, Wedgwood, England **$40-45**
Plate, dinner, Booth's, England **$40-45**
Plate, dinner, Cambridge, blue pattern on clear glass...... **$40-50**
Plate, dinner, flow blue, Royal Doulton **$50-75**
Plate, dinner, Japan **$10-15**
Plate, dinner, Mandarin patt., Copeland, England.......... **$35-40**
Plate, dinner, Paden City Pottery **$45-50**

Pepper pot, ca. 1870, England, 4" h., each (ILLUS. of four different styles) **$90-100**

Pepper shaker, figural Toby, "Prestopan," unmarked, Scotland, 5 1/4" h. **$225- 250**

Pitcher, cov., 5 1/2" h., Buffalo Pottery **$150-175**

Pitcher, 7" h., "Chicago Jug," ca. 1907, Buffalo Pottery, 3 pt. **$150-175**

Pitcher, 5 1/2" h., Ridgways, England **$50-75**

Pitcher, 6 3/4" h., cylindrical, restaurant ware, Buffalo China, 1920s **$200-250**

Pitcher, 7 1/2" h., stoneware, tan & brown w/molded designs trimmed in blue, Doulton Lambeth, late 19th c. **$175-200**

WILLOW WARES

Plate, dinner, restaurant ware, Jackson............................ **$15-20**

Plate, dinner, Royal China Co. **$5-10**

Plate, dinner, Royal Wessex, England, modern................. **$6-9**

Plate, dinner, scalloped rim, Allertons, England........... **$30-35**

Plate, dinner, unmarked, England, ca. 1870.......... **$35-40**

Plate, luncheon, square, Johnson Brothers, England.......... **$12-15**

Plate, luncheon, Wedgwood, England............................ **$15-20**

Plate, luncheon, Worcester patt. **$20-25**

Plate, child's, 4 1/2" d., Japan **$10-15**

Plate, 7 1/2" d., Arklow, Ireland **$15-20**

Plate, grill, 10" d., Japan **$18-20**

Plate, 10 1/4" d., paper, Fonda **$1-2**

Platter, 9 x 11", gold trim, dark blue handles, Coronaware .. **$125-150**

Platter, 9 x 11", rectangular, Wedgwood & Co., England **$100-125**

Platter, 8 1/2 x 11 1/2" l., oval, scalloped rim, Buffalo Pottery **$80-100**

Platter, 9 x 12" l., oval, American **$15-18**

Platter, 9 x 12" l., oval, Japan **$20-25**

Platter, 9 x 12" l., rectangular, Allertons, England....... **$100-125**

Platter, 11 x 14" l., oval, Johnson Bros., England................. **$40-45**

Platter, 11 x 14" l., rectangular, Buffalo Pottery............. **$150-175**

Platter, 11 x 14" l., rectangular, Holland............................ **$20-25**

Platter, 15 x 19" l., rectangular, well & tree, ca. 1890, unmarked, England....................... **$250-275**

Platter, 20 1/2" l., oval, English, late 19th - early 20th c. **$250-300**

Prestopan, figural toby-shaped, for salt, pepper, vinegar or oil, each **$100-125**

Pudding mold, England, 4 1/2" h. **$20-25**

Place card holder, unmarked, England, ca. 1870s, 2 1/2" d. **$85-100**

Plate, grill, 10" d., Japan **$18-20**

Platter, 11 x 14" l., rectangular, ca. 1880s, unmarked, England ... **$100-150**

Salt & pepper shakers, footed hexagonal shape w/ pointed top, Japan, 6 1/2" h., pr. **$25-30**

Relish dish, rectangular w/wide flaring tab handles, late 19th c. **$100-125**

Soap dish, oval slab-type, Burleigh, England............................ **$45-50**

Teapot, cov., miniature, lobed ovoid body, domed inset cover w/finial, C-scroll handle, serpentine spout, gold line decoration on handle, spout, rim & finial, Windsor China, England, modern, 3 3/4" h. **$15-20**

Spoon rest, Japan **$35-40**
Sugar bowl, cov., Buffalo Pottery **$40-50**
Sugar bowl, cov., Ridgways, England **$30-35**
Tablecloth, Simtex **$40-45**
Tea cozy, Blue Willow fabric, modern **$40-45**
Tea set, stacking-type, teapot, creamer & sugar, Japan **$80-100**
Tea tile, ca. 1900, unmarked, England, 6" sq. **$50**
Tea towel, souvenir of Historic Charleston, 16 1/2 x 26".. **$10-15**
Teapot, cov., child's, E.M. & Co., England **$75-85**
Teapot, cov., child's, Japan. **$30-35**
Teapot, cov., child's, Made in Occupied Japan **$35-40**
Teapot, cov., Homer Laughlin **$40-50**
Teapot, cov., restaurant ware, Sterling China................. **$50-60**
Teapot, cov., round, Buffalo Pottery, 1909 .... **$200- 225**
Teapot, cov., individual, Moriyama, Made in Japan, 4 1/2" h. . **$50-60**
Teapot, cov., Sadler, 4 3/4" h. **$35-40**
Teapot, cov., enamelware, unmarked, 7" h............. **$40-50**
Toothbrush holder, Wedgwood, England, 5 1/4" h............ **$70-80**
Tray, round, brass, 6" d. **$25-30**
Tumbler, clear glass, Johnson Brothers, England, 6 1/4" h. **$5-7**
Tumbler, frosted glass, 5" h. **$10-12**
Vegetable bowl, cov., round, Societe Ceramique, Holland **$75-100**

Tea set, child's, Japan, service for four **$125-150**

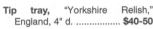

Tip tray, "Yorkshire Relish," England, 4" d. **$40-50**

Spill vase, pearlware, deeply waisted shape, unmarked, early 19th c., 4" h. **$175-200**

Tea set, Double Phoenix, Japan, service for two **$175-200**

WILLOW WARES

Wash pitcher, bulbous ovoid body w/wide scalloped spout, sponged border, 7 3/4" h. **$150-175**

Toby jug, w/Blue Willow jacket, unmarked, England, 6" h. **$250-300**

Wash pitcher & bowl, Royal Doulton, the set........... **$400-500**

Vegetable bowl, cov., round, Buffalo Pottery **$150-175**

Vegetable bowl, cov., square, ca. 1900, unmarked, England **$125-150**

Other Colors

Charger, gaudy coloring, cobalt blue scalloped border, Ridgways, England, 14" d. **$175-200**

Cup, purple, handleless, unmarked, England **$50-60**

Plate, dinner, gaudy coloring, Ridgways, England, 1920s **$50-70**

Cup & saucer, black, unmarked, England, early 20th c., the set **$35-40**

Pitcher, 5" h., red, "Old Gustavsberg," Sweden ... **$40-50**

Platter, 9 1/2 x 11 3/4", oval, multi-colored, Newport **$40-50**

Zsolnay

This pottery was made in Pecs, Hungary, in a factory founded in 1862 by Vilmos Zsolnay. Utilitarian earthenware was originally produced with an increase in art pottery production from as early as 1870. The highest level of production employed over 1,000 workers. The Art Nouveau era produced the most collectibles and valuable pieces in today's marketplace. Examples are displayed in every major art museum worldwide. Zsolnay is always well marked and easy to identify. One specialty was the metallic Eosin glaze. With over 10,000 different forms created over the years and dozens of glaze variations for each form there is always something new in Zsolnay being discovered. Today the original factory size has been significantly reduced, with pieces being made in a new factory.

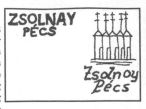

Cachepot, wide squatty flat-bottomed form w/a wide flat mouth, Shape #7140, gres (stone) body molded w/a repeated band of elk, metallic green & red Eosin glaze decoration, designed by Sandor Apati Abt, round raised factory mark, ca. 1903, 4 1/4" h. **$12,500-15,000**

Candelabra, three-light, Romanesque style, a tapering conical foot molded w/buttons, crosses & scrolls below the paneled stem trimmed w/buttons & supporting a pair of upturned arms ending in candle sockets flanking the large center cupped candle socket, Pyrogranite w/Eosin & polychrome decorations, Shape #2732, ca. 1890, 18 1/2" h., pr. (ILLUS. of one)................................. **$8,500-9,500**

Ewer, wide low domed & reticulated base divided into petal-form panels, swelled cylindrical & reticulated neck w/oval reserves below the widely rolled & pierced rim, ornate scroll-pierced dragon-form handle, decorated in blue & red enamel against a creamy yellow ground, impressed on bottom "Zsolnay Pecs 2042," remnants of paper label, 9 1/2" h. **$1,265**

Garden seat, molded as a large mushrom w/smaller mushrooms below on the molded base, majolica-glazed Pyrogranite, incised factory mark, originally had a matching table, ca. 1888, 18" h., garden seat **$4,500-6,500**

ZSOLNAY

Lamp, table-model, electric, Shape #6161, figural Art Nouveau design, the base modeled as a tall tapering ribbed plant stem w/leaf handles decorated w/a green & gold iridescent Eosin glaze, the large red flower-form top enclosing the electric socket, round raised factory mark, ca. 190, 14 1/2" h. .. **$15,000-20,000**

Pitcher, 7 1/2" h., bulbous fluted body w/a cylindrical neck, a wide mid-body band decorated w/domed & pierced buttons. small bottoms around the rim of the neck, the angled handle also trimmed w/buttons, a shriveled dark brown over yellow glaze, Shape #992, incised factory mark, ca. 1882 .... **$200-300**

Pitcher, 8 1/4" h., Art Nouveau style, Shape #6102, bulbous tapering smooth melon- form body tapering to a wide arched & pointed spout, a large figural handle in the shape of a satyr glazed in red & black, the body w/ a green & gold iridescent marbled Eosin glaze, round raised factory mark & artist mark of an acorn for Lajos Mack, ca. 1900 .... **$12,500-14,500**

Smoking set on tray, narrow oblong form molded at each end w/the reclining figure of an Art Nouveau mermaid, the center mounted w/three hexagonal containers of varied sizes, one for cigars, one for cigarettes & the third for matches, covered in a iridescent blue lustre glaze w/green & gold highlights, bronze glaze on mermaids, impressed mark, 10 x 11 1/2" **$4,370**

Pitcher, 13" h., cov., decorative Ivory Ware lid, dragon form handle & spout, cream ground w/gilt trim, incised & applied decoration of dragon & gargoyle copying 18th-c. designs, printed Zsolnay factory mark, incised form number 2994, ca. 1889 .... **$600-800**

Tazza, an oblong quatrefoil foot w/a central pedestal in a dark metallic blue Eosin glaze mounted at each point w/a figural standing angel w/a majolica glaze in gold & orange, all supporting the wide shallow dished top dish w/a metallic gold & green & blue Eosin glaze, round raised factory mark, ca. 1906, 11" d. **$12,500-15,000**

Umbrella stand, tall, slightly waisted cylindrical form w/rolled rim, the sides decorated w/dark golden iridescent fish swimming in iridescent swirls of dark blue, purple & gold, impressed "Zsolnay - Pecs - 4036 - 21," ca. 1900, 26 3/4" h. **$14,400**

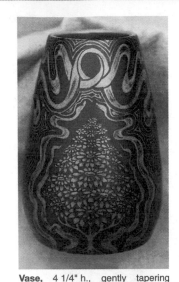

Vase, 4 1/4" h., gently tapering swelled cylindrical form w/a flat rim, decorated in an Art Nouveau design w/undulating ribbons framing flowering trees, Shape # 5330, dull Eosin glaze in shades of brown & yellow, painted factory mark, a design found in many sizes & variations, ca. 1898 .... **$1,750-2,500**

Vase, 8 1/2" h., in the Persian taste, bottle form w/a wide tapering ovoid body tapering to a tall slender cylindrical neck, the neck decorated w/an overall iridescent gold & blue florette design, the shoulder decorated w/ogival blue & gold cartouches alternating w/long pendant lappets in dark brown, blue & gold, on a copper lustre ground, printed five churches mark, ca. 1891-95 .... **$1,140**

Vase, 22" h., palace-type, flaring foot & tall slender ovoid body tapering to a short slightly flaring cylindrical neck, white ground w/ overall ornate colorful exotic birds & flowers decoration painted under- glaze on a high-fired porcelain faience, applied ornate gilt-brass lion head & ring handles, signed by Julia Zsolnay, ca. 1881 (ILLUS. of one)...... **$6,500-7,500**

Vase, 9 3/4" h., cylindrical body tapering to short, flared neck, painted w/landscape scene of trees, sunset, clouds & flowers, brilliant Eosin glazes, round raised Zsolnay factory mark, incised form number 8196, ca. 1909 .... **$12,500-15,000**

Vase, 10 3/4" h., ovoid body tapering in at neck, which tapers further to short molded rim, decorated w/three spotted leopards around body, silver metallic leaves w/red early Deco decorations, signed by Sándor Pillo-Hidasy, round raised Zsolnay factory mark, incised form number 8589, ca. 1912 .... **$20,000-25,000**

> Examine every object carefully before buying. Check for chips, cracks, hidden repairs and other defects that will lower value.

CHRISTMAS COLLECTIBLES

Starting in the mid-19th century, more and more items began to be manufactured to decorate the home, office or commercial business to celebrate the Christmas season.

In the 20th century the trend increased. Companies such as Coca-Cola, Sears and others began producing special Christmas items. The inexpensive glass, then plastic Christmas tree decorations began to appear in almost every home. With the end of World War II the toy market moved into the picture with annual Santa Claus parades and the children's visits to Santa.

In the 21st century, this trend continues, and material from earlier Christmas seasons continues to climb in value.

Bubble light shade, conical paper decorated w/the Three Wise Men against a dark blue ground, also found in other designs, designed to fit onto tree bubble lights, made by the Sail-Me Company, Chicago, ca. 1930s, each **$30-45**

Candy container, bendable figure of Father Christmas wearing a red & white crepe paper outfit & w/a bisque mask face produced by Heubach, holding a sack & bundle of twigs & seated on a simulated wood log that forms the container, Germany, early 20th c., overall 9" h. **$1,035**

Doll, Father Christmas, made by John Wright, red felt outfit w/ white underclothing, molded mask face, carrying a cross staff & basket, original wrist tag, 18" h. **$1,553**

Tree ornament, blown glass, a gilt top ball w/a patriotic spread-winged American eagle above a large red bell, Germany, early 20th c., 4 1/4" h. **$130**

Ornament, a molded realistic pear in yellow w/a touch of red covered w/ clear beading, large attached green fabric leaves, Germany, ca. 1910 .... **$200-250**

Pull-toy, cast iron, Santa Claus seated in a large ornate white & gold sleigh pulled by two white reindeer on red wheels, very fine condition, Hubley, early 20th c., 16" l. **$2,300**

Tree ornament, blown glass, small red horn, Germany, ca. 1920s, 2 1/2" l. **$30**

Hallmark Ornaments

1973 **Angel,** yarn...................... $21
1973 **Betsey Clark** glass ball, 1st in series.................................... $95
1973 **Mr. Santa,** yarn $25
1974 **Norman Rockwell** glass ball $46
1974 **Raggedy Ann & Andy** glass balls, set of 4 .... $75
1974 **Soldier,** yarn................... $10
1975 **Adorable Raggedy Ann** $95
1975 **Currier & Ives** satin ball .. $15
1975 **Marty Links** glass ball....... $8
1975 **Santa,** w/sleigh............... $75
1976 **Betsey Clark** satin balls, set of 3 .... $28
1976 **Reindeer,** handcrafted $85
1976 **Rudolph & Santa** satin ball $22
1976 **Santa,** handcrafted.......... $75
1976 **Twirl About Soldier** $32
1977 **Antique Car** $23
1977 **Betsey Clark Truest Joys of Christmas** glass ball, 5th in series.................................... $175
1977 **Drummer Boy,** acrylic..... $28
1977 **Peanuts** glass ball........... $58
1978 **Joan Walsh Anglund** satin ball.................................... $18
1978 **Panorama Ball** $65
1978 **Peanuts** satin ball $42
1978 **Schneeberg Bell** $85
1978 **Skating Raccoon** (reissued in 1979)..................................... $48
1979 **Christmas Collage** glass ball $20
1979 **Christmas Heart** $45
1979 **Rocking Horse,** cloth..... $10
1979 **Santa's Motorcar,** 1st in "Here Comes Santa" series.......... $400
1979 **The Bellswinger,** 1st in "Bellringers" series $250
1980 **A Cool Yule,** 1st in "Frosty Friends" series $400
1980 **Betsey Clark Cameo** $22
1980 **Caroling Bear** $45
1980 **Disney** satin ball............. $15
1980 **JOY,** acrylic....................... $8

Tree topper, figural, a celluloid angel doll w/blonde hair & silvered paper wings & ribbon headband, light pink paper dress, ca. 1930s .... **$95** →

1975 Raggedy Ann yarn **$24**

1975 Santa, w/squirrel on shoulder **$125**

1977 "Happy Holidays" House, dated **$48**

CHRISTMAS COLLECTIBLES

1981 Rocking Horse, 1st in series, dated $400

1984 Santa's Deliveries, Santa at wheel of truck loaded w/Christmas trees, 6th in "Here Comes Santa" series $55

1988 Buttercup, 1st in "Mary's Angels" series $21

1991 Claus & Co. Railroad series: four train car ornaments & trestle $35

1982 Old Fashioned glass ball, decorated w/scene of children putting up Christmas decorations $25

1984 Victorian Dollhouse, 1st in "Nostalgic House" series ... $100

1989 Frosty Friends, 10th in series $30

1980 Skating Snowman $35
1981 Baby's First Christmas $21
1981 Calico Kitty, cloth $15
1981 Divine Miss Piggy (The) $50
1981 Friendly Fiddler (The) $53
1981 Rooftop Deliveries, 3rd in "Here Comes Santa" series $275
1981 St. Nicholas, tin $23
1982 Cowboy Snowman $35
1982 Jingling Teddy $15
1982 Jogging Santa $20
1982 Locomotive, tin, 1st in series $425
1982 Peeking Elf $20
1982 Santa & Reindeer $30
1982 Spirit of Christmas (The) $85
1982 Teacher glass ball............ $5
1983 Angel Messenger $37
1983 Heart, acrylic................ $25
1983 Old Fashioned Santa $42
1983 Skiing Fox $12
1984 "12 Days of Christmas" Partridge, 1st in series $75
1984 Katybeth, porcelain........ $10
1984 Muffin $15
1984 Polar Bear Drummer $10
1984 Sister Bell $12
1984 Uncle Sam, pressed tin .. $20
1985 Ice Skating Owl $8
1985 Kit the Shepherd $13
1985 Rainbow Brite & Friends glass ball............................. $10
1985 Spirit of Santa Claus (The) $55
1985 Sugarplum Cottage, lighted $15
1986 Dasher, 1st in "Reindeer" series................................... $55
1986 Old Fashioned Santa $30
1986 Paddington Bear $20
1986 Soccer Beaver $13
1987 Icy Treat $9
1987 Jack Frosting $25
1987 Let It Snow $12
1987 Wee Chimney Sweep $10
1988 Filled With Fudge $15
1988 Purrfect Snuggle $12
1988 Son $20
1988 Wonderful Santacycle (The) $22
1989 Baby's First Christmas $35
1989 Old World Gnome $10
1989 Rudolph the Red-Nosed Reindeer $45
1989 Strollin' Snowman $10
1990 Air Santa $5
1990 Santa's Ho-Ho-Hoedown $40
1990 Snoopy & Woodstock ... $12
1991 Friendly Fawn................. $5
1991 Sister $11
1992 Fast Finish $5
1992 Sky Line Train, set of 4... $40
1993 Dollhouse Dreams $22

CLOCKS MARKET REPORT

Various types of clocks have been used for thousands of years. Early clocks, such as sundials, water clocks, and marked candle clocks, relied on the calibration of predictable rates, such as the sun's movement, the flow of water through a hole, or melting of wax. Clocks with hands and numbered dial were first used in Europe around the 13th or 14th century. Continuing developments, such as the spring-regulated escapement and pendulum-driven mechanism led to increasing accuracy. Today, of course, we have digital clocks and atomic clocks that are automatically regulated via a radio signal from a cesium atomic clock. While our modern timepieces are more accurate and less susceptible to the environment, what antique clocks lack in precision, they compensate for in beauty.

Kenneth Markley, owner of Old Timers Antique Clocks (www.oldtimersclocks.com) in Camp Hill, Pennsylvania, said "clocks in the $400 to $600 price range are selling well, but higher priced items are sluggish." While porcelain clocks sold well a few years ago, wood ones are favored now, especially solid walnut Victorian models. He says no one in the clock market is exactly sure why the porcelain clocks have lost favor, except that perhaps their earlier popularity priced them out of the market. Royal Bonn porcelain clocks typically go for more than $1,000.

Markley explained that to current buyers, practicality and convenience are just as important as looks. Buyers prefer smaller shelf and wall clocks because they fit better in modern homes, and 8-day and 30-day clocks sell much better than the 30-hour clocks because people don't want to have to wind their clock every day. American models like Seth Thomas, Waterbury, New Haven, Gilbert and E.N. Welch sell much better than European ones, likely because they are more available and affordable and because they appeal more to American aesthetic tastes. Seth Thomas is perhaps the most common of all American makers since it produced a city series of 102 models representing most of the major cities of the world at the time, and some collectors specialize in those city-series clocks.

Markley commented that he sells a number of clocks through his Web site because of his reputation for accuracy, completeness, and his return policy. "It can be frustrating to buy through eBay because sellers often don't know much about the clocks they sell, give inaccurate or incomplete information, and often don't allow returns. While many antiques are fragile and need to be handled with care, clocks are especially susceptible to mishandling and neglect. Plus, they have complicated movements so they should be handled and sold by professionals, who can make sure they are in perfect condition." He credits his success to his experience, his reputation, and to providing a selection of clocks in a wide range of styles and prices so he can offer something for everyone.

Auction Houses
R.O. Schmitt (www.roschmittfinearts.com)
Tom Harris (www.tomharrisauctions.com)
Mark of Time (www.markoftime.com)
Fontaines (www.fontainesauction.net)
Horton's (www.hortonsantiqueclocks.com)

CLOCKS

Banjo clock, mahogany, the round molded top frame topped by a small cast- metal eagle & enclosing the painted metal dial w/Roman numerals, the long narrow neck fitted w/a reverse-painted glass panel & flanked by long pierced C-scroll brackets, the lower rectangular pendulum box w/a glass panel reverse-painted w/a naval battle centered by an American eagle & shield, eight-day brass weight- driven movement, New England, ca. 1820, restored, 31 1/2" h. **$1,763**

Banjo clock, Willard (Simon), Roxbury, Massachusetts, Federal style, inlaid mahogany case w/a top round brass molded bezel enclosing a white painted dial w/ Roman numerals & an eight-day brass weight-driven movement, lower case w/white églomisé tablet & pendulum box tablet inscribed "S. Willards Patent," both framed by mahogany cross-banding & stringing w/flanking pierced brass brackets, old finish, ca. 1815, 32 1/4" h. (restoration) **$1,955**

Grandfather clock, Durfee (Walter), Providence, Rhode Island, Chippendale-Style oak case w/a broken-scroll pediment w/three brass ball finials above an arched glazed door opening to a steel & brass dial w/Roman numerals & two subsidiary dials, flanked by spiral-twist turned column, the tall waist w/a tall glazed door topped by a carved fan & flanked by free-standing spiral-twist columns, the projecting paneled base w/small spiral-twist turned columns at each corner & raised on front paw feet, w/a three-train movement w/ chiming bells & gongs, late 19th - early 20th c., 93" h. **$8,813**

Grandfather clock, Rittenhouse (Benjamin), Philadelphia, Pennsylvania, Chippendale carved cherrywood, broken swan's neck pediment above an arched glazed door, engraved brass dial inscribed "BENJAMIN RITTENHOUSE - FECIT 1790," w/second hand, date hand & moon phase dial, the door below flanked by quarter-columns above ogee bracket feet, ca. 1780, 11 x 19 1/4", 8' 3" h. **$17,250**

Grandfather clock, English, quarter-sawn oak, Georgian style, the broken-scroll pediment centered by a brass ball w/small eagle finial above the arched glazed door w/a top scene of a lady in a flowing dress holding a sickle above the white-painted dial w/ Roman numerals & floral painted spandrels, small colonettes at each front corner, the tall narrow body w/a long pointed arch door w/quarter- round fluted corner columns above the stepped out base section on bracket feet, brass works w/a second hand & calendar movement, rich color, mellow finish, w/weights, pendulum & winder, minor paint flaking, age splits in base w/some replacements, late 18th - early 19th c., 81" h. **$2,030**

Grandfather clock, Herschede (Frank) Clock Co., Cincinnati, Ohio, Gothic Revival style mahogany & mahogany veneer case, steel dial w/Arabic numerals, moon phase movement, large weights & large pendulum, octagonal block front feet, early 20th c. **$3,650**

Grandfather clock, Renaissance Revival style, carved & ebonized oak case, ornately carved case w/a high arched crest over an arched door flanked by carved scrolls & opening to a steel & brass dial w/ Arabic numerals & moon-phase dial, the tall body w/a tall door w/ an oval glass pane surrounded by ornate carving & opening to weights & a brass pendulum, a deep carved serpentine lower case w/a center figure flanked by leafy scrolls, heavy base molding raised on paw feet, movement by JJE, retailed by Tiffany & Co., New York City, late 19th c., 107" h. **$22,325**

Grandfather clock, Federal style, cherry case, arched scroll-carved crest on conforming molded cornice above the matching glazed door flanked by free-standing colonettes, opening to a white-painted dial w/Roman numerals & a painted moon phase, the narrow body of the case w/quarter-round columns at the sides flanking the line-inlaid door, stepped-out lower case w/band inlay & a shaped apron & short French feet, old refinish, ca. 1810, 12 x 15", 86" h. **$3,500**

Grandfather clock, Morris (Benjamin), Reading, Pennsylvania, Federal style, walnut & figured walnut case w/a broken- scroll pediment w/inlaid rosettes & three turned wood urn-form finials above the arched glass door opening to a moon phase dial over the white painted dial w/Roman numerals & floral-painted spandrels, flanked by slender corner colonettes, the waisted section w/chamfered corners & a tall, narrow arched door w/inlaid keyhole escutcheon above the stepped out tall lower section on simple French feet, w/ weights, pendulum & key, minor pieced repairs & replacements, 90" h. **$7,475**

Grandfather clock, Renaissance Revival-style, walnut case, the hood w/fruit & scroll carving, the round face w/painted stylized sun w/brass hands as stylized rays, weight-driven movement, the case open w/bobbin-turned columns on acanthus bases topped by carved female faces, the columns flanking a carved grotesque, the base w/fruit & scroll carving, ca. 1900, Germany, 79" h. **$1,955**

Grandfather clock, Twiss (J. & H.), Montreal, Canada, Federal country-style case, painted & decorated pine, the broken scroll pediments centered by a brass ball finial w/eagle above an arched glazed panel flanked by slender colonettes & opening to the painted dial w/Roman numerals, an urn & basket of flowers & gilt spandrels & signed "I. Twiss Montreal," long center case w/a single door above the stepped out base w/a molded edge & scalloped apron, original graining & yellow line & leaf accents, brass works & finials not original, feet replaced, after 1821, 10 1/2 x 17 5/8" h., 84" h. **$1,725**

Grandfather clock, Herwick (William), North Carolina, Federal style inlaid mahogany case, the molded broken-scroll pediment above an arched frieze band w/line inlay over the set-back arched door opening to a painted dial w/Roman numerals & a moon phase dial, the stepped-out lower case on small French feet, signed indistinctly, untouched & unrestored, early 19th c. . . **$8,750**

CLOCKS

Shelf or mantel clock, china case, the upright ovoid china body decorated w/transfer- printed red blossoms on leafy stems, cobalt blue flow blue leaftip bands around the base & top & dark blue molded lion head & ring side handles, a large round dial w/a gilt-metal bezel & door opening to the face w/Roman numerals and time & strike winding holes, mounted on a scroll-molded cast-metal base & a gilt- metal & ceramic disc cap, ca. 1890s **$1,950**

Shelf or mantel clock, Louis XVI-Style mantel clock, gilt-bronze & cut glass, the upright case w/beveled glass sides & front framed in gilt-brass w/an arched crest & base rail decorated w/ floral swags, a shell crest & berry-form finials, the top mounted w/a cut crystal & gilt-brass urn-shaped finial, the sides flanked by cut crystal columns w/cut crystal finials & raised on blocks & pointed peg feet, S. Marti two-train movement, retailed by Le Roy, Paris, France, late 19th c. **$2,350**

Shelf or Mantel clock, Ansonia Clock Co., Ansonia, Connecticut, ornate Royal Bonn "La Mine" model china case, the tall upright arched case w/waisted sides molded at the top w/a central shell flanked by long open scrolls w/further scrolls down the sides & across the base w/incurved scroll feet, painted a deep magenta at the top w/pale yellow in the center shading to dark green at the base, decorated on the front w/large h.p. white & magenta blossoms & green leaves, the large brass bezel around the porcelain dial, Arabic numerals, open escapement, eight-day movement, time & strike, ca. 1900, 6 1/4 x 11" , 13 1/2" h. ....$1,000-$1,200

Brewster & Ingrahams, Bristol, Connecticut, Kirk's patent movement, beehive form rosewood case w/molded frame & round molding around the round white signed dial w/black Roman numerals, the lower pane reverse-painted w/an image of Ballston Springs, eight-day time & strike rack & snail movement w/original brass springs, age cracks to dial paint, key escutcheon repaired, pendulum a later Seth Thomas type, hands are old but incorrect for this model, ca. 1845, 19" h. **$560**

Shelf or Mantel clock, Ansonia Clock Co., Ansonia, Connecticut, ornate Royal Bonn "La Mine" model china case, the tall upright arched case w/waisted sides molded at the top w/a central shell flanked by long open scrolls w/further scrolls down the sides & across the base w/incurved scroll feet, painted a deep magenta at the top w/pale yellow in the center shading to dark green at the base, decorated on the front w/large h.p. white & magenta blossoms & green leaves, the large brass bezel around the porcelain dial, Arabic numerals, open escapement, eight-day movement, time & strike, ca. 1900, 6 1/4 x 11" , 13 1/2" h... **$750-800**

COCA-COLA ITEMS

Coca-Cola promotion has been achieved through the issuance of scores of small objects through the years. These, together with trays, signs and other articles bearing the name of this soft drink, are now sought by many collectors. The major reference in this field is *Petretti's Coca- Cola Collectibles Price Guide*, 12th Edition, by Allan Petretti (Antique Trader Books). An asterisk (*) indicates a piece that has been reproduced.

Advertising handbook, for Coca-Cola distributors, stiff covers & wire spiral binding, many colorful pages, ca. 1935-55, excellent condition, 9 1/2 x 12" **$578**

Booklet, "50th Anniversary Coca-Cola 1886-1936 - Coca-Cola Bottlers Advertising Price List," w/red Coca-Cola 50th anniversary button logo, 1936, 16 pp., very good condition, 11 x 15" **$550**

Bookmark, 1898, celluloid, heart-shaped, black & white image of a beautiful woman w/glass in center, red wording "Drink Coca-Cola - Delicious ... - 5¢ - Refreshing" in border, 2 3/8 x 2 3/4" **$1,760**

Calendar, 1921, roll-down type, color illustration of young woman wearing dark blue & white outfit & hat sitting in garden setting amid pink & yellow flowers & holding glass of Coke, metal band at top, portion of calendar pad for November at bottom, framed, 16 1/2 x 36" **$900**

Can, cylindrical color-printed metal w/fitted flat red top, various action sports scenes around the sides w/Coca-Cola advertising in the background, 1990, 6" h. **$10**

Clock & sign, countertop neon light-up style, a round clock dial at the top in black on white w/"Drink Coca-Cola" in red on a stepped frame above a long rectangular sign in red banded w/chrome & featuring a white neon tube around a yellow circle w/a six-pack of Coca-Cola & white wording "Drink Coca-Cola - Take home a carton," domed clock cover may be a replacement, some motors & transformers updated, minor paint & edge wear, 1930s **$13,750**

Clock counter sign, light-up type, brass colored metal, square clock w/white face & dark green number panel w/gold Arabic numerals, attached at side to panel reading "Drink Coca-Cola" in white lettering on red ground, all on base w/white front edge reading "Have a Coke" in green lettering, a Price Makers decal on back, 19 1/2 l., 8 1/2" h. **$840**

COCA-COLA ITEMS

Cooler, rectangular, red embossed tin advertising panels on all four sides, legs that have been cut down just above lower case storage rack, metal tag reads "The Coca-Cola Company Cooler Patented March 4, 1930. Mfg. by Glascock Bros. Mfg. Co. Muncie, IN," no top, 23 1/2 x 31 1/2", 31 3/4" h. **$374**

Counter sign, light-up waterfall type, brass colored frame, square panel w/waterfall effect reading "Pause and Refresh" in gold on black ground w/green top & bottom borders, attached at side to panel reading "Drink Coca-Cola" in white lettering on red ground, all on base w/white front edge reading "Please Pay When Served" in green lettering, Price Manufacturing label on rear, rare, 19 1/2" l., 9" h. **$1,898**

Counter sign, reverse printed transfer on glass in wooden base, rectangular, reads "Drink Coca-Cola" in white lettering on bright red ground, the rear w/original paper decal reading "Price Bros. The Sign of Quality Chicago, NY," the wooden base w/attached white panel reading "Coke" in red, 5 x 12" **$460**

Door knobs, cast brass, each w/the Coca- Cola logo in the center, ca. 1913-15, set of two **$1,320**

Festoon, die-cut cardboard, Verbena, yellow verbena garlands surround picture of woman drinking Coke in center & "Drink Coca-Cola - Delicious and Refreshing" in white on green-bordered red boxes at center & each end, 1932, w/original envelope, minor flaws & spots, extends to over 9' **$1,100**

Sign, color-printed paper, long, narrow, rectangular banner style, a large half- length of Santa Claus at the left w/two six-packs of Coke on the right below the white wording "Almost everyone appreciates the best...," 1955, matted & framed **$440**

Leaded glass shade, hanging-type, wide cylindrical flat sides w/panels formed by narrow bands of green slag glass enclosing deep ruby glass inset w/the Coca-Cola name in white glass script, the wide angled top & flaring crown band composed of white glass section, metal band at crown stamped "Property of The Coca-Cola Company - To Be Returned On Demand," 1920s, one piece of green slag broken other very good condition, 16" d. **$4,030**

Ring, 50 year service commemorative, custom-made in 14k yellow gold w/ten diamond chips, openwork design w/a relief- cast bottle of Coca-Cola framed by laurel wreath, light wear, size 8 1/2-9, ca. 1930- 50 .... **$1,650**

String holder, lithographed tin, composed of two low curved panels, the front printed in yellow & red w/a color picture of a six-pack in the center, reads "Take Home Coca-Cola In Cartons," 1940s, only minor flaws, 12 16" **$2,530**

Thermometer, Masonite, rectangular, the red & white Coca-Cola button at the top above a color picture of a bottle beside a long thermometer in white, dark & light green ground w/"Thirst knows no season" at the bottom, 1944, only minor marks & soiling, 7 x 17" **$523**

Trolley sign, cardboard, printed in color w/a pretty young woman reclining in a hammock & holding up a glass of Colca-Cola, sepia-toned background, reads across the bottom "Have a Drink of Coca-Cola - Deliciously Refreshing," 1912, matted & framed, minor edge marks & crimps, 11 x 20 1/2" **$11,550**

Thermometer, round w/domed glass, black letters & red & white center logo on white ground read "Drink Coca-Cola Be Really Refreshed!," Pam-type dial, 1959, only minor marks, few minor bends to metal face, 12" d. **$935**

Thermometer, porcelain, oblong, round logo in gold, red & white at the top reading "Drink Coca-Cola" above a long dark green center panel printed in yellow "Thirst knows no season" next to the thermometer & over a yellow & green silhouette of lady drinking from bottle, Canadian, ca. 1939, few small chips, clear-coated w/some touch-up, tube appears to be a replacement, 5 1/2 x 18" ... **$715**

Thermometer, round, red center w/gold outline of Coke bottle & "Drink Coca-Cola" in white lettering, surrounded by green border w/black degree marks & numerals, black hand for indicating temperature, marked at bottom "Pam Clock Co. Mt. Vernon, New York 48," 12" d. **$518**

Thermometer, tin, die-cut bottle-shaped, reads "Coca-Cola - Trade Mark Registered - Bottle Pat'd Dec. 25, 1923," small thermometer at the bottom, small marks & minor wear, 1930s, 5 x 17" **$275**

Thermometer, tin, "Drink Coca-Cola - Delicious and Refreshing," red ground circle above thermometer & black-on-white silhouette of girl drinking from bottle in circle below, 1939, minor marks, some edge chinks, 6 1/2 x 16" ... **$358**

Tray, 1905, serving, oval, large center color picture w/a half-length portrait of Lilian Nordica leaning one arm on a pedestal that holds an early bottle of Coca-Cola & reading "Drink Carbonated Coca-Cola In Bottles - 5¢", gold border band w/leaf design, only minor flaws, 13" l. **$6,600**

Thermometer, tin, vertical oval form w/a thin gold border band, red background & large Coca-Cola bottle framing thermometer, complete w/gold hanging string & tassel in original box, 1938, 7 x 16" **$1,210**

Toy truck, route delivery type, red w/yellow bottle holder in truck bed, marked "Every Bottle Coca-Cola Sterilized," No. 171 Metalcraft w/rubber wheels, 1932, some wear & soiling, 11" l. **$880**

Tray, 1941, serving, tin litho, rounded rectangular shape, center panel w/color illustration of young woman wearing babushka, short red skirt & white ice skates sitting on a log at rink's edge against wooded backdrop & holding bottle of Coke, the gilt-trimmed red rim w/"Drink Coca-Cola" in yellow lettering at both top & bottom, American Art Works, 10 1/2 x 13 1/4" **$237**

Tray, 1933, serving, rectangular, horizontal view of Johnny Weismuller & Maureen O'Sullivan (Hollywood's Tarzan & Jane), average condition w/some chips & nicks, 10 1/2 x 13 1/4" **$715**

Tray, 1910, serving, rectangular, Hamilton King Girl above "Drink Delicious Coca-Cola" in lower right corner & "The Coca-Cola Girl" in left corner, reproduced, few semi-gloss areas on face, minimal crazing & rim nicks, 10 1/2 x 13 1/4" **$2,200**

Tray, 1916, serving, rounded rectangular shape, center w/color illustration of young woman wearing wide-brimmed hat & cream-colored dress seated under a tree near pink cut roses while holding a glass of Coke & looking back over her shoulder at viewer, "Drink Coca-Cola" in light blue letters at top, decorated gilt rim, edge wear, 8 1/2 x 19" **$220**

•Beware of the vast amount of fake, reproduction, and fantasy Coca-Cola items on the market. This collectible category is one of the most heavily reproduced in the antiques and collectibles industry.

•A fake is a copy that is intended to deceive. A reproduction is a copy not intended to deceive but can sometimes be mistaken for genuine (or altered by a dishonest person). A fantasy is piece designed to look like an antique but was never originally produced.

Vending machine, Cavalier Model CS-72- A, upright style w/narrow two-pane door at front left, white & red, ca. 1960, 57" h. ... **$1,610**

COMIC BOOKS MARKET REPORT

According to Maggie Thompson and Brent Frankenhoff of *Comics Buyer's Guide* magazine (www.cbgxtra.com), the current economic climate has prompted a flurry of activity. The Certified Guaranty Company, the only major third-party grading service in the comics industry, has seen "an incredible volume of comics in the last year because people are cleaning out their basements and attics to turn their comics into cash," Frankenhoff said.

The vintage comics hobby can be divided into three commonly recognized eras (although the exact dates are widely debated): the Golden Age (1938 to 1949), Silver Age (1956 to 1971) and Bronze Age (mid 1970s to mid 1980s). Comics from the mid '70s and later are fun to collect but are too common to appreciate significantly in value.

The comics hobby is largely show driven, with numerous national, regional and local shows. The largest is the annual Comic-Con convention in San Diego. The four-day show in July hosts more than 100,000 attendees and dealers. These shows aren't just for those with deep pockets; vintage comics are available for collectors at all levels. For instance, low-end comics can be purchased for a dollar or less, making them a bargain compared to brand new releases, which sell for $3. They're a great deal for those who just want collect for nostalgia or to introduce their children to reading. Comics in this category are often the tame animal character comics, like *Tom and Jerry*, which are suitable and appealing to beginning readers. "It's a way to get kids to read for pleasure rather than thinking of reading only as a school assignment. It's never too early to start," Thompson said, recalling that she recently came across a comic she bought when she was just three-and-a-half.

Mid-range comics can go for $25 to $50 and high-end from $100 to $500. With a few exceptions, vintage Marvel comics with superhero characters command the top prices. For example, in March 2009, a *Superman Action Comics #1* (the holy grail of comic book collecting) in mid-grade condition sold at auction for $317,000. Original art comic strip art is at the pinnacle of the hobby, though, because they are one-of-kind pieces. Black and white daily *Peanuts* strips by Charles Schulz generally sell for at least $10,000 each, and his color Sunday strips sell for far higher.

While counterfeits aren't a huge problem in the comics field because of the difficulty and expense of duplicating them, there are occasional problems. One notable example is the reprints of *Action Comics #1* made in the 1970s. The publisher went to great lengths to identify them as reprints, producing them in oversize form and adding a cardstock outer cover identifying the issue as a reprint. Unfortunately, dishonest collectors have removed the outer cover and sold them to naive buyers who don't realize they are much bigger than the originals. Also, the first issue of *Teenage Mutant Ninja Turtles* was deliberately counterfeited because it was much easier to reproduce its black and white pages than standard four-color-plate comics.

Thompson and Frankenhoff's advice: "Ask a lot of questions. Good dealers will take time to answer them. Unscrupulous dealers will just take your money. If you haven't decided on a category to collect, go to a show and buy a wide variety of lower-end comics. Then decide what works for you. Keep the ones you like and trade or sell the rest. Use the trade-up system to improve the quality of your collection; buy lower-grade comics as placeholders, purchase better copies when they become available at the right price, and then sell your lower-grade copies to finance future purchases."

Auction Houses
Heritage (www.ha.com)
Diamond Galleries (www.diamondgalleries.com)

COMIC BOOKS

Comic books, especially first or early issues of a series, are avidly collected today. Prices for some of the scarce ones have reached extremely high levels. Prices listed below show a range for copies from "Good" to "Mint" condition.

Looney Tunes - Merrie Melodies Comics, #2, cover image of Bugs Bunny kissing Porky Pig, 1941 .... **$600-3,000**

Master Comics, #116, Fawcett Publications, w/Tom Mix & Captain Marvel, Jr., early 1950s **$75-175**

Minute Man - The One Man Army, #1, Fawcett Publications, anti-Nazi cover, 1941 ..... **$800-3,000**

Our Army at War, #164, Presents Sgt. Rock's 6 Battle Stars, DC, giant 80 page edition, 1960s **$75-300**

Rangers Comics, #33, Fiction House Magazines, 1947 .... **$100-300**

Richie Rich, #7, Harvey Comics, 1961 .... **$100-400**

Evel Knievel, Marvel Comics/Ideal toy Corp., unnumbered give-away, 1974...................... **$20-60**

Fantastic Four (The), #4, Marvel Comics, first Sub-Mariner appearance, 1962.... **$1,200-6,000**

X-Men, #14, Marvel, first appearance of The Sentinels, 1965 .... **$150-600**

COMPACTS & VANITY CASES

A lady's powder compact is a small portable cosmetic make-up box that contains powder, a mirror and puff. Eventually, the more elaborate compact, the "vanity case," evolved, containing a mirror, puffs and compartments for powder, rouge and/or lipstick. Compacts made prior to the 1960s when women opted for the "au natural" look are considered vintage. These vintage compacts were made in a variety of shapes, sizes, combinations, styles and in every conceivable natural or man-made material. Figural, enamel, premium, commemorative, patriotic, Art Deco and souvenir compacts were designed as a reflection of the times and are very desirable. The vintage compacts that are multipurpose, combined with another accessory—the compact/watch, compact/music box, compact/fan, compact/purse, compact/perfumer, compact/lighter, compact/cane, compact/hatpin—are but a few of the combination compacts that are not only sought after by the compact collector but also appeal to collectors of the secondary accessory.

Today vintage compacts and vanity cases are very desirable collectibles. There are compacts and vanities to suit every taste and purse. The "old" compacts are the "new" collectibles. Compacts have come into their own as collectibles. They are listed as a separate category in price guides, sold in prestigious auction houses, displayed in museums, and several books and many articles on the collectible compact have been written. There is also a newsletter, Powder Puff, written by and for compact collectors. The beauty and intricate workmanship of the vintage compacts make them works of fantasy and art in miniature.

For additional information on the history and values of compacts and vanity cases, readers should consult *Vintage and Vogue Ladies' Compacts* by Roselyn Gerson, Collector Books.

Bakelite compact, back w/the top of the lid decorated w/rhinestones, the interior features a mirror & powder well, w/a black carrying cord & three long tassels, center tassel contains a black Bakelite tube containing perfume, the other two tassels contain lipsticks marked "Paris" **$450**

Bakelite is a plastic invented by Dr. Leo Baekland in the early 20th century. It produces a distinct formaldehyde odor when rubbed or held under hot water. This odor can be used to distinguish between genuine and fake Bakelite.

Bakelite compact, round dark green marbleized Bakelite case, the lid decorated w/pink carved Bakelite roses & painted green leaves, interior holds a beveled mirror & powder compartment, plastic ring carrying chain w/finger ring **$125**

Black enamel compact, oblong, Zodiac design designed by Erte, featuring Sagittarius, the cover w/outside rim enhanced w/rows of clear crystals framing a black star-studded silhouette of a centaur, the figure centered on a blue flowered cloud w/bow & arrow, Estee Lauder **$90**

Bicolor 18k gold & diamond compact, the case decorated w/a woven design of diamonds in three shades of gold, the thumbpiece bead-set w/full-cut diamonds, opening to a mirrored compartment, signed by Bulgari, No. 6489, w/black fabric sleeve, 2 1/4" d. **$2,233**

Black seude & brass vanity bag, bolster- shaped, "Noir Danseuse" model, a compact fitted into the lid, silk-lined interior, the top of the lid decorated w/an openwork brass silhouette of a dancing female designed to resemble Josephine Baker, w/carrying handle w/tassel **$550**

Enameled compact & lipstick set, antique vermeil sterling silver enameled pieces, the oblong compact w/engraved gilt banding centering an oval panel painted w/two lady musicians framed by dark green & black panels, the matching long rectangular lipstick w/a similar enameled scene & a blue cabochon stone on the latch, the compact w/a gilded interior w/ a beveled mirror, the lipstick tub opens to reveal a small mirror, lipstick $150 & powder compact (ILLUS. of compact & lipstick) **$750**

Brass compact, two-sided model on black silk braid cord, one side opening to powder compartment, the other side holding rouge compartment, both lids w/mirror inside, two pull-out rouge sticks on either side of cord, a center lid between the cord attachments unscrewing to reveal perfume compartment **$120**

Enameled mesh vanity bag w/silvertone metal cover, multicolored pink, green & brown embossed enamel design, metal oblong vanity cover opens to reveal compartments for powder, rouge & comb, complete w/ carrying chain, "El sah" imprint on attached interior metal tag, Whiting & Davis **$450**

Enameled   brooch/pendant compact, round, cover decorated w/applied blue enamel design enhanced w/crystals, removable pin decorated w/an enlarged version of design on lid, Volupte **$300**

Estee Lauder compact, "Golden Age" design, rectangular brushed goldtone, lid embossed w/an Art Deco style face of a lady, 1994 .... **$80**

Whiting & Davis is known for its products made of mesh material. Before 1909, when the automatic mesh making machine was invented, mesh had to be hand linked, making it very costly. Whiting & Davis capitalized on the automation and became the industry leader in mesh fashion accessories.

Fabric compact, figural, designed to resemble a large picture hat, the lid covered w/fabric resembling beading & mother-of-pearl petals on flowers, trimmed in pink velvet, the reverse in black silk **$325**

Flamand-Fladium goldtone compact- bracelet, a wide bangle bracelet decorated w/ large pierced stars & centered at the top w/an onyx disk set by gold stars & framed w/a braided rope-form band, onyx lid opens to the compact, signed "Claudine Cerola," France **$375**

Fabric-covered goldtone & enamel compact, round shape w/carrying strap, black enamel & goldtone rim, red floral fabric covering front & back & forming carrying strap, the interior w/ powder well, the front lid w/sleeve for lipstick & pocket for comb behind decorative bow, Vanity **$175**

Flato goldtone compact & lipstick, the flat goldtone compact decorated w/small good luck symbols centered by an applied wishbone, in a black case w/a sleeve at the side for the matching lipstick tube **$225**

Gold plate carryall, textured polished goldtone lid decorated w/bands of black enamel flanking cartouche of black enamel, the gilded interior w/powder & rouge compartments & well for mini-perfume bottle, the center mirror flanked by two lipstick tubes, a cigarette compartment behind mirror, mesh carrying chain, Dermey (ILLUS. open & closed) **$450**

Goldtone & enamel compact, round, the lid decorated w/profile of woman's face, a rose & a star on dark blue & black background, goldtone decorations over the top & around rim, silvertone bottom, Karess **$150**

Various types of rouge have been used since ancient times, such as juice from crushed beets and red berries. Modern rouge is made from colored powder, making it much more practical to use.

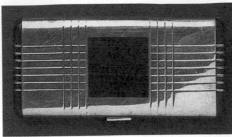

Gold, silver gilt & enamel compact, Art Deco style, long rectangular case in gold incised w/thin bands & centered by a black enamel square w/further trim at each end, opening to a mirrored interior w/lipstick & two compartments, diamond thumbpiece, hallmark of Cartier, Paris & French guarantee stamps **$1,998**

Goldtone decorated vanity, model of an Air Express package w/a blue ground, white & black name tag & a red & white "Rush - Railway Express" sticker, a raised goldtone cord, interior opens to mirror, powder & rouge compartments **$125**

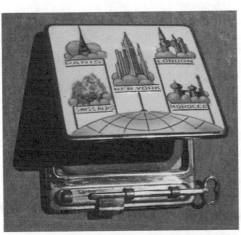

Hingeco Vanities, Inc. compact, "sardine can" style, white enameled metal lid decorated w/colorful scenes of Paris, London, New York, the Swiss Alps & Morocco, a key on bottom of lid pulls out & turns to open compact (ILLUS. open) **$250**

Goldtone vanity bag, round, filigree compact set w/blue stones on front of lid, top opening reveals interior bag w/shirred pockets, black silk carrying cord w/metal tassel, antique **$550**

Ivorene vanity set: goldtone lipstick tube, round plastic compact in hatbox presentation box & rectangular hinged rouge case; w/carved decorations of figures on a swing applied to lipstick & on lids of compact & rouge case, the lids also w/foliage decoration around rims & imprinted initials "L.D.," interior of compact w/ mirror & powder compartment, Lilly Dache "Loving Touch," the set **$300**

Polished silvertone compact, round, Art Deco style, the cover decorated w/an enamel design of circular motifs in shades of pink, plum & violet, Estee Lauder **$125**

Rare round cork compact, goldtone metal decorated w/a blue & orange abstract enamel design **$150**

Silvertone & enamel compact, round, made to resemble a spinning roulette wheel, silvertone ground decorated w/black enamel outer lid centered w/red, black, green & white numbered sections, interior reveals powder puff w/Zephyr logo **$350**

Richard Hudnut "le Debut" enameled vanity, an octagonal compact w/the stepped lid centered by blue enamel & a stylized white blossom, joined by a tango chain finger ring to a matching lipstick tube, compact opens to powder & rouge compartments separated by a mirror, in the original fitted presentation box **$250**

Whiting & Davis vanity bag, silvertone "El- sah" mesh enameled in a lattice design in shades of green, yellow & white, comes w/a carrying chain & a Van Dyke-style bottom edge, top of compact mesh lid enameled w/pink & green flowers, compact opens to a round lidded powder well, "El-sah" imprint on attached interior metal tag, early 20th c. **$450**

Silvertone pendant/compact, oblong, cut- off corners, white enameled cover decorated w/ black silhouette of period lady, back opens to reveal metal mirror & powder well, complete w/silvertone chain **$125**

Volupté compact, "Petite Boudoir," silvertone model of a vanity table w/collapsible cabriole legs, a mirror on the outside top of lid, interior w/powder compartment & signed puff, complete w/original presentation box (ILLUS. of compact & box) **$175**

DECOYS

Decoys have been used for years to lure flying water fowl into target range. They have been made of carved and turned wood, papier-mâché, canvas and metal. Some are in the category of outstanding folk art and command high prices.

Black Duck, Cobb Island, Virginia, carved wood w/old used repaint, inlet head w/tack eyes, crack in head, small cracks in underside, worn area on lower side, large carved "A" on underside, presumably for Arthur Cobb, last quarter 19th c. **$2,000**

Black Duck, Elmer Crowell, East Harwich, Massachusetts, carved wood w/lifted head pose, original paint w/strong feathering & minor wear, worn area on top of head, several tiny shot marks, oval brand on underside, first quarter 20th c. **$3,250**

Black Duck, Mason Decoy Factory, Detroit, Michigan, carved wood w/ original paint w/minor wear, crack in underside, Challenge grade **$1,300**

Bluebill drake, Mason Decoy Factory, Detroit, Michigan, carved wood w/snakey head & very wide bill, original paint w/some wear, several small cracks & shot marks, Premier grade **$1,300**

Bluebill hen, Elmer Crowell, East Harwich, Massachusetts, carved wood w/crossed wing tips & fluted tail, near mint original paint, rectangular stamp on underside, second quarter 20th c. . **$19,000**

Bluebill hen, Mason Decoy Factory, Detroit, Michigan, hollow-carved wood w/strong original paint w/ average wear, crack runs through neck, some paint flaked on back, Premier grade, 1896- 1924 .... **$1,500**

Bluewing Teal drake, carved & painted wood, Mason factory, Challenge grade, original paint w/ minor to moderate flaking & wear, several tiny dents & shot marks, branded "DWH" **$8,250**

Brant, carved wood w/old repaint w/some wear, the bill a late replacement, some deterioration to wood on head, characteristic split-tail carving, unknown carver, Eastern Shore Virginia, late 19th - early 20th c. **$800**

Bufflehead drake, Mason Decoy Factory, Detroit, Michigan, carved wood w/superb original paint w/ only minor wear & discoloration, couple of minor shot marks, Premier grade, only second example known, branded "Manning," last quarter 19th c. **$17,000**

Canada goose, Ben Schmidt, Detroit, Michigan, hollowed from underside, detachable head w/ small metal plate at neck seam, crack in tail, second quarter 20th c. **$5,500**

Canada goose, Ira Hudson, Chincoteague, Virginia, carved wood, old working repaint, filled & unpainted crack in bottom, tight fracture to neck, chew marks on end of bill, first half 20th c. **$1,100**

Canada Goose, James Whitney, Falmouth, Maine, large oversized carved & painted wood, natural flaw in wood on back now plugged, branded w/name of maker **$150**

DECOYS

Canada goose, Marcel Dufour, Verdun, Quebec, Canada, swimming position, head turned slightly, original paint, shot marks (ILLUS. right) **$1,100**

Canada goose, Sam Soper, Barnegat, New Jersey, swimming pose, hollow-carved w/good feather detail, original paint w/ good patina, minor wear, repair to crack in neck, early **$2,200**

Canvasback drake & hen, Augustus Moak, Tustin, Wisconsin, carved & painted wood, hollow-carved w/ original paint w/minor discoloration & wear, several small dents, hend w/slightly turned head, second quarter 20th c., pr. **$5,225**

Canvasback drake & hen, Mason Decoy Factory, Detroit, Michigan, carved wood w/repaint in the Mason style, both w/professional repairs to bills & a thin crack in the bottom, Premier grade, Back Bay model, 1896-1924, pr. **$700**

Canvasback drake, Ed Phillips, Cambridge, Maryland, original paint in black w/white midsection, red neck & head, grey bill, early second quarter 20th c. (ILLUS. top w/Ed Phillips redhead drake) **$2,475**

Canvasback drake, Lee Dudley, Knott's Island, North Carolina, humpback "classic" style w/"V" wing carving, original paint w/some overpaint removed, branded "ELM" for E.L. Mayer, vice president of Morse Point Gunning Club & Pocahontas Fowling Club, very rare, professional repair to bill, ca. 1900 .... **$25,300**

Canvasback drake, Ward Brothers, Crisfield, Maryland, 1932-36 model, original paint **$10,450**

Goldeneye drake, Mason Decoy Factory, Detroit, Michigan, hollow-carved wood w/old repaint to white areas showing some wear & flaking, tight factory-filled crack on back, some wear to edges of tail, Premier grade, 1896-1924 .... **$2,950**

Canvasback hen & drake, Ken Anger, Dunnville, Ontario, Canada, original paint, pr. **$4,620**

Goldeneye drake, Ward Brothers, Crisfield, Maryland, "Fat Jaw" model, head turned approximately 20 degrees & lifted slightly, dry original paint w/alligatored surface, old replaced glass eyes, ca. 1918 (ILLUS. left) **$28,600**

DECOYS

Gray Coot, Mason Decoy Factory, Detroit, Michigan, carved wood w/some working overpaint taken down to original surface, apparent repair to chip on tail, original "Challenge" stamp, Challenge grade, 1896-1924 .... **$1,800**

Gull, standing position, relief wing carving w/crossed wing tips, old black overpaint removed to show original paint, Long Island, New York, ca. 1900 .... **$12,650**

Mallard drake, carved & painted wood, very thin shelled, light weight w/serrated mandibles & good bill carving, original paint w/minor shrinkage & wear, slight roughness on tail edge, minor structural wear, Ontario, Canada, last quarter 19th c. **$10,725**

Mallard drake, Elmer Crowell, East Harwich, Massachusetts, carved wood w/head turned about 30 degrees & slightly lifted, tail feather carving, fine blended original paint w/good patina, underside never painted, pre-stamp, first quarter 20th c. **$15,000**

Mallard drake, Mason Decoy Factory, Detroit, Michigan, carved wood w/original paint w/minor discoloration & wear, professional tail chip repair, Premier grade w/Premier stamp on underside, first quarter 20th c. **$2,100**

Merganser drake, carved & painted wood, Mason factory, Challenge grade, taken down to original paint w/minor wear, numerous dents & shot marks, some old neck filler replaced, first quarter 20th c. **$3,575**

Merganser drake, George Huey, Friendship, Maine, carved & painted wood, fine dry original paint w/patinated surface, bill broken off & reattached, carved into bottom "Builder, G.R. Huey" w/a carved flying bird, 20th c. **$13,750**

Merganser drake, George Huey, Friendship, Maine, large red-breasted body w/slightly turned inlet head attached to body w/ small wooden dowel, carved eyes, "G R HUEY" carved in underside, original paint, second quarter 20th c., professional repair to bill **$11,275**

Old squaw, Gus Wilson, South Portland, Maine, w/characteristic carved eyes & raised shoulder & wings, dry original paint, swivel heads, rare, second quarter 20th c., pr. **$5,500**

Pintail drake, Elmer Crowell, East Harwich, Massachusetts, three-quarters size, carved wood w/ slightly turned head, near mint original paint w/blended feather painting, hairline surface crack on side of neck, some sap bleeding, rectangular stamp on underside, early 20th c. **$4,500**

Pintail drake, Mason Factory, Detroit, Michigan, hollow body, original paint w/crazed & crackled surface, original feathering still visible, thin crack in tail secured from bottom w/two small nails, first quarter 20th c. **$9,900**

Red-breasted Merganser drake, Miles Hancock, Chincoteague, Virginia, carved wood w/unusual preening pose, original paint, several tight checks in body, second quarter 20th c. **$900**

DISNEY COLLECTIBLES

Scores of objects ranging from watches to dolls have been created showing Walt Disney's copyrighted animated cartoon characters, and an increasing number of collectors now are seeking these, made primarily by licensed manufacturers.

ALSO SEE *Antique Trader Toy Price Guide*.

Alice in Wonderland film, 35mm Eastman Co. story reel w/original film tin w/original blue paper label, 1950s, rusting on the tin ... **$575**

Big Red comic book, "Walt Disney's Big Red," Gold Key Comics, color cover of Big Red & boy, 1962 .... **$10-35**

Black Hole book, "Walt Disney Productions - The Black Hole - A Press-Out Book," filled w/cut-outs of figures & space ships to reenact the movie, Whitman Publishing Co., 1979, 10 x 14" **$30**

Cinderella movie cel, watercolor on celluloid portrait of the evil stepmother, Lady Tremayne, 1949-50, 8 x 8" **$403**

Bambi cel, limited edition showing Bambi & his forest friends & Thumper teaching Bambi his first word, from an edition of 500 w/a certificate of authenticity from Disney Art Editions, background 12 x 15" **$1,093**

Donald Duck toy, windup tin, Donald the Drummer, Donald sways back & forth & nods & drums, Line-Mar, Japan, 6" h. **$210**

Ferdinand the Bull toy, key-wind tin, walking Ferdinand w/fabric flowers in his mouth, marked "Japan - Walt Disney Productions," 1938, all original w/box, 5 1/2" l., 4" h. **$360**

Fantasia pre-production sketch, pastel on paper, a scene of two centaurettes frolicking, in shades of green, yellow & blue, 1940, matted & framed, 7 x 11" **$1,315**

Fantasia movie premier program, large format souvenir-type printed on the cover w/a large black title panel surrounded by colored sketches of various characters from the movie, virtually mint, 1940, 9 1/2 x 12 1/2" **$225**

Goddess of Spring (The) production drawing, red & pencil sketch of Hades (dressed as the Devil) offering a crown to Persephone, the Goddess of Spring, a Silly Symphony production, 1934, 5 1/2 x 6 1/4" **$288**

Jiminy Cricket (from Pinocchio) figurine, ceramic, colorful, 2 3/4" h. **$10-20**

Goofy cartoon drawing, "Tennis Racket," 1948, pencil sketch of Goofy ready to play tennis, image 3 1/4 x 6" **$259**

Lady and The Tramp movie storyboard drawing, black on paper, Lady being held up to look into the baby's crib, 7 x 14 1/2" **$288**

Lady and The Tramp movie cel, gouache on full celluloid, Lady seated & looking surprised, 1955, image 3 1/2 x 4 1/2" **$660**

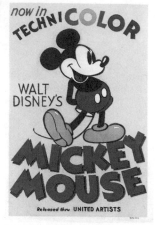

Mickey Mouse poster, for a color cartoon, a bright yellow background printed w/a large image of Mickey & colorful wording reading "now in Technicolor - Walt Disney's Mickey Mouse - Released thru United Artists," one-sheet, 1935, linen- backed, 27 x 41" **$14,350**

Mickey Mouse cartoon drawing, "Mickey's Garden," 1935, pencil sketch of Mickey entangled in a giant snake-like hose, image 5 1/2 x 9" **$978**

Mickey Mouse cartoon drawing, "Society Dog Show," 1939, pencil sketch of Mickey being ejected from the dog show, image 5 1/2 x 6 3/4" **$403**

Mickey Mouse Explorers Club Outfit, boxed set w/gun belt revolver, binoculars, etc., near mint, slight damage to box, box 10" sq. **$345**

Mickey Mouse figure, celluloid nodder, flattened standing figure of Mickey w/a nodding head, holding a square banjo, on a blue round base, excellent original paint & rare paper label reading "Mickey Mouse Copt. 1928, 1930 by Walter E. Disney," made in Japan, 7" h. **$805**

Mickey & Minnie Mouse figures, ceramic, Mickey holding flowers to give to Minnie, decorated in dark blue, black, white & yellow, American Pottery Co., w/original stickers, 6" h., pr. **$300-500**

Mickey Mouse toy, windup tin, Mickey Mouse Ferris Wheel, colorful printing w/the head of Mickey at the side of the base, other Disney characters on the baskets, by Chein, mechanism replaced, other restoration, 17" h. **$230**

Minnie Mouse doll, cloth & felt, her large head w/black felt ears, pie wedge eyes & a black wide-open mouth, her black body w/skinny limbs, the hands w/ large white gloves, the feet w/ large red felt shoes, retains about 90% of original paper tag on the chest, head looks repaired & sewn on, 1930s, 10" h. **$690**

Pinocchio movie cel, painted celluloid scene of Cleo the goldfish w/bubbles against a dark blue ground, Courvoisier set-up, w/original mat label, ca. 1940, overall 3 x 3 1/2" **$1,150**

Mickey Mouse cartoon cel, production cel w/Mickey standing on a large stage, unknown film, hand-prepared background, signed by Frank Thomas & Ollie Johnston, ca. 1940s, background 13 x 15" **$2,070**

Pluto toy, pull-type w/bell, lithographed paper on wood figure of a racing Pluto pulling a four-wheeled platform w/bell, three small lithographed cardboard figures of Mickey Mouse are detached from the platform & one is missing, early 1930s, overall 20 1/2" l. **$1,898**

DISNEY COLLECTIBLES

Pluto cartoon cel, painted celluloid showing a wistful Pluto seated bside a stream, on a reproduction background, ca. 1940s, background 7 x 8 1/2" **$805**

Winnie The Pooh and The Blustery Day movie cel, watercolor on celluloid, a half- length portrait of Tigger, on a stock Art Corner reproduction background, cell stapled to ground, Art Corner gold seal on the back, background 10 x 11 3/4" **$403**

Sleeping Beauty movie cel, a forest landscape w/a small figure of Briar Rose walking w/her basket, gouache on celluloid applied to an airbrushed background, 1959, 1 1/2 x 3" **$837**

Pluto toy, windup tin, "Drum Major," seated Pluto holding a horn, cane & bell, Line Mar, Japan, replaced ears, 5 1/2" h. **$201**

Snow White & the Seven Dwarfs production drawing, pencil sketch showing a half-length portrait of the Queen disguised as the old hag, w/studio stamp, 1937, image 5 1/4 x 7 1/4" **$633**

DOLLS MARKET REPORT

According to Dawn Herlocher, author of *200 Years of Dolls, Identification and Price Guide*, the antique and vintage doll market is down, as it is in most collecting categories. In the past, "doll collectors have been driven by exuberance, but in the current economic climate, they are more cautious." Herlocher speculates that dolls have been harder hit than some other collecting categories because they're less practical than categories like glass, ceramics, jewelry, and furniture.

The economy isn't the only thing that has affected the doll market, Herlocher explained. "eBay and Internet charlatans hurt the doll business by artificially inflating prices and creating a fake market." For example, five years ago, collectors could find 1960s Blythe dolls at garage sales and flea markets for $3 to $4. But recently they were selling for $2,700, which she believes has skewed their true value relative to the rest of the doll market.

Herlocher added that low-end dolls, which sell for $500 and below, are "wonderfully diverse, with a wide variety of manufacturers and materials, such as hard plastic." Mid-range dolls, such as French and German bisque dolls made before World War I, run $600 to $1,200. High end dolls sell for $1,500 to $30,000 or more.

High-end dolls are still selling, but not as fast as they used to. Mid range and lower are in even more of a slump. "Although the top and bottom of the market have traditionally gone up and down over the years, the mid range has stayed consistent, except for the last year," she said.

Doll collectors used to be older women, but that has changed in recent years. More than half the collectors are now younger women. Herlocher attributes the change to women developing an interest in collecting after buying dolls on QVC. They start with those dolls and eventually want to own antique dolls. She said that there aren't any antique dolls or doll makers that are dominating the market. Interest runs the gamut and is governed by personal taste and preference.

Bubbles do occur in the market from time to time. This year has seen increased interest in the Barbie doll because of her 50th anniversary. Events like these often cause '50s and '60s dolls to fluctuate, but antique dolls will always sell because there will always be more demand than supply. Herlocher pointed out that this is a good time to expand a collection, and this opportunity will eventually come to an end. Once the economy recovers, demand will increase, and prices will resume their upward trend.

Auction Houses
Theriaults (www.theriaults.com)
McMasters Harris Auction Co. (www.mcmastersharris.com)
Alderfer (www.alderferauction.com)
James Julia (www.jamesdjulia.net)
Morphy (www.morphyauctions.com)

Also see: Barbie Dolls & Accessories

A.M. "Just Me," marked "Just Me - Registered - Germany - A. 310/3/0.M." on back of head,bisque socket head w/blue sleep eyes to side, single-stroke brows, painted lashes, closed mouth, blonde mohair wig, five-piece composition body w/bent right arm, wearing factory original organdy dress w/red collar & trim, original underclothing, cotton socks & black leatherette shoes, tip of right little finger missing, 11" **$2,600**

A.M. (Armand Marseille) bisque socket head toddler, marked "1894 - A.M. 3/0 DEP," set blue eyes, single-stroke brows, open mouth w/four upper teeth, original blonde mohair wig, jointed wood & composition body, wearing all original outfit of light blue lace-trimmed print dress, lace-trimmed bonnet, underclothing, black cotton socks w/garters attached to chemise, original handmade shoes, minor repair on neck socket, 11" **$400**

A.M. bisque head "Fany" girl, marked "AM Fany 231," blue sleep eyes, closed mouth, blonde mohair wig, composition ball-jointed child's body w/ straight wrists, wearing white dress, white bonnet w/blue ribbon, socks & shoes, pinkie missing on right hand, 15 1/2" **$5,175**

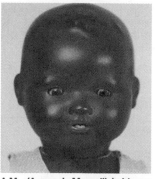

A.M. (Armand Marseille) bisque socket head black baby, marked "AM Germany 351/6.K.," brown sleep eyes, open mouth w/ two teeth, painted molded hair, jointed composition body, wearing replacement clothes, left thumb & right forefinger broken, neck worn, needs restringing, 20" **$661**

A.M. bisque socket head baby, marked "A.M. - Germany - 351./4.K.," solid dome, blue sleep eyes, softly blushed brows, open mouth w/ two lower teeth, lightly molded & painted hair, composition bent- limb baby body, wearing antique baby gown & slip, diaper, new sweater & bon-net, 16" ... **$200**

A.M. bisque socket head girl, marked "A. 18 M." on back of head, bisque socket head w/blue sleep eyes, molded & feathered brows, painted lashes, open mouth w/ four upper teeth, long brown h.h. (human hair) wig, jointed wood & composition body, wearing antique child's dress w/eyelet trim & many tucks, underclothing, knit socks, black leather shoes, missing real lashes, some repair on body, minor cracks in finish, 39" **$1,200**

A.M. Googlies, marked "Germany - 323 - A. 11/0 M." on back of heads, bisque socket heads w/blue sleep side-glancing eyes, single-stroke brows, painted lashes, closed smiling mouths, original blond mohair wigs, crude five-piece bodies w/unfinished carton torsos, molded & painted socks & shoes, wearing ethnic-type costumes, the boy in black pants, red wool vest front w/gold buttons, black velvet jacket w/red embroidery & black silk top hat, the girl in black dress w/blue embroidered apron w/yarn flower decorations, black neck scarf, original underclothing, replaced bow in hair, 7", pr. **$1,800**

Alexander (Madame) Jane Withers, marked on back of head & on original dress tag, all-composition w/ brown sleep eyes w/real lashes, closed mouth, original brown mohair wig, five-piece jointed body, wearing print dress w/pink collar & cuffs, replaced underwear combination, original socks & black oilcloth snap shoes, original black velvet beret, w/extra peach organdy dress, eyes cloudy, ca. 1936, 19" **$1,210**

Alexander (Madame) Jacqueline, marked "Alexander - 10©61" on head, "'Jacqueline' - by Madame Alexander" on tag on seam of slip, vinyl head w/brown sleep eyes w/ blue shadow, real lashes, feathered brows, closed mouth, pierced ears, rooted hair, hard plastic body jointed at hips & knees, vinyl arms w/jointed elbows, adult figure, high heel feet, wearing original white satin gown w/matching cape, taffeta slip & panties, stockings, high heeled shoes, "diamond" bracelet & ring, pearl necklace, purse & earrings w/pearls & "diamond," some stains, one pearl missing from right earring, 21" **$450**

DOLLS

Alexander (Madame) Maggie walker, marked "Madame Alexander - All Rights Reserved - New York U.S.A." on dress tag, hard plastic head w/walking mechanism, blue sleep eyes w/ real lashes, feathered brows, closed mouth, original wig, five-piece hard plastic body w/walking mechanism, wearing blue & white taffeta dress w/white collar & cuffs, white taffeta slip & panties, original stockings, black center-snap shoes, 17" **$700**

Alt, Beck & Gottschalck bisque socket head baby, marked "No. 5 - 1322 - 50," blue sleep eyes, two-tone single stroke brows, open mouth w/two upper teeth & molded tongue, antique blonde mohair wig, jointed composition baby body, wearing fine antique baby dress w/lace bodice, tucks & lace inserts on skirt, antique bonnet, new underclothes, left little finger replaced, 18" ... **$385**

Alt, Beck & Gottschalck bisque socket head girl, marked "911-8," set brown eyes, open-closed mouth w/white space between lips, pierced ears, original blonde mohair wig, jointed composition body w/straight wrists, separate balls at shoulders, elbows, hips & knees, wearing a faded blue silk dress, white lace-trimmed blouse, slip & pants made of old fabric, antique black socks, black leather side-snap shoes, small chip on upper rim of right eye, 16" **$825**

Averill (Georgene) "Bonnie Babe" doll, marked "Copr. by Georgene Averill 7005/365 2/0, Germany," bisque head w/painted hair, blue glass eyes, open smiling mouth w/tongue & two bottom teeth, five-piece cloth body w/swivel arms & legs, composition arms, 13" **$518**

American Character "Toni" lady, marked "An American Character Doll" on box label, all-vinyl fashion lady w/blue sleep eyes, rooted brown hair, fully jointed including at waist, high heel feet, wearing a rose gown w/double pleated skirt, panties, stockings, black high heel shoes, pearl necklace, rhinestone earrings, in original box w/extra clothing purchased separately, 1950s, 14" **$300**

Averill (Georgene) Nurse Jane, molded cloth, character from the Uncle Wiggily stories, wearing original costume w/blue duster cap, blue & red floral-printed dress & white apron, very minor face soiling, 13" **$316**

Babyland Rag, unmarked, cloth head w/flat face, h.p. features, blushed cheeks, strip of human hair sewn across forehead at bonnet line for bangs, cloth body stitch jointed at shoulders, elbows, hips & knees, stitched fingers, wearing antique, possibly original faded blue dress w/lace- trimmed bodice, matching bonnet, antique underclothing, pale blue cotton socks, black leather doll shoes w/buckles, hole on outside of left foot, 1 1/2" split on seam of torso, fingers missing some stitches, 30" **$1,850**

Bergmann (C.M.) bisque socket head girl, marked "C.M. Bergmann - Simon & Halbig - 13 1/2" on back of head, blue sleep eyes, molded & feathered brows, painted lashes, open mouth w/four upper teeth, pierced ears, original h.h. brunette wig, jointed wood & composition body, wearing pale green taffeta dress, lace bonnet, antique underclothing, socks & center-snap leatherette shoes, repair at neck socket of body, 29" **$500**

Bisque head lady w/wardrobe, unmarked, dark blue stationary eyes, closed mouth, cup & saucer neck, original light blonde braided mohair wig, kid body w/ball-jointed knees, bisque lower arms, 18", w/red leatherette trunk w/tray & variety of clothing including cream-colored dress w/green trim, black silk jacket, black & grey striped silk princess dress, pink cotton skirt, purple wool bodice w/black & white trim, skirts, jacket, undergarments, rubberized overshoes, hair accessories & jewelry, original high button leather boots, France, ca. 1870 .... **$9,400**

Bahr & Proschild bisque socket head baby, marked "678 - 7 - BP [in heart] - Made in - Germany" on back of head, stamped "Made in Germany" in red on lower back, blue sleep eyes, painted lashes, open mouth, antique mohair wig, composition bent limb baby body, wearing pale pink baby dress, new underclothing, socks & shoes, missing tip of left little finger, 15" **$275**

Consider combining a vacation with your collecting interests. Attend antique shows such as ones in Atlantic City, N.J., Brimfield, Mass., or Round Top, Texas, or even the Aloha Flea Market at the Aloha Stadium in Honolulu. These destinations will provide sightseeing as well as shopping opportunities.

Bru bisque socket head girl, impressed "Bru Jne 1" mark, brown paperweight eyes, closed mouth w/tongue tip, pierced ears, blonde wig, bisque shoulder plate w/molded bosom & scalloped kid trim, full kid body w/bisque lower arms, wearing original deep maroon silk dress w/brocaded anemone pattern, matching hat, small maroon silk & lace-trimmed parasol, red net stockings & brown leather shoes marked "BRU JNE" in oval, ca. 1880, some wear to clothing, 11 1/4" **$24,675**

Bru Jne. bisque head girl, impressed "2," light blue threaded reset paperweight eyes, molded tongue, antique blonde mohair wig, kid Bru body w/bisque lower arms, jointed at the elbows, paper label at back of torso from a New Jersey doll hospital, wearing a simple white cotton dress, comes w/a newer elaborate dress, some restoration to lower right eyelid, cabinet-sized, 13" **$9,488**

China shoulder head lady, so-called "Currier & Ives" style, marked "5" on back of shoulder plate, stamped "Made - in - Germany" on left front of torso, painted blue eyes, single-stroke brows, closed mouth, molded black hair w/short wavy bangs & long curls worn behind ears & falling to shoulders, pink cloth body w/china lower arms & lower legs, molded black boots w/blue tassels, wearing old red & black plaid dress w/white lace bodice, underclothing, repair to left ankle, 17" **$500**

Dolley Madison china shoulder head lady, unmarked, painted blue eyes, brown single-stroke brows, closed mouth, heavily rouged cheeks, pierced ears, molded & painted blonde hair w/ molded ribbon & bow, cloth body w/leather lower arms, striped lower legs w/leather boots, wearing black velvet two-piece outfit w/lace trim, torso re-covered, arms replaced, right boot patched & repaired, 24" **$725**

Bye-Lo Baby, marked "Copr. by - Grace S. Putnam - Made in Germany," stamped on front of body "Bye-lo Baby - Pat. Appl'd for - Copy. By - Grace - Storey - Putnam," also blue button w/"Bye-Lo Baby - reg. U.S. Pat. Off. - Patent Applied for - K and K - Copyright 1922 - by Grace Storey," original dress tag reading "Bye-Lo Baby - None Genuine Without Signature - Grace Story Putnam," solid dome bisque flange head, blue sleep eyes, closed mouth, lightly molded & painted hair, cloth body w/celluloid hands, wearing original baby dress & lace-trimmed bonnet, 10" head circumference, 11" **$358**

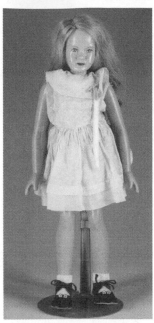

Dora Petzold girl, molded composition head w/painted blue eyes & red closed mouth, blonde wig, all-original w/velvet clothing & blue leather shoes, some distressing to painted hat & cuffs, Germany, ca. 1920s, 20" h. **$1,265**

E.D. bisque head girl, marked "E. 9 D.," blue paperweight eyes w/ mauve eye shadow, a full, well-defined closed mouth, jointed composition body, light brown h.h. (human hair) wig, wearing a French-style fancy newer dress & lace- trimmed hat, antique baby blue leather shoes, some peppering on bisque, France, 21" **$1,725**

Dewees Cochran "Cindy" girl, composition head w/painted eyes & mouth, composition body w/ jointed shoulders & hips, long blonde hair, wearing a print cotton dress & black shoes w/white socks, cracks to four fingers, minor foxing & chip to left leg, 14 1/2" **$403**

Effanbee "Patsy Ruth," marked "Effanbee - Patsy Ruth" on head, "Effanbee - Durable - Dolls" on tag on dress & on metal heart bracelet, composition head w/brown sleep eyes, closed "rosebud" mouth, original h.h. wig, composition body wearing original silk dress, socks & leatherette T- strap shoes, eyes cloudy, dress fragile & deteriorating, 26" **$800**

Effanbee "Lovums," marked "Effanbee - Lovums - © - Pat. No. 1.283.558" on back of shoulder plate, composition shoulder head w/brown sleep eyes w/ real lashes, open mouth w/two upper & two lower teeth, molded tongue, molded & painted hair, cloth mama doll body w/non-working crier, composition arms & lower legs, wearing original white organdy baby dress & bonnet, slip, undershirt, socks, leatherette baby shoes w/pompons, pink baby jacket w/embroidered collar, in original box marked "Lovums - Trademark - Reg. - An - Effanbee - Durable - Doll - The Doll With - The Golden Heart - 6022," 25" .. **$675**

Gaultier (Francois) bisque socket head lady, marked "F. 3. G.," brown paperweight eyes, feathered brows, closed mouth w/accented lips, pierced ears, brown mohair wig on cork pate, jointed wood & composition body w/straight wrists, separate balls at shoulders, elbows, hips & knees, redressed in an ecru two-piece outfit trimmed w/black braid & pale green, straw bonnet w/ feather trim, underclothing, socks & old shoes, 12" **$3,575**

DOLLS

Hallmark Susan B. Anthony doll, stuffed cloth, wearing a long blue dress & a red, white & blue sash reading "Votes," house-form box cover includes the story of Susan B. Anthony, sold in Hallmark stores, 1979, in original box, doll 6 1/2" h. **$7**

Hartman (Karl) bisque socket head girl, marked "30.5 - K/4" inside large "H" on back of head, brown sleep eyes, molded & feathered brows, painted lashes, open mouth w/four upper teeth, replaced synthetic wig, jointed wood & composition body, redressed in drop-waist blue dress w/lace bodice trim & ribbon belt, antique underclothing, socks & old fabric shoes, some touchups, old tape residue on lower torso, 24 1/2" **$225**

Use a natural deodorizer to remove odors from articles that can't be washed. Sweet wormwood, also known as Sweet Annie, is a bushy herb easily grown from seed. Place sprigs of the herb in a closed container with the object. It may take several months, but the odor should disappear.

Handwerck (Heinrich) bisque socket head girl, marked "Germany - Heinrich - Handwerck - Simon & Halbig - 7" on head, "Heinrich Handwerck - Germany - 7" stamped in red on back, blue sleep eyes, molded & feathered brows, open mouth w/accented lips & four upper teeth, pierced ears, original brown h.h. wig, jointed wood & composition Handwerck body, wearing antique white child's dress, antique underclothing, cotton socks, black patent leather shoes, left knee ball replaced, 32 1/2" **$1,025**

Hertel, Schwab & Co. "Patsy" baby, no visible marks, solid dome bisque head w/brown sleep eyes w/real lashes, soft brows that match molded & painted baby-type hair, closed "rosebud" mouth, five-piece composition toddler body, wearing baby-style smocked dress, matching panties, socks & shoes, body repainted, 18" **$1,400**

Hartman (Karl) bisque socket head girl, marked "28.5 - K/0" inside large "H" on back of head, brown sleep eyes, heavy feathered brows, painted lashes, open mouth w/four upper teeth, replaced mohair wig, jointed wood & composition body, wearing blue lace-trimmed organdy dress, underclothing, socks & replaced shoes, small chips, size of body may be slightly large for head, 22 1/2" **$200**

Heubach (Gebruder) bisque head character lady, Model 7926, blue glass eyes, stiff turned neck, cloth lady-style body w/long, slender bisque arms (replaced?), open mouth w/four upper teeth, dirty blonde mohair wig w/black bead tiara, wearing elaborate deep red fashion-style gown w/train, lady collar & black trim, 21" ... **$1,610**

Hertel & Schwab bisque head googlie, marked "165/4," blue set googlie eyes, single-stroke brows, open closed smiling mouth, pink cheeks, replacement blonde wig, jointed composition baby body, wearing older baby clothes & bonnet, comes w/remainder of original wig, small hairline to rear of head, 13" **$1,783**

Hertel, Schwab & Co. all-bisque girl, marked "208 - 5" on back of head & "Made in Germany" on the back & "208 - 5" on legs, head w/ stiff neck, blue sleep eyes, open/ closed mouth w/white space between lips, brown mohair wig, all-bisque body jointed at shoulders & hips, molded & painted white socks & black one-strap shoes, redressed in pink silk crepe dress w/lace trim, matching hat, slip & pants made from antique fabric, 7" **$220**

Heubach (Ernst) bisque socket head girl, marked "Heubach Koppelsdorf - 417 8/0 - Germany" on back of head, blue sleep eyes to side, feathered brows, tiny painted upper lashes, open mouth w/two upper teeth, antique mohair wig, five-piece composition body w/unfinished torso, wearing blue blouse w/ white dots, matching bonnet, white pinafore, underclothing, original socks & leatherette shoes w/pompoms, 12" **$975**

Huret bisque socket head character girl, impressed "MA" & "HURET" on head, dark blue stationary glass eyes, closed mouth, pink cheeks, long blonde wig, composition & wood child body, wearing ribbed aqua silk dress & bonnet, France, late 19th - early 20th c., paint flaking on hands, tiny chip at neck hole, 16" (ILLUS. right w/Huret character lady) **$7,638**

Ideal "Toni," marked "P-91 - Ideal Doll - Made in U.S.A." on head, "Ideal Doll - P- 91" on back, "Genuine Toni Doll - with ny-lon wig - Made by Ideal Novelty & Toy Co." on dress tag, hard plastic head w/blue sleep eyes w/ real lashes, single- stroke brows, closed mouth, original wig, five-piece hard plastic body wearing tagged red & yellow pique dress w/embroidery, attached half slip w/matching panties, socks, original red center-snap shoes, hair repinned & w/net, 15" **$235**

DOLLS

Ideal Shirley Temple, marked "11 - Shirley Temple" on head, "Shirley Temple - 11" on back, "Genuine - Shirley Temple - Doll - Registered - [illegible]" on dress tag, composition head w/blue sleep eyes w/real lashes, feathered brows, open mouth w/six teeth, original mohair wig, five-piece composition child body wearing original red & white organdy coin dot dress from movie "Stand Up and Cheer," underwear combination, rayon socks, center-snap leatherette shoes, tiny crack over left eye, minor crazing, socks replaced, 11" **$575**

Jumeau (E.) bisque socket head girl, marked "1907 - 10" on back of head, shoes marked "9 - Paris [bee] - Depose," blue paperweight eyes, heavy feathered brows, open mouth w/six upper teeth, accented lips, pierced ears, brown h.h. wig, jointed wood & composition body w/jointed wrists, wearing antique white dress w/tucks & lace inserts & trim, underclothing made w/ antique fabric, tiny inherent firing line on back neck rim, flake at left earring hole, repainted hands, left thumb broken & reglued, left second finger replaced, shoes worn w/half of right sole missing, bows & buttons replaced, 23" **$880**

Jumeau bisque head "long face" girl, blue paperweight eyes, feathered brows, closed mouth, blonde wig, composition body, wearing fancy ivory colored dress, buff-colored shoes marked "12" & socks, comes w/pale blue bonnet, blue silk dress w/ivory cape & bonnet, parasol, wire rimmed hat & white shoes marked "12," plaster has been added to eyes, slight repair to body at neck, 26" **$13,225**

Jumeau bisque head 1st series portrait doll, marked "2/0" on head, hazel almond-shaped eyes, feathered brows, closed mouth, pierced ears, honey-colored replacement wig, repainted original eight ball jointed body, newer replacement clothes, 14 1/2" **$8,625**

Jumeau (E.) bisque socket head portrait girl, marked "7" on back of neck, the blue stamped mark "Jumeau - Medaille d'Or - Paris" on lower back under repaint, head w/fine pale coloring, set blue threaded eyes, two-tone feathered brows, closed mouth w/accented lips & small white space between lips, pierced ears, replaced cork pate w/antique brown h.h. wig, jointed eight-ball composition body w/straight wrists, wearing antique low- waisted dress w/lace trim, wide antique ribbon below waist, new underclothing & socks, antique leather shoes, grey velvet hat, body poorly repainted, clothing fragile, 19" **$7,425**

Jumeau bisque head portrait doll w/wardrobe, indecipherable mark on head, body stamped "Jumeau Medaille d'Or Paris," almond-shaped hand-cut eyes w/blue spiral irises, closed mouth, original skin wig, fully articulated eight- ball composition body, 14", w/wardrobe trunk containing original & added items, most commercially made, including seven dresses & a coat, three hats, a bonnet, undergarments, leg warmers, muff, accessories, dark brown ankle-strap shoes & white leather shoes marked "Jumeau," ca. 1880 .... $28,200

Jumeau bisque socket head portrait lady, large blue paperweight eyes, feathered brows, closed mouth, large applied ears, slightly double chin, brown wig, fully articulated wooden body, wearing aubergine silk satin dress & ribbon-trimmed peaked hat, brown leather shoes marked "Jumeau," model associated w/Jumeau production for 1876 exhibition, 27" .. **$22,325**

K [star] R (Kammer & Reinhardt) bisque socket head character boy, marked "K*R - Simon & Halbig - 115 - A - 42," blue sleep eyes, feathered brows, closed pouty mouth, antique short brown mohair wig, jointed wood & composition toddler body w/ diagonal hip joints, jointed at shoulders, elbows, wrists & knees, wearing fine knit outfit w/ maroon sweater & cap w/tassel, white knit pants, black socks & leather sandals, 16" **$3,520**

K [star] R (Kammer & Reinhardt) bisque socket head character girl, marked "K [star] R - 114 - 23," painted blue eyes, single-stroke brows, closed pouty mouth, mohair wig in coiled braids, five-piece composition body w/molded & painted white socks & brown two-strap shoes, wearing original factory chemise trimmed w/red embroidery, 8 1/2" **$1,175**

Kathe Kruse girl, all-stockinette, molded face w/painted blue eyes & red lips, blonde wig, body w/jointed shoulders & hips, outfit w/original paper hang tag, signed on left foot "Aug. 22, 1955," near mint, 14 1/2" **$390**

DOLLS

Kestner (J. D.) bisque socket head girl, impressed "111" on upper torso & back of upper legs, brown sleep eyes, closed mouth, rosy cheeks, original blonde curly mohair wig w/blue hair ribbon, kid-lined swivel neck, peg-jointed limbs, the right hand molded in closed fist, left hand open, wearing molded pink high-heeled boots w/four straps, green banded ribbed stockings w/lacy imprint at top, ca. 1880, 8 1/2" **$8,225**

Kestner (J.D.) bisque socket head girl, marked "(?) made in - Germany 0 - 143," brown sleep eyes, feathered brows, open mouth w/four upper teeth, original auburn mohair wig, composition Kestner body w/straight arms, jointed at shoulders, hips & knees, wearing possibly original white dress trimmed w/tucks & lace, original underclothing, white cotton socks, white leather shoes, lace-trimmed bonnet, arms have been restrung w/elastic through composition at shoulders, 8 3/4" **$825**

Kley & Hahn bisque socket head baby, marked "K & H (in banner) - Germany - 572-6," set blue eyes, feathered brows, open mouth w/tongue that falls back in w/a weight, antique short blonde mohair wig, composition baby body, wearing antique white baby dress, underclothing made w/ antique fabric, socks & booties, chip & flake at hole on back of head, 14 1/2" **$248**

Kestner Kewpie, marked "Ges. gesch. - O'Neill. J.D.K. - 10" on back of head, solid dome bisque socket head w/topknot, oversized brown glass eyes set to side, dash brows, painted lashes, closed smiling mouth, five-piece chubby composition body w/"starfish" hands, wearing old white underwear w/crocheted trim, peach organdy dress w/new blue silk ribbon trim, front of torso & bottom of left foot repainted, touchups to both heels, right shoulder, left fingers, toes worn, 10" **$4,600**

Kestner Kewpie, bisque socket head w/brown set eyes, closed smiling mouth, ball jointed composition body w/"starfish" hands, finger replaced on right hand, pinkie missing on left, 12" **$9,200**

Kling bisque shoulder head lady, marked "144-9" on back of shoulder plate, painted blue eyes, closed mouth, pierced ears, elaborate molded blonde hair w/ black comb, molded lace collar w/ decorative trim, cloth body jointed at shoulders, hips & knees, leather lower arms, printed lower legs, leather boots, redressed in gown of antique fabric, antique underclothing, repairs on leather arms, edges of boots & toe of left boot worn, 24" **$1,100**

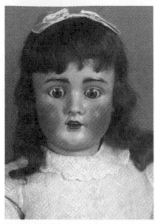

Konig & Wernicke bisque socket head girl, marked "4711 - 105," blue sleep eyes, molded & feathered brows, open mouth w/ outlined lips & four upper teeth, replaced red h.h. wig, jointed wood & composition body w/ opening in side for crier (most parts missing), wearing antique child's dress w/white net overlay over blue, new underclothing, socks & shoes, right eyeball cracked, minor firing lines over ears, possible old body repaint, 42" **$1,210**

Lenci Series 110 felt socket head girl, marked "Lenci" on bottom of left foot, painted features of brown side-glancing eyes, pouty closed mouth, blonde wig, wearing peach dress w/applied felt flowers & matching pink & yellow wide- brimmed hat & pink shoes, Italy, ca. 1930s, head loose in socket, small moth hole to shoe, 23" **$805**

Look for identifying marks on a doll at the base of the back of the head. To ensure the entire mark is visible, the hair may need to be pulled out of the way.

Lenci "400 D" girl, illegible mark on bottom of right foot, marked "Lenci Turin - (Italy) - Di E. Scavini - Made in Italy - 400/D - Pat. Sept. 8-1921 - Pat. N. 142433 - Bte S.G.D.G. X87395 - Brevetto 501-178" on paper tag, pressed felt swivel head w/painted brown eyes to side, single- stroke brows, painted upper lashes, closed mouth, applied ears, original long mohair wig, cloth torso w/felt arms & legs, individually stitched fingers w/middle fingers together, stitched & tinted toes, wearing light green felt dress, original underclothing, silk stockings to hips, black leather shoes, blue-green felt cape-coat & matching hat, some soil & fading, 16" **$850**

Mary Hoyer Doll Mfg. Company girl, composition, red mohair wig, handmade red knit ski outfit w/skis & poles, slight chip to lip paint, 14" **$489**

Lenci pressed felt socket head girl, molded face w/brown side-glancing eyes & red lips, blonde mohair wig, wearing a light blue felt coat w/dark blue trim & triangular patches around the hem, a matching hat, lightly soiled, few moth holes, 13" **$450**

"Mascotte" bisque head girl, marked "Mascotte" & "Bebe Mascotte Paris" on body, amber paperweight eyes, closed mouth, possibly original brown h.h. wig on cork pate, ball-jointed body, wearing antique shoes, replacement clothing, France, minor wear to fingertips & joints, 29" **$2,645**

DOLLS

Morimura Brothers bisque head baby, blue sleep eyes, open mouth w/upper teeth, short light brown wig, voice box in head, composition baby body, wearing newer blue baby dress & lacy bonnet, Japan, ca. 1918, 15" **$230**

Parian shoulder head lady, unmarked, untinted shoulder head w/painted blue eyes w/red accent lines, single-stroke brows, closed mouth w/accent line between lips, pierced ears, molded & painted cafe au lait hair w/ molded blue tiara trimmed in gold, molded braid across top, on lower sides & down middle of back of head, old cloth body w/red leather boots as part of legs, wearing white dotted Swiss & lace dress, antique underclothing, new arms by Emma Clear, three beads on tiara repaired by Charles Buysse, 24" **$1,900**

S.F.B.J. bisque socket head Jumeau mold girl, marked "S.F.B.J. - Paris - 9," blue sleep eyes w/real lashes, feathered brows, open mouth w/four upper teeth, pierced ears, replaced brown h.h. wig, jointed wood & composition body, wearing a fragile antique silk dress w/lace trim, hat, antique underclothing, socks & leather shoes, eyes crossed & in need of repair, 20" **$880**

Petterssen (Ronnaug) Norwegian ethnic dolls, marked "Made in Norway - Vare- Marke - Ronnaug Petterssen" on paper tags on clothing, celluloid socket heads w/painted blue eyes, single-stroke brows, closed mouths, original h.h. blond wigs, five-piece celluloid bodies, wearing original wool & felt Norwegian ethnic costumes, the girl in red felt skirt, white cotton blouse w/lace trim, black felt jacket, red felt bodice w/ gold decorative pins & beading, red felt ribbons w/embroidery, underclothing, black stockings & black felt shoes, a gold crown w/red felt backing on her head, the boy in white cotton shirt w/ gold decorative pin at neck, black wool pants w/embroidery, red wool jacket edged in green w/ decorative buttons, black felt top hat, white stockings & black felt shoes, some small moth holes on girl's skirt, girl's right cuff missing, 17", pr. **$1,000**

"Queen Anne" wooden doll, painted features, black pupil-less eyes, stylized line & dot brows, dots for lashes, closed mouth, carved ears, nailed-on woven dark brown h.h. wig, wooden upper arms & upper legs, carved hands & feet, wearing cream-colored silk flowered Watteau-style gown of period fabric w/ coral-colored stomacher, long silk stockings, silk slippers from dress fabric, England, ca. 1780, 17 1/2" **$5,875**

Schmidt (Bruno) bisque socket head character "Wendy," marked "BSW 537 (in heart below) 2033," brown sleep eyes, molded & brushed eyebrows, finely molded closed mouth, antique blonde mohair wig, jointed composition body, wearing old, if not original, dress w/collar & cuffs, blue shoes & socks, small restoration to one finger on each hand, rare, 23" h. **$36,225**

Schoenhut wooden socket head character boy, marked "Schoenhut Doll - Pat. Jan. 17th 1911 - U.S.A. - & Foreign Countries" on oval label on back, painted brown intaglio eyes, open/closed smiling mouth w/ four upper teeth, brown h.h. wig, wooden body spring-jointed at shoulders, elbows, wrists, hips, knees & ankles, nicely redressed in white pique Schoenhut-style sailor suit w/blue collar, cuffs & low belt, new socks & old replacement shoes, touch-up on cheeks, 21" **$660**

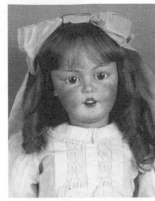

Simon & Halbig bisque socket head character girl, marked "S & H 1279 - DEP - Germany - 14 1/2," blue sleep eyes w/molded & feathered brows, open mouth w/accented lips & triangle accent on lower lip & upper teeth, pierced ears, replaced brown h.h. wig, jointed wood & composition body, wearing an antique child's dress & slip, pants made from antique fabric, new socks & shoes, hands repainted, 32 1/2" **$2,860**

Steiner bisque head girl, marked "Fre A 17 Steiner," blue paperweight eyes, closed mouth, replacement brunette wig w/ long curls, straight-wristed body, body repainted, later clothing, 24" **$2,013**

Shirley Temple doll, marked "Ideal Doll - ST-12," all-vinyl, head w/ sleep eyes, rooted curly hair w/ original set & ribbon, wearing original Scottie dress of white pique w/red & white striped trim, original cotton panties, original white socks & black vinyl shoes, unplayed-with, in original marked box, ca. 1957, 12" **$250**

Steiner Figure A bisque socket head girl, marked "J. Steiner - Bte. S.G.D.G. - Paris - Fre A7," also stamped on left hip "Le Petit Parisien - Bebe Steiner," lovely blue paperweight eyes, multi-stroke brows, closed mouth, replaced brown synthetic wig w/replaced pate, jointed composition body w/ straight wrists & short stubby fingers, redressed in lavender silk dress w/lace overlay, matching new undergarments, socks & new maroon leather shoes, lower legs are old German replacements, 14" **$3,080**

Swaine & Co. bisque socket head girl, marked "DIP - 1 - Geschutzt - S. & Co. - Germany," squinty brown sleep eyes, closed mouth, original blonde mohair wig, jointed wood & composition body, wearing factory chemise, new pants & slip & new socks & shoes, small hairline at back of crown, replaced old legs don't match, 11" **$385**

• French and German dolls of the 19th and early 20th century are prized for their superb artistry.
• Dolls with original clothing, especially with full wardrobes and accessories, command premium prices.
• Closed-mouth dolls can be significantly more valuable than open-mouthed dolls.

Thullier (A.) bisque head baby, marked "A4T," amber paperweight eyes, feathered brows, closed mouth, jointed kid body, bisque hands, replaced clothes but original marked shoes & socks, small damage to right knee joint, missing cork pate & wig, right hand missing thumb, 13 1/2" **$19,550**

Thullier (A.) bisque head girl, marked "A. 14 T" on head, large blue paperweight eyes, feathered brows, closed mouth w/protruding upper lip, light brown h.h. wig, original jointed composition body, wearing antique blue mariner's outfit of pleated skirt & sailor-style top & hat & antique shoes marked "Bebe Jumeau 12," body repainted, 30" **$21,275**

Vogue "Ginny," marked "Vogue Doll" on back, all-hard plastic, blue sleep eyes w/painted upper lashes, closed mouth, original brown wig in braids, body w/ jointed shoulders & hips, wearing original blue print dress w/ yellow trim & zipper up the back, matching panties, original white socks, blue leatherette snap shoes, blue straw hat w/yellow daisy on top, also original dress & wrist tags, ca. 1953, near mint **$1,595**

Vogue "Toddles" Little Red Riding Hood, marked "Vogue" on back of head & back, all composition, blue painted side-glancing eyes, red lips, original blonde mohair wig in original set, jointed shoulders & hips, wearing original white dress w/Vogue tag & matching panties, original white rayon socks, red leatherette center snap shoes, red jersey cape w/print lining, light crazing on face & body, 7 1/2" **$303**

Wax head man, the poured wax shoulder head w/set blue eyes, real hair eyebrows, mustache & goatee inserted into the wax, h.h. inserted into wax for hair, well detailed facial features & ears, on a cloth body w/poured wax lower arms & legs, wearing an original chemise, white shirt w/ "JH" cross-stitched on lower right side of bottom, separate collar, tie made of ribbon, grey vest w/buttons, matching grey jacket & pants, leather high button boots, straw hat, generally excellent condition, 19th c., 19" h. **$1,210**

Wax head lady, reinforced poured wax shoulder head w/blue glass eyes, multi-stroke brows, painted upper & lower lashes, shapely closed mouth, original blonde mohair wig, cloth body w/wax over composition lower arms & legs w/brownish black boots w/pink tassels, stockings w/ lace garters, wearing a wonderful original gold silk brocade gown, lace gloves & shawl, flower hair decoration, antique underclothing w/three half slips, repairs to shoulder plate & around neck, some fading on face, a few cracks, legs restitched at hips, dress deteriorated, 19th c., 27" **$440**

FIREARMS MARKET REPORT

It's impossible to discuss the state of the antique firearms market without putting it in context with what's taking place in the modern firearms market. Certain segments of modern firearms are seeing a tremendous increase in prices and numbers of sales prompted primarily by a change in presidential administration, which could bring tighter gun control. Some buyers fear that if they don't purchase guns now, they may not be able to later. Whether those fears are well founded or not remains to be seen. Time will tell.

The antique and vintage gun market is less volatile and is being affected primarily by the economy rather than politics. According to Kevin Michalowski, editor of *Gun List* magazine, many buyers are purchasing antique guns instead of investing in the stock market because they believe it's a better investment. While auction houses have seen a decline in the overall number of sales in some cases in the past year, certain types of guns have seen great demand and sky-high prices. These weapons include Colt Walker pistols, Colt single-action pistols, Winchester lever-action rifles, and guns with verifiable provenance. Another category that is doing well is German World War II military firearms with all-original parts, especially Class 3, such as machine guns and sniper rifles.

Michalowski cautioned that before purchasing a weapon it's a good idea to have it appraised by an expert to verify authenticity, condition, provenance if any, and value, and to buy only from reputable dealers or auctions houses. Michalowski added that there are some in the field who are proficient in selling fakes or altered weapons. An excellent resource on fakes and reproductions is the *Gun Digest® Book of Firearms Fakes and Reproductions*, by Rick Sapp, available at krausebooks.com. It features 300 color photos and gives readers the warning flags they need to know to spot alterations and includes an extensive list of appraisers.

State and Federal Firearms Laws

Strict state and federal laws apply to those who buy and sell guns. For more detailed information, see the NRA Web page at www.nraila.org/gunlaws. That page provides a state-by-state listing of laws, as well as the article "Citizen's Guide to Federal Firearms Laws," which gives a clear, concise summary of federal gun laws.

eBay Policy

Following is eBay's current firearms policy: "eBay prohibits members from listing firearms, ammunition, as well as certain parts and accessories. Any part or accessory that is required for a gun to fire is not permitted."

Auction Houses
Rock Island (www.rockislandauction.com)
James Julia (www.jamesdjulia.net)
Dumouchelle www.dumouchelle.com)
JC Devine (www.jcdevine.com)
Manions (www.manions.com)
Kull and Supica (www.armsbid.com)
Mohawk Arms (www.militaryrelics.com)
Cowans (www.cowanauctions.com)

FIREARMS

Carbine, Gallager Civil War standard percussion model, .54 cal., pinched front sight & two-position flip rear sight, straight grip walnut stock w/smooth steel carbine buttplate, sling bar & ring on left side of wrist, patchbox containing a spare nipple on right side of butt, round barrel 22 1/2" l. **$2,415**

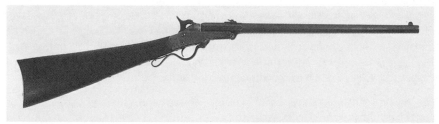

Carbine, Maynard Second Model Civil War percussion model, martially-marked, .50 cal., pinched front sight, two-leaf three- position rear sight, stock without patchbox, date 1865, barrel w/90% bluing, buttstock w/several small crude scratched drawings, octagonal to round 20" barrel **$2,645**

Carbine, Sharps & Hankins saddle ring model, .52 cal., missing sights, the lever catch & a chunk of the stock, also missing sling swivel on stock, main spring broken, round barrel 19" l. **$690**

Carbine, Spencer Model 1865 model, .50 cal., "ESA" cartouche on left side of stock behind sling ring bar, traces of finish, round barrel 20" l. **$2,128**

Carbine, Starr Civil War percussion model, .54 cal., unusual configuration w/a stepped round barrel w/blade front side & two-position flip rear sight, small forearm w/straight stock & semi-crescent carbine brass buttplate, usual markings on lockplate & top tang, no original finish, barrel 20 3/4" l. **$2,013**

Musket, Colt Special Model 1861, .58 cal., dated 1863 on lockplate, overall rust brown patina, w/bayonet w/ broken locking ring, partially octagonal barrel 40" l.. **$1,323**

Musket, Harpers Ferry Model 1842, .69 cal., barrel dated 1852, faint inspector mark, overall grey patina, w/ bayonet, barrel 42" l. **$978**

Musket, Mason Model 1863, .58 cal., barrel dated 1863 on the lock, nipple welded into place, rear side & swing swivels missing, ramrod & bayonet replacements, moderate to heavy pitting, stock repaired, barrel 48" l.
.... **$633**

Musket, Ohio surcharage German model, .74 cal., barrel dated 1831, lockplate engraved "Saarn." & "OHIO" stamped at the wrist & left side of stock, correct 18 3/4" l. bayonet, rear sling swivel missing, rust brown patina on barrel, bayonet rusted, partially octagonal barrel 41 1/4" l. **$1,158**

FIREARMS

Revolver, Colt Model 1849 pocket type, .31 cal., one-piece walnut grip, octagonal barrel w/two-line New York address marking, small brass front sight, silver plated trigger guard & back strap, fine condition, Serial No. 24484, barrel 4" l. **$1,035**

Revolver, Colt Model 1860 Army model, .44 cal., rare early Army model w/Navy frame, round barrel, rebated cylinder w/"Colt's Patent" on left side of frame, brass trigger guard & back strap w/the left flat of the trigger guard stamped "36 CAL," Navy-sized one-piece walnut grips, no original finish, one of frame pins missing, barrel 7 1/2" l. ... **$5,175**

Revolver, Colt Model 1878 DA model, .45 cal., blued finish w/7 1/2" l. barrel, attached ejector rod, black hard rubber grips & a lanyard loop in the butt, refinished, 90 percent of old reblue, right grip w/large chip in heel, Serial No. 11734 .... **$633**

Although Samuel Colt (1814-1862) didn't invent the revolver, he was largely responsible for its refinement and widespread production and distribution, similar to Henry Ford's role in producing an automobile for the masses. A capstan, or rotating winch on a ship, inspired Colt to create an improved revolver mechanism that used a ratchet system to advance the cylinder and lock it in place until the cylinder was advanced again.

Revolver, Colt single-action, handle w/applied bone plaques, one side carved w/a steer head, produced in 1891, 10 1/8" l. **$1,725**

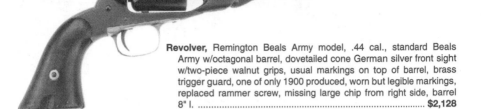

Revolver, Remington Beals Army model, .44 cal., standard Beals Army w/octagonal barrel, dovetailed cone German silver front sight w/two-piece walnut grips, usual markings on top of barrel, brass trigger guard, one of only 1900 produced, worn but legible markings, replaced rammer screw, missing large chip from right side, barrel 8" l. **$2,128**

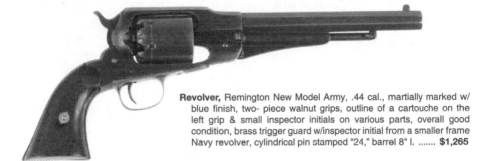

Revolver, Remington New Model Army, .44 cal., martially marked w/ blue finish, two- piece walnut grips, outline of a cartouche on the left grip & small inspector initials on various parts, overall good condition, brass trigger guard w/inspector initial from a smaller frame Navy revolver, cylindrical pin stamped "24," barrel 8" l. **$1,265**

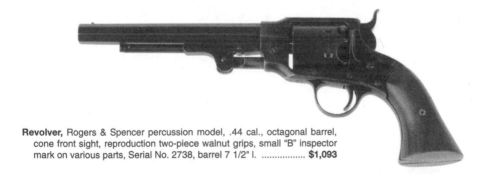

Revolver, Rogers & Spencer percussion model, .44 cal., octagonal barrel, cone front sight, reproduction two-piece walnut grips, small "B" inspector mark on various parts, Serial No. 2738, barrel 7 1/2" l. **$1,093**

Rifle, Frank Wesson tip-up model, .38RF cal., tang sight missing, barrel sights replacements, oil-stained stock, octagonal barrel 24" l. **$460**

Rifle, Maynard Model 1873 Improved Hunters No. 8 single-shot model, .35-30 cal., blued finish, pinched front sights w/two position V-notch rear sight, straight stock w/carbine-type smooth steel buttplate, octagonal to round 26" barrel **$1,035**

Rifle, Remington rolling-block military model, .50/70 cal., standard markings on upper tang, action w/the New York safety but no markings, bayonet & ramrod replaced, round barrel 36" l. **$518**

Rifle, Robbins, Kendall & Lawrence Model 1842 Mississippi, .54 cal. dated 1847 on the lockplate, "WAT" cartouche on left side of stock, spare nipple in patchbox, overall greyish brown patina, round barrel 33" l. **$1,955**

Rifle, Springfield Model 1855 Cadet model, .60 bored out cal., barrel & lock dated 1869, overall grey patina, ramrod a short replacement, stock including forearm tip 49 1/2" l. **$1,438**

FIREPLACE & HEARTH ITEMS

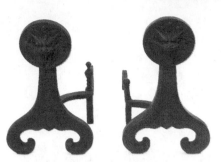

Andirons, Arts & Crafts style, cast iron w/a bronzed finish, the round disk top molded w/a ferocious dragon head raised on a flat tapering shaft spreading into C-scroll front feet, square curved log holder, original patina, replaced finials at rear, early 20th c., 12 x 27", 19" h., pr. **$720**

Andirons, Arts & Crafts Prairie School design, wrought & cast, a slender square upright w/a hammered square cap centered by a small dome & raised on a bracketed scroll base & projecting in front of a heavy hammered upright w/a bold knob finial on arched legs & w/rear log holder bar, original patina, early 20th c., 13 x 24", 24" h., pr. **$540**

Bellows, Arts & Crafts style, the sides carved w/a intricate leafy tree framed by the motto "The wind of prosperity to you," original leather & finish, 10 x 27 1/2" ... **$210**

Tinder lighter, flintlock-type, brass, iron & wood, a curled wooden pistol-form handle w/a brass & iron flintlock striking mechanism attached to a front arched brass support below a cylindrical candle socket, probably English, early 18th c., 3 1/2 x 5 1/4", 6 1/2" h. **$2,880**

Andirons, Arts & Crafts style, cast iron, figural top designed as pheasants atop flaring wrought legs, slender log bar, original patina, early 20th c., 20" h., facing pr. **$1,020**

Andirons, cast iron, figure of George Washington standing & leaning on a draped column, a book in one hand & his tricorn hat in the other, on a tall plinth-form base w/drapery & star trim, stepped block feet, repainted, 19th c., 9 1/4 x 14 1/4", 21 1/2" h. . **$633**

Furniture Dating Chart

American Furniture
Pilgrim Century – 1620-1700
William & Mary – 1685-1720
Queen Anne – 1720-50
Chippendale – 1750-85
Federal – 1785-1820
Hepplewhite – 1785-1800
Sheraton – 1800-20
Classical (American Empire)
– 1815-40
Victorian – 1840-1900
Early Victorian – 1840-50
Gothic Revival – 1840-90
Rococo (Louis XV) – 1845-70
Renaissance Revival – 1860-85
Louis XVI – 1865-75
Eastlake – 1870-95
Jacobean & Turkish Revival
– 1870-90
Aesthetic Movement – 1880-1900
Art Nouveau – 1895-1918
Turn-of-the Century
(Early 20th Century) – 1895-1910
Mission-style
(Arts & Crafts movement) – 1900-15
Colonial Revival – 1890-1930
Art Deco – 1925-40
Modernist or Mid-Century – 1945-70

English Furniture
Jacobean – Mid-17th Century
William & Mary – 1689-1702
Queen Anne – 1702-14
George I – 1714-27
George II – 1727-60

George III – 1760-1820
Regency – 1811-20
George IV – 1820-30
William IV – 1830-37
Victorian – 1837-1901
Edwardian – 1901-10

French Furniture
Louis XV – 1715-74
Louis XVI – 1774-93
Empire – 1804-15
Louis Philippe – 1830-48
Napoleon III
(Second Empire) – 1848-70
Art Nouveau – 1895-1910
Art Deco – 1925-35

Germanic Furniture
Since the country of Germany did not exist before 1870, furniture from the various Germanic states and the Austro-Hungarian Empire is generally termed simply "Germanic." From the 17th century onward, furniture from these regions tended to follow the stylistic trends established in France and England. General terms are used for such early furniture, usually classifying it as "Baroque," "Rococo," or a similar broad stylistic term. Germanic furniture dating from the first half of the 19th century is today usually referred to as Biedermeier, a style closely related to French Empire and English Regency.

FURNITURE

AMERICAN FURNITURE TERMS

CHAIRS

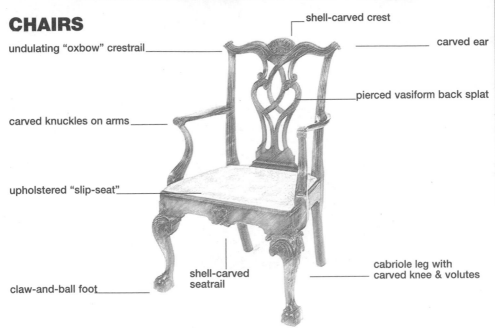

shell-carved crest

carved ear

undulating "oxbow" crestrail

pierced vasiform back splat

carved knuckles on arms

upholstered "slip-seat"

cabriole leg with carved knee & volutes

shell-carved seatrail

claw-and-ball foot

Chippendale Armchair

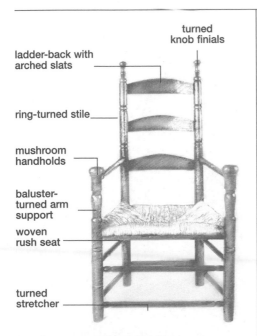

turned knob finials

ladder-back with arched slats

ring-turned stile

mushroom handholds

baluster-turned arm support

woven rush seat

turned stretcher

Early American "Ladder-back" Armchair

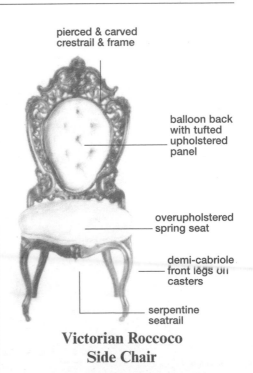

pierced & carved crestrail & frame

balloon back with tufted upholstered panel

overupholstered spring seat

demi-cabriole front legs on casters

serpentine seatrail

Victorian Roccoco Side Chair

CHESTS & TABLES

pierced brass pull

shaped molded edge

pierced brass keyhole escutcheon

graduated drawers

beaded drawer dividers & stiles

straight bracket feet

serpentine front

Chippendale Chest of Drawers

leather-covered top with tack trim

corbel

mortise & tenon through-construction

medial shelf

Mission Oak Library Table

FURNITURE PEDIMENTS & SKIRTS

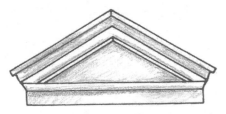

Classic Pediment

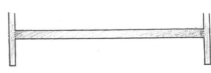

Plain Skirt

Broken Arch Pediment

Arched Skirt

**Bonnet Top with
Urn & Flame Finial**

Valanced Skirt

**Bonnet Top with Rosettes & Three
Urn & Flame Finials**

Scalloped Skirt

FURNITURE

FURNITURE FEET

Trestle Foot

Pad Foot

Block Foot

Slipper Foot

Spade Foot

Snake Foot

Tapered or Plain Foot

Spanish Foot

FURNITURE

FURNITURE FEET

Ball Foot

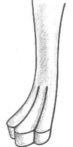

Trifid Foot

Bun Foot

Hoof Foot

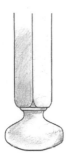

Turnip Foot

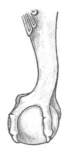

Claw-and-Ball Foot

Arrow or Peg Foot

Paw Foot

FURNITURE MARKET REPORT

Thomas Perry, owner of One of a Kind Antiques (www.oneofakindantiques.com) in Essex, Connecticut, said "No matter what period, good quality sells. It's finding the pieces in excellent condition that's the challenge." Perry has no trouble selling quality pieces of all styles: 18th century, Renaissance, Arts & Crafts, Art Deco, Modern, and others. He believes high quality, utilitarian goods are timeless and will always be in demand.

Perry's sales are strong in the $1,500 to $30,000 range, as his clientele aren't shopping for bargains, but for high-end pieces that will increase in value over time. He attributes his success to the expertise and reputation he has built over more than 30 years in the business and the fact that he was one of the first to have an online store, establishing his in 1995 at the very beginning of the Internet revolution.

Perry sells from both a brick-and-mortar and an online store, with 90 percent of his business done online now. The Internet allows him to do business all over the country and cater to the preferences of various geographical areas. For example, European pieces are popular in the southern states like Louisiana, and Victorian styles are favored in the Midwest.

He no longer does shows. While furniture can sell at shows, he said it can be hard to sell large pieces at them. The cost per square foot of booth space for large pieces can be prohibitive. Plus, it can be a challenge to move them in and out of the show and for customers to get those pieces home.

"Inexperienced buyers benefit by developing a personal relationship with a knowledgeable, trusted dealer who can give them reliable information and good advice," he said. This can be done via phone and e-mail, so a Web site isn't necessarily an obstacle to that. Good service, loyalty, and repeat business isn't dependent on physical distance but on attentiveness to the customer. Providing a diverse range of antiques is also important. In fact, he thinks the reason some shows struggle is that they are too narrow and specialized.

Perry predicts that high-caliber furniture will remain good sellers regardless of the economy because there will always be people with money who are looking for superior furnishings.

Eron Johnson of Eron Johnson Antiques (www.eronjohnsonantiques.com) in Denver, Colorado, agrees that top notch antiques are doing well. Buyers who can afford large houses are looking for antiques like large chandeliers and 10 to 12 foot dining tables that fit the scale of their homes.

He noted that the demographics of antique furniture sales have changed dramatically over recent years. The collector segment of the market is gone. At all levels of the market, decorating, rather than the historical importance of antiques, is the driving force. "No one cares anymore about how old pieces are or where they came from. What they're concerned about is whether the color of a piece will match their decor, how it will fit in a space, and whether the drawers work. They are interested in utilitarianism and pizzazz." For instance, they want flat top desks they can use for computers. Mirrors and bookcases move because they're practical.

Aesthetics are important, too. "What appeals to this generation is the styles that they're seeing in magazines and movies," Johnson said. "Modernism is strong, and Italian sells because it is visually stimulating. Quirky and interesting shapes are in, safe standard shapes are out. Exotic Anglo-Indian and Portuguese pieces are popular as they have cross-cultural elements. Restrained Asian designs do well because they work well with contemporary and modern."

Because decorating, rather than collecting, is dominating the market, many buyers rely on interior decorators to help them select pieces that will complement their living spaces. Sometimes the decorators come in with the owners, sometimes they pre-shop for the clients and narrow the options down to several choices, and the owners come in later to make the final selection.

Current buyers don't think of antiques as untouchable works of art to be treated with reverence the way the previous generation did. Twenty or thirty years ago, it would have been considered sacrilege to cut up an antique to make it more user friendly. Today's buyers, however, are willing to alter non-investment grade cabinets to install a sink or cut down legs to make them fit a room better.

Interestingly, both Perry and Johnson, while located on opposite sides of the country, sell nationally and internationally through the Internet, so neither is limited by the particular antiques preferences of their locales. Johnson sells 80 percent of his stock through the Internet and a significant portion overseas to Australia, England and western Europe. He also sells Asian pieces to China, Taiwan, Korea and Japan. He considers the Internet an indispensable asset and believes this is a must to survive, as "no single area will generate enough business for a dealer to depend only on local sales."

Auction Houses
Cincinnati Art Galleries (www.cincinnatiartgalleries.com)
Charlton Hall (www.charltonhallauctions.com)
Dumouchelle (www.dumouchelle.com)
Doyle New York (www.doylenewyork.com)
Garth's (www.garths.com)
Flomaton (www.flomatonantiqueauction.com)
Freeman's (www.freemansauction.com/home.asp)
John Moran (www.johnmoran.com)
Leslie Hindman (www.lesliehindman.com)
Neal (www.nealauction.com/indexnet.html)
New Orleans Auction Galleries (www.neworleansauction.com)
Weschler's (www.weschlers.com)
Ivey-Selkirk (www.iveyselkirk.com)

FURNITURE

Furniture made in the United States during the 18th and 19th centuries is coveted by collectors. American antique furniture has a European background, primarily English, since the influence of the Continent usually found its way to America by way of England. If the style did not originate in England, it came to America by way of England. For this reason, some American furniture styles carry the name of an English monarch or an English designer. However, we must realize that, until recently, little research has been conducted and even less published on the Spanish and French influences in the area of the California missions and New Orleans.

After the American revolution, cabinetmakers in the United States shunned the prevailing styles in England and chose to bring the French styles of Napoleon's Empire to the United States and we have the uniquely named "American Empire" (Classical) style of furniture in a country that never had an emperor.

During the Victorian period, quality furniture began to be mass-produced in this country with its rapidly growing population. So much walnut furniture was manufactured that the vast supply of walnut was virtually depleted and it was of necessity that oak furniture became fashionable as the 19th century drew to a close.

For our purposes, the general guidelines for dating will be: Pilgrim Century - 1620-85, William & Mary - 1685-1720, Queen Anne - 1720-50, Chippendale - 1750-85, Federal - 1785-1820, Hepplewhite - 1785-1820, Sheraton - 1800-20, American Empire (Classical) - 1815-40, Early Victorian - 1840-50, Victorian - 1840-1900.

Bedroom Suites

Art Deco, stepped vanity, five-drawer chest of drawers, bedside table, double bed & bench; bird's-eye maple, simple classic squared design w/narrow curved metal pulls & large upright round off-center mirror on dressing table, dated & marked "1936 - Triangle Brand - Crane & McMahon," the set **$288**

Art Deco: bedstead, two tall two-door cabinets fitted w/drawers, a pair of nightstands, a side table, a shelving unit & a mirrored vanity table & stool; lacquered & painted creamy white, simple rectangular forms, designed by Jules Bouy for Carlos Salzedo, ca. 1931, cabinets 17 1/2 x 20", 4' 6" h., the set **$4,780**

Classical style: double sleigh bed, large rectangular ogee-framed mirror, chest- of-drawers & commode: all mahogany & mahogany veneer, the chest w/two small handkerchief drawers w/wooden knobs on the rectangular top above a long ogee-front drawer slightly projecting above the lower case w/three long flat drawers w/turned wood knobs flanked by tall ogee pilasters ending in heavy C- scroll feet, the commode w/a white marble backsplash & rectangular marble top above a long serpentine drawer above a pair of paneled doors over the serpentine apron & casters, ca. 1840, the set **$978**

Louis XV-Style: double bed & two-door armoire; mahogany marquetry, each of undulating outline, the bed w/the head- and footboard ornately decorated w/leafy scrolls, urns & other classical designs in light inlay all bordered by brass bands w/gilt-brass mounts on the top rails & on the legs, serpentine siderails, the armoire w/an arched crest w/gilt-brass scroll mount above a pair of tall cupboard doors w/tall beveled mirrors, delicate marquetry band above the doors & on the drawer across the bottom, demountable, original finish, France, ca. 1890, armoire 20 x 50", 96" h., the set (ILLUS. of bed).............. **$15,000**

Arts & Crafts style: double bed, tall chest of drawers, wardrobe, nightstand, dressing table & bench & free-standing mirror; oak, each piece w/the main panels decorated w/a rectangular reserve enclosed by an arch & leaftip design, cabinet pieces w/vertical panels, doors w/long flat wrought-iron strap hinges & ring pulls in the shape of inverted hearts, original finish, ca. 1915, England, wardrobe 16 x 48", 78" h. (ILLUS. of part) **$2,000**

Renaissance-Style: bed, chest-of-drawers, cheval mirror, two-door armoire, pair of nightstands; burled elm & walnut, the large armoire w/a widely flaring stepped cornice w/blocked ends over a dentil- carved band above a frieze band w/lion mask carved blocks at the sides & a scroll-carved center panel flanked by narrow burl panels, all above the tall burl- paneled doors flanked by side pilasters carved w/angel heads, fruit clusters & scallops, blocked & stepped base on carved grotesque mask front feet, the other pieces w/ matching details, Italy, ca. 1900, bed 74 x 87", 71" h., armoire 31 x 80", 91" h., the set (ILLUS. of armoire)...................... **$4,830**

Victorian Aesthetic Movement substyle: double tester bed, wardrobe & washstand; walnut & burl walnut, the high- backed headboard supporting a half- tester w/an ornate stepped crown-form crestrail w/a pierced lattice band & quarter-round cut corner ears, the headboard w/a matching crestrail over an arched rectangular burl panel over lower burl panels, the low footboard w/a flat crestrail over a row of sunbursts; the wardrobe w/a matching crestrail above a pair of tall burl panel doors over a pair of base drawers; the washstand w/a matching crestrail above a square mirror swiveling between tall uprights above a white marble backsplash & rectangular top over a case w/a single long drawer over two small drawers beside a small paneled door, refinished, ca. 1880, bed overall 10' 5" h., the set **$7,500**

Victorian Aesthetic Movement substyle: half-tester double bed, chest of drawers, washstand & knockdown wardrobe; walnut & burl walnut, the high-back bed w/a large half-tester w/a gently arched crestrail centered by a narrow rectangular panel of leaf carving over a long frieze of leaf carving, the headboard w/a matching carved crestrail above large burl veneer panels & twist-carved colonette, low footboard w/flat crestrail over matching carved panels, the other pieces w/matching crestrails, the chest of drawers & washstand w/carved uprights flanking large square beveled swiveling mirrors over rectangular pink marble tops, the chest case w/a row of three drawers over two long drawers, the washstand w/two long drawers over a pair of paneled doors, the wardrobe w/tall doors w/beveled mirrors, original hardware & finish, ca. 880, bed 64 x 85", 10' h., the set (ILLUS. of bed, chest & washstand) **$35,000**

Victorian Aesthetic Movement substyle: high-backed double bed, chest of drawers & washstand; oak, each piece w/a flat-topped crestrail w/dentil carving over a band of leafy scrolls centered by a small shield & flanked by rounded scroll- carved corner ears, the headboard w/a further bands of dentil carving over a narrow rectangular leaf-carved panel flanked by square panels w/carved rosettes, a matching low footboard, the chest of drawers & washstand w/swiveling mirrors, original hardware, refinished, ca. 1890, bed 58 x 78", 6' 6" h., the set (ILLUS. of bed) **$2,800**

Victorian Aesthetic Movement substyle: high-backed double bed, chest of drawers & washstand; quarter-sawn oak, the bed & chest w/a flat flaring crestrail over a thin beaded band over a grapevine- carved band flanked by knob finials, the bed w/carved side pilasters flanking a large rectangular raised panel, the low footboard w/round fan-carved corners over a rectangular panel over a band of grapevine carving; the chest crestrail raised on narrow uprights w/pilasters flanking the large rectangular beveled mirror above the rectangular top over a case w/two small & one long raised panel drawers over a single long drawer over a shorter drawer beside a small square cupboard door all flanked by pilasters; the washstand w/a rectangular grey marble top above a case w/a single long drawer over two drawers & a square door, original hardware, original finish, ca. 1890, bed 60 x 78", 7' h., the set **$4,000**

Victorian Aesthetic Movement substyle: high-backed double bed, chest of drawers & washstand; walnut & burl walnut veneer, the bed & chest w/high ornate crestrails w/a pierced sunburst center crest above a wide panel centered by a pierced lattice panel centered by a carved florette flanked by triangular raised burl & leaf-carved panels, the bed w/long rectangular burl veneer panels, the chest w/flat uprights w/candleshelves flanking the large square swiveling mirror above the rectangular white marble top on the case w/a row of three burl veneer drawers over two long burl veneer drawers, flat apron, washstand w/white marble tall splashback on a case w/a long narrow burl panel drawer over two burled drawers & small door, flat apron, original fancy brass hardware, refinished, ca. 1880, chest overall 7' 8" h., the set **$3,500**

Victorian Eastlake substyle: double half-tester bed, a marble-topped chest of drawers w/mirror, a marble-topped washstand w/ mirror; walnut & burl walnut, the half-tester on the bed w/a stepped angular cornice w/panels carved w/stylized flowers between corner blocks, flat serpentine brackets supporting it above the high headboard w/a matching carved cornice, the lower flat-topped footboard w/floral-incised arched & burl panels above rectangular panels, the other pieces w/ matching crests, white marble tops & arrangements of drawers w/stamped brass pulls w/angular bails, marble on chest w/old repair & cracks, ca. 1880, bed 63 1/2 x 79 1/2", 8' 3" h., 3 pcs. (ILLUS. of bed only).......... **$7,188**

Victorian Eastlake substyle: double bed, chest of drawers & washstand; walnut & burl walnut, the bed & chest w/high backs topped w/a wide molded crestrail w/a carved central roundel & pointed carved corner ears above a scallop-cut frieze band, the bed headboard w/stepped narrow panels of burl & a matching low footboard, the chest w/a large swiveling square mirror flanked by small quarter-round shelves at the base of the side supports above the rectangular top over a case w/a row of three drawers over two long drawers; the washstand w/a marble splashback over a case w/a long narrow drawer over two small drawers beside a small raised-panel door, original narrow rectangular brass pulls, ca. 1880, chest 21 x 42", 6' 8" h., the set **$6,500**

The word "antique" can be defined in several ways. Purists define antiques as objects made before 1820. Objects made before this time were generally handmade. After the Industrial Revolution began around 1820, however, many objects were machine made.

The U.S. Customs Offfice, for purposes of determing import tax, defines an antique as an object that is at least 100 years old. This means that each year another year's worth of objects officially become antiques.

While many objects from the early 20th century are not officially anitques yet, some consider them antiques because of their quality and desirability.

BEDROOM SUITES

Victorian Faux Bamboo: double bed, chest of drawers, octagonal side table & pair of side chairs; turned wood & bird's- eye maple, the high-backed bed w/a tall rectangular headboard w/a top low gallery of bamboo-turned spindles above the bird's-eye maple headboard w/a large oval recessed panel, the bamboo- turned side stiles topped w/large ball finials, the side rails w/bamboo-turned trim & the low footboard matching the highboard, the chest of drawers w/a large oval mirror swiveling between bamboo-turned uprights above the rectangular case w/three long graduated drawers, attributed to R. J. Horner & Co., New York, New York, ca. 1875, bed 60 x 81", 68" h., the set (ILLUS. of the bed).......................... **$13,800**

Victorian Eastlake substyle: half-tester double bed, two-door armoire, chest-of- drawers & washstand; walnut & burl walnut, each w/a high stepped crestrail carved w/scrolls & flanked by tapering block corner finials above a narrow dentil & block band, the washstand w/a large rectangular mirror swiveling between up-rights above the rectangular red marble top w/a high splashback over a case w/two long narrow burl-paneled drawers slightly stepped-out above a pair of burl- paneled cupboard doors, molded base on casters, bed 62 x 74", 92 1/2" h., washstand 18 x 32 1/4", 78 1/2" h., the set (ILLUS. of washstand).... **$4,370**

Victorian Golden Oak style: double bed, chest of drawers, chiffonier & washstand; oak & oak veneer, the high-backed bed w/a double-arch crestrail centered by a carved shell over large C-scrolls & smaller leafy scrolls, a plain low footboard; the chest w/a serpentine crestrail w/small shell & scroll carving curves down to form an oblong tall frame around a large beveled mirror swiveling between S-scroll uprights w/scroll-carved trim over the rectangular top w/serpentine edges over a conforming serpentine case w/a pair of drawers over two long drawers over a serpentine apron & short legs w/paw feet; the tall chiffonier w/a matching rectangular serpentine frame around a long rectangular beveled mirror of S-scroll uprights above a serpentine top over a case w/a pair of drawers over a stack of four long drawers, serpentine apron & paw feet; the washstand w/a towel bar supported by S-scroll scroll-carved uprights over the serpentine top & case w/a long drawer over two small drawers beside a small door, on paw feet, refinished, ca. 1900, bed 6' h., the set **$4,000**

Antiques are the orginal recyclables. Reusing antiques not only saves them from ending up in the landfill, it reduces the amount of raw materials consumed for new goods. Plus, antiques are typically better quality than new and are sometimes less expensive. Why purchase a new piece of furniture made from particle board when you can buy a solid-wood piece at a local auction for less than new? Finally, antiques preserve history for future generations.

Victorian Golden Oak style: high-backed double bed & chest of drawers; oak, the headboard w/a central shell-and-scroll- carved low crest on a slightly serpentine crestrail above a scroll-carved cluster on the wide plain backboard, the low footboard w/a rod crestrail over a scroll- carved cluster; the chest of drawers w/a large rectangular beveled mirror in a molded frame w/matching crestrail, swiveling between S-scroll supports w/scroll-carved trim above the rectangular top w/a double-serpentine front over the conforming case w/a pair of drawers over two long lower drawers, serpentine apron & simple curved legs, original brass hardware, original dark finish, ca. 1900, bed 58 x 78", 6' h., 2 pcs. .. **$1,400**

Victorian Golden Oak style: high-backed double bed & chest of drawers; quarter- sawn oak, each piece w/a flat molded crestrail centered by an arched scroll- carved crest, the headboard w/a large flat panel decorated w/delicate leafy scroll carving w/matching carving on the low footboard, the chest of drawers crest above a large oblong beveled mirror swiveling between S-scroll scroll-carved supports over a rectangular top w/serpentine edges over a double-serpentine case w/a pair of drawers over two long drawers over simple curved feet, refinished, ca. 1900, bed 58 x 78", 6' 6" h., 2 pcs. **$2,750**

Victorian Golden Oak style: high-backed double bed, chest of drawers & washstand; each piece w/a serpentine crestrail centered by a shell carved over leafy scrolls on a wide half-round rail; the bed headboard w/half-round columns flanking a rectangular molding panel w/a scroll-and-cartouche crest, the low footboard w/a matching raised panel; the chest w/columnar uprights flanking an arched rectangular beveled swiveling mirror over a rectangular top over a case w/a pair of projecting drawers over two long graduated bow-front drawers flanked by half-round columns over paw feet; the washstand also w/columnar uprights flanking a narrow rectangular beveled mirror over a towel bar, the rectangular top over a pair of projecting drawers over a single long bow-front drawer over a pair of bow-front doors all on paw feet, original dark finish, ca. 1895, bed 58 x 78", 7' 7" h., the set **$8,500**

Victorian Golden Oak style: high-backed double bed, chest of drawers & washstand; oak, the headboard w/a slightly serpentine crestrail over delicate leafy scroll carving above plain panels, the chest w/a matching crestrail over flat uprights flanking a large rectangular swiveling mirror above the rectangular top over a case w/three long drawers, flat apron; the washstand w/a towel bar on uprights above the rectangular top & case w/a long drawer over two small drawers & a small door, refinished, ca. 1910, chest of drawers overall 6' 6" h., the set **$1,600**

Victorian Renaissance Revival substyle: bed & chest of drawers; walnut & burl walnut, the bed w/ a tall headboard w/a palmette & leafy scroll crest flanked by scrolled ears above an arched molding w/roundel above a tall rectangular burl panel flanked by half-round ring-turned columns & bars flanked by lower arched burl panels & short blocked & baluster- turned side stiles, the low footboard w/a raised & arched center crest over long burl panels & ring-turned rails, the chest of drawers w/similar carving & a tall arched mirror above a drop-well case w/white marble tops, ca. 1875, bed 68 x 85", 106" h., the pair (ILLUS. of bed)....... **$12,650**

Victorian Renaissance Revival substyle: bed, chest of drawers & washstand; walnut & burl walnut, the bed & chest topped by a carved pediment centered by an angel head over panels above scrolls, the chest w/a mirror w/ panels & candle shelves above a top w/three sections w/faux black marble painted tops, pairs of small drawers flank the center well above a drawer over a molded base, washstand marble top re-placed, bed 65 x 84", 95 1/2" h., chest- of-drawers 24 x 57 1/2", 95" h., the set (ILLUS. of chest of drawers) **$8,050**

Victorian Renaissance Revival substyle: high-backed double bed & chest of drawers; walnut & burl walnut, each piece w/a high crestrail centered by a large pointed palmette-and-scroll-carved crest flanked by pierced leafy scrolls over an angled pediment w/burl panels, the headboard w/further shaped burl panels flanking a large roundel flanked by urn-form finials all above three tall narrow molded panels, the lower footboard w/a peaked top over matching burl panels & angled paneled legs, the chest w/scroll-cut sides flanking the tall rectangular mirror above the drop-well white marble top over a case w/pairs of small drawers over two long drawers all w/raised burl panels, original black pear-shaped drops, 1870s, bed 58 x 78", 8' h., 2 pcs. **$5,800**

Victorian Renaissance Revival substyle: double bed, chest of drawers & washstand; walnut, the high-backed bed & chest w/tall broken-scroll arched crests centered by carved fruit finials above shaped raised burl panels, the bed w/a low arched footboard w/raised fruit & scroll carving, the chest w/an arched molding below the crest over a tall arched mirror flanked by shaped sides w/small candle shelves & raised burl panels above the drop-well white marble top w/stacks of four small drawers flanking two longer center drawers; the washstand w/an arched white marble splashback over a long narrow single drawer over a pair of arched-panel doors, original black pear-shaped drawer pulls, ca. 1875, refinished, chest overall 8' h., the set **$3,500**

Victorian Renaissance Revival substyle: high-backed double bed & chest of drawers, walnut & burl walnut, each w/a tall ornately carved broken-scroll crestrail centered by a large palmette & fruit-carved finial over further carved scrolls & a blocked crestrail, the headboard w/half-round columns below the blocked rail flanking a very tall raised burl panel flanked by shorter side panels below urn-form finials palmette-carved drops, the low footboard w/a flat crestrail over an arrangement of raised burl panels, the chest of drawers w/a similar design of columns & scroll-carved sides flanking a tall beveled mirror w/a paneled top above the white marble drop-well top, the side sections w/ outset beveled corners above a conforming section w/two small burl paneled drawers above two long burl paneled drawers flanked by slender side columns, original T-form pulls, refinished, ca. 1875, bed 58 x 78", 8' 6" h., pr. (ILLUS. of chest of drawers)......... **$7,500**

Victorian Renaissance Revival substyle: canopied double bed & mirrored armoire; ebonized beech, the bed headboard w/a crestrail w/a scroll-carved plaque and classical female mask, spindled galleries between stiles w/turned finials, above a frieze band over a panel, the footboard w/a top rail above two panels centered by roundels & flanked by columns, the bed w/a giltwood canopy frame, Napoleon II Era, France, ca. 1860, bed 60 x 82", 72" h. (ILLUS. of bed) ... **$11,213**

Victorian Renaissance Revival substyle: high-backed double bed & chest of drawers; walnut & burl walnut, each w/a matching crestrail w/peaked leafy scroll center bracket crest w/burl panel above an arched molding over further burl & molded panels flanked by brackets, the headboard w/block-and-roundel corner finials above block-molded sides flanking long narrow panels, the low arched footboard w/a central diamond-shaped burl panel flanked by shaped panels over long rectangular panels & heavy square blocked legs; the crest on the chest above a tall arched rectangular mirror flanked by paneled sides w/small candle shelves & scroll-carved lower sides above the drop-well top w/white marble tops, two small drawers at each side above two long lower drawers w/raised burl panels & original pulls, refinished, ca. 1875, bed 58 x 78", overall 7' 10" h., 2 pcs. (ILLUS. of chest of drawers).. **$6,500**

Victorian Renaissance Revival substyle: high-backed double bed & chest of drawers; walnut & burl walnut, the bed w/a tall palmette-and-scroll-carved center crest flanked by scrolls above the molded broken-arch pediment above triangular raised burl panels over a wide section w/scroll-carved sides flanking a large center oval burl panel surrounded by small triangular raised burl panels all flanked by urn-form finials on the block- carved sides flanking three tall vertical rectangular panels, the low footboard w/matching carving & panels; the chest of drawers w/a matching crest above wide tapering scroll-carved sides w/candle shelves flanking a tall rectangular mirror over the drop-well white marble top, the case w/ pairs of small burl drawers over a single long drawer w/raised burl panels flanking a center roundel, ca. 1875, original finish, bed 60 x 80", 8' 4" h., 2 pcs. (ILLUS. of bed) **$6,500**

Before buying any large pieces of furniture, measure your wall and floor space to make sure they will actually fit. Also take photos of your rooms with you on your shopping trips to help you visualize how your prospective antiques will look in their intended places.

Victorian Renaissance Revival substyle: high-backed double bed & chest of drawers; walnut & burl walnut; each piece w/an extremely ornate crest w/a large urn finial above a broken-arch raised center pediment flanked by turned T-form spindles above a heavy molded arch flanked by large angled side pediments w/fanned ears, the headboard w/a large arched burl center panel flanked by smaller rectangular panels each separated by short heavy turned columns on blocked brackets separating further burl panels, the lower arched footboard w/panels, a roundel & columns matching the headboard, the ornate chest crest above columns & blocks flanking the long rectangular mirror flanked by two side compartments w/square inset marble tops supporting a block & column w/a round disk shelf, each compartment w/a shaped & carved molding over three small drawers, refinished, ca. 1870, bed 68 x 80", 9' h., 2 pcs. **$25,000**

Victorian Renaissance Revival substyle: high-backed double bed & chest of drawers; walnut & burl walnut, the headboard w/a very high arched crest topped by a full-figure carved cupid w/quiver flanked by small dolphins above carved scrolls all above a large arched burl panel flanked by detailed urn corner finials above three molded arched panels, the low footboard w/an arched crestrail over three arched burl panels flanked by rounded corners w/burl panels, the chest of drawers w/a matching finial & crestrail over a tall arched mirror flanked by scroll-carved sides w/burl panels & candle shelves over the drop-well top w/white marble, the rectangular raised side section w/chamfered corners above a conforming case w/a stack of three burl-paneled drawers at each side flanking the low center section w/a concave front over a conforming long burl-paneled drawer, original pulls, refinished, ca. 1870, bed 58 x 78", 9' h., 2 pcs. **$25,000**

Victorian Renaissance Revival substyle: queen-sized bed & chest of drawers; walnut & flame-grained cherry veneer, both pieces w/matching crestrails centered by a long rectangular flaring block-form crest above scroll cutouts over a small arched cherry burl panel flanked by a broken-arch pediment, the headboard w/shaped scroll-carved sides centering a large burl cherry panel, a matching low footboard & deep side boards; the chest crest above a large rectangular mirror flanked by shaped supports w/small rounded shelves over the rectangular white marble top & a case of three long burl-paneled drawers, all on flattened bun feet, original finish, ca. 1880, chest overall 8' 7" h., 2 pcs. **$4,500**

Victorian Rococo substyle: high-backed double bed & chest of drawers; carved mahogany, the chest of drawers w/a very high superstructure topped by a Prince-of-Wales plumes carved finial over a broken-arched pediment w/scroll-pierced panels above wide pierced scroll-carved sections supporting two half-round shelves on each side & flanking a tall arched swiveling mirror, the rectangular white marble top w/a serpentine front & outset chamfered corners above a conforming case w/four long bow-front drawers w/ornate scroll-carved panels & pulls, molded bow-front apron; the bed head-board w/a pierced & scroll-carved finial on the wide arched & molded crestrail above a wide arched flame veneer panel flanked by heavy side posts w/large urn-form finials, low footboard w/raised scroll-carved corners & arched center crest above a cartouche-carved roundel, deep side rails, by Mitchell & Rammelsburg Co., Cincinnati, Ohio, ca. 1850-60, bed 62 x 80", overall 9' h., pr. (ILLUS. of chest) **$10,000**

Victorian Rococo substyle: high-backed double bed & chest of drawers; carved rosewood, the bed headboard w/a pierced arched crest carved w/ leafy vines w/an exotic bird perched at each side over the stepped crestrail above the backboard w/scroll carving flanked by stiles w/urn-form finials, the lower footboard w/scroll carving centered by an oval knob above two panels, low corner boards; the chest w/a superstructure w/pierced-carved branches w/an exotic bird on each side & resting on square plinths w/round candle shelves enclosing a swiveling mirror, the marble top w/a serpentine front above a case w/ three drawers w/carved pulls flanked by canted front corners w/carved scrolls, apron, Mitchell & Rammelsberg Co., Cincinnati, Ohio, ca. 1855, original finish, bed 64 x 82", 8' 6" h., pr. **$20,000**

Distressing is the natural wear and tear that appears on furniture surfaces. It occurs naturally over the life of the piece through everyday use. It adds to its charm and helps authenticate that a piece is genuinely old.

BEDROOM SUITES

Victorian Rococo substyle: high-backed double bed & chest of drawers; feather- grained walnut; the high bed headboard w/an arched crest w/ornately carved scrolls on an open C-scroll above the arched crestrail w/further scrolls above a large oval grained panel flanked by narrow arched rectangular panels between the serpentine stiles w/further scroll carving, the low footboard w/a raised, arched center w/fruit-and-flower carving & curved low corner posts; the chest w/a tall superstructure w/a high pierced scroll-carved crest & upturned corners over a tall rectangular mirror w/serpentine top swiveling between ornate shaped & scroll-carved uprights above the rectangular white marble top over a case w/two long, deep drawers decorated w/raised banded panels w/scroll carving, serpentine apron w/scroll carving between bun feet, labeled "O. P. Merriman, Baltimore," original finish, ca. 1860, bed 64 x 82", 6' 6" h., pr. (ILLUS. of bed) **$8,500**

Victorian Rococo substyle: highback double bed & chest of drawers w/mirror; carved walnut, the bed headboard w/an arched scroll-bordered crestrail topped by pierced carved scrolls centering a cartouche above a curved burl panel & a pair of carved urn finials flanking a round panel & serpentine sides, the lower footboard w/an arched crest w/ scrolls over raised panels & scrolls between quarter-round corners, the chest w/an arched crestrail w/ cartouche over the arched mirror flanked by shaped sides w/small candle shelves above the white marble top w/a bowed front over a case w/three long drawers w/ burl veneering & leaf-carved pulls, rounded front corners, original finish, ca. 1860, bed 64 x 83", 100" h., the set................ **$12,000**

Victorian Rococo substyle: high-backed double bed, chest of drawers & washstand; carved rosewood, the bed headboard w/a large arched & peaked pierce- carved crest composed of ornate scrolls centered by a Prince of Wales plumes finial above the arched & molded crestrail above raised burl panels over three small pierced-carved panels above three tall arch-topped veneer panels all flanked by block-and-scroll-carved stiles, the low arched footboard w/three arched veneer panels centered w/a scroll-carved cluster, curved & paneled corner boards; the chest w/a tall superstructure w/a pierced crest matching the bed above pierced & scroll carved uprights w/small half-round shelves flanking a tall, swiveling arched- topped rectangular mirror, the rectangular white marbled top w/ projecting canted corners above columns flanking a conforming case w/ three long drawers decorated w/raised oval banding & fruit- carved pulls, the washstand w/a rectangular white marble top over a case of three long drawers, Mitchell & Rammelsberg Co., Cincinnati, Ohio, ca. 1860, original finish, bed 64 x 84", overall 9' 6" h., the set (ILLUS. of bed)......... **$35,000**

Homeowners should make sure all their property is insured against fire, theft, and natural disater. Standard household policies generally do not cover antiques and collectibles. A rider or separate policy will likely be needed for these items. For those who have considerable value in their antiques and collectibles, it may be worth hiring a professional appraiser.

Also, be sure to inventory and photograph property that is not appraised because insurance reimbursement will not be made for property that isn't claimed. In the aftermath of a loss, when coping with stress, it can be difficult to try to recall all the contents of a home. It is much easier to do this before a loss occurs.

Beds

Classical low-poster bed, mahogany, matching head- and footboards w/curved tops w/scrolled ends above pairs of rectangular burl veneer panels, ropetwist posts w/large knob finials above blocked sections on heavy tapering ovoid legs, brass bolt covers, refinished, ca. 1830s, 58 x 76", 45" h. **$1,200**

Classical low-poster bed, mahogany, the flat-topped headboard w/a knob-ended bar over delicate applied bronze cupids flanking swags, acanthus leaf & ribbed knob carved side posts w/small bronze pineapple finials & heavy acanthus- carved turned legs, matching foot posts joined by a rail, original finish, ca. 1840, 60 x 80", 5' h. **$2,400**

Classical low-poster bed, mahogany, the gently arched headboard w/scroll-cut end flanked by ornate baluster-turned & leaf-carved sections topped by acorn finials, matching foot posts joined by a wide rail, bulbous tapering ovoid legs, brass bolt covers, probably original finish, ca. 1840, 40 x 74", 42" h. **$800**

Classical tall-poster bed, mahogany, the arched & scroll-carved headboard over two large rectangular flame veneer panels flanked by tall knob-, ring- and acanthus leaf carved tall posts w/knob finials, matching foot posts, short baluster- turned legs, original brass bolt covers, original dark finish, ca. 1835, 58 x 80", 7' h. **$5,500**

BEDS

When bidding at auction, don't bid early and tip your hand. Enter the bidding late, and with authority to intimidate competitors. They will likely think you are willing to spend more than you really will and back off.

BEDS

Classical tall-poster canopy bed, mahogany, a large rectangular canopy w/a deep frame & wide flaring cornice supported on four matching slender spiral-twist turned posts topped by pineapple carving & ending in a ring-turned section w/an acanthus leaf-carved section, all supported on short ring- and, rod-turned legs ending in ball feet, the high headboard w/ scroll-cut top ending in rosettes, early 19th c., 62 x 82", 122" h. **$51,750**

Classical tall-poster canopy bed, mahogany, a large rectangular canopy w/a deep frame & wide stepped & flaring cornice supported on four matching slender ring- and baluster-turned posts, all supported on ring- and baluster-turned legs ending in ball feet, the headboard w/flat rolled crest, made in Louisiana, ca. 1825, excellent surface, 60 x 81", 104" h. **$14,950**

Classical tall-poster canopy bed, tiger stripe maple & mahogany, a large rectangular canopy w/a deep frame & flaring cornice supported on four matching slender ring- and rod-turned posts, all supported on ring- and rod-turned legs, the high headboard w/scrolled crest, ca. 1825, fitted w/later rails but original rope rails available, associated canopy w/ mosquito netting, 60 x 80", 98" h. **$6,038**

Classical tall-poster canopy bed, walnut, a large rectangular canopy w/a deep frame & wide flaring cornice w/rounded corners added later; supported on four matching slender ring- and baluster- turned posts, all supported on ring- and baluster-turned legs, the headboard w/scroll-cut crest, made in Louisiana, ca. 1825, 56 x 81", 100" h. **$19,550**

Classical tall-poster tester bed, mahogany, a wide cove-molded rectangular tester frame raised on columnar posts, an arched headboard w/a cartouche- and- scroll-carved finial, wide side & foot rails, short ring-turned feet, original finish, ca. 1840, 60 x 78", 9' h. **$2,500**

Classical Revival tall-poster bed, mahogany, high flame veneer headboard w/flat crestrail w/knob ends above cutout scrolls flanked by leaf-carved spiraling posts w/ ring-turned & pineapple finials, matching foot posts joined by a turned leaf-carved upper rail & a flat lower rail, short heavy tapering turned legs w/bun feet, original finish, ca. 1890-1910, 56 x 76", 6' h. **$1,500**

Classical Revival tall-poster bed, mahogany, the high flat-topped headboard w/scroll trim over a leaf-carved band w/roundel above a rectangular panel w/ beaded molding, flanked by posts w/baluster- and ring-turned leaf-carved sections below tall tapering reeded sections w/ carved knob finials, matching shorter footrails joined by a wide rail, tapering reeded short legs, late 19th c., 60 x 78", 6' h. **$1,500**

Classical Revival tall-poster bed, mahogany, the wide arched headboard centered by a pair of large delicate cutout scrolls, heavy paneled tapering side posts w/flattened knob finials, matching foot posts joined by a paneled narrow upper rail & gently arched lower rail, heavy C-scroll feet, original finish, ca. 1890- 1910, 60 x 80", 5' 6" h. **$1,000**

Classical Revival tall-poster bed, mahogany, the wide headboard w/a broken- scroll crestrail centered by a pointed knob finial & flanked by rope-twist-turned posts w/knob-turned finials, the slightly shorter foot posts joined by a ropetwist-, knob- and ring-turned rail above a wide scroll-ended lower rail, short knob-turned feet, refinished, early 20th c., 58 x 78", 5' h. **$850**

Classical-Rococo transitional tall-poster bed, mahogany, the high arched headboard w/ ornate carved scrolls flanked by tall posts formed by a cluster of four columns topped w/a ball finial, shorter matching foot posts, serpentine scroll- trimmed siderails & footrails, possibly original finish, ca. 1845, 66 x 84", 6' h. **$4,500**

Classical tall poster canopy bed, walnut, a large rectangular canopy w/a deep frame & wide flaring corners supported on four matching slender paneled posts w/ring turned sections & a tapering top section all supported on short ring-, rail- and knob-turned legs, the two-paneled headboard w/scroll-cut top w/a blanket roll w/turned acorn end finials, second quarter 19th c., 65 x 86", 109" h. **$4,370**

Colonial Revival tall-poster bed, mahogany, the high broken-scroll headboard w/turned center finial flanked by slender leaf-carved baluster- and ring-turned posts w/carved pineapple finials, matching foot posts joined by a turned & leaf- carved upper rail & flat lower rail, short legs w/claw-and-ball feet, original finish, full-sized, early 20th c., 58 x 78", 6' h. **$2,400**

Federal tall-poster bed, mahogany, the headboard w/an arched crestrail over two rectangular panels flanked by tall slender ropetwist columns w/carved pineapple finials, matching foot posts joined by a rail, ropetwist legs on original brass feet, original bolt covers, original finish, ca. 1820s, 60 x 80", 7' 8" h. .. **$7,500**

The Federal period in the United Sates was a time of patriotism and anti-British sentiment after the Revolution. Consequently, French styles were preferred.

BEDS

Victorian cottage-style tall-poster bed, walnut, a flat-topped headboard w/scroll- carved sides over a row of short spool- turned spindles above a spool-turned rail, flanked by tall spool-turned posts, matching foot posts joined by a spool- turned upper rail & flat lower rail, tall spool-turned legs, original finish, mid- 19th c., 58 x 76", 6' h. **$1,200**

Federal Revival tall-poster twin-sized beds, mahogany, the wide flat head-board w/a narrow flat crestrail w/scrolled ends flanked by slender tapering reeded posts topped by stylized plume finials, matching foot posts joined by a knob- turned reeded upper rail & a flat bottom rail, early 20th c., 42 x 74", 5' 6" h., pr. **$1,800**

Mission-style (Arts & Crafts movement) three-quarters bed, oak, the headboard w/a crestrail above four wide vertical slats flanked by gently tapering posts continuing to form legs, the matching footboard slightly shorter, cleaned original finish, unsigned Gustav Stickley, Model No. 923, 46 1/2 x 78 1/2", 46 1/2" h. **$2,400**

Federal tall-poster bed, mahogany, the high shaped headboard topped by a baluster- and ringed-turned bar w/acorn terminals, slender baluster- and ring-turned posts w/baluster-turned finials, matching foot posts joined by a lower rail, bulbous turned & tapering legs, original finish, made in New Orleans, ca. 1825-35, 60 x 80", 7' 6" h. **$10,500**

Victorian Golden Oak bed, the high squared headboard w/a heavy rounded crestrail centered by a pointed & scroll- carved crest over a wide section w/a del-icate large panel of applied leafy scrolls flanked by squared stiles w/simple scroll carving, the low footboard w/a heavy rounded crestrail over delicate scrolling, original dark finish, ca. 1900, 58 x 78", 80" h. .... **$1,400** →

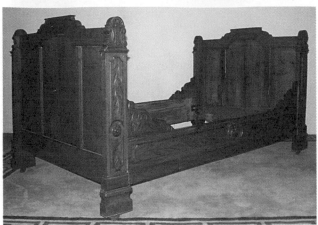

Victorian country-style double bed, carved butternut, high matching head- and footboards w/stepped crestrails over three wide panels flanked by flattened posts carved at the top w/a cornucopia above raised leaf-carved panels centered by a roundel, wide side rails w/scroll-carved top brackets & long raised panels carved w/leafy vines & centered by a carved roundel, heavy block feet, original finish, ca. 1870s, 56 x 76", 4' h. **$750**

Victorian Golden Oak "Murphy" bed, a high scalloped & scroll-carved crestrail above the rectangular top of the conforming case, the wide flat paneled & scroll- carved front folds out to expose the bed springs & mattress, original finish, ca. 1900, closed 20 x 50", overall 5' 4" h. **$650**

Victorian Golden Oak "Murphy" bed, wardrobe-style, the tall case w/a serpentine crestrail, delicate leafy scroll carving on the door-like panel enclosing an arched beveled mirror, the tall side panels w/rod cornices above tall slightly serpentine panels over flat panels, paneled & shaped side panels, full front folds down to expose the bed mattress & springs, patent-dated 1886, refinished, 22 x 60", 7' h. **$1,250**

Victorian Golden Oak child's bed, demountable, the high headboard w/a serpentine top w/carved scroll trim above a raised oval scroll band, side stiles w/scroll-carved ears, matching lower footboard, deep slatted side rails, original finish, ca. 1900 24 x 48", 40" h. **$500**

Saw marks are useful clues to furniture age. If the saw marks along the edge of a piece of wood are curved, the wood was cut by a circular saw and the furniture made after 1840.

Victorian Gothic Revival half-tester bed, mahogany, the rectangular bow-fronted tester frame cut w/repeating low Gothic arches & cutout trefoils, raised on tall baluster-turned & paneled posts w/Gothic arch brackets, the tall headboard w/a gently arched scroll-carved crestrail over three tall Gothic arch flame veneer panels, the low footboard w/a serpentine crestrail over three arched panels between heavy paneled legs w/urn-form finials & raised on knob feet, refinished, ca. 1840, 60 x 80", 9' 9" h. .. **$5,500**

BEDS

Victorian Renaissance Revival tall-poster child's bed, walnut, the arched & scallop-cut headboard over a row of short turned spindles between rod-and-baluster-turned tall posts w/ball finials, matching foot posts joined by a low gently arched footboard, heavy baluster-and ring-turned legs, brass bolt covers, old refinish, ca. 1870s, 42 x 76", 5' 4" h. **$600**

Victorian Rococo bed, carved rosewood, the arched headboard w/a high arched crestrail pierced & carved w/heavy scrolls centered by an oval button, heavy rounded columnar legs w/flattened urn-form finials, the side- and foot rails w/scroll- carved corner brackets & cartouche- carved aprons, shorter columnar footboard legs w/matching finials, refinished, ca. 1860, 68 x 80", 5' h. **$6,500**

Victorian Rococo bed, carved rosewood, the high headboard w/a tall broken-arch crest composed of ornate carved scrolls & pierced scroll panels centered by a turned urn finial, the arched crestrail above a simple paneled board flanked by matching turned urn corner finials, the lower arched footboard w/matching turned finials, wide sideboards, probably New York City, ca. 1855, original finish, 60 x 80", 6' h. **$2,800**

Victorian Rococo bed, carved rosewood, the very tall headboard w/an extremely ornate crest, a wide arched & pierced & scroll-carved crest centered by a full-figure seated putti above an arched molding over further elaborate leafy scroll & flower carving above three tall rectangular panels w/arched & serpentine tops flanked by heavy paneled side posts w/disk-turned finials, the low arched footboard w/further ornate scroll carving flanked by heavy panel legs w/disk finials, heavy disk-turned feet, ca. 1850s, 64 x 82", 8' 10" h. (ILLUS. of complete bed).............................. **$10,000**

Victorian Rococo bed, chestnut & walnut, the high headboard w/an arched, stepped crestrail topped by a scroll- carved cartouche finial above a central scroll-carved cartouche over an oval raised band, blocked top corners w/knob- turned finials, the matching low footboard w/curved leg panels, refinished, ca. 1860, 58 x 78", 5' h. **$950**

Victorian Rococo country-style bed, cherry & mahogany, the high arched headboard w/an ornate scroll-carved crestrail over the tall panels flanked by rod-turned posts w/ring-turned finials, low foot posts joined by narrow rails, original finish, ca. 1850s, 56 x 76", 6' h. **$1,000**

Victorian Rococo half-tester bed, carved rosewood, the rectangular half-tester w/a deep frame w/a coved cornice over a band of delicate scroll carving w/rounded projecting corners w/further detailed carving, supported by ornate scroll brackets above heavy columnar posts flanking the high arched headboard w/a scroll- carved central cartouche & scroll trim over a raised burl panel, the low footboard w/a serpentine top & a lower vine- carved panel flanked by short heavy paneled legs w/knob finials, refinished, Philadelphia, ca. 1855, 66 x 84", overall 10' h. **$18,000**

Victorian Rococo substyle high-backed bed, carved rosewood, the headboard w/a high arched broken-scroll pediment w/pierced scrolls below the large floral-carved cartouche over a simple arched crestrail & panel, the square sideposts topped by tall paneled posts w/large ring- and knop-turned finials, the simple arched footboard w/simple molded panels & curved corners w/scrolls & curved panels, the deep siderails w/molded rectangular panels, scroll-carved end feet, formerly a half-tester bed now reduced in height, probably from New Orleans & the shop of Prudent Mallard, ca. 1855, 69 1/2 x 87", 84 1/2" h. **$19,995**

Fine Rococo Revival mahogany bed, carved mahogany, the high arched headboard topped by a large carved shell crest above a large knob & floral swags & scroll-carved edging above a long rectangular burl panel w/cut-corners, the ring- and rod-turned head posts topped by disk-turned finials, the low footboard w/a low arched top above raised panels flanked by rounded corners w/ floral carving, original side rails, old surface, posts now shortened, mid-19th c., 70 x 83", 87 1/2" h. **$4,600**

Victorian Rococo Revival substyle bed, gilt-decorated black lacquer, double-size, the arched serpentine headboard w/a molded edge decorated w/gilt trim above the smooth panel decorated under the arch w/a band of delicate gold florals & chinoiserie designs including birds & arabesques, simple serpentine stiles above the blocked legs w/block feet, the low footboard w/a heavy flat molded crestrail & tapering blocked corner posts w/half-round spindles above the stepped block feet, probably Philadelphia, ca. 1850-60, 66 x 78", 4' 9" h. **$1,380**

Benches

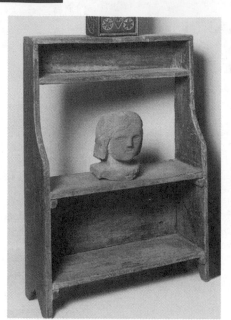

Bucket (or water) bench, pine, a long rectangular top shelf w/a three-quarters gently arched gallery, bookjack ends w/scalloped front edges above the open lower shelf, refinished, minor damage, 19th c., 11 x 37", 32" h. **$374**

Bucket (or water) bench, painted wood, a narrow rectangular top above a low open shelf flanked by curved sides & two lower shelves, bootjack ends, worn red paint, some damage, 19th c., 10 x 30", 44" h. **$460**

Handmade screws, dating before the early 1800s, have irregular threads and frequently have off-center slots. Machine-made screws, made after 1810, are more uniform and have centered slots.

Country-style bench, carved pine, the long, thick rectangular top above a wide apron carved to resemble fringe, on simple ring-turned legs, pegged construction, wax finish, 19th c., 14 1/2 x 59 1/2", 18" h. **$805**

Country style bench, hardwood, a long flat crestrail above a spindled back flanked by square stiles continuing to the rear legs, shaped open arms on low turned supports flanking the long plank seat, ring- and rod-turned tapering front legs, 19thc. 71" l..... **$1,016**

Kneeling bench, painted wood, long narrow rectangular top w/narrow side aprons, short bootjack legs, original worn green paint, possibly Shaker-made, 19th c. 7 x 30" l., 8 1/2" h.. **$403**

Bookcases

Country-style bookcase, table-top model, painted pine, the rectangular top w/a narrow coved molding above a pair of tall raised panel doors w/replaced brasses above a single long drawer across the bottom w/butterfly brasses, old red paint w/traces of black, some paint touch up, 19th c., 9 x 38 1/2", 36" h. **$920**

Mission-style (Arts & Crafts movement) bookcase, oak, the long rectangular top above three tall 8-pane glazed doors opening to three wooden shelves, paneled sides w/through-tenon construction, flat front apron, fine original finish, original hardware, Stickley Brothers Model No. 4774, unsigned, 12 x 59", 52" h. **$3,480**

Mission-style (Arts & Crafts movement) bookcase, oak, the rectangular top w/a low gallery w/through-tenons above a single wide 16-pane glazed door opening to three shelves, flat base w/through-tenons & low arched side bootjack feet, original iron hardware, original finish, signed by Gustav Stickley, Model No. 715, 13 x 35", 57" h. **$6,600**

Mission-style (Arts & Crafts movement) bookcase, oak, the long rectangular top w/through-tenons in the low three-quarters gallery, the case w/three tall 12-pane glazed doors opening to shelves, the flat base w/through-tenons above arched feet, original copper hardware, recoated original finish, burn damage to top leg edge, L. & J.G. Stickley Model 331 1/2, from the Onondaga Shops, early 20th c., 12 x 73", 57" h. **$5,400**

Bureaux Plat

Directoire bureau plat, brass-mounted fruitwood, the rectangular top overhanging an apron fitted w/two small drawers, raised on square tapering fluted legs, Southern France, early 19th c., 27 1/2" h. **$1,380**

Louis XV-Style bureau plat, ormolu- mounted hardwood, the rectangular top w/serpentine sides decorated w/elaborate inlay surrounding the writing surface, the serpentine floral-inlaid apron fitted w/three hand-dovetailed drawers, the cabriole legs w/ elaborate female head ormolu mounts, traces of original gilding, France, early 20th c., separations & chips to veneer, 31 x 63", 32" h. **$1,980**

Museums sometimes sell items they no longer need in their collections to raise money for purchasing other objects. Items sold by a museum are known as "deaccessioned" pieces.

Louis XV-Style bureau plat, ormolu- mounted kingwood, the rectangular top w/rounded corners fitted w/an ormolu border band enclosing the rectangular writing surface w/old gilt-tooled black leather, the shaped apron on one side fitted w/three drawers w/ornate ormolu pulls & mounts, large ormolu mask mounts at the knee of each cabriole leg ending in ormolu sabots, in the manner of Charles Cressent, France, late 19th c., 31 x 54 1/2", 29" h. **$4,140**

→

Empire Revival bureau plat, gilt bronze- mounted mahogany, the rectangular top inset w/gilt-tooled green leather within a wooden frame above the case w/a pair of small cross-banded drawers flanking a single long drawer, each mounted w/a long pierced scrolling brass, the square tapering legs headed by gilt carved Egyptian masks & palmettes & ending in a gilt paw foot, France, ca. 1900, 30 x 55", 30 1/2" h. **$1,380**

Louis XV-Style bureau plat, mahogany, kingwood & parquetry, the shaped rectangular top w/an inset leather writing surface & ormolu banding above an apron w/three drawers each inset w/diamond pattern parquetry panels & fitted w/scrolling ormolu mounts, on cabriole legs headed by ormolu mounts & ending w/ormolu foot mounts, France, third quarter 19th c., 31 1/4 x 57 1/2", 32 3/4" h. **$575**

Louis XVI-Style bureau plat, burlwood & mahogany, the rectangular top w/a large leather inset above a simple apron w/a long diamond panel inlay flanked on each side by pairs of matching smaller drawers, gilt-metal & carved ebonized wood panels atop the square tapering legs ending in brass caps, France, ca. 1900, 32 x 55 1/2", 29 1/2" h. **$1,725**

Louis XVI-Style bureau plat, ormolu- mounted kingwood, the rectangular top w/serpentine ormolu edging around an inset leather writing surface, the serpentine apron w/fine banded veneering, two narrow drawers w/an ormolu escutcheon or pull separated by a long pierced scroll mount from the single long central drawer, the reverse apron fitted w/matching faux drawers, raised on simple cabriole legs w/ornate scroll & floral mounts at the knees & ending in leaf & scroll metal sabots, France, late 19th c., 31 1/2 x 56 1/2", 30" h. ... **$5,060**

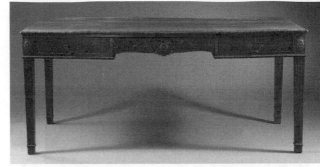

Louis XVI-Style bureau plat, mahogany, the rectangular top w/a floral-carved edge above an apron fitted w/a central foliate-carved drawer flanked by plain drawers w/bail pulls, simple square fluted tapering legs, France, ca. 1900, 32 x 68", 30" h. **$2,185**

Napoleon III bureau plat, brass-inlaid ebonized wood, the serpentine rectangular top centered by elaborate brass inlay & brass edge banding above an apron fitted w/one end drawer & brass banding on the serpentine edges, on cabriole legs headed by large ormolu shields & scrolls & ending in feet w/ormolu mounts, France, third-quarter 19th c., 31 1/2 x 51 1/2", 30" h. .. **$2,530**

Louis XVI-Style bureau plat, ormolu- mounted mahogany, the rectangular top w/a brass-bound border enclosing a yellow leather writing surface, one apron fitted w/pairs of small drawers w/ormolu mounts flanking a single center drawer over the kneehole opening, the corner blocks fitted w/ormolu swag drops, on tapering reeded legs w/ormolu mounts & ending in brass foot caps, France, early 20th c., 30 x 60 1/2", 30" h. **$920**

Cabinets

Apothecary cabinet, mahogany veneer & stained pine, a narrow long rectangular top above an arrangement of 20 small drawers w/mahogany veneered fronts, each w/reverse-painted glass labels & glass pulls, w/ paper label reading "W.K. Westlake Chemist, Oxford," old dark stain, possibly built-in, 19th c., some damaged or missing labels, 10 x 53 1/2", 24 3/4" h. (ILLUS. top with larger apothecary cabinet) **$578**

Apothecary cabinet, walnut, a long narrow rectangular top above a arrangement of 32 small square dovetailed drawers w/reverse-painted glass labels & glass knobs, 19th c., 12 x 75 3/4", 34 1/2" h. (ILLUS. bottom with smaller apothecary cabinet).. **$1,035**

Cellarette (wine cabinet), Federal style, inlaid walnut, two-part construction: the upper section w/a nearly square hinged top opening to a deep well above a single flush drawer below, the front decorated w/a line-inlaid panel w/inlaid fans in each corner & centered by an inlaid rayed pat-erae below the inlaid diamond keyhole escutcheon; the lower section w/a molded edge above an apron w/two small square drawers flanking a wider central drawer w/an oval brass, raised on slender square tapering legs, late 18th - early 19th c., 20 x 22", 41 1/2" h. **$4,560**

China cabinet, Arts & Crafts style, oak, Prairie School influence, thin rectangular top above the tall case w/a pair of glazed doors w/copper pull opening to three wooden shelves, glass sides, raised on a shoefoot trestle base, carved design on the posted, original finish, early 20th c., 15 x 52", 60" h. **$1,200**

Cellarette (wine cabinet), Federal-Style, inlaid mahogany, two-part construction: the upper section w/a rectangular hinged top opening to a divided interior, the front w/a line-inlaid large panel centered by a small oval enclosing a spread-winged eagle; the later lower section w/a single drawer w/oval brass raised on square tapering legs w/inlaid accents, late 19th c., top w/old repair, 16 x 22", 41 3/4" h. **$1,035**

China cabinet, Federal-Style, inlaid mahogany & mahogany veneer, two-part construction: the rectangular breakfront top w/a narrow cornice above a dentil-carved band over a conforming case w/two tall narrow glazed side doors flanking the wider center glazed door, all w/semi-circular & diamond-shaped panes; the stepped out lower section w/a bowed center section above a stack of three deep drawers w/ veneer banding & round brass pulls flanked by tall narrow veneer-banded cabinet doors, flat conforming base, one pane missing, minor edge damage, 20th c., 19 x 50", 80 1/2" h. **$575**

China cabinet, Arts & Crafts style, oak, the rectangular top w/a low back rail above a case fitted w/a single tall single-paned glazed door over a band of diamond lattice leaded glass & opening to four wood shelves, the door flanked by tall narrow leaded glass panels topped by stylized fleur de lis motifs in blue slag glass & above diamond lattice leaded panel at the bottom, matching side panels, narrow serpentine apron above short stile legs, original dark finish, marked w/original paper label of the New England Furniture Company, early 20th c., one cracked glass segment, 14 x 42", 58" h. **$1,920**

China cabinet, Mission-style (Arts & Crafts movement), oak, the rectangular top overhanging the tall case w/a pair of tall glazed cuboard doors opening to three glass shelves, glass side panels, flat base raised on shoefoot base, fine original finish, Michigan Chair Company, 16 x 44", 56" h. **$1,020**

Collector's cabinet on stand, Oriental style, parcel-gilt black lacquer, two-part construction: the upper cabinet w/a rectangular top, sides & pair of doors richly decorated w/scenes of flowers & birds, the doors w/molded panels decorated w/landscapes in heavy gold enamel & mounted w/brass fitting, opening to an interior composed of 12 drawers of varying sizes each w/ornate flower & insect decoration; the lower stand section made in Europe & features similar decoration, the cabinet made in Japan, ca. 1850, some brass loose, minor wear, 21 x 40 1/4", 62" h. **$12,650**

CABINETS

Dental cabinet, walnut, three-tiered design, the top teir w/a narrow rectangular top w/a low three-quarters gallery above a pair of open compartments flanking a small tambour-lidded center compartment opening top slots, the middle tier stepped-out w/free-standing corner columns flanking a large tambour door opening to 22 small drawers, the bottom tier w/two pairs of small drawers flanking a square central drawer above two short rectangular raised panel doors, raised side panels, lock replaced, back loose, late 19th c., 17 3/4 x 45 1/2", 58 3/4" h. **$978**

Music cabinet, Arts & Crafts style, inlaid mahogany, the superstructure w/a small flat crest above a rectangular arched mirror flanked by four small posts forming a gallery fitted w/small quarter-round shelves over mother-of-pearl & wood in-alid circle & band Arts & Crafts motifs, the break-front rectangular top above a conforming case w/a center stack of five shallow drawers above two high open compartments, all flanked on each side by two ornately inlaid narrow panels, each side w/three open compartments, serpentine narrow apron raised on slender square legs ending in square feet, original finish, England, early 20th c., 16 x 34", 52" h. **$3,900**

China cabinet, Rococo Revival style, mahogany, arched serpentine center crestrail w/a carved cartouche flanked by ornate carved scroll bands above a pair of arched glazed doors open to a mirrored back & fixed shelves above three long serpentine-front drawers, each side w/a shorter cabinet w/serpentine short cornice over a narrow conforming glass door & ends backed by a mirror above paneled front & sides; serpentine scroll-carved apron raised on four front cabriole legs w/scroll feet, original finish, France, early 20th c., 22 x 72", 7' h. **$1,800**

Side cabinet, Victorian Renaissance Revival substyle, marquetry-inlaid & bronze-mounted rosewood, the large case w/a central shell-carved crest over a marquetry-inlaid panel, the projecting central cupboard door w/a panel framed by marquetry banding, the base edged in Greek key marquetry, the back of the cabinet marked in heavy ink "Elbio 4565," attributed to Pottier & Stymus, New York City, ca. 1875, 20 x 61", 5' 1" h. ....**$!6,100**

Chairs

Arts & Crafts "Morris" armchair, oak, unusual form w/a tall adjustable upholstered back w/ cut-out design at each top corner, flat notched arms on bracketed & splayed legs, refinished, new upholstery, early 20th c., 42" h. **$720**

Arts & Crafts style barrel-backed rocker, oak, the wide U-form crestrail above numerous flat slats supported by heavy back styles & wide tapering front supports continuing to from the legs, wide apron w/arched front seatrail, recovered leather cushion seat, single flat front stretcher, refinished, replaced rockers, unsigned Plail Furniture Company, early 20th c., 32" h. **$1,080**

Baroque-Style armchair, carved walnut, the tall arched back upholstered in tapestry trimmed w/roundhead nails, long scrolling open arms w/incurved arm supports above the wide tapestry-upholstered seat, the front cabriole legs headed by finely carved cherub heads w/wings & ending in claw-and-ball feet, cabriole rear legs w/paw feet, all joined by a scroll-carved X-stretcher, France, late 19th c., wear to upholstery, 48" h. **$2,300**

Chippendale country-style commode armchair, walnut, the bold oxbow crest above canted stiles & a vasiform splat, shaped & scroll-tipped open arms on shaped armrests above the upholstered slip seat, a very deep apron w/a serpentine bottom edge, on slightly tapering square legs, mortise & pin construction, attributed to Lancaster County, Pennsylvania, late 18th c., 45 1/2" h. **$2,530**

Charles II armchair, walnut, the tall rectangular base w/a blossom- and foliate- carved frame around a caned panel flanked by block- and spiral-twist stiles topped by small ball finials, shaped open arms w/scroll grip raised on spiral-turned supports above the carved & caned trapezoidal seat above a wide flat foliate- carved front stretcher, raised on block- and spiral-turned legs joined by a spiral- turned H-stretcher & raised on ball feet, England, late 17th c., 47" h. **$1,763**

Chippendale armchair, carved mahogany, the ox-yoke crestrail w/ scrolled ear centered by a carved shell above the pierced vasiform splat, serpentine open arms ending in scroll-carved hand grips above incurved arm supports, wide upholstered slip seat w/a flat seatrail centered at the front by a carved shell, cabriole front legs w/ shell-carved knees ending in claw-and-ball feet, canted turned rear legs, descended in the Stevenson Family, Philadelphia, ca. 1770, 40 7/8" h. **$36,000**

CHAIRS

Federal "fancy" side chairs, painted & decorated, the narrow rolled crestrail above a narrow rectangular panel of caning & a thin lower rail, the caned seat raised on bamboo-turned outswept front legs & backswept rear legs, overall original light yellow paint decorated w/stenciled & h.p. black scrolls & leaves, newer seat caning, some paint loss & insect holes, early 19th c., 32 1/2" h., pr. **$604**

Chippendale side chair, carved mahogany, scalloped & scroll-carved crestrail above a wide slit-carved splat centered by scroll carving above the upholstered slip seat, square legs joined by flat box stretchers, retains old & possibly original finish, New York City, 1765-85, 38 1/2" h. **$6,573**

Federal armchairs, carved mahogany, the flat curved crestrail above three slender carved slats flanked by downswept open arms above the upholstered seat w/a gently bowed seatrail, carved, turned & tapering front legs & canted square tapering rear legs, Philadelphia, 1800-10, 33 1/4" h., pr. **$17,925**

Federal country-style side chairs, painted & decorated, a wide curved & arched crestrail above a narrow medial rail above four short knob-turned spindles all flanked by flaring tapering stiles, wide shaped plank seat, canted ring-turned front legs & plain turned rear legs joined by box stretchers, old dark brown paint w/white floral decoration of the rails & black & white line detail, two w/minor restoration, first half 19th c., 32 1/4" h., set of 6 (ILLUS. of one).................... **$690**

Country-style side chairs, painted & decorated, the wide slight curved crestrail w/rounded ends above a simple vasiform splat flanked by simple turned stiles, plank seat raised on simple turned & canted legs joined by box stretchers, original dark red paint w/h.p. flowers & leaves on the crestrail & splat, some wear, first half 19th c., 32 1/4" h., set of 6 (ILLUS. of one)................ **$633**

CHAIRS

Federal dining chairs, carved mahogany, the gently arched & molded crestrail & stiles frame four slender carved slats w/flared tops raised above the over-upholstered seat, square tapering fluted front legs & canted rear legs joined by box stretchers, possibly Salem, Massachusetts, 1790-1810, set of 8 (ILLUS. of one) **$15,600**

Federal side chairs, carved mahogany, the delicate rectangular back centered by a tall rectangular frame centered by a slender pierced, urn-form splat, over-upholstered seat on turned tapering front legs & canted square tapering rear legs, Philadelphia, 1800-10, 36" h., pr. **$1,793**

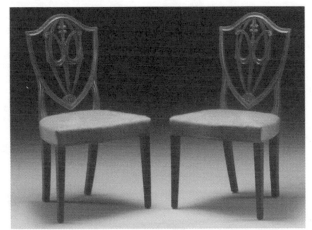

Federal side chairs, carved mahogany, the shield-back centered by a pierced oval splat trimmed w/carved drapery swags, over-upholstered seat on square tapering front legs & canted square rear legs, Salem, Massachusetts, 1790-1810, 38 3/8" h., pr. **$13,145**

Mission-style (Arts & Crafts movement) "Morris" armchair, oak, the angled adjustable back w/four carved slats & a wide crestrail w/incurved top edge, above flat arms above five vertical slats, seat w/rope foundation & no cushion, original finish, decal mark of Gustav Stickley, Model No. 332, replaced pegs, 39" h. **$9,000**

Mission-style (Arts & Crafts movement) armchair, oak, the low squared back w/three vertical slats above the flat arms above three side slats, attributed to Cortland, refinished, ca. 1910, 35" h. **$540**

Marks can be as confusing as they are helpful in identifying antiques. For example, one might misread a lightly branded mark on a piece of Gustave Stickley furniture as "Huckle" or "Huckley" because the "S" and "T" overlap. Learn to recognize valuable items for their merits as well as their marks.

CHAIRS

Mission-style (Arts & Crafts movement) armchair, oak, the squared back composed of six vertical slats above flat open arms mortised to the front legs & supported by brackets, recovered leather seat, recoated original finish, signed w/the "The work of..." label of L. & J.G. Stickley, Model No. 816, 39" h. **$570**

Mission-style (Arts & Crafts movement) rocking chair w/ arms, oak, the squared back w/ five vertical slats over the curved flat arms over four slats, deep apron arched at the front, worn original leather cushion, original finish, paper label of the Harden company, 37" h. **$660**

Mission-style (Arts & Crafts movement) side chair, oak, the squared back w/a V- form crestrail above five splats raised above the hard leather seat, square legs joined by wide flat front & rear rungs & pairs of narrower rungs on each side, original finish, red decal mark of Gustav Stickley, Model No. 354 1/2, 36" h. **$780**

> Patina is the natural accumulation of wax and dirt on antique over time. In past generations, patina was considered grime to be removed, and countless items were refinished, forever removing their original finish. Today, patina is valued because it retains the historical significance of the item, helps establish its age, and embues it with a beautiful mellow look and individual character.

Mission-style (Arts & Crafts movement) child's armchair, oak, the squared back w/three horizontal slats above flat arms raised on square front legs, original seat w/worn leather, wear to original finish, signed w/red decal mark of Gustav Stickley, Model No. 344, early 20th c., 26" h. **$275**

Mission-style (Arts & Crafts movement) rocking chair w/ arms, oak, unusual high back w/heavy stiles & crestrail w/key & tenon construction above the flat open arms, original leather cushions in the back & seat, original finish, signed by paper label of Barber Brothers, 42" h. **$660**

Mission-style (Arts & Crafts movement) side chair, oak, the tall back centered by nine slender square spindles raised above the recovered seat above five slender square spindles on each side & flat box stretchers, original finish, red decal mark of Gustav Stickley, minor wear, 49" h. **$1,020**

Mission-style (Arts & Crafts movement) side chair, oak, the tall back w/an arched crestrail above three flat slats raised above the recovered leather seat, square legs joined by box stretchers, recoated original finish, "The Work of..." label of L. & J.G. Stickley, 37" h. **$450**

Queen Anne side chair, carved birch & maple, the tall back w/ a bold arched & scroll-carved crestrail above a tall vasiform splat flanked by gently backswept molded stiles, woven rush seat, cabriole front legs ending in pad feet, square rear legs, all joined by slender turned stretchers, early 18th c., 47" h. **$2,032**

Queen Anne side chair, walnut, the serpentine crestrail w/corner ears above a scroll-carved splat & slightly curved stiles over the upholstered slip seat, cabriole front legs ending in trifid feet, old finish, good color, some repair & replacements, mid-18th c., 39 1/4" h. **$1,668**

Pilgrim Century bannister-back armchair, the tall back w/a triple-arched crestrail over five half-spindles flanked by turned stiles w/bulbous turned finials, simple turned sloping arms joining knob-topped front knob-turned front legs, ring- and baluster-turned front rungs, plain turned side & rear rungs, old surface, possibly Rhode Island, ca. 1690-1710, restoration, 40" h. **$3,055**

Queen Anne side chair, carved walnut, the arched crestrail w/ rounded corners continuing to shaped stiles flanking the tall scroll-carved splat, upholstered compass-seat w/cabriole front legs ending in pad feet & turned, canted rear legs, Philadelphia, 1735-50, 42 1/2" h. **$7,170**

Queen Anne side chair, walnut, the spooned crestrail above a vasiform splat & raked chamfered stiles over the upholstered balloon slip seat, cabriole front legs ending in pad feet joined to the chamfered raking rear legs by block-, baluster- and ring-turned stretchers, Boston, ca. 1740-60, refinished, minor imperfections, 40" h. **$6,463**

CHAIRS

Queen Anne side chairs, painted hardwood, the tall back w/a molded scroll- carved crestrail above raking vasiform splat & molded stiles above trapezoidal rush seats, front block- and baluster- turned legs joined by a knob-turned rung & ending in Spanish feet, plain double rungs on each side, raking square rear legs, old reddish brown surface, New England, first half 18th c., minor imperfections, 42" h., pr. **$3,055**

Shaker rocking chair w/arms, the tall "ladderback" w/four graduated slats between turned stiles w/acorn finials, shaped open arms w/mushroom caps, replaced woven tape seat, turned legs on stretchers joined by box stretchers, wear to dark finish, impressed "6," stenciled label "Shaker's Trademark, No. 6, Mt. Lebanon, N.Y.," late 19th - early 20th c., 42" h. **$633**

Windsor "arrow-back" armchair, painted & decorated maple, original overall grain painting, the tall back w/a flat crestrail h.p. w/yellow flowers & green leaves above a lower rail w/matching decoration over a row of five tall arrow slats, scrolled open arms above two arrow slat, thick plank seat on canted bamboo-turned legs joined by a flat front stretcher & simple turned side & back stretchers, possibly Ohio, first half 19th c., 45" h. **$1,035**

Windsor "bow-back" armchair, painted hardwood, the arched back rail above six spindles above a medial rail above baluster- and ring-turned spindles & continuing to form the curved arms, wide seat raised on ring- and knob-turned front legs & turned rear legs joined by an H- stretcher, made by Waters & Barrett, Cincinnati, Ohio, patented September 23, 1873, original red paint decorated w/black striping & floral details on the arms & seat front, minor paint loss, small pieced repair & splits, 43" h. **$748**

Windsor "bow-back" writing-arm armchair, painted wood, the bowed crestrail above seven turned spindles extending through the medial rail that curves to form a shaped arm on one side & a wide oblong writing surface on the other side, each arm above a spindle & ring- and baluster-turned arm support w/the writing arm supported by two additional spindles, the wide saddle seat above a single small drawer, raised on canted baluster- and ring-turned legs joined by a swelled H-stretcher, old worn white paint w/green trim, New England, possibly Vermont, 1790-1810, 37" h. **$18,000**

Windsor "bowback continuous arm" armchair, the high arched crestrail curving down to form the narrow flattened arms, nine tall slender back spindles & a pair of rear brace-back spindles, a single short spindle under each arm & a canted baluster- and ring-turned arm support, shaped saddle seat raised on canted baluster-, ring- and rod-turned legs joined by a swelled H-stretcher, old black paint, signed "Samler N York," New York, late 18th c., 36 1/2 h. **$4,780**

Windsor "bowback" armchairs, elm & oak, the bowed crestrail above a central pierced vasiform splat flanked on each side by four slender spindles, resting on a medial rail curving around to form the arms & above another pierced vasiform splat flanked by spindles, turned incurved arm supports above the wide oblong shaped saddle seat, slender cabriole front legs ending in raised pad feet joined by incurved stretchers joined by simple turned box stretchers to the canted rear legs, England, late 18th c., 36" h., pr. **$2,645**

Windsow "low-back writing-arm" armchair, the low U-form crestrail raised din the center & continuing on one side to a flattened curved arm w/scroll-carved hand grip, the other side continuing to a wide oblong writing surface above a small drawer, simple turned back spindles & bamboo-turned arm & writing shelf supports, wide plank seat raised on canted bamboo-turned legs joined by a bamboo-turned H-stretcher, old dark finish, minor edge wear, 18th c., 29" h. **$2,645**

Windsor "comb-back" armchair, stained wood, the top back w/ a curved crestrail above eight spindles attached to the U-form center rail continuing to form the scrolled arms, the lower back w/ plain turned spindles & baluster- and ring-turned spindles under each arm, wide seat, raised on baluster- and rod-turned front legs, turned rear legs, joined by an H-stretcher, old red stain, r attributed to Philadelphia area, late 18th c., 46 1/4" h. ... **$3,738**

Windsor "continuous arm" armchair, painted, the arched crestrail curving down to form narrow arms all over slender turned spindles, shaped saddle seat on canted baluster- and ring-turned legs joined by a swelled H-stretcher, old black paint, 37 1/2" h. **$2,760**

Chests & Chests of Drawers

Blanket chest, country-style, painted & decorated, the rectangular top w/a molded edge opening a deep well & till w/a walnut lid, the dovetailed case on a molded base w/simple bracket feeet, original wood graining resembling crotch grain mahogany, minor edge damage, some wear, first half 19th c., 19 x 38", 22" h. **$633**

Blanket chest, Chippendale country-style "dower" type, painted pine, the rectangular top w/molded edges opening to a well & goold tulip strap hinges & lock, two drawers at the bottom w/simple bail pulls & a butterfly brass keyhole escutcheon, molded base w/a half-round center drop & simple bracket feet, original blue paint, the front decorated w/two panels of potted six-petaled flowers framed by columns, a central scene of a Colonial man standing among plants, original brasses, attributed to Pennsylvania, edge loss to drawers, pieced repairs, base replaced, 18th c., 24 x 53", 28" h. **$4,715**

Blanket chest, painted & decorated pine, the hinged rectangular top w/breadboard ends opening to a lidded till, the dovetailed case decorated w/original dark red paint, h.p. & stenciled w/row of hearts wrapping around the front corners, the front h.p. w/a pair of facing perched birds above eight-petaled flowers centered by a leaf sprig & tulip on a leafy stem, in shades of yellow & green, molded flat base, Mahantongo Valley-style, Pennsylvania, early 19th c., wear, bottom side moldings old replacements, may have had cleated feet, 15 1/2 x 38 1/2", 14" h. **$3,335**

Chippendale "bowfront" chest of drawers, cherry, the rectangular top w/a bowed front & molded edges above a conforming case w/four long graduated drawers flanked by fluted quarter round columns, molded base on scroll-cut ogee bracket feet, original oval brasses w/two missing, old refinishing, minor repairs to feet, late 18th - early 19th c., 26 x 42", 37" h. **$2,530**

Chippendale "reverse-serpentine" chest of drawers, mahogany, the rectangular top w/molded edges & a reverse-serpentined front edge projecting over a conforming case w/four long graduated drawers w/butterfly brasses & keyhole escutcheons & blocked ends, the conforming base molding over fancy scroll-cut returns & a central drop raised on short claw-and-ball front feet, Salem, Massachusetts, 1760-80, 22 3/4 x 41 3/4", 22 3/4" h. **$27,485**

Blanket chest, painted & decorated poplar, opening to a well & lidded till, dovetailed case w/base mold & turned knob feet, original smoke graining, some paint loss & touch ups, attributed to Pennsylvania, first half 19th c., 20 x 41", 24" h. **$403**

Chippendale legs were made in six basic forms: the lion's paw, the ball and claw, the late Chippendale, the Marlborough, the spade, and the club.

Chippendale "serpentine-front" chest of drawers, carved birch, the rectangular top w/molded edges & a serpentine front overhanging a conforming case w/four long graduated drawers w/simple bail pulls & small brass keyhole escutcheons, molded apron centered by a small fan-carved pendant & raised on scroll-cut short claw-and-ball front feet, replaced brasses, refinished, probably Newburyport, Massachusetts, ca. 1760-80, minor imperfections, 21 x 35 1/2", 34 1/2" h. **$7,638**

Chippendale chest of drawers, cherry, the rectangular top w/a molded edge overhanging the case w/four long graduated drawers w/simple bail pulls & urn-shaped brass keyhole escutcheons, molded base w/gadroon-carved band along central apron, on scroll-cut ogee bracket feet, probably Connecticut, 18th c., old finish, replaced brasses, one foot reglued, 18th c., 20 1/4 x 38", 36 1/2" h. **$6,900**

Chippendale tall chest of drawers, birch, the rectangular top w/a deep coved cornice abouve a case w/six long graduated drawers w/butterfly brasses & keyhole escutcheons, molded base w/ simple bracket feet, attributed to New Hampshire, salmon-tinted red wash, some imperfections, late 18th - early 19th c., 19 x 38", 51 1/2" h. **$1,150**

Chippendale tall chest of drawers, maple, the rectangular top w/an ogee cornice above a stack of six long thumbmolded graduated drawers w/brass butterfly pulls & keyhold escutcheons, high scroll-cut bracket feet, New England, 18th c., replaced brasses, pieced repairs, 19 x 41", 55" h. .. **$1,955**

Chippendale tall chest of drawers, walnut, the rectangular top above a deep flaring cornice over a row of three drawers above a stack of five long graduated drawers each w/butterfly brasses & keyhole escutcheons, quarter-round fluted colonettes down the sides, molded base on tall scroll-cut ogee bracket feet, Pennsylvania, 1760-90, 23 3/4 x 44 1/2", 67" h. **$11,400**

Chippendale tall chest of drawers, walnut, the rectangular top w/a wide flaring coved cornice above a row of three small drawers over a pair of drawers above three deep graduated drawers all w/ simple bail pulls & oval brass keyhole escutcheons, fluted quarter columns down each side, molded base w/tall scroll-cut ogee bracket feet, original brasses, dust boards, old refinishing, small pieced repairs & one foot facing & two spurs replaced, late 18th c., 23 1/2 x 43", 68 1/2" h. .. **$6,038**

Classical "bowfront" chest of drawers, carved mahogany & mahogany veneer, the scrolled backboard above the rectangular bowfront top w/ovolu corners above a conforming case of four long graduated beaded drawers w/rosette & ring pulls & brass keyhole escutcheons, flanked by quarter-engaged ring- and spiral-turned posts carved w/flowers & acanthus leaves on punchwork continuing down to ring- and baluster-turned legs w/peg feet, scalloped apron, old replaced brasses, Massachusetts, ca. 1825, imperfections, 20 1/2 x 45", 41 1/2" h. **$2,938**

Classical country-style chest of drawers, cherry & bird's-eye- maple, rectangular top w/veneer edging above a single long deep drawer w/a bird's-eye maple front & two turned wood knobs, projecting above the long graduated matching drawers flanked by ring-turned columns, raised on ring- and rod-turned legs, ca. 1830-40, 20 3/8 x 39", 40 1/2" h. **$1,380**

Classical storage chest, mahogany & mahogany veneer, a rectangular top above an upper case w/a row of three narrow drawers w/small turned wood knobs above a single long deep drawer w/wood knobs projecting above the lower cabinet w/a pair of paneled cupboard doors flanked by columns w/carved capitals, on turned knob front feet, shrinkage crack in top, other minor cracks & veneer loss, ca. 1840, 22 3/4 x 47 1/4", 47" h. **$920**

Classical child's chest of drawers, cherry & bird's-eye maple veneer, a gently arched scroll-ended crest rail atop a two- drawer compartment atop the rectangular top over a long veneered drawer w/turned wood knobs projecting over three long matching graduated drawers flanked by baluster- and rope-turned columns, heavy baluster-turned legs, some knobs original, pieced repairs, crestrail replaced, attributed to New England, ca. 1820-30, 16 1/4 x 31", 38 1/2" h. **$2,070**

Classical Revival chest of drawers, mahogany & mahogany veneer, the superstructure w/a peaked crestrail joined by tall flat uprights flanking a large rectangular swiveling mirror, raised above the rectangular top over a long deep top drawer overhanging two long drawers all w/stamped brass pulls, the lower drawers flanked by ring-turned columns all raised on heavy carved front paw feet, original dark finish, late 19th c., 45" w., 6' 4" h. **$529**

Country-style chest of drawers, painted poplar & chestnut, the rectangular top w/an arched, scallop-cut back crest above a row of three curved-front drawers w/white porcelain pulls above four long graduated paneled drawers w/matching pulls, the frame painted in red & the small drawers w/yellow & brown graining, the long drawers w/raised red panels against the grained ground, the top long drawer stenciled "L 1886 H," straight apron w/pieced repair, on replaced ring- and knob-turned black- painted legs, attributed to Pennsylvania, similar to Soap Hollow chests, ca. 1886, 22 x 39", 54" h. **$2,760**

Federal chest of drawers, cherry & figured cherry, the rectangular top above a pair of drawers over three long graduated drawers all w/oval brasses, narrow serpentine apron & simple bracket feet, secret compartment behind one drawer, refinished, replaced brasses, 22 x 44", 43" h. **$1,208**

Federal chest of drawers, walnut, the rectangular top above a case w/four long graduated drawers w/old silver plated oval pulls, serpentine apron & tall French feet, early 19th c, backboards renailed, good color, age split in one end, 17 1/4 x 36", 38 3/4" h. **$1,725**

William & Mary-Style chest on frame, oak, two part construction: the upper section w/a rectangular top w/molded edges above a pair of drawers over three drawers each divided into two geometric panels, small butterfly brasses & keyhole escutcheons; the lower section w/a molded molding & flat apron raised on baluster-turned front legs & flat rear legs all joined by box stretchers, old marriage w/some reconstruction, 18th - 19th c., 22 x 38", 58 1/2" h. **$633**

Federal child's chest of drawers, walnut, the rectangular top above a case w/a pair of drawers w/lion head & ring pulls above three long graduated drawers w/matching pulls, serpentine apron & tapering French feet, warm refinish, pieced repairs, early 19th c., 9 5/8 x 22 1/2", 22" h. **$1,265**

William & Mary furniture is generally heavy and bulky, and features multiple turnings, exaggerated moldings, and round or oval feet.

CRADLES

Cradles

Low cradle on rockers, walnut, dovetailed construction w/an arched & canted headboard & lower footboard flanked by scroll-carved sides w/heart-shaped rope holes, on deep arched rockers, early 19th c., 24 1/2 x 40 1/2", 22" h. **$460**

Victorian Renaissance Revival "trestle-style" cradle, carved walnut, the cradle w/eight pierced slats on each side decorated w/circle carvings, the ends w/pierced scroll carving & applied decorative molding, supported by an iron hanger at each end & hanging between turned posts above the trestle-style framed w/flattened serpentine legs joined by a flat cross stretcher, ca. 1870, one leg w/repaired split, 19 1/4 x 41", 38 1/2" h. **$300-500**

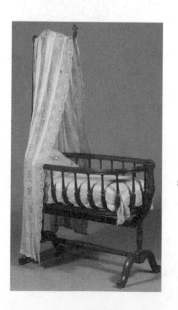

Swinging cradle on frame, walnut, a tall S-curved drapery bracket on a turned support extending to a yoke from which swings a cradle w/curved & turned side spindles, swinging on a trestle base w/ arched end legs, w/lace-trimmed drapery & bedding, old repairs, late 19th c., 23 1/2 x 48", 74" h. **$1,035**

Windsor cradle on rockers, painted wood, an oval bentwood crestrail above twenty- four ring-turned slanted canted side spindles above the oval base, raised on canted baluster-, ring- and rod-turned legs w/inset rockers & jointed by box stretchers, old white paint over earlier colors, early 19th c., 17 1/2 x 39 3/4", 22" h. **$518**

Country-style cradle with tester on rockers, yellow pine, mortise & peg construction, the rectangular tester frame supported on heavy paneled posts continuing to form the corner posts & square legs ending in inset one-board rockers, the deep cradle sides w/a zig-zag open bar design, simple half-round headboard, tester & cover have age but not original, from a Mississippi collection, reputedly slave-made, old refinishing, 19th c., 22 x 42", 51 1/2" h. **$575**

> Caution: Be very careful when using antique cradles. Be certain a baby's head can't fit through side spindles or slats or be trapped between the mattress and side of the crib.

Cupboards

Corner cupboard, Chippendale barrel- backed architectural-type, painted pine, one-piece construction, the flat top w/a stepped cornice w/a center keystone & wide fluted pilasters down the sides, the large arched opening w/an interior sawtooth-cut molding flanking four curved & shaped open shelves above a lower case w/a pair of short raised panel cupboard doors w/ H-hinges, flat apron, plastered interior & old blue paint, repairs & some restoration, 18th c., 21 x 59", 86" h. **$5,290**

Corner cupboard, country style, cherry, one-piece construction, the flat top w/a narrow molding continuing down the outside edges of the case, a pair of tall 8- pane glazed doors opening to three shelves above a pair of doors each w/four raised panels, serpentined apron, painted interior, removed latches, refinished, first half 19th c., 21 x 50", 84" h. **$1,380**

Corner cupboard, Federal country-style, painted pine, one-piece turkey-breast form, the sharply pointed triangular top above a conforming case w/a pair of tall 8-pane glazed doors opeing to three shaped shelves, molded waist molding above a pair of raised panel cupboard doors opening to a shelf, molded base on simple bracket feet, mortise, pin & square nail construction, old blue paint, early 19th c., some edge loss, repair & paint touch-up, 28 1/2 x 47", 81" h. .. **$5,780**

Corner cupboard, Federal country-style, poplar, two-piece: the upper section w/a cornice above a pair of 6-pane doors opening to two shelves; the lower section w/a mid-molding above a pair of drawers w/turned wood knobs flanked by small blocks w/ roundels above a pair of doors, scroll-cut apron w/ simple bracket feet, first half 19th c., 30 x 59", 79" h. **$1,840**

Corner cupboard, Federal country style, cherry, the flat top w/a narrow molding above a pair of full-length two-panel cupboard doors w/diamond inlays in the center of the inner rails, scroll-carved apron on high bracket feet, later robin's-egg blue interior paint, made in Louisiana, early 19th c., 23 x 42", 68" h. **$79,500**

Corner cupboard, Federal country-style, walnut, one-pieceon, the top w/a coved cornice above a pair of 8-pane doors opening to three shelves w/olive green paint above a pair of raised panel cupboard doors, early 19th c., 25 x 56", 82 1/2" h. **$2,185**

CUPBOARDS

Corner cupboard, Federal country-style, walnut, two-part construction: the upper section w/ a flat top & narrow dentil- carved cornice above a pair of tall 8-pane glazed cupboard doors opening to three shelves; the lower section w/a mid-molding above a pair of tall paneled cupboard doors, raised on scroll-cut bracket feet, probably Virginia, first half 19th c., one glass pane cracked, 21 1/2 x 47", 86" h. **$3,450**

Hanging cupboard, country-style, walnut, the dovetailed case w/ a rectangular top w/a narrow molding continuing around the other three edges, a long paneled door w/an old brass knob opens to three shelves, old dark finish, 19th c., 10 1/4 x 18 1/2", 30" h. **$460**

Linen press, Chippendale style, mahogany, two-part construction: the upper section w/a rectangular top w/a narrow flaring cornice above a pair of molded panel cupboard doors opening to three linen slides; the lower section w/ a hinged slant top w/two simple bail pulls opening to a desk fitted interior w/small drawers above a lower case w/a pair of drawers over two long drawers, all w/ simple bail pulls, narrow base molding on scroll-cut bracket feet, one desk drawer signed "J. McCormick" in pencil, Virginia, 1787-1791, 21 x 49", 81" h. **$9,560**

Corner cupboard, Federal style, cherry, two-part construction: the upper section w/a flat top & narrow cornice above a single tall 12-pane glazed door opening to three shelves; the lower section w/ a mid- molding above a pair of tall paneled cupboard doors opening to shelves, simple low bracket feet, Pennsylvania, early 19th c., 21 x 42", 7' 1" h. **$1,175**

Linen press, Chippendale country-style, cherry, two-piece construction: the upper section w/a flaring stepped cornice above a pair of large doors opening to a divided interior; the stepped-out lower section w/four graduated drawers w/ brass bail pulls & keyhole escutcheons, molded base on scroll-cut bracket feet, old replaced drawer pulls, late 18th - early 19th c., 21 1/2 x 43", 72 1/2" h. **$5,463**

Pie safe, walnut & pine, the rectangular top above a pair of tall doors fitted w/six punched tin panels w/a central pinwheel & quarter round corners, doors open to an interior divided into two shelves on each side, matching tin panels down each side, on ring- and baluster-turned legs w/ knob & peg feet, second half 19th c., 22 x 49", 57" h. **$1,955**

Linen press, Neo-Classical style, mahogany & mahogany veneer, two-part construction: the upper section w/a rectangular top w/a recessed stepped cornice above a plain frieze band above a pair of large paneled cupboard doors flanked by colonettes w/engine-turned gilt bronze capitals & bases; the lower section w/a mid-molding over a pair of shorter paneled doors opening to a series of half drawers & flanked by blocked pilasters, molded base w/projecting block feet, Holland, early 19th, 25 x 62 1/2", 94" h. **$9,200**

Step-back wall cupboard, Federal country-style, cherry, two-piece construction: the upper section w/ a deep flaring & stepped cornice above a pair of 6-pane cupboard doors w/arched top panes flanking three fixed center panes, opening to two shelves, all above a pie shelf; the lower stepped-out case w/the rectangular top above a row of three drawers w/turned wood knobs above a pair of paneled doors flanking two reeded pilasters & flanked on the sides w/half-round turned columns, flat base on small ball feet, interior painted ivory, older replaced knobs, age splits on side, minor pieced repair, early 19th c., 21 x 61", 87" h. . **$4,313**

Step-back wall cupboard, Federal country-style, painted wood, two-part construction: the upper section w/a rectangular top w/ a deep flaring molded cornice above a pair of 6-pane glazed cupboard doors opening to two shelves above an arched pie shelf; the projecting lower section w/a row of three drawers w/small turned wood knobs over a mid-molding above a pair of two-panel cupboard doors w/small turned knobs, original red surface, pulls probably original, New England, first half 19th c., some repairs, 23 1/2 x 57 1/2", 85" h. .. **$4,994**

Step-back wall cupboard, country-style, walnut, two-piece: the upper section w/a narrow cornice above a pair of 8-pane cupboard doors opening to three shelves; the lower section w/a pair of drawers slightly projecting over a pair of paneled cupboard doors, first half 19th c., 20 1/2 x 47", 85 1/2" h. **$1,840**

Step-back wall cupboard, Federal style, carved mahogany & mahogany veneer, two-part construction: the upper section w/ a molded broken-scroll pediment w/brass rosettes at the end of each scroll flanking a raised section decorated w/a gilt-carved pineapple & acanthus leaf design all flanked by spherical brass corner finials, the flat molded & reeded cornice above a pair of 6-pane glazed cupboard doors opening to two shaped shelves; the lower stepped-out section w/a long thin pull-out tray drawer above a row of three narrow drawers above a pair of cupboard doors w/recessed crossbanded panels opening to shelves, all flanked by narrow reeded pilasters ending in carved acanthus leaves, raised on acanthus leaf-carved front hairy paw feet & square rear feet, replaced round brasses, possibly Bergen County, New Jersey, ca. 1825-35, refinished, restorations, 21 1/2 x 48", 103 1/2" h. .. **$7,638**

CUPBOARDS

Step-back wall cupboard, painted & carved wood, two-part construction: the upper section w/a rectangular top w/a deep flaring stepped cornice above a pair of hinged 6-pane glazed doors centered by three glass panels & flanked by roundels & shaped reeded panels w/cock-beaded surrounds at the sides above the low arched pie shelf; the stepped-out lower section w/a row of three small drawers flanking two longer drawers all w/ simple bail pulls above a pair of raised panel cupboard doors w/exterior hinges flanking a long center reeded panel w/a roundel, molded base w/simple bracket feet, overall old red paint w/white borders & free-hand black designs, the lower doors w/yellow painted hearts w/scallop & line borders, Pennsylvania, early 19th c., imperfections, restoration, 23 1/2 x 66", 91 1/2" h. **$16,450**

Step-back wall cupboard, poplar & pine, one-piece construction, the rectangular top w/front molding continuing down the sides & flanking three open fixed shelves, the stepped-out lower sectoin w/a tall narrow flat dodors w/thumb-latches, layers of paint ending in older red, flat base, some edge wear, paint touch-up, 19th c., 17 1/2 x 43 1/2", 82" h. **$2,645**

> Antique purists want furniture in as-found condition, with no restoration done. Others prefer to have furniture repaired, refinished, and ready for use in their home. If restoration is done on a valuable piece of furniture, it should be performed by an expert who can minimize loss in value.

Wall cupboard, country-style, painted & decorated pine, the rectangular top w/a molded front rail w/canted corners above a conforming case w/a pair of tall two-panel doors above a mid-molding over two drawers at the bottom, flat molded base, each door panel h.p. w/an urn of flowers or a landscape scene within red & white herringbone frames, side & center vertical stiles w/ornate C-scrolls in color on a blue ground, similar scrolls & floral swags across the bottom drawers, Switzerland, 19th c.. **$7,175**

Desks

Chippendale slant-front desk, cherry & figured cherry, the narrow rectangular top above a hinged slant front opening to an interior fitted w/an arrangement of blocked drawers, scalloped pigeonholes & document boxes, the lower case w/four long graduated thumbmolded drawers w/brass butterfly pulls & keyhole escutcheons, molded base w/a small carved central drop & scroll-cut short cabriole legs ending in raised pad feet, old refinishing, glueblocks renailed, 18th c., 21 x 41", 45" h. **$8,050**

Country-style stand-up desk, walnut, a narrow rectangular top above the hinged slant-top writing surface opening to a dovetailed compartment projecting over the lower case w/a pair of tall paneled doors w/turned wood knobs, simple bracket feet, attributed to Virginia, old finish, age splits & minor edge loss, 19th c., 24 1/2 x 36 1/2", 50" h. **$805**

Federal "fall-front" writing desk, figured mahogany, the upper section w/a narrow rectangular top w/a brass rail above a wide two-panel hinged fall-front opening to an interior fitted w/ central letter dividers flanked by six pigeonholes above three small drawers w/ivory pulls, the stepped-out lower section w/a pair of drawers w/lion head & ring brass pulls, raised on slender ring-turned & reeded legs ending in baluster-turned feet on small brass knobs, New York City, descended in the Gardiner Family, 1800- 20, 23 1/4 x 33", 61" h. **$2,640**

Country-style school desk, painted pine, the top w/a short three-quarters gallery above a wide hinged lift-top opening to an interior fitted w/six pigeonholes, deep arched apron on long slender octagonal legs, old green paint w/stenciled flower on central apron & decorative trim on the legs, some wear & stains, mid-19th c., 19 1/4 x 28 1/4", 33 1/2" h. **$978**

Empire-Style cylinder-front desk, mahogany & mahogany veneer, a long narrow rectangular white marble top above a row of three short drawers above the cylinder front opening to a pull-out baize-lined writing surface & a variety of drawers & pigeonholes, the lower case w/a long central drawer flanked by pairs of smaller drawers, each side fitted w/a pull-out writing surface, raised on double-baluster- and ring-turned legs w/ormolu paw foot mounts on the front legs, France, mid-19th c., 27 1/2 x 56", 47 3/4" h. **$2,070**

Federal country-style child's slant-front desk, cherry, a narrow top above the hinged slant front opening to five pigeonholes, the case w/three graduated drawers w/small brass pulls, ring- and knob-turned legs, paneled ends, early 19th c., 13 x 18 3/4", 21 1/2" h. **$6,038**

> People sometimes naively claim that a piece of their furniture came to America on the Mayflower. No pieces from the Mayflower have been documented, and given the cramped quarters on the ship, and the need for transporting essential survival items like food, tools and other supplies, It's unlikely that any furniture made the trip.

DESKS

Late Victorian roll-top desk, oak, a rectangular top w/a low three-quarters gallery above the C-scroll top opening to an interior fitted w/small drawers & pigeonholes & a leather-inlaid writing surface, the lower case w/three stacks of paneled drawers flanking the knee opening, brass drawer pulls, late 19th - early 20th c. **$3,055**

Queen Anne country-style child's slant- front desk, maple & chestnut, the rectangular top above a hinged slant front opening to an interior fitted w/ pigeonholes & small drawers, the case w/three long graduated drawers w/butterfly brasses & keyhole escutcheons, simple bracket feet, old brown & olive green graining over old red paint, interior written inscription dating the piece to 1772, one end w/ paint removed, replaced brackets on pigeonholes, 18 1/2 x 30", 32 1/2" h. **$3,450**

Mission-style (Arts & Crafts movement) partner's desk, the long rectangular top above a deep apron w/two blind drawers on each side, raised on heavy square legs joined by cross-form supports & joined by a medial shelf w/key & tenon construction, original finish, Joseph P. McHugh & Company, New York, New York, some stains in top, chip to lower stretcher, early 20th c., 36 x 72", 29" h. **$1,320**

Rococo-Style desk, painted & decorated, the rectangular top w/serpentine edges above a case w/two stacks of concave- front drawers flanking a long bowfront drawer over the kneehole opening, raised on six cabriole legs, painted w/an antiqued green ground decorated on the top, sides & each drawer w/ scroll-framed white panels filled w/colorful flowers, Venice, Italy, early 20th c., some paint loss & scuffs, 26 x 48 1/2", 30 1/2" h. **$863**

Victorian "Davenport" desk, carved & burl walnut, the top w/a shaped & slanted lift- lid w/tooled leather writing inserts over a fitted interior, the sides installed w/five working & four opposing faux drawers, paneled front w/ floral- and leaf-carved cabriole supports, on extended feet on casters, some veneer repairs, England, ca. 1850, 21 5/8 x 23", 31" h. **$1,150**

Victorian lady's desk & side chair, faux bamboo bird's-eye maple, the desk w/an ornate stepped superstructure w/a tall central panel w/bamboo-turned trim & spindles framing a small shelf over a rectangular mirror flanked by short side panels w/ matching bamboo-turned trim & open shelves supported on bamboo-turned columns, the hinged slanted leather-inset writing surface opening to a fitted interior, bamboo-turned edge trim, corner brackets & legs joined by a bamboo-form H-stretcher, the matching bamboo-turned chair w/caned seat, late 19th c., desk 22 1/2 x 32", 4' 7" h., 2 pcs. **$3,738**

Victorian desk, Renaissance Revival substyle, walnut & walnut veneer, the rectangular top w/notched corners inset w/ green beize above an apron w/a long burl-paneled drawer & a small swing-out side inkwell w/ porcelain knob, raised on pairs of heavy squared supports joined by a pierced upper stretcher above the trestle base w/arched end legs & a stepped stretcher w/small center spindles, top tilts for use as drafting table, made by H. Closterman, Cincinnati, Ohio & patent-dated "February 12, 1878," refinished............................ **$715**

Victorian Renaissance Revival 'patent' desk, Renaissance Revival substyle, walnut & ebonized wood, the high upright blocked & scroll-carved crest w/a high center section w/a pair of short pilasters flanking a burl-veneered block w/roundel & flanked by narrow raised burl panels, the rectangular top above a narrow frieze w/raised burl panels over a pair of large round-topped hinged doors w/rectangular burl panels above longer arched burl panels & two fitted brass letter slots, the doors swing open to expose a very ornate interior trimmed w/bird's-eye maple & composed of numerous small drawers, pigeonholes, slots & original cardboard boxes, one door w/an applied metal plaque inscribed "Manufactured by - The Wooton Desk Co. - Indianapolis Ind. - Pat. Oct. 6 1874," fold-down writing surface w/original green fabric, Extra Grade, minor losses, 28 x 36 1/4", 68" h. **$23,000**

William & Mary country-style slant-front desk, painted pine, a narrow top fitted w/a long rectangular lid over the wide slanted top w/butterfly hinges & rose head nails opening to an interior fitted w/four drawers & eight pigeonholes w/yellow & red paint, flaring molded molding raised on ring-, baluster- and block-turned legs ending in knob feet & joined by a baluster- and ring-turned H- stretchers, old green paint, attributed to Pennsylvania, some pieced repairs & edge damage, first half 18th c., 27 1/2 x 39", 33" h. **$2,300**

Dining Room Suites

Colonial Revival style: dining table w/two leaves, six chairs, a sideboard, small server & a china cabinet; Jacobean design in walnut & burl walnut, the case pieces w/flat tops over slightly angled fronts, the sideboard & server w/a pair of arched carved central doors w/ring pulls flanked by slightly angled matching doors, the china cabinet w/a large arched carved door above a long carved drawer all flanked by angled side panels, boldly turned knob-, ring- and block-decorated legs on bun feet, the case pieces w/open base shelves w/serpentine fronts, made in Rockford, Illinois, ca. 1920s, table 45 x 66" plus leaves, sideboard 44" l., the set **$863**

Colonial Revival style: dining table, six chairs, a sideboard & a china cabinet; Jacobean design in walnut & burl walnut, the china cabinet w/a tall arched top above a geometrically glazed door above a long deep drawer w/banded carving & burl, the sideboard w/similar details & a case w/two long center drawers flanked by end doors, all the pieces raised on heavy turned legs w/very large central knobs & small bun feet all joined by H- stretchers, ca. 1920s, the set **$2,070**

Colonial Revival: dining table, sideboard, server, china cabinet & five side chairs & one armchair; inlaid mahogany & mahogany veneer, the Chippendale-style chairs w/an arched shell-carved crestrail over pierced carved vasiform back splat, overupholstered seat on cabriole legs; the oval extension dining table raised on heavy C-scroll legs ending in bun feet, the two-part D-form china cabinet w/the upper section centered by a large curved door w/a large oval reserve w/inlaid floral decoration, matching details on the long sideboard & small server, Rockford Republic Furniture Co., ca. 1920s, the set **$10,450**

Modern Style: dining table & four "Mira" chairs; walnut, the table w/a square top supported on a simple pedestal on a cross-form foot, each chair w/a wide curved crestrail above seven spindles over a triangular saddle seat, three simple turned & canted legs, by George Nakashima, ca. 1965, table 26 1/4 x 32", 26" h., chairs 27 1/4" h. **$14,340**

Victorian Baroque-Style: round table w/six leaves, twelve chairs, tall china cabinet, sideboard & server; oak, each piece with elaborate carving, the rounded expandable dining table w/carved apron above a heavy turned round leaf-carved center post flanked by four ornately carved winged griffins below spiral-turned support legs, each chair w/a high arched carved crest & spiral-turned stiles flanking an oval caned back panel over the caned seat on turned legs & stretchers, the china cabinet w/a high crest carved w/pierced scrolls & a center cartouche above a leaf-carved corner & scroll-carved frieze band centered by a mask carving over two tall glazed cupboard doors flanked by spiral-turned side stiles, deep molded & carved base, dark original finish, ca. 1880s, the set (ILLUS. of china cabinet) **$25,000**

Modern Style: drop-leaf dining table & six dining chairs; birch w/a champagne finish, the table w/a rectangular top flanked by wlde D-form drop leaves & raised on a set of three arched pedestal legs, Model M197G by Heywood-Wakefield, together w/Heywood-Wakefield chairs Model M553A w/a curved back crest above a cross-form splat between the canted stiles above the upholstered seat, squared tapering legs, ca. 1950-53, the set (ILLUS. of part) **$431**

William & Mary Revival: oval table, five side chairs & one armchair; oak, each chair w/a tall back w/a yoked crest centered by a pierced scroll crest above a large pierce-carved splat enclosing an oval upholstered panel, upholstered slip seat on a carved seatrail & S-scroll front legs joined by a curved H-stretcher to the rear legs, the oval table w/a scroll-carved apron, raised on four large flat leg panels w/shell, floral & scroll carving centered by a caned oval panel & drop-down supports at each end, w/six leaves, original finish, late 19th c., table 54" l., 30" h., armchair 46" h., the set **$3,500**

DRY SINKS

Dry Sinks

Painted & decorated poplar, the long arched splashback above a long well above a case w/ a pair of large paneled cupboard doors above simple bracket feet, old dark brown graining over an amber-colored ground, evidence of earlier red, interior w/two shelves painted light green, wear, door latch missing, 19th c., 17 3/4 x 45", 36" h. **$575**

Painted pine & poplar, a narrow rectangular shelf atop the raised backboard flanked by shaped sides on the long well above a pair of drawers w/turned wood knobs over a pair of paneled cupboard doors opening to two shelves, simple bracket feet, old yellow paint over earlier colors, signed in pencil in one drawer "Thos. Underwood, Clark Co. Ohio, August 10, 1881," 18 x 42", 41" h. **$4,025**

Pine & tiger stripe maple, a long, deep rectangular well above a case w/a pair of drawers w/wooden knobs over a pair of paneled cupboard doors w/ original butt hinges & a cast-iron latch, bracket feet, old refinish, second half 19th c., 19 x 52", 33" h. **$800**

Cherry, the rectangular hinged top opens to a well above a pair of paneled cupboard doors w/brass H-hinges & brass latches, simple bracket feet, mid-19th c., sink lining missing & replaced w/a plywood panel, 20 x 36 3/4", 33 3/4" h. **$690**

Some people have the misconception that anything that is old is valuable, and the older it is, the more valuable it is. Age alone, however, is no guarantee of value. A much more important factor is quality of design and workmanship. A modern exquisitely designed and executed object made of high quality material will almost certainly be more valuable than a comparable poorly designed and crafted object of poor quality material made a hundred or more years ago. Poor quality then is still poor quality now. Age will not increase its value.

Hall Racks & Trees

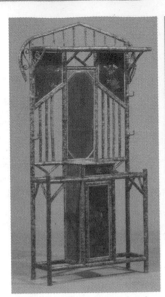

Hall rack, Arts & Crafts style, oak, a large rectangular central mirror framed by wide oak slats & outer narrow beveled panels, flat side slats each mounted w/two original iron coat racks, original finish, early 20th c., 37" l., 21" h. **$960**

Hall rack, Arts & Crafts style, oak, a long rectangular mirror in a wide oak frame, flat top & bottom rails w/tapering molded side rails topped by angled blocks, each end mounted w/two original metal coat hooks, original dark finish, early 20th c., 37" l., 26" h. **$300**

Hall tree, Victorian faux-bamboo style, the top mounted w/a curved & peaked cornice composed of faux-bamboo rods over slender spindles above a rectangular projecting shelf composed of matching rods, the upper back decorated w/a pair of lacquered paint-decorated panels flanking a tall slender beveled mirror & large faux-bamboo spindles above a small square projecting shelf over a small drawer & a tall narrow door all flanked by open umbrella racks formed by faux-bamboo rods, the upper sides each mounted w/three metal hanging hooks, ca. 1880s, 12 x 44", 80" h. .. **$1,495**

Antique mirrors are wavy and have thinner glass than modern mirrors. To evaluate the thickness of the glass, touch the tip of a key to its surface. If the tip of the reflected key is much closer to the actual key than it is if touched to a modern mirror, it is likely antique.

Hall rack, Arts & Crafts style, oak, the wide flat rectangular frame deeply carved w/a repeating design of scrolled leafy florals, a pair of fancy scrolled metal coat hooks at each end, original black finish, replaced mirror, early 20th c., 40" l., 29" h. **$570**

Highboys

Queen Anne "bonnet-top" highboy, carved cherry, two-part construction: the upper section w/a broken-scroll bonnet top centered by a slender fluted post topped by an urn-carved & flame-turned finial, matching corner blocks & flame finials, the case w/a pair of small drawers flanking a deep shell-carved drawer over a stack of four long graduated drawers all w/butterfly brasses & keyhole escutcheons, fluted pilasters down the sides; the lower section w/a mid-molding above a case w/a pair of narrow drawers over a pair of deep drawers flanking a small shell-carved & blocked center drawer above a conforming apron w/two drops, raised on cabriole legs w/scroll-carved returns & ending in raised pad feet, top & base married, Long Island, New York, 18th c., 20 1/2 x 41 1/2", 92" h. **$9,000**

Queen Anne "bonnet-top" highboy, carved mahogany, two-part construction: the upper section w/a broken-scroll pediment centered by a tall plinth w/ an urn- and flame-turned finial & corner plinths w/matching finials above a pair of short drawers flanking a deep center drawer w/a large carved fan above four long graduated drawers w/butterfly pulls & keyhole escutcheons; the lower section w/a molded edge above a long narrow drawer over a row of three drawers, the center one fan-carved, shaped & valanced apron raised on slender cabriole legs ending in pad feet, brasses appear to be original, old refinish, probably Massachusetts, 1786, pencil inscription inside upper case reads "made by Horace Smith, Sept. 9, 1786," minor restoration & imperfections, 22 x 42", 88" h. **$23,500**

Queen Anne "bonnet-top" highboy, cherry, two-part construction: the upper section w/ a tall scrolled pediment centered by a pointed brass finial above four small drawers flanking a deep fan-carved center drawer above four long graduated drawers, all w/butterfly brasses & keyhole escutcheons; the lower section w/a mid-molding above a narrow long drawer over a row of three deeper drawers, the center one fan-carved, scalloped apron w/ two drops, cabriole legs ending in pad feet, dark stain, Kittery Point, Maine, old brasses, minor losses & splits, 18th c., 20 1/2 x 39", 83 1/2" h. **$5,750**

Queen Anne "flat-top" highboy, maple w/burl veneer, two-part construction: the upper section w/a rectangular top w/a deep flaring & stepped cornice above a pair of drawers over three graduated drawers all w/brass butterfly pulls & keyhole escutcheons; the lower section w/a wide mid-molding above a pair of deep drawers flanking a shallow central drawer, arched & scalloped apron w/turned drop finials, tall cabriole legs ending in pad feet, refinished, pieced repairs, 21 1/4 x 38 1/2", 64" h. **$1,265**

→

Love Seats, Sofas & Settees

Settee, child's Windsor "step-back" style, mixed wood, the long narrow stepped crestreail above numerous slener bamboo-turned spindles flanked by bamboo- turned stiles, bamboo-turned arms above two turned short spindles & a canted bamboo-turned arm support, long plank seat w/rounded corners raised on six splayed bamboo-turned legs joined by bamboo-turned stretchers, refinished, early 19th c., 15 1/2 x 46", 32" h. **$1,495**

Settee, Queen Anne Revival, mahogany, the high rectangular upholstered back flanked by scrolled upholstered arms & the over-upholstered seat, raised on three front cabriole legs ending in pad feet & joined by simple turned H-stretchers to the square canted rear legs, England, late 19th - early 20th c., 52" l., 41" h. **$4,025**

The term "style" refers to a characteristic design or form, while "period" refers to the era or time in which a style was first introduced.

Settee, Georgian-Style, mahogany, a double chair-back with the shield-shaped sections each enclosing a pierced fanned splat & joined by a center scrolled & slated splat, shaped open arms on incurved arm supports above the spring- upholstered seat, narrow molded seatrail on square tapering legs, minor nicks, England, late 19th - early 20th c., 44 1/2" l., 36 1/2" h. **$1,150**

Settee, Louis XVI style, beechwood, the thin molded & slightly arched crestrail w/notched ends flanked by reeded, curved styles curving to the padded closed arms flanking the upholstered back, cushion seat above a thin molded bowed front seatrail raised on four turned & fluted tapering front legs, France, ca. 1790, 64" l. **$6,463**

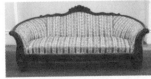

Sofa, Classical-Victorian Rococo transitional style, mahogany, the long serpentine & arched crestrail centered by a flower- and scroll-carved crest, crestrail curves forward over the deep rolled upholstered arms w/leaf-carved arm supports, long deep serpentine seatrail further carved w/scrolled leaves, raised on leafy scroll- carved front feet on casters, ca. 1840-50, 75 1/2" l., 33" h. **$805**

LOVE SEATS, SOFAS & SETTEES

Settee, Windsor "sack-back" style, the very long slender bowed crestrail above numerous slender turned spindles continuing down through the medial rail that curves to form the flat shaped arms on pairs of spindles & baluster- and ring- turned canted arm supports, the long plank seat raised on eight canted baluster- and ring-turned legs joined by three swelled H-stretchers, old finish, label of John DeWitt, New York City, 1797, 22 x 81", 37" h. **$31,200**

Sofa, Classical style, mahogany & mahogany veneer, the long serpentine crestrail w/a wider center section w/a carved rosette at each end, above the upholstered back flanked by S-scroll upholstered arms w/ front rails ending in a carved rosette & continuing into the long molded seatrail raised on winged paw front feet, some minor wear, ca. 1830, 80 1/2" l., 37" h. **$1,265**

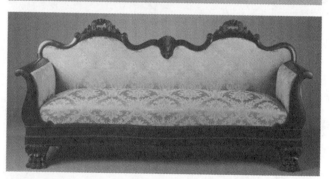

Sofa, Early Victorian transitional style, carved mahogany, the double-arched crestrail centered by a carved shell & w/two pierced arched & scroll-carved crests above the long upholstered back flanked by outswept upholstered arms above the deep upholstered seat on a deep flat seatrail raised on heavy paw- carved front feet, ca. 1840-50, 81" l. . **$1,035**

Sofa, Federal style, inlaid mahogany, the narrow crestrail centered by a low long raised & fluted panel above the upholstered back flanked by stepped & curved reeded arm rails on the closed upholstered arms, long over-upholstered seat, raised on four square tapering front legs w/ inlaid bellflower drops & banded ankles on casters, canted square rear legs on casters, New York City, 1790-1810, 75" l., 37 1/2" h. **$4,200**

Sofa, Victorian Renaissance Revival style, walnut & burl walnut, the long narrow stepped crestrail centered by a high point & pierce-carved crest & trimmed w/narrow burl panels & roundels all above the wide upholstered back flanked by large round bolster-style upholstered arms w/round fancy pierce-carved front supports on narrow blocks above the flat molded & burl-inlaid seatrail w/a narrow arched center drop panel, heavy disk- and knob-turned legs, seat fitted w/a long cushion & added pillows, ca. 1875, 75" l., 48 3/4" h. **$805**

Sofa, Federal-Style, mahogany & mahogany veneer, the long flat crestrail inlaid w/a light wood band above the upholstered back flanked by downswept upholstered arms w/scrolled hand grips raised on reeded baluster-turned arm supports, a long cushion seat above the flat seatrail w/a light wood band of inlay, raised on four turned, reeded & tapering front legs on ball & peg feet, square canted rear legs, minor veneer damage, 20th c., 66 5/8" l., 32 1/4" h. **$978**

Sofa, Mission-style (Arts & Crafts movement), oak, the low wide back raised joined to low arms each over five vertical slats, deep seatrail mortised through the front legs, recovered leather cushions, fine original finish, red decal mark of Gustav Stickley, Model No. 225, 31 x 78", 29" h. **$10,800**

• Good buys can sometimes be found in the last hours of a show from a dealer who hasn't had strong sales or doesn't want to haul a large item home.

• If you have the space, including high ceilings, buying an extra-large piece of furniture may be less costly than buying the same form in standard scale. Most people are downsizing their dwelling in these tough economic times, and large scale furniture is not in high demand.

MIRRORS

Mirrors

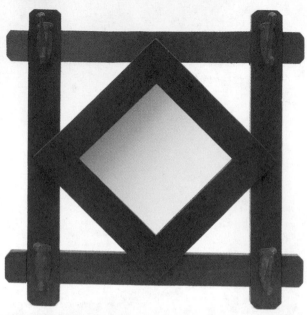

Arts & Crafts wall mirror, oak, the wide flat diamond-shaped frame mounted within a flat square cross-cornered outer frame, each corner mounted w/ original iron coat hooks, early 20th c., refinished, 27" w. **$450**

Classical wall mirror, giltwood, the tall rectangular frame w/florette corner blocks joined by half-round ring- and knob-turned columns, a large rectangular upper panel w/a raised panel enclosed a basket of fruit & leaves in bold relief, mirror streaked & flaking, minor edge flakes, some wear to gilding, ca. 1825-35, 17 x 36 1/4" **$345**

Country-style shaving mirror, hanging- type, mahogany, the narrow rectangular top fitted w/an arched back crest w/a hanging hole above a rectangular beaded panel framing the old mirror, projecting shaped lower sides flanking a small shelf over an open compartment, varnish mottling, early 19th c., 7 3/4 x 11 1/8", 22 1/2" h. **$764**

Federal wall mirror, gilt gesso, the flat flaring crest w/blocked ends above a row of large spheres & a plain frieze over a reverse-painted upper tablet showing a sepia tone rural landscape w/cottage framed by a wide green band within a wide white band decorated w/a brown leafy vine, a long rectangular mirror below, all flanked by half-round spiral-carved columns w/acanthus leaf-carved capitals, blocked bottom corners & a plain rail, probably New England, ca. 1810-15, minor restoration, 17 1/2" w., 30 3/4" h. **$499**

Speckles and dark marks in old mirrors are accepted as signs of age, and unless the silvering loss is major will not detract from the value. Because flaking is caused by dampness, mirrors should be kept in a dry environment. Resilvering is seldom recommended.

MIRRORS

Chippendale wall mirror, mahogany & giltwood, the high arched scroll-cut & incised crest centered by a giltwood phoenix or heron, a parcel-gilt liner, scroll-cut shaped base pendant, early glass & early dark-stained surface, probably England, ca. 1780, 16" w., 36 1/2" h. **$1,265**

Classical wall mirror, gilded & black-painted wood, rectangular frame w/turned split-baluster borders & corner blocks w/rondels, a reverse-painted rectangular tablet at the top showing a lady standing under draperies, leaftip & blossom borders, rectangular mirror plate, New England, minor imperfections, ca. 1830, 16 x 32" **$748**

Federal wall mirror, inlaid & parcel-gilt mahogany, the curved & gilded swan's-neck cresting surmounted by a gilded urn w/wheat ears & flowers, the crest & pendant inlaid w/oval reserves, flanked by giltwood drapery, old refinish & regilding, New York City, 1790-1810, 24 1/2" w., 5' 2" h. (restoration, losses) **$3,105**

George I-Style mirror, gilt gesso & giltwood, the beveled rectangular mirror plate w/swan's-neck cresting centering a shell, w/ scrolled ears & pendent foliage, the shaped pendant w/a central shell, missing candlearms, England, 19th c., 22 x 41" **$3,450**

Mission Style (Arts & Crafts Movement) wall mirror, oak, rectangular w/inverted-V crestrail, two-color glass, original finish, Lifetime Furniture Co., similar to Model No. 512, 48 3/4" l., 28 1/4" h. **$489**

Queen Anne wall mirror, mahogany & giltwood, the high arched scroll-cut & incised crest centered by a giltwood phoenix or heron, a parcel-gilt liner, scroll-cut shaped base pendant, early glass & early dark-stained surface, probably England, ca. 1780, 16" w., 36 1/2" h. **$1,725**

Regency, giltwood & part-ebonized, a convex mirror plate within a beaded frame mounted w/ spherules, the pendant w/a leaf spray flanked by foliage & continuing to exotic serpentine beasts, missing cresting, losses, England, early 19th c., 47" d., 4' 7" h. **$7,475**

Federal-Style girandole wall mirror, giltwood, the wide round concave frame trimmed w/a ring of spheres enclosing a convex round mirror, the crest mounted w/a large spread-winged eagle flanked by arched leafy scrolls, the base w/a curved gadrooned & rayed drop, minor losses to gilt, eagle slightly loose, second half 19th c., 22 1/2" w., 36 1/2" h. **$1,495**

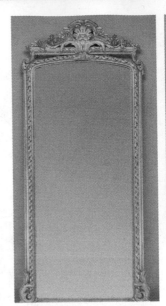

Napoleon III pier mirror, giltwood, the tall arched mirror within a bead & ropetwist frame surmounted by an arched swan's-neck pediment over striated acanthus leaves issuing scrolling foliate garlands, France, third quarter 19th c., 44" w., 8' 4" h. **$881**

Neoclassical overmantel mirror, giltwood, the stepped rectangular plate within gilt ropetwist banding surmounted by an urn-form finial issuing scrolling acanthus leaves above a mask of a beauty flanked at the stepped sides by birds w/elaborately curled tails, Italy, late 18th c., 4' 5" l., 35" h. **$3,819**

Parlor Suites

Art Nouveau style: settee, armchair & side chair; carved giltwood, the settee w/a long serpentine crestrail centered by a pierced scroll-carved crest & w/fanned scroll round corners enclosing the upholstered back, open serpentine arms curving into the narrow serpentine scroll- carved seatrail enclosing the upholstered seat, long C-scroll outswept front legs on scroll & peg feet on casters, the chairs w/matching frames, some rubbing to gilt, fabric worn, France, ca. 1890s, settee 51 1/2" l., 37 1/2" h., 3 pcs. **$600**

Empire Style: sofa, two open-arm armchairs & two side chairs; ormolu-mounted mahogany, each piece w/a rolled crestrail flanked by molded stiles w/ormolu leaf mounts flanking the raised upholstered back panel, squared open arms w/large figural gilt sphinx armrests above the over-upholstered seats, the flat se-atrails w/a slender ormolu leaf band mount w/corner rosettes above front legs formed by winged gilt griffins & ending in a gilt paw foot, square canted rear legs, France, late 19th c., sofa 63" l., the set **$26,290**

Louis XVI-Style: two sofas, two open-arm armchairs & two side chairs; carved giltwood, the sofa w/a long narrow & gently arched crestrail centered by carved scrolls atop the rectangular frame enclosing a tapestry-upholstered back featuring scenes from "The Fables of Fontaine," padded open arms w/incurved & reeded arm supports above the tapestry-upholstered seat w/a narrow gently arched molded seatrail raised on four turned tapering & reeded front legs ending in knob-and-peg feet, the chairs of match-ing design, France, late 19th c., 6 pcs. (ILLUS. of one sofa) **$6,613**

Modern style: two armchairs & a corner table; bent ashwood w/faux bamboo turnings, each w/a light framework enclosing a square back cushion & seat cushion & supported on a box stretcher base w/U- form front stretchers, the two-tier table w/an incurved upper shelf above the round-cornered top supported on faux bamboo legs joined by curved stretchers & a lower shelf, marked by Heywood-Wakefield, ca. 1955, the set $316

Victorian Renaissance Revival substyle: sofa, one armchair & four side chairs; ebonized beechwood, the sofa w/a long narrow gently arched crestrail centered by carved crossed torches & a quiver tied w/a ribbon & bow, the raised back frame w/ rounded lower corners framing the tufted upholstery back, open padded arms w/incurved arm supports above the long gently curved upholstered seat on a conforming three-section seatrail w/a small carved shell centering each, raised on disk-turned and fluted tapering legs, the chairs w/matching shield-shaped backs, France, ca. 1860-70, sofa 70" l., 43" h. (ILLUS. of the sofa) $1,840

Victorian Renaissance Revival: sofa & armchair; ormolu-mounted ebonized wood, the sofa w/a raised central tufted back section w/a narrow arched crestrail centered by a carved shell crest all flanked by the lower curved upholstered back sections ending in closed arms w/gilt-bronze & metal putto busts & leaves flanking the long tufted upholstered seat on a gently curved seatrail w/gilt incised trim & a central drop, on tapering front legs ending in hoof-style feet, square canted rear legs all on casters, the matching armchair w/the crestrail centered by a round copper-plated panel flanked by a small recumbent gilt-bronze figural putto, worn original tufted upholstery, signed by Pottier Stymus, New York, New York, ca. 1875, sofa 70" l., 36 1/2" h., two pcs. $4,600

PARLOR SUITES

Victorian Renaissance Revival: sofa & two side chairs; walnut & burl walnut, the sofa w/a long gently curved tufted upholstery back centered by a gently arched central crestrail w/a peaked finial over an oval medallion carved in the image of a female face over narrow burl panels & urn-form corner finials, closed upholstered half-arms w/arm supports carved as female heads, serpentine seatrail trimmed w/oval burl panels, on tapering disk-and-baluster-turned front legs on casters, the matching chairs w/ similar carved crests & incurved back stiles, refinished, newer upholstery, ca. 1870s, attributed to John Jelliff, Newark, New Jersey, sofa 70" l., the set .. **$2,500**

Victorian Renaissance Revival: walnut; sofa, armchair & two side chairs, the sofa w/a long tufted upholstery back within a rectangular frame w/rounded top corners, the crestrail centered by a scroll- and ribbon-carved crest, open padded arms on incurved arm supports, long oblong upholstered seat w/a carved apron raised on turned trumpet front legs on casters, the chairs w/matching frames, refinished, new brocade upholstery, attributed to Alexander Roux, New York City, ca. 1870, sofa 70" l., the set **$6,000**

Victorian Rococo substyle: sofa, armchair & two side chairs; pierce-carved & laminated rosewood, the long sofa w/double high chair backs flanking a lower long arched central back section, the central section w/a high arched serpentine crestrail ornately pierce-carved w/scrolls & centered by large carved face w/a leaf- form tongue, the high arched chair backs w/higher matching serpentine carved crestrail also centered by carved faces, padded incurved arms on heavy pierced & scroll-carved sides, the long serpentine seat w/a scroll-carved serpentine seatrail centered by a carved face, on demi-cabriole front legs w/leaf-carved feet on casters, canted square reeded legs on casters, each chair w/a high arched back matching the sofa backs, attributed to Charles Boudoine, New York City, ca. 1855, sofa 82" l., 42 1/4" h., the set **$29,900**

Victorian Rococo: sofa, armchair & four side chairs; carved rosewood, the sofa w/a long upholstered serpentine back w/a narrow conforming crestrail w/low carved crests, padded & closed upholstered arms w/incurved arm supports, long serpentine seatrail w/a carved trim above four demi-cabriole front legs, matching chairs w/shaped balloon backs, original finish, ca. 1860, sofa 66" l., the set **$2,300**

Victorian Rococo: sofa, armchair & two side chairs; carved rosewood, the sofa w/an oval medallion w/tufted upholstery in the center below a floral-carved crest & curved crestrails continuing down to form the closed half-arms w/incurved arm supports, long serpentine seat w/a serpentine floral-carved seatrail on four demi-cabriole front legs on casters, the matching chairs w/shaped balloon backs, possibly original needlepoint upholstery, ca. 1865, original finish, sofa 72" l., the set **$3,000**

Wicker: love seat & armchair; each piece w/a wide tightly woven rolled crestrail curving down to form the outswept rolled arms over tightly woven sides, the upper back w/a padded brown leather panel over a tightly woven panel, leather-upholstered seats, deep tightly woven & gently arched aprons, original natural finish, both signed w/a Heywood-Wakefield plaque, early 20th c., love seat 25 x 41 1/2", 36 1/2" h., 2 pcs. **$1,380**

Secretaries

SECRETARIES

Classical secretary-bookcase, mahogany & mahogany veneer, two-part construction: the upper section w/a rectangular top w/a deep ogee cornice w/rounded corners above a pair of tall geometrically- glazed cupboard doors opening to three shelves above a row of three narrow drawers; the projecting lower section w/a fold-out writing surface above a long drawer over a pair of paneled cupboard doors, deep base molding raised on scroll-cut bracket feet, ca. 1840, 22 x 42", 87" h. **$4,313**

Country-style secretary, chestnut, butternut & pine, two-piece construction: the upper section w/ a wide rectangular top w/a deep stepped cornice overhanging a pair of short rectangular two-panel doors above a flat fall-front opening to an interior w/three open compartmenbt s above an arrangement of seven small drawers & a small compartment; the lower section w/three long graduated drawers w/turned wood knobs, flat base raised on bulbous turned feet, good color w/old finish, attributed to the Shakers, second half 19th c., 19 1/2 x 42 1/2", 71 1/2" h. **$3,220**

Federal secretary-bookcase, birch & flame birch, two-part construction: the upper short section w/a rectangular top w/a narrow molded cornice above a pair of long rectangular paneled doors opening to an interior w/a shelf above rows of small drawers & pigeonholes, a row of three small drawers w/small round brass pulls below the doors; the lower section w/a gently slanted fold-out writing surface above a single long drawer projecting above two long graduated drawers flanked by ring- and spiral-turned columns, drawers w/oval brasses & keyhole escutcheons, flat base w/blocked ends raised on ring-, knob- and baluster- turned legs ending in peg feet, warm dark refinishing, New Hampshire, ca. 1820- 30, old replaced brasses, minor damage & age splits, 40 3/4" w., 56 5/8" h. **$2,300**

←

Federal country-style secretary-bookcase, maple, two-part construction: the upper section w/a rectangular top & widely flaring flattened cornice above a pairs of two-pane cupboard doors w/scallop- cut points at the top of each pane, opening to two shelves; the lower section w/a hinged slant-top opening to an interior fitted w/pigeonholes & small drawers above a case w/ three long graduated drawers w/ butterfly brasses, scalloped apron & bracket feet, replaced brasses, front foot facings replaced, early 19th c., 18 1/2 x 41 1/2", 77" h. **$2,760**

Federal secretary-bookcase, carved & inlaid mahogany, two-part construction: the upper section w/a high broken-scroll pediment w/scroll-pierced scrolls flanking a central block w/an urn-turned finial above a narrow veneer-paneled frieze band above a pair of tall geometrically-glazed doors opening to three wooden shelves; the stepped-out lower section w/a stack of five long graduated drawers w/line-inlaid panels, oval brasses & diamond-shaped inlaid keyhole escutcheons, serpentine apron continuing to tall outswept French feet, Maryland, 1790-1810, 23 1/4 x 42 1/2", 97 1/4" h. **$26,400**

Sideboards

The Arts & Crafts movement was in vogue between roughly 1880 and 1910. It sought to oppose the mass production of the Industrial Revolution and restore the ideals of quality and pride in handcraftsmanship. Arts & Crafts furniture featured straight, clean lines and relied heavily on oak. Famous designers included William Morris. Elbert Hubbard, and Gustave Stickley.

Arts & Crafts server, oak, the rectangular top w/molded edges & a low three-quarters gallery raised on four tapering square legs joined by a medial shelf over a pair of drawers w/original brass pulls & an open bottom shelf, original finish, some separation in top, early 20th c., 21 x 46", 41" h. **$1,320**

Mission-style (Arts & Crafts movement) dining table, oak, expansion-type, the wide round top w/a flat apron raised on a heavy center split octagonal pedestal w/four blocked extension feet, w/five original leaves, original finish, signed w/decal mark of Hastings, closed 54" d., 29" h. **$2,280**

Victorian Renaissance Revival style sideboard, burl & ebonized wood veneer w/ormolu trim & elaborate inlaid panels, the long rectangular top w/four stepped-out blocks along the front above a conforming case w/a row of three long very shallow ornately inlaid drawers separated by blocks above a lower case w/two three-pane cabinet doors each opening to two mirrored-back shelves, the large central door w/burl banding around a raised central panel ornately inlaid w/mythical beasts among delicate inlaid leafy scrolls & colonettes, the three door separated by four slender ring-turned free-standing columns above large projecting blocks raised on bun feet, glass panes at each end of the case, third-quarter 19th c., missing a piece of molding & one replacement, 18 1/2 x 78", 45 1/2" h. .. **$5,405**

Stands

Bookstand, oak, Arts & Crafts style, the rectangular top overhaning flat tapering sides w/bootjack feet joined by a V-form book trough w/ key & tenon construction, branded signature of L. & J.G. Stickley, refinished, 15 x 24", 25" h. **$570**

Candlestand, Federal country-style, curly maple & cherry, the rectangular tilting single board curly maple top w/notched corners raised on a columnar turned cherry pedestal on a tripod base w/spider legs, refinished, glued repairs to legs, late 18th - early 19th c., 18 1/2 x 23 3/4", 27" h. **$748**

Magazine stand, Mission-style (Arts & Crafts movement), oak, the rectangular top shelf w/a three-quarters gallery above three lower shelves flanked by double-slat sides, peaked apron on each side of the base, original finish, branded mark of Charles Limbert Furniture Company, 12 1/2 x 16", 43" h. **$440**

Plant stand, Mission-style, oak, small round top supported on corbels & a slender four-part pedestal continuing to flaring feet, original finish, branded mark of Charles Limbert Furniture Company, early 20th c., 14" d., 32" h. **$2,040**

Magazine stand, Mission-style (Arts & Crafts movement), oak, the nearly square top shelf w/a three-quarters gallery above two lower shelves w/double- slat sides, original finish, possible light recoat on top shelf, sugned & number by Stickley Brothers, Model No. 4600, 13 x 16", 31" h. **$1,320**

Candlestand, country-style, pine, a square top on a chamfered post atop a cross- form base, New England, late 18th c., im-perfections, 13 1/2" w., 29 3/4" h. **$881**

Plant stand, Arts & Crafts style, oak, the rectangular trough top fitted w/a zinc liner & faced on each side w/a caned panel, square legs joined by a medial shelf w/incurved sides, refinished, replaced cane, early 20th c., 13 x 31", 15" h. $270

Washstand, Classical country-style, painted & decorated pine, the rectangular hinged top opening to a well, the upper case w/a small drawer in the lower corner above a single paneled door w/wood knob flanked by serpentine front stiles, old yellow & ochre vinegar grain painting, some minor paint ware, 19th c., 16 1/4 x 29", 33" h. $230

Plant stand, Mission-style, oak, the small square top supported on a square tapering column atop a square base raised on short through-post feet, original finish, metal tag mark of Stickley Brothers, Model No. 133, some stains in top, 13" w., 34" h. $1,020

Federal one-drawer stand, stained maple, the rectangular top overhanging an apron w/a single drawer w/small turned wood knobs, on tall slender ring- and baluster-turned legs ending in knob- and peg feet, old reddish finish, top warped & w/age split, early 19th c., 15 1/2 x 19", 27 3/4" h. $345

Picture stand, Victorian Renaissance Revival substyle, easel-type, gilt-incised & ebonized-accented walnut, the tall tapering front frame topped by a large carved palmette finial above an arched panel w/rosettes flanking a central gilt classical Minerva head above three slats above the lower panel w/a hinged arched folio rack decorated w/a large black scroll-trimmed cartouche, a curved & pierced front apron on scrolled front legs, a plain fold-out rear support rack, ca. 1875, 28 1/2" w., 6' 1/2" h. $2,530

Plant stand, Oriental, carved hardwood, the round dished top above a scroll-pierced apron raised on three lion head-carved cabriole legs ending in paw feet & joined by a pierced lower shelf, China, late 19th - early 20th c., 16" d., 40" h. $200-400

Federal two-drawer stand, mixed hardwood & mahogany veneer, the rectangular top w/a band of burl inlay above a pair of drawers w/flame grained mahogany veneer & original rectangular brasses, drawers flanked by narrow veneer bands above the tall slender square tapering legs, top drawer w/fitted interior, Mid-Atlantic States, early 19th c., 18 1/4 x 23", 27 3/4" h. $575

Stools

Windsor stool, mixed woods, the small oval top raised on three canted baluster-turned legs joined by a swelled T-form stretcher, remnants of black paint, some loss & make-do repairs using wrought nails, late 18th - early 19th c., 12" w., 16 3/4" h. **$184**

George II-Style footstool, carved walnut, rectangular upholstered slip seat above a deep burl apron raised on four cabriole legs w/shell-carved knees & ending in pad feet, late 19th - early 20th c., 16 x 21 1/2", 20" h. **$660**

Mission-style (Arts & Crafts movement) footstool, oak, the rectangular top w/replaced leather supported on four corner legs w/ through-tenion flat stretchers, recoated original finish, signed w/Gustav Stickley paper label, Model No. 300, 16 1/2 x 20 1/2", 15" h. **$728**

Victorian Gothic Revival stools, oak, a rectangular top above a line-incised apron raised on molded square legs w/carved quatrefoil corner brackets, England, mid-19th c., 13 1/2 x 18", 18" h., pr. (ILLUS. of one) **$805**

Regency gout stool, mahogany, an upholstered & rolled top over scrolled sides carved w/honeysuckle vines, on bulbous knob feet, England, early 19th c., 12 3/4 x 18", 10 1/2" h. **$1,610**

TABLES

Tables

Art Deco coffee table, birch veneer & ebonized wood, the thick rectangular top decorated w/a checkerboard design in birch veneer, flat curved ebonized legs, unmarked, refinished, 24 x 48", 13 1/2" h. **$540**

Arts & Crafts lamp table, oak, the round top above a narrow apron supported by four square legs joined by X-form through-tenon stretchers supporting a small round shelf, refinished, early 20th c., 26" d., 30" h. **$450**

Art Nouveau work table, mother-of-pearl & fruitwood-inlaid, the rectangular hinged bird's-eye maple top w/serpentine edges opening to a fitted interior above the apron w/one drawer on a scalloped serpentine border & inlaid w/multicolored butterflies & foliage, raised on tall slender turned supports joining the rectangular medial shelf w/serpentine edges, raised on slender turned & tapering outswept legs, Europe, late 19th - early 20th c., 15 x 21", 22" h. (ILLUS. right with Dutch Classical work table) **$529**

Classical work table, fruitwood marquetry- inlaid mahogany, the rectangular hinged top opening to a fitted interior above two drawers, the drawer fronts & case sides finely inlaid w/flowering leafy vines, raised on lyre-form end supports, atop an inlaid medial shelf w/incurved edges, all supported on ball feet, Holland, early 19th c. (ILLUS. left with Art Nouveau work table) **$1,410**

Arts & Crafts library table, oak, the oval top overhanging tapering brackets & rounded aprons in the front & back, gently canted legs joined by the tapering side boards pierced w/two tapering pierced openings, an inset medial shelf, original finish, branded mark of Charles Limbert Furniture Company, Model No. 146, 30 x 45", 29" h. **$2,760**

> Antiques can be gently cleaned without removing patina, but the method depends on the material being cleaned. Wood, metal, jewelry, ceramics, glass, and silver each have special needs. Before doing any cleaning, consult a dealer or expert. If in doubt, don't clean at all.

Arts & Crafts library table, oak w/original dark finish, the oval top raised on four heavy square legs joined by two open shelves, the lower one w/two compartments & flanked by slatted sides, lightly over-coated finish w/some wear, unsigned, Michigan Chair Company, early 20th c., 27 1/2 x 44", 28 1/2" h. **$720**

TABLES

Chippendale tea table, carved mahogany, the round tilt-top w/a scallop-carved edge raised on an urn-form turned & reeded column resting on a tripod base w/cabriole legs ending in claw-and-ball feet, England, 18th c., 33 1/2" d., 28 1/2" h. **$1,998**

Classical parlor center table, mahogany & mahogany veneer, the large rounded & faceted black & gold marble top above a deep conforming ogee apron raised on a heavy paneled urn-form pedestal atop a cross-form base raised on heavy C-scroll feet on casters, New York City, ca. 1835, 40" w., 31 1/2" h. **$7,475**

Classical parlor center table, mahogany & mahogany veneer, the square white marble top w/ serpentine sides above a conforming apron, raised on a square tapering paneled pedestal resting on a cross-form platform w/ scrolled block feet on casters, ca. 1830, some veneer damage, 31" w., 29" h. **$633**

Classical game table, mahogany & mahogany veneer, the rectangular fold-over top w/rounded corners raised on a heavy turned & acanthus leaf-carved pedestal supported by four arched, molded & outswept legs ending in brass paws on casters, Boston, in the manner of Timothy Hunt, ca. 1825, 17 7/8 x 36", 28" h. **$4,380**

Classical parlor center table, mahogany & mahogany veneer, the rectangular black & gold marble top w/serpentine molded edges above a deep conforming apron raised on four heavy S-scroll squared legs raised on casters & joined by a cross-form medial shelf, Boston, ca. 1830, 30 x 37", 30 1/4" h. **$2,990**

Classical pier table, gilt-stenciled mahogany & mahogany veneer, the rectangular white marble top above a deep coved apron decorated w/gilt-stenciled palmette corner designs & a central stencil of leafy scrolls, the front supported on heavy acanthus leaf-carved curved supports ending in large paw feet resting on round blocks flanking a tapering serpentine medial shelf backed by a large rectangular mirror, short ring-turned & gadrooned front legs w/small knob feet, attributed to Anthony Quervelle, Philadelphia, ca. 1820, 20 x 42", 38 1/2" h. **$54,000**

A pier table was designed to rest against a wall between two windows and typically had a narrow mirror, or pier glass, above it.

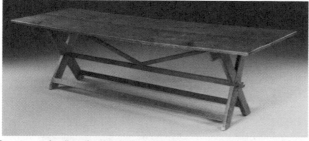

Country-style "sawbuck" table, pine, the very long rectangular top overhanging heavy X-form end legs joined by angled braces & long slender stretchers, American, late 18th - early 19th c., 34 x 113", 29" h. **$6,573**

Country-style kitchen table, cypress, the wide rectangular top overhanging an apron fitted w/a long drawer w/a carved wood pull, raised on square legs beveled at the base & joined by an H-stretcher, natural weathered finish, made in Louisiana, mid-19th c., 49 x 64", 31" h. **$14,950**

Classical work table, cherry, the rectangular two-board top overhanging a case w/a pair of beaded drawers w/turned wood knobs over a long drawer w/turned knobs, all flanked by half-round columns w/ring-turning & pineapple & spiral segements, a serpentine front apron, a large carved oval starburst on each of the sides, on ring- and spiral-twist turned legs ending in knob & peg feet, alligatored finish, knobs old replacements, attributed to Bopes Corner, Fairfield County, Ohio, early 19th c., 20 1/4 x 25 1/2", 29 1/2" h. **$5,750**

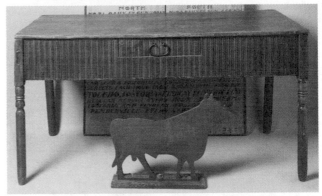

Country-style kitchen table, pine, the long rectangular one-board toop w/a border of diamond inlays above a deep reeded apron mortised through the turned round legs, a small single apron drawer w/a wrought-iron bail handle, old finish, some edge damage, a leg needing repair, 19th c., 26 3/4 x 57 1/2", 30 1/2" h. **$1,265**

Country-style dining table, curly maple, rectangular top flanked by wide hinged D-form drop leaves, the apron fitted w/a drawer at one end, raised on slender ring-turned tapering legs ending in ball & peg feet, good color, minor wear, 20 1/2 x 40" plus 14" w. leaves, 29" h. **$920**

Chippendale Pembroke table, mahogany, a boldly grained wide rectangular top flanked by two narrow hinged drop leaves above an apron w/an end drawer w/a butterfly brass, square legs w/inside chamfered corners joined by shaped flat cross-stretchers, old finish, original brass, Connecticut River Valley, ca. 1780, 34 3/4 x 35", 27" h. (top slightly warped) **$2,875**

Country-style tavern table, walnut, the wide rectangular two-board top w/original cleats & scrubbed surface widely overhanging the deep apron fitted w/a short & long drawer each w/a brass knob, one w/escutcheon plate & lock, square tapering molded legs, mortise & tenon construction w/pegs, some repairs including drawer runners, Pennsylvania, 18th c., 36 x 60 1/2", 28" h. **$1,150**

Chippendale tea table, walnut, wide round dished top tilting above a birdcage platform on a vase- and ring-turned pedestal continuing to the tripod base w/cabriole legs w/paneled knees & ending in pad feet on platforms, old refinish, Pennsylvania, ca. 1780, 35 1/2" d., 28 1/2" h. (minor imperfections) **$2,300**

TABLES

Federal card table, mahogany & mahogany veneer, the half-round hinged top w/projecting ovolu corners above a conforming top w/serpentine sides, bowed front apron & ovolu corners above reeded round corners, raised on tall slender tapering ring-turned & reeded legs on peg feet, some top wear, late 18th - early 19th c., 17 1/2 x 37", 30 1/2" h. .. **$1,093**

Federal country-style game table, painted & decorated walnut, the rectangular fold- over top w/serpentine edges above a conforming top overhanging an apron w/a single long drawer w/ two bail pulls, raised on slender square tapering legs, good wood graining in red & yellow, top w/ original green paint imitating felt or leather w/black banding, one swing-out support leg, replaced brasses, minor paint wear, early 19th c., 17 1/2 x 36", 29" h. **$1,725**

Federal country-style side table, curly male, narrow rectangular top flanked by narrow drop leaves, on square tapering legs, good figure & old mellow finish, top reset, age crack in leg, pieced repair in apron, missing one leaf slide, early 19th c., 13 x 24 1/4", 26 3/4" h. **$1,610**

Federal country-style dining table, curly maple, the rectangular top w/a single wide drop leaf on one side, flat apron & slender square tapering legs, good color, screw replaced, early 19th c., closed 13 1/2 x 42", 28 1/2" h. .. **$1,265**

Federal country-style game table, painted & decorated wood, the rectangular fold- over top w/ rounded front corners above an apron w/a single long drawer w/ round brass pulls & gold striping to simulate inlay, on swelled ring-turned slender legs, original grain painting in putty & vinegar painting in shades of brown & gold, original surface, norther New England, 1815- 25, imperfections, 17 3/4 x 36", 29" h. **$2,938**

Federal dining table, mahogany, the rectangular top flanked by wide half-round hinged drop leaves, the deep apron raised on ring-, knob- and spiral-turned legs w/knob feet on casters, a fifth swing- out support leg, ca. 1820s, 44 x 64 1/2" open, 29 1/2" h. **$805**

Federal dining table, mahogany, a rectangular top flanked by two wide half-round & slightly scalloped drop leaves above the apron, raised on four acanthus leaf- carved legs raised on casters, New York City, ca. 1825, 25 x 39 1/2" closed, 29 1/2" h. **$2,300**

Federal game table, cherry & inset burl panels, the half-round hinged top above a conforming base w/inset panels around the apron, on tall slender square tapering legs, one swings out for top support, good color, dark stain on underside, minor age splits, early 19th c., 17 1/4 x 35 1/2" closed, 28" h. **$1,208**

Federal dining table, mahogany, two-part construction, each D-form half w/a hinged rectangular drop leaf supported by a swing-out leg, raised on square tapering legs w/banded inlay at the ankles, ca. 1815-1825, open 80 1/2" l., 29" h. **$2,300**

Federal Pembroke table, inlaid mahogany, the rectangular top flanked by hinged drop leaves w/cut-corners above an apron w/ a single drawer w/an oval brass pull, square tapering legs w/ankle banding, some restorations, ca. 1800, 20 1/4 x 30 1/4", 29" h. **$1,800**

Federal Pembroke table, mahogany, the rectangular top flanked by D-form hinged drop leaves above an apron w/a single end drawer, raised on turned & reeded slender legs ending in tiny brass ball feet, New York City, 1780-1810, 24 x 34", 28 1/2" h. **$2,032**

Federal Pembroke table, mahogany, the rectangular top flanked by wide D-form notched drop leaves above an apron w/a single drawer at one end, raised on ring- and knob-turned legs raised on casters, New York City, ca 1825, 23 x 36", 29" h. **$2,185**

Federal Pembroke table, mahogany, the rectangular top flanked by two D-form hinged drop leaves above a narrow apron w/a small brass pull, raised on ring-turned reeded tapering legs ending in brass-cuffed cannon ball feet, attributed to Michale Allison, New York City, ca. 1810, 21 x 36", 29" h. **$2,115**

Technically, there are no antique coffee tables, as they weren't in use until the 1920s, and thus aren't 100 years old, the official definition of antique.

Federal game table, inlaid mahogany & bird's-eye maple, the rectangular fold-over top w/serpentine reeded edges & projecting from corners above a conforming apron, the front centered by an inlaid rectangular panel of bird's-eye maple, raised on tall slender reeded legs ending in swelled peg feet, Massachusetts, 1800-10, 16 3/4 x 35 1/2", 29 1/4" h. **$4,200**

Federal Pembroke table, inlaid mahogany, the rectangular top flanked by D-form hinged drop leaves above an apron w/one working & one faux drawer above a banded lower edge w/ contrasting inlaid stringing, raised on faux bamboo-turned legs w/ebonized turnings ending in casters, New England, ca. 1820, minor imperfections, 21 x 34", 28 3/4" h. **$588**

Hutch (or chair) table, grain-painted poplar, the wide rectangular top tilting above a seat opening to a storage compartment, graining on the base, rosehead nails, late 18th - early 19th c., 29 x 47 1/2", 30" h. **$1,150**

TABLES

Hutch (or chair) table, pine, the long four- board rectangular top w/rounded corners tilting above bootjack ends flanking a long seat above a serpentine apron, one side w/a peg hold, iron bail handles on each ends, wear, late 19th c., 42 x 88", open 29" h. **$4,225**

Mission-style (Arts & Crafts movement) side table, oak, the round top resting on flat cross braces & raised on tall slender square legs joined by cross stretchers fitted w/a small round shelf, Model No. 573, red & yellow decal mark of L. & J.G. Stickley, ca. 1912, 17 7/8" d., 27" h. **$1,554**

Mission-style (Arts & Crafts movement) dining chairs, oak, the flat crestrail above a single wide slat above the recovered spring seat, square legs joined by flat box stretchers, original finish, Lifetime Furniture Model No. 116, five side chairs & one armchair, 38" h., the set **$1,440**

Queen Anne country-style tea table, maple, the round top overhanging a deep apron w/a valanced skirt raised on four simple cabriole legs ending in pad feet, probably Massachusetts, ca. 1740-60, refinished, 25 3/4 x 32 1/4", 26 1/4" h. **$21,150**

Mission-style (Arts & Crafts movement) dining table, oak, expansion-type, the round divided top raised on four heavy square inset legs around a square split leg all joined by flat stretchers, original finish on base, top refinished, metal tag of Stickley Bros., Model No. 2404, w/two replaced leaves, closed 54" d., 29" h. **$1,920**

> Because wood shrinks across the grain over time, antique round tables aren't perfectly round. This can be a good test of whether an "antique" table is genuinely old.

Mission-style (Arts & Crafts movement) library table, oak, the rectangular top overhanging an apron w/a single long drawer w/a pair of original copper bail pulls, four square legs joined by a through-tenon medial shelf, refinished, unsigned Stickley Brothers, 26 x 40", 30" h. **$900**

Mission-style (Arts & Crafts movement) parlor table, oak, the fixed round top above a narrow apron & raised on four heavy square legs joined by through-tenon X-stretchers, worn original finish, unsigned L. & J. G. Stickley Model No. 544, some separation, early 20th c., 48" d., 29" h. **$1,080**

Queen Anne-Style dressing table, burl & curly maple, the rectangular top w/molded edges overhanging a case w/a long slender drawer over a pair of deeper drawers flanking a shallow center drawer all w/brass butterfly pulls, deeply scalloped apron w/drops, simple cabriole legs ending in pad feet, old finish, early 20th c., 17 x 30", 30" h. **$1,725**

Mission-style (Arts & Crafts movement) side table, oak, the wide rectangular top supported on bracket rails above pairs of flat supports & a lower stretcher supported by double key & tenon construction, on a shoefoot base, recoated original finish on base, top refinished, L. & J.G. Stickley Model No. 593, 29 x 48", 29" h. **$1,800**

Wardrobes & Armoires

Armoire, Spanish Colonial, fruitwood, the arched deep cornice flattened in the center, above a pair of tall two-panel doors, each panel centered by a raised diamond molding, flat base on shaped plank feet, 19th c., 16 x 47", 69 1/2" h. **$2,350**

Kas, (American term for Netherlands kast or wardrobe), ebonized & carved oak & rosewood, the rectangular top w/a deep widely flaring crest over a wide frieze band carved w/putti & scrolling leafy vines above a pair of tall cushion-paneled doors flanked by foliate-carved stiles, interior shelves & later drawers, heavy squatty bun feet, Holland, 17th c., 24 x 66", 88 1/2" h. **$2,233**

Wardrobe, Victorian Eastlake country-style, walnut, the rectangular top w/a flaring stepped cornice above frieze band carved w/roundels & inclsed leafy bands above a pair of tall paneled doors centered by a large rosette & incised leafy scrolls & blossoms, a pair of paneled drawers w/brass pulls at the bottom, flat molded base w/cutout apron & bracket feet, refinished, ca. 1885, 18 x 48", 7' 2" h. **$2,400**

Armoire, Louis XV-Style Provincial type, fruitwood, the rectangular top w/beveled front corners on the coved cornice above a paneled frieze band centered by a star-inlaid roundel over a pair of tall three-paneled doors w/long pierced brass latches, three-panel sides, serpentine carved apron on short scrolled legs w/upturned toes, France, late 19th c., 24 1/2 x 56", 7' 1" h. **$2,185**

Whatnots & Etageres

Etagere, Art Nouveau style, carved mahogany & marquetry, a high arched back crest w/a marquetry floral band above a top shelf flanked by curved sides above an ornately pierce-carved floral apron curving around the sides of the case & tapering to form a center stile, a large recessed compartment w/original pleated fabric above a lower case composed of a pair of tall tapering cupboard doors w/whiplash marquetry leaves & flowers & opening to a shelf, a flaring & scroll- carved base, designed & signed by Louis Majorelle, ca. 1900, France, 15 x 28 1/2", 5' 5" h. **$31,070**

Etagere, Art Nouveau style, mahogany, the tall back composed of a large oblong beveled mirror in a narrow frame w/a carved crest above a tall vertical rectangular lower mirror, all supported on an arrangement of two curved long front legs & two shorter straight rear legs w/various sized oblong open shelves down the front, ca. 1910 .... **$431**

Etagere, Regency Style, mahogany, an arrangement of four open shelves on graduated baluster-turned supports above a bottom shelf over a narrow drawer w/two round brass pulls, on turned peg feet on casters, England, last quarter 19th c., 17 7/8 x 22", 5' 1 3/4" h. **$2,070**

→

Etagere, Chippendale Revival style, carved mahogany, the scrolled pediment above a trelliswork half dome fronted by a pierced cartouche, the mirrored back divided by a shelf & over a pair of relief- carved doors, each side w/a shelf surmounted by finials, a glazed center door & two open compartments, on a base w/scroll-carved serpentine apron raised on short cabriole legs w/paw feet, in the manner of Edward and Roberts, London, England, ca. 1900, 13 x 51", 5' 10" h. **$5,463**

Etagere, Classical style, mahogany, a rectangular base cabinet w/ two cockbeaded drawers above bracket feet on casters, the top supporting four open shelves joined by graduated baluster-turned supports, Boston, ca. 1830, 18 x 23", 5' 2" h. .. **$1,725**

Victorians were fond of etageres because they could use them to display their large collections of knickknacks.

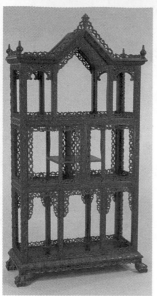

Etagere, Oriental, carved rosewood, the peaked top decorated w/an ornate scroll- carved crestrail above the molded cornice w/ turned corner finials & edged along the bottom w/further pierce-carved borders, supported on four slender carved supports to the top mirror-backed open shelves w/a pierce-carved gallery above five slender supports all framed by narrow pierced borders & centered by a small open shelf & backed by another mirror, all on four additional carved supports w/pierced upper borders atop the bottom shelf backed by a mirror, the flaring carved apron w/a low pierced gallery & base band, raised on carved paw feet, East Asia, early 20th c., 17 x 39", 5' 10 1/2" h. **$1,150**

Etagere, Victorian Aesthetic Movement style, cherry, corner-style, the tall case w/a rectangular top w/an arched serpentine three-quarters gallery w/short spindled front galleries above an open arrangement of small & larger shelves, a small mirror-backed door above a rectangular glazed door, all above another shelf w/a long rectangular glazed door beside an arched open shelf over a higher asymmetrical arrangement of three small drawers & staggered small shelves, slender knob-turned spindles throughout, flat base, American, ca. 1875-85 .... **$1,763**

Etagere, Victorian Rococo style, carved & pierced rosewood, two-part construction: the tall upper section w/a high arched & ornately pierce-carved crest decorated w/grapevines centering a large magnolia blossom above the tall arched central mirror flanked by three half-round graduated shelves each w/ornate scroll-carved brackets; the lower section w/a long white marble top w/serpentine sides & small rounded projections above a conforming case w/serpentine scroll-carved drawer over a mirrored cupboard door flanked by concave apron panels over an open shelf above the plinth base, each side shelf supported by baluster- or columnar-turned supports & backed by a mirror, the serpentine apron w/a scroll-carved cluster in the center panel, attributed to John H. Belter, New York City, ca. 1855, 16 1/2 x 59", 8' 2" h. **$52,900**

Shop owners are in a better position to offer a price reduction on a particular item because they have purchased the antique, prepared it for sale and priced it. Antique mall owners and managers, because they don't usually own the merchandise, cannot ordinarily give discounts without approval of the seller.

Whatnot, Victorian country style, walnut, two narrow rectangular shaped & graduated open shelves joined by pairs of baluster-turned spindles above a rectangular compartment w/a fall front opening to a small writing surface & interior fitted w/small drawers & pigeonholes, raised on two larger matching open shelves supported on matching spindles & turned feet, ca. 1870-80 .... **$250-400**

Etagere, Victorian Rococo style, rosewood- grained hardwood, the tall superstructure w/a high arched & pierce-carved crest w/an acanthus leaf cartouche over a tall arched mirror flanked on each side by four graduated quarter-round open shelves w/S-scroll supports & pierce- carved back brackets, the mirror above a molded rectangular panel flanked by scroll brackets on a half-round marble- topped base w/ serpentine molded edges above a conforming apron w/a central drawer & trimmed w/carved scrolls & raised on four cabriole legs ending in scroll feet, ca. 1850s, 52" w., 7' 6" h. ... **$3,450**

Etagere, Victorian Rococo style, walnut, the upper section composed of three graduated & shaped open shelves supported by cut-out & molded serpentine brackets, each shelf w/a pierced back crest & gallery, the lower cabinet w/an oblong top above a conforming case w/a pair of cabinet doors w/pierced fretwork panels, serpentine apron above knob-turned feet, ca. 1850-60, 16 x 35", 6' 1" h. **$690**

Etagere, Victorian Rococo substyle, carved rosewood, the tall superstructure w/a wide arched scroll-carved & pierced crest above a half-round narrow serpentine top shelf raised on slender S-scroll carved front supports & flanked by S-scroll carved side flanking a mirrored back all above a matching larger lower shelf & mirrored back resting on the half-round serpentine-edged sienna marble top above a conforming cabinet base w/a serpentine-fronted scroll-carved top drawer above a conforming wide door centered by an oval panel, flanked on each side by two open quarter-round shelves w/scroll-carved brackets, the deep conforming apron w/ ornate scroll carving, ca. 1850-60, 20 3/4 x 49 1/2", 73 1/2" h. **$8,050**

Whatnot, William IV, mahogany, the rectangular top w/a low three-quarters gallery raised on slender ring-turned supports over three more open shelves w/matching turned supports, raised on trumpet- turned feet, England, second quarter 19th c., 16 1/4 x 23 1/2", 6' 10" h. **$1,955**

←

Etageres, Chinese Chippendale-Style, carved mahogany, in the form of tall pagodas, a top cupola shelf over four graduated open shelves each w/ a full pierced gallery, the upright w/blind fret carving, raised on cabriole legs ending in paw feet, late 19th - early 20th c., 20 1/2" sq., 70" h., pr. **$4,140**

←

GARDEN FOUNTAINS & ORNAMENTS

Ornamental garden or yard fountains, urns and figures often enhanced the formal plantings on spacious lawns of mansion-sized dwellings during the late 19th and early 20th century. While fountains were usually reserved for the lawns of estates, even modest homes often had a latticework arbor or cast-iron urn in the yard. Today garden enthusiasts look for these ornamental pieces to lend the aura of elegance to their landscaping.

Models of Great Danes, cast iron, each seated on a rectangular plinth, brown patina, 19th c., 43" h., pr. **$1,150**

Models of lions, bronze, each seated roaring male lion w/head turned, fine verdigris patina, 19th c., 18 x 38", 28" h., pr. **$4,140**

Sundial, the dark patinated metal dial raised atop a weathered octagonal limestone pedestal base, England, second quarter 19th c., base 20" w., overall 4' 6 1/4" h. **$5,060**

Fountain, cast iron, Victorian-style, the top w/a figure of a standing putto holding a shell that issues the water, seated atop a wide shallow fluted basin raised on a fluted pedestal flanked by three figural dolphins on a trilobed fluted platform base, painted white, 26" d., 47" h. **$748**

Models of lions, cast iron, after Antonio Canova from the Tomb of the Arch-Duchess Maria Christina in Vienna, each recumbent animal on a rectangular base, cast in two sections, remnants of old ochre paint, New York, New York, mid- 19th c., 16 x 39", 19" h., pr. **$8,338**

Urns, cast iron, a wide shallow rounded & gadrooned bowl w/a flaring annulated & egg-and-dart rim, raised on a waisted & fluted pedestal on a square stepped base, old white paint, England, 19th c., 38 1/2" d., 39" h., pr. (ILLUS. of one) **$1,495**

GLASS MARKET REPORT

Reyne Haines, co-owner of the Web site Just Glass (www.justglass.com), said "the lower end of the market has been hit the most, the middle has been hit or miss, and the top end has done exceptionally well." She added that "now is the time to buy, and that those who don't buy now will regret it when the recession ends." She has found that good buys typically appreciate 10 to 15 percent in 12 to 18 months.

Depression glass prices have been down 20 percent online, but have been doing well at shows. Victorian glass is slower because it's perceived as "Grandma's glass," which is too old for the younger generation who want to buy what is nostalgic for them. These 20- to 40-year-olds like Mid-century Modern, either because they remember it themselves or they remember their parents having it. Tiffany and Steuben also continue to be strong.

Several factors affect trends in glass. One is the publicity gained from a major museum display or book being released, or article written, such as the *Robb Report* in the *Wall Street Journal*, or a celebrity collecting a certain category.

Another factor is geography. Haines gave the illustration of her hometown of Houston, Texas. The city is too new to have accumulated a lot of antique glass. Stalwart makers like Tiffany, however, can be readily found on the East coast. Art Deco is prevalent in Florida, especially Miami, as the city architecture was heavily influenced by Art Deco. Modernism is popular in California.

As in many areas of antiques and collectibles, fakes and reproductions are a huge problem. While many of the lower-end fakes are easy to spot, some of the higher-end items are getting better, as the counterfeiters are willing to spend more time in their craft because profit margin is much higher. "While a lot of fakes are coming from China, a lot is still being made in our own back yard," Haines said.

Haines warns novices to "work with someone who is an expert. Just as you would have a mechanic look at a car before you buy it, you would be wise to have a trained eye examine a piece of glass before investing in it." However, there are some simple things you can do to weed out the most obvious flaws, including running your fingers lightly over the surface to check for roughness or chips, holding it up to a light to check for cracks, and examining it with a black light to find glass that has been cut down, filed down or filled in. Black lights are relatively inexpensive and are a good investment. She added that buyers should be wary of signatures, as they are the easiest thing to fake. "Don't buy the signature. Buy for the glass itself. The signature should be the last thing you consider."

Auction Houses
Green Valley Auctions (www.greenvalleyauctions.com)
Cincinnati Art Galleries (www.cincinnatiartgalleries.com)
Early (www.earlyauctionco.com)
Heckler (www.hecklerauction.com)
John Moran (www.johnmoran.com)
James Julia (www.jamesdjulia.net)
Seeck Auction Company (www.seeckauction.com/results.htm)
Treadway Toomey Gallery (www.treadwaygallery.com)

GLASS

Agata

Agata was patented by Joseph Locke of the New England Glass Company in 1887. The application of mineral stain left a mottled effect on the surface of the article. It was applied chiefly to the Wild Rose (Peach Blow) line but sometimes was applied as a border on a pale opaque green. In production for a short time, it is scarce. Items listed below are of the Wild Rose line unless otherwise noted.

Creamer, Green Opaque, wide tapering ovoid body w/pinched spout, applied handle, 4 1/2" h. **$1,000-1,250**

Creamer, squatty bulbous body w/wide cylindrical short neck, applied handle, 3 3/4" h. **$1,750-2,200**

Pitcher, 7" h., bulbous ovoid body tapering to a squared slightly flaring neck, applied handle, fine overall oil spotting **$6,325**

Bowl, 5 1/4" d., 2 1/2" h., deep gently flaring sides w/a ten-ruffle rim, good color & spotting ... **$546**

Celery vase, bulbous base tapering slightly w/a gently flaring rim, green opaque ground decorated w/lacy gold trim on the rim & shoulder, 6 7/8" h. $985

Cruet w/original stopper, green opaque, spherical body tapering to a slender neck w/tricorner rim, applied green handle & facet-cut green stopper **$1,650**

Finger bowls & underplates, deep round upright ruffled bowls & matching ruffled underplates, fine mottling, set of 6 .... **$7,920**

Lemonade glass, tall slightly tapering form w/small applied pink loop handle near the base **$688**

Pitcher, 7" h., bulbous ovoid body tapering to a short squared neck, applied reeded pink handle, uniform mottling **$4,500**

Spooner, deeply ruffled lavender rim, 4 1/2" h **$1,800-2,400**

Toothpick holder, green opaque, bulbous body tapering gently to a slightly flared rim **$990**

Toothpick holder, cylindrical w/square rim, good mottling **$1,100**

Toothpick holder, ovoid body tapering to a short cylindrical neck................................. **$1,760**

Toothpick holder, cylindrical w/ a tricorner incurved rim, fine mottling, 2" h. $750

Toothpick holder, green opaque, squatty ovoid body tapering to a widely flaring rim, decorated around the rim w/a band of blue mottled stain w/a gold border band, 2 1/4" h. **$950**

Toothpick holder, squatty ovoid base tapering to a flaring rim, green opaque ground decorated w/lacy gold trim on the rim & shoulder **$1,150**

Tumbler, cylindrical, deep raspberry shading to creamy pink, decorated w/oily mottling & blue spotting, 2 1/2" d., 3 7/8" h. $750

Tumbler, nicely mottled, sticker of Maude B. Feld, 3 3/4" h. $750

Tumbler, cylindrical, green opaque, strong rim mottling, sticker of Maude B. Feld, 3 3/4" h. **$675**

Tumbler, cylindrical, scattered blue 'oil spots' on a finely mottled surface, 3 3/4" h. $750

Vase, 6 1/4" h., green opaque, fourteen-rib gently tapering ovoid body w/flared rim, New England Glass Co. $650

Vase, 8 1/4" h., bottle-form, ovoid body tapering to a tall slender 'stick' neck, good mottling on the lower half............................ **$798**

Vase, 6 1/4" h., Green Opaque, ovoid body tapering to a flaring rim, minor wear **$575**

Vase, 4 5/8" h., ovoid body w/four deeply dimpled sides tapering to an upright flaring crimped four-point rim, New England ...**$1,380**

Vase, 8" h., bottle-form, bulbous ovoid body tapering to a tall slender 'stick' neck, excellent gold & blue spotting, New England **$1,955**

Water set: tankard pitcher & six tumblers; the tall pitcher w/applied handle, fine coloring, tumblers 3 3/4" h., pitcher 8 3/4" h., the set **$9,150**

Amberina

Amberina was developed in the late 1880s by the New England Glass Company and a pressed version was made by Hobbs, Brockunier & Company (under license from the former). A similar ware, called Rose Amber, was made by the Mt. Washington Glass Works. Amberina-Rose Amber shades from amber to deep red or fuchsia and cut and plated (lined with creamy white) examples were also made. The Libbey Glass Company briefly revived blown Amberina, using modern shapes, in 1917.

Bowl, 4 1/2" d., 3 1/2" h., Plate Amberina, deep squatty round tapering sides below the flaring flat rim **$4,600**

Bowl, 7 3/4" d., 2 1/2" h., wide shallow round form, ridged bottom resembling a snowflake surrounded by diamond quilted designs, fuchsia rim shaded to amber, attributed to the New England Glass Co. **$316**

Creamer, rounded squatty base w/sharply tapering cylindrical sides to a tricorner rim, Inverted Thumbprint patt., applied amber handle, 4 1/2" h. **$460**

Bowl, 7 1/2" d., Plated Amberina, low rolled sides w/five crimps **$7,188**

Bowl, 10 1/2" l., Reverse Amberina, Diamond Quilted patt. in a rounded heart-form bowl w/a rolled & tightly crimped rim, a curved, looped clear applied thorn handle at one side, late 19th c. **$550**

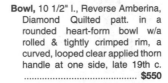

Bowl, 7 3/4" d., Plated Amberina, low rounded form w/five-lobed sides **$8,050**

Butter dish, cov., wide flat-topped flaring cylindrical top w/an applied curl finial, Inverted Thumbprint patt., on a deeply ruffled fuschia base, 7 1/2" d., 5" h. **$575**

Cruet w/original stopper, spherical body tapering to short pedestal base & to a slender cylindrical neck w/a high, arched spout, Inverted Thumbprint patt., blue floral enamel decoration, applied angled amber handle & amber facet-cut stopper, 7 3/4" h. . **$688**

Cruet w/original stopper, Plated Amberina, bulbous body tapering to a cylindrical neck w/tricorner rim, applied amber handle, facet-cut amber stopper, 6 3/4" h. **$3,968**

Cruet w/original stopper, Plated Amberina, bulbous body tapering to a cylindrical neck w/tricorner rim, applied amber handle, facet-cut amber stopper, 7 1/4" h. **$6,900**

AMBERINA

Goblets, a round foot & slender stem w/a swelled top supporting a large bulbous knop below the deep rounded bowl w/a flat rim, deep red to amber bowl, w/a typed note indicating they may have come from the New England Glass Co., 8 1/2" h., pr. **$518**

Ice cream set: large shallow oblong bowl in a fancy footed silver plate stand & twelve 5 3/4" w. square side dishes; pressed Daisy & Button patt., very minor roughage to large bowl & chip on one side dish, large bowl 9 1/4 x 17" l., the set **$2,185**

Pitcher, 9 1/2" h., tankard-type, Diamond Quilted patt., tapering cylindrical body w/a pinched spout & applied amber handle, New England Glass Co. **$750- 1,000**

Punch set: cov. punch bowl & eight punch cups; the large footed bowl w/a rounded base & wide cylindrical sides, fitted w/a wide domed cover w/a tall panel-cut pointed finial, the sides enameled w/a large bouquet of large, colorful flowers, matching cylindrical cups w/applied amber handles & white-enameled blossoms, one enameled flower petal w/a chip, roughness at edge of ladle opening in cover, some gilt wear, late 19th c., bowl 8" d., 14" h., the set **$805**

Vase, pressed upright square form, Stork patt., designed by Joseph Locke, New England Glass Co. **$2,000-2,800**

Punch cup, Plated Amberina, rounded tapering cup w/applied amber handle, 2 1/2" h. . **$2,875**

Vase, 5" h., jack-in-the-pulpit type, wide squatty flat-bottomed body w/optic ribbing below the widely flaring upturned neck, circular trademark on base for Libbey Amberina (ILLUS. bottom row, center)............................. **$690**

Vase, 5 1/2" h., egg-shaped w/tricorner rim, on three applied amber reeded feet, Diamond Quilted patt., ground pontil **$578**

Vase, 6 5/8" h., lily-form shape, delicate optic ribbing, swirled fuchsia rim shading to amber, small scratch inside body .. **$230**

Vase, 10" h., a squatty compressed base below the tall cylindrical sides w/a widely flaring crimped & ruffled rim, Optic Swirl patt. **$300**

←

Vase, 6" h., lily-form w/tricorner rim, New England Glass Co. ... **$532**

Vase, 10 3/4" h., lily-form, ruffled rim, ground pontil & signed by Libbey, ca. 1917 .... **$575**

Vase, 12 1/2" h., flora-form, a round foot below a hollow stem knop supporting the tall slender optic ribbed body w/a widely flaring deeply ruffled rim, signed by Libbey ca. 1917 ... **$1,000-2,400**

Vase, 8" h., lily-form, tall slender body w/rolled flaring rim, teardrop enclosed in lower stem, round foot, unmarked Libbey, ca. 1917 .... **$275**

AMBERINA

Water set: 8 3/4" h. pitcher & five cylindrical 4 1/2" h. tumblers; the pitcher w/an ovoid body & cylindrical neck, ornate enameled w/designs of flowers, butterflies & insects, applied reeded amber handle, each tumbler w/enameled insect decoration, some wear to gold trim, the set **$600**

The Libbey glass company of Toledo, Ohio, became known as the glass capital of the world in large part because in 1903, one of its employees, Michael Owen, invented a revolutionary glass making machine that dramatically increased production and profits. Libbey is still in business and has plants in multiple locations.

Animals

Americans evidently like to collect glass animals. For the past sixty years, American glass manufacturers have turned out a wide variety of animals to please the buying public. Some were produced for long periods and some were later reproduced by other companies, while others were made for only a short period of time and are rare. We have not included late productions in our listings and have attempted to date the productions where possible. Evelyn Zemel's book, *American Glass Animals A to Z*, will be helpful to the novice collector. Another helpful book is *Glass Animals of the Depression Era* by Lee Garmon and Dick Spencer Collector Books, 1993.

Boxer dog, lying, clear, American Glass Co., 4 3/4" h. (ILLUS. left)
.... **$55**

Donkey, clear, Heisey Glass Co., 5" l., 6 1/2" h. **$350**

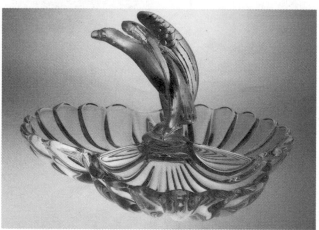

Eagle, three-part relish dish, clear, Cambridge Glass Co., 8" w. **$85**

Goldfish, vertical, clear, Fostoria Glass Co., 4" h. **$175**

Elephant, covered dish, black, Co-Operative Flint Glass, 7" h.
.... **$155**

Horse, Clydesdale, clear, Heisey Glass Co., 7" l. **$475**

Horse, rearing, satin clear, Fostoria Glass Co., 7 3/4" h. **$65**

Owl, book end, clear, Fostoria Glass Co., 7 1/2" h. **$170**

Mallard, wings down, clear, A. H. Heisey & Co., 4 1/2" h. (ILLUS. right with other Mallard) **$325**

Pheasant, tail up, Twilight, Tiffin Glass, No. 6042-1, 17" l. **$850**

Parlour Pup, Scottie, amber, Imperial Glass Co., 2 1/2" h. **$28**

Plug horse "Oscar," clear, A. H. Heisey & Co., clear, 1941-46, 4" l., 4" h. **$125**

Seal, large w/ball, clear, New Martinsville Glass Co., 7" h. **$58**

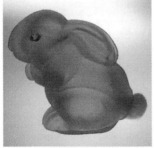

Rabbit cotton dispenser, ears back, Paden City Glass, hollow pink satin, painted eyes, 5" h. **$175**

Ringneck pheasant, clear, A.H. Heisey & Co., 1942-53, 11" l., 4 3/4" h. **$115**

Swordfish, clear, ribbed fin, Duncan & Miller Glass Co., 5" h. **$200**

Polar bear, clear, Fostoria Glass Co., 4 5/8" h. **$65**

Woodchuck, caramel slag, Imperial Glass Co., 4 1/2" h. **$52**

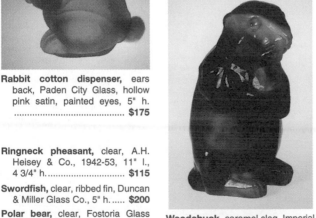

Swan, Pall Mall patt., solid back, clear, Duncan & Miller, 3" l. . **$58**

Appliquéd

Simply stated, this is an art glass form with applied decoration. Sometimes master glass craftsmen applied stems or branches to an art glass object and then added molded glass flowers or fruit specimens to these branches or stems. At other times a button of molten glass was daubed on the object and a tool pressed over it to form a print in the form of a raspberry, rosette or other shape. Always the work of a skilled glassmaker, applied decoration can be found on both cased (two-layer) and single layer glass. The English firm of Stevens and Williams was renowned for the appliquéd glass they produced.

Vase, 4 3/4" h., 3 3/4" d., spherical clear body tapering to a short flared mouth trimmed in gold, the sides enameled overall w/delicate blue & white flowers & butterflies w/gold trim, three rigaree bands down the sides continuing to form claw feet **$200-225**

Vases, 13" h., stick-type, shaded Rubina Verde cylinder w/ overshot decoration & an applied band of lime green icicling near the top & another band forming the base, ca. 1880s, pr. **$1,000-1,500**

Vase, 11 1/4" h., 7" d., bulbous tapering pale lavender body w/an applied blue pointed scalloped rim, bands of blue rigaree down the sides alternating w/applied inverted dolphins up the sides & forming feet, late 19th c. **$400-425**

Bowl, 6" d., 3 7/8" h., wide cylindrical form w/a swelled bottom, pale blue opaque w/an overshot background & applied amber rigaree around the rim & applied green leaves on purple stems w/ blue & red & white & red applied blossoms **$195**

Box, rounded base in yellowish opalescent fitted w/gilt brass scroll feet & hinged collar fittings w/a wide domed cover applied w/amethyst branches & green leaves w/a red flower & bud, 5 5/8" d., 4 1/4" h. **$450**

Ewer, baluster-form w/widely flaring crimped & ruffled rim, opaque white body w/applied amber rim, loop handle & three long leaves in green, amber & cranberry & an amber acorn under the handle, 3 1/4" d., 8" h. **$110**

Vase, 12 1/2" h., 6 1/2" d., tall waisted ovoid sapphire blue body w/clear appliqued spines down the sides & clear feet, ornate colored enamel ribbon decoration w/pink & white flowers, further crystal applied around rim **$265**

Vases, 9" h., a footring below a spreading base on the tall cylindrical optic ribbed body, applied clear rigaree around the rim & large clear salamander crawling up the side, late 19th c., pr. **$259**

Vase, 16" h., 5" d., tree-trunk form, a slender cylindrical rich orangish red body w/white opalescent thorns & applied w/slender vaseline branches & greenish leaves up the sides w/pink bell-like flowers on the sides & at the base, swirled greenish applied feet, gilt trim **$550**

Vase, 6 3/8" h., 5 1/8" d., sapphire blue bulbous body tapering to a short cylindrical neck, applied clear ruffled rim band & three pointed feet, decorated w/a gold bird in flight & colored flowers & leaves **$150**

Vase, 14 1/4" h., 5 1/4" d., squatty swelled squared base tapering to a tall cylindrical body in pink opalescent, applied w/vaseline opalescent large blossoms & leafy vine **$425**

Vase, 12 1/2" h., 6 1/2" d., ovoid dark blue body tapering to a flaring rim w/an applied clear band, applied down the sides w/three long spiny rigaree bands alternating w/ panels enameled in color w/wide ribbons & pink & white flowers, raised on applied pointed clear feet **$325-350**

Vase, 3 1/4" h., 3" d., miniature, cylindrical w/flaring crimped & pulled rim in shaded cased pink, clear applied leaves & feet applied in rows, late 19th c. **$115**

BACCARAT

Art Glass Baskets

Popular novelties in the late Victorian era, these ornate baskets of glass were usually hand-crafted of free-blown or mold-blown glass. They were made in a wide spectrum of colors and shapes. Pieces were highlighted with tall applied handles and often applied feet; however, fancier ones might also carry additional appliquéd trim.

Spatter, rounded body w/flaring crimped rim pulled into points, arched applied clear thorn handle, yellow & pink spatter, white lining, 6" d., 6" h. **$165-185**

Bluerina, round foot below the widely flaring, flattened Hobnail patt. rim w/two sides pulled up, tall applied clear twisted thorn handle, 9 1/2" h. **$633**

Spatter glass is made by adding chips of colored crushed glass to the surface of molten glass. The glass is rolled smooth, and sometimes a layer of clear glass is applied over it.

Baccarat

Baccarat glass has been made by Cristalleries de Baccarat, France, since 1765. The firm has produced various glassware of excellent quality as well as paperweights. Baccarat's Rose Tiente is often referred to as Baccarat's Amberina.

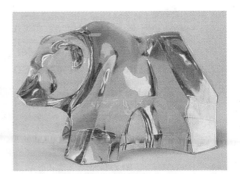

Ice pail, footed deep bell-form body w/incurved looped side handles, opaline & cobalt blue cut-overlay w/ an acid-etched Bacchic figures on the front & back, surrounded by scrolling foliage & anthemions, the rims & handles trimmed w/classical designs trimmed w/gold, ca. 1867, 10" h. **$10,200**

Model of a bear, colorless crystal, a stylized walking animal, signed on the bottom & side, 11" l. **$2,300**

Blown Three Mold

This type of glass was entirely or partially blown in a mold and was popular from about 1820 to 1840. The object was formed and the decoration impressed upon it by blowing the glass into a metal mold, usually of three—but sometimes more—sections hinged together. Mold-blown glass actually dates back to ancient times. Recent research reveals that certain geometric patterns were reproduced in the 1920s; some new pieces, usually sold through museum gift shops, are still available. Collectors are urged to read all recent information available. Reference numbers are from George L. and Helen McKearin's book, *American Glass*.

Pieces are clear unless otherwise noted.

Decanter w/no stopper, geometric, bulbous ovoid body w/large diamonds enclosing diamond point panels, tall cylindrical neck w/applied sloping collared mouth w/ring, large pontil scar, possibly Keene Marlboro Street Glassworks, Keene New Hampshire, 1820-30, medium yellowish green, some interior brownish residue, pt., GII-43 .... **$4,760**

Decanter w/no stopper, geometric, bulbous body tapering to a tall neck w/applied collared mouth, pontil scar, probably Parks, Edmunds & Parks glasshouse, Kent, Ohio, 1820-40, aqua, faint interior stain, 5 1/4" h., GII-6 .... **$4,200**

Decanter, cylindrical body w/ beveled edges, the lower body w/vertical ribs, the upper body w/crisscross diamond design, shoulders tapering to narrow neck w/flared rim, neck ground to accept a stopper, pontil scarred base, apple green, Keene, New Hampshire, ca. 1815-35, 7" h., GII-28 .... **$3,360**

Decanter w/no stopper, geometric, bulbous ovoid body w/a tapering neck & sheared mouth, pontil scar, Keene Marlboro Glassworks, Keene, New Hampshire, ca. 1820-40, brilliant yellowish olive, pt., GIII-16 .... **$840**

Decanter w/original blown stopper, geometric, bulbous sides w/a wide band of diamonds below swirled ribbing up the neck, swirled rib stopper, pontil scar, clear, tiny flake at edge of lip, 10 1/4" h., GIII-2, type 1 ..... **$202**

Model of a top hat, geometric, flared tooled rim, pontil scar, Boston & Sandwich Glass Co., ca. 1820-40, cobalt blue, 2" d., 2 5/8" h., GIII-25 .... **$1,344**

Bohemian

Numerous types of glass were made in the once-independent country of Bohemia and fine colored, cut and engraved glass was turned out. Flashed and other inexpensive wares also were made; many of these, including amber- and ruby- shaded glass, were exported to the United States during the 19th and 20th centuries. One favorite pattern in the late 19th and early 20th centuries was Deer & Castle. Another was Deer and Pine Tree.

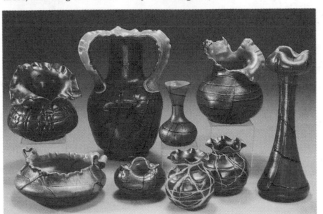

Bowl, 4 1/4" d., 2 3/4" h., squatty round shaped w/three-crimp rim, salmon pink iridescence decorated overall w/random aubergine threading, Rindskopf factory, ca. 1900 (ILLUS. bottom row, second from left)... **$173**

Chalice, blown moss green w/a widely flaring round, ringed foot & ringed knop stem below the tall cylindrical bowl applied w/ prunts around the bottom, the sides enameled in color w/the figure of a working man holding a small train under one arm & a raised torch in the other, framed w/a white scroll banner & green leafy branches, late 19th c., 9" h. **$180**

Bowl, 7" d., 3 1/4" h., wide squatty form w/incurved sides w/a ruffled rim, iridescent green decorated w/overall random violet threading, supported on a three- footed embossed gilt-metal frame, Pallme-Konig factory, ca. 1900 (ILLUS. bottom row, far right).................................... **$345**

The Pallme-Konig company of Czechoslovakia was formed by Ignaz Pallme-Konig in Austria in the late 1700s. Around 1900, the firm merged and became Palme-Konig and Habel. During the Art Nouveau period, the company was known for its iridized glass featuring glass trails that formed a network. Its glass is sometimes mistaken for Loetz glass.

Vase, 3 3/4" h., footed squatty bulbous body tapering to a sheared & rolled & ruffled wide collar, olive green randomly threaded w/burgundy bands, attributed to Pallme-Konig **$316**

Vase, 5" h., footed squatty bulbous body tapering to a wide crimped rim, swirled ruby & aqua body w/a wide band of pointed gold panels around the neck trimmed w/ white enamel, gilded applied loop shoulder handles, gold wear & minor scratches **$633**

Vase, 6 1/2" h., a wide waisted cylindrical form w/a widely flaring four-lobed rim, iridescent verre de soie ground applied around the sides w/amethyst vines dotted w/leaf pods, the base nestled into a bronzed metal dish flanked by nude kneeling children all set upon a thin round brown & white marble base, attributed to the Pallme-Konig firm, base 9" d. **$207**

Vase, 12 3/4" h., squatty bulbous base below the tall cylindrical sides w/a widely flaring folded rim pulled into four points, wine red decorated w/dark iridescent blue, green & gold pulled designs, attributed to the Rindskopf firm **$260**

Vase, 6" h., ringed pedestal base w/small urn-shaped vase, pink cased in white w/an overall pulled green Aventurine decoration, Rindskopf factory, ca. 1900 (ILLUS. top row, far left with other vases) **$173**

Be wary of any group that attempts to capitalize on the popularity of the *Antiques Roadshow* television program by using "Roadshow" in its name. Dishonest dealers may try to buy antiques at these events. Appraisers working at the real *Antiques Roadshow*, however, will not try to purchase items that people bring to the shows, as it is unethical for them to buy items they have appraised.

Bride's Baskets & Bowls

These berry or fruit bowls were popular late Victorian wedding gifts, hence the name. They were produced in a variety of quality art glasswares and sometimes were fitted in ornate silver plate holders.

Cased bowl, apricot shaded to white interior w/a fancy tri-ruffled & fluted rim, white exterior, fitted in a fancy silver plate frame marked by the Rockford Silver Plate Co., small size, bowl 5 1/2" d., overall 5 1/2" h. **$161**

Satin glass, deep round bowl w/ molded lobes around the lower half & a flaring, crimped & ruffled rim, shaded pink mother-of-pearl satin Herringbone patt. cased in yellow, the exterior h.p. w/large fern- like leaves & flowers, raised on an ornate silver plate stand w/ loops, leaf sprigs & floral swags above the domed round foot, stand marked by the Meriden Britannia Co., ca. 1880s, 11" d. **$1,840**

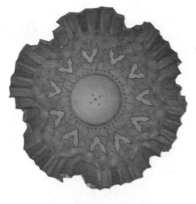

Cased bowl, apricot shaded to white satin interior, ruffled & crimped rim, enameled band of white spearpoints around the interior joined by delicate yellow enameled webbing, white exterior, 10" d., 3" h. **$225-250**

Cased bowl, deep blue satin interior w/flaring fluted sides pinched-in at one side & tightly crimped, enameled w/swags of small white blossoms w/ yellow leaves, small pink buds & green leaves, applied clear edging, white exterior enameled w/a yellow & white bug, 10 1/2" d., 4" h. **$275-300**

Cased bowl, turquoise blue interior & deep shaded pink exterior, wide cylindrical body w/a squared crimped & ruffled rim, fitted in a fancy silver plate frame w/figural cherries applied to the high arched handle, marked by Meriden, two leaves missing on frame, ca. 1890s, bowl 4" h., overall 10 1/2" h. **$345**

Bristol

A number of glasshouses operated in Bristol, England over the years and they produced a variety of wares. Today, however, the generic name Bristol refers to a type of semi-opaque glass, often accented with ornate enameling. Such wares were produced in England, Europe and America in the 19th and early-20th centuries.

Cracker jar, cov., cylindrical pale green body finely decorated w/a scene of a stork standing among cattails & water plants, silver plate rim, bail handle & cover w/ strawberry finial **$220**

Finger bowl, narrow footing under the deep rounded upright sides w/a flat rim, clambroth w/colored enamel floral & leaf sprigs around the sides, 19th c., 4 1/2" d., 3" h.
.... **$33**

Vases, 10 3/4" h., footed ovoid body tapering to a short, wide cylindrical neck, matte creamy ground h.p. w/a bust portrait of a young Victorian boy w/curly light brown hair & wearing a blue smock or a young Victorian girl w/long curly brown hair & wearing a pink smock, speckled gold trim, artist-signed, late 19th c., pr.
.... **$748**

Burmese

Burmese is a single-layer glass that shades from pink to pale yellow. It was patented by Frederick S. Shirley and made by the Mt. Washington Glass Co. A license to produce the glass in England was granted to Thomas Webb & Sons, which called its articles Queen's Burmese. Gundersen Burmese was made briefly about the middle of the 20th century, and the Pairpoint Company is making limited quantities at the present time.

Bowl, 3" h., three small yellow peg feet supporting the squatty bulbous body tapering to the widely flaring ruffled rim, satin finish, attributed to Thomas Webb & Sons, minor polishing on feet
.... **$230**

Bowl, 3 1/2" d., 2" h., miniature, waisted cylindrical sides enameled w/yellow & white mums on meandering leafy stems, satin ground, Mt. Washington
.... **$633**

Caster set: two shakers & a bottle fitted on a silver plate stand; the cylindrical ribbed shakers w/silver plate caps, the matching bottle w/the original facet-cut stopper, the stand w/a round flat base w/a lightly ruffled rim, a tall central wire handle w/a large hoop top fitted below w/three rings to hold the shakers & bottle, frame marked by Pairpoint, Mt. Washington, overall 7 1/2" h., the set **$1,093**

Bowl, 9 1/2" d., 2 3/4" h., footed wide shallow form w/an upright crimped rim, probably Mt. Washington
.... **$175-225**

Cracker jar w/brass rim, cover & bail handle, footed cylindrical form, unusual form, Thomas Webb & Son **$800-1,000**

Model of a pig, good detail, satin finish, 1 1/8" l. **$460**

Cracker jar w/original silver plate rim, cover & ornate bail handle, barrel- shaped, enameled w/a delicate band of leafy branches & pine cones, attributed to Thomas Webb, 6" h. **$1,020**

Cruet w/original stopper, squatty melon- ribbed body tapering to an arched spout, pointed ribbed hollow stopper & applied yellow handle, decorated w/delicate flower & leaf sprigs, ca. 1885 .... **$2,500-3,000**

Rose bowls are designed to hold fresh flower petals to release a perfume-like fragrance.

Rose bowl, eight-crimp rim, egg-shaped, raised on three applied yellow peg feet, glossy finished h.p. w/pinecones, rare **$650-750**

Pitcher, 7" h., mold-blown Hobnail patt., tapering cylindrical body w/applied yellow handle, satin finish **$2,500-3,000**

Toothpick holder, squatty bulbous base tapering to a wide squared neck, decorated w/pansies, satin finish **$650-850**

BURMESE

Vase, 3 3/4" h., miniature, a squatty bulbous base below the cylindrical sides below the flaring ruffled & crimped rim, satin finish, Thomas Webb & Sons **$403**

Vase, 6 1/4" h., slender baluster form w/a gently flared flat rim, enameled w/cascading slender branches supporting lavender blue flowers & green leaves, Thomas Webb **$1,035**

Vase, 7" h., double gourd-form w/ spherical bottom & tall stick neck, h.p. w/flying black birds, satin finish **$1,500-2,000**

Vase, 9 1/2" h., footed gently swelled cylindrical body w/a narrow shoulder tapering to the low cylindrical neck, h.p. ivy decoration, Queen's Burmese, signed **$1,000-1,500**

Vase, 11" h., chalice-form, ringed pedestal base below the tall flaring cylindrical body w/a ruffled rim, satin finish, Pairpoint Corp., ca. 1920s **$600-800**

Vase, 16" h., tall ovoid body tapering to a short cylindrical neck, upright gold loop shoulder handles, finely painted w/a detailed "Garden of Allah" scene w/Arabs, camels & pyramids, retouched where one handle attached to body .. **$7,188**

CAMBRIDGE

Cambridge

The Cambridge Glass Company was founded in Ohio in 1901. Numerous pieces are now sought, especially those designed by Arthur J. Bennett, including Crown Tuscan. Other productions included crystal animals, "Black Amethyst," "blanc opaque," and other types of colored glass. The firm was finally closed in 1954. It should not be confused with the New England Glass Co., Cambridge, Massachusetts.

NEAR CUT — TUSCAN — C

Caprice Pattern

Candleholders, pressed Alpine Caprice patt., No. 72, two-light, Moonlight Blue, 6" h., pr. **$225**

Bowl, 12 1/2" d., No. 61, crimped rim, footed, Caprice patt., Moonlight Blue (ILLUS. w/other Caprice pieces)... **$165**

Rose bowl, pressed Caprice patt., No. 236; Moonlight Blue, 6" d. **$145**

Crown Tuscan Line

Candy dish, cov., Sea Shell patt., shell-shaped, gold trim, 6" h. **$78**

A cigarette box, even if no longer used for its original purpose, can still make a beautiful table accent and hold various items such as candy.

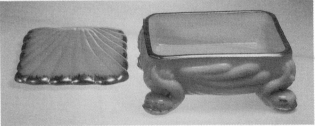

Candlestick, Statuesque Line, figural nude **$135**

Cigarette box, cov., rectangular Sea Shell shape w/dolphin feet, gold trim, 4 3/4" l., 3 3/4" h. **$82**

CAMBRIDGE

Etched Rose Point Pattern

Basket, squared upturned sides, footed, two-handled, Gold Encrusted, 6" w. **$55**

Cocktail, No. 3500, Crystal, 3 oz. (ILLUS. right with sherbet) ... **$40**

Compote, 5" h., No. 3500/148, Crystal **$65**

Miscellaneous Patterns

Baskets, applied crystal handle, No. 119, amber, 7" w. **$65**

Beverage set: footed ball pitcher & four footed half-round tumblers; deep amethyst, Crystal ball stopper on jug, jug 6 oz., the set **$150-200**

Candlestick, one-light, No. 627, etched Grape patt., green, 4" h. **$35**

Candle blocks, Cambridge Square patt., clear, 2" w., 2 1/2" h., pr. **$26**

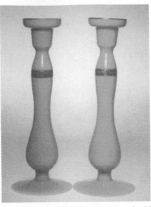

Candlestick/vases, Azurite w/gold band, 9 1/2" h., pr. **$125**

Candlesticks, one-light, No. 3121, w/bobeches & prisms, Crystal, 7 1/2" h., pr. (ILLUS. of one) **$145**

Compote, open, 5" d., 7 1/2" h., etched Diane patt., Crystal, fitted in a Farberware chrome frame **$68**

Compote, 6" w., 6 1/4" h., Mt. Vernon line, w/ball stem, two handles, Crystal **$32**

Console set: 11 1/2" flared bowl & pair of 3 1/2" h. one-light candleholders; Decagon patt. etched Cleo patt., Dianthus Pink, the set (ILLUS. w/flower frog) **$220**

Figure flower holder, Two Kids, Crystal, 9 1/4" h. **$195**

Relish, cov., oblong, five-part, w/dome cover, No. 397, Royal Blue, 12" l. **$450**

Carnival

Earlier called Taffeta glass, the Carnival glass now being collected was introduced early in the 20th century. Its producers gave it an iridescence that attempted to imitate that of some Tiffany glass. Collectors will find available books by leading authorities Donald E. Moore, Sherman Hand, Marion T. Hartung, Rose M. Presznick, and Bill Edwards.

Acanthus (Imperial)

Bowl, 8" to 9" d., purple, deep sides **$215**
Bowl, 8" to 9" d., smoky **$55**

Advertising & Souvenir Items

Bowl, "Bernheimer Brothers," ruffled, Many Stars patt., blue **$2,100**

Bell, souvenir, BPOE Elks, "Parkersburg, 1914," blue **$2,300**
Bowl, "Dorsey & Funkenstein Fine Furniture," ruffled, amethyst **$625**
Bowl, souvenir, "Brooklyn Bridge," marigold, unlettered **$1,400**
Bowl, souvenir, "Brooklyn Bridge," ten-ruffle rim, marigold **$170**
Bowl, souvenir, "Millersburg Courthouse," ice cream shape, amethyst w/radium finish.... **$750**
Bowl, souvenir, "Millersburg Courthouse," purple **$800**
Bowl, souvenir, BPOE Elks, "Detroit, 1910," purple, two-eyed Elk (Millersburg) **$3,000**
Bowl, souvenir, BPOE Elks, "Detroit, 1910," ruffled, green.......... **$725**
Card tray, "Isaac Benesch 54th Anniversary," marigold, Holly Whirl patt............................ **$65**
Mug, souvenir, "Granger's Picnic," Near-Cut patt., marigold....... **$75**
Plate, "Spector's Department Store," marigold, Heart & Vine patt., 9" d.................................... **$750**

Apple Tree

Tumbler, white........................ **$150**

April Showers (Fenton)

Vase, 7 1/2" h., purple **$80**
Vase, 8" h., green.................... **$90**
Vase, 8" h., marigold **$55**
Vase, 11" h., blue **$100**
Vase, 12" h., vaseline............. **$250**

Basket (Fenton's Open Edge)

Aqua, w/two rows, two sides turned up **$45**
Blue **$25**
Celeste blue **$550**
Green **$95**
Green, jack-in-the-pulpit shape **$155**
Ice blue small square-shaped **$130**
Ice green, large square-shaped **$155**
Marigold **$30**
Powder blue, jack-in-the-pulpit shape **$75**
Purple **$80**
Red **$325**
Red ruffled edges................. **$135**
Red, jack-in-the-pulpit shape.. **$145**
Smokey lavender, two-sides up **$45**
White, large size, ruffled rim **$65**
White, 6" **$275**

Basket or Bushel Basket (Northwood)

Aqua opalescent, 4 1/2" d., 4 3/4" h. **$250**
Blue, 4 1/2" d., 4 3/4" h. **$95**
Green eight-sided.................. **$200**
Green 4 1/2" d., 4 3/4" h......... **$150**
Ice blue, ... **$450**
Ice blue, eight-sided **$250**
Ice green, 4 1/2" d., 4 3/4" h... **$115**
Lavender slag, 4 1/2" d., 4 3/4" h. **$125**
Marigold, 4 1/2" d., 4 3/4" h..... **$55**
Purple **$160**
Sapphire blue 4 1/2" d., 4 3/4" h. **$450**
White, eight-sided **$55**
White, 4 1/2" d., 4 3/4" h. **$125**

Basketweave (Fenton) - see Basket (Fenton)

Beaded Cable (Northwood)

Rose bowl, purple, Rayed interior **$35**

Big Fish Bowl (Millersburg)

Green, round, scalloped rim, radium finish, 8" d., 2 1/4" h. **$850-1,000**

Blackberry (Fenton)

Basket, open-edged, ruffled, amber **$225**
Basket, open-edged, ruffled, amethyst................................ **$35**
Basket, open-edged, ruffled, blue **$35**
Basket, open-edged, ruffled, green **$125**
Basket, open-edged, ruffled, marigold **$18**
Vase, 7" h., whimsey, open edge, marigold **$2,100**

Blackberry Spray

Hat shape, aqua, crimped rim, flattened out **$95**
Hat shape, red, two sides turned-up, cherry tones **$225**

Blackberry Wreath (Millersburg)

Bowl, 5" d., ruffled rim, green w/ radium finish........................ **$60**
Bowl, 5" d., ruffled rim, marigold w/ radium finish........................ **$25**
Bowl, 7" d., ruffled rim, marigold w/ radium finish........................ **$30**

Brooklyn Bridge - see Advertising & Souvenir Items

Bushel Basket - see Basket (Northwood) Pattern

Butterfly & Berry (Fenton)

Bowl, 8" to 9" d., white, master berry, four-footed.............. **$650**
Vase, 9" h., green.................... **$85**

CARNIVAL

Butterfly & Fern (Fenton)

Pitcher, water, blue $425

Captive Rose

Bowl, 8" d., amethyst, three-in-one edge $60
Bowl, 8" to 9" d., blue, 3-in-1 edge $95
Bowl, 8" to 9" d., green, 3-in-1 edge $65
Bowl, 8" to 9" d., green, candy ribbon edge $115
Bowl, 8" to 9" d., purple, candy ribbon edge $65

Plate, 9" d., green $400

Cobblestones Bowl (Imperial)

Marigold, 8-9" d., ruffled rim .. $145

Coin Dot

Rose bowl, amethyst, large $15

Concord (Fenton)

Plate, 9" d., marigold $500

Constellation (Dugan)

Compote, white $35

Corinth (Westmoreland)

Vase, 9" h., aqua, jack-in-the-pulpit $55
Vase, 10" h., aqua, jack-in-the-pulpit (small chip) $125

Corn Vase (Northwood)

Green $700
Green, corn stalk base $650
Ice blue $1,700
Ice blue, corn stalk babse, very dark color, rare $4,900
Ice green $300
Ice green, corn stalk base $225
Marigold, plain base, dark color $800
Purple $600
Purple, plain base $275
White $200
White, corn stalk base $245

Cosmos

Sauce dish, green, ice cream-shaped, radium finish $20

Cosmos & Cane (U.S. Glass Co.)

Tumbler, honey amber $35

Daisy & Drape Vase (Northwood)

Amethyst, turned in $700
Aqua opalescent, flared out $300-375
Blue w/electric iridescence, flared out $1,400
White, turned in $65-90

Ice blue, turned in $1,800

Daisy & Plume

Compote, green $45
Compote, marigold $30
Compote, purple $55
Rose bowl, blue, three-footed $475
Rose bowl, green, stemmed $50
Rose bowl, green, three-footed $125
Rose bowl, marigold, stemmed $35
Rose bowl, marigold, three-footed $125
Rose bowl, purple, stemmed ... $50
Rose bowl, purple, three-footed $125

Dandelion (Northwood)

Mug, aqua opalescent $250
Mug, marigold $85
Water set: tankard pitcher & 6 tumblers; marigold, 7 pcs ... $550

Deep Grape Compote (Millersburg)

Marigold, round shape $1,700

Diamond & Daisy Cut (aka Maylower or Floral & Diamond Band)

Pitcher, water $45
Tumbler, marigold $60

Diamond Lace (Imperial)

Water set: pitcher & 5 tumblers; purple, 6 pcs $400

Diamond Point Columns Vase

Vase, 7 1/2" h., squatty shape, blue $95
Vase, 10 1/2" h., purple $225
Vase, 11" h., green $65
Vase, 16" h., blue $40

Double Star or Buzz Saw (Cambridge)

Cruet w/stopper, marigold, large, clear stopper, 6" $75
Cruet w/stopper, green, large, 6" $175

CARNIVAL

Double Stemmed Rose (Dugan)

Bowl, celeste blue, ruffled, dome-footed, epoxy on back........ **$215**
Bowl, light marigold, domed foot, 3-in-1 edge **$25**
Bowl, purple, deep round shape, domed foot **$85**
Plate, white, domed foot, rare shape **$75**
Plate, 7" d., powder blue, very rare **$1,100**

Dragon & Lotus (Fenton)

Bowl, 8" to 9" d., green, ruffled **$50**

Bowl, 8" to 9" d., green, three-in-one edge **$70**
Bowl, 8" to 9" d., marigold, ruffled **$35**
Bowl, 8" to 9" d., peach opalescent, three-in-one edge............... **$450**
Bowl, 8" to 9" d., ruffled rim, collared base, green **$95**
Bowl, 8" to 9" d., ruffled rim, collared base, peach opalescent **$300**
Bowl, 9" d., blue, ice cream shape, collared base........................ **$80**

Bowl, 8" to 9" d., ruffled rim, collared base, red w/cherry tones .. **$850**

Dragon & Strawberry Bowl/ Dragon & Berry (Fenton)

Bowl, 9" d., deep sides, blue, minor nick on base **$250**

Drapery (Northwood)

Candy dish, tricornered, ice blue **$155**
Rose bowl, aqua opalescent **$300**
Rose bowl, blue..................... **$135**
Rose bowl, ice blue **$275**
Rose bowl, marigold.............. **$250**
Vase, 8 1/2" h., variant **$35**
Vase, 8 1/2" h., variant **$100**

Embroidered Mums (Northwood)

Bonbon, white, stemmed....... **$525**
Bowl, 8" to 9" d., ruffled rim, ribbed back, blue........................... **$400**
Bowl, 8" to 9" d., ruffled rim, ribbed back, horehound **$500**
Bowl, 8" to 9" d., ruffled rim, ribbed back, ice blue **$350**

Fantail

Bowl, 9" d., blue, footed, ice cream shape **$625**
Bowl, 9" d., marigold, footed, ice cream shaped **$95**

Farmyard (Dugan)

Bowl, purple, ruffled rim **$2,750**

Bowl, three-in-one edge, purple **$5,750**

Fashion (Imperial)

Creamer, marigold **$40**
Pitcher, water, marigold **$150**
Pitcher, water, purple.......... **$1,100**
Punch bowl & base, smoky, 12" d., 2 pcs.................................. **$3,000**
Punch cup, marigold.............. **$15**
Punch cup, smoky.................. **$45**

Punch set: 12" d. bowl, base & 6 cups; marigold, 8 pcs. **$275**
Rose bowl, marigold................ **$30**
Rose bowl, marigold, large...... **$65**
Tumbler, marigold **$20**
Tumbler, purple **$200**
Tumbler, smoky...................... **$100**

Feather & Heart (Millersburg)

Tumbler, amethyst **$50**
Tumbler, marigold **$25**

Fenton's Flowers Rose Bowl – See Orange Tree Pattern

Fine Rib (Northwood & Fenton)

Vase, 10" h., amber (Fenton) ... **$65**
Vase, 10" h., aqua (Fenton)...... **$85**
Vase, 10" h., lime green w/marigold overlay (Fenton).................. **$80**
Vase, 10" h., red (Fenton) **$150**

Finecut & Roses (Northwood)

Candy dish, aqua opalescent, three-footed........................ **$125**
Candy dish, ice blue, three-footed **$135**
Rose bowl, ice blue **$105**

Fisherman's Mug

Purple **$50**

Fleur De Lis (Millersburg)

Bowl, 8" to 9" d., ruffled rim, collared base, green **$295**

Floral & Grape (Dugan or Diamond Glass Co.)

Pitcher, water, blue **$225**
Water set: pitcher & 6 tumblers; purple, 7 pcs........................ **$225**

Flowers & Frames

Bowl, ruffled, dome-footed, purple **$125**

Flute (Imperial)

Toothpick holder, green **$35**
Toothpick holder, marigold **$25**
Toothpick holder, purple **$35**

Four Pillar Vase (Northwood)

Aqua opalescent, 9" h., shaped **$200**
Aqua opalescent, 11" h............ **$85**

Fruits & Flowers (Northwood)

Bonbon, aqua opalescent, stemmed, two- handled...... **$400**
Bonbon, blue w/electric iridescence, stemmed, two-handled....... **$105**
Bonbon, blue, stemmed, two-handled **$225**
Bonbon, green, stemmed, two-handled **$150**
Bonbon, ice blue, stemmed, two-handled **$350**
Bonbon, ice green, stemmed, two-handled **$500**
Bonbon, marigold, stemmed, two-handled **$85**
Bonbon, purple, stemmed, two-handled **$100**
Bonbon, white, stemmed, two-handled **$175**
Bowl, 7" d., ruffled rim, Basketweave exterior, ice green **$175**

Good Luck (Northwood)

Bowl, 8" to 9" d., emerald green, ruffled **$2,000**

Bowl, 8" to 9" d., blue, piecrust edge, ribbed back............... **$225**
Bowl, 8" to 9" d., blue, ruffled, ribbed back.................................... **$195**
Bowl, 8" to 9" d., purple, ruffled, Basketweave back **$165**

Bowl, 8" to 9" d., blue, piecrust rim, ribbed back......................... **$200**
Bowl, 8" to 9" d., blue, ruffled rim, ribbed back......................... **$300**
Bowl, 8" to 9" d., marigold, piecrust rim, ribbed back.................. **$135**
Bowl, 8" to 9" d., purple, ruffled rim, ribbed back......................... **$250**
Plate, 9" d., ribbed back, green **$1,600**
Plate, 9" d., ribbed back, ice blue w/ dark color & stretchy iridescence, minor nick on cleat of horseshoe **$5,400**
Plate, 9" d., ribbed back, marigold w/pink iridescence.............. **$900**

Grape & Cable (Northwood)

Bonbon, two-handled, blue w/ electric iridescence **$100-175**

Banana boat, banded rim, stippled, blue w/slag effect **$450**
Banana boat, ice green **$650**
Berry set: master bowl & 6 sauce dishes; green, 7 pcs. **$145**
Bonbon, two-handled, stippled, aqua opalescent.............. **$2,800**
Bonbon, two-handled, stippled, purple **$175**
Bowl, 8" to 9" d., piecrust rim, stippled, ribbed back, aqua opalescent........................ **$2,000**
Bowl, 8" to 9" d., piecrust rim, variant w/plain back, purple **$225**
Bowl, 8" to 9" d., variant, stippled, ribbed back, aqua w/marigold overlay................................ **$500**
Bowl, 8" to 9" d., variant, stippled, ribbed back, sapphire blue **$1,200**

Bowl, berry, 9" d., ice green **$1,150**

Punch bowl & base, marigold, 14" d., 2 pcs. **$800**

Plate, 6" d., turned-up handgrip, purple **$75**
Plate, 9" d., stippled, variant w/Old Rose Distillery advertisement, green.................................... **$400**
Plate, 7 1/2" d., turned-up handgrip, purple **$150- 175**
Punch set, master: 17" bowl, base & 12 cups; marigold, 14 pcs. **$2,500**
Punch set: 14" bowl w/round top, base & 6 cups; purple, 8 pcs. **$700**
Punch set: 14" bowl, base & 8 cups; marigold, 10 pcs................ **$500**
Sauce dish, blue w/electric iridescence, rare................... **$85**
Sweetmeat jar, cov., blue, very rare................................. **$1,800**

Water set: pitcher & 6 tumblers; purple, 7 pcs. **$250**

Grape & Gothic Arches (Northwood)

Water set: pitcher & 5 tumblers; marigold, 6 pcs..................... **$95**
Water set: pitcher & 6 tumblers; blue, 7 pcs........................ **$550**

CARNIVAL

Grape Arbor (Northwood)

Hat shape, blue $65
Hat shape, white $40
Tumbler, marigold $10
Tumbler, white......................... $65

Grape Delight

Rose bowl, six-footed, purple.. $85
Rose bowl, six-footed, white
.... $45-60

Grape Leaves (Northwood)

Bowl, 9" d., horehound, ruffled
.... $20
Bowl, 9" d., green, ruffled $25

Grape Wreath (Millersburg)

Bowl, 7" d., variant, 3-in-1 edge,
amethyst w/radium finish...... $75
Bowl, 8" d., ruffled rim, green w/
radium finish......................... $65

Heart & Vine

Plate, 9" d., amethyst............. $250

Heart & Vine (Fenton)

Bowl, 8" to 9" d., emerald green
.... $450

Hearts & Flowers (Northwood)

Bowl, 8" to 9" d., piecrust rim, ribbed
back, blue.......................... $525
Bowl, 8" to 9" d., piecrust rim, ribbed
back, lime green............. $1,000
Bowl, 8" to 9" d., piecrust rim, ribbed
back, white......................... $300
Bowl, ruffled w/ribbed back, ice
blue, light iridescence........ $145
Bowl, ruffled w/ribbed back, purple
.... $300
Bowl, 8" to 9" d., piecrust rim,
marigold, dark color........... $650

Bowl, 8" to 9" d., ruffled rim, ribbed
back, ice blue $275
Bowl, 8" to 9" d., ruffled rim, ribbed
back, ice green.................. $475
Bowl, 8" to 9" d., ruffled rim, ribbed
back, marigold.................... $225
Bowl, 8" to 9" d., ruffled rim, ribbed
back, white $175
Compote, aqua opalescent on
butterscotch, ruffled rim...... $425
Compote, blue, ruffled rim...... $300
Compote, green, ruffled rim
.... $1,800
Compote, ice blue, ruffled rim
.... $425
Compote, ice green, ruffled rim
.... $500
Compote, marigold on custard,
ruffled rim, very rare........ $4,500
Compote, marigold, ruffled rim
.... $105
Compote, powder blue opalescent
ruffled rim, very rare........ $2,200
Compote, Reninger blue, ruffled
rim, very rare..................... $500
Compote, white, ruffled rim ... $135
Compote, 6 3/4" h., ice blue .. $300
Compote, 6 3/4" h., marigold... $95

Compote, 6 3/4" h., blue $325

Compote, 6 3/4" h., powder blue
opalescent $3,250

Compotes are footed bowls
with stems used to serve fruit,
nuts, etc. They are also known
as comports.

Plate, 9" d., ice blue $1,100

Heavy Grape (Dugan, Diamond Glass or Millersburg)

Bowl, 6" d., lime green, deep sides
.... $20

Heavy Grape (Imperial)

Plate, 7" to 8" d., green............ $25
Plate, 7" to 8" d., purple $145
Plate, chop, 11" d., marigold.... $70
Plate, chop, 11" d., white $550

Hobnail (Millersburg)

Tumbler, blue $400
Tumbler, marigold $1,100

Holly Sprig - See Holly Whirl Pattern

Holly Whirl or Holly Sprig (Millersburg, Fenton & Dugan)

Bowl, 7" w., tricornered, marigold
w/radium finish $95
Bowl, 8" to 9" d., marigold....... $45
Card tray, two-handled, green . $35
Nappy, tricornered, peach
opalescent (Dugan)............. $30

Holly, Holly Berries & Carnival Holly (Fenton)

Bowl, 8" to 9" d., blue w/silvery
iridescence, three-in-one edge
.... $40
Bowl, 8" to 9" d., blue, very flat w/
three-in- one edge................ $75
Bowl, 8" to 9" d., lime green, three-
in-one edge $65
Bowl, 8" to 9" d., ruffled, amber
.... $145
Bowl, 8" to 9" d., ruffled, powder
blue w/marigold overlay $85
Bowl, 8" to 9" d., ruffled, white
.... $60

Bowl, 8" to 9" d., ice cream shape, blue **$55**

Bowl, 8" to 9" d., ice cream shape, red **$3,300**

Compote, ruffled rim, light aqua w/ marigold overlay................... **$75**
Dish, hat-shaped, purple opalescent, 5 3/4".................................... **$150**
Dish, hat-shaped, red, crimped rim, 5 3/4".................................... **$185**
Plate, 9" to 10" d., clambroth ... **$95**

Homestead - see Nu-Art Homestead Plate

Horse Heads or Horse Medallions (Fenton)

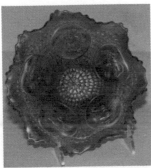

Bowl, 7" to 8" d., footed, ruffled rim, green **$225**

Bowl, amethyst, footed, ruffled **$625**
Bowl, jack-in-the-pulpit shaped, marigold **$125**
Bowl, 7" d., ice cream shape, marigold **$30**
Bowl, 7" to 8" d., ruffled rim, marigold **$115**
Bowl, jack-in-the-pulpit shaped, flattened, amber **$45**
Bowl, jack-in-the-pulpit shaped, lime green w/marigold overlay ... **$225**
Plate, 7" to 8" d., marigold **$130**

Imperial Grape (Imperial)

Bowl, 8" to 9" d., amber **$15**
Plate, 6" d., green **$30**
Plate, 6" d., purple.................. **$105**

Inverted Strawberry (Cambridge)

Tumbler, amethyst **$85**
Tumbler, marigold **$135**

Inverted Thistle (Cambridge)

Bowl, 6" d., round, green **$115**

Juin Line (India, 1930+)

Vase, 5" h., molded Left Hand design, marigold.................. **$45**
Vase, 6" h., molded Elephant design, marigold **$20**
Vase, 8 1/2" h., molded Elephant design, marigold..................... **$5**
Vase, 9" h., molded Fish design, marigold **$20**

Kittens (Fenton)

Bowl, round rim, marigold...... **$105**
Bowl, ruffled rim, marigold **$85**
Cup & saucer, blue............. **$1,050**
Cup & saucer, marigold......... **$125**
Dish, four sides turned-up, marigold **$85**
Dish, turned-up sides, blue **$600**
Dish, two sides turned-up sides, blue **$255**
Toothpick holder, marigold **$85**

Leaf & Beads (Northwood)

Nut bowl, aqua opalescent, handled, footed **$1,300**
Nut bowl, blue, handled, footed **$225**
Rose bowl, marigold............... **$95**
Rose bowl, white **$200**

Rose bowl, aqua opalescent **$200**

Leaf & Flowers or Leaf & Little Flowers (Millersburg)

Compote, miniature, green w/ radium finish...................... **$375**
Compote, miniature, ruffled, amethyst w/radium finish.... **$200**
Compote, miniature, ruffled, marigold w/radium finish **$185**
Compote, miniature, sherbet-shaped, amethyst w/radium finish................................. **$145**
Compote, miniature, sherbet-shaped, marigold w/radium finish **$135**

Leaf Chain (Fenton)

Bowl, 7" d., ruffled rim, white ... **$45**
Plate, 9" d., white **$215**

Leaf Columns Vase (Northwood)

Lime green, 10" h. **$250**

Leaf Rays Nappy

Purple, Nebraska souvenir **$30**
White **$50**

Lined Lattice Vase

Purple, 10" h. **$70**
White, 10" h. **$50**

Little Stars Bowl (Millersburg)

Bowl, 7" d., ruffled, amethyst **$105**

Lotus & Grape (Fenton)

Bonbon, two-handled, marigold **$15**
Plate, 9" d., amethyst **$1,150**

CARNIVAL

Many Fruits (Dugan)

Punch bowl & base, purple, 2 pcs.
.... $850
Punch set: bowl, base & 6 cups;
marigold, 8 pcs................... $250

Many Stars (Millersburg)

Bowl, 8" to 9" d., ruffled, blue,
fine satin iridescence, very rare
.... $3,500
Bowl, three-in-one edge, green w/
radium finish........................ $800
Bowl, 8" to 9" d., ruffled rim crimped
into a six-point star, marigold w/
radium finish........................ $350
Bowl, 8" to 9" d., ruffled, marigold
.... $450

Mayan (Millersburg)

Bowl, 8" to 9" d., ice cream shape,
green..................................... $30

Memphis (Northwood)

Berry set: master bowl & 7 sauce
dishes; purple, 8 pcs. $500
Fruit bowl set: bowl, base & 6
individual bowls; purple, 8 pcs.
.... $500
Punch set: bowl, base & 7 cups;
marigold, 9 pcs................... $200

Milady (Fenton)

Tumbler, marigold $65
Tumbler, purple $125

Millersburg Courthouse Bowl - See Advertising & Souvenir Items

Millersburg Peacock - See Peacock & Urn Pattern

Morning Glory (Millersburg & Imperial)

Vase, 4 3/4" h., miniature, flared out,
purple $350
Vase, 5 1/2" h., miniature, flared,
marigold $35
Vase, 5 1/2" h., miniature, flared,
smoky $60
Vase, 5 1/2" h., miniature, non-
flared, marigold $30
Vase, 5 1/2" h., miniature, purple
.... $105
Vase, 12" h., funeral, marigold
.... $300

Multi-Fruits - See Many Fruits Pattern

Nesting Swan (Millersburg)

Bowl, 9" d., ruffled, purple $225
Bowl, 9" d., ruffled rim, amethyst w/
radium finish........................ $180
Bowl, 9" d., ruffled rim, amethyst w/
satin finish $200
Green, diamond-shape bowl w/
crimped rim, green w/radium
finish, rare $700

Nippon (Northwood)

Bowl, 8" to 9" d., ruffled rim,
Basketweave exterior, ice green,
minor nick on seam of base .. $200
Bowl, 8" to 9" d., ruffled rim,
Basketweave exterior, white
.... $150
Bowl, 8" to 9" d., piecrust rim, ribbed
back, ice blue $180
Bowl, 8" to 9" d., piecrust rim, ribbed
back, white $115
Plate, 9" d., Basketweave exterior,
green $1,100
Plate, 9" d., Basketweave exterior,
marigold $400

Nu-Art Homestead Plate (Imperial)

Amber $1,800

Orange Tree (Fenton)

Bowl, 7" d., ruffled, white $45
Bowl, 8" to 9" d., ruffled, white
.... $75
Bowl, ice cream shape, blue.. $200
Creamer, blue, individual size.. $55
Dish, whimsey w/ruffled rim made
from a sherbet, marigold $75
Hatpin holder, blue $245
Hatpin holder, marigold.......... $95
Loving cup, amethyst, rare color
.... $650
Loving cup, green $225

Loving cup, blue $325

Loving cup, marigold............. $105
Loving cup, white, heat checks in
handles................................. $205
Mug, amethyst $35
Mug, brick red, scarce............ $105
Mug, light amethyst................. $25
Plate, 9" d., flat, blue, tree trunk
center $450
Plate, 9" d., tree trunk center, blue
.... $300
Plate, 9" d., tree trunk center,
marigold $95
Plate, 9 " d., tree trunk center,
clambroth $50
Powder jar, cov., blue........... $100
Punch set: bowl, base & 7 cups;
blue, 9 pcs............................ $375
Shaving mug, blue................... $25
Shaving mug, red slag w/silvery
iridescence, very rare........ $425
Sugar bowl, open, individual size,
white..................................... $40

Oriental Poppy (Northwood)

Tumbler, green......................... $35
Tumbler, marigold $23
Tumbler, purple $40
Tumbler, white....................... $105
Water set: pitcher & 6 tumblers,
purple, 7 pcs................... $1,250

Pansy and Pansy Spray (Imperial)

Bowl, 8" to 9" d., ruffled rim, purple
.... $45

A loving cup is a large, two-
handled cup often shared
among guests at weddings,
banquets and feasts. It is
used for ceremonial purposes,
and symbolizes unity, love, or
comraderie.

CARNIVAL

Panther (Fenton)

Bowl, 5" d., footed, red $625

Bowl, 5" d., footed, ruffled, marigold $30
Bowl, 5" d., footed, white $300

Peach (Northwood)

Spooner, white $65
Sugar bowl, cov., white $85

Peacock & Grape (Fenton)

Bowl, 8" d., ice cream shape, marigold, spatula-footed....... $20
Bowl, 9" d., ruffled, amethyst ... $50
Bowl, 8" d., spatula-footed, blue $50
Bowl, ruffled, spatula-footed, lime green opalescent................ $250
Plate, 9" d., flat base, marigold $350

Plate, 9" d., collared base, marigold $1,750

Peacock & Urn (Millersburg, Fenton & Northwood)

Bowl, ruffled, mystery-type, green (Millersburg) $285
Bowl, three-in-one edge, mystery-type, marigold (Millersburg) $200
Bowl, 7 1/2" d., "shotgun," ruffled, green................................. $325

Bowl, 8" to 9" d., ruffled rim, white (Fenton)............................... $95
Bowl, 9" d., ruffled, blue (Fenton) $250
Bowl, 9" d., ruffled, purple (Fenton) $300
Bowl, 9" d., ruffled, white $450
Bowl, 9 1/2" d., berry, purple (Millersburg) $450
Bowl, 10" d., ice cream shape, amethyst w/radium iridescence (Millersburg) $1,300
Bowl, 10" d., ice cream shape, aqua opalescent (Northwood) $25,000
Bowl, 10" d., ice cream shape, blue (Northwood) $1,200
Bowl, 10" d., ice cream shape, blue, stippled (Northwood)...... $1,400
Bowl, 10" d., ice cream shape, green (Northwood) $1,850
Bowl, 10" d., ice cream shape, ice blue (Northwood)............... $850
Bowl, 10" d., ice cream shape, ice green (Northwood) $1,500
Bowl, 10" d., ice cream shape, marigold (Millersburg) $350

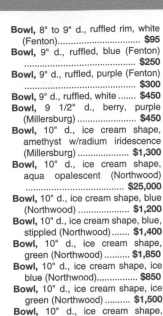

Bowl, 10" d., ice cream shape, marigold, Northwood $300

Bowl, 10" d., ice cream shape, purple $750
Bowl, 10" d., ice cream shape, stippled, Reninger blue (Northwood) $1,150
Bowl, 10" d., ruffled, made from master ice cream bowl, marigold $425
Bowl, master ice cream, stippled, marigold (Northwood)......... $750
Bowl, master, blue (Millersburg) $2,500
Bowl, master, green (Millersburg) $650
Compote, ruffled rim, aqua (Fenton)............................. $155
Hat shape, jack-in-the-pulpit style, white............................... $405
Ice cream dish, marigold, small $80
Ice cream dish, blue, small (Northwood) $125
Ice cream dish, green, small (Northwood) $650

Ice cream dish, green, small $220

Ice cream dish, ice blue, small $275
Ice cream dish, ice green, small $275
Ice cream dish, purple, small .. $85
Ice cream dish, white, small.. $175
Ice cream set: large bowl & 6 small dishes; amethyst, 7 pcs. (Northwood) $1,500
Plate, 9" d., marigold (Fenton) $210
Sauce dish, blue (Millersburg) $800
Sauce dish, green (Millersburg) $250
Sauce dish, marigold (Millersburg) $150
Sauce dish, purple (Millersburg) $95

Peacock at the Fountain (Northwood)

Bowl, fruit, blue $550
Bowl, fruit, marigold w/light color $135

Bowl, master ice cream-shape, blue w/electric iridescence $2,100

CARNIVAL

Bowl, orange, three-footed, marigold **$300**

Bowl, 6" d., blue w/great iridescence, flattened-shape **$650**
Pitcher, water, white **$300**
Sauce dish, blue, ice cream-shaped **$60**
Sauce dish, green, ice cream-shape **$350**
Tumbler, blue **$50**
Tumbler, blue w/eletric iridescence **$45**
Tumbler, ice blue.................... **$215**
Tumbler, purple **$50**
Water set: pitcher & 4 tumblers; marigold, 5 pcs................... **$420**

Peacock Tail (Fenton)

Compote, marigold w/radium finish, variant, 6" d., 5" h................ **$95**

Peacocks on Fence (Northwood Peacocks)

Bowl, 8" to 9" d., piecrust rim, plain back, white **$325**
Bowl, 8" to 9" d., piecrust rim, ribbed back, blue........................ **$375**
Bowl, 8" to 9" d., piecrust rim, ribbed back, purple........................ **$325**
Plate, 9" d., ribbed exterior, blue **$550**
Plate, 9" d., ribbed exterior, ice green **$375**
Plate, 9" d., ribbed exterior, marigold w/pink iridescence............. **$400**
Plate, 9" d., ribbed exterior, white **$300**

Bowl, 8" to 9" d., ruffled rim, ribbed back, aqua opalescent **$700**

Bowl, 8" to 9" d., ruffled rim, ribbed back, blue, electric highlights **$525**

Bowl, 8" to 9" d., ruffled rim, ribbed back, marigold **$165**

Plate, 9" d., rlbbed exterior, ice blue **$1,110**

Plate, 9" d., ribbed exterior, purple **$450**

Persian Garden (Dugan)

Bowl, 11" d., ice cream shape, white.............................. **$130**
Fruit bowl & base, white, 2 pcs. **$625**
Plate, 6" to 7" d., marigold **$35**
Plate, 6" to 7" d., purple **$210**

Persian Medallion (Fenton)

Bonbon, two-handled, blue...... **$25**
Bonbon, two-handled, green **$75**
Bonbon, two-handled, red **$300**
Bowl, 10" d., green, three-in-one rim **$135**
Compote, emerald green, crimped rim, 6 1/2" d., 6 1/2" h......... **$250**
Compote, purple, crimped rim, 6 1/2" d., 6 1/2" h.................. **$185**
Compote, green, crimped rim, 6 1/2" d., 6 1/2" h.................. **$235**
Hair receiver, marigold **$25**
Plate, chop, 10 1/2" d., blue... **$275**

Bowl, 8" to 9" d., red, ruffled rim **$1,000**

Peter Rabbit (Fenton)

Bowl, 8" d., green, ruffled ... **$1,100**

Plate, 9" d., blue **$6,500**

Pony

Bowl, 8" to 9" d., six-ruffle rim, aqua **$525**
Bowl, 8" to 9" d., ten-ruffle rim, marigold **$40**

CARNIVAL

Poppy (Northwood)

Pickle dish, blue $155
Pickle dish, green.................. $350
Pickle dish, marigold $105

Poppy Show (Northwood)

Bowl, 8" to 9" d., white $185
Plate, 9" d., blue w/electric
    iridescence...................... $1,550
Plate, 9" d., white $350

Poppy Show Vase (Imperial)

Marigold, dark color.............. $325
Marigold, pastel color $700

Primrose Bowl (Millersburg)

Amethyst, ruffled rim, radium finish
.... $85
Green crimped rim, radium finish
.... $95

Question Marks

Compote, crimped edge, marigold
.... $20

Raspberry (Northwood)

Compote, ruffled rim, white ... $275
Pitcher, milk, purple $220
Tumbler, purple $75
Water set: pitcher & 6 tumblers;
    purple, 7 pcs...................... $550

Rays & Ribbons (Millersburg)

Bowl, 8" to 9" d., crimped rim, green
    w/radium finish $125

Ripple Vase

Marigold, 7" h. $35
Purple, 8 3/4" h. $85
Purple, 11" h. $75
Purple, 12" h. $80

Rosalind (Millersburg)

Bowl, 10" d., ruffled, green .. $140
Compote, small, ruffled, purple,
    6" d. $500

Rose Show

Bowl, 9" d., , ruffled rim, marigold,
    minor nick on rose.............. $275

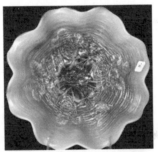

Bowl, 9" d., aqua opalescent
.... $1,000
Bowl, 9" d., ice green $800
Bowl, 9" d., ruffled rim, ice blue,
    minor nick in pattern........... $375

Plate, 9" d., amethyst $800
Plate, 9" d., blue..................... $500
Plate, 9" d., marigold............. $550
Plate, 9" d., white, turned-up edges
.... $175

Round Up (Dugan)

Bowl, 9" d., deep sides, 3-in-1 rim,
    white................................... $105
Bowl, 9" d., low ruffled sides, peach
    opalescent.......................... $205
Plate, 9" d., blue.................... $200

Rustic Vase

Amethyst, funeral, 19" h. $900
Blue, 6" h., whimsey jardiniere
    made from funeral mold vase,
    flared out, fine iridescencd, crack
    in base............................. $4,000
Blue, 7" to 12" h. $60
Blue, 15" h................................ $75
Blue, 16" h.............................. $150
Blue, funeral, 18" h., 5" base.. $950
Blue, funeral, 18" h., w/plunger
    base, rare......................... $1,700
Blue, funeral, 19" h................. $700
Green, 6" h. to 10 1/2" h........... $80
Green, 16" h. $250
Marigold, 6" to 10 1/2" h. $40
Marigold, 15" h. $85
Marigold, 16" to 21 1/2" h., 5 1/2"
    base $95
Marigold, funeral, 19" h., marigold
.... $600
Purple, 6" to 10 1/2" h.............. $70
Purple, 15" h. $150
White 16" h., crimped edge...... $75
White funeral, 19" h. $2,000
White, 15" h., white w/touch of sun-
    colored lavender................. $115

"S" Repeat (Dugan)

Tumbler, marigold in dark color
.... $525

CARNIVAL

Scales

Bowl, 7" d., blue opalescent, ruffled $45
Bowl, 7" d., marigold on milk glass, ruffled $35

Scroll Embossed

Bowl, 9" d., purple, ruffled rim, File patt. on exterior $240
Sauce dish, purple, ruffled rim, File patt. on exterior, 5 3/4" d. $50

Singing Birds (Northwood)

Mug, blue $65
Mug, purple $35
Pitcher, purple $275
Tumbler, purple $60

Water set: pitcher & 6 tumblers; green, 7 pcs. $725

Springtime (Northwood)

Tumbler, green $100

Stag & Holly (Fenton)

Bowl, 8" d., footed, ice cream shape, blue $95
Bowl, 8" d., footed, ice cream shape, marigold $75
Bowl, 10" to 11" d., three-footed, ruffled, blue $150

Star of David (Imperial)

Bowl, ruffled, green $150
Bowl, ruffled, marigold $150
Bowl, ruffled, purple $250

Star of David & Bows (Northwood)

Bowl, 7" d., dome-footed, green $175
Bowl, 7" d., dome-footed, marigold $100
Bowl, 7" d., dome-footed, purple $125

Strawberry (Fenton)

Bonbon, two-handled, amber .. $25
Bonbon, two-handled, blue $80
Bonbon, two-handled, green . $225
Bonbon, two-handled, ice green opalescent $300
Bonbon, two-handled, marigold $30
Bonbon, two-handled, red $800
Bonbon, two-handled, vaseline $55

Strawberry (Millersburg)

Compote, marigold, ruffled $145

Strawberry (Northwood)

Bowl, 8" to 9" d., blue, stippled, piecrust rim $900
Bowl, 8" to 9" d., green, ruffled, Basketweave exterior $155
Bowl, 8" to 9" d., marigold, ruffled, Basketweave exterior $75
Bowl, 8" to 9" d., piecrust rim, plain back, lavender $185
Bowl, 8" to 9" d., ruffled, Basketweave exterior, purple $75
Bowl, 8" to 9" d., stippled, ruffled, purple $300
Bowl, ice blue, stippled, piecrust rim $7,000
Bowl, 9" d., green, piecrust rim $200
Bowl, 9" d., marigold, piecrust rim $100
Bowl, 9" d., purple, piecrust rim $195
Plate, 9" d., green $250
Plate, 9" d., marigold $150
Plate, 9" d., purple $225
Plate, stippled, ice blue $12,000
Plate, stippled, ice green... $15,500

Swan Nesting - see Nesting Swan

Swirl Hobnail (Millersburg)

Cuspidor, marigold $525
Rose bowl, amethyst $275

Swirl Hobnail (Millersburg)

Rose bowl, marigold.............. $175

Ten Mums (Fenton)

Bowl, large, footed, three-in-one edge, green $125
Water set: pitcher & 6 tumblers; marigold, 7 pcs................ $1,100

Thin Rib Vase (Fenton & Northwood)

Blue w/electric iridescence, 11" h., Northwood $185
Green, 14" h. $155
Ice blue, 11" h. (Northwood).. $135
White, 13" h. (Northwood)...... $200

Three Fruits (Northwood)

Bowl, 8 1/2" d., stippled, piecrust rim, ribbed exterior, blue $250
Bowl, 9" d., ruffled, plain back, light horehound $275
Bowl, 9" d., ruffled, stippled, spatula-footed, lime green $450
Bowl, 9" d., stippled, ruffled, ribbed back, white $200
Bowl, 9" d., stippled, ruffled, ribbed exterior, aqua opalescent ... $800
Bowl, 9" d., stippled, ruffled, ribbed exterior, marigold w/pumpkin iridescence $325
Plate, 9" d., stippled, ribbed exterior, blue w/electric iridescence . $850
Plate, 9" d., stippled, ribbed exterior, marigold $275

Plate, 9" d., green, Basketweave exterior $105

Tree Trunk Vase (Northwood)

Aqua opalescent, 9" to 12" h.
.... **$900**
Blue, 10" h............................. **$100**
Blue, 8" to 10" h. **$225**
Blue, 13 1/2" h........................ **$900**
Green, 10" h. **$125**
Green, 12" h. **$300**

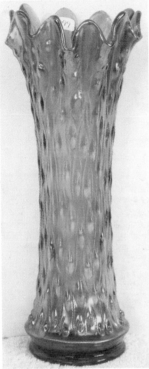

Green, 13" h. **$1,600**
Green, 22" h., funeral.......... **$3,000**
Ice blue, 10" h........................ **$265**
Ice blue, 8" to 10" h. **$750**
Ice green, 12" h. **$450**
Ice green, 22" h., funeral **$8,500**
Marigold, 10" h. **$240**
Marigold, 11" h. **$85**
Marigold, 12" h. **$175**
Marigold, 12" h., funeral-type,
    elephant foot, very rare ... **$9,000**
Purple, 8" to 11" h. **$100**
Purple, 12" h. **$90**
Purple, 13" h. **$350**
Purple, 18" h., funeral **0000**
Purple, 22" h., funeral **$2,500**
White, 10" h. **$95**
White, 11 1/2" h. **$1,300**
White, 9" h. **$325**

Tulip Scroll Vase (Millersburg)

Green, 12" h. **$150**

Vintage or Vintage Grape

Bowl, 8" to 9" d., marigold (Fenton)
.... **$15**
Epergne, green (Fenton) **$115**
Fernery, footed, blue (Fenton)
.... **$35**
Fernery, footed, marigold (Fenton)
.... **$25**
Plate, 7" d., green (Fenton)...... **$55**
Sauce dish, marigold, radium finish
    (Fenton)................................ **$20**

Whirling Leaves Bowl (Millersburg)

Green, 9" d., ruffled rim, radium
    finish..................................... **$75**
Marigold, tricornered, 9 1/2" w.
.... **$225**
Purple, 9 1/2" w., tricornered,
    crimped rim, radium finish, minor
    flake on edge...................... **$700**

Wide Panel (Northwood)

Epergne, four-lily, green **$900**
Epergne, four-lily, purple..... **$1,100**
Epergne, four-lily, white (chip on
    base near small lily) **$1,200**

Wild Strawberry (Northwood)

Plate, 6" to 7" d., w/handgrip, green
.... **$95**

Wishbone (Northwood)

Bowl, 8" to 9" d., footed, purple
.... **$150**
Bowl, 8" to 9" d., footed, white
.... **$215**
Bowl, 10" d., piecrust rim,
    Basketweave exterior, white
.... **$350**

Wreath of Roses

Punch set: bowl, base & 6 cups;
    Vintage interior, green, 8 pcs.
.... **$375**
Punch set: bowl, base & 8 cups;
    Persian Medallion interior, green,
    10 pcs........................... **$1,100**
Rose bowl, amber (Dugan) **$35**
Rose bowl, marigold (Dugan).. **$30**
Rose bowl, purple (Dugan)...... **$55**

Zig Zag (Millersburg)

Bowl, 10" d., three-in-one rim,
    amethyst w/radium finish.... **$155**

Zippered Loop Lamp (Imperial)

Sewing, marigold, large **$375**

- Auctioneers generally strive to include only items of lower value in box lots and sell items of greater value or interest separately, if this will benefit the seller. But the task often falls to inexperienced workers who may not recognize valuable items. This is why savvy auction-goers don't dismiss box lots as junk.

- Small items have a way of getting misplaced at country auctions. If you're interested in a particular item, keep your eye on it. Unscrupulous buyers may try to help themselves by moving items from one box lot to another.

- Be wary when an auctioneer says, "This looks like it's ... ." Judge for yourself an item's merits. Don't take the auctioneer's word as fact. He is human and capable of making mistakes.

- If you find an antique or collectible priced significantly less than normal, consider the possibilities. The dealer may not know the fair market value of the item, or it may not be his specialty. The dealer may have acquired the item at an unusually low price. The dealer may have had the item for a long time and wants to be rid of it. It may be damaged or not in top condition. An extremely low price is an indicator that the item might be a reproduction or fake.

- Antique shop owners face a stigma when it comes to liquidating their inventory at auction. Antiques that have been offered in a shop tend to sell for less than normal prices at auction. That's good news for customers who have admired something offered in a shop, but at a price they felt they could not afford. If the dealer, however, was widely known and highly regarded for finding great items, the inventory could sell at a premium price.

CENTRAL GLASS WORKS

Central Glass Works

From the 1890s until its closing in 1939, the Central Glass Works of Wheeling, West Virginia, produced colorless and colored handmade glass in all the styles then popular. Decorations from etchings with acid to hand-painted enamels were used.

The popular "Depression" era colors of black, pink, green, light blue, ruby red and others were all produced. Two of its 1920s etchings are still familiar today, one named for the then President of the United States and the other for the Governor of West Virginia - these are the Harding and Morgan patterns.

From high end Art glass to mass-produced plain barware tumblers, Central was a major glass producer throughout the period.

Ash receiver, cov., Frances patt., green, 5" d., 2 3/4" h. **$125**

Bowl, 5 1/2" sq., No. 1450, flat rim, black (ILLUS. w/cup & saucer & plate)
.... **$24**

Candleholder, one-light, Frances patt., green, 4" h. **$42**

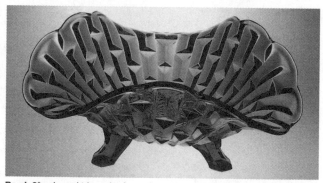

Bowl, 9", crimped triangular form, three- footed, Frances patt., amber . **$65**

Candlestick, Chippendale patt., three-handled, clear, 8 1/2" h.
.... **$75**

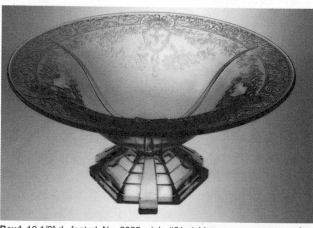

Bowl, 10 1/2" d., footed, No. 2025, pink, #61 etching **$75**

Candlestick, one-light, Chippendale patt., w/cutting, crystal, 6 1/2" h. **$35**

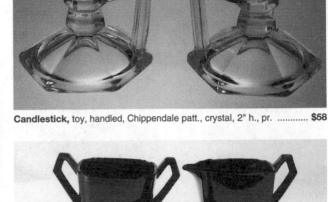

Candlestick, toy, handled, Chippendale patt., crystal, 2" h., pr. **$58**

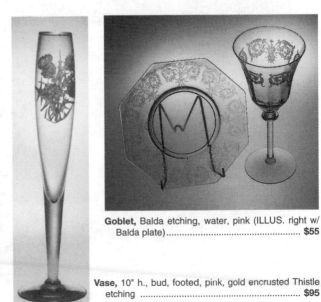

Creamer & open sugar on handled tray, No. 1450 patt., black, 3 pcs. **$75**

Vase, 8" h., fan-shaped, gold-encrusted Dunn's Parrot etching, black **$175**

Goblet, Balda etching, water, pink (ILLUS. right w/ Balda plate) **$55**

Vase, 10" h., bud, footed, pink, gold encrusted Thistle etching **$95**

Vase, 10" h., flat bottom w/cylindrical sides flared & deeply ruffled at the top, Frances patt., Orchid **$150**

Vase, 10" h., Morgan etching, footed bud vase, black w/gold encrusted etching.................................. **$325**

Cranberry

Gold was added to glass batches to give this glass its color on reheating. It has been made by numerous glasshouses for years and is currently being reproduced. Both blown and molded articles were produced. A less expensive type of cranberry was made with the substitution of copper for gold.

Pitcher, 8 1/2" h., ovoid molded twelve- lobed body w/a triangular crimped rim w/arched spout, applied frosted clear reeded handle **$50-100**

Pitcher, 8 3/4" h., ovoid Optic Ribbed patt. body w/a round neck & crimped rim, decorated w/enameled large colorful flowers & leaves, applied clear handle, minor flaws **$88**

Butter dish, cov., footed squatty round base w/an applied skirt band of clear rigaree, flattened domed cover w/optic ribbing & an applied clear twisted leaf finial, 19th c., 6 1/2" d. (minor edge flakes)................................. **$193**

Cologne bottle w/swirl flame stopper, the corset-form body molded w/four ribs & tapering to a rim applied w/a marked sterling silver band embossed w/a single leaf, 9 1/2" h. **$110**

Cracker jar w/silver plate ruffled rim, cover w/grape finial & swing bail handle, bulbous melon-lobed body covered in a white crackle finish, 5" h..... **$374**

Pitcher, 9" h., ovoid body & a tall upright lobed neck, striped Polka Dot patt., applied clear handle w/a pressed fan at the upper terminal, West Virginia Glass Co., three broken bubbles on interior **$143**

Overshot glass was produced by adding tiny bits of clear glass to a glass article being formed and then melting them to smooth them. It was originally done to cover flaws in the glass.

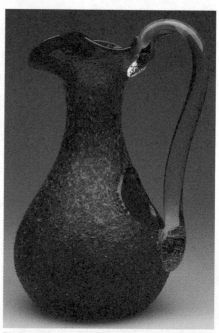

Pitcher, champagne-type, 10 1/4" h., Overshot decoration on the bulbous sharply tapering body w/a wide triangular rim, an indented ice bladder at the lower back, applied long arched clear handle, Boston & Sandwich Glass C. **$550**

Crown Milano

This glass, produced by Mt. Washington Glass Company late in the 19th century, is opal glass decorated by painting and enameling. It appears identical to a ware termed Albertine, also made by Mt. Washington.

Cracker jar w/original silver plate rim, cover & bail handle, the bulbous melon- lobed body in dark peach w/a sienna band around the top, decorated in gold & natural colors w/a design of leaves & berries around the body, the cover decorated w/an embossed crab design, base signed "CM 522," 6 1/2" d., 5 1/4" h. **$1,320**

Reverse

Ewer, nearly spherical body w/a small white cylindrical neck below a blue & gold cupped rim, white ropetwist entwined handle & band from neck to shoulder, the main body w/a shaded & mottled blue ground decorated to represent water & coral w/applied gilt fish, shells & coral, 10" h. **$9,200**

Creamer, bulbous melon-lobed body w/an attached silver plate rim, spout & handle, creamy ground h.p. w/flowers & leaves in tan, rose & green, signed **$750-1,000**

Mustard pot w/hinged silver plate cover & handle, a bulbous lobed body w/each white lobe bordered by pink & h.p. w/tiny blue forget-me-nots w/green leaves, domed petaled cover w/knob finial, slight silver wear, two flower dots missing, 2 3/4" h. **$690**

Jardiniere, wide bulbous flat-bottomed body w/a wide short cylindrical neck, almond white ground decorated around the body w/colorful pastel pansies among grey & tan lacy medallions, pink gold-trimmed neck, marked, 10" d., 7" h. **$750**

Ewer, wide squatty bulbous body tapering to a short neck w/a rim spout, gilt reeded scroll shoulder handle, the white sides enameled around the shoulder w/heavy gilt scrolls & a lattice design on a pale yellow ground all highlighted w/a clusters of pink flowers, Crown Milano mark, 6 1/2" h. **$2,500-3,000**

Pitcher, 9" h., jug-shaped, a very wide bulbous ovoid body w/a short divided neck w/a wide arched neck & a coiled snake handle trimmed in gold, the sides decorated overall w/a peach & pale green scrolling ground decorated w/heavy gilt florals & applied beaded trailing around the sides, Crown Milano mark **$4,485**

Rose bowl, eight-crimp rim, pale blue shaded to white satin ground, h.p. shaded maroon orchid w/long green & yellow leaves, unsigned, 4" d. **$250-300**

CROWN MILANO

Syrup pitcher w/original silver plate rim, domed cover & handle, bulbous melon- lobed body, creamy ground h.p. w/clusters of tan, rose & green flowers w/pale yellow shadow flowers, rare **$1,500-2,000**

Vase, 10 1/2" h., footed bulbous spherical paneled form w/a small cylindrical neck flanked by applied gold ribbed snail-form handles, creamy ground h.p. w/large gold & tan acorns & oak leaves **$2,500-3,000**

Vase, 7 1/2" h., cylindrical, blue wash decoration w/heavy gold floral design, white interior, gold detailing on wavy rim, marked "1556/1210" on base, original silver plated holder stamped "P" in diamond & "Pairpoint Mfg. Co." **$550**

Vase, 4 1/2" h., wide squatty bulbous body w/the top centered by a short small cylindrical neck, almond brown ground decorated overall w/scattered heavy gilt spider mum blossoms & light brown shadow blossoms.... **$825**

Vase, 5 3/4" h., squatty bulbous body tapering to a short ribbed flaring & scalloped neck, creamy ground h.p. w/red poppies, blue & green leaves & delicate gold roundels **$2,000-2,500**

Vase, 12" h., tall ovoid melon-ribbed body tapering to a slender twisted stick neck, small ribbed gold loop shoulder handles, h.p. w/medallions of gold dragons surrounded by gold flower, leaves & stems w/raised gold outlines, creamy ground **$2,588**

Vase, 11 3/4" h., tall slender conical body w/a flaring, gently ruffled rim, glossy white ground decorated around the rim & base w/delicate gilt scrolls & four bands of three large gold prunts applied up around the lower body, marked **$950**

Vase, 5" h., footed squatty bulbous ovoid body w/lightly molded swirled ribs up the sharply tapering sides to small neck w/a four-lobed upturned rim, decorated w/tan shadow ferns overlaid w/ gold fern fronds outlined w/raised gold, gold-trimmed rim, unmarked **$770**

Vase, 9" h., footed ovoid body tapering to a ringed neck & deep cupped rim, white ground decorated overall w/shadow flowers in light green & mauve, h.p. w/large stylized mauve, purple, white & green flowers outlined in gold **$2,703**

Vase, 12 1/2" h., footed wide squatty round lower body tapering to a very tall swelled stick neck, creamy ground h.p. w/an overall ornate gold floral decoration, signed **$1,200-1,500**

Vase, 12" h., bulbous ovoid melon-lobed body tapering to a tall slender twisted cylindrical neck w/ flared rim, golden applied arched & reeded handles at the base of the neck, the body decorated in pastel fall colors w/large teasel leaves & floral buds against a biscuit ground, gold scrolls & pink blush on the neck, marked, ... **$2,200**

Cup Plates

Produced in numerous patterns beginning more than 170 years ago, these little plates were designed to hold a cup while the tea or coffee was allowed to cool in a saucer. Cup plates were also made of ceramics. Where numbers are listed below, they refer to numbers assigned to these plates in the book *American Glass Cup Plates* by Ruth Webb Lee and James H. Rose. Plates are of clear glass unless otherwise noted. A number of cup plates have been reproduced.

L & R-148A, round w/thirty bull's-eye scallops, large flower sprig in the center, Midwestern, very rare, soft blue, 3" d. **$1,210**

L & R-227, round w/seventy-two even scallops, large flower blossom in center, leaf & blossom border, Philadelphia area, extremely rare, bright deep green, loss of two scallops, 3 3/8" d. **$7,150**

L & R-425, Hearts, round w/nine large scallops w/hearts between, quatrefoil of four hearts in the center, small diamonds in inner band, unrecorded, chip on large scallop, 3 3/8" d. **$3,850**

L & R-582 Jenny Lind, round w/ fifty-six even scallops, electric blue, possibly unique, only minor tipping, 3 3/4" d. **$1,980**

L & R-610-A, sailing ship, twenty-three bold scallops, Boston & Sandwich Glass Co., brilliant dark blue, chip to reverse rim, light tipping, 3 5/8" d. (ILLUS. left with other sailing ship cup plate) **$88**

L & R-677A, Eagle, scalloped rim, spread-winged American eagle looking right in the center w/an arch of stars above, palmette & rosette rim, medium blue, rim chips, 3 1/4" d. (ILLUS. far left with blue cup plates)....................... **$441**

Cut

Cut glass most eagerly sought by collectors is American glass produced during the so-called "Brilliant Period" from 1880 to about 1915. Pieces listed below are by type of article in alphabetical order.

Baskets

Bonbon, short round base w/flaring scalloped rim, two sides turned up & notched handle, decorated w/large & small hobstars.... **$425**

Bonbon, short round base w/flaring serrated rim, two sides turned up & annealed double-notched handle, decorated w/hobstars & fans, possibly Pairpoint, 4 x 6 1/4", 5" h. **$480**

Libbey-signed bonbon, No. 53 patt. on No. 761 blank, short round base w/flaring serrated rim, two sides turned up & annealed triple-notched handle in flattened arch shape, bottom w/16-point hobstar, sides decorated w/hobstars, fans, crosscut diamonds & panels, signed "Libbey" w/saber, 4 x 6 1/4", 5 1/4" h. **$495**

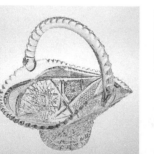

Pairpoint, "Cactus," 12" h. **$1,595**

Bottles

Carry a small flashlight when attending early morning antique markets, especially late in the summer or fall when it's barely daylight when the gates open. Under these conditions examine an object carefully with a flashlight before purchasing. Hairline cracks are difficult to see in poor light.

Water, Meriden presentation bottle w/bulbous base tapering to slender cylindrical neck, sterling silver top w/flared rim, decorated w/four suspended 24-point hobstars whose center hobs are cut w/double-miter cane, the hobstars alternating w/vesicas filled w/hobdiamond hexad & crosshatched bow ties, the bottom w/a large suspended 24-point hobstar, silver top marked "sterling" w/ Wilcox trademark of intertwined "WSW," 1904, 6 1/4" d., 7 3/4" h. **$575**

Lady's flask, basketweave design, sterling holder & screw flip lid, marked by Tiffany & Co., 6" h. **$500**

Jug, Hoare's Monarch patt., triple-notched side strap handle, 15" h. **$3,750**

Whiskey w/original stopper, overall deep cutting of hobstars, fans, cross-hatching w/same cutting on stopper, neck w/eight flutes separated by zipper cutting, cut hobstars around lip, 13 3/4" h. **$295**

Basket w/cut-all-over geometric pattern, short round base w/ flaring scalloped rim, two sides turned up & annealed double-notched handle, decorated w/ large & small alternating hobstars & crosscut diamond design, 7 1/4 x 9 3/4", 9" h. **$775**

Bowls

Hawkes, 11 3/4" x 8 1/4" oval, "Kohinoor," clear **$2,700**

Hobstars, low round shape, the sides deeply cut w/hobstars of various sizes & cane, 5" d., 1 2/3" h. **$165**

Napoleon's hat, J. Hoare & Co., w/scalloped rim, decorated w/hobstars & crosscut diamonds in geometric patterns, 8 3/4 x 13", 4" h. **$1,575**

Tuthill-signed, round shape w/scalloped rim w/notched edge, decorated w/geometric cutting consisting of four 24-point hobstars, four 20-point hobstars, 5- and 7-rayed fans, clear & crosshatched bow ties & four hobnail-filled kites, 8" d., 3 1/4" h. **$425**

Boxes

Glove box, rectangular, w/metal rims on body & lid, the body w/slightly bulbous sides decorated w/diamond design, the hinged lid decorated w/hobstars & beaded vesicas, attributed to Empire Glass Co............ **$1,525**

Powder box, tall bulbous form w/hinged lid, the body decorated w/24 concave, elongated cuts around circumference, the lid covered w/an elaborate 8-point hobstar formed w/double miters & flashed w/7- rayed fans, metal collar has been resilvered **$550**

Dresser box, square w/notched corners, the cover cut in the center w/a large sunburst framed by a wide Harvard-cut border, banded stepped bottom, 7" w. **$330**

Dresser box, square w/notched corners & hinged cover, the top cut in a circle of hobstars, the sides cut w/stars within squares, a rayed star in the base, 5" w. **$275**

Dresser box, hinged glass cover, round flattened top & tapering cylindrical low sides cut w/ hobstars alternating w/zipper cutting, C.F. Monroe Co., 6 1/2" d., 4 1/4" h............... **$585**

Glove box w/hinged cover, long narrow rectangular form w/notched corners, the top w/ etched floral designs, the base cut w/hobstars, crosshatching & fans **$1,350**

Jewelry box, rectangular w/rounded corners, hinged flat top w/silver plate mountings, cut overall w/large hobstars alternating w/zipper-cut panels & fans **$2,450**

CUT

Butter Dishes & Tubs

• Because auctioneers usually attempt to start bidding at the value of the item they are selling, it's probably not wise to enter the bidding at that point. When no one opens the bidding at that level, the auctioneer will quickly seek a lower starting bid and work up to the sale price.

• If the item at auction is a desirable piece and the opening price asked for by the auctioneer is fair, a bidder can sometimes be successful by bidding that amount immediately. Known as a preemptive bid, the strategy is to shut out competing bidders, especially those who were hoping for a bargain.

Covered dish, domed cover & underplate w/dam, both decorated w/hobstars & fans, the plate w/serrated edge, the lid w/faceted knob handle, rare **$430**

Candlesticks & Candleholders

Libbey, Plain Flute patt., signed "Libbey" w/saber mark, 10" h., pr. (ILLUS. of one).................. **$750**

Russian-cut, 6"-d. domed base decorated w/fans & groups of hobstars in vesicas, 6-sided fluted stem w/round ball at base, 10 1/2" h. **$795**

Tall candlestick, 5"-d. base decorated w/24-point hobstar, teardrop stem decorated w/ hobstars, crosscut diamonds & fans, beveled neck w/flared rim, 14 1/4" h. **$1,175**

Champagnes, Cordials & Wines

Wine glass, cranberry cut to clear bowl w/ horizontal bands of decoration, the lower portion of the clear stem decorated w/ inverted teardrop design conforming to shape of the stem itself, the circular base w/24-point rayed star, 2 1/4" d. bowls, 5" h., each (ILLUS. of two) **$395**

Sherry glasses, strawberry diamond & fan design, notched stem & rayed foot, cranberry cut to clear, set of 4 .... **$1,000**

Wine glasses, Hawkes-signed, bowl cut w/a raised diamond border, circles & spheres above the beaded stem & square foot, 6 1/2" h., set of 5 .... **$173**

Wine glasses, double-mitre & cross-cut hobnail design, cranberry cut to clear, rayed bases & notched stems, 5" h., pr. **$400**

Wine glass, Dorflinger, No. 1216 patt., emerald cut to clear bowl w/clear stem **$375**

←

Compotes

Elmira Cut Glass Co., No. 33 patt., 1906- 1910, 9" h. **$195**

Hawkes-signed, cov., footed, disk base w/rayed design, short knobbed stem, short squat body decorated w/panel of alternating Xs & bull's eyes, rayed collar, lid tapering to flattened faceted knob **$775**

Monroe, Tempt patt., 8 x 11" **$795**

Tazza-style, footed, widely flaring form, scalloped rim w/serrated edge, round base w/24-point hobstar, bowl decorated w/ alternating kite-shaped panels of hobstars & Russian cut design, 8 3/4" d., 7 1/2" h. **$675**

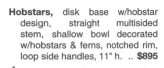

Hobstars, disk base w/hobstar design, straight multisided stem, shallow bowl decorated w/hobstars & ferns, notched rim, loop side handles, 11" h. .. **$895**

←

CUT

Creamers & Sugar Bowls

Creamer & sugar bowl w/notched handles, slightly waisted shapes deeply cut w/hobstars, C-form handles, pr. **$225**

Decanters

Decanter w/hobstar design, ovoid body w/cylindrical neck w/spout, faceted flattened ball stopper, C-form notched handle, the body decorated w/hobstars & fans **$375**

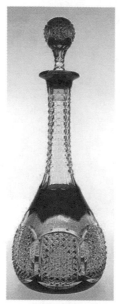

Flashed, ovoid base tapering to long slender neck w/flared lip, purplish to clear, the body w/horizontal band of crosscut diamonds in panels, w/pattern matched stopper, the bottom w/deeply cut 32- point rayed star, 15" h. **$925**

Hawkes, ship's decanter, Flutes patt. **$575**

Ice Tubs

Blackmer, Crescent patt. ice tub, w/underplate **$1,450**

Hoare (J.) & Co., Rookwood patt. ice tub, 7 1/2" d., 5 1/2" h. **$650**

Unger Bros., Larrissa patt. ice tub, 6" d., 3 1/2" h., 5+" h. including handles **$550**

Teepee shape, body cut overall w/starred buttons, hexagonal buttons w/cross-hatching, neck cut w/step cutting, 13" h. **$295**

Ship's decanters were designed to be short and squatty with a low center of gravity to prevent tipping in rough weather.

Clark signed, bulbous ovoid body tapering to a tall panel-cut neck w/a flattened rim, cut w/large buzzstars alternating w/fan cutting, compressed ball stopper w/matching cutting, 11" h., pr. **$358**

Decanter, short squatty bulbous body centered by a tall cylindrical neck w/a flaring notched spout, sides cut in hobstars w/cross-cut diamonds in hob points, triple-notched handle, 32-point hobstar in base................................. **$550**

Jars

Cigar jar, Dorflinger, Marlboro patt., 6" d., 9 1/4" to top of stopper **$1,650**

Presentation jar, cov., cylindrical form decorated in pattern similar to Ribbon Star, sterling silver repousse lid by Gorham, lid w/Gorham mark followed by "sterling-D- 3897," a sideways M & an indistinguishable mark, also bears information that "JEEBI" won the annual regatta at the Knickerbocker Yacht Club in 1903, 5 3/8" d., 6" h. **$1,775**

Miscellaneous

Lamps

Boudoir lamp, Egginton (O.F.), Virginia patt. w/6 1/2"-d. peaked mushroom shade, 13" h. **$1,350**

Table lamp, 12" d. mushroom dome from which 40 notched prisms hang, two horizontal bulbs, flared base, overall cut geometric pattern, rewired & resilvered, new set of notched prisms, 22" h. **$4,050**

Finger bowl & underplate, Straus, bowl & plate both w/scalloped rim w/notched edges, decorated w/stars, hobstars & crosscut diamonds, pr. **$400**

Perfumes & Colognes

Elmira Cut Glass Co. perfume, No. 33 patt., 4" d., 6 3/8" h. **$450**

Libbey-signed cologne, Corona patt., signed "Libbey" w/saber mark, 4 1/2" d., 6 1/2" h. ... **$475**

Cologne, hobstars alternating w/ notched prisms, facet-cut stopper **$350**

Cologne, Hawkes' Venetian patt., cut diamonds, fans & vesicas, facet-cut stopper, 3 1/2" d., 6 1/2" h. **$345**

Cheese, cov., the domed cover w/facet-cut knob handle above sides cut w/hobstars, the dished base w/a center cut hobstar surrounded by hobstar & fan cutting, plate 8" d., 2 pcs.... **$460**

Cut

Pitchers & Jugs

Hobstar pitcher, tall ovoid form tapering out slightly to shoulder, high arched spout, annealed handle decorated w/series of parallel miters cut at 45-degree angle to handle's vertical axis, body cut all over w/hobstars, fans & cane vesicas, an 8-point hobstar on bottom, 11" h. **$525**

Libbey jug, Harvard patt., 8" h. **$395**

Jug-form, cut w/pinwheels, fans, strawberry diamonds & a central star, notched spout & thumbprint-cut applied handle, 10" h.... **$105**

Water, pedestal-based, ovoid body tapering to a flaring plain neck w/rolled spout, applied handle, the body cut w/narrow flutes above & below a medial band of strawberry diamond, possibly early Dorflinger, 10 1/2" h. **$358**

Pitcher, jug-form, ovoid shape w/ flared three-sided scalloped rim, large notched C-form handle, body decorated w/fans & stars, a 24-point rayed star on base, 5 3/4" d., 7 1/2" h. **$495**

Tankard, Wreath patt., waisted cylindrical shape w/notched angled rim & wide spout, notched applied handle, cut in hobstars w/panels of large cane cutting, 10" h................................... **$143**

Plates

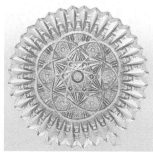

7" d., Libbey-signed, Ellsmere patt. **$775**

Parsche cake plate, Propeller patt., footed **$875**

7" w., square w/scalloped edge, decorated w/four vesicas radiating from central point to each of the far corners, w/curved major miters outside the square bottom & straight major miters inside the bottom square, the bottom square divided into squares, triangles, four-sided kites & another four-sided geometric figure **$295**

8" d., w/notched scalloped edges, decorated w/ten 16-point hobstars in teardrop- shaped miter outline surrounded by flashed miters, the 24-point central hobstar also surrounded by some flashed mi-ter cuts, the hobstar w/8-point radiants in hobstar points & crosshatching infills between outside of points **$395**

A vesica is shape formed by the intersection of two circles.

Punch bowls

Clark, Mercedes patt., 14" d., 11 1/2" h., signed **$4,950**

One-piece punch bowl, notched scalloped rim, sides decorated w/8-pointed hobstars & crosscut diamonds, bottom w/large hobstar, 6" h., 12" d. **$795**

Many quality American made goods are no longer affordable, but it is possible to purchase these items on the secondary market, often for less money than it costs to buy new. The most inexpensive way to furnish a home is by buying at auctions.

Two-piece punch bowl, bowl on stand flaring out at bottom, both w/scalloped, notched edge, decorated w/very large 32-point hobstars separated by vesicas filled w/two double-miter 8-point hobstars separated by clear bow ties w/triple-miter outlines, the peg w/a 16-point hobstar, 13" h., 14" d. **$2,475**

Punch Bowls, Cups & Sets

Punch bowl & base, deep bulbous bell- shaped bowl w/a flaring scalloped & notched rim, the sides cut w/large hobstars alternating w/panels cut w/four-part horizontal diamonds cut w/hobstars & fans above pairs of triangular panes above a blazing star & fans, matching flaring pedestal base, minor edge roughness, 12" d., 12" h. **$863**

Punch bowl & base, deep rounded bowl w/a scalloped & notched rim, the sides cut w/large diamonds cut w/alternating strawberry diamond or hobstars separated by an upper cut chevron band above inverted cut fans, short flaring pedestal base w/a ropetwist top rim, minor edge roughness on base & bowl, 14" d., 11 1/2" h. **$518**

Punch bowl & base, Harvard patt., deep rounded bowl w/scalloped & notched rim, knop pedestal & flaring base w/scalloped rim, chips to bowl & base, 12" d., 13 3/4" h., 2 pcs. **$460**

Punch bowl & base, Glenwood patt., the deep rounded bowl w/a low scalloped & spearpoint rim above cut puntiess over crosscut panels alternating w/hobstars, matching flaring pedestal base, minor edge roughness, 12" d., 9" h. **$805**

Punch bowl & base, Harvard patt., rounded bowl w/lightly notched rim, knop pedestal & flaring base w/scalloped rim, slight edge roughness, 10" d., 12" h., 2 pcs. **$575**

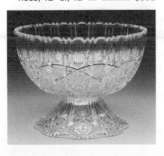

CUT

Punch cups

Dorflinger lemonade cup, No. 20 patt., handled, 3" h., 2 1/4" d. **$80**

Roman punch glass & plate, Russian cut decoration, w/ notched edge on plate & cup, pr. **$295**

Salt & Peppers

Master salt dip, Hawkes or Dorflinger, Marlboro patt. **$245**

Rose Bowls

Clark, Baker's Gothic patt., 7" **$650**

Egginton (O.F.), Creswick patt., 5 3/4" h., 7" d. **$725**

Hobstar, bottom decorated w/24-point hobstar within six points filled w/fine diamond, the sides w/ hobstars & strawberry diamonds, 6" h., 7 1/4" d. **$775**

Trays

Bread tray, J. Hoare, Marquise patt. **$525**

Empire round tray, Atlantic patt., 14" d. **$995**

Hoare (J.)-signed ice cream tray, Champion patt., ca. 1896, 10 3/8 x 17" **$1,295**

CUT

Vases

Baluster vase, 9 1/2" h., baluster-form body w/scalloped rim, decorated w/fans, stars, & vertical flutes **$375**

Shouldered vase, 12" h., cylindrical form tapering out slightly at shoulder, the neck w/horizontal step cutting, the flaring rim w/ deep scallops, decorated w/three large pinwheels & six 16-point hobstars, the various motifs separated by notched miters, the base featuring a 24-point rayed star **$795**

Tall vase, 14" h., cylindrical shape tapering out at shoulder, neck w/step cutting, scalloped rim slightly tapered out, the body decorated w/cane vesicas, fans, hobstars & strawberry diamonds, the 3 1/2" d. base w/hobstar **$1,475**

Trumpet vase, 18" h., w/9" d. scalloped notched rim, 7" d. base w/24-point hobstar, body decorated w/8-point hobstars w/ crosshatched buttons **$1,850**

Clark (T.B.) & Co., 14" h., "American Beauty," clear..................... **$795**

Hoare, (J.) & Co., 12" h., "Marquise," clear **$1,250**

DAUM NANCY

Daum Nancy

This fine glass, much of it cameo, was made by Auguste and Antonin Daum, who founded a factory in 1875 in Nancy, France. Most of their cameo and enameled glass was made from the 1890s into the early 20th century.

Cameo bowl, 5 1/2" w., squared shallow form in frosted clear overlaid w/reddish brown & cut w/ large oak leaves, applied w/three brightly colored cabochon insets, signed **$1,725**

Cameo ceiling fixture, a wide mushroom-shaped inverted shade in shaded grey to yellow ground overlaid in deep amethyst & cut w/a wide border of stylized flowers & leaves, signed, suspended from gilt-metal chains & ceiling plate, ca. 1900, shade 16" d. **$8,913**

Cameo cruet w/original stopper, bulbous ovoid body tapering to a short cylindrical neck w/a small pinched spout, round disk stopper & applied shoulder handle, frosted clear ground cameo-etched w/delicate flowering stems & long leaves trimmed w/gilt, etched signature on the side, one nick on upper rim of stopper, overall 7" h. **$1,495**

Cameo powder box, cov., squared squatty body w/rounded corners fitted w/a low domed cover, mottled white & pink cover & mottled white to greenish yellow base, cameo out & enameled w/bright deep rose red small blossoms on slender leafy stems, base rim polished & w/a pin nick on design, inside rim nicks on cover, cameo signature on the base, 4" w., 2 1/2" h. **$1,840**

Cameo vase, 4" h., miniature, ovoid body tapering to a flat mouth, a colored ground cameo-etched & enameled w/rosehips & leaves down from the rim, signed in cameo **$900**

Cameo glass is made by carving into multiple layers of colored glass to create a design in relief. Cameo glass is at least as old as the Romans, who produced the famous Portland Vase. Englishman John Lockwood inspired a revival of cameo glass in 1876 when he created a reproduction of the Portland Vase.

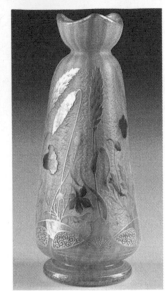

Cameo vase, 5 3/4" h., a round cushion foot tapering to a trumpent-form body w/an irregular shaped rim pulled into a spout at one side, mottled yellow shaded to motted dark brown cameo-etched w/wild orchids on tall leaft stems w/a flying bee, enameled in shades of pink, green, black & gold, signed on the bottom, some wear to gilding on the foot **$8,625**

Cameo vase, 6" h., footed tapering cylindrical body w/a cupped top pulled into three points, a mottled orange shading to green ground cameo-cut & enameled w/colorful flowers & field grasses, gilt trim & oblong panels of tiny scrolls around the lower body, signed in gilt **$5,290**

Cameo vase, 8" h., footed ovoid body tapering sharply to a narrow cylindrical neck, deep bluish green shading to a frosted ground cameo-etched w/a wreath of small leaves decorated w/green & yellow enamel & encircling a black enameled scene illustrating the Aesop fable of "The Crow and the Fox," gilt signature on the bottom **$3,220**

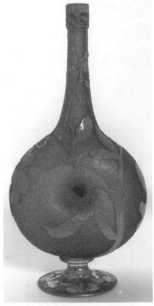

Cameo vase, 13" h., disk foot & short stem supporting the flattened round body tapering to a tall stick neck, frosted pink overlaid w/opalescent white & carved w/undulating leaves, stems, flowers & sweet pea pods in pale green outlined in gold, gold-lettered mark, pre-1900 .... **$7,475**

Cameo vase, 17 1/2" h., a cushion foot below the very tall cylindrical body, mottled shaded light to dark blue to brown ground, cameo cut & enameled w/brown leaves & stems below white-petaled flowers & buds **$10,350**

Cameo vase, 8 3/4" h., a small cushion foot below the bulbous tapering lower body centered by a tall swelled cylindrical neck, greyish blue & yellow mottled overlaid in vitrified green & orange & cut w/tall leafy stems supporting a white padded wheel-carved daffodil, signed in intaglio, ca. 1900 .... **$3,910**

Center bowl, a wide black disk foot supporting a very wide shallow flaring round bowl in mottled & swirls russet & brown w/gold foil inclusions. carved signature on the base, early 20th c., 12 1/4" d. **$374**

Cruet w/original stopper, spherical body w/a cylindrical neck & pinched spout, applied strap handle & flattened disk stopper, mottled yellow & orange etched & enameled w/red poppies on gold- trimmed green leafy stems, signed in gold enamel, ca. 1900, 6 1/2" h. (ILLUS. center with tumbler & vase) **$4,600**

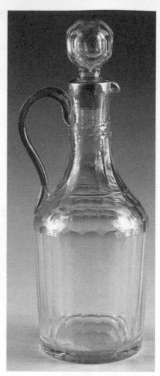

Decanter w/original facet-cut stopper, clear cylindrical panel-cut body w/a rounded shoulder tapering to the panel- cut neck w/a small rim spout, round panel-cut stopper, long applied C-scroll handle, trimmed in gold & signed in gold, 10" h. **$345**

Vase, 4 1/2" h., upright rectangular form, blue & grey mottled etched & enameled w/a continuous summer lakeside landscape in greens, yellows & browns, signed in black enamel, ca. 1900 .... **$2,070**

Vase, 4 1/2" h., upright rectangular form, grey internally decorated w/amethyst & yellow mottling, etched & enameled w/green leafy stems w/reddish orange berries, signed in cameo, ca. 1900 .... **$2,300**

Vase, 8 1/4" h., a cushion foot below the slightly swelled cylindrical body w/a flared flat rim, mottled grey, blue & amber etched & enameled w/a continuous winter village landscape w/snow-covered trees, homes, churches & windmills, signed in black enamel, ca. 1910 .... **$6,325**

Vase, 4 1/4" h., squatty ovoid pillow-form body in mottled orange & yellow, etched & enameled w/a continuous winter landscape in shades of brown, black & white, signed in black enamel, ca. 1900 (ILLUS. bottom row, center)
.... **$4,025**

Vase, 4 3/4" h., slightly swelled cylindrical form w/a flat rim, mottled mustard yellow etched & enameled w/wild violets & leaves, signed **$1,783**

Vase, 6" h., cushion foot supporting a flaring cylindrical body, mottled grey & blue etched & enameled w/a lakeside landscape, signed in black enamel, ca. 1900 . **$3,565**

Vase, 10" h., cushion foot tapering to a tall flaring body, yellow & orange w/mottling, etched & enameled in color w/a crocosmia arising from leafy green stems, signed on the base in script "Lorrain," 1927-32
.... **$374**

de Vez & Degué

The Saint-Hilaire, Touvier, de Varreaux and Company of Pantin, France used the name de Vez on its cameo glass early in the 20th century. Some of the firm's examples were marked "Degué" after one of its master glassmakers. Officially the company was named "Cristallerie de Pantin."

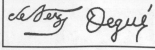

Cameo bowl, rectangular flat base w/flaring ends & arched wide sides, pastel green ground overlaid in dark raisin & green cameo etched w/a scene of a castle in the foreground beside a lake w/sailboats & mountains in the distance, signed "deVez," 4 1/4 x 12", 6 1/2" h. **$1,840**

Cameo vase, 3 1/2" h., miniature, round base flaring to a squared flat rim pulled into four points, mottled pale yellow, blue & rust red ground overlaid in red & black & cameo-carved w/a landscape w/large fir trees in the foreground & a lake & mountains in the distance, signed "de-vez" in cameo, minor rim roughness **$420**

Cameo vase, 7 1/2" h., tapering cylindrical body, pale opal yellow ground overlaid in cobalt blue & dark brown & cameo- carved w/a landscape of a village ter-raced above a fortress & framed by mountains, deVez cameo signature, tiny bruise in pattern, rim polishing **$633**

Cameo vase, 12" h., ovoid body tapering to a short cylindrical neck, mottled & shaded deep amber to cream to pale blue & overlaid in rose & burgundy, cameo-cut w/large flowers blossoms on tall leafy stems, signed in cameo "deVez," ca. 1910 .... **$2,415**

Shot glass, slender slightly tapering cylindrical shape in dark green shaded to clear intaglio-cut w/stylized flower blossoms & leaves, signed "Degué," two chips on inner lip, 2" h. **$144**

Intaglio cutting or incising is carving that is sunken below the surface. It is the opposite of relief carving.

Duncan & Miller

Duncan & Miller Glass Company, a successor firm to George A. Duncan & Sons Company, produced a wide range of pressed wares and novelty pieces during the late 19th century and into the early 20th century. During the Depression era and after, they continued making a wide variety of more modern patterns, including mold-blown types, and also introduced a number of etched and engraved patterns. Many colors, including opalescent hues, were produced during this era, and especially popular today are the graceful swan dishes they produced in the Pall Mall and Sylvan patterns.

The numbers after the pattern name indicate the original factory pattern number. The Duncan factory was closed in 1955. Also see ANIMALS.

Basket, applied handle, American Way patt., clear, 7 1/4 x 11 1/4" **$55**

Candleholders, one-light, Hobnail patt., clear, 3 3/4" h., pr. **$28**

Champagne, Dover patt., ruby bowl w/clear stem (ILLUS. right w/water goblet)........................... **$20**

Compote, 5 1/2" d., 4 3/4" h., etched First Love patt., clear **$45**

Decanter w/stopper, Hobnail patt., clear, 12 oz. (ILLUS. w/four tumblers) **$60**

Fernery, four-footed, rectangular, Spiral Flutes pattern, green, 6 x 9 1/2" $295

Goblet, Alden patt., blue, 6 1/2" h. $24

Goblet, Indian Tree etching, clear, 7 3/4" h. $30

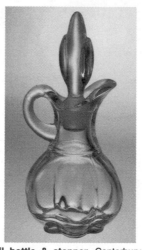

Oil bottle & stopper, Canterbury patt., crystal, 3 oz. $32

Plate, 14 1/2" d., Sculptured Line, Dogwood patt., blue opalescent $295

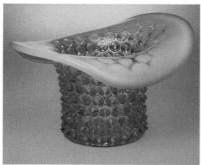

Model of top hat, Hobnail patt., blue opalescent, 2 1/2" h. $34

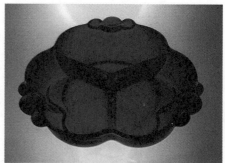

Relish, three-part, Canterbury patt., ruby, 7 1/2" w. $45

Plate, 9 1/2" d., Early American Sandwich patt., crystal **$40**

Vase, 5 1/2" h., Sanibel patt., footed, blue opalescent **$325**

Vase, 7" h., flared, Hobnail patt., pink opalescent **$125**

Vase, 8" h., cornucopia-shaped, Three Feather patt., clear w/ cutting **$55**

Vase, 10 1/2" h., footed, Venetian No. 126 patt., ruby.............. **$225**

Basket, Hobnail patt., applied handle, blue opalescent, 9 x 14" **$200**

Relish dish, Sylvan patt., two-part, milk white w/ green handle, 8 1/2" l. **$125**

DURAND

Durand

Fine decorative glass similar to that made by Tiffany and other outstanding glasshouses of its day was made by the Vineland Flint Glass Works Co. in Vineland, New Jersey, first headed by Victor Durand Sr. and subsequently by his son, Victor Durand Jr., in the 1920s.

Vase, 8 1/8" h., simple gently tapering cylindrical body w/a thin flat rim, overall gold iridescence over the marigold body, base marked "V. Durand - 1722-8" in applied silver **$431**

Vase, 8 1/2" h., gently tapering cylindrical body w/rounded shoulder & short flaring neck, overall orangish gold exterior iridescence decorated w/random bands of gold iridescent threading, interior in yellow shading to gold iridescence, minor loss of threading **$630**

Vase, 10" h., footed slender ovoid body w/a thin flared lip, dark blue iridescent ground decorated w/ a random silvery blue & purple iridescent heart & vine design, unsigned **$1,840**

Vase, 12" h., round foot & short stem in gold iridescence supporting the tall gently flaring trumpet-form body, the exterior in antique ivory decorated w/scattered bicolor leaves in blue & gold & covered w/overall gold threading, base marked w/Durand signature & "20120-12," some threading missing **$2,070**

Bowl-vase, bulbous slightly ovoid simple form in striated iridescent blue, signed "Durand - 1995-4," minor scratches, 4" h. **$259**

Some online auction reserves may be exceptionally high because the seller is testing the waters to determine what a piece is worth before selling it elsewhere.

Lamp, table model, the baluster-form gold iridescent body wrapped in fine golden threads, fitted w/an ornate cast-metal cap & paneled gilt-metal base w/foliate trim, base marked "M.S. Co. Des. Pat. #0154," w/cloth shade & finial, minor loss to threading, glass body 11 1/4" h., overall 22" h. **$575**

Fenton

Fenton Art Glass Company began producing glass at Williamstown, West Virginia, in January 1907. Organized by Frank L. and John W. Fenton, the company began operations in a newly built glass factory with an experienced master glass craftsman, Jacob Rosenthal, as their factory manager. Fenton has produced a wide variety of collectible glassware through the years, including Carnival. Still in production today, its current productions may be found at finer gift shops across the country.

William Heacock's three-volume set on Fenton, published by Antique Publications, is the standard reference in this field.

Basket, No. 203, Diamond Optic, Mulberry w/clear applied handle **$150**

Bowl, 10 1/2" d., oval footed, dolphin handles, No. 1608, black **$145**

Bonbon, heart-shaped, handled, Ruby Snow Crest, 6 1/2" d. **$58**

Candleholder, one-light, No. 318, Cameo Opalescent, 3" h. (ILLUS. top w/three other colors) **$28**

Cologne bottle & stopper, No. 192, Aqua Crest, 5" h. **$125**

Candleholders, Diamond Lace patt., cupped, blue opalescent, 4" d., 2" h., pr. **$65**

FENTON

Goblet, a deep ruby foot below the knopped stem & large bell-shaped bowl in deep ruby cased in white & decorated w/a design of overall ruby vines & heart leaves, artist signed by Dan Fitty & dated 2004, impressed mark "DLF Fenton," 5 3/4" h. **$150**

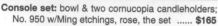

Console set: bowl & two cornucopia candleholders; No. 950 w/Ming etchings, rose, the set **$165**

Decanter w/stopper, No. 1934, w/pressed floral stopper, ruby **$185**

Deviled egg plate, figural hen cover, oval, milk glass w/amethyst head, 12 1/2" l. **$365**

Vase, 4" h., Crystal Crest, hat-shaped, double crimped rim **$45**

Tray, lemon, center-handled, Tangerine Stretch glass, 6" d. **$65**

Vase, 6" h., crimped, Bubble Optic patt., Blue Overlay $70

Vase, 10" h., tall ovoid body w/a low rolled rim, molded Dogwood patt. made from a Consolidated mold, pink cased in milk glass, ca. 1980 .... $125

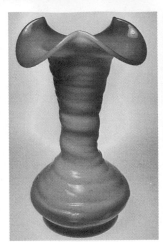

Vase, 6 1/2" h., three-crimp rim, No. 186, Peach Blow $48

Vase, 8 1/4" h., limited edition, h.p. underwater scene, Custard $245

Vase, 6" h., footed bulbous lower body w/flared upper body ending in a widely flaring crimped & ruffled rim, Shape #1925, Coin Dot patt., cranberry opalescent $78

Vase, 19" h., footed, swung, Hobnail patt., milk glass $35

Vase, 6" h., Hobnail patt., footed, trumpet- form w/flaring ruffled rim, milk glass $15

Vase, 9" h., footed Melon-lobed body w/a tall ringed neck w/a widely flaring crimped & ruffled rim, Peach Crest, Shape #192A $45

Vase, 10 1/2" h., deep rose mother-of-pearl satin glass in the Raindrop patt., small foot below the widely flaring bulbous body w/the wide shoulder tapering to a short trumpet neck w/widely flaring crimped rim, second half 20th c. $104

Fostoria

Fostoria Glass company, founded in 1887, produced numerous types of fine glassware over the years. Its factory in Moundsville, West Virginia, closed in 1986.

Almond dish, footed, Alexis patt., crystal **$15**

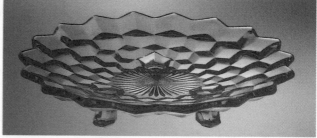

Bonbon, American patt., three short feet, Canary, 7 1/2" d. **$22**

Bowl, 11" d., footed console, No. 2333, blue **$75**

Bowl, 10 1/2" d., 5 1/2" h., low footed, Colony patt., clear ... **$75**

Bowl, 12" d., No. 2362, Brocade Grape etching, flared, green **$85**

Cake stand, American patt., round, clear, 10" d. **$165**

Candleholder, three-light, No. 2383, Rose **$38**

Candleholders, one-light, Heirloom patt., clear opalescent, 3 1/2" h., pr. **$48**

Candlestick, one-light, Mayflower etching, clear, 4" h. (ILLUS. right w/two-light candlestick)... **$36**

Candlestick, two-light, No. 2447, Wisteria, 5" h. **$75**

Candlesticks, one-light, Navarre etching, Baroque blank, No. 2496, clear, 4" h., pr. (ILLUS. of one, left w/compote & champagne)...................... **$45**

Candlesticks, one-light, No. 239 5 1/2, Fern etching, Ebony, 5" h., pr. (ILLUS. of one).............. **$145**

Candy dish, cov., footed flaring optic ribbed base w/molded scroll handles at the bottom, low pyramidal cover w/knob finial, Green, 5 1/2" h. **$50**

Chalice, cov., Windsor Crown patt., yellow, 8 1/2" h. **$55**

Champagne, Contrast line, black foot & stem, white bowl, 5 3/4" h. **$28**

FOSTORIA

Cocktail icer, June etching, non-etched liner, Topaz, 2 pcs. **$98**

Console set: rolled edge bowl & two low candlesticks; Oak Leaf Brocade etching, No. 2375 1/2, clear, the set **$175**

Goblet, Shirley etching, clear **$30**

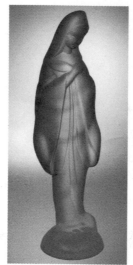

Figure of Madonna, crystal satin, 10" h. **$75**

Decanter & stopper, No. 4101 shape, Rose **$82**

Vanity box, three-piece, No. 2289, Canary, set **$275**

Goblet, Argus patt, blue (ILLUS. left with sherbet) **$20**

Fry

Numerous types of glass were made by the H.C. Fry Company of Rochester, Pennsylvania. One of its art lines was called Foval and was blown in 1926-27. Cheaper was its milky-opalescent ovenware (Pearl Oven Ware), made for utilitarian purposes but also now being collected. The company also made fine cut glass.

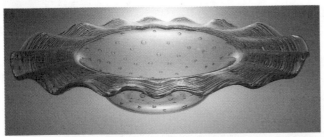

Bowl, 14" l., oval shape, light blue w/controlled bubbles in bowl & blue threading in wavy rim, polished pontil **$245**

Goblet, water, "Skyscraper Stem," crystal **$55**

Creamer & open sugar bowl, Foval, creamy opalescent body w/applied dark blue handles, pr.. **$350-450**

Goblet, water, Panel Optic, Art Deco pressed stem, green, 7 1/2" h. **$25**

Pitcher, 10" h., footed, wide panel w/four bulges, amber **$85**

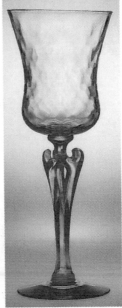

Goblet, water, pink bowl & foot, green "Cactus" stem **$175**

GALLÉ

Gallé

Gallé glass was made in Nancy, France, by Emile Gallé, a founder of the Nancy School and a leader in the Art Nouveau movement in France. Much of his glass, both enameled and cameo, is decorated with naturalistic motifs. The finest pieces were made in the last two decades of the 19th century and the opening years of the 20th.

Pieces marked with a star preceding the name were made between 1904, the year of Gallé's death, and 1914.

Cameo powder box, cov., low tapering round base in frosted pale green ground overlaid in purplish brown & cameo- carved w/sprigs of leaves & berries, engraved signature on the cover, cameo signature on the base, 4" d., 2 3/8" h. ... **$1,093**

Don't pass up a deal on an antique when you are traveling because you don't want to have to transport it. Dealers may be willing to pack and ship it for you to make a sale.

Cameo powder box, cov., squatty round base, frosted white w/ mottled amber & green overlaid in golden yellow, the cover cameo carved w/a daffodil & tall leaves, the base carved w/leaves, cameo signature, 5 1/4" d., 2 3/8" h. **$1,093**

Cameo vase, 8 3/8" h., flat-sided spherical base tapering to a very tall slender stick neck w/a cupped rim, mottled pale yellow & green ground overlaid in dark olive green & brown & cameo-carved w/a grasshopper & grasses on the base w/stems wrapping up the neck, cameo signature **$1,725**

Cameo vase, 9 3/8" h., 4 1/2" d., a wide round foot tapering to a slender stem & narrow ovoid body tapering to a rolled rim, mottled blue & white ground overlaid in very dark blue & cameo-cut w/tall fir trees, signed in cameo, ca. 1910 .... **$3,120**

Cameo vase, 7 1/16" h., footed slender tapering cylindrical body w/a flaring mouth, grey mottled w/peach & overlaid in purple, cut w/two flowering plants, signed in cameo, ca. 1900 .... **$1,092**

Vase, 4 3/4" h., 4 3/4 x 6 3/4", bulbous low oval shape tapering to short rolled neck, translucent yellow acid-etched & enameled in color w/a butterfly & blue & yellow flowers, ca. 1910 .... **$6,000**

Vase, 12" h., "Lion of Lorraine" design, rum-colored blown tapering ovoid body w/a flaring flat rim, raised on three applied rum-colored peg feet & w/two large rigaree bands of rum up the sides & around the rim, finely enameled overall w/scattered flowers in gold, maroon & blue & w/a dark blue griffin near the bottom, signed "E. Gallé Nancy Déposé" **$2,588**

Vase, 9 1/2" h., footed crystal flattened, flaring rectangular body w/a narrow angled shoulder to a rectangular neck, the side intaglio-carved w/a finely detailed portrait of a semi-nude woman wearing a flowing transparent gown, signed on the base "E. Gallé Nancy Déposé" **$1,725**

Vase, 15 7/8" h., 7 1/4 x 10 1/2", a thick oval foot supporting a bulbous flattened ovoid body w/ optic ribbing in clear smoky glass tapering to a short flaring neck, enameled overall w/detailed clusters of long dark & light blue leaves on thin stems accented by a long slender insect, engraved "E. Gallé Nancy 1993," ca. 1895 .... **$10,800**

Cameo Vase, 7" h., round foot below the ovoid body tapering slightly to the molded flat mouth, mottled citrine yellow & frosted ground w/an applied blown-out design of deep purple leaves suspending long pale pods, molded signature **$5,405**

Handel

Lamps, shades and other types of glass by Handel & Co., which subsequently became The Handel Co., Inc., were produced in Meriden, Connecticut, from 1893 to 1941.

Boudour Lamp, 7" w. hexagonal domed shade, reverse-painted w/a large blue parrot perched on a leafy branch w/pink flowers, shaded bright yellow to clear background, shade signed "Handel," on a bronzed metal base w/a slender paneled stem & a flaring hexagonal base, overall 14" h. **$4,312**

Humidor, cov., a round foot below the four-sided bulbous glass body w/a painted green to reddish brown ground decorated w/a brown transfer-printed scene of two squirrels on a log, a bronzed metal rim w/flat cover w/a large figural pipe handle **$672**

Tray, metal-mounted opalware glass dish h.p. w/red collared pug dog, signed by artist "Bauer," mounted on base, "4091/S" w/ partial Handel Ware shield mark, 4 3/4" h. **$633**

Tobacco Jar, cov., wide cylindrical body w/rounded base & shoulder, silver plated hinged fitting w/ a domed glass cover w/wide knob handle, opal molded glass decorated w/raised leafy gilt scrollwork against a green shading to mahogany brown ground centered by a bust portrait of a Native American chief in a feathered headdress, base marked w/Handel shield mark, 7 1/4" h. **$1,495**

Vase, 10 1/2" h., "Teroma" line, round foot & slender base on the tall flaring ovoid body w/a wide flaring neck w/a ruffled rim, frosted ground decorated in dark maroon & green w/a h.p. tropical scene w/tall palm trees, signed "Handel Teroma 4214" .. **$1,783** →

Heisey

Numerous types of fine glass were made by A.H. Heisey & Co., Newark, Ohio, from 1895. The company's trademark, an H enclosed within a diamond, has become known to most glass collectors. The company's name and molds were acquired by Imperial Glass Co., Bellaire, Ohio, in 1958, and some pieces have been reissued. The glass listed below consists of miscellaneous pieces and types. Also see ANIMALS.

Almond dish, handled, Octagon patt., Moongleam (light green), 3" w. . **$28**

Ashtray w/match holder, No. 360, Flamingo (pink), 6" d. **$75**

Almond set: six individual footed almonds & one 6" w. master; Medium Flat Panel, Flamingo (pink), set **$175**

Ashtray, Lodestar patt., Dawn (light grey), 5" d. **$98**

Banana split dish, footed, Greek Key patt., clear **$45**

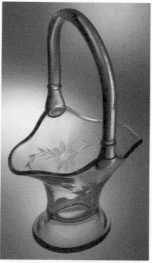

Basket, No. 463, crystal w/cutting, 9" h. **$295**

Basket, No. 466, crystal w/cutting, 8" w. **$325**

Bowl, 11" d., Empress patt., flared shape, dolphin feet, Sahara **$125**

Cocktail shaker, rooster head stopper, Barcelona cut, crystal, 14" h. **$175**

Candleholders, toy one-light, Patrician patt., clear, 4 1/2" h., pr............. **$89**

Cocktail, figural horse head stem, clear **$365**

Cruet w/original stopper, oil-type, Yeoman patt., Moongleam, 2 oz. **$80**

Oil cruet & stopper, Pleat & Panel patt., Moongleam, 3 oz. **$80**

HEISEY

Cup & saucer, Stanhope patt., clear w/black plastic knob in handle **$32**

Marmalade jar, cov., No. 341 Puritan, crystal, 4" h. **$85**

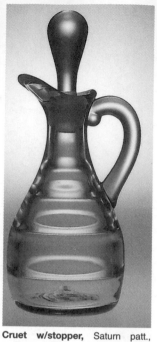

Cruet w/stopper, Saturn patt., Zircon (blue green) w/clear stopper **$650**

Decanter w/stopper, Ridgeleigh patt., clear, 1 pt. **$250**

Candleholder-vase, one-light, two-piece, Ipswich patt., square foot, flaring rim hung w/twelve prisms, clear, 10" h. **$155**

Candlesticks, two-light, Trident patt., Sahara, pr. (ILLUS. of one).. **$250**

Candlesticks, toy-size, one-light, Patrician patt., clear, 4 1/2" h., pr... **$85**

Imperial

From 1902 until 1984 Imperial Glass of Bellaire, Ohio, produced hand made glass. Early pressed glass production often imitated cut glass and may bear the raised "NUCUT" mark in the interior center. In the second decade of the 1900s Imperial was one of the dominant manufacturers of iridescent or Carnival glass. When glass collecting gained popularity in the 1970s, Imperial again produced Carnival and a line of multicolored slag glass. Imperial purchased molds from closing glass houses and continued many lines popularized by others including Central, Heisey and Cambridge. These reissues may cause confusion but they were often marked.

IMPERIAL

Candlewick

Ashtray, eagle, No. 1776/1, milk glass, 6 1/2" **$65**

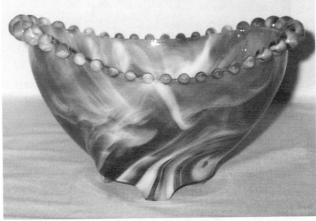

Bowl, 8 1/2" l., caramel slag, a long oval flaring bowl w/beaded rim, tapering to a three-toed base, No. 400/182 .... **$425-475**

Cigarette box, cov., rectangular base w/large beads around bottom, flat fitted mirrored copper-colored top w/an applied cluster of clear grapes, No. 40/135 .... **$125-150**

Bowl, 9" d., No. 400/74SC, square, crimped bowl, four-toed, ruby **$325**

A nappy is a a a small shalllow dish or bowl with sloping sides.

Nappy, No. 400/1F, shallow round bowl raised on a turned wood pedestal base **$75-100**

→

IMPERIAL

Compote, 10" h., crimped, three-bead stem, No. 400/103, clear w/h.p. pink roses & blue ribbons **$260**

Toast plate w/glass dome lid, No. 400/123, clear, 8" d., 2 pcs. **$425**

Cape Cod

Wine carafe & stopper, footed, handled, No. 160/185, crystal **$220**
→

> Visit antique shops, malls, shows and museums to study antiques in person and learn to recognize quality. Your experience will reward you later in spotting overlooked deals and avoiding fakes and reproductions.

←
Decanter w/stopper, square, No. 160/212, clear **$75**

Free-Hand Ware

Vase, 9 1/4" h., bulbous ovoid lower body tapering to a cylindrical neck w/a very wide rolled rim, overall blue & white pulled-feather design decorated w/orange iridescence, iridescent orange interior, unsigned **$920**
→

←
Vase, 7 1/4" h., footed baluster-form w/a widely flaring rim, cobalt blue exterior decorated w/an iridescent orange design of random threading & heart-shaped leaves, unsigned **$978**

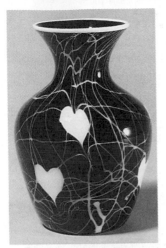

Vase, 6 1/2" h., flat-bottomed wide ovoid body tapering to a trumpet neck, cobalt blue ground decorated overall w/random white threading & heart-shaped leaves **$500**

Vase, 7" h., ovoid body tapering to a short rolled neck, green iridescent ground decorated w/ trailing burgundy hearts & vines, cobalt blue rim band **$460**

Vases, 9 1/8" h., simple baluster-form body w/a trumpet neck, draped chartreuse festoons down the sides against a dark iridescent ground w/bronze, green & purple highlights, citron yellow interior, pr. **$805**

Miscellaneous Patterns & Lines

Candy dish cov., low, flat, three-part, No. 1961/110, clear, 9" d. **$36**

Mug, Big Shot patt., ruby, 4 1/2" h. **$35**

Pillow box, cov., Cathay Line, jade green, 4" x 8" **$18**

Sherbet, Chroma patt., dark green, 4 1/2" h................................. **$18**

IMPERIAL

Bowl, Cathay Line, figural Phoenix, No. 5026, clear satin, marked "Virginia B Evans" in script **$295**

Console set: compote & two candlesticks; all w/figural elf stems, satin milk glass, the set **$195**

Candlestick, single-light, Cathay Line, figural Candle Servant (female), No. 5035, clear satin, marked "Virginia B Evans" in script **$295**

Flower bowl, Cathay Line, model of a Chinese junk, No. 5010, clear satin, marked "Virginia B Evans" in script **$225**

Plate, 8" w., Blaise patt., pink **$15**

Punch bowl, footed, pressed, No. 292 line, crystal, 10" d. **$120**

Shoppers shouldn't expect to receive a discount on purchases of $20 or less. A dealer may decide to give a customer a discount for buying multiple items, like postcards, even if they cost only a few dollars each. However, an antique mall manager likely will not allow a discount on several inexpensive items each belonging to different dealers.

Rose bowl, Molly line, black w/silver deposit floral decoration, 5" h. **$75**

Tumbler, flat, Marine Lamp patt., ruby w/gold decoration **$26**

Vase, Fu Wedding, No. 5016 Cathay Line, octagonal body w/embossed design, clear satin, marked "Virginia B Evans" in script **$275**

Sugar, open, Katy Blue patt., blue opalescent **$38**

Kew Blas

In the 1890s the Union Glass Works, Somerville, Massachusetts, produced a line of iridescent glasswares closely resembling Louis Tiffany's wares. The name was derived from an anagram of the name of the factory's manager, William S. Blake.

Vase, 7 1/4" h., gently tapering cylindrical body w/a rounded shoulder to the short flaring & scalloped neck, platinum iridescent wave designs on a gold iridescent background w/emerald green dragging design on the lower half, signed on the bottom **$575**

Vase, 8 1/4" h., flora-form w/a cushion foot tapering to a very slender stem supporting a bulbous ovoid upper body w/a short flared neck, overall gold iridescence w/flashes of red, purple & green, signed on the polished pontil **$403**

Vase, 8 5/8" h., waisted cylindrical body w/a low flaring mouth, the white rim above the dark green iridescent body decorated w/ golden scrolls & pulled-feather designs, signed, ca. 1905 .... **$1,434**

LACY

Lacy

Lacy Glass is a general term developed by collectors many years ago to cover the earliest type of pressed glass produced in this country. "Lacy" refers to the fact that most of these early patterns consisted of scrolls and geometric designs against a finely stippled background that gives the glass the look of fine lace. Formerly this glass was often referred to as "Sandwich" for the Boston & Sandwich Glass Company of Sandwich, Massachusetts, which produced a great deal of this ware. Today, however, collectors realize that many other factories on the East Coast and in the Pittsburgh, Pennsylvania, and Wheeling, West Virginia, areas also made lacy glass from the 1820s into the 1840s. All pieces listed are clear unless otherwise noted. Numbers after salt dips refer to listings in *Pressed Glass Salt Dishes of the Lacy Period, 1825-1850*, by Logan W. and Dorothy B. Neal. Also see CUP PLATES and SANDWICH GLASS.

Bowl, 10 5/8" d., 2 1/2" h., Gothic Arch & Palm with Chevron Rim patt., clear, probably Boston & Sandwich Glass Co., 1835-50, one rim chip w/loss to scallop, loss of scallop & two point, several tipped points **$770**

Creamer, Gothic Arch & Palm patt., molded handle, translucent fiery opalescent blue, Boston & Sandwich Glass Co., 1835-45, 4" h. **$358**

Dish, oval, Beaded Medallion & Urn patt., lobed sides w/scalloped rim, Boston & Sandwich Glass Co., 1835-45, 5 3/4 x 8", 1 3/4" h. **$77**

Dish, round, Anchor & Shield patt., rope table ring, even scalloped rim, possibly Providence Flint Glass Works, 1830-40, partial loss of four scallops, 8" d., 1 1/2" h. **$242**

Dish, rectangular w/notched corners, Double Peacock Eye patt., variation w/ no background stipping on ends, plain cross bars in center, even scalloped rim w/inner beads, Boston & Sandwich Glass Co., very minor flaking, Boston & Sandwich Glass Co., 1835-50, 9 1/8 x 12 1/8", 2" h. (ILLUS. right) **$330**

Dish, round, Peacock Eye patt., center w/three concentric rings of beads around a rope-framed eye, clear, Boston & Sandwich Glass Co., 1830-45, minor tipping, 10 1/2" d., 2 3/8" h. (ILLUS. left) **$468**

Dish, oval, Beaded Medallion & Urn pat., central design of tiny flower bracketed by beaded scrolls & stylized leaves, each side & end w/a beaded medallion from which extends scrolled flowers, each corner lobe w/a scroll-handled urn, shaped plain even scallop rim, Boston & Sandwich Glass Co., 1835-45, colorless, chip under rim w/loss of one scallop, 5 7/8 x 8", 1 3/4" h. (ILLUS. center) **$88**

Tray, oblong, Butterfly patt., central design of butterfly & beaded bull's-eyes, shoulder w/fleur-de-lis, pinwheels & fans, serpentine rim, Boston & Sandwich Glass Co., 1835-45, colorless, loss of one tiny scallop, 6 1/8 x 9 1/8", 1 3/8" h. (ILLUS. right) **$231**

Window pane, rectangular, Gothic Arch patt., design comprised of six individual arches, scrolls & rosettes at the top, faintly signed "Bakewell" on the back, Pittsburgh Flint Glass Manufactory, 1830-45, colorless, broken into two pieces, several edge chips, 4 7/8 x 6 7/8" (ILLUS. left) **$1,100**

When searching for an antique mall in which to sell, consideration should be given to its hours of operation and marketing. An antiques dealer once observed, "If you are open 10 to 5 on weekdays, you are catering to the unemployed." An antique mall should be open weekends and at least one evening each week to ensure that people who work long hours can have access during their time off. They also need to advertise locally and in trade publications.

Lalique

Fine glass, which includes numerous extraordinary molded articles, has been made by the glasshouse established by René Lalique early in the 20th century in France. The firm was carried on by his son, Marc, until his death in 1977 and is now headed by Marc's daughter, Marie-Claude. All Lalique glass is marked, usually on or near the bottom, with either an engraved or molded signature. Unless otherwise noted, we list only those pieces marked "R. Lalique," produced before the death of René Lalique in 1945.

R. Lalique France N° 3152

R. LALIQUE
FRANCE

R LALIQUE
FRANCE

Bowl, 12" d., "Ondines," wide shallow form w/a flat rim, molded in medium relief w/a band of swirling mermaids around the border, clear opalescent, engraved "R. LALIQUE - FRANCE," introduced in 1921 .... **$3,107**

Box, cov., "Cleones," low cylindrical round base w/slightly domed cover, amber, the cover molded w/beetles among fern leaves, signed in block letters "R. Lalique France," two small chips on cover rim **$1,093**

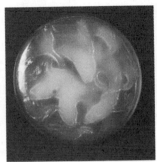

Box, cov., "Grande Cyprins," low cylindrical base w/slightly domed cover, opalescent, the cover molded w/swirling fish, signed in block letters "R. Lalique France," 10" d., 2" h. **$3,163**

Charger, "Ormeaux," frosted clear molded around the wide sides w/overlapping leaves, stenciled block mark "R. Lalique France," 13 5/8" d. **$547**

Paperweight, figural, "Moineau sur Socle, Ailes Overtes" (Sparrow on base, open wings), frosted clear model of a bird, introduced in 1929, inscribed "R. Lalique," 4" h. **$374**

Lamp, table model, "Suzanne," frosted opalescent molded in full relief as a nude dancer w/ outstretched arms holding lengths of drapery, w/gilt-bronze base & silk shade, molded "R. Lalique," inscribed "France," ca. 1925, 8 7/8" h. **$19,120**

Perfume bottel w/stopper, "Le Jade," flattened ovoid snuff bottle-form molded w/a jungle bird design in bright green crystal, matching stopper, marked "Le Jade - Roger et Gallet Paris - R. Lalique," 3 1/4" h. **$2,185**

Perfume bottle w/ith original stopper, "Arys," flattened wide tapering sides pressed w/a feather design, the pointed stopper w/a matching design, bottle & stopper patinated in light blue, original sticker on the side reads "Faisons un Reve ARYS," signed on the base in raised letters "ARYS - R. Lalique," flake on bottle lip, 4 3/4" h. **$805**

Jewelry suite: necklace & bracelet; "Dahlias," each formed by bands of molded frosted clear glass in a petal design, the necklace w/ adjustable spacer, the bracelet extendable, pr. **$1,725**

LALIQUE

LALIQUE

Perfume bottle with original stopper, "D'Orsay," tall slightly tapering square deep amber bottle w/a molded figure of a standing woman wearing a long gown at each corner, the flattened square stopper molded w/florals, signed on the foot "Ambre D'Orsay -Lalique," 5" h. **$1,495**

Vase, 6 5/8" h., "Gui," small foot below the wide nearly spherical body w/a small flat mouth, emerald green molded overall w/berried mistletoe branches, signed in block letters "R. Lalique France," Model No. 948 .... **$2,300**

Vase, 6 1/8" h., "Cogs et Raisins," slightly swelled cylindrical frosted clear body w/a flat rim, molded in low-relief w/a continuous design of pairs of confronting longtailed roosters perched beneath scrolling grapevines heavy w/fruit, inscribed "R. Lalique," introduced in 1928 .... **$1,150**

Perfume bottle with original stopper, "Duflores," frosted & clear colorless body molded in the shaped of overlapping blossoms, dotted blossom-form stopper, R. Lalique etched signature, 3 1/2" h. **$690**

Vase, 6 3/4" h., "Formose," large spherical body on a tiny footring & w/a small, short cylindrical neck, translucent white w/a pale blue tint, molded in medium and low relief w/an overall design of large Japanese goldfish w/long delicate tails & fins, retains traces of original aquamarine patina, molded mark, introduced in 1924 .... **$2,040**

Vase, 7 1/4" h., "Orsin," spherical body w/short flaring rim, clear stained overall in light blue, molded w/overall knobs resembling a sea urchin, signed in block letters "R. Lalique, France" **$1,560**

Vase, 6 1/2" h., "Ibis," widely flaring trumpet form w/eight panels of narrow vertical ribs w/an impressed head of wheat at the base of each panel, clear w/light blue patination, signed "R. Lalique - France" **$1,020**

Vase, 7 1/4" h., "Danaides," footed wide ovoid body w/a wide flat rim, molded around the sides w/standing nude maidens each holding a large urn on her shoulder & pouring water from it, clear w/blue patination, signed "R. Lalique" **$4,140**

Vase, 7" h., spherical body tapering to a small neck, dark blue molded overall w/fern leaves, signed "R. Lalique France No. 996" **$2,875**

Vase, 7 1/2" h., "Coquilles," footed swelled cylindrical body w/a small cylindrical neck, frosted clear w/an overall light blue stain, molded overall w/overlapping seashells, signed in block letters "R. Lalique" **$1,495**

Vase, 7 3/4" h., "Ajaccio," flat-bottomed wide trumpet-form body, deeply molded around the base w/a band of recumbent sleeping impalas below overall graduated stars against a dark blue patinated background, signed "R. Lalique - France" **$2,300**

Vase, 8" h., "Plumes," flat-bottomed wide squatty bulbous body tapering sharply to a small cylindrical neck, molded overall w/swirling ostrich plumes, clear w/ a dark reddish brown patination, signed "R. Lalique" **$2,160**

Vase, 8 1/2" h., "Domremy," flat-bottomed wide ovoid body w/a rounded shoulder & short flaring neck, molded overall w/large spherical flower tops on spiney leafy stems, clear w/light blue patination, signed "R. Lalique - France" **$1,720**

Vase, 9 1/2" h., "Monnaie du Pape," footed wide ovoid body w/a short cylindrical neck, deep reddish amber molded overall w/silver dollar plant, introduced in 1914, embossed mark "R. Lalique" **$4,600**

Vase, 10" h., "Penthievre," nearly spherical body w/a small flaring neck, blue, inscribed "R. LALIQUE," introduced in 1926 .... **$19,120**

Vase, 10" h., "Perruches," bulbous ovoid body w/a low flat mouth rim, electric blue molded w/fourteen pairs of love birds perched on flowering branches, frosted & polished to enhance the design, signed "R. Lalique - France," introduced in 1919 .... **$11,950**

Vase, 10 1/2" h., "Archers," ovoid body w/short neck, archers shooting at birds, signed "R. Lalique" **$11,500**

Vase, 13 1/4" h., "Lezards et Bluets," ovoid body w/a small cylindrical neck, molded in relief w/lizards & flowers, blue, molded "R. LALIQUE," inscribed "France," introduced in 1913 .... **$28,680**

Le Verre Francais

Glassware carrying this marking was produced at the French glass factory founded by Charles Schneider in 1908. A great deal of cameo glass was exported to the United States early in the 20th century and much of it was marketed through Ovingtons in New York City.

Cameo vase, 12 3/4" h., thick cushion foot supporting the tall ovoid body w/a short flared neck, mottled citron ground overlaid in orange shaded to dark brown & cameo-carved w/tall arched stylized flower clusters in the Art Deco style, signed on the foot **$2,243**

Cameo vase, 13 5/8" h., cushion foot & knop stem tapering to a very tall slender ovoid body w/a short flared neck, yellow ground overlaid w/deep orange shading to dark purple & cameo-carved in the Art Deco style w/berried vines w/domino-like flowers, inscribed signature, nick in mid- body **$1,955**

Cameo vase, 13 3/4" h., Art Deco style, round cushion foot in mottled orange & purple tapering to a slender stem supporting a tall cupped upper body, frosted clear shading to pale yellow ground overlaid in mottled purple & cameo-cut w/tall stylized thistle- like blossoms on leafy stems, etched signature on the foot **$2,875**

Cameo Lamp, "Escargot" patt., 8 1/2" d. domical shade in deep yellow overlaid w/dark brown shaded to orange & cameo-cut w/ a design of large snails on arching foliage, raised on a matching urn- form base w/a knopped stem & round orange foot w/another snail, engraved signature on the foot, overall 13" h. **$5,160**

Cameo vase, 13 3/4" h., Art Deco style, large cushion foot supporting a flaring body topped by a large trumpet neck, the upper & lower angled sides cameo-cut w/narrow knobby stripes, the orange medial band etched w/ stylized flowerheads, dark blue neck, signed in script........ **$2,645**

Cameo vase, 11" h., footed spherical body tapering to a widely flaring low trumpet neck, mottled peach & yellow ground overlaid w/deep orange shading to deep purple & cameo-carved around the bottom w/a band of grass issuing a band of very slender stems topped by bold five-petaled blossoms, signed "Le Verre Francais- France" **$3,360**

Legras

Cameo and enameled glass somewhat similar to that made by Gallé, Daum Nancy and other factories of the period was made at the Legras works in Saint Denis, France, late in the 19th century and until the outbreak of World War I.

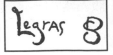

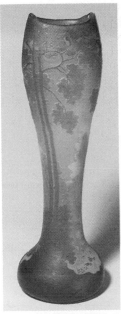

Cameo vase, 21 1/2" h., tall shouldered tapering cylindrical form in lime green internally decorated w/mottled pumpkin, cameo-etched w/a stylized design of towering black trees w/enameled dark orange, red & yellow leaves against a multi-rayed setting sun on a textured ground of cascading ice, cameo-signed, ca. 1905 (ILLUS. far left) **$2,415**

Cameo vase, 21 1/2" h., tall shouldered tapering cylindrical form in lime green internally decorated w/mottled pumpkin, cameo-etched w/a stylized design of towering black trees w/enameled dark orange, red & yellow leaves against a multi-rayed setting sun on a textured ground of cascading ice, cameo-signed, ca. 1905 (ILLUS. second from left) **$2,530**

Cameo vase, 22" h., tall slender tapering cylindrical body w/a small cupped mouth, mottled butterscotch opaque ground cameo-etched w/various seaweeds & shells enameled in shades of purple & green, signed in enameled cameo, ca. 1900 (ILLUS. far right) **$1,150**

Cameo vase, 24" h., tall slender ovoid body in mottled white & brown overlaid in a deep crystal paperweight finish & etched w/a design of stylized birds & leafy flowers decorated w/dark sepia enamel, signed in intaglio, ca. 1920 (ILLUS. second from right) **$1,955**

Cameo vase, 23 3/4" h., bulbous cushion vase tapering to a tall ovoid upper body w/the rim pulled into two points, mottled yellow & green ground overlaid in dark green & cameo-carved w/a forest scene w/tall leafy trees in the foreground, dense brush w/a view of a waterway, cameo signature **$2,530**

Cameo vase, 4" h., 3 1/4 x 4 1/4", flat-bottomed straight-sided oblong form w/the flat rim pulled into a small point at each end, thick cream ground overlaid w/mottled green & orange & carved w/ thin stems w/nasturtium leaves & enameled red blossoms, ca. 1910 .... **$1,920**

Cameo vase, 5 7/8" h., round-based tapering cylindrical body w/a bulbed top, a mottled orange & red upper body shading to dark mottled purple, a design of a foggy low river valley cameo cut in the foreground w/a tall weathered tree enameled in brown w/green leaves & grass below, a swollen river below, signed in enamel on the side **$633**

Loetz

Iridescent glass, some of it somewhat resembling that of Tiffany and other contemporary glasshouses, was produced by the Bohemian firm of J. Loetz Witwe of Klostermule and is referred to as Loetz. Some cameo pieces were also made. Not all pieces are marked.

Bowl-vase, squatty bulbous body tapering to a four-lobed rim, arched reeded applied handles from the rim to lower body, overall gold iridescent oil spot decoration, unsigned, 4 1/2" h. **$510**

Lamp base, paperweight style w/"Titania" finish, bulbous tapering gourd-form, internally decorated w/random silver in the upper half & emerald green around the lower half, w/electric fittings, 8" h. **$460**

Vase, 4 5/8" h., pinched & undulating cylindrical form w/ flared mouth, peach decorated overall w/salmon & silvery blue wavy iridescent bands, the base further decorated w/silver overlay leafy scrolling vines & a silver rim band, signed on the bottom **$2,070**

Vase, 7 1/8" h., footed wide squatty bulbous lower body tapering sharply to the widely flaring neck, apricot ground decorated overall w/horizontal silvery blue wavy bands & applied w/nine long raindrop prunts applied down the sides in dark blue w/silvery iridescent stripes, engraved script signature in the polished pontil **$11,500**

Vase, 5 1/2" h., 6 1/2" d., wide cylindrical tree trunk-style form w/a cushion foot, deep random ruffling on the rim, tooled lines & indentations around the sides, gold w/an overall iridescent finish w/platinum oil-spot decoration **$690**

Vase, 6 3/4" h., footed ovoid body tapering to a short cylindrical neck, satin mother- of-pearl "Federzeichnung" design in dark brown w/lighter swirls, enameled w/fine gold tracery & gilt trim, late 19th c. **$1,668**

Vase, 7 1/4" h., slightly flaring cylindrical body w/pinched-in sides & a pinched & ruffled rim, bronze ground decorated overall w/swirling silvery blue iridescent bands, signed on the pontil "Loetz Austria" **$2,530**

Vase, 7 1/2" h., squared tapering bulbous body w/a flat rim, clear w/overall bright gold oil spot iridescence, signed on the base "Loetz Austria" **$575**

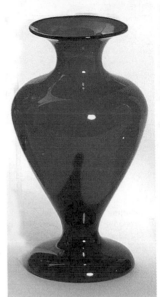

Vase, 8 1/2" h., "Tango" type, wide cushion foot below the wide ovoid body w/a flaring trumpet neck, tangerine orange above pulled amethyst bands around the lower section, signed on the base "Czechoslovakia," ca. 1920s **$288**

Vase, 9 1/2" h., tapering conical lower body below the large bulbed neck w/a flaring rim, green w/an overall Papillon style platinum ribbon decoration, the bottom decorated w/a wide band of silver overlay scrolling leaves & blossoms, glass signed **$2,990**

Vase, 9 1/2" h., wide cylindrical body w/a narrow angled shoulder & wide flat mouth, overall textured green ground w/blue iridescent oil spot decoration & seven applied gold iridescent figural seashell prunts, ca. 1909 .... **$3,910**

Vase, 10" h., tall cylindrical form w/ pinched- in & twisted design below the widely flaring inverted three-lobe neck, amethyst w/overall silvery blue oil spot iridescence, unsigned............................ **$720**

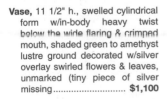

Vase, 11 1/2" h., swelled cylindrical form w/in-body heavy twist below the wide flaring & crimped mouth, shaded green to amethyst lustre ground decorated w/silver overlay swirled flowers & leaves, unmarked (tiny piece of silver missing **$1,100**

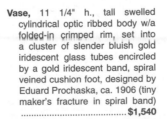

Vase, 11 1/4" h., tall swelled cylindrical optic ribbed body w/a folded-in crimped rim, set into a cluster of slender bluish gold iridescent glass tubes encircled by a gold iridescent band, spiral veined cushion foot, designed by Eduard Prochaska, ca. 1906 (tiny maker's fracture in spiral band) **$1,540**

LOETZ

Vase, 10 1/4" h., Papillon style, a tapering ovoid body w/a gently flaring wide cylindrical neck, ruby red decorated overall w/silvery blue oil spot decoration & enclosed by openwork pewter Art Nouveau looping vines, long looping & undulating pewter handles down the sides from the rim to the base, metal w/impressed number 4530 .... **$2,185**

Vase, 11 1/4" h., Neptun (sic) line, bulbous ovoid base tapering to a ruffled cupped rim, molded w/ slender vertical vining, dark blue w/green iridescence, ca. 1906 .... **$425-525**

Vase, 11 1/2" h., modeled as a large upright seashell supported on leaves of seaweed continuing to a foot composed of leaves, iridescent gold "Candia Diaspora Silveriris" finish on the shell, the leaves in clear w/an iridescent finish, ca. 1898 .... **$3,450**

Vase, 12" h., a tall stylized bulbed flower form in cobalt blue w/a blue iridized finish supported by swirled gold iridescent leaves & round foot, ca. 1910 .... **$3,795**

Mont Joye

Cameo and enameled glass bearing this mark was made in Pantin, France, by the same works that produced pieces signed de Vez.

Vase, 14 1/8" h., tall slender trumpet-form in frosted marine green finely enameled w/spiked white & pink flowers on gold stems, band of lacy gold scrolls around the rim, mounted in a scroll-cast gilt metal base w/a round white marble foot **$460**

→

Vase, 13" h., elongated acorn-form body w/a short wide mouth w/ a flattened flaring rim, heavily scale-textured emerald green decorated around the shoulder & base w/heavily gilt Art Nouveau style oak leaves & silver acorns, signed............................. **$2,200**

Layaway plans are still accepted by many antique shop owners, especially among those who do not accept credit cards. Occasionally, the dealer will charge a fee for a layaway purchase.

Moser

Ludwig Moser opened his first glass shop in 1857 in Karlsbad, Bohemia (now Karlovy Vary, in the former Czechoslovakia). Here he engraved and decorated fine glasswares especially to appeal to rich visitors to the local health spa. Later other shops were opened in various cities. Throughout the 19th and early 20th century lovely, colorful glasswares, many beautifully enameled, were produced by Moser's shops and reached a wide market in Europe and America. Moser died in 1916 and the firm continued under his sons. They were forced to merge with the Meyer's Nephews glass factory after World War I. The glassworks were sold out of the Moser family in 1933.

Bowl, 2 5/8" h., an oblong cranberry form w/a flaring & pointed-crimp rim, an applied gold-painted clear branch handle at one end, raised on four heavy pointed gilt-trimmed root-form feet, the interior decorated w/a gold vine enameled w/strawberries & florets, minor gilt loss **$374**

Bowl, 8 3/4" d., 3 5/8" h., wide flat bottom w/shallow rounded sides w/a flat rim, light amethyst w/optic-ribbed design, decorated on the exterior w/gilded sprigs of moss w/enameled florets & three butterflies, the interior w/a brown enameled beetle crawling on a mossy sprig, minimal gold wear **$345**

Bowl, 15 1/2" l., 5" h., long oblong form w/optic-ribbed sides tapering slightly to a flat rim, amethyst shaded to clear, the sides engraved w/large blossoms & buds, fine acid-etched signature, barely visible bruise on rim **$805**

Cameo vase, African Safari patt. from the "Animor" series, ovoid body tapering to a ringed neck w/flared rim, a chartreuse textured ground cased in garnet red & cameo cut around the sides w/a pair of reticulated giraffes, a rhinoceros, a grazing water buffalo, all beneath several palm trees & flying birds, upper & lower red rings, all accented w/gold, signed in the gilded grass "Moser Karlsbad" & the artists' initials "R.W." & "LMK" **$5,520**

MOSER

Chalice, a round flat-topped rainbow diamond-quilted bowl enameled w/delicate gold leafy vines, supported on two gilt squatty knops above the tall flaring clear ringed pedestal stem trimmed in gold, signed, minimal wear, 8 1/8" h. **$575**

Chamberstick, a domed foot below the baluster-form stem below a wide deep bowl- form drip pan centered by the cylindrical socket w/a flattened rim, a long C-scroll gilt handle from rim of pan to stem, pale blue w/heavy paneled gold designs & gold florals on the drip pan & garlands around the foot, annealing lines where handle meets drip pan, 4 5/8" h. **$288**

Ewer, dark blue, round low domed foot w/a short stem supporting a bulbous body tapering to a very tall slender cylindrical neck w/a flared arched spout, applied amber handle, the body decorated overall w/ enameled branches of blue, yellow & brown swirling oak leaves & lacy gold stems w/ a large applied flying bird in color on the front, late 19th c., chip & one area of repair on foot, 17 3/4" h. ... **$3,565**

Goblet, a round foot supporting a very tall slender stem w/upper ball knob below the bell-shaped bowl, clear foot & stem finely enameled w/delicate florals & gold, the deep cranberry bowl enameled overall w/lacy gold scrolls & tiny blossoms, berries & leaves in blues, greens & pinks, minor gold wear, 7 7/8" h. **$460**

Pitcher, 8 1/2" h., bulbous ovoid optic ribbed body w/a short neck below the wide cupped rim w/pinched spout, applied clear handle, body in clear shaded to deep green at the base & enameled w/large white, pink & purple poppies on leafy green stems, nearly invisible heat check at handle, minor fogginess **$547**

Goblets, a domed ringed foot supporting an ornate ringed & bulbed stem supporting a deep rounded bowl, champagne color, the bowls ornately decorated w/tiny exotic flowers on scrolling vines enameled & filled in w/silver & lilac lustre, gold decoration down the stem also trimmed w/applied prunts, an overall wash of mother- of-pearl lustre, 7 1/4" h., set of 10 .... **$2,645**

Scent bottle w/original brass cap & finger ring, tusk-form, cranberry decorated around the top w/a wide band of gold enameled w/tiny blossoms, the sides decorated w/gold fern leaves, some gold wear, 3" l. **$546**

Vase, 3 1/8" h., miniature, three gold scroll feet supporting the squatty bulbous body tapering to a flared & scalloped rim, overall gold decorated w/purple & blue sprigs of blossoms w/green leaves, slight gold wear **$230**

Vase, 4 3/4" h., footed bulbous six-lobed clear body w/a short flaring neck, each lobe ornately engraved w/delicate florals around a ruby-flashed oval reserve in each lobe further engraved w/a floral bouquet, gold trim, signed on the base **$420**

Urn, cov., wide baluster-form panel-cut body w/a matching domed cover w/pointed finial, the shoulder, neck & cover border decorated w/acid-etched gold bands of Greek warriors, signed "Moser Karlsbad," ca. 1925, 14" h. **$920**

Vase, 5 1/4" h., slightly tapering cylindrical body in cranberry applied w/three clear handles, decorated w/heavy scrolling gold top band w/spearpoints around the base, trimmed overall w/small multicolored blossoms, signed on the side, some gold wear on lip, late 19th c. **$300-500**

Vase, 6" h., a spherical cobalt blue body w/a short flared & scalloped neck, overall delicate gilt-decorated wheel-carved flowers & leaves, three applied amber rigaree bands down the side, raised on three amber scroll feet, etched signature, late 19th c. **$259**
➜

Vase, 2 3/4" h., miniature pillow style, gold tightly coiled scroll feet supporting the flattened rounded cranberry body w/an arched rim, the sides colorfully enameled w/stylized floral vines & insects, signed & numbered on the bottom **$575**

Vase, 5" h., the ovoid egg-shaped optic-ribbed body w/a five-crimp rim & raised on three gilt peg feet, in pale teal shaded to clear & ornately decorated overall w/gold scrolls & floral vines, minimal wear **$460**

MOSER

Vase, 6" h., fan-shaped, three applied gilded scroll feet supporting a round ball below the tall flattened & fanned sides, pale teal ornately enameled overall w/ vines & stylized flowers attracting butterflies, design continuing on the ball-form base, minuscule rim nicks **$633**

Vase, 11" h., footed flaring cylindrical body w/a wide waisted neck, deep cobalt blue decorated around the lower body & neck w/gold-outlined panels, the upper body w/a gold band of Grecian figures, signed on the bottom "Moser Carlsbad," some minor enamel wear, late 19th c. **$259**

Vase, 8" h., wide bulbous tapering cylinder w/a widely flaring rim, amber acid-cut w/a continuous frieze of elephants under palm trees on a grassy plain w/birds in the sky, three fluted bands around the base, highlighted overall w/gilt, incised mark "Moser - Karlsbad," the base inscribed "Made in - Czecho-Slovakia - Moser - Karlsbad," ca. 1925 ....**$1,725**

Vase, 7 1/2" h., squatty bulbous optic- ribbed base below the cylindrical sides opening to a widely flaring & crimped rim w/ upturned back, amethyst w/an applied clear rim band, decorated in colored enamels on the side w/a portrait of a maiden against a stenciled background, executed in Theodore Rossler's enamel "color cake" technique, late 19th c. **$196**

Vase, 12" h., a domed flaring pedestal base supporting a large urn-form body, emerald green very ornately enameled w/delicate gold florals & leafy scrolls centered by a large oval medallion enameled in color w/a bust portrait of a beautiful woman, unmarked, base reattached w/a metal fixture, ca. 1900 .... **$546**

Vase, 12 7/8" h., three clear applied stylized figural salamander feet supporting the flared base tapering to the tall cylindrical optic-ribbed body, deep amethyst shading to clear, enameled w/ large yellow & purple irises above tall leafy green stems, trimmed in gold, tiny chips on feet & rim **$374**

Vase, 8 3/4" h., slightly flaring cylindrical form, emerald green acid cutback w/an overall stylized design of large tulip-like blossoms & leaves, signed "Moser" & "MM" **$1,100**

Vase, 11" h., a round foot & short ringed stem supporting a tall slightly flaring cylindrical body w/a narrow shoulder tapering to a wide trumpet neck, amber decorated overall w/colored enameled flowers, a tree, bee & bird, early 20th c., script signature **$385**

Vase, 6" h., upright paneled oblong body inset in a gilt-metal pierced base & pierced framework w/ the figure of an Art Deco-style dancing lady on each side, pr. **$1,100**

Mt. Washington

A wide diversity of glass was made by the Mt. Washington Glass Company of New Bedford, Massachusetts, between 1869 and 1900. It was succeeded in 1900 by the Pairpoint Corporation. Miscellaneous types are listed below.

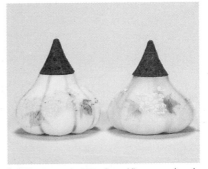

Jewelry box w/hinged cover, squatty bulbous base ornately molded w/leafy scrolls trimmed in gold & brown framing smooth panels decorated w/pink florals on a green ground, metal neck & cover fittings, bottom marked "4652-1219," 7 1/2" d., 5 3/4" h. **$1,150**

Salt & pepper shakers, figural figs, one w/a pale blue ground h.p. w/white blossoms & green & brown leaves, the other with a white ground w/pink lines on the ribs & h.p. pinl blossoms w/green & brown leaves, 2 1/2" h., pr. **$460**

Salt shaker w/original metal cap, cockle shell-shaped, pale pink ground h.p. w/lavender, green & tan leaves & tiny white blossoms, scarce form **$750-850**

Sugar shaker w/original metal lid, egg- shaped, painted dark pink to yellow Burmese-like background decorated w/yellow & brown daisies & green leaves, 7" h. **$350-500**

Lamp, miniature, "Dresden" ware, squatty bulbous paneled base tapering sharply to the brass fitted w/burner, shade ring & matching paneled ball shade, milk white h p. w/colorful delicate flowers **$750-1,000**

Cracker jar, cov., barrel-shaped, cased rose satin exterior decorated overall w/pale blue blossoms outlined in yellow enamel, white interior, silver plate rim, floral-embossed domed cover & twisted rope bail handle, 7 1/2" h............................. **$523**

Vase, 3 3/4" h., "Lava," footed squatty bulbous body tapering sharply to a widely flaring neck, black ground w/scattered bright bits of glass in red, blue, green & white, glossy finish **$2,645**

Vase, 8" h., eight-ribbed body w/a flared rim, colored base w/green thistle decoration outlined in gold in the Verona manner.......... **$201**

Flower frog, mushroom-shaped, the wide domed top in pale shaded blue satin enameled w/delicate colored florals, the top raised on a slender trumpet foot, 5" d., 3 1/4" h. **$338**

New Martinsville

The New Martinsville Glass Manufacturing Company operated from 1900 to 1944, when it was taken over by new investors and operated as the Viking Glass Company. In its time, the New Martinsville firm made an iridescent art glass line called Muranese along with crystal pattern glass (included ruby-stained items) and, later, the transparent and opaque colors which were popular during the 1920s and 1930s. *Measell's New Martinsville Glass 1900-1944* covers this company's products in detail.

Bowl, 11 1/2" l., oval, Janice patt., blue **$70**

Creamer & open sugar, No. 38, amber, pr. **$28**

Model of swan, "sweetheart" shape, w/cutting, clear, 6" l. **$32**

Ashtray, figural, model of a wheelbarrow, clear, 4 x 5 1/2" **$24**

Tumbler, No. 38 Hostmaster patt., Old Fashion, cobalt blue **$24**

Candleholder, one-light, No. 415 Flame patt., clear, 5" w., 6 1/2" h. **$25**

Candlestick, No. 34 Addie patt. w/ Lions etching, pink, 3" h. **$35**

Pitcher 4 1/2" h., figural "Wise Owl," green satin w/ enamel decoration **$65**

Opaline

Also called opal glass (once a name applied to milk-white glass), opaline is a fairly opaque glass with a color resembling the opal; however, pieces in such colors as blue, pink, green and others also are referred to now as opaline glass. Many of the objects were decorated.

Vase, 14 1/2" h., baluster-form, translucent white ground w/the trumpet neck trimmed in gold, the shoulder painted w/a band of birds perched in branches within gilt scrolls above a ruby "jeweled" trellis, the body w/three arched panels painted w/scenes of gallants at various leisure pursuits in garden landscapes, within a "jeweled" surround & above small panels of flowers all on a scrollwork design dark blue ground, knopped stem & stepped round foot banded in gold, probably Baccarat, France, ca. 1845 .... **$1,434**

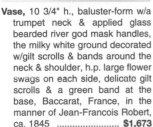

Vase, 10 3/4" h., baluster-form w/a trumpet neck & applied glass bearded river god mask handles, the milky white ground decorated w/gilt scrolls & bands around the neck & shoulder, h.p. large flower swags on each side, delicate gilt scrolls & a green band at the base, Baccarat, France, in the manner of Jean-Francois Robert, ca. 1845 .... **$1,673**

Jean-Francois Robert developed enamels with a low melting point for decorating crystal. A gifted artist, Robert worked for Sevres as a porcelain decorator and then decorated opalines for Baccarat from 1843 to 1855.

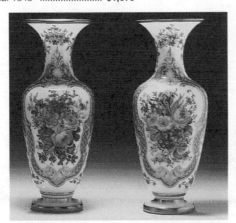

Vases, 15 1/2" h., footed baluster-form w/a tall trumpet neck, very pale bluish white ground, finely painted front & back w/a rich bouquet within a foliate trellis cartouche in gold & dark blue surmounted by a shell, the reverse w/trailing pelargonium vine, gilt-banded foot, probably Baccarat, in the manner of Jean-Francois Robert, ca. 1845, pr. **$5,019**

Vases, 15 3/4" h., ringed base & ovoid body tapering to a tall trumpet neck, milky white ground painted on the front & back w/large, long ribbon-tied colorful pendent floral swags within a foliate gilt border, gilt rim & foot bands, probably Baccarat, in the manner of Jean-Francois Robert, ca. 1845, pr. **$5,378**

Paden City

The Paden City Glass Manufacturing Company began operations in Paden City, West Virginia, in 1916, primarily as a supplier of blanks to other companies. All wares were handmade, that is, either hand-pressed or mold-blown. The early products were not particularly noteworthy, but by the early 1930s the quality had improved considerably. The firm continued to turn out high quality glassware in a variety of beautiful colors until financial difficulties necessitated its closing in 1951. Over the years the firm produced, in addition to tablewares, items for hotel and restaurant use, light shades, shaving mugs, perfume bottles and lamps.

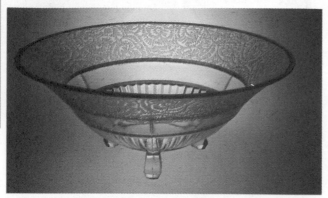

Bowl, 11 1/2" d., flared, three-footed, Glades patt., Frost etching, clear **$48**

Candlesticks, Nerva patt., crystal, 6" h., pr. **$45**

Candy dish, cov., low flat, No. 210 Regina patt. w/cutting, Green **$54**

Bowl, 12" l., Maya patt., oval, handled, light blue **$65**

Candlestick, two-light, No. 2000 Mystic, light blue **$75**

Cocktail shaker, cover & rooster stopper, Eleanor etching, clear, 3 pcs. **$145**

Candlesticks, two-light, Crow's Foot (No. 890) line, round, red, pr **$180**

Compote, open, 11" d., footed, Party Line (No.191) line, clear **$35**

Server, swan-necked center handle, Gazebo etching, Line 1504, clear, 10" d. **$75**

Creamer, Crow's Foot patt., milk glass, w/silver overlay **$65**

Decanter w/ stopper, tilt cordial style ruby body w/ silver overlay, clear stopper, Glades patt., 12 oz. **$95**

Decanter w/stopper, Popeye & Olive patt., ruby w/silver overlay, crystal shot glass stopper **$245**

Plate, 9 1/2" d., Gadroon patt., ruby (ILLUS. left with sherbet) **$25**

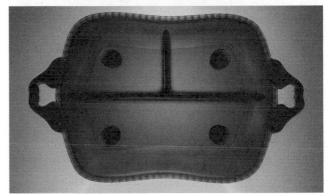

Relish dish, three-part, Gadroon patt, Mulberry, 8 x 10" **$55**

Tumbler, footed, Party Line patt., pink, 12 oz. **$15**

Vase, 8" h., etched Lela Bird patt., ovoid, ebony **$175**

PAIRPOINT

Pairpoint

Originally organized in New Bedford, Massachusetts, in 1880 as the Pairpoint Manufacturing Company on land adjacent to the famed Mount Washington Glass Company, this company first manufactured silver and plated wares. In 1894, the two famous factories merged as the Pairpoint Corporation and enjoyed great success for more than forty years. The company was sold in 1939 to a group of local businessmen and eventually bought out by one of the group who turned the management over to Robert M. Gundersen. Sub-

sequently, it operated as the Gundersen Glass Works until 1952 when, after Gundersen's death, the name was changed to Gundersen-Pairpoint. The factory closed in 1956. Subsequently, Robert Bryden took charge of this glassworks, at first producing glass for Pairpoint abroad and eventually, in 1970, beginning glass production in Sagamore, Massachusetts. Today the Pairpoint Crystal Glass Company is owned by Robert and June Bancroft. They continue to manufacture fine quality blown and pressed glass.

Candlesticks, a round foot & disk stem supporting a tall hollow baluster-form stem below the applied cylindrical candle socket w/a flattened rim, sulfur yellow, the stem & base engraved w/lush pods on a vine w/florets scattered around the sockets, 10 1/8" h., pr. **$633**

Candlesticks, tall blown baluster-form w/a cylindrical socket & flattened rim, clear optic ribbed design w/dark blue swirls, 12" h., pr. **$1,200-1,800**

Compote, open, 5" h., 8" d., the widely flaring & gently ruffled bowl w/a wide cobalt blue border around spirals in clear & blue, on an applied clear stem & foot **$780**

Compote, open, 6" d., cut overlay, Lincoln patt., a shallow wide round bowl in cobalt blue cut to clear, on a tapering facet-cut stem & star-cut round foot **$650-750**

Vase, 12" h., blown chalice-form, the cobalt blue ovoid body w/a flaring rim supported by a clear controlled bubble connector to the cobalt blue foot **$450-650**

Tazza, Fine Arts line, a rib-cut cylindrical flaring amber glass bowl mounted in a swag-cast brass-plated metal holder supported by a figural putto standing on a square onyx platform w/a cast brass-plated border, signed, ca. 1920s, 10" h. **$500-750**

Pate de Verre

Pate de Verre, or "paste of glass," was molded by very few artisans. In the pate de verre technique, powdered glass is mixed with a liquid to make a paste which is then placed in a mold and baked at a high temperature. These articles have a finely pitted or matte finish and are easily distinguished from blown glass. Duplicate pieces are possible with this technique.

Bowl, 3 1/2" h., flat-bottomed flaring bulbous shape w/a scalloped rim, molded up the sides w/four large locusts in amber & dark blue against the mottled green & blue ground also molded w/yellow & green pine cones & green pine needles, signed on side of foot "A. Walter Nancy" **$8,913**

Paperweight, figural, an oblong thick brown-streaked white base topped by a large molded mottled dark greyish black mouse, side of rock engraved w/circular "DeCorchemont" mark, France, early 20th c., 2 1/4" l. **$1,438**

Picture frame, rectangular w/a wide flat border molded w/large stylized red & blue blossoms on a white ground, rectangular metal band around the picture opening, signed on top left "G. Argy-Rousseau," 4 x 4 3/4" **$3,278**

Bowl, 6 3/4" d., 3 1/2" h., figural, flat-bottomed w/wide flattened flaring sides in deep terra cotta, a large black amethyst model of a large iguana molded on the rim, signed "Berge SC - A. Walter Nancy" **$345**

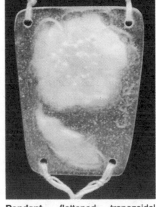

Pendant, flattened trapazoidel shape w/a mottled clear ground molded w/a large white flower w/yellow stamens, white cord at bottom holes & hanging cords at the top, signed "G.A.R.," 2 1/4" l. **$1,150**

Pendant, butterfly design, pierced square w/blue, green, reddish orange wings against colorless & clear ground, inscribed "GAR" in design, G. Argy-Rousseau, 2 1/8 x 2 1/4" **$2,415**

Paperweight, figural, round, molded w/a green rodent w/large blue eyes, resting on a mottled pink base, impressed round mark "DeCorchemont," ca. 1920s, 4" d. **$2,280**

Night light, round thin ribbed cast-iron foot supporting the swelled cylindrical body w/a wide cylindrical cast-iron rim fitted w/a flat cover w/a tiny melon-shaped finial, deep mottled green, red & yellow molded w/large roses & leaves around the upper body, side molded "G. Argy-Rousseau," & "France" on the top rim, original metal hardware, overall 7 1/2" h. **$4,680**

Pendant, oval form cast in the shape of a cicada in colors of raspberry pink & mulberry blue, molded monogram of Gabriel Argy-Rousseau, 2 1/2" h. **$1,150**

Vase, 11 3/4" h., "Libations" patt., simple ovoid body tapering to a short wide flared rim, mottled deep orange & yellow ground, a wide raised center band composed of rows of wheel-like devices in orange, yellow & charcoal flanking a large rectangular vertical panel enclosing a half-length portrait of a female carrying a water jug on her shoulder done in shades of dark orange, deep yellow & charcoal, signed on the side "G. Argy-Rousseau" & "France" on the bottom, ca. 1920s, drill hole in bottom **$14,950**

Vase, 6 1/4" h., Art Deco style, swelled cylindrical body w/a short cylindrical neck flanked by large inward-scrolled molded handles w/notched border design, the body molded w/full-length narrow incised triangular panels w/zig-zag borders, in rich brown shaded to magenta & pink w/orange highlights at the top, signed on the side "G. Argy-Rousseau" **$4,920**

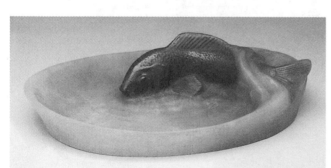

Vide poche (figural dish), flat-bottomed shallow oval dish in mottled yellowish green molded in relief at one end w/a deep green fish, signed "Berge SC - A. Walter Nancy," 5 x 7 1/2" **$6,038**

Glass has been known to crack after being removed from a heated building in freezing weather. To avoid this, pack the glass in bubble wrap and several layers of paper. Don't place the package on the floor of the car where the heater will blow warm air on it. Back home, don't unwrap the item until it has returned to room temperatture.

Vase, 6" h., slightly swelled cylindrical body molded around the top w/geometric scrolls, mottled purple, red, brown & peach, signed on the side "G. Argy- Rousseau," ca. 1920s **$6,038**

Peach Blow

Several types of glass lumped together by collectors as Peach Blow were produced by half a dozen glasshouses. Hobbs, Brockunier & Co., Wheeling, West Virginia, made Peach Blow as a plated ware that shaded from red at the top to yellow at the bottom and is referred to as Wheeling Peach Blow. Mt. Washington Glass Works produced an homogeneous Peach Blow shading from a rose color at the top to pale blue in the lower portion. The New England Glass Works' Peach Blow, called Wild Rose, shaded from rose at the top to white. Gundersen-Pairpoint Co. also reproduced some of the Mt. Washington Peach Blow in the early 1950s and some glass of a somewhat similar type was made by Steuben Glass Works, Thomas Webb & Sons and Stevens & Williams of England. New England Peach Blow is one-layered glass and the English is two-layered.

Another single-layered shaded art glass was produced early in the 20th century by the New Martinsville Glass Mfg. Co. Originally called "Muranese," collectors today refer to it as "New Martinsville Peach Blow."

Gundersen - Pairpoint

Compote, open, 7 1/4" d., 6 3/4" h., a round foot & slender baluster-shaped stem below a twisted knop below the wide shallow bowl w/a six-ruffle rim, satin finish **$288**

Mt. Washington

Toothpick holder, cylindrical w/a tricorner rolled-in rim, glossy finish, ca. 1885, 2 1/8" h. **$275**

New England

Finger bowl, rounded base w/deep cylindrical sides, deep raspberry w/band of white at base, satin finish, 4 1/4" d., 2 5/8" h. **$230**

Vase, 9" h., lily-style, round foot & tall very slender stem to the flaring & inwardly- folded tricorner rim, deep rose to white, satin finish **$173**

Cruet w/original stopper, squatty bulbous body tapering to a cylindrical neck w/tricorner rim, applied pink handle, white hollow ball stopper, deep color w/glossy finish **$1,200-1,500**

Creamer, squatty bulbous lightly ribbed body tapering slightly to a wide flat rim w/pinched spout, applied handle, decorated w/leafy branches of asters, 2 1/2" h. **$495**

PEACH BLOW

New England continued

Punch cup, deep rounded bowl w/applied reeded white handle, satin finish, 2 3/4" h. **$150**

Whiskey tumbler, cylindrical, satin finish, 3 1/2" h. **$330**

Vase, 9 1/2" h., lily-form w/a round foot & tricorner rolled rim, attributed to New England Glass Co. **$850**

Vase, 6" h., lily-type, deep rose shading to white **$600-750**

Pitcher, 8" h., water-type, bulbous ovoid body tapering to a squared rolled neck, applied amber handle, glossy finish **$1,500-2,200**

Wheeling

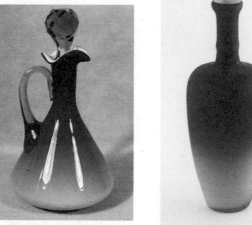

Cruet w/original facet-cut amber ball stopper, sharply tapering conical body w/a cylindrical neck & tricorner rim, applied amber handle **$1,250-1,750**

Morgan Vase, 8" h., Wheeling Peach Blow, ovoid body w/tall slender ringed neck, deep ruby to yellow w/satin finish, ca. 1886 .... **$1,200-1,500**

Vase, 7" h., bottle-form, bulbous base tapering to a tall stick neck w/an applied band of amber rigaree around the lower neck, glossy finish **$900-1,200**

Vase, 10" h., ovoid body tapering to a short trumpet neck, satin finish .... **$1,500-2,200** →

Vase, 3 1/2" h., Wheeling Peach Blow, bulbous ovoid body w/a short cylindrical neck, deep ruby shading to yellow, ca. 1886 .... **$325-375** ←

Quezal

In 1901, Martin Bach and Thomas Johnson, who had worked for Louis Tiffany, opened a competing glassworks in Brooklyn, New York. The Quezal Art Glass and Decorating Co. produced wares closely resembling those of Tiffany until the plant's closing in 1925.

Bowl, 6" d., squatty bulbous tapering sides w/a wide low rolled rim, golden brown iridescent ground w/silvery blue iridescent pulled-feather decoration, light blue iridescent interior, signed on the pontil "Quezal N.Y." **$2,300**

Toothpick holder, small bulbous body w/deeply pinched-in sides below the short widely flaring neck, overall gold iridescence w/magenta highlights, signed, 2 3/8" h. **$518**

Vase, 2 1/4" h., miniature, a footed squatty flaring ribbed body w/ an angled shoulder below the four-petal rolled rim, overall gold iridescence w/reddish pink highlights, tiny short scratches on rim, signed **$460**

Vase, 4 1/8" h., miniature, a round cushion foot below the slender stem flaring to a wide ruffled rim, overall gold iridescence w/ magenta highlights, engraved "Quezal K597" **$1,035**

Vase, 6" h., bud-type, a round foot below the very slender gently flaring sides to a bulbed shoulder & widely flaring flattened & gently ruffled rim, overall gold iridescence w/amethyst highlights, signed on the bottom.......... **$518**

Vase, 4 1/4" h., 3 3/4" d., flattened squatty round bottom centered by a tall trumpet neck, the bottom on opal decorated w/golden iridescent lappets & green & gold triple-hooked designs, the neck in golden iridescence, signed on pontil **$3,450**

Vase, 5 7/8" h., sweet pea-type, the round cushion foot tapering to a slender stem below the widely flaring six-petal rim, green w/ gold iridescence pulled feathers on a white ground up the sides, gold iridescent interior, engraved "Quezal 285" **$1,725**

QUEZAL

Vase, 6" h., footed squatty bulbous body tapering to a large trumpet neck, opal ground decorated w/green, white & gold pulled feathers alternating down from the rim & up from the base, orange iridescent interior, signed on the pontil **$1,380**

Vase, 6 3/4" h., flora-form, a round foot below a slender stem & widely flaring & deeply ruffled body, exterior w/a cream & green pulled-feather design, gold iridescent interior, iridescent green & gold zipper foot, signed on bottom **$3,163**

Vase, 10" h., stick-form w/flared rim, overall dark blue iridescence, signed **$800**

Vase, 13" h., jack-in-the-pulpit style, a wide cushion foot below the tall slender stem issuing a widely flaring ruffled & upturned rim, overall amber iridescence w/rings of pink & green, signed on the bottom "Quezal G562" ... **$9,200**

Vase, 9 3/4" h., baluster-shaped w/a trumpet neck & cushion foot, iridescent gold neck above the shoulder decorated w/pulled & swirled emerald green & opal white design above iridescent gold pulled leaves continuing down over the foot, #C268, signed.............................. **$3,850**

Vase, 14 1/4" h., 6 1/4" d., flat-bottomed ovoid shape tapering to a short flaring neck, the bottom half decorated w/a band of wide pulled feathers in green & gold, the shoulder decorated w/large five-petal green blossoms on a cream ground w/random gold threading with gold heart-shaped leaves, signed, ca. 1908 .... **$17,925**

Vase, 10 1/2" h., tall slender baluster-form w/short trumpet neck, overall blue iridescent finish, signed **$1,375**

Vase, 18 1/2" h., a rounded domed bronze foot base w/entwined snakes supporting a very tall slender trumpet-form vase w/a gently ruffled rim, vase w/overall bright gold iridescence, glass signed, bronze base marked "Copyright 1913..." **$3,163**

Satin

Satin glass was a popular decorative glass developed in the late 19th century. Most pieces were composed of two layers of glass with the exterior layer usually in a shaded pastel color. The name derives from the soft matte finish, caused by exposure to acid fumes, which gave the surface a "satiny" feel. Mother-of-pearl satin glass was a specialized variety wherein air trapped between the layers of glass provided subtle surface patterns such as Herringbone and Diamond Quilted. A majority of satin glass was produced in England, Bohemia and America, but collectors should be aware that reproductions have been made for many years.

Bowl, 6 1/2" d., 4 7/8" h., deep rounded form w/deeply ruffled rim, shaded dark blue to white mother-of-pearl Diamond Quilted patt., framed by three heavy clear frosted branch legs, white lining **$325- 375**

Pitcher, 6 3/8" h., spherical body w/wide cylindrical neck w/wide arched spout, shaded pink mother-of-pearl Diamond Quilted patt., applied frosted clear handle **$259**

Sugar shaker w/original top, ovoid body, peach mother-of-pearl Peacock Eye patt., signed by Thomas Webb, minor dents in top, 5 1/4" h. **$719**

Sugar shaker w/original top, swelled cylindrical form, shaded apricot mother-of- pearl Coin Spot patt., delicate floral enameling, rare, 5 1/2" h. **$750-1,200**

Vase, 8" h., ovoid body tapering to a short ringed tapering neck, shaded dark blue to dark rose mother-of-pearl Swirl patt., attributed to Stevens & Williams, England **$900-1,200**

Tumbler, cylindrical, shaded dark blue mother-of-pearl Diamond Quilted patt., colorful enameled pink flowers on leafy stems, 3 7/8" h. **$375-450**

Vase, 8 1/2" h., bulbous base w/tall cylindrical sides & a four-lobed rolled & crimped rim, rainbow mother-of-pearl Diamond Quilted patt., deep colors, Mt. Washington Glass Co. ...... **$1,500 -2,000**

Vase, 7 3/4" h., bulbous body w/ pinched-in sides below a short, white cylindrical neck, shaded amethyst to white exterior enameled w/white prunus blossoms on brown stems, the neck decorated w/a gold enamel band, lined in white, unsigned by numbered "III/115," England, late 19th c. **$345**

SPATTER

Spatter

This variegated-color ware is similar to Spangled glass but does not contain metallic flakes. The various colors are applied on a clear, opaque white or colored body. Much of it was made in Europe and England. It is sometimes called "End Of Day."

Pitcher, 8" h., bulbous body w/a molded spiral swirl design & a round neck w/small pinched spout, blue w/overall delicate white spatter, applied blue handle, possibly Phoenix Glass Co. **$220**

Pitcher, 8 1/2" h., ovoid eight-lobed bod w/a star-shaped neck, horizontal butterscotch & white bands, colorful enameled floral decoration, clear applied handle, Phoenix Glass Co., slight wear to gilt trim **$303**

Pitcher, 8 3/4" h., bulbous body tapering to a cylindrical neck w/squared flaring crimped rim, cranberry & white spatter in clear, applied clear handle **$143**

Pitcher, 9" h., tapering ovoid body w/a tall cylindrical neck & deeply ruffled & crimped triangular rim, cranberry & white spatter in frosted clear, applied frosted clear reeded handle, Phoenix Glass Co., minor rim flaw **$121**

Pitcher, 8 3/4" h., bulbous ovoid body tapering to a cylindrical neck w/a downturned crimped & ruffled rim, cased colorful Rib Optic spatter w/overall silver mica flecks, applied frosted white rim band & applied ribbed clear handle **$253**

Spoon holder, ovoid body w/the mount fitted w/a silver plate collar flanked by fancy arched handles, overall dense red & yellow spatter cased in white, 5 1/2" h. **$55**

Cracker barrel w/original brass rim, cover & bail handle, barrel-shaped, white interior cased w/a swirling spatter design in shades of root beer, pink, maroon & white, tiny orange & blue enameled trim near rim, late 19th c., inside rim chip, 5 1/8" h. **$173**

Pitcher, 7 1/2" h., bulbous body w/molded spiral swirl design below the tall squared neck, multicolored pink, maroon & white spatter cased in white, applied clear frosted handle............. **$165**

Steuben

Aurene

Compote, open, a flat round foot & swelled stem supporting a deep rounded bowl w/gently flaring sides, rich gold iridescence w/ pink & blue highlights, signed "Steuben Aurene 2360," 5 1/2" d., 5" h. **$288**

Vase, 8 1/2" h., wide bulbous ovoid body tapering to a short flaring neck, overall blue iridescence w/purple highlights, base signed, Shape No. 2683 .... **$1,265**

Celeste Blue

Vase, 11" h., footed large bulbous urn-form body w/a narrow neck & wide low flaring rim, unsigned **$518**

Potpourri jar, cov., a round foot & short stem supporting the flaring trumpet-form body w/a bulbous lower section, fitted w/a domed cover w/a pointed knob finial & three small spaced holes, overall rich blue iridescence w/green, gold & purple highlights, signed on bottom "Aurene 2824," original paper label reading "Aurene Glass Controlled by Haviland & Co.," 5 1/2" h. **$1,495**

Cluthra

Bowl, 15" d., 8" h., a deep widely flaring inverted conical form w/a flat rim, white w/overall clear bubbles, resting in a scrolling wrought-iron Art Deco style holder, Shape No. 6169, scratches on interior......... **$2,070**

Rosaline

Creamer, miniature, squatty bulbous Rosaline body tapering to a wide mouth w/an arched spout, applied Alabaster handle, ground pontil, unsigned, 1 3/4" h. **$259**

Vase, 6 1/4" h., wide bulbous ovoid body tapering to a short flaring neck, iridescent royal blue ground decorated around the shoulder w/ an applied band of creamy woven vines w/heart-shaped leaves, signed on the base, Shape No. 6299, original serrated paper label on pontil reads "Steuben Glass Works, Corning, New York 6 - 6299," few minor surface scratches **$3,565**

Pomona Green

Candlesticks, a flaring optic ribbed foot supporting an optic ribbed baluster-shaped double-knobbed stem below the ovoid socket w/a wide flattened rim, Steuben fleur-de-lis mark on one, 10" h., pr. **$575**

TIFFANY

Tiffany

This glassware, covering a wide diversity of types, was produced in glasshouses operated by Louis Comfort Tiffany, America's outstanding glass designer of the Art Nouveau period, from the last quarter of the 19th century until the early 1930s. Tiffany revived early techniques and devised many new ones.

Pitcher, 5 3/4" h., "Lava," wide tapering cylindrical body w/a small pinched rim spout, applied gold iridescent handle, the sides decorated w/gold slender hatch-mark stripes w/thin rings of gold threading around the base, engraved "L.C. Tiffany - Favrile 5610C," ca. 1908 .... **$5,975**

Vase, 2 1/8" h., miniature, a short wide mouth & wide squatty bulbous shoulder tapering sharply down, dark iridescent green ground decorated around the shoulder w/platinum iridescent leaf-like designs, signed "L.C.T. V3785" **$2,040**

Candle lamp, the gold iridescent base w/a flaring base tapering sharply to a swirled rib cylindrical standard supporting a cupped top holding the green glass candle w/ a green pulled-feather design & gilt-metal top fitting, the matching gold iridescent open-topped umbrella shade w/a ruffled rim, original chimney w/gold iridescent finish, original metal hardware stamped "The Twilight," shade & base marked "L.C.T.," shade w/chip at top, lamp drilled & electrified, overall 15" h. ... **$1,725**

Vase, 4 1/8" h., "Cypriote," tapering ovoid body w/a flat mouth, overall swirled iridescent gold on a pebbled ground, engraved "L.C. Tiffany - Favrile 2080K," ca. 1916 .... **$9,560**
Vase, 4 1/8" h., "Millefiore," footed bulbous body tapering to a tall cylindrical neck, millefiore canes set randomly among swirling silver iridescent vines against a dark greenish blue iridescent ground, engraved "L.C.T. V4601," ca. 1904 (ILLUS. with two other Tiffany vases)............................. **$4,183**
Vase, 4 1/8" h., bulbous tapering ovoid body w/a closed rim, turquoise blue iridescent ground applied w/swirled random blobs of red & green among threads of green, engraved "L.C.T. E2101," ca. 1896 (ILLUS. with two other Tiffany vases).. **$13,145**

Inkwell w/hinged bronze neck & cap, footed squatty round waisted well in iridescent blue w/silver & blue iridescent pulled-feather decoration, signed on bottom "L.C.T. H205," 5 1/2" h. **$6,038**

Vaseline

This glass takes its name from its color, which is akin to that of petroleum jelly used for medicinal purposes. Originally manufacturers usually referred to the color as "canary." We list miscellaneous pieces here.

Table set: cov. butter dish, creamer, spooner & celery vase; Petticoat patt., gold trim, ca. 1900, the set **$206**

Vase, 7 1/2" h., opalescent, central thorny stem w/two attached bud vases & applied feet, England, late 19th c. **$255**

Dish, ooted, Shadow patt., ruffled & widely flaring shallow sides on a domed foot, Coudersport Glass Co., 7 1/2" d., 3 1/4" h. **$65-70**

Venetian

Venetian glass has been made for six centuries on the island of Murano, where it continues to be produced. The skilled glass artisans developed numerous techniques, subsequently imitated elsewhere.

Stemware & tableware set: composed of seven 4" cordials, 10 - 5 7/8" h. wine glasses, 11 - 5 5/8" h. water goblets, 11 - 6 1/2" d. plates & 11 - 4" d. bowls & a pair of footed compotes, 9 1/8" d., 5 3/8" h.; all free-blown ruby glass w/paneled bowls on the stemware w/ornate gilt rim bands & clear ribbed & swirled stems accented w/minute red & green jewels, late 19th c., the set (ILLUS. of part) **$2,233**

Wall sconces, blown & applied, each w/a central coupe centered by a blown candlestick w/a baluster-form stem & deep cupped socket issuing slender blown curled canes each holding a glass ring & floral pendant alternating w/slender canes w/ colorful glass blossoms & long downswept serrated clear & pink leaves, the coupe also issuing two lower serpentine candle arms ending in clear cupped sockets w/a crimped pink rim band & further applied colored blossoms & a bottom pendant in crimped pink glass, rectangular backplate of mahogany, electrified, in the 18th c. taste, ca. 1900, probably by Salviati & Company, 19" w., 24" h., pr. **$3,910**

Wave Crest

**WAVE CREST
WARE**

Now much sought after, Wave Crest was produced by the C.F. Monroe Co., Meriden, Connecticut, in the late 19th and early 20th centuries from opaque white glass blown into molds. It was then hand-decorated in enamels and metal trim was often added. Boudoir accessories such as jewel boxes, hair receivers, etc., predominated.

Box w/hinged lid, Pansy blown-out mold, dark green low flaring box & domed cover molded w/a large pink & amethyst pansy blossom, original metal fittings, signed on base, 4" w., 2 3/8" h. **$863**

Box w/hinged lid, Helmschmeid Swirl mold, decorated w/white & purple lilacs w/pale pink leaves, original metal fittings, unsigned, 6" d., 4 1/2" h. **$575**

Box w/hinged lid, long rectangular form molded w/borders of scrolls, pistachio green ground around gilt scroll-bordered white reserves decorated w/delicate daisies, original metal fittings, signed w/red banner mark, 4 x 7", 5" h. **$1,438**

Box w/hinged lid, Helmschmeid Swirl mold, satin crystal h.p. overall w/green holly branches w/red berries, 7" d., 4" h. **$1,150**

Cracker jar, cov., Helmschmeid Swirl mold, pink ground decorated around the top w/white daisies & green leafy stems, ruffled silver plate rim, domed cover & bail handle, 7 1/4" h. **$431**

Box, Baroque Shell mold, blackened base & cover border centering a faintly outlined bust portrait of a Victorian lady wearing a large fancy hat, body highlighted w/ sponged gold, wide gilt-metal fittings, 5 1/2" d., 3" h. **$550**

Dresser box w/hinged cover, Egg Crate mold, alternating turquoise & white panels decorated w/pink-stemmed yellow flowers, four footed embossed brass base, 5" w, 5 1/2" h. **$1,265**

Dresser box w/hinged cover, Egg Crate mold, shaded dark brown to tan ground decorated w/yellow & white mums, ornate ruffled brass collar & brass base w/scroll feet molded w/ cupid faces, marked, 6 3/4" w., 6 3/4" h. **$3,795**

Humidor w/hinged cover, barrel-shaped, molded w/bands of delicate scrolls, pale blue ground decorated on the cover w/pink & maroon flowers, the side panel painted in large letters w/"Cigars" framed w/delicate florals, 9 1/2" h. **$1,200-,750**

Jewelry box w/hinged cover, Baroque Shell mold, white ground decorated on the cover w/small pink & white blossoms & green leafy stems, brass fittings, unsigned, 7" d. **$345**

Letter holder, Egg Crate mold, upright rectangular shape w/brass scroll-trimmed rim band, shaded white & pink ground decorated w/red, white & pink flowers & pale green leaves, 4" h. **$403**

Muffineer, Helmschmied Swirl mold, bulbous ovoid shape w/original silver plate lid, h.p. w/large white & deep rose blossoms & green leaves, unmarked, 3 1/8" h. **$345**

Vase, 5 1/2" h., cylindrical w/large molded leafy scrolls around the bottom, raised on a pierced gilt brass footed base, white ground decorated w/yellow, brown & white daisies & leafy stems **$450-550**

Salt & pepper shakers, Helmschmeid Swirl patt., one w/alternating white & pink panels, the other w/white & shaded yellow panels, each w/ blossom & leaf decoration in the white panels, ca. 1900, 2 1/4" h., pr. **$200-250**

Vase, 12" h., large ovoid body w/a wide short cylindrical neck, white top & bottom bands w/gilt trim, long large open scroll handles down the sides **$2,300**

Webb

This glass is made by Thomas Webb & Sons of Stourbridge, one of England's most prolific glasshouses. Numerous types of glass, including cameo, have been produced by this firm through the years. The company also produced various types of novelty and "art" glass during the late Victorian period. Also see BURMESE & ROSE BOWLS.

Cameo rose jar, cov., bulbous ovoid body w/a citron yellow mother-of-pearl ground cased in crimson & finely etched w/ large apple blossoms & leaves trimmed in gold, gilt-metal filigree collar & domed cover, 8 3/4" h. **$22,425**

Cameo vase, 7 1/2" h., three-color type, citron yellow cased in red & white & etched w/large roses on leafy branches, signed "Tiffany & Co. Paris Exposition 1889 Thomas Webb & Sons Gem Cameo" **$3,278**

Cameo vase, 5" h., footed spherical body below a tall slender 'stick' neck w/a ruffled, flared rim, deep pink cased on white & cut w/a design of fern fronds & grass blades, glossy finish **$193**

Cameo vase, 4 3/4" h., in the Japonesque taste, ovoid body tapering to ringed cylindrical neck w/flared rim, wheel-cut w/ flowers & dragonflies revealing embedded swimming foil fish & a caged foil canary, the ground stipple-finished & gilt, the neck heavily enameled w/floral banding, enameling probably by J. Kretschman & the gilding by Jules Barbé, impressed on the pontil w/segmented fan-frammed reserve centering "Webb" **$23,000**

Cameo vase, 8 1/4" h., footed ovoid body tapering to a low widely flaring flattened neck, dark blue overlaid in white & etched w/large daisy-like flowers, the reverse w/two cameo-etched bees & a butterfly, signed "Thomas Webb & Sons Gem Cameo" **$1,438**

Cameo vase, 6" h., 6" d., footed low wide cushion-form body tapering to a trumpet neck flanked by two carved elephant head handles, ivory cased in white & etched w/ an overall delicate flower & scroll design outlined in heavy gold, signed on the base "Thomas Webb & Sons Limited" **$2,243**

Cameo vase, 8" h., a round foot supporting the bulbous ovoid body w/a short neck & wide cupped rim, Prussian blue overlaid in white & etched w/an elaborate Passion flower decoration, leaf & spearpoint etched bands around the foot & leaf & lappet w/fleur-de-lis bands around the neck, signed "Thomas Webb & Sons" **$10,063**

Cameo vase, 9 1/2" h., ovoid body tapering to a wide cylindrical neck, deep red overlaid in white & cameo cut around the sides w/leafy flowering vines, a band of pointed leaves around the neck, unsigned **$2,530**

Cameo vase, 11 1/2" h., bulbous double- gourd form body, deep rose to grey ground overlaid in white & etched w/large Passion flowers on leafy stems, stippled floral band at the top, Gem Cameo **$10,350**

Cameo vase, 8 1/4" h., small knob feet support the squatty bulbous lower body decorated around the base & top w/cameo- cut bands w/florette diamonds & triangular enameled in gold & pink, the main body decorated w/five large oval cameo- cut panels w/a feathered leaf & link design decorated in heavy gold & separated by a continuous undulating band of green leafy vines, the lower body centered by a tall cylindrical neck decorated w/four tall pointed arch panels each carved w/spiraling vines of green leaves & pink & yellow blossoms, the panels surrounded by heavy gold borders carved w/scrolling acanthus leaf vines, decorated by Jules Barbé, signed "Thomas Webb & Sons - Gem Cameo" **$9,775**

Cameo vase, 5 1/4" h., pilgrim flask-form, a domed foot w/flattened rim supporting a wide flattened round body tapering to a short cylindrical neck w/flared rim, applied pink handles from rim to shoulder, the body in duBarry pink cut to white w/a solitary dragonfly above meadow grasses, white beaded enamel decoration on the rim & foot, glossy finish **$743**

Cameo vase, 7" h., bottle-form w/a spherical base centered by a tall cylindrical neck, simulated ivory ground etched w/ivy above berries on leafy vines enhanced by sepia coloration, semicircular base mark "Thos. Webb & Sons" **$743**

Cameo vase, 11" h., the ovoid body tapering to a tall stick neck, frosted yellow ground cased in white & cut w/an overall design of vining morning glory blossoms, a butterfly on the reverse, banner mark on base, interior w/faint silhouetted bubble under design **$1,265**

Vase, 5 3/4" h., Rainbow mother-of-pearl satin Dewdrop patt., alternating stripes of pink & blue, decorated overall w/dainty gilt flowers & leaves, registry mark **$440**

Iced tea tumbler, shaded deep rose pink to pale pink cased satin, bubble encased in mid-body, polishing to edge of rim, 5 5/8" h. **$173**

Cameo vase, 5" h., footed spherical body below a tall slender 'stick' neck w/a ruffled, flared rim, deep pink cased on white & cut w/a design of fern fronds & grass blades, glossy finish **$193**

WESTMORELAND

Westmoreland

In 1890 Westmoreland opened in Grapeville, Pennsylvania, and as early as the 1920s was producing colorwares in great variety. Cutting and decorations were many and are generally under appreciated and undervalued. Westmoreland was a leading producer of milk glass in "the antique style." The company closed in 1984 but some of their molds continued in use by others.

Candleholder, three-light block, Paneled Grape patt., milk glass **$170**

Candleholders, tall, one-light, No. 1012 Line w/cutting, clear, 7 1/2" h. **$48**

Cheese dish, cov., round, Paneled Grape patt., milk glass, 7" d. **$58**

Candlesticks, dolphin-form standard w/a petal-form socket, hexagonal foot, green, 9" h., pr. **$168**

Compote bowl, 13" d., flared & high footed, Sawtooth patt., Golden Sunset **$75**

Candy container, figural Mantel Clock patt., Brandywine Blue, 2 1/2" w., 3" h. **$27**

Compote, 5 1/2" d., 3 1/2" h., open stem, Lotus patt., Flame red **$30**

Compote, 7 1/2" h., 8" d., ball stem, spray- cased black, amber stain, cut to clear **$150**

Compote, 9 1/4" d., Princess Feather patt., Golden Sunset **$68**

Ivy ball, footed, English Hobnail patt., milk glass, 6 1/2" h. ... **$26**

Pitcher, Paneled Grape patt., footed, crystal w/ruby stain, 1 qt. **$145**

Pitcher, 9" h., tankard-type w/ ringed base & stag horn-shaped handle, milk glass w/a painted brown background decorated w/a black decal decoration of a monk playing a violin, early 20th c. **$145**

Bowl, 9 1/2" d., scalloped rim, American Hobnail patt., blue opalescent............................ **$50**

Basket, English Hobnail patt., high arched handle, clear, 5" w..... **$24**

Candleholders, low one-light, Ring & Petal patt., Bermuda Blue, 3 1/2" h., pr...$36

INDIAN ART & ARTIFACTS

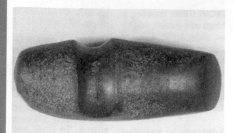

Adz-ax, Hohocom, hand-worked stone, 7 1/2" l. **$345**

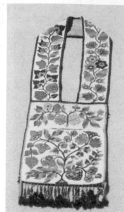

Bandolier, Chippewa, fine beadwork in floral vining design in shades of pink, blue, turquoise, green & yellow against white beaded background, the back lined w/cotton & edged w/red wool braid, fringes of tubular glass beads & yarn pompoms suspended along bottom, 14 1/4 x 17 3/4", 41" h. **$1,725**

Blanket, Navajo, hand-loomed chief's blanket decorated w/ diamonds & stripes in shades of red, brown & tan, small damages in center & along edge, 4'4" x 7'4" **$4,370**

Blanket, Navajo, Yei design, tightly woven in handspun wool, in natural ivory & deep brown bands, centering a single standing female figure wearing a brown dress & vibrant red shoes, only normal wear, 20th c., 16 x 30" **$316**

Bowl, Santa Clara, pottery, blackware w/a deeply incised serpent & arrow design around the body, signed "Madeline Sta Clara," by Madeline Naranjo, 8" d., 5 1/2" h. **$575**

Bowl, San Ildefonso, pottery, blackware squatty bulbous form w/a wide flat mouth, matte swag & leaf design around the mouth, signed "Maria and Julian," ca. 1940, 4" d., 3" h. **$748**

Cradleboard & beaded cover, Chippewa, toy-sized, the slightly tapering rectangular wooden back w/a heart cut-out at the top, a lovely curved bow & heart pierced decoration on the backboard, all painted in a muted green, the beaded cover finely decorated w/ large pink & blue flowers & green leafy stems again a black velvet background, glued break along backboard, ca. 1860, 6 x 14" **$1,438**

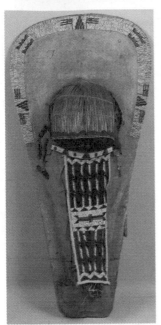

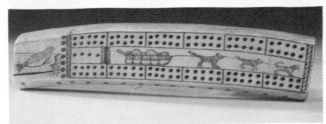

Cribbage board, Inuit, carved ivory, flattened tusk engraved w/a dog sled & seal on one side & a cityscape, possibly Nome, Alaska, on the other, inscribed "Nome Alaska 1903," 8 3/4" l. **$575**

Cradleboard, Ute, large tapering oblong backboard stained yellow for a girl, a beaded band arching acrosss the top in white & colors featuring rare American flag designs, finger-like rows of beading on the flap covering the laces done on early red & blue strouding w/red 'white hearts,' navy black unstable beads, greasy yellow & green beads, Transmontane style used from 1860-80, red stroud trade cloth beaded in black & white at hood edge, the cross flap at top of the opening geometrically beaded w/ later beads such as cut metallic, orangey red 'white hearts' & translucent blue & green, attached to it is an umbilical fetish bead wrapped in white heart reds & blue w/brass bead drops, a weasel claw amulet, a miniature brass shoe sold & a small Victorian key, fringe at the back, replaced laces, perhaps in the 1880s, good provenance, 39" l. **$6,900**

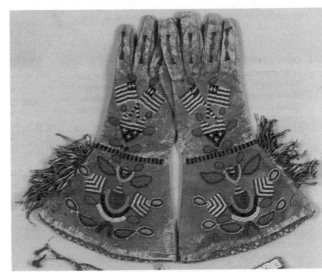

Gauntlets, Plateau, beaded leather, the top finely beaded w/tiny seed beads in many shades to from lance-shaped finger stripes, patriotic falgs & shields on the top of the hands & bright stylized floral designs on the cuffs, cloth interior of cotton homespun, work of an Umatilla, Nez Perce or Yakima master craftsman, very early Pendleton Roundup-type wear, worn binding & slight insect damage, patch at right thumb, 19th c., 8 1/2" w., 13 1/2" l., pr. **$1,495**

Favorite traditional Zuni designs include water-related animals like frogs, tadpoles, and the "rain bird." Other common designs are dragonflies, deer, and flowers.

Jar, Zuni, pottery, wide bulbous form w/a wide flat rim, painted in red ochre & black on typical white slip w/relief figures of frogs & a swirling stylized floral design, ca. 1880-1900, 7 1/2" d., 6" h. **$6,900**

Jar, San Ildefonso, pottery, blackware, widely flaring round bottom half w/a sharply tapering shoulder decorated w/a feather design around the wide flat mouth, signed "Tonita," 7" d., 4 1/4" h. **$460**

Kachina, Hopi, "Citulilu," deriving from Zuni word for rattlesnake, wearing yellow case mask w/ rattlesnake painted on forehead, w/long black snout, red tongue & fan- shaped crest of turkey tail feathers, 7 5/8" h. **$780**

Kachina, Hopi, "Sio Heimis Ta Amu," "Zuni Kachina's Uncle," wearing green squash- shaped case mask w/black band painted across eyes, tubular mouth, 9 3/4" h. **$920**

Kachina, Hopi, "Tungwup," "The Whipper," wearing black case mask w/protruding eyes, large curved horns & long beard & carrying yucca whip in right hand, repair to horns, 7 1/8" h. ... **$780**

Moccasins, Southern Plains, child-size, natural leather decorated w/ bands of turquoise, black, pink & red beads, several areas missing bead strings, 8 1/2" l., pr. . **$403**

Model of a canoe, Woodlands, birch bark, traditional design w/wrapped seams, orange rim band & painted stylized blossoms, ca. 1940, 22 3/4" l., 6 1/2" h. **$345**

Necklace, Navajo, "squashblossom" design in silver & turquoise, 15" l. **$288**

Olla, Acoma, pottery w/bulbous shape & short rimless neck, short foot, decorated w/black & off-white geometric designs w/red accents to upper neck, base & inside of neck, 12" d. at widest point, 11" h. **$4,600**

Olla, Laguna, pottery, large squatty bulbous shape tapering to a wide flat mouth, decorated w/orange parallelograms pendant from the rim, stylized birds & leafed berry designs, checkered & foliate medallions separated by Chaco-scroll designs, red band on interior & at base, portion of rim missing, rim repair, small puncture hole on girth, first half 20th c, 13 1/2" d., 11 1/2" h. **$11,500**

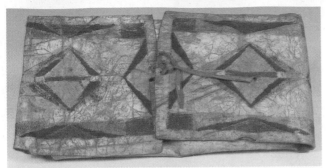

Parfleche case, Crow, natural ground w/polychrome geometric designs in mustard yellow, sky blue, red & deep green in symmetrical pattern, 19th c., some areas of repolychroming, 14 x 27" closed **$635**

Pipe bag, leather, turquoise trim decorated w/red, white & blue opposing American flags & other similarly colored designs, 9" end fringe w/tin cone beginnings, overall 4 1/2 x 23" **$403**

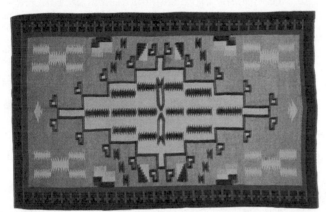

Rug, Navajo, Ganado or Klagetoch area, central elongated diamond design in hand-carded natural, black & grey wool w/double dye red border design, ca. 1930, stains, wear, 4' 4" x 6' 7" **$1,380**

Rug, Navajo, Western Reservation, a large zigzag diamond center design flanked by smaller diamond & cross designs, in natural, dark brown & light brown, ca. 1930, 57 x 75" **$200-400**

Rug, Navajo, Ganado-style, handwoven wool, three-band border in shades of brown & beige, center panel a deep red w/design in same colors as border radiating from red & black "X" in center, ca. 1930, small early repair, some soiling, 57 x 81" **$1,955**

The Navajo originally made utilitarian blankets with few patterns and colors. Only after they began trading with American setlers did they begin making the more elaborate designs.

IVORY MARKET REPORT

Dealers and collectors need to be knowledgeable about state, federal, and international laws concerning ownership, transportation, sale, and purchase of ivory and other animal products. Products made from ivory include carvings, scrimshaw, jewelry, chess pieces, piano keys, inlays for furniture, and netsuke. While some people may believe the sale of ivory is completely banned, it is not. It is, however, closely regulated and violations can result in severe penalties. Legal ivory includes products made from ivory before 1989 (pre-CITES ban). Ivory does not have to be antique (100 years old) to be legal, just pre-1989. It can be traded legally within the United States but cannot be imported or exported.

This area could prove to be an exceptionally promising for dealers because fewer people are willing to research and keep up with regulations. Those who are willing to do their homework are likely to have much less competition than in other areas.

Some Animal Products Covered by Law

African elephant ivory (AEI), hippo tusks, and warthog tusks are among the products covered by laws such as the Endangered Species Act, the African Elephant Conservation Act, and the Lacey Act. Marine mammal products are covered by even stricter regulations, such as the Marine Mammal Protection Act. Items in this category include whale teeth, walrus tusks, and narwhale tusks.

Some Animal Products Not Covered by Law

Elk antlers and ox bone may be sold domestically or internationally with no restrictions. The same is true with mammoth tusks because the species isn't endangered, it's extinct, so regulations to protect them would be irrelevant.

Regulations

Laws covering ivory and similar products are too extensive to cover here. The Web site www.gustavus.com/heidi/laws.html gives a good summary, but for complete, current, official information, consult the following sources:

State

Many states, such as California, have regulations in addition to federal and international laws. Consult the Department of Fish & Wildlife or Game Department in your state for specific information.

Federal

The U.S. Fish and Wildlife Service is the primary federal agency in charge of enforcement of laws concerning land animals. Visit www.fws.gov/le and read the *Importers/Exporters* and *Laws, Treaties, and Regulations* sections. Laws governing marine mammals are enforced by the National Marine Fisheries Service (see www.nmfs.noaa.gov/regulations.htm)

International

CITES (The Convention on International Trade in Endangered Species of Wild Fauna and Flora) is an international treaty that governs trade in animals and plants. Visit the CITES Web site at www.cites.org

eBay Policies on Ivory

As of January 1, 2009, eBay banned sales of almost all forms of ivory (including legal ivory) on its site. eBay only allows listings of "items created before 1900 that contain a trace amount (less than 5%) of actual ivory. Examples may include antique furniture or musical instruments with ivory inlay. To list these items, the seller must include a picture of the actual item and a clear and prominent disclaimer that specifically states that the item was created prior to 1900." See eBay's complete policies on animal and wildlife products at http://pages.ebay.com/help/policies/wildlife.html.

AntiqueSpider.com Policies on Ivory

AntiqueSpider is an online auction site that allows the sale of legal ivory and ivory-related products. See the Antique Spider website at www.antiquespider.com for more information about its policies. In addition, Antique Spider offers free appraisals (ivory-related items only) and has no listing fees.

Tips and Precautions

1. Certain states may require dealers to obtain a special license.

2. Sellers should be scrupulously accurate in identifying and describing the items they are selling, use precise terms, and provide multiple photos from various angles.

3. Buyers should be knowledgeable about fakes and reproductions. For an excellent article about distinguishing real ivory from fake, visit www.asian-arts.net/oriental-treats/fake.htm

4. For expensive items, it may well be worth the expense of having a USPAP-compliant appraisal done by a specialist appraiser.

5. Buyers and sellers should be aware that customs and postal officials may be suspicious of even legally sold and shipped animal items, which could result in shipping delays and possibly even confiscation because of misidentification by an authority.

Note: This article provides only general information about buying and selling ivory and ivory related products. It is not intended to give legal advice.

IVORY

Figure of a Buddhist Immortal, a tall gently curved tusk carved as the figure of a bearded man wearing long robes & holding a large flowering branch, mounted on a round black wood base, Oriental, mid- 20th c., 13 1/2" h. **$575**

Figure of elderly woman, finely carved standing w/her vest colored brown & her hair detailed in black, char mark on underside, on a turned wood base, Japan, late 19th - early 20th c., 10 1/2" h. (ILLUS. far right with figure of man & boy & three Buddist Immortals) **$1,093**

Figure of man & young boy, Okimono- type, man standing carrying various items, the small boy standing beside him, Japan, late 19th - early 20th c., 7 1/2" h. (ILLUS. far left with figure of elderly woman & three Buddhist Immortals) **$748**

Figures of Buddhist Immortals, each a tall slender figure, one standing holding a ring & a cat, one w/praying hands holding a brush & the third standing holding a gong & strikers, finely carved w/details highlighted in black, each on a carved teak base, Oriental, late 19th - early 20th c., 11 1/2" h., set of 3 (ILLUS. center with figure of elderly woman and man & boy) **$1,898**

Floral bouquet in vase, carved in the round as an arrangement of realistic peonies overflowing a rectangular vase decorated w/an engraved butterfly & calligraphy, raised on an oblong carved wooden base, China, late 19th - early 20th c., 10 1/2" l., 6" h. **$1,150**

Ivory has been used to create both art and utilitarian articles throughout history. Besides its well-known use in piano keys and billiard balls, the ancient Greeks and Romans used ivory in statues to form the whites of the eyes. Some Asian cultures used ivory as containers because of its ability to retain an air-tight seal. Others carved intricate seals into ivory to stamp official documents.

Figures of angels, each standing female figure w/enameled wings & other metal adornments, each playing w/infants, Europe, late 19th c., some decoration missing, one w/damage to infant, other w/damage to a wheel at the base, 5 1/2" h., pr. **$3,450**

JEWELRY MARKET REPORT

According to C. Jeanenne Bell G.G., an *Antiques Roadshow* appraiser and author of a number of books, including *Answers to Questions About Old Jewelry 1884-1950*, *The Collectors's Encyclopedia of Hairwork Jewelry*, *How to be a Jewelry Detective*, and *Warman's Antique Jewelry*, following are a few of the styles that are in demand: costume jewelry, large necklaces, large stones, Art Deco, Art Nouveau, and men's cufflinks. White metals, like white gold, which go well with sterling silver are popular. Many buyers looking for affordable fashion are turning to sterling silver with an overlay of 18K gold, which can run from eighty to several hundred dollars. Bold colors, such as orange, hot green, and solid turquoise colors are also in style.

Hair jewelry is an antique form that can be quite valuable. Although it originated as mourning pieces given in remembrance of a loved one's death, it developed into a broader art form and was used as love tokens in brooches, necklaces, bracelets, and even watch chains. Hair jewelry faded away as photographs became more popular as keepsakes.

Bell advises novice buyers to stay away from eBay because many listings aren't accurate or complete. Beginning buyers should instead rely on trusted, expert dealers who will stand behind what they sell. She also cautions inexperienced shoppers not to be fooled by confusing markings. For instance, some people have mistaken a piece of jewelry marked 18K HGE to mean that it is solid 18K gold and that HGE is a maker's mark. Actually HGE means "heavy gold electroplate," so the piece wouldn't be worth anywhere near what a solid piece of 18K gold is worth.

Knowledgeable buyers can find the best deals at flea markets, garage sales, and similar venues where novice sellers are most likely to offer their jewelry. Shops and estate sales are far more likely to have screened out the best pieces. To avoid inadvertently selling valuable jewelry at firesale prices, Bell recommends that anyone who inherits jewelry ask about its history and value and write that information down to accompany it in the jewelry box and pass it along with the item if it is sold or gifted. This will help ensure that the new owners give the jewelry the proper value and care it deserves.

"Price is subjective and value is transient," said Bell, to explain why she doesn't think buying jewelry strictly for investment is a good idea. "Diamonds have an especially high markup, so it is difficult to make money on them," she added. "It's better to invest in your own enjoyment, so buy what you like rather than for investment," she concluded.

Auction Houses
Skinner (www.skinnerinc.com)
Dumouchelle (www.dumouchelle.com)
Doyle New York (www.doylenewyork.com)
Freeman's (www.freemansauction.com/home.asp)
Leslie Hindman (www.lesliehindman.com)
Weschler's (www.weschlers.com)
Ivey-Selkirk (www.iveyselkirk.com)

JEWELRY

Antique (1800-1920)

Armlet, gold (14k) & sapphire, Art Nouveau style, slender design enclosing delicate scrolling bellflower designs bezel-set w/ three round sapphires, marked by Burstow, Kollmar & Co., interior circumference 8 3/4" d. **$353**

Bracelet, enamel & gem-set 14k gold, bangle-type, the narrow openwork band designed as polychrome enameled pansy blossoms interspersed w/scrolling leaves mounted w/circular-cut sapphires & seed pearl highlights, mark of Krementz & Co., Newark, New Jersey, 19th c., interior circumference 7 1/8" **$2,115**

Bracelet, gold (14k), bangle-type, hinged entwined tapering gold loop engraved w/floral & foliate designs, mark of L. Fritzsche & Company, Newark, New Jersey, dated 1908, interior circumference 7" **$646**

Bracelet, gold (15k), bangle-type, the top half w/applied bead & wirework designs, Edwardian era, early 20th c., English assay mark, interior circumference 6 3/8" **$828**

Bracelet, sapphire & diamond, bangle-type, hinged, the ring bezel-set w/five circular- cut sapphires interspersed w/diamond- set leaf & vine designs, platinum-topped 14k gold mount, interior circumference 6 1/2".................... **$1,175**

Bracelets, diamond & tricolor 14k gold, bangle-type, the thin hinged bangle mounted at the top w/a large cupped flower blossom centered by an old mine- cut diamond & flanked by buds & vines, marked "Pat. Nov. 4 '79," pr. **$2,585**

Brooch, malachite & 22k gold, the malachite cabochon mounted within a leaf & acorn frame, 2" l. **$323**

Brooch, pietra dura & 18k gold, oval frame enclosing a design of a bouquet of forget- me-nots, roses & lily-of-the-valley, mount w/applied wiretwist accents, 19th c., 1 3/4" l. **$529**

Bracelet with locket, garnet, diamond & enameled 18k gold, centered by a navette-shaped step-cut garnet framed by rose-cut diamonds & blue enamel scrolls, completed by a flexible fancy link gold bracelet, later safety chain w/evidence of solder, 6 5/8" l. **$1,058**

Bracelet, diamond & pearl, bangle-type, the narrow band set w/small old mine-cut diamonds, centered at the top by a button pearl flanked by two large old European- cut diamonds, diamonds weighing about 1.82 cts., French guarantee stamp, interior circumference 6 1/4" **$2,233**

Bracelet, diamond, turquoise & gold, bangle-type, the very narrow band set w/rose-cut diamonds & centered by a prong-set oval turquoise cabochon, silver-topped 18k gold mount, inscribed & dated 1883, French guarantee stamps & mark of the maker, interior circumference 6 3/4" **$1,410**

Bracelet, emerald, diamond, seed pearl & 14k gold, bangle-type, two thin open bands swelling at the upper half & mounted w/ an arrangement of alternating starbursts & leaf clusters, each starburst mount outlined in black enamel around a ground of rose-cut diamonds centered by an emerald, the leaf clusters set w/seed pearls, interior circumference 6 1/4" **$881**

Bracelet, gold & ruby, bangle-type, the narrow band w/delicate engraved scrolls & set w/three small rubies, unmarked, early 20th c. **$173**

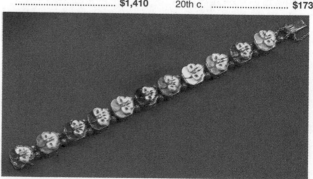

Bracelet, enameled 14k gold & diamond, slide-type, composed of links each mounted w/a small enameled pansy, each in a different color & each centered by a tiny diamond, 7 3/8" l. **$999**

Bracelet, enameled 15k gold, bangle-type, hinged, the domed round top enclosing a compartment, centered by a dark blue enameled dome decorated w/gold stars, surrounded by numerous gold border bands decorated w/applied beads & ropetwist accents, the wide gold side bands further decorated w/a raised fine wirework design of oblong loops & beads, original fitted box for a London jewelry, minor dents, interior circumference 6 1/2" **$2,350**

Bracelet, gold (14k) & tracery enamel, bangle-type, belt buckle style w/a delicate mesh ground & delicate black & white enamel on the buckle, adjustable length, small solder repair, second half 19th c. **$588**

Bracelet, gold (14k), sapphire & seed pearl, Art Nouveau style, composed of small openwork oval & double-band links alternately bezel-set w/circular-set sapphires or seed pearls, by Birks, 7 3/4" l. **$1,058**

Bracelet, gold (18k), diamond & enamel, slide-type, the wide mesh strap completed by a buckle set w/nine old mine-cut diamonds weighing about 3.20 cts., green enamel highlights & engraved foliate accents & fringe .. **$3,819**

Bracelet, lapis lazuli & 18k gold, composed of three cage-set lapis beads alternating w/engraved ball spacers, completed by an engraved cylindrical & trace links ending w/two small lapis beads, Rome, Italy assay marks, 7 1/4" l. **$2,293**

Bracelet, malachite & 15k yellow gold, the center w/a large oval malachite cabochon flanked by small oval malachite cabochons each framed w/ applied bead- and ropetwist accents & engraved floral motifs, completed by a wide woven gold bracelet w/geometric banding, w/a later detachable extender, 19th c., 6 1/8" l. **$764**

Bracelet, turquoise & 14k gold, buckle-style hinged bangle, the wide gold band mounted at the top w/a large pointed buckle & trimmed down the center w/a band of small cabochon turquoise, Victorian, interior circumference 5 7/8" **$940**

Turquoise is a phosphate of copper and aluminum and is frequently uncovered in copper mines.

Bracelet, seed pearl, diamond & platinum, bangle-type, hinged, the upper half set w/four-row sections of seed pearls separated by small diamond-set bars, millegrain accents, early 20th c., mark of Alsopp & Alsopp, interior circumference 6 1/2" **$1,528**

Bracelet, tourmaline & 14k gold, Arts & Crafts style, composed of links set w/oval yellow, green & pink cabochon tourmalines w/notched bezels alternating w/scrolling leaf links, signed by Edward Oakes, early 20th c., 7" l. **$8,813**

Bracelets, gold (14k) & black tracery enamel, bangle-type, belt buckle style w/a finely stippled ground & delicate black enamel on the buckle, second half 19th c., enamel loss, small interior dents, 5 3/4" circumference, pr. **$558**

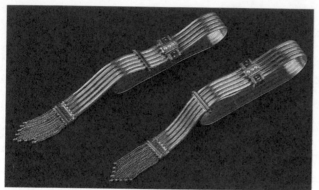

Bracelets, enameled 18k gold & seed pearl, slide-type, each w/a flat ribbed band mounted w/a slide band trimmed w/black tracery enamel & centered by a row of three seed pearls, the end w/a delicate black enamel Greek key band above foxtail fringe, adjustable to 8 1/2" l., pr. **$2,468**

Brooch-clip, citrine, diamond & gold, centered by a large rectangular fancy-cut citrine w/ cut-corners within a conforming frame set w/a narrow band of rose-cut diamonds, a delicate diamond-set ribbon at the top flanked by a pair of large diamonds, a triangular cluster of six larger diamonds at the bottom edge, platinum-topped 18k gold mount, European hallmarks, possibly Belgium, early 20th c., 1 1/8 x 1 3/4" **$2,820**

Although beryl and chrysoberyl have similar names, they are different gemstones and are unrelated.

Brooch-pendant, amethyst, seed pearl & 15k gold, an oblong bar decorated w/applied wire, bead & scrollwork accents centered by a very large circular fancy-cut amethyst, the bar suspending delicate trace link chains set w/seed pearls, 19th c. **$264**

Amethyst is a form of quartz. Its name means "not intoxicated." The Greeks and Romans believed that drinking from a vessel made from amethyst would prevent drunkenness.

Brooch-pendant, amethyst, chrysoberyl & 14k yellow gold, the large oval blossom-form brooch composed of 10 oblong petal w/applied gold ropetwist trim & set w/a foil-backed oval-cut amethyst, the oval center w/a ring of smaller amethysts centering a chrysoberyl, suspending three fine mesh chains suspending a matching round pendant set w/a ring of round-cut amethysts centered by a single cut chrysoberyl, back w/a hair compartment & a portrait of a little boy, evidence of solder on the back, 19th c., 2 3/4" l. **$588**

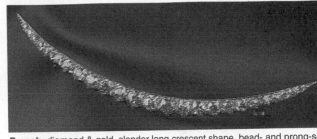

Brooch-pendant, diamond & 14k gold, designed as an eight-arm starburst centered by a prong-set old European-cut diamond, a single old mine-cut diamond mounted between each arm, w/an 18k gold trace link chain, brooch 1 1/4" d. **$441**

Brooch, diamond & gold, slender long crescent shape, bead- and prong-set w/a graduated row of old European-cut diamonds weighing about 3.03 cts., platinum-topped 18k gold mount, mark of Marcus & Co., early 20th c. **$3,290**

> Because of the diamond's unique structure, very few impurities can contaminate it.

Brooch, diamond, pearl & 14k gold, a delicate garland openwork mount set overall w/small old single- and mine-cut diamonds, a large pearl suspended in the center w/two pearls along the bottom & a pearl-tipped drop below, silver-topped 14k gold mount, 19th c. **$588**

Brooch, diamond, pearl & gold, the fanned openwork mount w/the frame set w/rose- cut diamonds accented w/a row of pearls across the top, silver-topped 18k gold mount, French import stamp **$1,880**

Brooch, diamond, sapphire & 14k gold, a delicate openwork bow & ribbon design, the lower bow set w/old mine-cut diamond mélée & suspending a pear- shaped sapphire drop, long curled ribbons further set w/mine-cut diamonds & terminating in a single diamond, extending above the bow & framing a ring of diamonds enclosing a pront-set circular- cut sapphire, Russian maker's mark & guarantee stamps, 19th c., in a box for R. J. Spearing, 1" l. **$1,645**

Brooch, enamel & silver-gilt, a round enameled picture of a grey & white kitten on a guilloché enamel ground, silver-gilt mount, Edwardian era, England, early 20th c., 1 3/8" d. **$881**

Brooch, enamel, freshwater pearl & diamond, Art Nouveau style, in the form of a swimming swan w/a freshwater pearl forming the body, bass taille enameled neck, resting amid gold water lilies & leaves, a circular-cut diamond & gold leaf in its beak, hallmark of Krementz & Co., Newark, New Jersey **$9,400**

Brooch, enamel, 14k gold & pearl, a long narrow oval dark blue guilloché enamel plaque centered by a single pearl & bordered by a ring of seed pearls, gold mount, in fitted London jeweler's box, 19th c., 1 1/2" l. **$206**

ANTIQUE (1800-1920)

Brooch, enameled 14k gold & diamond, Art Nouveau style, designed as a large & smaller pansy blossom both enameled in dark purple w/a yellow & brown center set w/an old European-cut diamond, curled rope-twined gold stems, illegible marker's mark, 1 1/2" l. **$588**

Brooch, enameled 14k gold & diamond, Art Nouveau style, designed as a realistic orchid enameled in pale yellow & pink, the lip set w/a single old European-cut diamond, mark of Whiteside & Blank, 1" l. **$823**

Brooch, enameled 14k gold & diamond, designed as a curved heart-shaped ropetwist frame enclosing a flower bouquet w/a purple & pink pansy centered by a small diamond, a six-petal pink & white blossoms w/a center diamond & two clusters of small forget-me-not blossoms, 1" l. **$294**

Brooch, enameled 18k gold, seed pearl & diamond, an oblong twisted gold rope frame enclosing a small purple, lavender & yellow-enameled pansy centered by a small diamond beside a cluster of three enameled forget-me-not blossoms each centered by a tiny seed pearl, 1 1/4" w. **$323**

A cabochon is a stone that has been shaped and polished rather than faceted.

Brooch, enameled silver-gilt, Renaissance Revival style, a pair of openwork scrolls ending in large palmette leaves flanking a round central medallion enameled in color w/a profile bust portrait of a lady in Renaissance dress, late 19th c., 2" l. **$300-500**

Brooch, enameled silver, Art Nouveau style, designed as a stylized winged Egyptian scarab enameled w/plique-a- jour in brown & green in the wings & champlevé enamel in green, yellow & black in the body, flanked by horizontal stylized lotus blossom bars enameled in shades of green, early 20th c. 1 5/8" l. **$588**

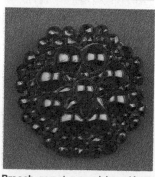

Brooch, garnet, a round domed form set by round garnet cabochons framed by a band of pear- and rose-cut garnets, silver-gilt mount, 1 1/2" d. **$382**

Brooch, freshwater pearl, diamond & 18k gold, Art Nouveau style, designed as a flower stem, the gold leafy stem mounted w/a blossom & bud formed by freshwater pearls, the blossom centered by an old European-cut diamond, 1 3/8" l. **$382**

Brooch, hardstone, paste & 15k gold, Judaic design, the blue paste ground inlaid w/a hardstone & goldstone glass Star of David, the wide gold frame decorated w/applied gold bead & ropetwist designs, center not original to mount, evidence of solder **$705**

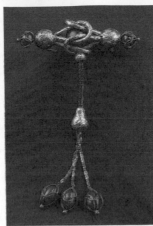

Brooch, landscape agate, diamond & gold, a narrow top pin bar suspending a squared arrangement of four square agates each bordered by tiny rose-cut diamonds & joined by thin diamond-set bars & centering a smaller matching agate, suspending two thin straight links supporting a pendant composed of two more small diamond-framed agates, silver- topped 18k & 14k gold mount, evidence of solder, 1 1/4 x 2 3/4" **$4,994**

Brooch, lapis lazuli & 18k gold, the top bar centered by entwined engraved gold band enclosing a lapis sphere, flanked by engraved gold balls & cage-set lapis spheres, suspending a slender fancy link chain supporting an engraved gold sphere further supporting three link chains each ending in a cage-set lapis bead, Rome, Italy assay marks **$1,410**

Brooch, malachite, seed pearl & 14k gold, designed as two malachite cubes decorated w/clusters of tiny seed pearls & joined by a gold bar centered by a band of seed pearls, all topped by a palmette & scroll crest, missing clasp, second half 19th c. .. **$323**

Brooch, moonstone, seed pearl & gold, Art Nouveau style, a large domed round bezel-set moonstone mounted in the center of a delicate four-lobed openwork platinum-topped gold mount, four seed pearls frame the moonstone & four small square-cut synthetic sapphires trim the mount, hallmark of Allsopp & Allsopp **$1,293**

Brooch, painted ivory & 18k gold, the oval ivory top h.p. w/a scene of an amorino reposing on a fallen cross before a mountainous landscape & distant town, gold frame & mount, French guarantee stamp, 19th c. **$881**

A seed pearl is a small, often imperfect pearl.

Brooch, painted enamel & seed pearl, mourning-type, an oval plaque painted in sepia tones w/a scene of two ladies mourning at an obleisk composed of applied enamel plaques, seed pearls & gold wirework on a grassy mound formed of clipped hair, within a bright-cut 14k rose gold mount, the back inscribed & dated 1795, original fitted red leather oval hinged box, one seed pearl detached, late 18th - early 19th c., 1 3/4" l. **$3,819**

Brooch, pearl & gem-set 14k yellow gold, a stylized butterfly form composed of delicate scrolling filigree mounted w/14 bezel-set rubies, three emeralds & centered by a cultured pearl, one small spot of filigree damage, early 20th c. **$460**

Brooch, pearl & 18k gold, a barbell form gold mount w/fine wirework & applied florets across the center, the round terminals set w/later added freshwater pearls, Continental hallmarks, second half 19th c., 3" l. . **$353**

ANTIQUE (1800-1920)

Brooch, pietra dura, the oval black stone ground set w/a spray of white flowers & buds on a green leafy stem, gold ropework frame, boxed, Victorian, 1 1/2 x 2 1/4" **$323**

Brooch, pink sapphire, diamond & gold, designed as a ring formed by a looping ribbon set w/old European-cut diamonds, each loop framing a prong-set circular-cut pink sapphire, diamonds weighing about .77 cts., platinum-topped 14k gold mount, ca. 1915, 1 1/8" d. **$940**

Brooch, silver, 14k gold, synthetic ruby & diamond, Art Nouveau style, a thin rectangular frame enclosing an openwork design of stylized three-petal blossoms set w/pear-cut synthetic rubies & stylized fanned leaves set w/ rose-cut diamonds, gold mounts, 1 7/8" l. **$764**

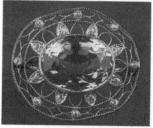

Brooch, pink topaz, diamond & platinum, an oval openwork mount composed of delicate wirework set w/a band of small full- cut diamonds w/a band of pointed dia- mond-set petals around the large central oval fancy-cut pink topaz, millegrain accents, Edwardian era, early 20th c., replaced 14k gold pin stem, 1" l. **$4,230**

Brooch, sterling silver, silver narrow round pin frame w/two side tabs enclosing a round swiveling silver medallion w/a crest on one side & a scene of The HMS Hampshire on the other, made in Birmingham, England, 1909, 1 3/4" w. **$92**

Cameo brooch, agate & 18k gold, the cameo w/a profile bust of a woman, the ornate gold framed w/engraved designs, French guarantee stamp, 1 3/4" l. **$1,410**

Buckle, diamond & 14k gold, Art Nouveau style, the rectangular frame w/a repeating design of scrolls set w/bezel-set old mine-cut diamonds, signed "S. Sons," 1" l. **$705**

Cameo brooch, carved agate, seed pearl & 18k gold, the large oval carved white to black agate w/a large profile bust of a classical lady, gold border & a frame of seed pearls, mark of French maker & guarantee stamps, 1 3/4" l. **$800-1,200**

Cameo brooch, carved coral, a central Bacchante face enclosed by a wide frame of carved grapevine & scrolls, 14k gold mount, evidence of solder at pin stem, 19th c., 2" l. **$1,293**

Cameo brooch, carved hardstone, seed pearl & 14k gold, a large oval cameo w/the bust profile of a classical woman in white carved to black, framed by a ring of seed pearls, gold mount, 19th c., 1 7/8 x 2 1/4" **$881**

Cameo brooch/pendant, hardstone, seed pearl & 14k gold, the oval cameo w/a dark ground & relief-carved profile bust of a Renaissance lady, framed by split seed pearls, gold mount, 19th c., 1 5/8" l. **$588**

Cameo cuff buttons, gold (14k) & hardstone, a pair of oval hardstone cameos of bearded gentleman mounted in elaborate oblong gold mounts, in a Kirkpatrick box, second half 19th c., each 1 1/8" l., pr. **$558**

Cameo pins, carnelian agate & 18k gold, each round cameo finely carved w/the head of Janus, simple gold band frame, formerly cuff buttons, 19th c., 7/8" d., pr. **$764**

Cameo ring, carved hardstone, 18k gold & diamond, the oval white carved to red cameo carved w/a scene of Zeus as an eagle bearing Ganymede to Mt. Olympus, a narrow border band of bead-set single-cut diamonds, size 5 .... **$1,528**

Cameo ring, onyx & 18k rose gold, the oval cameo top carved w/a profile bust of a helmeted warrior, simple gold frame & ribbed shank, 19th c., size 3 3/4 ..... **$250- 350**

ANTIQUE (1800-1920)

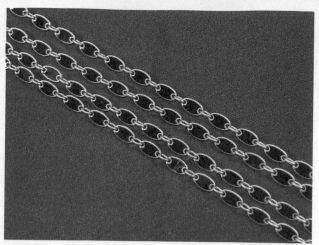

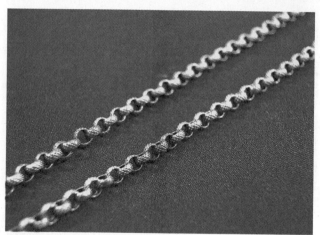

Chain, enameled 18k gold, composed of small navette-form black enameled links, some losses, 19th c., 62" l. **$764**

Chain, gold (18k), composed of round trace links textured w/stars on a stippled ground, completed by a flattened box clasp w/bright-cut floral engraving, 19th c., 25" l. **$411**

Chain, gold (18k), composed of sections w/a pair of teardrop-shaped openwork links filled w/scrolls centered by a round openwork link w/scrolls, the groups alternating w/section of smaller chain links, French guarantee stamp, 56" l. **$1,528**

Chain, platinum & 18k gold, composed of alternating fancy links completed by a box clasp, ca. 1910, 30 1/2" l. . . **$823**

Choker, gold (10k), turquoise & seed pearl, composed of two parallel link chains joining narrow oval gold plaques set w/a row of four small cabochon turquoise & two seed pearl accents, a large ornately scrolling central gold plaque set w/bands of small cabochon turquoise & seed pearls, evidence of solder, late 19th - early 20th c., 13" l. (ILLUS. of part)............................... **$450**

Cuff buttons, moss agate, rectangular agate top w/an inclusion resembling a leafless tree, a narrow rectangular beaded gilt-metal frame & findings, late 19th c., 7/8" l., the set **$353**

Cuff link, platinum-topped gold, enamel & sapphire, mark of Later & Sons, England, Edwardian era, early 20th c., 1/2" l., pr. **$823**

Cuff buttons, tortoiseshell & 14k gold, each w/the inlaid monogram "S" & a Greek key border, pr. **$129**

Cuff links, gold (10k), Art Nouveau style, each designed as the head of a woman among rushes w/a full-cut diamond accent, one w/a dent, 3/4" l., pr. **$176**

Cuff links, gold (18k), Art Nouveau style, the top of each decorated w/the head of a veiled maiden, boxed, the set..................... **$235**

Earrings, gilt-metal, Etruscan Revival style, the oval hoops w/bead- and ropetwist accents, three fancy-cut black glass highlights, reverse w/dents, second half 19th c., 1 7/8" l., pr. **$147**

Cuff links, diamond & 14k gold, each circular engine-turned double link centering an old European-cut diamond & w/a ropetwist border band, Edwardian era, early 20th c., platinum-topped 14k gold mounts, pr. **$382**

Cuff links, enameled 18k gold & diamond, each oval blue enamel link bead-set w/an old mine-cut diamond fleur-de-lis & joining a flattened blue enamel button, Edwardian era, early 20th c., pr. **$1,116**

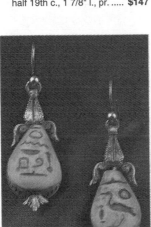

Earrings, faience & 18k gold, Egyptian Revival style, pendant-style, the gold foliate top suspending a yellow faience teardrop etched in green w/ stylized hieroglyphics, French guarantee stamps, glaze wear, 1 1/4" l., pr. **$588**

Cuff links, enameled gold, each round flat double link centered by a design of floral swags on an engine-turned ground, a narrow border band of black enamel, platinum-topped 14k gold, mark of Wordley, Allsopp & Bliss, Newark, New Jersey, early 20th c., 3/8" d., the pair **$764**

Cuff links, gold (14k), each double oval link decorated in low-relief w/a steeplechase scene w/a horse & jockey, European assay mark, ca. 1910, pr. **$1,645**

Cuff links, moonstone & 18k gold, each w/a round disk top fitted w/a moonstone carved w/a moon face, joined by a trace link chain to a gold sphere, Edwardian era, early 20th c., 5/8" d., pr... **$1,528**

Earrings, diamond, the wire loop fitted w/a small bezel-set diamond suspending a larger rose-cut diamond, 14k gold mount, pr. **$1,175**

Earrings, gold (14k), a gold bead decorated w/fine wirework & a fanned & wirework top, second half 19th c., 1 1/8" l., pr. **$1,175**

Moonstone derives its name from the unique way it reflects light internally through various alternating layers.

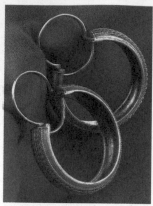

Earrings, garnet, diamond & 18k gold, pendant-type, the top w/an oval cabochon garnet in a gold wirework frame, suspending to graduated round garnet cabochons each centered by an inset gold starburst set w/old mine- and rose-cut diamonds, 14k gold tops, 1 1/2" l., pr. **$1,998**

Earrings, gold (14k), a basket-form bead decorated w/fine wirework below a smaller suspended bead & palmette & bar top, second half 19th c., some tarnish, 1" l., pr. **$1,645**

Earrings, gold (14k), Etruscan Revival style, a three-quarters ringlet applied w/delicate wirework, second half 19th c., 1 1/4" d., pr. **$1,175**

Earrings, gold (18k), pendant-type, a small top suspending a very long textured gold teardrop pendant encircled near the base w/a band of stylized blossoms & w/a floral terminal, later tops, 1 3/4" l., pr. **$823**

Locket & chain, bicolor gold (14k), the shaped flower-decorated lockket set w/seed pearl highlights & applied bead & wirework, the chain composed of ribbed oval banded links w/a double integral closure, second half 19th c., locket 2" l., chain 19 1/2" l. **$1,293**

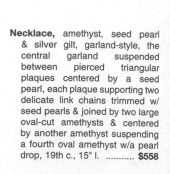

Necklace, amethyst, seed pearl & silver gilt, garland-style, the central garland suspended between pierced triangular plaques centered by a seed pearl, each plaque supporting two delicate link chains trimmed w/ seed pearls & joined by two large oval-cut amethysts & centered by another amethyst suspending a fourth oval amethyst w/a pearl drop, 19th c., 15" l. **$558**

ANTIQUE (1800-1920)

Necklace, coral & 14k gold, composed of reddish orange coral beads graduating in size, completed by a box clasp, 17" l. **$1,116**

Necklace, cut-steel fringe-style, composed of faceted studs & navettes, later jump ring closure, 19th c., 15" l. **$294**

Pendant-locket, gold (14k), holds a watercolor on ivory picture of a lady standing by a classical temple & votive figure w/anchor & clipper ship, paint loss, first half 19th c., 1 1/4 x 1 3/4" **$206**

Pendant, amethyst & diamond, composed of prong-set round and pear-shaped amethysts interspersed w/rose-cut diamonds, 14k gold & silver mount, ca. 1900, suspended from a later 18k gold chain, overall 18" l. **$646**

Pin, black opal, diamond, enamel, 18k gold & platinum, a diamond-shaped frame centering a large bezel-set oval broadflash black opal, the frame composed of curved intersecting bands on each side w/large gold scale-design bands alternating w/smaller bands set w/old European- cut diamond mélée, green enamel accents, hallmark of Bailey, Banks & Biddle, No. 37930 .... **$7,931**

Necklace, ceramic & 14k gold, composed of 31 ancient ceramic scarabs & tablets w/ hieroglyphs, joined by fancy triangular & cylindrical 14k gold links, chips and losses, 42" l. ... **$823**

Necklace, citrine, seed pearl & 14k gold, fringe-style, a fine trace link chain centered by a section of fine openwork floret & navette links accented w/ seed pearls & suspending thirteen graduated fancy links each suspending a pear-shaped faceted citrine, American-made, ca. 1915, 14 3/4" l. **$4,406**

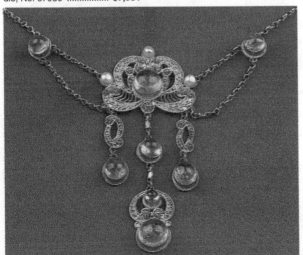

Necklace, emerald, seed pearl & 18k gold, fringe-style, a delicate trace link chain w/T-form clasp suspending an ornate pendant design w/the chain set on each side w/a framed round emerald cabochon suspending another delicate chain, a central ornate cartouche-form plaque composed of gold filigree, fine ropework, beads & florets & centered by a large round emerald cabochon & three seed pearl edge accents, the cartouche suspending three drops, two short ones w/an open gold scroll link above an emerald cabochon & the longer central one w/a fine link chain w/another round emerald cabochon above an openwork rounded gold scroll fitted w/ a small round emerald cabochon above a large round emerald cabochon, 16 1/2" l. **$2,115**

Necklace, gold (14k), composed of 61 plain round gold beads, strung on a foxtail chain, second half 19th c., minor dents, 16 3/4" l. **$358**

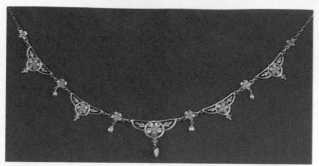

Necklace, freshwater pearl & 18k gold, Art Nouveau style fringe-type, a delicate trace link chain suspending a front band of five half-round openwork links decorated w/a floret flanked by leaves & alternating w/small floret links each suspending a tiny freshwater pearl, mark of a French maker & guarantee stamps, 16 1/4" l. **$1,058**

Necklace, gold (18k), Etruscan Revival style, fringe-type, composed of gold cylindrical small links & beads suspending a fringe of arched plaques & florets w/applied bead & wirework accents, completed by an oval box clasp, mid-19th c., 16 3/4" l. **$7,931**

Necklace, garnet, composed of 19 round links centered by a round cabochon garnet surrounded by a ring of rose-cut almandite garnets, suspending a large oval drop center by an oval garnet cabochon surrounded by three rings of rose-cut almandite garnets, gilt mount, w/a leather presentation sleeve, 19th c., 13 1/2" l. **$2,115**

Necklace, gold (15k), Etruscan Revival style, composed of 50 gold beads each applied w/fine wirework & strung on a foxtail chain, second half 19th c., 15" l. ... **$1,528**

Necklace, gold (15k), Etruscan Revival style, composed of 59 beads applied w/fine wirework accents, strung on a foxtail chain, 19th c., 14 1/8" l.
.... **$1,175**

Necklace, gold, Etruscan Revival style, composed of 37 gold beads w/applied bead & wirework decoration, strung on a foxtail chain completed by a hinged double-ring clasp, inscribed & dated 1878, 16" l. **$3,173**

Necklace, seed pearl & 9k gold, composed of delicate openwork gold starburst links set overall w/seed pearls & suspending a larger matching starburst pendant, completed by a fancy link chain, English hallmarks, Victorian, 16 3/4" l. **$1,410**

Necklace, tourmaline & gem-set 9k gold, fringe-style, a fine link chain suspending a varied band of round & oblong gems including pink & green tourmalines w/the large central stone suspending a teardrop aquamarine & round peridot, ca. 1910, 15 3/4" l. **$1,645**

Necklace, turquoise & silver-gilt, designed as a flexible thin ring decorated w/five graduated five-petal blossoms & two tiny florets all pavé-set w/tiny cabochon turquoise beading, each large flower w/a central pearl, 19th c., 17 1/2" l. **$4,406**

Pendant-brooch, seed pearl, diamond & 14k gold, the rounded form composed of fancy S-scroll arms each set w/graduating seed pearls, all centered by an old European-cut diamond, two pearls missing, 1 1/8" d. ... **$823**

Pendant-brooch, seed pearl, diamond & 14k gold, designed as a bunch of pearl grapes w/ golden, rose & silver overtones suspended from a leafy gold vine set w/two old mine-cut diamonds **$1,880**

Pendant-brooch, garnet, the triangular top pin mounted w/ rose-cut garnets, suspending a large round brooch composed of eight small florets centered by a larger central floret all set w/numerous rose- and pear-cut garnets, compartment in the back, European hallmarks, missing three garnets, 2 1/4" l. **$323**

Pendant-locket, seed pearl, enamel, diamond & 18k gold, the flat disk centered by a small starburst set w/ small mine- and rose-cut diamonds surrounded by bass taille dark blue enamel, a border of seed pearls, the back w/a locket compartment, replaced pin stem, 1 1/2" d. **$823**

ANTIQUE (1800-1920)

Pendant-locket, gold (14k), Etruscan Revival style, designed as an ancient amphora suspended from an arched bar & tall loop booth decorated w/fine beading & wirework, the amphora w/inward-scrolled shoulder handles above a central band of palmettes, decorated overall w/fine beading & wirework, opening to reveal a compartment, 19th c., 2 1/4" l. **$1,998**

Pendant-necklace, amethyst & 14k gold, the oval gold pendant w/an inner filigree band encloses a large oval-cut amethyst, suspended from a chain composed of small spade-shaped openwork links w/ a fancy-cut amethyst accent, 19th c., overall 15 3/4" l. **$1,410**

Pendant-necklace, diamond, pearl & bicolor 18k gold, a long slender chain composed of navette-form links w/an old European-cut diamond & suspending an off-white pearl w/a single-cut diamond cap, completed by a bow-form clasp, diamonds weighing about 4.40 cts., two diamonds chipped, 16 1/2" l. **$2,820**

Pendant-necklace, black opal, green chalcedony & gold, Arts & Crafts style, a delicate looping link gold chain suspending an oblong delicate openwork gold pendant w/scroll & band design centered by a large oval black opal w/green hues, seed pearl highlights, suspending three flexible teardrop chalcedony drops, made by James Winn & signed, early 20th c., overall 16 1/4" l. **$6,463**

Pendant-necklace, plique-à-jour enamel, Jugendstil (Germanic Art Nouveau), stylized bird-like design w/scrolled wings & fanned tail composed of green & deep red enamel, a band of tiny seed pearls along the top & a central square-cut green glass stone, suspended from a trace link chain, silver gilt mount, mark of Carl Hermann, Pforzheim, early 20th c., overall 17" l. (ILLUS. of pendant)............................. **$999**

Pendant-necklace, gold (18k), composed of 59 engraved gold beads suspending a shield-shaped gold pendant w/a central oval surrounded a raised double circle & bar design, an arched top & pointed palmette base w/small colonettes at the sides, applied bead & wirework accents, completed by an S-form closure, a locket compartment in the back, original fitted box, 17 1/4" l. (ILLUS. of part)................ **$4,348**

Pendant-necklace, turquoise & 15k gold, Art Nouveau style, a sideways-set oval turquoise cabochon accented w/four seed pearls suspending two plain link & seed pearl chains ending in small oval turquoise cabochons, on a trace link chain, early 20th c., overall 15 1/2" l. **$646**

Pendant-pin, enameled 14k gold & diamond, Art Nouveau style, in the form of a pansy blossom enameled in pink over yellow w/deep rose accents around the center set w/an old mine-cut diamond, mark of A.J. Hedges, 1" w. **$1,645**

Pendant, gold (18k), seed pearl & enamel, designed as double foxtail chain tassels topped by black enamel & seed pearl accents, missing on pearl, 19th c. **$499**

Pendant, micromosaic & 18k gold, a narrow ribbed gold framed w/ three pointed knobs enclosing a micromosaic design of the Greek letters Chi & Rho represented a Christian symbol, frame w/ applied bead accents, hanging loop at the top, inscribed date of 1887, missing two tessera, 1" l. **$1,175**

Pendant, pietra dura & 18k gold, the oval lapis lazuli plaque inlaid w/ polychrome hardstones depicting four white doves drinking at a fountain, within a delicate scrolling gold floral framed w/applied bead & wirework, suspended from a delicate 14k gold trace link chain, overall 18" l. **$1,528**

Pendant, platinum, moonstone intaglio & diamond, an oval moonstone carved in intaglio w/a scene of a cherub holding a torch, delicate openwork foliate platinum frame bezel- and bead-set w/old single- cut diamonds, Edwardian era, early 20th c., 1 3/4" l. **$4,994**

Pin, enameled silver, a flat rectangular bar finely enameled w/a row of colorful perched birds, solder at pin stem, 19th c. **$1,116**

ANTIQUE (1800-1920)

Pendant, sterling silver & enamel, the long slender barred sides end in an oblong mount enameled in dark blue w/two round buttons, a teardrop-shaped drop enameled in mottled green & blue, Birmingham, England hallmarks & date letter for 1908, mark of maker possibly JF, 2 3/4" l. **$294**

Pin, enameled 18k gold & diamond, Art Nouveau style, designed as curled green-enameled leaves encircling a pink-enameled iris blossom highlighted w/a diamond & the profile bust portrait of an Art Nouveau maiden, mark of Krementz & Co., Newark, New Jersey **$1,528**

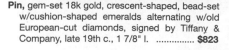

Pin, gem-set 18k gold, crescent-shaped, bead-set w/cushion-shaped emeralds alternating w/old European-cut diamonds, signed by Tiffany & Company, late 19th c., 1 7/8" l. **$823**

Pin, enameled 18k gold & diamond, Egyptian Revival style, a round flat disk centered by a profile bust portrait of an Egyptian goddess in champlevé enamel, rose-cut diamond accents, decorative engraved background, French guarantee marks, late 19th - early 20th c., 1 1/4" d. **$1,058**

Pin, gem-set 14k gold, Art Nouveau style, the round gold disk molded w/a profile bust portrait of Lady Liberty & a fasces, enclosed by an outer thin ring mounted w/ three small rose-cut diamonds alternating w/three rubies . **$353**

> In the early Middle Ages, diamond cutting was crude. Diamonds were cut with few facets, and in Medieval paintings, diamonds appear black because they had little sparkle. Consequently, colored gemstones like rubies were preferred.

Pin, enameled 18k gold, round, painted in polychrome w/a bust portrait of a gypsy lady wearing rose-cut diamond earrings, 19th c. **$646**

Pin, gold (14k), Art Nouveau style, modeled as a winged serpentine griffin w/a cabochon ruby eye, the back w/a pendant hook, late 19th - early 20th c., 1 1/2" l. **$411**

Ring, emerald, diamond & gold, the rectangular top centered by a row of three emerald-cut emeralds framed by old mine- and European-cut diamonds, 14k gold mount, size 6 1/4 ... **$1,175**

Ring, colored diamond, diamond & 14k gold, prong-set w/a brown old mine-cut diamond approximately 1.10 cts. framed by smaller clear old mine-cut diamonds, gold mount, later shank, size 8 .... **$1,880**

Ring, emerald, diamond, enamel & 18k gold, the top prong-set w/a large emerald-cut emerald surrounded by 14 old mine-cut diamonds weighing about 1.12 cts., foliate-decorated shoulders w/black enamel trim, 19th c., enamel wear, size 7 1/2 .... **$1,763**

Ring, enamel & diamond, wide domed top centered by a starburst bead- and bezel- set w/old European-, single-, and mine- cut diamonds on a dark blue enamel ground, border band further set w/diamonds, platinium-topped 14k gold mount, engraved highlights, blue enamel shoulders, size 5 1/2 ..... **$2,115**

Ring, gem-set 14k gold, snake-form, the coiled serpent w/engraved scales set w/a circular-cut blue sapphire on the top of the head & w/ruby eyes, dated 1916, size 9 .... **$999**

Ring, gold (14k), Shakudo-style, the round top tablet decorated w/a flower on a stem, 19th c., size 6 1/2 .... **$353**

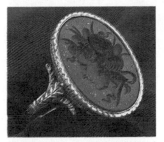

Ring, lapis lazulis & 18k gold, oval flat lapis intaglio cut w/a classical figure, open gallery & foliate shoulders, size 6 1/2 ..... **$1,293**

Ring, platinum & diamond, the long openwork top w/crossed bands & a central leaf sprig bezel & bead-set w/old European-cut diamonds, ca. 1915, size 5 1/2 .... **$999**

Ring, ruby intaglio & 18k gold, the gold mount set w/an oval ruby plaque incised w/Masonic symbols, London hallmarks & letter date for 1905, size 7 1/2 .... **$1,645**

Ring, rose gold (14k), memorial-type, the almond-shaped gold frame w/ a finely beaded edge enclosing a sepia tone inkwork images of a mourning lady standing beside an urn & monument, engraved shoulders, Georgian period, England, ca. 1780, minor loss to inkwork, size 10 1/4 .... **$529**

Ring, ruby & diamond, a long rectangular top composed of radiating bands alternating old European-cut diamonds & cal-ibré-cut rubies, shank w/engraved floral & leaf designs & set w/old single-cut diamond accents, diamonds weighing about .83 cts., platinum-topped 14k gold mount, ca. 1915, size 3 1/2 .... **$881**

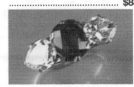

Ring, ruby, diamond & gold, the top set w/a pair of faceted pear-shaped diamonds weighing 1.29 & 1.44 cts. flanking a cushion-cut ruby, signed by Tiffany & Co., ca. 1915, platinum & 18k gold mount, size 6 1/2 .... **$66,975**

ANTIQUE (1800-1920)

Ring, sapphire, diamond & 18k gold, the oblong top centered by a cushion-cut blue sapphire flanked by old mine-cut diamonds, engraved shoulders, size 8 1/2 .... **$2,468**

Stickpin, moonstone, diamond, enamel & gold, the top in moonstone carved as a man's head wearing a cap & collar set w/rose-cut diamonds & trimmed w/purple guilloché enamel, 14k gold mount, Edwardian era, early 20th c. **$2,938**

Watch chain & locket fob, platinum & 14k rose gold, the chain composed of small curb links, suspending a small flattened round locket engraved w/a rayed design, 19th c., the set .. **$2,350**

Ring, sapphire, diamond & 18k gold, twin- stone style, the top prong-set w/an old pear-cut diamond weighing about 2.18 cts. & a matching pear-cut blue sapphire, the openwork foliate shoulders bead-set w/old European- and mine-cut diamonds, size 6 1/2 .... **$24,675**

Stickpin, reverse-painted crystal & 14k gold, the round top w/a domed crystal reverse-painted w/the head of a chestnut horse, gold frame & pin, signed by Marcus & Co. **$382**

> Chalcedony was often used to make seals, as hot wax would not stick to it.

Watch fob, chalcedony & 14k gold, a large oval carnelian & milk chalcedony tablet mounted within a scroll-decorated oval revolving frame w/a scalloped leaf top band & forked crest suspended from a large ring connected to a faceted & engraved openwork bar link chain, 19th c., 9" l. **$1,293**

Ring, ruby & diamond, the top centering a cushion-cut ruby surrounded by rose-cut diamonds & circular-cut rubies, silver-topped 18k gold mount, 19th c., size 3 3/4 .... **$1,880**

Stickpin, hardstone cameo & 14k gold, the cameo top carved w/a profile bust of a classical elder, gold frame & shank, 19th c., 1 1/8" l. **$382**

Stickpin, shell cameo & 14k rose gold, the oval cameo head carved as a figure of a satyr leaping at a leaping goat, gold frame & pin **$294**

Watch chain, gold (14k.), composed of multiple interlocking oval links, 43 3/4" l. **$823**

Watch chain, gold (14k), Art Nouveau style, composed of alternating navette & oval links, late 19th - early 20th c., 12k gold jump ring, 30" l. **$764**

Watch chain, gold (14k), composed of curb links w/a later chain extender & gold-filled clasp, 16 1/2" l. **$294**

Watch chain, gold (18k), Art Nouveau style, composed of navette-form links w/wirework scrolls, 56 1/2" l. **$705**

Watch fob, amethyst & 18k gold, set w/an intaglio-engraved amethyst w/a floral & leaf design in a gold mount, 1 1/4" l. **$382**

Sets

Brooch & earrings, angelskin corla & 14k gold, the brooch carved as a scallop shell centered by the head of a cherub & suspending three spiral shell drops, each earring w/a matching design, second half 19th c., brooch 1 3/8" l., earring 1 1/2" l., the set **$1,880**

Cameo brooch-pendant & a pair of pins, hardstone, the brooch-pendant set w/a large oval cameo depicting the figures of Hector & Andromache within a pierced 18k gold & platinum mount, each cameo pin w/a seated figure of the widowed Andromache, boxed, mid-19th c., the set **$2,468**

Cameo brooch & earrings, carved shell & 14k gold, the oval brooch carved w/three profiles of classical figures within a twisted gold mount, matching earrings w/a single cameo bust, late tops, second half 19th c., the set **$353**

Choker & brooch, onyx, seed pearl & 14k gold the choker composed of slightly curved rectangular onyx plaques each centered by a seed pearl, the matching round onyx brooch also centered by a pearl, good mounts, second half 19th c., choker 14 1/2" l., brooch 1 1/4" d., the set **$294**

Cross pendant & earrings, seed pearl & 14k gold, the wide flat gold cross pendant lined in the center w/bands of seed pearls, the small matching earrings each centered by a pearl, 19th c., the set **$1,410**

ANTIQUE (1800-1920)

Cuff links & shirt studs, mixed-metal 18k four-color gold, in the Japonesque taste, each piece designed as a flat rectangular plaque w/each decorated w/a raised design of a stork amid reeds, pair of cuff links & three shirt studs, Tiffany & Co., New York, ca. 1880s, the set (ILLUS. of part)............................ **$5,288**

Earrings & cuff buttons, pietra dura, the pendant-type earrings composed of two round graduated gold rings joined by S- scroll links & each enclosing a pietra dura scene of a flying bird, matching cuff buttons, mid-19th c., boxed, the set **$881**

Brooch & earrings, gold (14k) & amethyst, the brooch designed as a ringed knot set w/a spray of amethyst berries, applied wire-twist decoration, a glass compartment on the back, the earrings of similar design, Victorian, the set **$1,410**

Necklace, pendant, & earrings, turquoise & 18k yellow gold, the cross-form pendant w/rounded arms set w/teardrop-shaped turquoise-set teardrops & a central ring, the necklace composed of graduated circular turquoise & wirework florette links, matching teardrop-shaped earrings, 19th c., boxed, small losses, 19th c. **$4,700**

Brooch & earrings, pink coral, the brooch of squared shape boldly carved in the center w/the head of a classical lady framed by leafy roses & carved at each side w/another classical profile, suspending three carved coral teardrops, the longest central one carved w/a classical head, the matching earrings w/the small top carved as a classical head suspending a larger tapering carved plaque carved w/another classical head & suspending three carved coral teardrops, 14k yellow gold mounts, Victorian, the set **$2,350**

Brooch & Earrngs, pink coral & 18k yellow gold, each piece carved as a scallop shell centering a coral bead, w/original fitted box from Howard & Co., Victorian, the set **$2,115**

If you cannot attend an auction or bid online—and you trust the auctioneer— you may be allowed to leave an absentee bid. It will be bid in competitively. That is, even though you are willing to pay up to the limit of your bid, you may win the item at a lower amount.

Costume Jewelry (19th & 20th Century)

Costume Jewelry refers to jewelry made of inexpensive materials. It was originally designed to accessorize designer's clothing collections, and was meant to be discarded along with the clothing when it went out of style. Women saved this jewelry for its beauty, and today it is a very important collectible. It was inexpensive in its time, and was made in the most up-to-the-minute designs. Today collectors can pay more for certain costume jewelry than for some precious jewelry.

Bracelet, goldplate & glass, each link mounted w/a carved glass multicolored scarab, 1/2" w., 7" l. **$55-75**

Bracelet, goldplate & plastic, Art Deco Revival style, the plastic links w/geometric designs centered by a ball & alternating w/amber plastic circles, 1" w. **$55-75**

Bracelet, goldplate & rhinestone & faux pearl, composed of four metal disks w/a finely ribbed ground, each centered by a medieval design including a rampant lion, a Maltese cross, a crown & shield & a plumed crest, each accented w/ a different colored stone or faux pearl, joined by delicate looped links centered by a marquise-cut aqua rhinestone & accented w/faux pearls, signed "Coro," 1 1/8" w., 7" l. **$100-125**

Bracelet, goldplate & rhinestone, openwork links set w/red baguette rhinestone flowers w/clear pavé-set rhinestone centers, signed "Trifari," 5/8" w............. **$140-165**

Bracelet, goldplate chains & rhinestones, six chains attached to an oval center decorated w/ grey, clear & Aurora Borealis round & baguette rhinestones, signed "Hobé," 1" w....... **$85-110**

Bracelet, goldplate mesh & glass stones, the mesh band set w/ multicolored agate-style glass cabochon stones, signed "Sarah Coventry," 1" w., 6 1/2" l. **$55-75**

Bracelet, goldplate, bangle-type, child-sized, etched w/ initials, Victorian, 1/2" w. **$60-85**

Bracelet, goldplate, bangle-type, hinged, unadorned, signed "Bartek," 2 1/4" w. **$65-95**

Bracelet, goldplate, composed of interlocking "tank tread" links, w/safety chain, signed "Monet," 1 1/4" w............................ **$55-75**

Bracelet, goldplate, woven hair & crystal, the cross-form links w/a large cabochon crystal in the back, the front w/brown woven hair & a lock of reddish hair under glass, initials on the back, the front 1" w. **$135-165**

Bracelet, faux pearls & Lucite, composed of two strands of medium sized faux pearls on elastic, the top mounted w/large stylized clear Lucite flowers w/a faux pearl center, w/original paper hang tag reading "Adrée Creation by Coro" **$95-120**

Dress clip, white metal & rhinestone, Art Deco style, the long shield-shaped openwork mount w/a rounded tip, set overall w/pink rhinestones w/a large oval stone in the center surrounded by smaller round & square-cut stones, attributed to Miriam Haskell, 2 3/4" w., 2 3/4" h. **$225-250**

Bracelet, glass stone & silver plate, the wide flat handmade silver plate mount & findings set w/ten rows of square-cut red glass stones imitating rubies, unsigned, designed by Rose-Madeleine de Neuvielle for Yves Saint Laurent, France, ca. 1970, 7" l. **$657**

Dress clips, white metal, glass stone & rhinestone, Art Deco style, the long pointed shield-shaped mount centered by a large red oval glass cabochon above a pointed opening, the sides w/ geometric designs set w/clear round & baguette rhinestones, signed "TKF," an early Trifari mark, 1 1/2 w., 2 1/2" l., pr. **$275-300**

Earrings, glass stone & beads, pendant- type, the top w/a large oval clear faceted stone suspending five rows of tiny silver beads above larger faceted red Aurora Borealis beads, 3 3/4" l., pr. **$30-45**

Pin, enameled goldplate & rhinestone, designed as a pink & red enameled rose blossom pavé-set w/clear rhinestone accents, on a scrolling goldplate stem w/ green enameled leaves all further accented w/clear rhinestones, signed "Coro," 2 1/2 x 3 1/4" **$140-165**

Rhinestone is imitation diamond made from acrylic, glass, or rock crystal. Rhinestones derived their name from the rock crystals collected from the Rhine river in Germany.

Bracelet, plastic, amber wedge-shaped links alternating w/gold plastic spacers, on two rows of elastic, 1 5/8" w. **$30-45**

Bracelet, rhinestone & white metal, tennis- style, the flexible white metal band set w/rhinestones, 3/8" w., 6 3/4" l. **$30-45**

Bracelet, rhinestone, tennis-style, one row of flexible hand-set lavender rhinestones, 1/4" w. **$35-55**

Bracelet, sterling silver & carved glass, the silver links set w/ pink cabochon glass stones w/a carved white glass flower on each, the silver hallmarked, 1/4" w., 6 3/4" l. **$40-55**

Bracelet, sterling silver & glass, the hinged silver links mounted w/ large royal blue glass rectangles alternating w/royal blue glass carved face masks wearing ball earrings, Mexico, signed "JP - DFE," 1 1/4" w., 7" l..... **$175-200**

Bracelet, sterling silver, a silver chain suspending an enameled silver Pekinese dog charm, ca. 1935 .... **$50-70**

Bracelet, sterling silver, composed of "tank tread" style flexible links, made in Italy, 1/2" w., 7" l.... **$65-85**

Dress clip, red cinnabar & goldplate, a scalloped goldplate shield-shape centered by carved cinnabar w/flowers & a bird, China, 1 5/8" l. **$55-75**

Dress clip, white metal & rhinestone, the metal mount in a curved pointed ribbon design entirely pavé-set w/ clear rhinestones, signed "Creative," 1 3/8" h................................. **$30-45**

Dress clip, white metal, glass stone & rhinestone, Art Deco style, the openwork metal mount set w/pink opaque marquise-cut stones & small clear rhinestones, 2" h. **$55-75**

Dress clips, brass & glass bead, a brass shield decorated w/four rows of clustered pink glass beads in the center, 1 x 1 1/4", pr. **$55-75**

Dress clips, goldplate & glass stone, the goldplate mount in an inverted triangular shape, decorated w/ rows of deep blue, red & green cabochon stones, 1 1/2 x 2 1/4", pr. **$90-120**

Dress clips, goldplate, Retro style, designed as swirls around a central flower, 3/4 x 1 1/4", pr. **$45-65**

Dress clips, metal & rhinestone, the metal mount centered by a large oval red cabochon surrounded by clear marquise-cut rhinestones, 1 1/2", pr........................ **$85-115**

Dress clips, white metal, Art Deco style, triangular shape w/an embossed circle around three rows of swirls, 2" h., pr. **$50-70**

Earrings, enameled sterling silver, clip-on type, designed as a fan enameled in blue & green, Siam, 1 1/4" l., pr. **$45-65**

Earrings, glass bead, clip-on type, a round cluster of green Aurora Borealis beads, 1" d., pr. .. **$30-55**

Pendant watch, goldplate & rhinestone, a ball-shaped metal case decorated w/stars set w/tiny blue Aurora Borealis rhinestones, opens to a working watch, no chain............................ **$150-175**

Pendant-locket, goldplate & glass stone, decorated w/applied griffins & trimmed w/red, amber & blue cabochon glass stones, no chain, 1 1/2 x 1 3/4" **$25-40**

Pendant-scarf pin, white metal, designed as a snowflake centered by a coral-colored cabochon bead, 3" l. **$25-45**

Pendant, sterling silver & crystal, an 18" l. sterling chain suspending a 2" l. cut crystal drop, ca. 1930s **$55-80**

Pendant, sterling silver, the oval shape decorated w/a portrait of a 1920s woman wearing a locket, pendant 1 1/2" l., on a 16" l. chain............................... **$95-115**

Pendant, white metal & glass stone, the metal frame centered by a large stone that turns green, pink or blue depending on the mood of the wearer, ca. 1970s, on a 15" l. chain............................... **$25-40**

Pendant, white metal & rhinestone, designed as a leopard w/an articulated body in textured white metal, set overall w/clear rhinestone "spots," black rhinestone eyes, attributed to the estate of Eva Gabor, 7 1/2" l., on an 18" l. chain **$125-150**

Pin, Bakelite & goldplate, a very densely carved black Bakelite plaque w/raised flowers & leaves, set in a diamond- shaped metal frame, 2 3/8" l. **$170-195**

Pin, brass & glass stone, Art Nouveau style, the brass frame centered by a turquoise oval glass stone decorated w/two fleur- de-lis, 1 5/8 x 2 1/2" **$70-95**

Pin, crystal & goldplate, the oval openwork metal mount w/three-dimensional raised crystal flowers & leaf sprays, 2 1/4 x 3"..... **$175- 200**

Pin, enameled goldplate & rhinestone, designed as a bouquet of flowers enameled in pink, yellow, blue & beige, each flower w/a rhinestone center, 1 1/2 x 2" **$35-55**

Pin, enameled goldplate, crystal & rhinestone, designed as a flower spray, each flower w/a large oval red crystal center, green enameled leaves & clear crystals & rhinestone trim, unsigned designer quality, 2 3/4" w., 3 1/2" h. **$200-225**

Pin, enameled goldplate, model of a cat w/blue rhinestone eyes, set inside a circular frame w/yellow & green-enameled daisies & leaves, 1 1/2" d. **$30-45**

Pin, enameled metal, model of a "Stop" sign w/multicolored dangles including a white enameled turn sign, traffic lights & a yellow "Yield" sign, 1 1/4" w., 4" h. **$30-45**

Pin, goldplate & glass stone, transitional Art Nouveau-Art Deco style, the hexagonal mount decorated w/a large center red glass stone overlapped by goldplate leaves, unsigned Czechoslovakian, 1 1/4" w. **$55-75**

Pin, goldplate & rhinestone, an openwork crescent-shaped mount set w/large multi-colored marquise-cut rhinestones in red, green, clear, amber & blue, 2 1/2 x 2 1/2" **$55-75**

Pin, goldplate & rhinestone, designed as a flower basket w/multicolored rhinestone flowers, rare design, signed "Vogue," 2 x 2 3/4" **$300-500**

Pin, goldplate & rhinestone, designed as a flower set w/clear rhinestones w/a yellow center stone, yellow marquise-cut rhinestone buds on a long goldplate stem, signed "Staret," 2" w., 3 3/4" h. **$300-350**

Pin, goldplate & rhinestone, designed as an openwork flower arrangement in an antiqued finish goldplate vase, the flowers w/a large center purple crystal stone surrounded by red & purple marquise-cut & pearl-shaped rhinestones, clear rhinestone accents, signed "H. Pomerantz Inc. N.Y.," 2 1/4" w., 3" h. **$250-300**

Pin, goldplate & rhinestone, model of a bumble bee, the body set w/round red rhinestones, the wings & head set w/clear round rhinestones, signed "Ciner 1892," from a limited edition made for Ciner's 100th anniversary in 1992, w/original cloth pouch w/tag, 1 3/4" w., 1 1/4" h. **$150-175**

Pin, goldplate & rhinestone, the top designed as ornate openwork

Pin, enameled metal, figure of a sad boy clown standing & holding a white mask, wearing a dark yellow clown suit w/white polka dots, signed "Puccini," 1 x 2 1/2" **$95-120**

goldplate leaves centered by a large oval topaz rhinestone, suspending five ornate chains each supporting a large topaz stone, a heart or an ancient Egyptian design, signed "Lupe," 2 1/4" w., 5 3/4" l. **$200-225**

Pin, goldplate, glass stone & rhinestone, designed as a bouquet of nine flowers composed of large oval aquamarine stones, clear rhinestone trim on the flowers & long stems, 3" w., 5 1/8" h. **$370-395**

Pin, goldplate, glass stone & rhinestone, designed as a floral spray w/the flowers set w/beveled clear triangular glass stones, teardrop glass buds & small clear rhinestone flowers & trim, rare design, signed "Reinad," 2 3/4" w., 3 1/2" h. **$450-500**

Pin, goldplate, model of a cat reaching for a goldfish in a bowl, cat's tail moves, the fish hung w/a charm in the shape of an openwork bowl, 1 1/2 x 2 1/2" **$25-40**

Pin, goldplate, white metal & rhinestone, designed as a cluster of cherries on stems, the goldplated leaves set w/ clear rhinestones, the cherries

Pin, rhinestone & goldplate, the mount designed as a large rounded bouquet of flowers w/the multiple small blossoms edged in clear rhinestones around red, blue, green & amber marquise-cut & round rhinestones, a border of green marquise-cut rhinestone leaf clusters & green channel-set stone stems, signed "Staret," 2 3/4 x 3" **$300-350**

of textured white metal set w/ red rhinestones, unsigned but designer quality, 2 x 2".... **$65-90**

Pin, metal, crystal & glass stones, designed as an openwork star-shaped mount hand-set w/topaz-colored marquise-cut glass stones & centered by a large raised topaz-colored cabochon stone, signed "Fashion craft Robert," 3 1/2" d. **$175-200**

Pin, pewter, crystal & rhinestone, designed as a flower & leaf spray, the flowers set w/purple crystals & pink & turquoise rhinestones, pear-shaped crystal accents, signed "Kandell & Marcus, N.Y.," 2 1/2 x 4 1/4" **$175-200**

Pin, rhinestone & enameled white metal, the metal mount designed as flowers on a branch, the two flowers set w/oval emerald green rhinestones, the branch set w/ emerald green rhinestone buds & brown enameled stems, clear round rhinestone trim & on the ribbon at the base, unsigned Mazer, 3" w., 4" h. **$150-200**

Pin, rhinestone & goldplate, the openwork ribbon-form goldplate mount set w/purple, lavender, blue & clear large oval rhinestones & emerald- and square-cut clear rhinestones, signed "Staret," 3 3/4" w., 2 1/4" h. **$300-350**

MODERN (1920-1950s)

Modern (1920-1950s)

Art Deco

Jabot, rock crystal & 14k gold, designed as a gold arrow w/ engraved designs, the end set w/a rock crystal flat ring engraved & carved w/ flower & leaf designs, 2 7/8" l. **$784**

Jabot, platinum, jadeite & diamond, two oblong green jadeite tablets pierced & carved w/florals & leaves & attached at one end to a curved band set w/old mine- cut diamonds joined by a gold pin, millegrain accents .. **$940**

Earrings, platinum, diamond & emerald, pendant-style, a long open teardrop loop barrel-set w/ old European-, mine- and single-cut diamonds w/a small rectangular-cut emerald at the base of the loop above a suspended large European-cut diamond drop, millegrain accents, diamonds weighing about 3.52 cts., 1 7/8" l., pr. **$6,463**

Necklace, jadeite & 14k gold, composed of five oval carved & pierced green jadeite plaques, completed by abstract leaf-form links, makr of Wordley, Allsopp & Bliss, ca. 1930, 19 1/4" l. .. **$646**

Earrings, platinum, seed pearl & diamond, pendant-style, a round old European-cut diamond at top suspending a link of seed pearls ending in another diamond suspending a teardrop-shaped loop of pearls enclosing a small leaf swag w/millegrain accents & suspending another round European-cut diamond, boxed, pr. **$1,998**

Locket, jadeite, enamel & 14k gold, rectangular hinged black enamel case mounted w/a carved green jadeite plaque w/low- relief carving & framed by gold trimmed w/dark blue & green enamel, suspended from a paper clip-style chain, marks for Schanfein & Tamis & Carter, Howe & Co., overall 23" l. (ILLUS. of locket) **$2,233**

Pendant-necklace, platinum, pearl, diamond & emerald, the long oval flexible openwork pendant bead-set overall w/old European- and single-cut diamonds, centering a large white pearl framed by a circle of channel-set calibré-cut emeralds, suspended from a matching diamond link chain, diamonds weighing about 4.70 cts., millegrain accents, one emerald missing, overall 23 3/4" (ILLUS of part).............. **$24,675**

Pendant-necklace, diamond & platinum, the side chains composed of flexible links bead-set w/262 old European- and single-cut diamonds, suspending a long articulated tassel set w/160 old European-, five marquise- and three rose-cut diamonds, millegrain accents, diamonds weighing about 21.88 cts., later 14k gold pin stem, minor evidence of gold solder **$48,175**

Pendant, diamond & platinum, tassel-type, the long tapering trapezoidal openwork articulated mount bead- and bezel-set overall w/single-, rose- and old European-cut diamonds, suspending a fringe of seven marquise-cut diamonds, diamonds weighing about 6.85 cts., millegrain accents, suspended by a fancy link chain, missing seven small diamonds, overall 15 1/4" l. (ILLUS. of pendant) **$18,800**

Pendant, pate-de-verre glass, squared plaque molded w/a pine cone & needles in shades of dark purple & deep maroon, on a knotted purple silk cord w/tassel fringe, unsigned Argy Rousseau, France, ca. 1920s, overall 19 1/2" l. (ILLUS. of pendant) **$1,293**

Pendant, enameled & gem-set gold, Egyptian Revival style, centered by a turquoise cabochon scarab flanked by curved stylized winged vultures w/rose- cut diamond eyes, their bodies & the edges of the wings decorated w/champlevé & bass taille enamel in dark & light blue & brick red, suspended from a delicate trace link chain, evidence of prior findings, overall 15 1/4" l. **$1,998**

Pendant, emerald, diamond & platinum, designed w/curved bands above a lantern- style mount, the lantern designed centered by a triangular & trapezoidal step- cut emeralds framed & accented overall by old European-, marquise-, single-cut & briolette diamonds & diamond drops, diamonds weighing about 3.53 cts., millegrain accents, w/a trace link chain, evidence of solder, overall 15 1/4" l. (ILLUS. of pendant) **$17,625**

Ring, emerald & diamond, the rectangular top centered by a graduating bead-set line of five emerald-cut emeralds framed by a band of old mine- and single-cut diamonds, millegrain accents, scrolling openwork gallery & incised shank, size 8 ..... **$4,348**

Pin, diamond & platinum, circle-style, the simple ring bead-set w/19 full-cut diamonds weighing about 3.80 cts. **$3,290**

MODERN (1920-1950s)

Pin, pearl, garnet & 14k yellow gold, circle- style, the gold frame composed of scallop shell-form flutes each enclosing a single pearl, the outer rim set w/nine small garnets, ca. 1930, 1 3/4" d. **$460**

Ring, diamond & platinum, the long top centered by an old European-cut diamond weighing about 1.18 cts., flanked by two baguette diamonds & marquise-cut diamonds w/narrow borders of single-cut diamonds, other diamonds weighing about 2.22 cts., size 7 1/4 .... **$2,233**

Ring, diamond & platinum, the rectangular top box-set in the center w/a row of three old European-cut diamonds each weighing about .75 cts., framed by single-cut diamonds, pierced gallery, ca. 1940, size 9 .... **$4,700**

Ring, diamond & platinum, the rounded top centered by a large bezel-set old European-cut diamond weighing about .76 cts., flanked by small old mine- and European-cut diamonds, open gallery, other diamonds weighing about .86 cts., mark of Jung & Klitz, New York, New York, size 6 1/4 .... **$2,233**

Ring, diamond & platinum, the long navette- shaped top designed w/ a pointed group of diamond-set petals at each end flanking a large central full-cut diamond flanked by bands all set w/baguette & single-cut diamonds, diamonds weighing about .67 cts., w/ring guard, size 7 .... **$1,528**

Ring, diamond & platinum, the top centered by a large oval bezel-set rose-cut diamond weighing 2.75 cts., framed by a band of full-cut diamonds & diamond-set shoulders, engraved platinum mount, size 6 .... **$9,988**

Ring, diamond, ruby & platinum, the rounded curved top centered by a bead-set oval-cut ruby within an openwork mount bead-set w/16 old European-cut diamond mélée, diamonds weighing about 1.02 cts., millegrain accents, size 3 .... **$1,116**

Pin, diamond & 14k white gold, circle-style, bead- and bezel-set w/full-cut diamonds & square-cut green stones, mark of Theberath & Co., Newark, New Jersey **$176**

Ring, diamond & platinum, vertically set w/three old European- and mine-cut diamonds weighing about 1.40 cts., diamond mélée & French-cut blue stone accents, engraved mount, size 4... **$1,410**

Ring, ruby, diamond & platinum, centered by a large prong-set cushion-cut ruby flanked by old mine-cut diamonds, the raised scrolling mount w/full- and single-cut diamonds, engraved accents, diamonds weighing about .79 cts., size 6 1/2 .... **$705**

Ring, diamond, sapphire & platinum, the large almond-shaped top centered by a large cushion-cut blue sapphire weighing about 1.75 cts., flanked at each end w/ two large bead-set old European-cut diamonds, further decorated w/smaller diamonds & millegrain accents on the openwork mount, engraved shank, diamonds weighing about 2.60 cts., size 6 .... **$3,878**

Ring, emerald, diamond & platinum, the top bezel-set w/a large cabochon emerald flanked by small diamond baguettes, size 6 .... **$2,468**

Ring, emerald, diamond & platinum, twin- stone design, composed of two loops each ending in a top curl, one loop channel-set w/ emeralds ending in a loop prong-set w/a full-cut diamond, the other loop w/diamond mélée ending in a loop set w/ circular-cut emerald, by Oscar Heyman Company, Design No. 52270, ca. 1930s, size 6 .... **$4,818**

Ring, platinum, sapphire & diamond, the wide center band centered by a large full- cut diamond flanked by baguette & single-cut diamonds, each side w/two narrow bands, the first two channel-set w/small sapphires & the outer two further set w/small diamonds, diamonds weighing .87 cts., w/ ring guard, size 5 1/4 ..... **$3,173**

Ring, sapphire, diamond & 18k white gold, set w/a large fancy rose-cut Burmese blue sapphire weighing 5.61 cts., surrounded by a thin ring set w/micro-pavé full-cut diamonds, Villa, Milan, Italy, signed, size 5 1/4 .... **$10,575**

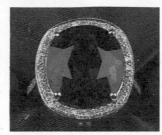

Ring, pink tourmaline, diamond & platinum, centered by a large prong-set cushion- shaped pink tourmaline weighing 15.76 cts., framed by a narrow ring & shoulders micropavé-set w/ full-cut diamonds, size 6 1/4 .... **$5,288**

Ring, platinum, diamond & colored diamond, the oblong top centered by a large bezel-set old European-cut diamond weighing about 2.04 cts., flanked by yellow marquise-cut diamonds & old European-cut diamonds, engraved shoulders, size 7 .... **$9,988**

Ring, sapphire, diamond & platinum, the domed top centered by a large prong-set cushion-shaped faceted blue sapphire, the open gallery & shoulders set w/18 old European-cut diamonds weighing about 1.10 cts., size 5 1/2 .... **$4,700**

Ring, sapphire, diamond & platinum, engraved shoulders, No. 52208, size 8 3/4 .... **$2,820**

Ring, platinum, coral & diamond, prong-set w/a piece-carved floral design oval coral plaque framed by diamond mélée & onyx half moons, open gallery, engraved shank, size 4 1/4 .... **$1,175**

Ring, ruby & diamond, the round top centered by a large prong-set cabochon ruby framed by two rows of single- and full-cut diamonds weighing about 1.88 cts., open scrolling gallery, silver & gold mount, India, ca. 1930, size 6 .... **$1,763**

Ring, sapphire, diamond & platinum, centered by a large sapphire cabochon framed by a band of baguette, triangular & single-cut diamonds, size 5 3/4 ..... **$3,290**

MODERN (1920-1950s)

Retro Style

Bracelet, bicolor 18k gold & diamond, buckle-style, the flat wide band composed of hexagonal links, centered by a tight fanned & scrolled ribbon cluster accented w/small diamonds, the arched buckle tip also set w/ diamonds, 7" l. **$1,116**

Bracelet, citrine, onyx & 14k gold, composed of squared bezel-set citrine cabochons joined by black onyx rings & ribbed gold links & long rectangular gold links, gold-filled jump ring closure, 7 1/2" l. **$1,140**

Bracelet, garnet, moonstone & 14k gold, composed of three spessartie garnet florets each centered by a bezel-set round moonstone & joined by double leaf-form gold links, mark of Wordley, Allsopp & Bliss, ca. 1940, 7 1/4" l. **$1,410**

Bracelet, gold (14k), composed of heavy tank track links, 8 1/2" l. .. **$2,115**

Bracelet, citrine, ruby & 14k rose gold, the top centered by a large rectangular step- cut citrine flanked by D-shaped brackets & scrolls set w/small bands of circular-cut rubies, completed by a double snake chain, 6 1/2" l. **$1,293**

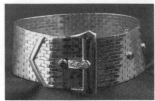

Bracelet, sapphire, diamond & 14k gold, buckle-style, the wide strap composed of brickwork links, the buckle set w/sapphire & full-cut diamonds, interior circumference adjusts to 6 1/4" **$1,401**

Brooch-pendant, citrine, diamond & 18k white gold, centering a large rectangular fancy-cut citrine framed by a scrolling mount bezel-set w/full-cut diamonds, diamonds weighing about 1.58 cts. **$1,058**

Ring, platinum, star sapphire, star ruby & diamond, the domed top set w/seven star sapphires & six star rubbies, , mark of Oscar Heyman, size 7 3/4 .... **$3,408**

Bracelet, gold (14k), composed of tank track-style links, 7 3/8" l. **$1,880**

Brooch, gold (14k), designed as an oblong pair of swirled rib leaves, American maker mark, signed by Cartier, No. 14848, 1 7/8" l. **$705**

Brooch, moonstone, sapphire & 14k gold, designed as a large gold bow centered by a large oval moonstone cabochon flanked at the top & bottom by a band of prong-set circular-cut blue sapphires **$999**

Brooch, rock crystal & gem-set 18k gold, designed as a floral spray w/the long gold leafy stems wrapped by a platinum & diamond ribbon & supporting a pair of rounded petaled rock crystal flowers centered by a blue sapphire surrounded by a ring of small cabochon rubies, two tall upper stems set w/cabochon sapphire berries **$705**

Brooch, sapphire & 18k gold, a rounded openwork shape set along one side w/four large bezel-set light blue cushion- and oval-cut sapphires, the other slde composed of two half-round arched bands set w/step-cut pink sapphires flanking a large oval pale blue sapphire, the center set w/a pair of small cushion-cut lavender sapphires flanking a square- cut pink sapphire & two bars set w/step- cut pink sapphires flanking a large cush-ion-cut light blue sapphire, French guarantee stamp, 2" l. ... **$4,406**

Clip, gem-set 14k gold, designed as a two- band ribbon formed into a teardrop design centered by a pear-shaped pink tourmaline cabochon framed by a ring of single-cut diamonds, three-band gold bracket at the top, signed by Cartier, tourmaline replaced **$600**

Dress clips, bicolor gold (14k), designed as a triangle composed of faceted gold links, each 1 7/8" l., pr. **$705**

Earrings, diamond & 18k gold, gold domed shape set w/scattered old European & full-cut diamonds in star designs, each 3/4" d., pr. **$940**

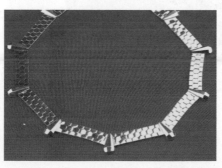

Necklace, gold (18k), composed of long flattened h o n e y c o m b links, interior circumference 14 1/2" **$2,938**

Twentieth Century Designer & Fine Estate Jewelry

Designer Pieces

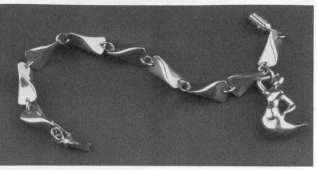

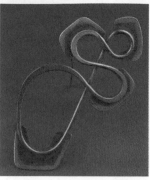

Bracelet, gold (18k), composed of abstract links suspending a mermaid charm, signed by Georg Jensen, boxed, No. 1104A, 7 3/4" l. **$2,115**

Brooch, copper & brass, designed as serpentine, looped brass wire bordered by copper elements, designed by Art Smith, signed, 2 1/4 x 4 1/2" **$1,998**

Ring, sterling silver & lapis lazuli, the oblong openwork scrolled leaf top bezel-set w/a large round center lapis cabochon framed by a ring of smaller lapis cabochons, signed by Georg Jensen, Denmark, size 6 1/4 .... **$588**

Before becoming a silversmith, Georg Jensen worked as a modeller at the Bing & Grondahl porcelain factory, but couldn't make enough money to support himself. After he opened his own silversmith shop, his earlier artistic training helped him become a world renowned designer.

Sets

Necklace & earrings, sterling silver, the necklace composed of stylized leaf links joined by double knop links, designed & signed by Georg Jensen, Denmark, necklace No. 96A, earrings No. 50B, earrings 5/8" l., necklace 16 1/2" l., the set **$1,410**

Bangle-type bracklet & earrings, diamond, emerald & 18k yellow gold, each piece in a stylized leaf form in gold, the hinged bracelet set w/six round full-cut diamonds & 18 round faceted emeralds; the clip-on earrings each w/two round full-cut diamonds & four round faceted emeralds, designed by Réné Borien, France, the set **$4,481**

Necklace & bracelet, gold (18k), "Connections" necklace & bracelet designed as interlocking circles, signed "Paloma Picasso & Tiffany & Co.," w/ original suede sleeve, necklace 16 1/2" l., bracelet 7 1/2" l., the set **$1,223**

Necklace & earrings, gold (18k yellow), the necklace composed of overlapping leaf-form rose petals, matching petal-shaped earrings, designed by Angela Cummings, Tiffany & Co., ca. 1979-80, necklace 15 1/2" l., the set **$6,463**

Miscellaneous Estate Pieces

Bracelet, gold (18k) & diamond, large S- form links joined by arched spacers bead-set w/full-cut diamonds, diamonds weighing about 4.35 cts., 7 1/2" l. **$1,645**

Bracelet, ruby, diamond & 18k white gold, the flat band closely set down the middle w/prong-set circular-cut rubies flanked by full-cut diamond bands & interspersed w/diamond flowers, 7 1/4" l. **$1,528**

Bracelet, tourmaline & 18k gold, designed as ring links alternating w/round disk links centered by alternating bezel-set pink & green cabochon tourmalines w/each suspending a flat heart-shaped pendant, 7 1/8" l. **$1,175**

Bracelet, turquoise, diamond & 14k gold, the flexible fancy ball-form links set w/scattered groups of cabochon turquoise & full-cut diamond mélée, 7 3/8" l. **$1,175**

Bracelet, gold (18k), composed of braided tiny bead chain, completed by a bar clasp, 7 3/4" l. (ILLUS. of part).................. **$999**

Bracelet, gold (22k) & sapphire, bangle- type, hinged open ring w/each end terminating w/an early Grecian bull head trimmed w/ornate wirework, the edges bezel-set w/round-cut sapphires, retailed by Zolotas, Greece, interior circumference 5 1/2" d. **$1,175**

Brooch, diamond & platinum, circle-style, a simple ring of prong-set full-cut diamonds weighing about 2.44 cts., 1 1/4" d. **$1,410**

Brooch, diamond & platinum, designed as a double-loop ribbon bow bead-set overall w/full-cut diamonds weighing about 2.17 cts., 1 1/2" l. **$999**

Brooch, diamond & 18k white gold, designed as a bow w/large loops above a flower head w/a leaf drop, prong-set overall w/full- and marquise-cut diamonds weighing about 4.65 cts. **$2,350**

TWENTIETH CENTURY DESIGNER & FINE ESTATE JEWELRY

Brooch, diamond, pearl & 14k yellow & white gold, model of a swan swimming in water, the water in white gold, the lower body of the swan in yellow gold, the high arched neck set w/round full-cut diamonds, the large outstretched wing formed by a freshwater pearl w/some blemishes, 2" l., 1 1/2" h. **$777**

Brooch, enameled 14k gold & diamond, a model of a frog w/a green enameled body, the bulging eyes pavé-set w/diamond mélée **$411**

Brooch, gemstone & 18k yellow gold, model of a ladybug, the six-legged mount in gold, the head & center body mounted w/a mélée of 48 round full-cut diamonds, the large wings decorated w/a mélée of 68 round faceted medium strong purplish pink sapphires & eight round faceted blue sapphires **$1,434**

Brooch, diamond, pink sapphire & 14k yellow & white gold, modeled as a flamingo- type standing bird, the feathers & body paved w/pink sapphires & diamonds on white gold, unmarked, 1" w., 1 3/4" h. **$863**

Brooch, gem-set & enameled silver-gilt, designed as a swimming duck w/a blue enameled head & seed pearl body, blue & red stone highlights, mark of the maker, 1 1/8" l. **$1,293**

Brooch, gold (18k yellow & white), ruby & emerald, figural, model of a curled fish w/long tail fins, set w/28 small full-cut emerald mélées & a ruby eye, marked "Italy 750" & an illegible maker's mark **$546**

Brooch, diamond, sapphire, emerald, black onyx & 18k white gold, in the shape of a stylized tadpole, the triangular head w/a black onyx snout inset w/small emerald eyes, the main body decorated w/a mélée of six light purplish red square-cut faceted sapphires, the border & tiny fins inset w/a mélée of 19 round full-cut small diamonds, the long tail inlaid w/a band of black onyx, 2" l. **$657**

Brooch, gem-set platinum & 18k gold, designed as a stylized flower w/three carved amethyst petals above smaller carved citrine petals, flanked by cabochon turquoise-set leaves all accented w/smaller leaves & buds set w/diamonds, 14k gold pin stem, 1 3/4 x 2" **$3,819**

Brooch, gold (18k), designed as two overlapping realistic birch-like leaves, mark of American maker, 1 x 2" **$411**

Before selling your jewelry, get two or three quotes from a jeweler who is a graduate gemologist. If any pieces are antique, take them to an antique dealer or appraiser who specializes in jewelry.

Brooch, green jadeite, diamond & 18k white gold, designed as a wickerwork basket w/an arched central handle trimmed w/a bow, filled w/small green jadeite fruits accented w/small diamonds, the basket completely bead-set w/ diamonds, 1 1/4" l. **$1,058**

Brooch, ruby, mabe pearl & 18k gold, designed as a stylized comical pirate w/the head formed by a mabe pearl, the clothing, peg-leg, arms & long sword in gold, the body set overall w/rubies & w/one ruby eye, the other eye a trillion-cut diamond patch, marked by maker, 1 3/4" h. **$1,763**

Earrings, gold (18k), clip-on type, each oblong piece composed of bands of small rounded shapes resembling a honeycomb design, signed "DM," 1 1/8" l., pr. **$529**

Brooch, platinum & sapphire, designed as a stylized floral spray w/a carved blue sapphire flower at the top center above a cluster of leafy stems tied by a ribbon & bezel-set overall w/small diamonds, each stem topped by a bezel-set circular-cut blue sapphire blossom **$1,058**

Earrings, diamond & 18k bicolor gold, clip- on type, designed as a X w/one side of smooth gold, the other pavé-set w/full-cut diamonds, 7/8" l., pr. **$999**

Earrings, diamond & 18k gold, clip-on type, wide comma shape w/a ground of tiny gold beads above a section pavé-set w/full-cut diamonds, diamonds weighing about 3.60 cts., pr. **$3,819**

Brooch, platinum, sapphire & diamond, openwork snowflake-like design, centered by diamond-form arrangement of large step-cut medium blue sapphires w/the outer border composed of alternating arches of small full-cut diamonds & sapphires, 1 7/8" w. **$7,638**

Brooch, ruby, diamond & gold, modeled as a long lizard w/its tongue out, the back bead-set down the center w/a line of graduating oval-cut rubies, the rest of the body set w/single-cut diamonds, clutching a cultured pearl in its mouth, silver- topped 18k gold mount **$1,880**

Earrings, diamond & 18k gold, clip-on type, square top pavé-set w/ sixteen princess- cut diamonds, diamonds weighing about 2.24 cts., pr. **$2,350**

Earrings, high-karat gold & seed pearl, pendant-type, each designed as a flower suspending a pavé drop flexibly-set within a seed pearl frame, India, 1 1/2" l., pr. **$499**

TWENTIETH CENTURY DESIGNER & FINE ESTATE JEWELRY

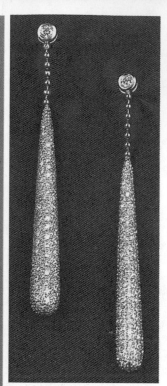

Earrings, diamond & 18k white gold, pendant-type, a small round top bezel-set w/a full-cut diamond above a tiny bead chain suspending a very long slender teardrop pavé-set w/full-cut diamonds, pr. **$1,293**

Earrings, emerald, diamond & 18k white gold, pendant-type, the top composed of a cluster of scrolling leaves set w/single- cut diamonds & suspending a straight line of diamonds above a squared drop w/a band of single-cut diamonds surrounding a square step-cut emerald, pr. **$999**

Earrings, gem-set 18k gold, clip-on type, two C-form gold bands prong-set w/circular-cut mélée including topaz, amethyst, garnet, aquamarine, periot & citrine, French import stamps, pr. **$441**

Earrings, emerald, sapphire & 18k gold, clip-on type, a domed round gold mount set overall w/a mixed arrangement of oval faceted & cabochon sapphires & emeralds, 3/4" d., pr. **$2,820**

Earrings, gold (18k) & amethyst, clip-on type, each formed as a tall serpentine gold leaf cluster trimmed w/circular-cut amethysts, pr. **$441**

Earrings, diamond & 18k white gold, clip-on type, each composed of five graduated & tapering bands each bead-set w/full-cut diamonds, diamonds weighing about 6.75 cts., 1 1/4" l., pr. **$4,700**

Earrings, sapphire, blue topaz & 18k white gold, clip-on type, modeled as a flower centered by a circular-cut sapphire framed by topaz, 3/4" d., pr................. **$764**

Earrings, jadeite, diamond & 18k gold, stud-type, composed of a cluster of green jadeite cabochons interspersed w/small full-cut diamonds, pr. **$705**

Earrings, diamond & platinum, dangle-style w/friction-style posts & backs, each centered by a cushion-cut diamond, both totaling 1.16 cts., framed by a mélée of 14 marquise-cut diamonds & 24 round full-cut diamonds, pr. **$5,975**

Earrings, lapis lazuli, diamond & 18k gold, pendant-type, a long ribbed lapis teardrop suspended from a diamond-set gold cap & a wide stepped gold top accented w/a pointed band of diamonds, pr. **$881**

Earrings, ruby & diamond, clip-on type, a long geometric design w/ruby cabochons boxed by diamond baguettes, 14k white gold mount, pr. **$1,645**

Earrings, ruby, diamond & 14k gold, clip-on type, rectangular top decorated at each end w/three bands of channel-set circular-cut rubies separated by a central cross set w/full-cut diamonds, pr. **$441**

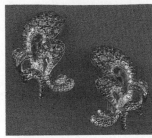

Earrings, ruby, sapphire, diamond & 18k white gold, clip-on type, each designed as a stylized butterfly viewed from the side w/the high arched & scrolling wing pavé-set w/rubies, diamonds & sapphires, 1 1/8" l., pr. **$1,293**

Earrings, sapphire, diamond & 18k white gold, pendant-type, the fanned gold top w/plain blades alternating w/blades bezel-set w/full-cut diamonds above a square-cut blue sapphire & loop supporting a diamond-set bar & a hexagonal gold mount centered by a fancy-cut sapphire, pr. **$1,645**

Earrings, South Sea Keshl pearl & gem-set 18k gold, stud-type, a large central silver pearl measuring about 8.90 mm. above a curved band of single-cut diamonds all framed w/scattered diamonds in a star design, 3/4" d., pr. **$1,175**

Earrings, South Sea pearl & 18k white gold, each composed of a single large pearl, pr. **$1,998**

Necklace, diamond, emerald & 14k yellow gold, 24 oval-cut emerald links each framed by 12 round diamonds & joined by 24 star cluster links each w/seven round diamonds, marked "14k BH," emerald total 10.26 cts., diamond total 10.6 cts., 15 3/4" l. **$6,900**

Necklace, gem-set multi-strand design, composed of strands of tumbled green tourmaline, green chalcedony, peridot & carnelian interspersed w/shaped 18k gold beads, 14k gold clasp, 16 1/2" l. **$940**

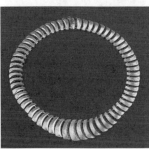

Necklace, gold (18k), fringe-type composed of flattened graduating curved bars, 16" l. **$2,468**

Pin, gold (18k) & reverse-painted crystal, the domed round crystal reverse-painted w/a large bumblebee, within a ribbed gold frame, 1" d...................... **$3,173**

Necklace, diamond & 14k yellow gold, composed of links w/ alternating square & round gold ropetwist frames each bezel-set w/a full-cut diamond, diamonds weighing about 4.00 cts., 17 1/2" l. $1,175

TWENTIETH CENTURY DESIGNER & FINE ESTATE JEWELRY

Necklace, pearl & diamond, two strands of 117 cultured pearls measuring 7 mm to 7.5 mm, in a light creamy rose color, a 14k white gold clasp mounted w/three round full-cut diamonds, strands 18" & 19" l. **$2,151**

Pendant, jadeite, the green stone carved & pierced in the form of gourds among leafy vines **$676**

Pin, turquoise & 18k gold, row of graduated penguins w/turquoise bodies, w/a red stone eye, 1 3/8" l. **$588**

Pendant-brooch,   diamond, emerald, ruby & 14k yellow gold, figural lion head in gold w/a curly mane, the eyebrows & snout set w/twelve diamond mélées, small emerald eyes & a ruby tongue, unmarked, pin missing on back **$374**

Pendant, peridot, diamond & 18k gold, designed as a large pointed oblong fruit set w/bands of peridot, the small textured gold buds issuing from the lower stem ringed w/full-cut diamonds **$529**

Pin, platinum & diamond, modeled as a long peacock feather w/an openwork eye, the stem bead-set w/full- and single-cut diamonds, mark of Krementz & Co., Newark, New Jersey, 2 1/4" l. **$764**

Necklace,   sapphire, diamond & 18k gold, composed of swelled & ribbed gold links centering a large three-band knot w/ each band centered by   cabochon sapphires bordered by bands of full-cut diamonds,   Italy, 18" l. **$4,994**

Pendant, diamond & white gold, model of a cross, set w/13 diamonds, w/a 16" l. chain marked "58514K T Italy," pendant 1/2 x 1" **$230**

Pin, amethyst, ruby & 18k gold, designed as a four-leaf clover w/each petal set w/a large heart-shaped amethyst centered by three marquise-cut rubies around a cultured pearl, curved gold stem, 1 7/8" l. **$940**

Pin, diamond & 14k gold, designed as an abstract sea gull trimmed by full-cut diamond mélée **$176**

Ring, amethyst & 18k gold, a pear-cut amethyst enclosed by a long scrolled gold oak leaf terminating in an acorn, size 6 .... **$235**

Ring, amethyst, diamond & platinum, the top centered by a large oval-cut amethyst framed by a ring of 20 small diamonds, size 5 . **$441**

Ring, aquamarine, diamond & 14k white gold, the top prong-set w/a large step-cut aquamarine framed by a band of small full-cut diamonds, size 7 1/2 .... **$881**

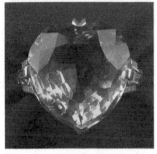

Ring, aquamarine, sapphire, diamond & platinum, the top prong-set w/a very large heart-shaped faceted aquamarine, flanked at the shoulders by tiny sapphire & diamond baguettes, size 7 .... **$3,055**

Ring, lady's fashion-type, ruby, diamond & 14k yellow gold, the top centered by a single oval faceted ruby weighing 1.67 cts., the wide tapering band set w/a mélée of 60 round full-cut diamonds w/a total weight of 1 ct., size 8 ..... **$1,554**

Ring, lady's fashion-type, sapphire, diamond & 18k gold, a four-prong to mount fitted w/a large 3/53 ct. emerald-cut blue sapphire, the tapering shank sides set w/ten straight-cut diamond baguettes, stamped mark "18K AP 430" **$2,300**

Ring, lady's fashion-type, sapphire, diamond & 18k yellow & white gold, the blossom-form top centered by a large oval blue sapphire weighing .75 cts. surrounded by petals set w/12 round-cut diamonds set in white gold, yellow gold band, marked "18k," size 7 .... **$460**

Ring, lady's fashion-type, white gold (18k) & tanzanite, three undulating tiers of mélée straight baguette diamonds alternating w/full-cut diamonds, all centered by a large 6.61 ct. oval faceted tanzanite **$2,032**

Ring, man's fashion-type, 14k yellow & diamond, figural, cast in the form of the head of a Germanic god wearing a swan-shaped crown centered by a single small diamond, 14k mark **$489**

Ring, man's fashion-type, 14k yellow gold, emerald, ruby & diamond, figural lion head w/ incised mane & facial details in gold, the eyebrows & snout set w/eight diamond mélées, emerald eyes & a ruby tongue, stamped 14k mark **$374**

Ring, man's fashion-type, emerald, diamond & 18k yellow gold, the top centered by one squared facet-cut emerald weighing 2.25 cts. surrounded by a mélée of 10 round full-cut small diamonds **$568**

TWENTIETH CENTURY DESIGNER & FINE ESTATE JEWELRY

Ring, man's fashion-type, emerald, diamond & platinum, mounted at the top w/one emerald-cut emerald weighing 1.99 cts. mounted at each corner w/a small round full-cut diamond **$418**

Ring, platinum, sapphire & diamond, the top centered by a large prong-set cushion- cut dark blue sapphire weighing 5.948 cts., flanked by shield-shaped diamonds weighing about .98 cts., size 4 1/4 .... **$10,575**

Ring, ruby, diamond & 14k gold, designed as an open rose centered by a circular- cut ruby, the petals accented by six full- cut diamonds, the shoulder w/leaf & scroll tendril designs, gold & platinum mount, size 8 ..... **$353**

Ring, platinum, rubellite & diamond, the top prong-set w/a long oval fancy-cut rubellite framed by a band of marquise- and full-cut diamonds weighing about 2.12 cts., one diamond missing, size 6 3/4 .... **$3,525**

Ring, rubellite, peridot & 18k gold, centering a circular-cut red tourmaline flanked by small bezel-set peridots in the gold mount, size 6 3/4 .... **$588**

Ring, South Sea pearl, diamond & platinum, prong-set w/a large South Sea pearl w/rose overtones measuring about 12.60 mm, flanked by bands of round-cut & baguette diamonds, size 7 3/4 .... **$764**

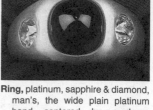

Ring, platinum, sapphire & diamond, man's, the wide plain platinum band centered by a large sugarloaf blue sapphire flanked by old European-cut diamonds weighing about .66 cts., size 8 .... **$6,463**

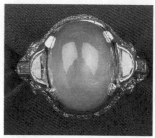

Ring, platinum, star sapphire & diamond, the top centered by a large oval star sapphire, the frame & shoulders bead- and bezel-set w/half moon, baguette & single-cut diamonds, size 6 .... **$3,055**

Ring, star sapphire, diamond & gold, man's, set w/a round sapphire weighing about 17.75 cts. flanked by tapering diamond baguettes, 14k white gold mount, size 6 .... **$881**

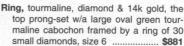

Ring, yellow sapphire, diamond & 14k gold, the oval top centered by a large cushion- cut yellow sapphire framed by a ring of full-cut diamonds weighing about 1.80 cts., abrasions on the sapphire, size 8 3/4 .... **$3,290**

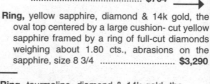

Ring, tourmaline, diamond & 14k gold, the top prong-set w/a large oval green tour- maline cabochon framed by a ring of 30 small diamonds, size 6 .... **$881**

KITCHENWARES

The Vintage Kitchen - 1850-1920

Crockery & Dishes

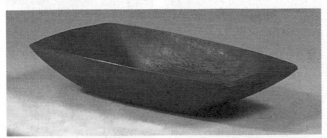

Bowl, carved black walnut, rectangular trencher style, gently curved base, carved end handholds, Shaker-made, Enfield, Connecticut, 19th c., age crack, 15 5/8 x 28 1/2", 6" h. **$441**

Bowl, carved burl, slightly oblong rounded form w/an integral rim handle w/finger ring hole, 19th c., 9 1/2" l. **$632**

Bowl, turned walnut burl, round w/a small flat bottom w/wide rounded sides & a thick molded rim, 19th c., 18 1/2" d. **$1,673**

Bowl, carved burl, wide well-rounded form w/tight small mottled grain, rich patina, 19th c., 14" d. **$1,207**

• Bid pooling is a scheme in which several bidders conspire to not compete against one another so items sell for less money. Items purchased by the pool are later distributed to the participants. To appear less conspicuous, participants sometimes bid in rotation. Bid pooling and other forms of bid rigging are criminal offenses.

• Conspirators involved in bid pooling will occasionally resort to interfering with competing bidders. One of the participants may position himself in front of competing bidder and attempt to engage in conversation to break his concentration. The way to counter this illegal practice is to notify the auctioneer immediately.

• If you and a friend are both interested in the same lot and you agree not to bid, you are not guilty of auction pooling. Only if money changes hands afterwards does an offense occur.

• Should friends who collect the same things go to shows and auctions together? It depends on how competitive they are. If both collectors want the same highly prized piece, their cooperation may end and turn into a confrontation.

Jar, cov., turned wood, squatty bulbous body w/incised rings tapering to a domed cover w/large button handle, varnish finish, attributed to Pease of Ohio, splits reinforced w/glue & a pegged hole in bottom, 19th c., 7" h. **$259**

Pitcher, blue & white pottery, embossed Cow patt., A.E. Hull Pottery Co., five sizes, rarest 5 3/4" h. to 9" h.............**$250-600**

Kitchen Utensils

Miscellaneous

Brazier, brass, two-part, a high domed cover ornately pierced w/delicate lattice swags, leaf bands & a lower Greek key band & topped by a tall turned finial, the stepped & widely flaring base w/a pierced Greek key apron & raised on tall flat legs w/paw feet, probably Europe, 19th c., 30" d., 32" h. **$1,495**

Bucket, cov., slightly tapering cylindrical form w/stave construction wrapped by three lapped bands, red-painted ground w/flat fitted black cover & black bands, red bentwood swing handle, painted in white on the side "C.R. Tartar," illegible lettering on handle, cover w/mark of "N. & J. Howe & Co. Fitzwilliam, N.Y.," 19th c., wear, bands loose, loss on handle peg, 13" d., 16" h. **$353**

Butter churn, lid & dasher, oak, stave construction w/five riveted steel bands, carved bottom, broom-handled dasher, 19th c., 19 1/2" h. **$288**

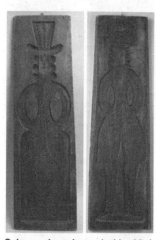

Cranberry scoop, wooden curved-bottom box w/a galvanized metal back & 22 long pointed wooden teeth, galvanized metal side straps, the flat top w/a rectangular wood frame enclosing a galvanized metal panel, low open top end brackets joined by front & back round grip bars, late 19th - early 20th c., 21" l., 10" h. **$200-250**

Cake board, double-sided, rectangular, one side carved w/a full-length figure of a man in 18th c. costume, the other side carved w/a matching figure of a woman, some worm holes, early, 10" w., 33" l. (ILLUS. of both sides) **$575**

Kettle stand, D-form cast brass top w/ornate pierced scroll & floral medallions around the skirt, raised on three wrought- iron cabriole legs ending in large penny feet, a decorative rosette missing on front, 19th c., 10 1/2 x 13", 13 1/2" h. **$460**

Teakettle, cov., brass, wide squatty bulbous body, 10" l. **$51**

The Modern Kitchen - 1920-1980

Crockery & Dishes

Egg Cups

Ceramic egg cups were a common breakfast table accessory beginning about the mid-19th century and were used for serving soft-boiled eggs. Ceramics egg "hoops" or "rings" were used for many years before the cup-form became common. Egg cups continue to be produced today, and modern novelty and souvenir types are especially collectible.

The descriptions and values listed here were provided by collector Dr. Joan M. George, who notes that values for older egg cups are based on their marks, rarity and recent sales results.

Bucket-style, color transfer-printed portrait of Princess Diana, commemorating her death, England, 1997 .... **$35**

→

Single w/attached saucer base, h.p. fruit decoration, Herend, Hungary, 1988 .... **$90**

Single, figural whistle-type, modeled as a small auto driven by a Teddy bear, Germany, ca. 1925 .... **$150**

Single, alphabet-type, printed w/"Q is for Quail," part of a line of dinnerware produced for children, Adderleys, England, 1939 .. **$55**

Single, boldly colored Imari patt. in dark blue, red & gold, Royal Crown Derby, England, ca. 1880s **$100**

Single, figural, brightly colored model of a peacock w/the cup on its back, Sarreguemines, France, ca. 1935 .... **$155**

Single, colorful floral decoration w/ h.p. gold trim, Limoges, France, 2002 .... **$55**

Single, brightly colored poppies on a cream ground, Aynsley, England, ca. 1930 .... **$45**

THE MODERN KITCHEN

Single, colorful floral design against a blue lattice background, bone china, Cauldon, England, ca. 1920s **$85**

Single, colorful floral wreath below various Italian names printed in black, unmarked, Italy, 1987 (ILLUS. of one)..................... **$20**

Single, decorated around the top w/pink floral swags below panels of raised blue dots, bone china, retailed by Ovington Bros., New York City, England, ca. 1900 .... **$65**

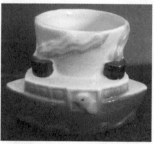

Single, figural whistle-type, modeled as a small orange ship w/a small chick passenger, Germany, ca. 1925 .... **$150**

Single, figural, modeled as the head of Stan Laurel of the Laurel & Hardy comedy team, Germany, ca. 1930 .... **$150**

Single, decorated w/flower blossoms & thin green leaf wreathes & swags, Limoges, France, ca. 1935 .... **$35**

Single, figural, head of Oliver Hardy of the Laurel & Hardy comedy team, Germany, ca. 1930... **$150**

Single, color transfer-print portrait of Queen Elizabeth II as a young girl, part of a set that includes Princess Margaret Rose, England, ca. 1937, each **$75**

Single, figural, model of a baby's head & shoulders, separate white insert for the egg, nicely detailed, unmarked, ca. 1925 .... **$100**

Single, figural, model of a boy's face w/fine detailing, unmarked, possibly France, ca. 1920 .... **$100**

Single, figural, modeled as a Flapper-style girl w/black curls, Goebel, Germany, ca. 1930 .... **$125**

Urn-shaped, h.p. floral decoration w/ gold trim, bone china, Copeland, England, ca. 1880 .... **$75**

Single, flaring cylindrical top w/molded rim, teal blue branch decoration, unmarked, Staffordshire, England, ca. 1885. .... **$75**

Single, Jasper Ware, applied white classical figures on six different colored backgrounds, Dancing Hours patt., Josiah Wedgwood, England, 1994 (ILLUS. of one) **$40**

Single, pink lustre base, cup printed in gold "A Present From Leigh," unmarked, England, ca. 1900 .... **$35**

Single, figural lady, part of a series individually named & clothed, modern, United States **$15**

Urn-shaped, color transfer of a bird perched on a flower, colored by hand, Copeland-Spode, England, ca. 1880 .... **$65**

Single, rare bisque example in peach w/a pink tinge, Locke, Worcester, England, 1886 .... **$80**

Kitchen Accessories

Napkin Dolls

Until the 1990s, napkin dolls were a rather obscure collectible, coveted by only a few savvy individuals who appreciated their charm and beauty. Today, however, these late 1940s and 1950s icons of postwar America are hot commodities.

Ranging from the individualistic pieces made in ceramics classes to jeweled Japanese models and the wide variety of wooden examples, these figures are no longer mistaken as planters or miniature dress forms. Of course, as their popularity has risen, so have prices, putting smiles on the faces of collectors who got in on the ground floor and stretching the pocketbooks of those looking to start their own collections.

Bobbie Zucker Bryson is co-author, with Deborah Gillham and Ellen Bercovici, of the pictorial price guide *Collectibles For The Kitchen, Bath & Beyond - Second Edition*, published by Krause Publications. It covers a broad range of collectibles including napkin dolls, stringholders, pie birds, figural egg timers, razor blade banks, whimsical whistle milk cups and laundry sprinkler bottles. Bryson can be contacted via e-mail at Napkindoll@aol.com.

Ceramic, figure of Uncle Sam, dressed in red, white & blue w/matching top hat, gold star buttons on vest, holding cloth American flag, Lillian Vernon Corporation, ca. 2003, 9" h. **$12**

Ceramic, figure of woman in hat, in dress w/yellow drop waist & purple skirt, yellow & purple hat w/upturned brim, marked "Cal. Cer. Mold," 12 1/2" h. **$65-85**

Ceramic, figure of woman w/black braids wearing light blue knee-length skirt & white top w/molded stays & blue cuffs, standing on leaf-covered base, one hand on hip, the other raised to head, 15" h. **$125-150**

Ceramic, figure of woman w/brown hair in a bun, wearing brown dress w/white collar & cuffs, holding green heart w/holes for toothpicks, 6 1/2" h. **$65-85**

Ceramic, figure of woman w/open mouth & yellow bobbed hair, wearing full-skirted gown in shades of green & matching headband, holding orange lily, handmade from Atlantic Mold, 11" h. **$65-75**

Ceramic, figure of woman w/ toothpick tray, brown hair, green lustre dress decorated w/pink roses, one arm holds a toothpick tray w/similar decoration on her head, pink bird perches on other arm, 10 1/2" h. **$75-95**

Ceramic, figure of woman w/black hair wearing lavender skirt & purple blouse w/gilt buttons & collar, purple hat, holding green unfurled umbrella behind back, slits in skirt for napkins, 10 3/4" h. **$90-110**

Ceramic, figure of woman w/long black hair wearing white dress w/gold neckline & cuffs & holding white & gold pitcher in both hands, applied lavender roses w/green leaves on one shoulder & on pitcher, glossy finish, handmade, 11" h. **$95-115**

Ceramic, figure of woman w/colonial-style hairdo, wearing period dress & holding large picture hat at side, all pink, marked "USA" on bottom, 12" h. **$50-60**

Ceramic, half doll, figure of milkmaid w/brown braids, wearing red dress w/white apron & polka dots, blue bow, blue & white cap, carrying buckets on yoke across her shoulders, on wire skirt-like base that holds napkins, marked "Davar Originals," 6" h. **$95-110**

Ceramic, half-doll, figure of woman w/black hair wearing green off-the-shoulder dress, on wooden stand w/wires to hold napkins, Goebel X97, ca. 1957, 8 1/4" h. **$225-250**

Wood, figure of woman w/jointed arms wearing dark pink dress w/ white flowers & bodice & black hat, marked "Artefatos Catarinenses Ltda., Ave. Argalo, 80-Sao Bento do Sul, Santa Catarina, N-94, Industria, Bruseleira," 6 3/8" h. **$60-75**

Reamers

Reamers are a European invention dating back to the 18th century. Devised to extract citrus juice as a remedy for scurvy, by the 1920s they became a must in every well-equipped American kitchen. Although one can still purchase inexpensive glass, wood, metal and plastic squeezers in today's kitchen and variety stores, it is the pre- 1950s models that are so highly sought after today. Whether it's a primitive wood example from the late 1800s or a whimsical figural piece from post-World War II Japan, the reamer is one of the hottest kitchen collectibles in today's marketplace - Bobbie Zucker Bryson

Ceramic, boat-shaped, yellow w/ black trim & white interior & cone, side w/image of anchor & word "Lemon" in black, 3" h. .. **$75-100**

Ceramic, figure of clown lying supine, the open mouth forming the spout, white w/yellow, red, blue & black trim, incised "6358," 4" d. **$135-175**

Ceramic, figure of Mexican man, teapot- shaped, two-piece, wearing bright orange jacket, yellow, orange, green & black serape & black pants, the yellow & orange cone forming his sombrero, one hand on hip forming handle, sitting next to green cactus that forms spout, 5 1/2" h. **$250-300**

Ceramic, model of green leaf holding the yellow cone, saucer-shaped, 4" d. **$30-35**

Ceramic, model of orange, two-piece, realistic w/green leaf spout & brown branch handle, white top & reamer cone, marked "Goebel," Germany, 4 1/2" h. **$65-75**

Ceramic, model of rose, pink flower on green leaves, stem forming handle, a rosebud forming the spout, marked "Erphila Germany," 1 3/4" h. **$200-250**

Ceramic, pitcher-shaped, two-piece, squat form w/lip & circular handle, white ground w/maroon & yellow flower design, gold trim, marked "Hand Painted Japan," 3 3/4" h. **$75-95**

Ceramic, saucer-shaped, one-piece w/lipped spout and shell-form handle, white ground w/pink & magenta flowers, green leaves & gold bead trim, marked "Hand Painted Japan" **$150-175**

Ceramic, saucer-shaped, one-piece, souvenir-type, w/spout & side handle, blue, rust & cream, w/painted image of Victorian woman w/parasol on one side of bowl & mass of flowers on the other, marked "Made in England, A Present From Dobercourt," 3 1/4" d. **$85-125**

Ceramic, saucer-shaped, light orange exterior w/dimpled finish, white interior & green loop end handle, marked "Czecho-slovakia," 3" h. **$40-50**

Ceramic, saucer-shaped, one-piece, white w/gold trim, w/figures of tree, swan, butterfly & flowerpot, marked "Made In France - Limoges France," 3 1/2" d. **$75-95**

Ceramic, saucer-shaped, two-piece, beige w/red, yellow, blue & tan trim, "Quimper Ivoire Corbell" patt., marked "Henriot Quimper France 1166," 2 3/4" h. **$200-250**

Ceramic, teapot-shaped, two-piece, decorated w/lavender & purple flowers on pink ground, marked "1990 LaVerne Hemmers," 5" h. **$20-30**

Ceramic, teapot-shaped, two-piece, off-white w/rose & blue floral band around the footed base, blue & rose pink trim on the reamer top, marked "Made in Japan," 5 3/4" h. **$55-65**

Ceramic, teapot-shaped, two-piece, white w/a blue sailboat scene around the base w/blue trim, marked "Germany" on the base, 3 1/4" h. **$60-75**

Ceramic, two-piece, wide tapering cylindrical base w/angled handles, off-white ground molded in relief w/three small yellow chicks jumping rope, blue & red thin border bands, marked "Japan," 4" h. **$55-65**

Ceramic, saucer-shaped, two-piece, beige w/red, yellow, blue & tan trim, "Quimper Ivoire Corbell" patt., marked "Henriot Quimper France 1166," 2 3/4" h. **$200-250**

Ceramic, boat-shaped, white w/gilt line trim, decorated w/rust-colored leaves & navy blue, small loop handle, 3 1/2" h. **$45-65**

Ceramic, two-piece, cylindrical body decorated w/multicolored flowers & gold trim on pale blue ground, spout & cone also pale blue & white w/gold trim, marked "Frances - Limoges," 3 1/2" h. **$160-185**

Ceramic, model of a swan, two-piece, off-white w/pink rose designs & green trim, 4 1/4" h. **$75-85**

Silver plate, two-piece, simple round shape base w/leaf-form tab handle, marked "Apollo EPNS, Made By Bernard Rice's Sons, Inc., 5230," 2 3/4" h. .. **$125-150**

Sterling silver, saucer-shaped, open tab handle, marked "Black Starr - Gorham Sterling 909," 4 1/4" d. **$225-275**

THE MODERN KITCHEN

String Holders

String holders were standard equipment for general stores, bakeries and homes before the use of paper bags, tape and staples became prevalent. Decorative string holders, mostly chalkware, first became popular during the late 1930s and 1940s. They were mass-produced and sold in five-and-dime stores like Woolworth's and Kresge's. Ceramic string holders became available in the late 1940s through the 1950s. It is much more difficult to find a chalkware string holder in excellent condition, while the sturdier ceramics maintain a higher quality over time.

Apple with worm, chalkware, "Willie the Worm," ca. 1948, Miller Studio **$45**

Cat, ceramic, white, full-figured on top of ball of string **$45**

Kitten wi/ball of yarn, ceramic, handmade **$40**

Mouse, ceramic, sitting, Josef Original **$85**

Bird, ceramic, in birdhouse, "String Swallow" **$45**

Cherries, chalkware, bunch on leafy stem **$125**

Dog, ceramic, Scottie, marked "Royal Trico, Japan" **$55**

Cabbage, ceramic, Japan **$95**

Cat, ceramic, head w/scissors held in plaid neck ribbon, Holt Howard **$30-50**

Dog, chalkware, Westie, bow at neck **$85**

Monkey, chakware, on ball of string **$300**

Father Christmas, ceramic, Japan **$95**

French chef, chalkware, w/scarf around neck **$85**

Indian w/headdress, chalkware, brightly colored **$150**

Lovebirds, ceramic, Morton Pottery **$35**

Mexican man, chalkware, head only, flower-trimmed hat **$60**

Snail, ceramic, dark brown **$20**

Tomato, ceramic **$35**

Elephant, ceramic, white w/gold tusks, pincushion on head, Japan **$35**
Clown, chalkware, "Jo-Jo," ca. 1948, Miller Studio **$125**

Woman, ceramic, full-figured, blue dress w/white & red flowers, Japan **$50**

Grapes, chalkware, bunch **$50**

THE MODERN KITCHEN

Tea Serving Accessories

People around the world have been drinking tea for centuries, and the brewing of the perfect cup has long been considered an art form. Tea balls, or infusers as they're sometimes called, were used to hold loose tea and hung into the pot or cup to properly steep. Most of the pieces came with a bottom or tray to catch the residual drips of water and tea. When tea bags came into common use and the potential of tea stains persisted, the decorative tea strainer was put into service as an acceptable receptacle even at the most elegant tables.

Ceramic, two-part tea strainer, white w/large deep rose red & pink h.p. roses & green leaves w/heavy bands of gold trim, 5" l., 1 1/2" h. **$40-55**

Ceramic, two-part tea strainer, white w/small dark blue flowers & blue border, 5" l., 1 1/2" h. **$25-30**

Ceramic, two-piece tea strainer, celadon green glaze, marked "Made in Japan," 6" l., 1 1/2" h. **$40-50**

Ceramic, two-piece tea strainer, the squared top w/pointed corners & a rectangular tab handle resting on a conforming flaring base, dark blue trim, small h.p. red blossoms & green leaves on the top, marked "Decora Ceramics Handpainted California," 4" l., 1 1/2" h. **$15-20**

Ceramic, two-piece tea strainer, the top molded as a pansy blossom in purple, yellow & pink w/a green leaf handle, white base, marked "Made in Japan," 4" l., 1 1/4" h. **$15-20**

Ceramic, two-piece tea strainer, white w/cobalt blue scalloped border trim & h.p. small blue flowers & green leaves, marked "Made in Japan," 6 1/8" l., 2" h. **$40-55**

Ceramic, two-piece tea strainer, white w/h.p. purple & pink flowers & green leaves w/gold trim, marked "Made in Japan," 5 7/8" l., 1 1/2" h. **$35-45**

Ceramic, two-piece tea strainer, white w/printed dark pink roses & green leaves, gold trim, marked "T-103," 3 5/8" l., 1 1/4" h. **$15-20**

Porcelain, two-piece tea strainer, deep yellow & dark brown h.p. decoration of red trees & gold trim, marked "Hand Painted Nippon," early 20th c., 4 7/8" l., 1 1/4" h. **$25-35**

Porcelain, two-piece tea strainer, Geisha Girl porcelain decorated w/a central landscape w/Geishas, trimmed w/panels of dark red w/ green, pink & blue highlights & ornate gold trim, ca. 1920s, 6" l., 1 1/2" h. **$95-125**

Porcelain, two-piece tea strainer, pale green, pink & yellow ground w/ornate overlaid gold flowers & beading, marked "Nippon Hand Painted," 6" l., 1 5/8" h. **$95-125**

LIGHTING DEVICES

Early Non-Electric Lamps & Lighting

Miniature Lamps

Our listings are generally arranged numerically according to the numbers assigned to the various miniature lamps pictured in the following reference books: Frank R. & Ruth E. Smith's book *Miniature Lamps*, now referred to as Smith's Book I (Smith I), and Ruth Smith's sequel, *Miniature Lamps II* (Smith II), and Marjorie Hulsebus' books, *Miniature Victorian Lamps* (Hulsebus I or H-II) and *Miniature Lamps of the Victorian Era* (Hulsebus II or H-II).

Clear, finger lamp embossed "Little Pearl" on font, Hornet sized burner, 2 7/8" h., Hulsebus I, Fig. 19 .... **$125-150**

Milk glass, finger-type, waisted cylindrical font w/h.p. florals around the font & pink on the top, Nutmeg burner, 3" h., Smith I, Fig. 39 .... **$100-115**

Blue, stem lamp w/optic ribs in font, Hornet sized burner, 6" h., Hulsebus I, Fig. 64 .... **$175-200**

Blue, finger-type, dark waisted font embossed "Little Buttercup," blue applied handle, Acorn burner, 2 3/4" h., Smith I, Fig. 36 .... **$115-125**

Amber, finger-type, cylindrical ribbed font w/attached basket w/ ring handle for holding matches, matching ribbed shade, Nutmeg burner, Atterbury & Co., ca. 1870s, 3 3/4" h., Smith I, Fig. 53 .... **$700- 750**

Milk glass, footed spherical font, base & chimney shade decorated w/a rust-colored vine design, called "Will-O'-the- Wisp" in early ad, Nutmeg burner, 7 7/8" h., Hulsebus II, Fig. 89 ... **$200-225**

Blue opaque, bulbous base & shade, both w/embossed flower & leaf decoration over a lattice field, clear chimney, Nutmeg burner, small flake on edge of shade, 7 1/2" h., No. 229 ... **$259**

Milk glass, footed bulbous font & ball shade painted light blue & decorated w/the color logo & inscription for the "Pan-American Exposition - 1901 - Buffalo, N.Y.," Nutmeg burner, 9" h., Smith I, Fig. 309 .... **$450-500**

Milk glass, squatty bulbous font & ball shade embossed w/scrolls & flowers & painted w/blue Dutch scenes, marked under base "Amsterdam," made by Pairpoint Mfg. Co., E.M. Boudoir burner, Junior size 11 3/4" h., Smith I, Fig. 331 .... **$500-550**

Blue cased satin, melon-lobed base & molded pansy design ball shade, Nutmeg-type burner, 7" h., Smith I, Fig. 389 ... **$1,150**

Milk glass satin, double-gourd ribbed base & ribbed domed shade, h.p. w/colored flowers, Nutmeg burner, clear glass chimney, 7 3/4" h., Smith I, Fig. 393 .... **$300-350**

Cased yellow, spherical body & domed shade in molded Pine Cone patt., glossy finish, made by Consolidated Lamp & Glass Co., clear glass chimney, 8" h., Smith I, Fig. 394 .... **$400-450**

Milk glass, brass foot supporting the squatty bulbous melon-ribbed font painted pink, w/colored flowers, matching ribbed ball shade & clear glass chimney, Nutmeg burner, 10" h., Smith I, Fig. 303 ....**$400-500**

Milk glass, footed bulbous font & ball shade painted light blue & decorated w/the color logo & inscription for the "Pan-American Exposition - 1901 - Buffalo, N.Y.," Nutmeg burner, 9" h., Smith I, Fig. 309 ....**$450-500**

Milk glass, a low disk-form round font tapering to the burner, ball shade, each painted deep maroon w/large shaded green leaves, Nutmeg burner, 7 1/2" h., Smith I, Fig. 312 ....**$325-350**

Lamps, Miscellaneous

Cranberry, optic ribbed cylindrical & ringed base & conical shade, early ad called it "Little Beauty," 8 1/4" h., Smith I, Fig. 439 .... **$375-400**

Amber, stem-type, Hobnail patt. font & flaring shade, Nutmeg-type burner, 7" h., Smith I, Fig. 477 .... **$425-475**

The "Gone with the Wind Lamp" is commonly associated with the Civil War era because of the 1930s movie *Gone with the Wind*. However, the lamp is actually a late Victorian design and was not in existence during the Civil War.

Argand lamp, gilt-brass, the round domed base cast w/leaves supporting the cut crystal baluster-form standard topped by a rolled crystal crown suspending long facet-cut prisms & centered by an upper gilt-brass post w/ two straight arms each ending in a metal font & burner fitted w/tall tulip-shaped shades, the upper shaft topped by another cut crystal section supporting a gilt-brass band suspending additional prisms, Johnston Brooke & Company, first quarter 19th c., electrified, 16" w., 22" h. **$3,910**

Gone-with-the-Wind table lamp, kerosene-type, the ball globe & matching squatty glass base molded in bold relief w/lion head masks alternating w/lobed panels, dark brown w/each smooth panel printed w/a desert oasis scene against a shaded yellow ground, cast-brass scrolling arched base, brass font shoulder & burner, late 19th c., non-electric, 14" h. **$575**

Cut-overlay banquet lamp, white cut to clear cut to blue alabaster, a stepped marble base trimmed w/brass supporting a tall waisted cylindrical standard cut w/ovals fitted w/a ringed brass connector to the inverted bell-shaped font cut w/bands of ovals, brass collar, attributed to Boston & Sandwich Glass Co., ca. 1870, very minor shedding to blue layer, upper most brass stem mount had leaves removed, 17" h. ... **$6,600**

Gone-with-the-Wind table lamp, kerosene-type, a leafy-scroll cast-brass base supporting the squatty bulbous milk glass font decorated w/large red mums & green leaves on a shaded deep blue ground, a matching ball shade on top, electrified, ca. 1900, 15" h. **$150-200**

EARLY NON-ELECTRIC

Hall lamp, gas-type, leaded glass & brass, a tall square form w/ each side composed of clear leaded segments centered by an amber & red cross design, metal corner finials & four arched top bars & drop center burner joined to hanging cap, ca. 1890s, electrified, 9" w., 24" h. **$633**

Hall lamp, kerosene-type, a high domical mold-blown optic swirled rib cranberry shade w/a domed base cap w/ring finial & a small brass top collar hung from chains, ca. 1900, overall 12" h. **$250- 350**

Sinumbra table lamp, gilt-lacquered bronze, the cut-and-etched clear tulip- form shade resting on a circular shade ring above a tall reeded vasiform standard w/a pair of foliate-cast handles, on a columnar stand joined to a square plinth base, mid-19th c., America or England, electrified, overall 33" h. **$2,185**

Banquet lamp, kerosene-type, a cylindrical decorated Longwy Pottery central body in blue decorated exotic birds & foliage in red, yellow, black, white & green, fitted w/a pierced cylindrical upper body & raised on a cylindrical bronze footed base w/a cut-out design of stylized leaves & flowers, fitted w/a brass burner & clear frosted ball shade acid-etched w/bands of urns, bands & scrolls, marked "H.G. Moehring," ca. 1880s, overall 23 1/2" h. **$748**

Banquet lamp, kerosene-type, an onion- shaped porcelain font decorated w/a painted blue Dutch windmill scene, raised on a tall swelled cylindrical matching pedestal on a fancy pierced brass foot, the stamped brass shoulder supporting a brass burner & ring for the matching decorated ball shade, clear chimney, Pairpoint-Limoges, ca. 1890, overall 35" h. **$633**

Alladin table lamp, Vertique patt., font & base in yellow moonstone, 13" h. **$441**

Electric Lamps & Lighting

Handel Lamps

The Handel Company of Meriden, Connecticut (1885-1936) began as a glass and lamp shade decorating company. It became a major producer of decorative electric lamps which have become very collectible today.

Boudoir lamp, 9 1/2" d. tapering pyramidial frosted glass shade fitted w/a metal cap, the shade exterior covered in a gold- wash & etched w/a delicated overall scrolling design, raised on a slender ribbed gilt-metal standard & round foot cast w/a design of triangles, shade signed "Handel 7271," some wear on gold wash, roughness to shade fitter, overall 13 1/2" h. **$345**

Table lamp, 16" d. domical leaded glass shade w/large caramel slag honeycomb bands above a wide floral border in shades of pink, white & mottled green, on a bronzed-metal slender lobed base w/embossed Handel mark, ca. 1910, overall 21" h. **$1,725**

Table lamp, 18" d. domical reverse-painted shade decorated around the border w/large clusters of deep red & pinks blossoms & green leaves, a background of low hills in deep purple & greenish yellow & w/tall slender trees in the foreground w/stippled green & yellow leaves, signed "7106 Handel R," raised on a bulbous tapering ovoid bronze base cast w/Art Nouveau looping & ending in four thick square feet, base w/worn Handel signature, one chip to shade rim, overall 27" h. **$4,888**

Table lamp, 18" d. domical reverse-painted shade decorated in the Jungle Bird patt., two large brightly colored macaws perched among tropical foliage, reverse w/a single macaw in flight, shade signed "Handel 6874," raised on a bronze Chinese-style base w/ a paneled ovoid body on a disk foot raised on openwork scrolls, 23" h. **$25,300**

Table lamp, 18 1/2" w. squared tapering open topped shade w/ each panel etched & enameled w/a Medieval knight & coat- of-arms, raised on a bronzed metal three- light candelabra-style base w/faceted glass stem & saucer base on paw feet, shade signed "Handel 7463," small heat fracture in one shade panel, ca. 1920, overall 26" h. **$1,495**

Table lamp, 19 1/2" w. octagonal leaded glass shade w/panels composed of amber slag glass w/a leaded applique of cattails on a bronzed base, shade & base both signed, overall 25" h. **$3,105**

Boudoir lamp, 7" d. domical shade w/zigzag rim, reverse-painted in the Jungle Bird patt., a pair of large red & blue macaws perched together on branches w/green tropical foliage in the background on a mottled green, yellow & red ground, on a bronzed metal base w/a slender ribbed stem on a disk foot w/a gadrooned edge, shade signed "Handel," overall 14" h. **$7,475**

Boudoir lamp, 7" w. hexagonal domed shade, reverse-painted w/a large blue parrot perched on a leafy branch w/pink flowers, shaded bright yellow to clear background, shade signed "Handel," on a bronzed metal base w/a slender paneled stem & a flaring hexagonal base, overall 14" h. **$4,312**

Table lamp, 24" w. domical octagonal bent- panel shade, mottled orange & red slag panels overlaid w/metal filigree pine trees above a narrow yellow slag border panel overlaid w/pine needles, overall 30" h. ... **$9,775**

Table lamp, 18" d. domical glass shade, reverse-painted in the Exotic Birds patt., the fancy birds in red, yellow & dark blue flying among dark blue leaves & clusters of large round, green & yellow blossoms, signed "Handel 7125 Palme," raised on a bronzed metal base w/a shallow urn supported on three slender legs & a center post above the round foot w/a lappet border band, three orange glass teardrops hanging from the top of the base w/a matching finial above the shade, overall 26 1/2" h. **$25,875**

Table lamp, 18" d. domical glass shade, reverse-painted w/a continuos landscape w/stately trees & shrubs along a waterway, in autumnal shades of orange, brown, green, yellow & blue, signed "Handel 7111," on a simple slender bronzed metal base signed "Handel," overall 23 1/2" h. **$5,462**

Table lamp, 18" d. domical glass shade, reverse-painted w/a continuous landscape of tall trees, meadows & hills under a dark stormy sky in shades of brown, chipped ice exterior, shade signed "Handel 6432 - HB," on a bronzed metal ovoid base w/four open loops at the top & cross-form feet, base rewired & probably repatinated, overall 23 1/2" h. **$6,038**

Table lamp, 18 1/2" d. octagonal bent caramel slag shade w/wide shaped border panels in green slag overlaid w/a pierced oak leaf design, raised on a simple ribbed bronzed metal base w/an octagonal foot, panel strips re-soldered at the crown, rewired, overall 23" h. **$2,588**

Table lamps, 18" w. domical octagonal bent-panel shade, ribbed white glass panels overlaid w/delicate rose vine filigree trimmed in yellow & green, simple bronzed metal base w/ lobed foot, shade signed "Handel 924457," base signed "Handel," overall 23" h., pr. (ILLUS. of one) **$10,350**

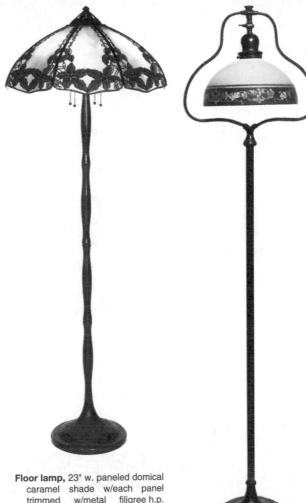

Table lamp, 18" d. domical reverse-painted shade decorated w/a tropical landscape w/plam trees flanking a lake w/the setting sun in the background, raised on a bronze tapering ovoid basketweave designed base w/ four projecting block feet, shade signed "Handel 6322" & diamond logo, base unsigned & w/copper patina worn off the main body, 25 1/2" h. **$6,900**

Floor lamp, 23" w. paneled domical caramel shade w/each panel trimmed w/metal filigree h.p. w/stylized green leaves, the tall slender bamboo-shaped standard & round foot w/a re-patinated bronzed finish, 64" h. **$7,800**

Floor lamp, 24" d. domical octagonal paneled yellow glass shade, each panel ornately decorated w/leafy bamboo stems, raised on a tall sender bamboo-shaped standard on a round leaf-molded foot, overall 61" h. **$7,475**

Floor lamp, the 10" d. reverse-painted domed shade in yellow w/a black border band painted w/ pink & yellow flowers, suspended from a bronzed metal harp raised on a tall, slender standard on a round foot, shade signed & numbered, cloth tag on the base, 57" h. **$2,640**

Reverse painting is painting applied to the back side of glass, with the finished work intended to be viewed from the front. This form of painting is challenging, as it not only requires the artist to produce a mirror image of the work (the view from the front will be reverse of how it is painted on the back), the artist must also apply the layers of paint in reverse order. In a standard painting, the background is laid down first, then the foreground on top of it. With reverse painting, however, the foreground layers must be painted first, followed by the background layers. Once the foreground has been covered by the background, the foreground can't be altered without removing both layers.

ELECTRIC LAMPS & LIGHTING

Pairpoint Lamps

Well known as a producer of fine Victorian art glass and silver plate wares between 1907 and 1929, the Pairpoint Corporation of New Bedford, Massachusetts, also produced a wide range of fine quality decorative lamps.

Boudoir lamp, 8" w. domical paneled "Portsmouth" patt. shade reverse-painted w/large red roses & green leafy stems against a ground of vertical tinted stripes alternating white & pale yellow, the exterior w/black outlining the designs, marked shade, on a slender gilt-metal baluster- form base on a stepped paneled foot also marked, needs rewiring, overall 14 1/2" h. **$748**

Boudoir lamp, 8" w. squared domical reverse-painted "Portsmouth" shade decorated w/purple flowers & green leaves outlined in black, raised on a squared baluster-form bronze base impressed w/red leaves, both shade & base signed, some wear to base, 16" h. **$3,163**

Radio lamp, composed of a large upright flat glass panel w/cut-corners reverse- painted w/bold & colorful stylized Art Deco florals in shades of blue, green, yellow, brown, red & orange, fitted onto a brass-plated metal ribbed base, base signed "Pairpoint E3035" w/diamond logo, overall 10 1/2" h. .. **$1,610**

Boudoir lamp, 6 1/2" d. "Puffy" shade in the Rose patt., large molded rose blossoms against a dark blue, green & brown ground, on a silvered cast metal tree trunk base, base signed w/Pairpoint logo & "B3079," overall 6 1/2" h. **$4,025**

Table lamp, 12" d. "Puffy" shade in the Grape patt., reverse-painted, raised on a cast-metal base w/molded grapes & leaves up the standard & around the foot, shade signed "Pat. Applied For," base signed w/Pairpoint logo & "B3010," overall 19" h. **$14,560**

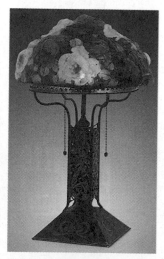

Table lamp, 12 3/4" d. "Puffy" shade in the Rose Bouquet patt., the large molded rose blossoms reverse-painted on a square base signed "Pairpoint 3054," overall 21" h. **$17,825**

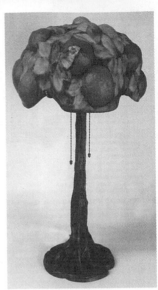

Table lamp, 13" d. domical closed-top reverse-painted "Florence" shade decorated w/turquoise blue striped background & red & yellow stylized floral designs, obverse of shade highlighted w/gold trimmings, on a silvered metal rectangular tapering standard on a rectangular foot w/pierced designs on four sides, base signed, small spot on rim of shade possibly ground, some wear to base finish, 19 1/2" h. **$3,163**

Table lamp, 13" d., domical "Puffy" reverse- painted "Poppy" shade, large molded shaded pink poppy blossoms among light & dark green leaves, raised on a three-arm ring atop a bronze base w/ the slender cylindrical standard cast w/flower & leaf clusters above the squatty disk foot w/four scroll feet, shade w/Pairpoint signature, base marked "Pairpoint 3093," 20" h. **$17,250**

Table lamp, 14" d. domical "Puffy" reverse- painted Orange Tree shade, raised on an unsigned tree trunk base, shade signed, overall 24" h. **$51,750**

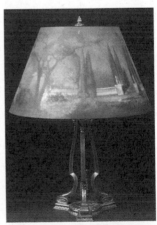

Table lamp, 14" d. domical "Puffy" shade in the "Stratford" shape w/a border of large roses & hummingbird against a lattice background in cream & pale blue, on a signed paneled trumpet-form bronze- metal base w/round gadrooned foot, No. D30441, 23" h. **$4,830**

Table lamp, 15 1/2" d. "Puffy" closed-top "Papillon" patt. shade, large red, yellow & black butterflies on red, yellow & pink roses & green leaves, on a signed tall slender bronzed-metal urn-form base w/three scroll legs resting on a tri-corner foot, No. B3011, 21 1/2" h. **$13,225**

Table lamp, 16" d. tapering conical reverse- painted "Seville" shade, decorated w/a continuous Italian garden scene in shades of orange, yellow, green, red & blue, raised on a gilt-metal base w/three serpentine legs flanking a central column all on a tripartite foot, No. D3084, minor flake, overall 21" h. **$3,335**

ELECTRIC LAMPS & LIGHTING

Table lamp, 17" d. domical reverse-painted "Exeter" shade decorated w/a continous sunset landscape w/green & yellow fields & black trees silhouetted against the deep orange, cream & purple sky, raised on a silver plate base w/a ring & leaf-cast section above a trumpet-form urn above the domed leaf-cast round foot, 21" h. **$2,875**

Table lamp, 18" d. domical reverse-painted "Carlisle" shade decorated in the Jungle Bird patt., painted on one side w/two exotic birds perched among tropical foliage, the other side depicts a single colorful bird resting on a branch w/another single bird among the tropical foliage, an usunusal design variation, painted in shades of deep red, yellow, blue, green & cream, raised on a bronzed base composed of three serpentine supports resting on a tripartite base, shade & base signed "Pairpoint Corp.," overall 21" h. **$5,750**

Table lamp, 18" d. domical reverse-painted "Touraine" shade decorated w/pastel blue & yellow flowers & medallions on a pale pink ground above a dark green border band painted w/scrolling leaves & birds in blue, pink & yellow, shade signed inside rim, on a signed silver plate base w/a tall slender ringed standard above a cup-shaped base w/scroll fit, pierced silver plat cap, 22 1/2" h. **$2,588**

Table lamp, 13" d. "Puffy" shade in the "Devonshire" shape, Hummingbird & Roses patt., reverse-painted in greens, yellows, reds & orange against a frosted ground, on a gold-washed cast-metal base w/a slender paneled & floral-cast standard on a square paneled foot, overall 21 1/2" h. **$9,200**

Table lamp, 14" d. "Puffy" shade in the Lilac Tree patt., reverse-painted w/pink & white blossoms against dark green leaves w/two yellow & red butterflies, gilt cast-metal baluster-form base w/floral garlands & leaf bands, shade signed "Pairpoint Corp.," base signed w/Pairpoint logo & "73," overall 22" h. **$21,840**

Table lamp, 16" d. "Puffy" shade in the "Chesterfield" shape, painted in vibrant sunset colors w/a Venetian harbor scene, the bronzed metal base w/a slender panel & floral-cast standard on a square paneled foot, base signed w/the Pairpoint logo & "B320," overall 22" h. **$7,475**

Tiffany Lamps

Candle lamps, a round stepped gilt-bronze foot supporting a tall cylindrical Favrile glass standard in white opal decorated w/an iridized blue pulled-feather design, an electric brass cap w/drip tray, metal fittings stamped w/logo & "Louis Tiffany Furnaces Inc. - 756," one standard w/hairline, 13" h., pr. **$2,070**

Desk kerosene-type lamp, 15 3/4" d. domical open-topped greenish yellow damascene shade signed w/initials, raised on bronze spider arms above the dome- topped cylindrical metal font fitted into a bulbous bronze base w/etched band & supported by a ring raised on three legs, oil canister stamped "Tiffany Studios - New York" w/Tiffany Glass & Decorating Co. monogram, ca. 1910 .... **$11,353**

Table lamp, "Acorn," 14" d. domical leaded glass shade, composed of an upper section of graduated striated green & white segments above a wide band of undulating acorns in green & orange striated segments, the border band w/three narrow bands of striated green & white segments, raised on a three-arm bronze base w/slender standard & round base w/wide ribs, shade signed "Tiffany Studios New York," base signed "Tiffany Studios New York" w/Tiffany Glass & Decorataing monogram, socket, support arms & ball appear to be modern replacements, several tiles w/hairlines, one acorn poorly replaced, shade slightly warped, overall 19 1/4" h. **$6,960**

Desk lamp, counterbalance style, a 14" d. domed blue iridescent damascene shade supported at the end of a high bronze S- scroll counterbalance arm on a slender stem & stepped domed base, shade engraved "L.C.T. Favrile," base stamped "Tiffany Studios - New York 416," ca. 1910, overall 14" h. **$17,925**

Table lamp, "Black-eyed Susan," 16" d. domical leaded glass shade decorated w/large yellow & brown daisies w/mottled light green leafy stems against a blocked ground of creamy white to mottled dark green, raised on a slender ribbed standard continuing into a wide disk base w/ribs ending in ribbed leaves, raised on small scroll feet, base stamped "D794 - 8" & Tiffany Glass & Decorating Co. monogram, overall 21 1/2" h. **$26,290**

Table lamp, "Apple Blossom," 25 1/8" d. domical leaded glass shade w/bronze openwork branch design at the top center surrounded by an overall design of mottled green leaves, mottled red buds & white & yellow blossoms, uneven edge, supported on a bronze tree trunk base, shade & base both w/stamped marks, overall 29 3/8" h. **$136,000**

ELECTRIC LAMPS & LIGHTING

Table lamp, "Daffodil," 16" d. domical leaded glass shade composed of segments forming long-stemmed yellow daffodils & long green & yellow stems & leaves against a white shaded to green background, on a bronze base w/a ribbon- wrapped standard above the scroll and lobe-decorated domed base on scroll tab feet, base signed "Tiffany Studios - New York 28615" & w/the TGD Co. monogram, overall 21" h. **$25,200**

Table lamp, "Drophead Dragonfly," 22" d. domical leaded glass shaded composed in the upper portion of elongated & oblong mottled dark & light green glass & amber tiles, the border band composed of a band of large green dragonflies w/red eyes, on a gilt-bronze Art Nouveau base w/a pod design on the standard & pierced leaf designs around the rounded base on small tab feet, shade stamped "Tiffany Studios - New York - 1507," base stamped "Tiffany Studios - New York - 397," overall 28 1/2" h. **$185,500**

Table lamp, "Greek Key," 16" d. domical leaded glass shade composed of mottled green panels above a wide Greek key border band in bright green & yellow bordered w/amber, shade signed "Tiffany Studios - New York," on a bronze base w/a long ovoid stem supported on three arms above the rectangular foot, base marked "Tiffany Studios - New York 444," overall 23 1/2" h. **$27,600**

Table lamp, Whirling Leaf," 18" d. domical leaded glass shade composed of an upper band of graduated mottled tan blocks above a wide band of swirling green leaves leaves on a mottled tan ground, the wide lower border composed of bands of rectangular tan blocks, raised on a three-spider above the bulbous tapering bronze teardrop base raised on a three-legged framework on a round disk foot, shade marked w/a Tiffany Studios tag, base stamped "Tiffany Studios New York 190," two cracked tiles, missing top cap, one leg restored, socket cluster probably a copy, overall 23" h. **$17,250**

Table lamp, "Lily," seven-light, a bronze lily pad base issuing seven slender upright arching stems each supporting a long flora-form golden iridescent shade, shades signed "LCT," base signed "Tiffany Studios-New York 385," overall 20" h. **$17,250**

Table lamp, "Linenfold," 19" w. twelve-paneled domical shade w/a pierced top plate, each panel w/emerald green linenfold glass trimmed at the top & bottom w/ clear frosted panels, on a gilt-bronze base w/a slender reeded standard above a round lobed foot, shade marked "Tiffany Studios - New York 1927 Pat. Apl'd For," base signed "Tiffany Studios - New York 26847," overall 23" h. **$24,150**

Table lamp, "Pansy," 16" d. domical leaded glass shade composed of graduated mottled pale yellowish green to dark green tile ground decorated w/a wide band of colorful pansies in shades of purple, yellow & green, supported on bronze arms above the slender standard w/fine reeding & loops above the wide rounded knobby base on small scroll feet, shade w/stamped tag, base stamped "Tiffany Studios - New York - 23617" & Tiffany Glass & Decorating Co. monogram, 22 1/2" h. **$50,190**

Table lamp, "Poppy," 20" d. conical leaded glass shade composed of red, fuchsia & purple striated blossoms & green mottled leaves against a striated yellow & orange ground, two narrow border bands in apple green & one in orangish yellow, on a slender simple bronze standard on a ribbed & dished base on tab feet, shade signed "Tiffany 8805," base signed "Tiffany Studios - New York," overall 25" h. **$89,500**

Table lamp, "Bellflower," 18" d. domical leaded glass shade composed of mottled light & dark green swirled leaves above a border band of red bellflowers, raised on a bulbous urn-form bronze base raised on four slender curved & reeded legs ending on a squared foot w/rounded corners, shaded marked w/Tiffany Studios tag, base stamped "Tiffany Studios New York 299714" & company monogram, overall 22" h. **$38,240**

Table lamp, "Geometric," 16 1/2" d. domical leaded glass shade composed of panels of graduated mottled yellow tiles w/a narrow border band of small tiles, raised on a slender paneled gilt-bronze standard w/a round foot, shade signed "Tiffany Studios New York - 1901," base signed "Tiffany Studios New York - 539," 21" h. **$10,350**

Table lamp, "Poinsettia," 15 3/4" d. domical leaded glass shade composed of an upper band of mottled deep orange & yellow tiles above a wide band of dark red & blue poinsettia flowers on green leafy stems, narrow bands of mottled orange & green at the bottom rim, raised on a bulbous ovoid bronze base w/lightly cast stylized leaves above foot composed of upright trumpet-form blossoms, shade signed "Tiffany Studios New York - 1557," base signed "Tiffany Studios New York - 26846" & company monogram, 18 3/4" h. **$59,750**

Table lamp, "Lemon Leaf," 18" d. domical leaded glass shade composed of an upper section of graduated mottled dichroic green & orange segments above a narrow band of swirled leaves, the drop border band composed of four bands of rectangular segments, raised on a slender ribbed & waisted standard on a domed ribbed base on ball feet, shade signed "Tiffany Studios New York 1470," base signed "Tiffany Studios New York 370," overall 23" h. **$29,900**

Table lamp, "Peacock," 18 3/4" d. domical open-topped leaded glass shade composed of colored glass segments forming twenty peacock eyes arranged in two rows the encircle the middle of the shade, each eye w/a sapphire blue center surrounded by teal & green segments surrounded by orange & green striated segments, the upper portion made entirely of rippled glass in amethyst shading to orange, the middle portion of the background graduated to feathers comprised of soft teal green & orange above two small horizontal bands of rippled glass over the apron continuing the feather design, raised on an original bronze peacock feather designed ovoid base tapering down to a scalloped bottom w/ each scallop enclosing a peacock feather eye, three-arm shade support, shade & base unsigned, overall 25" h.... **$120,750**

Authentic Tiffany lamps having leaded glass shades are more than 100 years old. Over the years the glass and lead may have moved due to heat from the lightbulbs and weight of the shade, causing glass to fall out. Replacing a lost piece of glass with a suitable match can be a challenge.

Desk lamp, 10" d., domical open-topped damascene shade in green iridescent w/rich blue & gold iridescent wavy lines, vertically ribbed w/a white interior casing, raised on a three-arm single-socket base bronze base tapering down to an artichoke-cast foot, gold patina, shaded signed "L.C.T.," base stamped "Tiffany Studios - New York - 445," replaced socket & minor wear on base, overall 16 1/2" h. **$4,560**

Lamps, Miscellaneous

Bradley & Hubbard table lamp, 20" d. umbrella-form leaded glass shade composed of radiating mottled green rectangular tiles above the wide drop border band w/red grape clusters alternating w/large green leaves, on a bronzed-metal footed inverted trumpet-form base embossed "Bradley & Hubbard" w/triangle mark, ca. 1910, 28" h. **$2,645**

Bigelow Studios boudoir lamp, the conical leaded glass shade w/an Art Nouveau design of blossoms around the top & leaves around the bottom edge, raised on a slender bronzed metal standard w/disk base & thin bun feet, based signed "Bigelow Studios," shade unsigned, early 20th c., top vent cap soldered to shade, 14" h. **$2,040**

Arts & Crafts table lamp, 18" d. domical caramel & green slag glass shade composed of alternating radiating graduated caramel slag & mottled green & amber tiles above the flattened drop edge w/uneven rim, raised on a bronzed metal base w/a slender tapering square standard w/stylized bamboo corner above the square pyramidal foot w/a large molded fleur-de-lis on each side, early 20th c., 22" h. .. **$978**

Daum Nancy table lamp, 12" d. domical etched & enameled shade decorated w/a continuous winter landscape w/large brown & black trees in the foreground of a snowy background in black, mottled brown & pale yellow, raised above a tall slender swelled matching glass base w/a flaring round foot, enameled mark w/the Cross of Lorraine, ca. 1905, overall 25 1/2" h. **$35,850**

Moe Bridges table lamp, 18" d. domical reverse-painted shade decorated w/an autumnal landscape w/a wide path winding through fields w/clusters of slender trees w/golden brown & green leaves, a lakeshore & high mountains in the distance, a pale yellow sky background, shade signed "Moe Bridges Co. 192," raised on a Moe Bridges bronzed metal tapering paneled base w/a paneled flaring foot, all w/incised angular lines, overall 22" h. **$3,163**

Heintz Art Metal boudoir lamp, a flat-bottomed squatty bulbous bronze base w/a mottled green & brown patina w/sterling silver decoration of large flowers on leafy stems, the conical metal shade w/four cut-out panels w/a floral design matching the base, shade lined in salmon colored silk fabric, early 20th c., shade 8 1/2" d., overall 9 1/2" h. . **$690**

Steuben banker's lamp, an oval footed bronzed metal base cast w/delicate scrolls centering a bulbed knob & tall slender shaft issuing two arched side arms each ending in an electric socket fitted w/a signed domed gold Aurene Stebuen shade, each shade 6 3/4" d., lamp overall 22" h. **$2,415**

Student lamp, double style, ornate brass leaf-cast slender standard & arched arms each suspending a socket w/a signed bell-form Quezal shade decorated in a gold & green pulled-feather design on a creamy white ground, the standard raised on a stepped black marble base, early 20th c., overall 18" h. **$1,080**

Fulper Pottery table lamp, the thick round base tapering to a slender slightly tapering shaped glazed in drippy green & black over a cream ground, signed, 20" h. **$600**

ELECTRIC LAMPS & LIGHTING

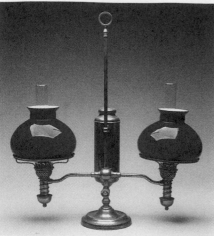

Student lamp, Harvard double-light, round ringed brass base supporting a tall central rod supporting the cylindrical fuel font & two projecting adjustable arms each ending in a burner & ring supporting a domed open-topped cased ruby glass shade, overall 22 1/2" h. **$1,955**

Arts & Crafts table lamp, iron & slag glass, the square tapering paneled shade w/an inward-scrolled metal crest above each panel inset w/a green slag glass panel, an arched & twisted metal bar runs from the top of each panel to the base & is fitted w/a heavy chain running down to the shade rim, raised above a deep square base w/a heavy ring handle on each side above the tightly scrolled feet, early 20th c., 15" w. shade, 19" h. ... **$390**

Leaded glass & Teco pottery table lamp, Arts & Crafts style, the tapering octagonial leaded glass shade w/wide tapering panels of iridescent & stained glass alternating w/narrower panels arranged in a chevron stylized floral design, the flat border panels composed of small glass pieces arranged in a brickwork design, raised on a bulbous ovoid Teco pottery base w/four deeply molded buttress handles down the side, fine mottled green glaze, Shape No. 288, designed by W. D. Mundie, originally designed as an oil lamp, original paper labels, base drilled for electricity, shade 15" w., overall 18" h. ... **$28,800**

Jefferson table lamp, 18" d. domical reverse-painted shade decorated w/a pretty landscape w/pairs of tall leafy trees & small wooded hills in the foreground & meadows in the distance, done in shades of yellow, blues, greens & brown, signed "2680 Jefferson Co. FH," raised on a rare large baluster-form glass base acid-etched w/a Chinese dragon design against a chipped-ice background & covered in a copper-colored patina, overall 24 1/2" h. **$1,725**

Pittsburgh table lamp, 14" d. domical reverse-painted shaded decorated w/a continuous border jungle landscape w/palm trees & flowers against a deep tan to yellow sky, raised on a copper-finished metal base w/a paneled & dimpled design, 22" h. ... **$1,150**

Duffner & Kimberly table lamp, 19" d. domical leaded glass shade, the upper shade w/graduated blocks of purplish brown slag glass above a wide border band of green fleur-de-lis & ribbons w/yellow ground, on a Duffner & Kimberly cast-metal base w/a tall reeded standard & a round foot cast w/oak leaves & acorns, overall 21 3/4" h. **$6,613**

Duffner & Kimberly leaded glass table lamp, 20" d. leaded glass shade w/a wide gently angled top & narrow drop border, the top composed of triangular & diamond-shaped mottled yellow & green slag glass w/dark green lobes around the top, the narrow border composed of an arrangment of rounded triangular mottled yellow & green slag tiles, raised on a slender bronzed tiered standard on a round ribbed foot, 24" h...................... **$3,450**

Slag glass table lamp, 18" d. octagonal umbrella-form caramel slag paneled shade w/the upper tapering panels decorated w/lattice filigree & the wide border panels decorated w/scroll & loop filigree, supported above a lighted octagonal base w/tapering rectangular caramel slag side panels decorated w/filigree bands above the loop-cast shaped base, ca. 1920, overall 25" h. **$1,150**

Wilkinson leaded glass table lamp, 18" d. domical leaded glass shade composed of a wide upper section of dark & light green mottled slag graduating blocks above a wide border band of stylized flowers in ruby, pink, & mottled green slag, raised on a gilt-metal base w/a slender paneled standard ending in scrolls atop the round foot **$3,450**

Other Lighting Devices

Chandeliers

Arts & Crafts, slag glass & patinated metal, hexagonal w/the long tapering caramel slag panels topped by a conforming slag glass crown top, each panel w/a flat wide border band set w/caramel slag overlaid w/a repeating pierced metal landscape design, original chain & ceiling cap, early 20th c., 24" w., overall 34" h. **$660**

Arts & Crafts, patinated metal & mica, English influence, the shade composed of tapering rectangular panels each centered by an intricate pierced metal overlay & lined w/mica panels, narrow pierced top & bottom panel trim, all joined to the slender center post by five long C-scroll arms topped by pierced panels joined to top smaller C-scrolls joining the hanging chain, original patina, early 20th c., 18" h., 22" w. **$780**

Leaded gllass, 24 1/2" domical shade w/an open flaring pointed petal green slag glass top, the upper sides composed of graduated green slag blocks above a repeating design of large pink bows atop white baskets overflowing w/deep red berries & joined by trailing dark green leaves, uneven rim, some repairs & replaced segments, some tight hairlines, late 19th - early 20th c., 16" h. **$403**

Leaded glass, Arts & Crafts design, 25" d. deep domical shade covered of yellow radiating panels at the top above the deep flattened sides decorated w/narrow vertical panels w/a stylized papyrus design in green, pink, amber & yellow alternating w/panels of large & small yellow panes, original chain & ceiling cap, early 20th c., shade 14" h. **$2,640**

Lanterns

Hall lantern, Arts & Crafts style, hammered iron & mica, the domed & paneled top above a cylindrical mica shade supported by flat iron bands each fanned at the bottom, original patina & mica, early 20th c., 6" d., 18" h. **$660**

Hall lantern, Arts & Crafts style, patinated iron, the pyramidal top w/pierced flat vent holes, each side inset w/a white slag glass panel w/an overlaid squared metal design, metal curled brackets at each corner, hinged door on one side, original patina, original chain & ceiling cap, early 20th c., 12" sq. overall 45" h. **$330**

Hall lantern, Arts & Crafts style, pierced bronzed metal, the pyramidal top w/a colored centered jewel framed w/a pierced design, the rectangular lantern w/starburst & fan-pierced sides each set w/five colored jewels, original patina, early 20th c., 8 x 11", 14" h. **$420**

Candle lantern, glass & wood, a primitive wooden frame w/one side forming a door, glass sides, domed tin top vent & wire bail handle, 19th c., 11" h. **$161**

Candle lanterns, hanging-type, grey painted tin, a hanging loop above a widely flaring conical tin shade w/a curved strap from side to side centered by a small candle socket, Shaker-made, Hancock, Massachuseets, mid-19th c., scattered paint loss & corrosion, 12 1/4" d., 11 1/4" h., pr. (ILLUS. of one) **$4,230**

Hall lantern, Art Deco style, wrought-iron & textured clear glass, the tall square iron frame enclosing pierced iron panels w/ stylized hunters & antelope, four arched & scrolled straps joined at the top below hanging ring, gilt-metal narrow open swag band around the base w/small reeded corner drops, designed by Edgar Brandt, glass possibly by Daum, w/original chain, ca. 1925, 10 1/8" w., 25" h. **$204,000**

MARBLES

End-of-day, mottled & swirled dark green & yellow w/reddish orange bands, segmented onion skin, 2" d. **$264**

Latticinio core, clear w/white latticinio core w/narrow yellow & red & blue & white outer bands, fine original surface, two very faint hits, 1 11/16" d. **$123**

Latticinio core, clear w/yellow latticinio core w/narrow red & white & blue & white outer bands, original surface, two tiny pecks, 1 11/16" d. **$134**

Onionskin, clear w/green, blue, red & white core, two hit marks, original surface finish, 1 9/16" d. **$123**

Onionskin, clear w/green, pink, blue & yellow core, slight wear, several faint hit marks, original surface, 1 3/4" d. **$258**

Onionskin, clear w/red, yellow & green core, very slight wear, original surface finish, 1 1/2" **$235**

Onionskin, four-panel style, two panels of red & yellow & two panels of blue & white, single pontil, original conidition, 1 7/8" d. **$690**

Open Ribbon Swirl, swirled bands in red, white, blue, yellow & green, outer bands in yellow & white, all original, no wear, 2 1/2" d. **$2,588**

Swirl, divided center w/bright swirls of orangish red, green, blue, white & yellow, some chips, 1 1/2" d. **$58**

METALS

Brass

Bed warmer, a round brass pan w/a hinged cover decorated w/a chased scrolling decoration & several small air holes, long well-turned baluser- and knob-turned handle in mustard yellow, red & black grain paint, pan 10" d., overall 40" l. **$345**

Door knocker, modeled as a spead-winged American eagle w/a shield on the breast & arrows or laurel branches in the talons, a long U-form knocker bar, early 20th c., 6 x 7" **$460**

Candlestick, Art Deco style, four-bobeche type, figural Pierrot stands on one foot on lobed base, arms & other leg outstretched, the bobeches balanced on extended foot, two hands & head, stamped w/"GRG" figural mark & "Germany," 9 x 10" **$173**

Palace jar, wide bulbous body w/a wide shoulder tapering to a short flaring neck, overall delicate chased designs of various deities within a scrolled field, India, early 20th c., 17" d., 16" h. **$414**

Coal hamper, English Arts & Crafts style, hammered brass w/stylized repoussé design to side panels, riveted corners & handles, inset lid, zinc liner, 14" sq., 16" h. **$460**

Samovar, a square base on knob feet supporting a two-part pierced pedestal below the large nearly spherical body w/large scroll & bar handles & a large spigot, a gadrooned top band w/large inserted top w/wooden knob handles flanking the tall ringed chimney, Imperial era, Russia, marked, 15" h. **$374**

Wax jack, a round brass base w/an ornate scroll projecting handle, centered by a slender round supporting a swiveling arm to hold the end of the spiraling band of wax, turned brass post finial, England, 18th c, 5 1/2" h. **$6,573**

BRASS

Wine bucket, cov., cylindrical shape w/angular turned mahogany side handles & finial lid, decorated w/vertical & horizontal bands of stamped fruit, Austria or Germany, 13 x 14" **$230**

Wood box, rectangular w/slant lid, two ladies head columns in front, & front paw feet, large lion head handles at sides, decorated w/ embossed images of rampant lions & eagles, 18 x 30", 21" h. **$403**

Copper

Bronze

Box, Arts & Crafts style, the rectangular flat top cast in relief w/a stylized sea horse on a textured background, original patina, signed by E.T. Hurley, early 20th c., 4 3/4" w. **$840**

Ashtray, Arts & Crafts style, hand-hammered floor model, the bowl-form top fitted w/a match box holder & raised on three slender legs continuing to the domed base, original patina, impressed mark of Dirk Van Erp, early 20th c., 31" h. **$1,680**

Bowl, hand-hammered, Arts & Crafts style, a small round footring supporting the very wide rounded sides w/a flat rim, original patina, impressed mark of Dirk Van Erp, 9" d. **$540**

Plate, hand-hammered, the center inlaid w/a starburst silver design, original patina, signed by Linossier, 6" d. **$240**

Plate, hand-hammered, the shallow center surrounded by a wide flat rim inlaid w/a mosaic serpentine & circle blue & green design, original patina, Mexico, illegible signature, 8 1/2" d. **$150**

Tray, hand-hammered, Arts & Crafts design, round w/a wide flanged rim, the center w/a large starburst design, the rim w/stylized floral & lappet leaf design, original patina, unsigned, early 20th c., 10 1/4" d. **$360**

Tray, hand-hammered, Arts & Crafts style, round w/a very wide flanged rim w/four high-relief stylized leaves alternating w/buttons, impressed number "17," unsigned, early 20th c., 7" d. **$390**

Cache pot, hand-hammered, Arts & Crafts style, a deep rounded bowl w/stepped rim mounted to two ring handles, raised on three serpentine legs, original patina, Stickley Brothers, early 20th c., 10" d., 9 1/2" h. **$420**

Vase, Arts & Crafts style, footed gently swelled cylindrical form tapering to a flat rim, the side applied w/a silver design of flying ducks above cattails, original patina, impressed mark of Silver Crest, No. 1051B, early 20th c., 13" h. **$270**

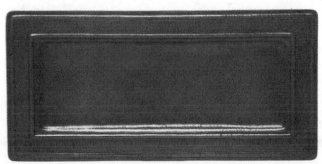

Tray, Arts & Crafts style, hand-hammered, long rectangular form w/a slightly indented center, the rim trimmed w/two thin bands, original patina, incised mark of Jarvie, 11" l. **$1,800**

Iron

Hinges, hand-wrought, a long strap w/a small rounded end & widely flaring curved forked stap w/a small rounded end, 14" w., 30 1/4" l., pr. **$115**

←

Game hook, hand-wrought, domed crown-form, S-scroll handing hook above four curved bands joining a horizontal ring suspending four four-prong hooks, scroll hanged added later, 19th c., 10 1/2" d., 12" h. **$201**

Because it is less expensive than silver, pewter was the main tableware in Europe until the development of porcelain.

Antique pewter contains tin, copper, antimony, and lead, with tin comprising 85 to 99 percent of the alloy. Modern pewter is made with at least 90 percent tin and only tiny amounts of lead, if any.

Antique pewter is heavier and tarnishes faster than modern pewter because of its lead content.

Pipe tongs, hand-wrought, a long spring handle opens the long thin tongs, w/a bowl cleaner & tamp, American or English, 18th c., some wear, 14 5/8" l. **$441**

↓

Pewter

Plate, round w/flat flanged rim, lion mark of John Skinner, Boston, last half 18th c., minor dents & wear, 8 7/8" d. **$881**

Porringer, round w/boss bottom & pierced flowered handle, eagle touch mark of William Calder, Providence, Rhode Island, first half 19th c., minor rim dents, wear, 5 1/4" d. **$499**

Porringer, round w/a boss bottom & pierced scrolled crown handle, raised marks of backwards "SG," minor wear, New England, late 18th - early 19th c., 5 3/8" d. **$470**

Porringer, round w/boss bottom & pierced flowered handle, anchor touch mark attributed to William Billings, Providence, Rhode Island, late 18th c., slight dents & wear, 5" d. **$382**

Porringer, round w/boss bottom & pierced flowered handle, eagle mark of William Calder, Providence, Rhode Island, first half 19th c., 4 1/8" d. **$499**

Sheffield Plate

Candlesticks, telescoping-type, round flaring fluted base tapering to an adjustable fluted stem below the fluted trumpet-form candle socket, marked "Mortons Patent," England, early 19th c., 8 1/4" h., pr. **$518**

Entree dishes, cov., rounded rectangular form w/a gadrooned edge, matching flat- topped domed cover w/detachable leafy scroll loop handle, engraved arms & crowned heart armorial, England, ca. 1815, 8 1/4 x 11 1/2", 5" h., pr. **$575**

Platter, round w/a wide applied acanthus leaf scroll & flower rim band, the center engraved overall w/elaborate rococo C- scrolls & acanthus leaves centered by a rampant lion crest, raised on three fluted acanthus scroll feet, ca. 1790, some wear, 24 1/2" d., 2" h. **$978**

Tea caddy, cov., Neoclassical style, tall oval & slightly flaring sides inlaid & chased w/silver bands & a crest, the concave curved shoulder around the domed cover w/knob finial, lock on the front, George III Era, England, ca. 1770, unmarked, 6 1/4" h. **$546**

Urn, cov., a large pointed spiral-twist finial on the stepped domed cover chased w/floral & gadrooned bands, resting on a double-handled squat urn-form body w/reeded & chased floral scrolls centering a cartouche w/a crest & motto, flaring round foot, unknown maker's mark, ca. 1760, some wear, base of one handle bent, 12" h. **$1,093**

Chambersticks, shallow dished round base w/gadrooned border, a curved side finger handle w/conical snuffer, the open-centered center shaft w/an urn-form candle socket w/a swirled gadrooned flattened rim, by Matthew Bolton, England, ca. 1785, some copper bleeding through, missing wick trimmers, 7" w., 4 1/4" h., pr. (ILLUS. of one) **$500**

Mirror plateau, the round concave table frame w/an ovolo base border band & a top cast shell & acanthus leaf rim band enclosing the mirror, Creswick mark on hinged mounts, Regency Era, England, ca. 1825, 17 3/4" d., 2 1/4" h......... **$1,035**

Silver

American (Sterling & Coin)

Salad serving set: long handled fork & matching spoon; sterling, Medallion patt., w/original fitted case, mark of Ball, Black & Co., New York, New York, ca. 1875, each 11 3/4" l., the set **$1,800**

Sauceboat, coin, deep oval body raised on hoof feet w/foliate joins, the body engraved w/rocaille, a leaf-capped C-scroll handle, reeded rim, a cartouche on each side, one engraved w/a coat-of-arms, the other w/script monogram, possibly American, ca. 1760, overall 7 1/2" l. **$960**

Sterling, which is 92.5 percent silver, has been the standard in England for hundreds of years. Coin silver is 90 percent silver and was produced in America from colonial times until just after the Civil War.

Sugar bowl, cov., coin, inverted double-bellied form, on a gadrooned round foot, the body engraved w/a flower-and-leaf garland & a monogram below the gadrooned rim, double-domed cover w/gadrooned band & cast bud finial, mark of Daniel Van Voorhis, New York City, ca. 1785, 8 1/2" h. **$21,600**

Sugar casters, cov., sterling, each w/a footed ovoid body chased in the form of a peacock w/a tall tail, the conical pierced cover w/a trellis & flowers design & a tiny figural peacock finial, mark of Wm. B. Durgin, Concord & Gorham Mfg. Co., Providence, Rhode Island, ca. 1910, 7 1/4" h., pr. **$3,600**

Sugar urn, cov., coin, a square foot & short pedestal support the deep cup-form body w/a low pierced gallery rim, pyramidal cover w/ urn-form finial, the body engraved w/a monogram, mark of Charles L. Boehme, Baltimore, ca. 1800, 10 1/2" h. **$3,600**

Monogrammed silver flatware is much more affordable than unmarked silverware. An entire set can be purchased for the price of a single place setting of new silver flatware.

English & Other

Teapot, cov., footed spherical body w/répoussé swirled ribbing below a wide shoulder band of ornate chased flowers & leaves, short cylindrical neck w/ruffled rim, hinged, domed & fluted cover w/squared wooden knob finial, fluted serpentine spout, C-scroll wooden handle, England, worn hallmarks, probably second half 19th c., overall 8" l. **$288**

Teapot, cov., footed squatty pear-shaped body w/a hinged high domed cover w/wooden knob finial, angled serpentine spout, C-scroll wooden handle, chased overall w/lambrequin, acanthus leaves & shells, engraved inscription on base, mark of Jan Verdoes, Haarlem, Holland, 1736, 6 1/4" h. **$1,554**

Teapot, cov., George I era, footed octagonal squatty pear-shaped body w/a domed hinged & paneled cover w/a wood disk finial, paneled scroll-cast serpentine spout, C-scroll wooden handle, one side engraved w/a coat-of-arms, crest & motto, base w/mark of John Hamilton, Dublin, Ireland, 1719-20, 6 1/2" h. **$53,775**

Teapot, cov., miniature, waisted cylindrical body w/flared shoulder & short neck w/fitted domed cover w/knop finial, flat C- scroll handle & angled straight spout, chased w/C-scroll & floral decoration, mark on base of James Goodwin, London, England, 1727, two solder marks on base, 4" h. **$518**

Cup, flared base & cylindrical sides w/high arched loop handle, the body engraved w/Art Nouveau flowers, gold-washed interior, Russian touch marks, 19th c., 3 1/2" h. **$345**

Teapot, cov., William IV era, fluted squatty bulbous body on four leaf-clad feet, the body chased & applied w/flowers & acanthus leaves, a leaf-clad serpentine spout & leafy scroll handle w/ivory insulators, domed hinged cover w/flowerhead finial, mark of Joseph & Albert Savory, London, England, 1836, overall 8 1/4" l. **$1,912**

Basket, oval footring w/pierced diamond & star designs below the deep flaring basket pierced overall w/delicate cross, dot & chevron design, serpentine narrow gadrooned rim band, twisted arched swing handle, mark of William Vincent, London, England, 1773-74, 8 3/4" l. **$863**

Cigarette box, cov., rectangular w/hinged cover, the sides decorated w/répoussé flying birds above turbulent seas, the cover decorated w/bold répoussé chrysanthemums & leaves, opening to a cedar-lined interior, raised on narrow bracket feet, Japanese Export, ca. 1900, 3 1/2 x 6 1/2", 3" h.................... **$1,955**

SILVER PLATE (HOLLOWWARE)

Silver Plate (Hollowware)

Card tray, four-lobed squared-shape tray decorated w/engraved flowers & insects, attached to round base by three legs & two applied leaf & flower supports, maker's name indistinct, 5 7/8 x 6 1/4".... **$175**

Centerpiece bowl, oblong shallow bowl w/wide pierced sides composed of a lattice & leaf design, supported by four full- figure kneeling cupids, mark of Christofle & Cie., Paris, France, ca. 1890, 20 1/2" l., 5 1/4" h. .. **$5,019**

Condiment holder, in the form of a woven basket containing three egg-shaped holders for salt & pepper shakers & mustard cup, w/spread-winged baby bird perched on rim, English, indistinct maker's mark on bottom, 5 1/2" h. **$1,295**

Jewelry casket, oblong form, the arched top w/two hinged covers flanked by arched sides w/a pierced design of flowers & leaves & raised on four leaf-sprig feet, a slender arched handle from side to side, mark of the Pairpoint Mfg. Co., portions of base reinforced & some leaves missing, 1890s, 6 1/2" l., 9" h. **$633**

Salt cellar, in the form of a dolphin carrying a shell on its back, rimmed base w/design depicting ocean waves, handle in the form of a ribbed leaf, 2 x 2 3/4 x 4 1/2" **$275**

Silver hollowware is generally made of silver plate (silver over copper) because these serving containers need the added strength and rigidity that copper provides.

Match holder, model of old oaken bucket w/two branch handles on sides, sitting on raised base ribbed for striking matches, 4" l. **$325**

Teakettle on stand, cov., Victorian, Orientalist taste, the decagonally paneled body tapering to a short neck w/thin pierced gallery & hinged domed & stepped cover w/spherical finial, a pointed Arabesque arch fixed overhead handle, serpentine spout, the panels engraved as arches enclosing ornate quatrefoils above a chain band, raised on a platform base w/a wide top & thin gallery around a narrower pierced & paneled pedestal enclosing the burner, the wide dished & paneled base w/short columns forming the feet, by Elkington & Company, Birmingham, England, 1854, overall 10 1/2" w., overall 8 1/2" h. **$1,150**

Serving station, heated-type, the round lazy Susan heated tray stand fitted w/a large central two-handled cov. soup tureen surrounded by three cov. round serving dishes, three shakers, three open footed salt dips w/cobalt blue glass liners, two cov. mustard pots w/cobalt blue glass liners & three tall shakers, each piece decorated w/a wide reeded band, tureen marked "Made in Sheffield, England," early 20th c., tray 27" d., the set **$1,610**

Teapot, cov., round flat base below the wide rounded lower body w/a gadrooned medial band below the tall tapering sides w/a flaring rim, hinged domed cover w/knob finial, tall slender serpentine spout, C-scroll handle, trademark w/a lion on either side of a shield above "Silverplated - Est. 1905," early 20th c., 9 1/4" w., 9 3/4" h. **$65**

Toothpick holder, figural, round stepped base holding figure of monkey holding staff & carrying on its back a basket w/basketweave decoration & rope twist rim, Meriden, 3 1/3" h. **$550**

Tea & coffee set: cov. teapot, cov. coffeepot, cov. sugar bowl, creamer & waste bowl; bulbous squared bodies w/each side decorated w/répoussé large leafy scrolls, squared necks & covers w/reeded button finials, hollow loop handles, Gorham Mfg. Co., Providence, Rhode Island, 1888, coffeepot 7" h., the set **$460**

Wine trolley, modeled as a cannon w/large scroll-trimmed open wheels & pierced scrolling handles joined by a turned bar, short cylindrical base w/beaded bands & a long serpentine side panel between the wheels, England, 19th c., 6 1/2 x 11 1/2", 8 3/4" h. **$1,265**

Teapot, cov., squatty bulbous boat-shaped body w/widely flaring flanged rim & hinged stepped, domed cover w/wooden disk finial, ribbed serpentine spout, pointed angular handle, the sides w/an ornate engraved floral cartouche enclosing a gift inscription dated 1911, marks for an English silver plate firm, 11 1/2" l., 5 3/8" h. **$85**

TIN & TOLE

Tin & Tole

Candle screen, told, upright arched & curved screen w/the black ground decorated w/a gold spread-winged eagle under a rising run, some wear, early 19th c., fitted for a light bulb w/a pewter lamp base, 6 1/4" w., 7 3/4" h.
.... **$1,150**

Mug, tole, tall cylindrical form w/wide strap handle, black asphaltum ground decorated w/large red fruit & curved yellow leaflets, possibly Berlin, Connecticut, early 19th c., 4 7/8" h. **$2,703**

Coal bin, tole, a rectangular domed cover on a tall square tapering bin raised on scrolling brass feet, fixed side handles w/turned wooden grips, decorated w/a green ground & gold border around a large reserve showing a fox hunting scene, England, late 19th c., 19" w., 19 1/2" h.
.... **$1,998**

Tea caddy, cov., tole, rectangular w/hinged lid & deep sides, the top & sides decorated w/a smoke decoration in black & cream w/ yellow border bands, the front h. p. w/an oval reserve in white bordered by black & decorated w/stylized pink flower & green leaves, early 19th c., minor paint loss, 2 1/3 x 3 5/8", 3 7/8" h.
.... **$705**

Plate warmer, tole, a domed top on an upright nearly square black cabinet w/a door w/a raised panel h.p. w/a floral bouquet & framed by gilt scrolls, metal fixed side handles, raised on molded cabriole metal legs w/paw feet, interior w/three shelves, England, late 19th c., 17 3/4" w., 30" h.
.... **$999**

Document box, cov., tole, the rectangular hinged domed cover w/a brass swing handle on an embossed oval plate decorated w/a border bands of yellow ropetwist & scallops, the front decorated w/a white band decorated w/stylized red flowers & green leaves, the dark asphaltum ground decorated around the sides w/yellow ropetwist & scallop borders, early 19th c., minor paint wear, 6 1/2 x 10 1/4", 7 1/2" h.
.... **$4,994**

> Tole painting is folk art that, in the U.S., was practiced primarily by German and Scandinavian immigrants beginning in the 18th century.

Storage box, cov., tole, low square form w/a hinged cover w/brass swing handle on an oval floral-embossed plate & decorated w/ leafy vines in yellow, opening to three interior compartments, the three sides decorated w/a white border w/flowers & buds in red, green & yellow all on a black ground, attributed to Connecticut Filley Tinshop, early 19th c., minor scattered paint wear, 11 1/4" w., 5 5/8" h. **$11,750**

MILITARIA MARKET REPORT

According to John Adams Graf, editor of *Military Trader* and *Military Vehicles* magazines (www.militarytrader.com), and author of Warman's Civil War, World War II and Vietnam books, "there has been some slowdown in the high end of the market in investment quality pieces such as $10,000+ Third Reich items." He thinks this may be because those who are buying these items are buying more for investment than for love of the hobby. Thus, with a tighter economy, these purchases are decreasing. The middle and lower-end items are holding steady, however, with no drop in volume or prices.

In it's early days, eBay was a great place to find quality memorabilia, but not anymore. "It's become a dumping ground," said Graf. eBay has also discouraged buyers by increasing its fees and instituting all-encompassing rules. For example, it bans Nazi-related materials like swastikas even though collectors typically want them for historical purposes, not because they are Nazi sympathizers. And because eBay bans all brass knuckles, World War I trench knives with brass knuckles formed in the handles are also banned. While these knives are historical items, eBay makes no distinction between them and modern brass knuckles sold as weapons. Graf predicts that "within two or three years, specialized collector-to-collector Web sites will emerge to replace the militaria segment of eBay."

Meanwhile, collectors are moving away from eBay and back to shows, where they can trade these items, conduct a hands-on inspection of artifacts, and develop a personal relationship with dealers. At the 2009 Show of Shows (www.sosovms.com) held in Louisville, Kentucky, all 1,600 dealer tables had been reserved six months in advance.

"One of the hottest areas of military memorabilia collecting is that of identified medals [medals that can be connected with the people who were awarded them]. This is especially true of medals that have engraved names that help verify their identification," Graf said. Collectors, however, should be aware that the 2006 Stolen Valor Act prohibits the unauthorized wear, manufacture, sale or claim (either written or verbal) of U.S. military decorations and medals. Graf speculates that one of the reasons this area is so hot is that the law has not been significantly enforced yet. Collectors who want to purchase military firearms should also be aware of gun laws (see the NRA Web page at www.nraila.org/gunlaws). Headgear such as helmets and visor caps remain popular. World War II collecting is still hot, but interest in Civil War artifacts has cooled off some.

Graf advises collectors to specialize in an area to get the most satisfaction and make the best investment of their money. He also recommends that they educate themselves before buying rather than after and to be patient. "If the seller doesn't offer a return policy, walk away. These things were produced in quantity, so you'll be able to find it again elsewhere. If you're willing to wait, good stuff will come up."

Auction Houses
Advance Guard Militaria (www.advanceguardmilitaria.com)
Manions (www.manions.com)
Wermacht Awards (www.wehrmacht-awards.com)
The Ruptured Duck (www.therupturedduck.com)
Wittman Militaria (www.wwiidaggers.com)
Hermann Historica (www.hermann historica.com)
Stewart Military Antiques (www.stewartsmilitaryantiques.com)

MILITARIA & WARTIME MEMORABILIA

Civil War (1861-65)

Ambrotype, sixth-plate, portrait of three Union soldiers, two seated & one standing, wearing four-button sack coats w/forage caps, attached pencil note, housed in leatherette case w/split hinge (some emulsion flaking) **$220**

Canteen, polychrome & gilt-painted tin, flattened round shape, one side painted w/a Civil War battle scene depicting several Union soldiers, one carrying an American flag, an officer on horseback, two injured Union soldiers & two injured Confederate soldiers, the reverse in black w/a gilt banner inscribed "G.A. Hanson - Co. H 51st Reg. Mass Vol. 1" above a later inscription "1861-1865 - G.A.R. 1884 - L.M. Thomson. Pt.," gilt border & spout, 8 5/8" d. (dents, small scattered paint losses) **$499**

Carte de visite, photo of Lieutenant Colonel Martin Tschudy, 69th Pennsylvania Infantry, killed at the battle of Gettysburg, shown seated w/his knees up, unknown photographer.................. **$1,760**

Carte de visite, photograph of Colonel Joshua Blackwood Howell (1806-64) of the 85th Pennsylvania Infantry, named a brigadier after his death in 1864, half-length portrait **$275**

Photograph, large albumen print of General Meade & his staff in front of a log cabin, inscribed in pencil on the back "At Hd Qtrs 1st Brig House March 1864," unknown photographer, image 7 1/4 x 9 1/2", mounted on larger board (minor foxing on board) **$3,025**

Confederate States note, $800 note printed in black & white w/ top center vignette, issued in Richmond, Virginia, May 19, 1863, redeemable after July 1, 1868, glued to substrate, some bleeding, foxing & creases, framed, 9 1/4 x 13 1/2" **$104**

Poster, recruitment-type, printed in black & white, the top w/a large patriotic vignette w/slogan banners & figures w/the American flag, recruiting Volunteers for Company B of Col. E.M. Gregory's Regiment, 22 x 30" **$3,850**

Tintype of a Union soldier, 1/6th plate, seated infantry man wearing his jacket, his infantry overcoat & Hardee hat placed on the table beside him, good strong image, cased **$431**

Revolver & holster, Union Arms Co. single- action pocket model, by Bacon Manufacturing Co., Serial No. 3002, five-shot, fluted cylinder, walnut grips, barrel 4 3/34" l., w/vintage leather holster, ca. 1860, the set ... **$460**

Tintype of a Union soldier, 1/6th plate, seated Union soldier holding a M1860 sword & wearing a belt w/eagle plate & sword knot form which hangs a holstered pistol, cased **$460**

Spanish-American War (1898)

Canteen, flated round form, used by a soldier, one side h.p. w/a scene of the wreckage of the Battleship Maine, the other side w/a scene of Manilla Bay, original leather strap & cork stopper **$431**

World War I (1914-1918)

World War II (1939-1945)

German Luger, 1942 BYF model, P.08 cal., Nazi markings, Serial No. 490, good condition **$575**

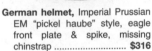

German helmet, Imperial Prussian EM "pickel haube" style, eagle front plate & spike, missing chinstrap **$316**

• Never dry fire an antique gun, allowing the hammer to hit the firing pin. People who do this at auctions and shows are quckly reprimanded. Don't fire antique firearms either, as this can be dangerous and can ruin a valuable antique. Buy a reproduction to fire instead.

• Do not attempt to do restoration work on a valuable antique weapon. Consult a professional restorer or conservator to ensure no permanent damage is done resulting in a loss of value.

Some auction-goers intentionally discourage competition by deriding an item before it sells. After making disparaging remarks about a valuable item and scaring away potential bidders, the detractor will often be the winning bidder at a reduced price. Recognize this ploy for what it is and decide for yourself how much you want to bid.

Novelty pinback button, a 7/8" d. celluloid button in white w/read wording "Let's All Pull Together," w/a string suspending a cardboard color cut-out of a hanging Hitler, unusual **$1,099**

MINIATURES (PAINTINGS)

Full-length portrait of a lady, watercolor on ivory, a scene of a lady wearing a red dress & kneeling in a garden setting & placing a swag of flowers on a monument topped by two white doves, in a round gilt-metal locket frame, American School, first half 19th c., minor foxing, unsigned, 1 3/4" d. **$646**

Half-length portrait of a lady, watercolor on ivory, seated lady facing forward, wearing a lacy cap tied w/a black & white ribbon, a wide white collar on her black dress w/pleated sleeves & bodice, tightly curled brown hair, wearing spectacles, American, first quarter 19th c., in a red leather-covered oval hinged frame, unsigned, 1 5/8 x 2 1/2" **$353**

Sailing ship, watercolor on ivory, a single- masted ship under full sail & flying an American flag, mounted in a narrow rectangular stamped gold-plated metal frame, American School, first half 19th c., minor fading, 3/4 x 1" **$2,233**

Half-length portrait of a gentleman, watercolor on paper, seated figure facing right, one arm resting on a chair back, brown hair brushed forward, wearing a brown coat w/mutton-leg sleeves & wide collar, black tie & striped vest, pencilled inscriptions identy sitter as Moses Waterhouse, dated 1839, in a period white-dotted green painted frame, foxing, toning, stain, 4 1/8 x 4 1/2" **$8,225**

Objects have been made in miniature for a variety of reasons: for children's playthings; for portability (such as a salesman's sample or a painting in a locket); and for a way to showcase the skill of an artist or craftsman.

MINIATURES (REPLICAS)

Blanket chest, curly maple, rectangular hinged lid w/molded edges opening to the well, dovetailed sides on a molded base w/scroll-cut ogee bracket feet & a center front foot, repair at one hinge, contemporary, 8 1/2 x 17", 9 3/4" h. **$374**

MOVIE MEMORABILIA

Posters

"Creature From The Haunted Sea," Filmgroup, 1960, starring Antony Carbone & Betsy Jones-Moreland, directed by Roger Corman, insert-size **$30-50**

"I Met Him in Paris," Paramount, 1937, starring Claudette Colbert, Melvyn Douglas & Robert Young, colorful portrait of Colbert at the top, one-sheet, linen- backed, 27 x 41" **$239**

"Indestructible Man," 1956, starring Lon Chaney, Jr., one-sheet, 14 x 36" **$115**

"Frankenstein Meets the Wolf Man," 20th Century-Fox Film Corporation/Terry-Toon Cartoons, 1938, linen-backed one-sheet featuring monochromatic illustration of the two characters grappling w/each other beneath the words "Fiend of Fury vs. Night-born Killer!" & at bottom a black & white photo of woman half-reclining & looking up, seemingly at action taking place in top of poster, the title in red-bordered white block letters across the center, cast Info in black in bottom right, all within red border, 27 x 41".............. **$1,150**

"Where Danger Lives," RKO, 1950, starring Robert Mitchum, three-sheet, linen-backed, 41 x 81". **$2,868**

"King Kong vs. Godzilla," Toho-Universal, 1963, U.S. release, large central scene of the monsters battling, one-sheet **$250-400**

"The 3 Worlds of Gulliver," Columbia Pictures, 1960, starring Kevin Mathews, group of scenes from the movie w/a tall figure behind, one-sheet **$35-50**

"The African Queen," United Artists, 1952, starring Humphrey Bogart & Katharine Hepburn, one-sheet, linen-backed, 27 x 41" **$1,673**

"The Astounding She Monster," American International, 1958, starring Robert Clarke, Kenne Duncan & Marilyn Harvey, dramatic image of scantilly clad She Monster, one-sheet, 27 x 41" **$450-750**

"The Dark Corner" 20th Century-Fox, 1946, starring Lucille Ball & Clifton Webb, one-sheet, 27 x 41" **$956**

"The Gorgon," Columbia Pictures, 1964, starring Peter Cushing & Christopher Lee, dramatic colorful scene w/the Gorgon head & other characters, yellow background, one-sheet **$65-95**

Collectors sometimes gripe when they are outbid by a dealer. However, a collector has the advantage and should be able to outbid a dealer, who must buy at a lower price to make a profit. Plus, dealers who buy at auction risk having their customers know what they paid for an item. Knowing the sale price gives the collector the leverage to bargain with the dealer.

"The Killer Shrews," American International, 1959, dramatic scene of rat-like tail & high heel, one-sheet, 27 x 41" ... **$200-300**

"The Lady from Shanghai," Colbumia, 1947, starring Rita Hayworth & Orson Welles, sexy full-length portrait of Hayworth, one-sheet, linen-backed, 27 x 41" **$2,868**

"The Lives of a Bengal Lancer," Paramount, 1935, starring Gary Cooper, Franchot Tone, Richard Cromwell & Sir Guy Standing, one-sheet, linen-backed, 27 x 41" **$2,868**

Miscellaneous

Game, "E.T. - The Extra-Terrestrial" game, board-type, Parker Brothers, 1982, complete in box **$10-15**

Magazine, "Famous Monsters of Filmland," dramatic cyclops image on cover, March 1964 .... **$35-75**

Game, "James Bond 007 Thunderball Game," board-type, Milton Bradley, 1965, complete in box **$35-50**

Game, "James Bond Secret Agent 007 Game," board-type, Milton Bradley, 1964, complete in box **$25-40**

Lunch box & thermos set, Benji, blue plastic w/color image of Benji, King Seely Thermos, 1974, the set **$10-25**

Golden Globe award, presented to Steve McQueen as World Film Favorite for 1969, awarded in 1970, 8 1/2" h. **$10,800**

Photograph, studio portrait of Douglas Fairbanks, by Preston & Duncan of Hollywood, autographed, ca. 1920s, 22 x 17" **$115**

Photograph, black & white image of Marilyn Monroe by Cecil Beaton, signed & inscribed in red ink "To Howard, luck and love, Marilyn Monroe," 1956, 7 1/4 x 8" **$9,000**

Photograph, portrait of Joan Crawford, by George Hurrell, inscribed by Crawford to Clark Gable, early 1930s, 11 x 14" **$2,629**

Photograph, studio portrait of Bela Lugosi, personally inscribed by Lugosi, early 1940s **$818**

Photograph, black & white publicity shot of the four leading stars of Casablanca - Humphrey Bogart, Ingrid Bergman, Paul Henreid & Claude Rains, signed in red ink by each actor next to their image, 1942, 8 x 10" **$8,400**

MUSICAL INSTRUMENTS

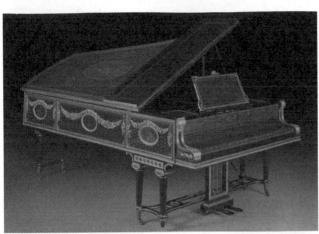

Grand piano, Louis XVI-Style, kingwood, mahogany, parquetry, marquetry & giltwood, the hinged top inlaid w/lozenge parquetry & centered by an oval reserve depicting foliage & insects, the border banded w/Vitruvian scrolling, the garland-hung sides decorated w/rosettes within lozenges, each panel centered by a framed oval reserve w/a foliate trophy, the music stand w/foliate & insects, signed "John Broadwood - & Sons - London," on six Ionic columnar tapering legs w/casters, England, ca. 1895, closed 59 1/2 x 101", 38 1/2" h. **$78,000**

Harp, child's, floor-type, painted wood, serpentine top above a fluted slender front column & tapering angled rear soundbox, impressed mark on base "PAT. FEB.17.74," old creamy white paint w/bronze-painted soundbox & details, ca. 1874, 21 1/2" w., 30 1/2" h. **$1,858**

> The harp is a favorite musical instrument in Celtic countries, and Ireland has used it as a political symbol for centuries.

Harp, floor-model, single-action w/a mahogany reeded column & burl veneer sound board, Egyptian Revival motifs of a rams' head, female forms & acanthus leaves, all brightly regilt, restored & regulated w/a partial replacement to the neck, signed "J. Erat Maker, Wardour Street, Soho, London 1248," ca. 1805-07, w/ burgundy cloth cover & wooden case, 35" w., 66" h. **$5,175**

Snare drum, painted wood, ceremonial- type, round w/ bentwood rims & body, painted w/an oval reserve centered w/ yellow lettering "Cadets 1786," & bordered in black letters w/the motto "Monstrat Viam" (It Points the Way), topped w/a label w/ black stenciled wording "From H. Prentiss 33 Court St. Boston," replacement heads & new rope included, for the First Corps of Cadets, an organization of the Massachusetts National Guard, 19th c., imperfections, 16 1/2" d., 17 1/2" h. **$3,525**

Hurdy gurdy, 23-key organ w/31 violin & flute pipes in front & bottom, front of case w/decorative inlay & marquetry w/mother-of-pearl & an embossed image of a Victorian lady, seven-tune pinned cylinder, original paper label listing tunes, hardwood case w/ beveled brass corners, in playing condition, Muzzio Organ Works, Glen Rock, New Jersey, ca. 1920s, replaced leather straps & wooden bottom frame, 15 1/2 x 17", 18" h. **$4,600**

NAUTICAL ITEMS

The romantic lure of the sea, and of ships in general, has opened up a new area of collector interest. Nautical gear, especially items made of brass or with brass trim, is sought out for its decorative appeal. Virtually all items that can be associated with older ships, along with items used or made by sailors, are now considered collectible, for technological advances have rendered them obsolete. Listed below are but a few of the numerous nautical items sold in recent months.

Lifeboat binnacle, brass, w/ gimbaled mounted compass & side oil lamp w/burner, marked by Coubro & Scrutton, Ltd., London, England, 9" h. **$323**

Sea chest, painted wood, rectangular hinged one-board top w/canted-form side brackets & inset strap hinges opening to a side till w/lock, dovetailed sides w/ molded base & rope end handles, old blue over older brown paint, old top crack, one rope handle broken, 19th c., 21 1/2 x 40", 16 1/2" h. **$390**

Sextant, ebony, brass & ivory, appears to be all intact w/three round lenses & four square lenses, brass wing arm w/ivory scale & ivory name plate, by Thomas Jones, Liverpool, England, some minor cracks & chips, missing two small screws on the back, old finish, 19th c., 9 1/2 x 10" **$288**

Ship half-model, carved & laminated wood, American, late 19th - early 20th c., 47" l., 7" h. **$2,708**

Ship model, carved & painted wood, model of the mid-19th c. fully-rigged clipper ship of the "Cutty Sark" class, finely executed w/all necessary deck equipment, belaying pins, anchors, winches, rudder, lifeboats in perfect scales, w/sisal ladders & running gear on an actual planked hull, Scotland, ca. 1900, 10 1/2 x 36 1/2", 28 1/2" h. **$1,150**

Ship model, the whaling ship "Lacoda, New Bedford," three-masted model constructed of wood in natural finish & white & black paint w/a copper-clad hull, seven small whaling boats attached, w/an old American flag & rigging, 19th c., 39" l., 33 1/2" h. **$4,025**

Ship model, pilot boat "Meteor" of Boston, steam & sail boat w/ fine woodwork including decks, lifeboats, masts & hull, hull painted red & black, desk is white & natural, in a fine wood & glass case, late 19th - early 20th c., model 31" l., 20" h. **$1,035**

Ship's bell, cast bronze, stamped on side "U.S.," 20th c., 9" h. **$118**

OFFICE EQUIPMENT

By the late 19th century business offices around the country were becoming increasingly mechanized as inventions such as the typewriter, adding machine, mimeograph and Dictaphone became more widely available. Miracles of efficiency when introduced, in today's computerized offices these machines would be cumbersome and archaic. Although difficult to display and store, many of these relics are becoming increasingly collectible today.

Pencil sharpener, cast iron & steel, marked "Specialty Mfg. Co. Decatur, Ill.," a round dished base centered by an angled adjustable steel sharpener, late 19th c., 4" l. (ILLUS. left Automatic sharpener) **$115**

Pencil sharpener, cast iron & wood, marked "Automatic Pencil Sharpening Co." rectangular wood base supporting a square container below a large flat vertical cutting wheel beside a small cylindrical neck for inserting the pencil, early 20th c., 5 1/2" h. (ILLUS. right with Specialty sharpener) **$172**

Cash register, National Cash Register Model 333, nickel-plated brass under later gold paint, early 20th c., 17 1/2" w. (ILLUS. on top of oak floor-style case) **$259**

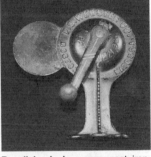

Pencil lead sharpener, cast iron, rotary type, upright style w/round disk-form top on flattened pedestal w/screw holes at the base, large side crank handle w/wooden grip, embossed "The Webster Pencil Sharpener - Patent June 21, '92 - F.S. Webster Co. New York, Boston, Chicago," 98 percent original japanning, rare........ **$172**

Corporate seal stamp, cast iron, plunge-type, tall upright scroll handle supported by an arched upright figural lion head & ending in a die-cut logo stamp, stamp marked "Brooklyn Majestic Theatre of New York," painted black w/gold trim, ca. 1885 .... **$205**

Cash Register, National Cash Register Model 91, ornate embossed bronze leaf-leaf case, original natural finish w/dark patina, early 20th c., 23" w. **$345**

PAPERWEIGHTS

New England Glass Company apple weight, figural apple in red, green & yellow laying on its side on a colorless cookie glass base, late 19th c., Massachusetts, 3" l. **$1,150**

New England Glass Company pear weight, figural pear in deep rose & yellow laying on its side on a colorless cookie glass base, late 19th c., Massachusetts, 3" l. **$604**

Orient & Flume "Cabbage Rose" weight, chartreuse matte ground decorated overall w/a large stylized golden iridescent cabbage rose design, designed by Dan Shura, engraved w/signature of the designer, company name & "May 1980 - 4/50 E," original Orient & Flume label, 3" d. **$288**

Bronze, model of a turtle, by E.T. Hurley, molded "ETH/0?6," fine original patina, early 20th c., 4 1/4 x 6 1/2"... **$1,840**

Baccarat, "Wallflower with Garland" weight, green, white & red arrowhead cane center w/six green leaves, stem & a red bud, garland of green, white & red canes alternating w/red & white stardust canes, star-cut base, 19th c., 2 3/4" d. **$2,420**

Perthshire "Bouquet Swirl" weight, clear glass set w/a colorful swirled floral bouquet w/yellow, blue & red & white flowers & green leafy stems on a band of black swirls & a cobalt blue ground, signature cane reads "1988-P," original paper label & fitted box w/numbered certificate, 3" d. **$345**

Clichy "Scattered Millefiori" weight, colorful bed of bright pastry mold, florettes & edelweiss canes including two Clichy roses on a clear ground, 19th c., 3 1/8" d.. **$1,760**

Sandwich "floral" weight, seven-petaled cobalt blue blossoms on eight green leaves w/pastel blue centered white millefiori canes around the edge, attributed to Nicholas Lutz, 2 1/2" d. **$489**

PAPIER-MÂCHÉ

Various objects, including decorative adjuncts, were made of papier-maché, which is a substance made of pulped paper mixed with glue and other materials, or layers of paper glued and pressed and then molded.

Tea caddy, a blockfront-shaped box w/a hinged cover, black ground, the top decorated w/ a h.p. landscape w/a castle, the front & sides w/bands of ornate scrolls composed of inlaid mother-of-pearl & h.p. floral clusters, top opens to a dividedd lidded interior, molded base on bun feet, ca. 1890, 5 1/2 x 7 3/4", 5" h. **$1,093**

Table, small occasional-type, the oblong top w/serpentine edges centered by mother- of-pearl inlaid florals, raised on a slender pedestal decorated w/gilt designs above the tripartite base on three scrolled feet w/further gilt decoration, late 19th c., 14 x 17", 25" h. **$1,475**

Tray, dished oblong shape w/bold serpentine sides, the center h. p. w/a large foral bouquet w/an exotic bird, a parcel-gilt trailing vine border band, now on a later stand, England, Regency era, early 19th c., 24 1/2 x 32" **$1,495**

Anyone selling antiques at a garage sale should not expect to receive price-guide prices. Garage sale shoppers want bargain prices. When selling to dealers, expect to get 40 to 60 percent of retail prices. To receive top prices, avoid the middleman and sell directly to other collectors.

Tray, oblong w/serpentine dished rim, black ground h.p. in the center w/a large floral bouquet & around the border w/leaf & blossoms clusters, in the manner of Jennens & Bettridge, England, mid-19th c., turned wooden stand of later date, 25 x 32 1/8", stand 16 1/4" h. **$1,160**

CZECHOSLOVAKIA

PERFUME, SCENT & COLOGNE BOTTLES

Decorative accessories from milady's boudoir have always been highly collectible, and in recent years there has been an especially strong surge of interest in perfume bottles. Our listings also include related containers such as pocket bottles and vials, tabletop containers & atomizers. Most readily available are examples from the 19th through the mid-20th century, but earlier examples do surface occasionally. The myriad varieties have now been documented in several recent reference books, which should further popularize this collecting specialty. Also see other glass categories.

Czechoslovakia

Perfume bottle & stopper, clear cut glass lay-down type, in the shape of a cornucopia w/a facet-cut stopper, ca. 1910, 4 1/4" l. **$200**

Perfume bottle & stopper, black cut glass bottle in a stepped cross-cut design & a small cylindrical neck, fitted w/a very tall flattened & pointed lilac stopper w/cross-cutting & a sprig of flowers, paper label reads "Irice - Made in Czechoslovakia," ca. 1920s-30s, 7 1/3" h. **$300-350**

Perfume bottle & stopper, clear cut glass pyramidal bottle w/a small neck, fitted w/a tall flat rectangular stopper w/an intaglio design of a troubador, ca. 1920-30s, 5 1/2" h. **$240-275**

Perfume bottle & stopper, rectangular block-cut clear crystal bottle w/a small neck fitted w/a large flattened block-cut red crystal stopper, no dauber, signed, ca. 1920s-30s, 4 3/8" h. **$285**

Authentic cut glass has a sharp feel to the edges, while molded glass is smoother. Cut glass is also heavier because it contains lead oxide. To create cut glass, rotating wheels of various sizes were used to cut complex patterns into the glass. One error could ruin a piece, so it required the abilities of a highly skilled artisan.

England

• Before hiring an auctioneer, attend one of his auctions and observe him in action. The auctioneer's performance at the sale is not the only consideration, but it is one of the most important. Does the auctioneer have command over the auction and does he work in a professional manner? Is the auction well-attended? If there is any question about the auctioneer's integrity, look for someone else.

• Whether you're selling a single item or an estate, always enter into a written contract with an auctioneer. The contract should list terms and conditions of the sale including commission rate, advertising and fees, and clarify responsibility for unsettled accounts, such as bad checks. The date, time and place of the auction must be specified. The contract should also specify when the seller will be paid.

Perfume bottle & stopper, satin glass, dusty pale blue w/a ring of bluish violet at the base, swelled ovoid body tapering to a short gilded neck w/gilt & blue ball stopper, highlighted overall w/gold beads, late 19th c., 5 3/4" h. (ILLUS. upper right with two Stevens & Williams satin glass perfume bottles) **$259**

Germany

Perfume bottle & powder box, porcelain, figural, designed as a lady in 18th c. dress in yellow w/green trim, her upper body lifts off to expose the powder box, her upper body forms the perfume bottle topped by a small metal crown-form stopper, ca. 1930s, 7 1/4" h. **$525**

Japan

Cologne bottle w/flower cluster stopper, Noritake china, Art Deco man wearing checkered cape, lustered sides, 6 3/4" h. **$470**

Cologne bottle & stopper, Grape & Cable patt. Carnival glass in marigold, Northwood Glass Co. **$150**
Cologne bottle & stopper, Grape & Cable patt. Carnival glass in purple, Northwood Glass Co. **$175**

Perfume bottle w/cap, Mt. Washington egg-shaped bottle, white opaque w/a pale beige ground h.p. w/irises in amethyst & blue, 4" h. **$1,438**

Cologne bottle w/original stopper, Star & Punty patt., paneled sides & stopper, canary, Boston & Sandwich Glass Co., ca. 1860, minor flakes, 6 1/8" h. (ILLUS. right with yellowish green Star & Punty cologne) **$286**
Cologne bottle w/original stopper, Star & Punty patt., paneled sides & stopper, yellowish green, Boston & Sandwich Glass Co., ca. 1860, minor flakes, 6 1/8" h. (ILLUS. left with canary Star & Punty cologne) **$440**

Perfume Bottle Makers

England

Stevens & Williams

Perfume bottle & stopper, satin glass, honey amber & bittersweet mother-of-pearl Swirl patt., spherical body w/a short flaring neck & matching ball stopper, creamy white interior, attributed to Stevens & Williams, England, late 19th c., 5 1/2" h. **$748**

Perfume bottle w/cap, satin glass, turquoise blue mother-of-pearl Swirl patt., spherical body w/a sterling silver collar & bulbous leaf-cast cap dated Birmingham, England, 1887, bottle attributed to Stevens & Williams **$633**

Thomas Webb

Scent bottle w/cap, cameo glass, lay-down type w/a pointed teardrop shape, deep red overlaid in white & cameo-carved w/water lilies & a dragonfly, original gold-washed metal screw-on cap w/répoussé designs, 3 1/4" l. **$3,335**

Gallé

← **Scent bottle w/cap,** cameo glass, bulbous creamy white ground overlaid in orange & cameo-carved w/large flowers & leafy vines, a silver band on the small neck w/hinged cap opening to the original glass stopper, raised on a silver foot band, silver marked "C & M" & rearing lion & "G" in a shield, signed in cameo on the side, 5 1/2" h. **$1,438**

Scent bottle w/cap, lay-down type w/long pointed teardrop form in deep red shaded to pink & enameled in gold & white w/a long leafy stem w/blossoms & a gold butterfly, minor gold wear, 6 1/2" l. **$690**

France

Baccarat

Perfume bottle & stopper, "Champs Élysées" by Guerlain, a Baccarat bottle in clear glass, figural design of a turle, a limited edition, w/orignal label, ca. 1904, original box not shown, 4 1/2" h. **$800- 1,250**

Daum - Nancy

Scent bottle & stopper, Daum - Nancy cameo glass, spherical white body tapering to a short neck w/a clear stopper w/faceted edges trimmed in gold, the body cameo-cut & enameled w/a leafy vine of shaded red flowers & buds framing a black & white enameled scene of a road leading to a village, base signed w/etched signature, very small old chip inside lip, small flake on corner of stopper, 3 1/4" h. **$2,185**

POLITICAL ITEMS MARKET REPORT

Al Anderson of Anderson Americana (www.anderson-auction.com) said Obama fever has been a huge driving force in the political collectibles market, bringing renewed interest and new collectors. "During Obama's campaign, membership in the American Political Items Collectors club (APIC) increased to its highest level in ten or twelve years." He sees a higher level of speculative buying than in the past, as people are expecting prices for Obama memorabilia to appreciate more than previous presidents because of the historic nature of his election. Obama posters from one series of 1,000 copies are still selling for $1,000 each. Obama posters from Bruce Springsteen concerts are popular, too.

Anderson saw some slowdown in political collectibles in November 2008, but within three months they had returned to normal levels. "Medium and high-end items are doing great, while the low end is weak." eBay sales have dropped off noticeably, he noted, which suggests that most eBay political items are at the lower end of the market. His prices have not been affected a great deal. "What recession?," he commented.

Some blue chip collectibles are appreciating quickly. For example, a pin by Clifford Berryman, the cartoonist who created the teddy bear associated with Teddy Roosevelt, sold for $6,800 in 2008. A pin in similar condition sold for $11,000 only nine months later. Anderson predicts that if the recession gets worse, lower-end items will drop more, but top level pieces will go higher as people turn to tangible investments.

A number of trends have developed in the last few years. Interest has grown for pre-presidential collectibles. A notable example is the pin from Obama's 1996 run for the Illinois state senate, which sold for $3,683. Only a few of these pins have turned up, since Obama was almost unknown then and no one anticipated him becoming President. This price is higher than anything generated by the Bushes, Clinton, Reagan, or Carter. Anderson commented that some people who didn't vote for Obama are collecting his material, which isn't normally the case, as people usually collect only the candidates they vote for.

Other growing categories include items from local offices like mayor, and causes like Women's Suffrage, World War II patriotic pins, and Vietnam anti-war pins. Anderson recalls with regret dumping Vietnam anti-war pins for $5, as they are now selling for $200 to $500. Collectors also like collectibles from one-day events, as they are produced in relatively limited quantities. Items related to Obama's announcement of his presidential candidacy in Springfield, Illinois, fall into this category.

The 1960s have proven to be the hottest era because of the political turmoil and the quantity of material made during that time. Kennedy items can sell for $5,000 or more. Ironically, Nixon's notoriety has made his collectibles sought after, too. Early- to mid-20th-century items, like Teddy Roosevelt and FDR can range from $5 to $10,000 depending on rarity. Nineteenth century items like Lincoln flags are some of the rarest and most desirable and can easily cost $10,000 or more.

Auction Houses
Heritage (www.ha.com)
Hakes (www.hakes.com)
Anderson Americana (www.anderson-auction.com)

POLITICAL ITEMS

CAMPAIGN

Campaign

Bandanna, 1904 campaign, Parker-Davis Republication presidential candidates, jugate-style design on cloth, pair of large American flags centered by a large star swag back above oval black & white portraits of the candidates above a red banner across the bottom reading "Good Government For The People," very minor staining, 22 x 23" **$187**

Banner, 1884 campaign, Blaine-Logan Republication presidential candidates, cotton cloth printed w/blue, white & red bands, the blue band w/white stars & the white band printed in black w/the candidates' names, minor soiling, 27 x 40" **$276**

Cane, 1896 campaign, Willian McKinley Democratic presidential candidate, hollow tin round head molded in relief w/a bust portrait of McKinley framed by "McKinley - 1896," wooden shaft, some denting & wear to head, 33" l. . **$205**

Banner, 1936 campaign, Alfred Landon, Republican presidential candidate, long swag-style cloth printed at each end w/blue stripes w/two white stars flanking two wide bands of red & white stripes, all centered by a dark blue square printed in color w/a portrait of Landon above sunflowers & w/crossed American flags behind, printed in white "For President - Alfred M. Landon," yellow cord fringe at bottom, some light aging & fading, very small hole in bottom left corner, 36" l. **$1,530**

Ferrotype token, 1872 campaign, jugate tintype photo portrait of Democratic candidates Horance Greeley & his running mate, Gratz Brown, in a rectangular brass frame stamped w/flowers, photo a bit light, 3/4 x 1" ... **$506**

Flag, 1860 campaign, Stephen Douglas & Herschel V. Johnson, Democratic presidential candidates, printed cloth American flag design w/the white stars arranged in rings, printed in blue w/"Douglas - Johnson," moderate fading, some damage at the top, 13 1/2 x 22" **$3,795**

Pin, 1864 campaign, Abraham Lincoln, silvered brass shield shape embossed w/the wording "Republican Invincibles," an oval paper photo of Lincoln in the center, original pin on back missing **$1,201**

Pennant, 1912 campaign, Woodrow Wilson, Democratic candidate, dark blue felt w/a printed color-tinted bust portrait of Wilson & "Our next President" in white, excellent conditioin, 23" l. **$213**

Pin, 1884 campaign, jugate-type, Blaine & Logan Republication presidential candidates, brass shield & tassel frame enclosing small cardboard photos of the candidates, 1 1/8 x 1 1/4" . **$248**

Pinback button, 1904 campaign, Theodore Roosevelt, colorful design of Roosevelt mounted on horseback wearing his Rough Rider outfit, American flag in the background on a hill printed in black "San Juan," black wording around the rim "Theodore Roosevelt - For President 1904," minor stain, 1 1/4" d. **$743**

Pinback button, 1908 campaign, jugate- type, Taft & Sherman, Republican presidential candidates, large round button printed in gold, dark & light blue & centered by a portrait of the Statue of Liberty illuminating oval photos of the two candidates, some minor fading, 1 3/4" d. **$2,444**

Poster, 1864 campaign, Abraham Lincoln & Andrew Johnson, white ground w/a large black central oval w/black & white portraits of Lincoln & Johnson at the top & bottom & oval triple portraits of Union generals at each side, printed across the bottom "The Defenders of Our Union," near mint, 19 x 24" **$1,091**

Poster, 1900 campaign, jugate-type for William McKinley & Theodore Roosevelt, white ground printed in red "Do You Read The Boston Journal - The Leading Republication Newspaper of New England...," large black & white photos of the candidates, some minor deterioration, 20 x 27" **$991**

Poster, 1920 campaign, jugate-type, Harding & Coolidge, Republican presidential candidates, printed in black on white on heavy cardboard w/a large racing train above oval portraits of the candidates, printed in black "U.S. Special - 'Let these two Lads off at Washington, D.C.,'" very minor edge imperfections, 14 1/2 x 22" **$463**

CAMPAIGN

Poster, 1960 campaign, coattail-type poster w/a black & white photo of John F. Kennedy & Congressional candidate Healey, red, white & blue background bands printed in white "Kennedy For President - Healey For Congress - Vote Democratic - Leadership For The 60's," 13 x 21" **$311**

Poster, 1944 campaing, jugate-type for Franklin Roosevelt & Harry Truman, white ground printed in red "Roosevelt - Truman" w/ large center sepia-tone photos of the candidates, near mint, 11 x 14 1/2" **$529**

Brooch, 1840 campaign of William Henry Harrison, sulfide, rectangular, gold tone metallic scroll-decorated frame holds image of log cabin w/"Harrison" above & "& Reform" below, all in white on lime green ground, rare vertical orientation, w/original pinback clasp, 7/8 x 1" .. **$1,794**

Cane, 1896 presidential campaign of William McKinley, a figural metal bust handle w/gilt finish, marked w/his name around the base, on a wooden shaft, top 3 1/8" h., overall 35 1/2" l. (ILLUS. of top) **$403**

Clock, 1896 campaign of William McKinley, mantel type, bronze-plated metal, rectangular central panel w/4" d. clock face w/Roman numerals, the date "1896" & Republican slogan "Sound Money," below which is a rectangular plaque reading "Protection - Prosperity," the central panel flanked by images of sailing ship on one side & factory machinery on the other, a 5" h. bust of McKinley topping all, molding at top & bottom, on rectangular wooden base, rare, about 15" h. **$1,497**

Cane, 1976 presidential campaign of Jimmy Carter, the molded metal handle in the shape of a large peanut w/the raised name of the candidate, painted in light & dark brown, on a brown-finished hardwood shaft, overall 33" l. **$196**

CAMPAIGN

Goblet, 1872 campaign of Ulysses S. Grant & Henry Wilson, blown glass, clear, w/incised bust portraits of the two candidates, one on either side, 3 1/2" d. bowl, short knobbed stem, 6" h. . **$991**

Flag, 1840 campaign of William Henry Harrison, printed silk, a square-shaped American flag w/a circle of white stars on blue in the upper left, the wide red & white stripes centered w/a sepia-colored wreath enclosing the name & bust of the candidate, the slogan "The Hero of Tippecanoe" in white stripes below, archivally framed, extremely rare, some very fine professional restoration to a few small holes, 27 x 28" **$10,189**

Newspaper, 1948 Harry Truman campaign, famous "Chicago Daily Tribune" error edition headlined "Dewey Defeats Truman," complete edition, near-mint condition, 16 1/2 x 23 1/2" **$892**

Magazine Inaugural souvenir edition, 1961, "Inaugural Spectacle" published by Life Magazine, packed w/photos & text recounting first hours of John F. Kennedy's presidency, w/ink inscription on front "To Mrs. Frank W. Burke, with very best wishes, John Kennedy" **$984**

Phonograph record & sleeve, 1924 Calvin Coolidge campaign, the gold-colored recording centered by a black & white portrait of Coolidge & titled "A Campaign Talk - 1924 - President Calvin Coolidge," near mint, the set **$168**

CAMPAIGN

Pin, 1896 McKinley & Hobart campaign, jugate type, stamped brass w/a spread-winged eagle above two oval openings w/a cardboard photo of McKinley & his running mate, Hobart, a shield & crossed flags at the bottom, fine condition, 1 1/4 x 1 1/4" **$271**

Pin, 1928 campaign of Al Smith, 2 1/2"-d. celluloid pin w/sepia portrait of Smith & encircling caption reading "For President - Alfred E. Smith" suspended on textured flag replica anchored by brass pinback bar & tucked into button's collet, the rear reading "The Whitehead & Hoag Co. - Newark, N.J. - Buttons, Badges, Novelties and Signs," overall 4" l. (ILLUS. front & back).......... **$604**

Pinback button w/hanger, 1912 campaign of Theodore Roosevelt, 2 1/4" d. button w/color portrait of Roosevelt flanked by words "Bull" & "Moose," "Theodore Roosevelt" at bottom, a brown composition moose, the symbol of Roosevelt's Progressive Party, hanging from a ribbon attached to the pin, rare, overall 5" l. **$3,850**

Pinback button, 1896 presidential campaign between William McKinley & William Jennings Bryan, round pinback type w/color caricature of McKinley wearing blue dress, short lacy pantalettes & Napoleonic hat & riding a hobby horse, the words "My 'Hobby'" in arch over illustration & "A Winner" beneath, rare, some moisture staining, minor surface blemishes, faint discoloration on reverse rim, 2 1/4" d. **$3,618**

Pinback button, 1904 campaign of Theodore Roosevelt, color illustration of saluting Roosevelt in Rough Rider regalia astride horse, a large flag planted on distant hill labeled "San Juan" in background, encircling caption reading "Theodore Roosevelt - For President 1904," marked w/copyright of Charles K. Cohn of Detroit, 1 1/4" d. **$685**

Pinback button, 1908 campaign of William Jennings Bryan, 2 1/2" d. button w/portrait of candidate in center, "For President - Wm. J. Bryan" around rim, w/flag ribbon suspended below, the original back paper insert stamped w/its maker, J.H. Shaw of Philadelphia, overall 5" l. **$498**

Pinback button, 1908 campaign of William Howard Taft, celluloid, center sepia portrait of Taft encircled by red & dark blue border w/gold scroll & bead decoration & gold shield w/flag center, 2 1/4" d. **$455**

Pinback button, 1940 Wilkie-McNary campaign, jugate type, blue printed bust photos of the candidates surrounded by American flag banners, scarce, 7/8" d. **$443**

Pinback button, 1924 campaign of Calvin Coolidge, black & white photo of Coolidge in center, a gold-trimmed red, white & blue border bearing words "Support the Coolidge Administration," 1 3/4" d. **$818**

Pitcher, 1840 campaign of William Henry Harrison, ceramic, decorated on one side w/ mulberry-colored illustration of candidate flanked by draped flags under words "The Country's Hope" & over "Harrison & Reform," the other side w/illustration of Harrison's campaign symbol, the log cabin, w/plaque hanging from front door reading "To let in 1841," below the shell- form spout a spread-winged eagle holding in its beak a banner reading "Union for the sake of Union," C-form applied handle, gold trim, 11" spout to handle, about 8" h. **$8,210**

Plate, 1840 campaign of William Henry Harrison, ceramic, w/log cabin & cider barrel trademarks of the campaign in the center, the scalloped rim ornately decorated w/basketweave design & floral garlands w/three oval bust portraits of Harrison in profile w/his name spelled out around the edges alternating w/three cartouches holding urns of flowers, the reverse w/logo inscription log cabin, repaired edge crack on back of rim, 6" d. **$613**

Plate, 1828 campaign of Andrew Jackson, china w/a center printed w/black & white bust portrait of Andrew Jackson framed by the wording "General Jackson - The Hero of New Orleans," narrow & white pink lustre band trim, near mint, very rare, 6 1/4" d. **$2,271**

Political box, 1876 campaign of Samuel J. Tilden & Thos. A. Hendricks, mechanical type, heavy brass, the top w/two oval openings for images protected by a thin sheet of mica, the windable paper scroll advancing to show side-by-side portraits of every president from George Washington to Ulysses Grant, in working order, only known example, 1 7/8 x 3 1/8", 1/2" h. **$2,444**

Poster, 1900 campaign of William Jennings Bryan, full color litho "Octopus" poster, a 9 x 12" portrait of McKinley w/scroll & laurel leaf border under banner reading "No Crown of Thorns - W.J. Bryan - No Cross of Gold" & flanked by flags, the top reading "The Issue - 1900 - Liberty - Justice - Humanity," the bottom reading "Equal Rights to All - Special Privileges to None" in red, w/many images & symbols throughout including gold Liberty Bell reading "1776," silver Liberty Bell reading "1900 - No Imperialism," crowing rooster, plowshare, Statue of Liberty, blindfolded Justice, a silver coin reading "Dollar of the Daddies," a smaller gold coin, uniformed men waving flags, robed female figure raising ax above image of octopus whose tentacles entwine various businesses, copyright 1900 by Neville Williams of Columbus, Ohio, lithographed by Strobridge of Cincinnati, Ohio, w/applied linen backing, 19 1/2 x 29 1/2" **$5,670**

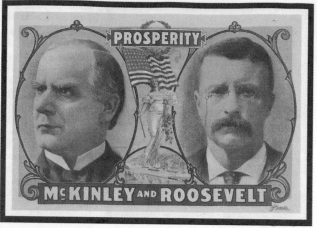

Poster, 1900 campaign of William McKinley & Theodore Roosevelt, full color litho, jugate portraits in oval scroll borders flanking figure of Liberty holding American flag standing over scene of bustling commerce, bold white lettering reading "PROSPERITY" in red panel at top, "MCKINLEY and ROOSEVELT" in red panel at bottom, 28 x 40" **$7,225**

Poster, 1932 campaign of Herbert Hoover, printed in black & white, artwork by Christy w/the large upper portrait showing the figure of Victory holding a wreath aloft & standing on the back of a large eagle, reading "the Dawn of Victory - Stand By Our President - Re-Elect Herbert Hoover," one small edge tear at bottom, unusual, 22 1/2 x 32" **$944**

Poster, 1960 campaign of John F. Kennedy & Lyndon Johnson, jugate type, cardboard w/a dark blue ground printed w/black & white photo of the candidate and white & red wording reading "Go Forward with John F. Kennedy & Lyndon B. Johnson - For Progress and Security - Vote Democratic," very minor color retouching, some minor creasing, 22 x 28" .. **$622**

Ribbon, 1860 campaign of Abraham Lincoln & Hannibal Hamlin, pink, w/fringed edge, reads "Prairie City - REPUBLICAN CLUB" over illustration of two hands clasped in unity under spread-winged eagle holding banner in its beak reading "United we stand - Divided we fall," bottom reading "For President - ABRAHAM LINCOLN - For Vice President - HANNIBAL HAMLIN!" 2 5/16 x 4 3/8" **$3,581**

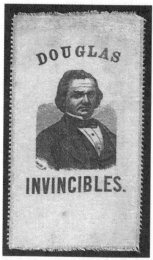

Ribbon, 1860 campaign of Stephen Douglas, white w/delicately scalloped edges on sides & original selvage across top & bottom edges, central black & white illustration of Douglas, "DOUGLAS" in arch over illustration & "INVINCIBLES" below, hint of water toning, 3 1/4 x 5 5/8" **$2,018**

Toothpick holder, 1904 campaign of Alton Parker & Henry Davis, milky opalescent pressed glass in the Ring & Beads patt., black w/portraits of the candidates & American flags, a flying eagle, American shield & their names, 2 3/8" h. **$818**

Stickpin, 1916 campaign of Charles Evans Hughes, celluloid, flag-shaped, w/black & white oval portrait of candidate alongside colored shield reading "For President," a red, white & blue flag & green laurel branch in the background, 7/8 x 1 1/8" flag on 2 3/8"-l. ball-topped stickpin **$498**

Streamers, 1876 campaign of Rutherford B. Hayes, three red, white & blue ribbons, one stenciled w/the name of the presidential candidate, Hayes, the second w/the name of his running mate, Wheeler, and the third "Garfield," for James Garfield (later president), then running for Congress, brown cord connecting them, each ribbon 2 x 14" **$190**

Non-Campaign

Bowl, glass, clear, round shape w/ bottom decorated w/frosted image of bust of U.S. Grant in profile, the sides reading "The Patriot and Soldier - Gen. Ulysses S. Grant," scalloped rim, 9 1/4" d. .. **$45-65**

Almanac, dated 1784 & printed & sold by Norman & White, Boston, 1783, the cover w/an engraved symbolic scene commemorating the American victory in the Revolutionary Ware, various symbolic figures standing around a small oval portrait of George Washington, cover image captioned "Washington - Victory doth thy Trumpets sound, who are with Laurels cover'd round!," 22 of 24 pp., trimmed close to right edge & bottom, original twine binding **$513**

Badge, tin shell-type pinback badge printed w/a sepia bust portrait of President Grover Cleveland, possibly a souvenir of his 1893 inauguration, worn gilt border band, 1 1/2 x 2" **$84**

Flag holder, ceramic, cone-shaped, red w/color bust of George Washington in oval framed w/ words "George Washington Bi-Centennial 1732-1932," 3" h. **$20-25**

Bust, bronze, figure of Abraham Lincoln, marked "Geo. E. Bisell Gorham Co. Founders 046, Copyrighted SC," 16 7/8" h. **$500**

Banner, painted & appliqued fabric, first displayed at the Great Central Sanitary Fair in Philadelphia in June 1864, the month Abraham Lincoln visited the Fair, a dark blue ground w/deep red border band, large gold wording across the top reading "Proclamation of Emancipation" above a large oval portrait of Lincoln flanked by anti-slavery medals & above an American eagle & shield, the lower half w/a large ribbon printed in gold "By The President of the United States of America" over another ribbon flanking the U.S. Capitol dome & reading "June 1864," fringe along the bottom & hanging ribbons at the top, extremely rare & unique, 68 x 69" **$123,258**

Cane, figural, the handle formed as a brass bust of President Franklin Roosevelt, his name at the front & also marked "Century of Progress," sold at the Chicago Century of Progress world's fair in 1933, on a black wooden shaft, top 2 3/4" h., overall 36" l. **$403**

Clock, bronzed cast metal, figural, Franklin Roosevelt beside a large ship's wheel enclosing a clock dial w/Arabic numerals & sweep seconds hand, "Roosevelt" molded below the wheel, the platform base printed "At the Wheel for a New Deal," w/original cord & plug, not running, early 1930s, 13 1/2" h. **$170**

Framed prayer, "Washington's Prayer for our Country," the words of the prayer flowing around an illustration of George Washington on bended knee w/ hands clasped as if in prayer, ca. 1970, 8 3/4 x 10 3/8" **$10-12**

Impeachment ticket, black-printed orange paper, large section reading "U.S. Senate - Impeachment of the President - Admit The Bearer - Gallery - April 2, 1868," for the impeachment trial of President Andrew Johnson, complete w/stub, minor spotting.. **$1,903**

Letter opener, sterling silver, flat curved blade printed w/a bust portrait of Ulysses Grant titled "Gen. Grant," the flat handle cast in the shape of a Grand Army of the Republic badge, possibly 1870s or 1880s, light wear, toned patina, 4" l. **$367**

Memorial textile, brown printed on tan cloth, a memorial for George Washington, depicting a large arched portico w/Washington standing on a pedestal in the center, a fort & harbor in the background & a memorial urn, flags & other patriotic emblems below him, tall obelisks flanking the portico, long memorial quote across the top, signed at the bottom "Printed & Published at Glasgow - C.G. 1819," small tears & holes, minor staining, pinned to card backing, in early 20th c. frame, image 19 1/4 x 24 3/4" **$2,645**

Photograph, imperial card-sized sepia- toned portrait of U.S. Grant seated beside a table, by A. Bogardus & Co., New York City, ca. 1880, beveled gilt edge w/only minor wear, 7 1/2 x 13" **$493**

NON-CAMPAIGN

Pin, gilt brass, a souvenir of the 1893 inauguration of Grover Cleveland, top pin bar reading "Souvenir," shield-shaped pendant stamped w/profiles of President & Mrs. Cleveland & "Courage - Consistency," 1 1/4 x 1 1/2" **$130**

Pitcher, creamware, early Liverpool jug- style, bulbous baluster shape w/rim spout & strap handle, transfer-printed in black on one side w/a military bust portrait of George Washington & the inscription "Washington crowned with laurels by Liberty," all above a draped flag, Liberty cap & American eagle, the reverse w/a printed design of a large sailing warship flying the American flag, probably 1790s, 7 3/4" h. **$6,356**

Plaque, metal w/bronze-colored finish, model of Liberty Bell under bust of Thomas Jefferson & crossed flags & reading "1776 - 1926 - Sesquicentennial," 6 1/2" h. **$20-25**

Plate, glass, clear, round shape w/ bottom decorated w/frosted image of bust of John F. Kennedy, 8" d. **$45-50**

Ribbon, paper, red, white & blue stars & stripes design w/bust of George Washington in oval at top, "1732 - Washington - 1799" at bottom, back reads "Fold back this flap and use for pinning to coat," 4" l. **$40-50**

Ribbon, woven silk, color design of an American eagle & shield at the top above a leafy wreath enclosing a bust portrait of a beardless Abraham Lincoln, woven at the bottom "A. Lincoln - President," made in Switzerland & signed "L. Chevre," probably celebrating his inauguration in 1861, some light yellowish staining, silk brittle w/several separations, 7 3/4" l. **$253**

Plate, porcelain, Spanish-American War commemorative, dark blue border band, the center w/American flags & the Statue of Liberty and portrait of President McKinley & other American military leaders, banner reading "A Souvenir of the Cuban War 1898," 12" d. . **$299**

POP CULTURE COLLECTIBLES

The collecting of pop culture memorabilia is not a new phenomenon; fans have been collecting music-related items since the emergence of rock and roll in the 1950s. But it was not until the 'coming of age' of the post-war generation that the collecting of popular culture ememorabilia became a recognized movement.

The most sought after items are from the 1960s, when music, art and society were at their most experimental. This time period is dominated by artists such as The Beatles, The Rolling Stones and Bob Dylan, to name a few. From the 1950s, Elvis Presley if the most popular.

Below we offer a cross-section of popular culture collectibles ranging from the 1950s to the present day. Also see: RECORDS.

Andy Warhol brogues, brown leather stamped on the insole in gold w/the mark of Ferragamo, splattered w/white, red, green & pink synthetic polymer paint, worn by Warhol in the mid-1980s, size 8, pr. **$7,800**

Andy Warhol necktie, burgundy, grey & white striped silk, labelled "Brooks Brothers," worn by Warhol in the 1970s, accompanied by a color photo of Warhol wearing the tie, 3 1/4 x 5 1/4" **$480**

Andy Warhol outfit, a pair of blue denim Levi jeans, the left leg splattered w/flecks of pink paint, the right leg splattered w/flecks of green paint, & a polo-necked sweater of black cashmere labeled "Halston," worn by Warhol in the 1980s, 2 pcs. **$960**

Andy Warhol sunglasses, metal frames w/yellow-tinted lenses, worn by Warhol in the 1960s, arms broken **$600**

Andy Warhol wig, silver & dark grey wig w/three strips of toupée tape applied to the inside, worn by Warhol in the 1980s **$10,800**

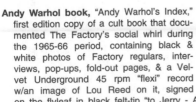

Andy Warhol book, "Andy Warhol's Index," first edition copy of a cult book that documented The Factory's social whirl during the 1965-66 period, containing black & white photos of Factory regulars, interviews, pop-ups, fold-out pages, & a Velvet Underground 45 rpm "flexi" record w/an image of Lou Reed on it, signed on the flyleaf in black felt-tip "to Jerry - Andy Warhol," record signed "to Denny - Andy Warhol," 1967, some 70 pp. (ILLUS. open) **$1,554**

POP CULTURE COLLECTIBLES

Andy Warhol tee shirt, black & white image of a torn Campbell's soup can label, back reads "Andy Warhol at Colorado State University, Fort Collins, Colorado 1981," faded siganture on the front $75-150

Andy Warhol flyer, yellow paper w/ black wording, advertising an Andy Warhol & rock band appearance at the Fillmore, two-sided w/a Los Angeles Times review printed on the back, May 1966, 5 1/2 x 8 1/2" $800-1,400

Aretha Franklin RIAA Gold Record, for her album "Lady Soul," marked the sale of one million dollars worth of this Atlantic Records long-playing record album, matted & framed, 16 x 21" $837

Beatles record carrier, Disk-Go Case, round yellow plastic w/white handle, printed black images of the band members, found in various colors, 1960s $175-400

Beatles game, "Flip Your Wig," Milton Bradley, 1964 .... $125-225

Beatles lunch box, vinyl, printed in black "The Beatles Kaboodle Kit," sepia printed photos of the band members & facsimile autographs, Standard Plastic, 1964 .... $300-800

Some show promoters charge an early buyer fee for admission to their show a few hours before opening the gates to the public. Customers must decide if the fee, which can be $20 or more, is worth the expense. Even with the advantage of shopping before the public arrives, the show may have been picked clean of bargains by dealers during the show setup. On the other hand, the savings realized by just one good purchase may more than cover the early buyer fee.

POP CULTURE COLLECTIBLES

Beatles lunch box, steel, blue background w/color-printed graphics, Aladdin, 1965 (ILLUS. left with matching thermos) **$350-800**

Beatles movie poster, "Help," United Artists, 1965, the heads of the four Beatles across the top, title & credits below on a yellow ground, one-sheet, linen-backed, 27 x 41" **$837**

Beatles record, "Love Me Do/P.S. I Love You," 45 rpm, framed w/original sleeve, Tollie #9008 .... **$80-250**

Beatles record, "Do You Want to Know a Secret/Thank You Girl," 45 rpm, framed w/original sleeve, VeeJay #587 .... **$75-160**

Program book, "Beatles (U.S.A.) Ltd." concert tour, 1964 .... **$45-60**

Beatles record album, "Songs, Pictures and Stories of The Fabulous Beatles," mono, VeeJay #1092, 1964 .... **$250-500**

Paul & Linda McCartney magazine, "Manchete," Brazilian magazine, April 1990, signed in black felt-tip pen by the couple, 9 x 12" **$478**

Beatles scrapbook, "The Beatles Scrap Book," colorful cover w/portraits, Whitman, 1964, 11 x 13 1/2" **$75-125**

Program book, "Beatles (U.S.A.) Ltd." concert tour, 1965 .... **$45-60**

Beatles autographs, blue fountain pen on paper, on a piece of Oberoi Intercontinental letterhead signed by all four band members while they were in India, 1967, 5 1/2 x 7" **$3,107**

Beatles beach hat, black graphics on white & dark blue cloth, found in various colors, 1964, each **$75-110**

Beatles concert tour program book, "Beatles (U.S.A.) Ltd.," color photo of the band members, framed w/a concert ticket, 1966 .... **$80-150**

Beatles guitar, Hofner bass guitar w/a violin-shaped body in a sunburst finish & a later-replaced mahogany neck signed by John Lennon, Paul McCartney & George Harrison as well as Chet Atkins, Jim Reeves, Chubby Checker, Cliff Richard & Joe Frasier, each signature later carved into the wood, guitar ca. 1959, signed in 1964, overall 41" l. **$7,170**

Beatles cup, ceramics, tall slightly tapering shaped printed in black, white & blue w/pictures of the band members, made by Washington Pottery, England, 1960s, 4" h. **$75-150**

→

Beatles guitar, toy-type, "Beatles New Sound Guitar," hard plastic in white printed w/black & white portraits & red & black trim, by Selcol, England, 1964, 23" l. **$350-625**

Beatles linen, large rectangular cloth printed in the center w/large portraits of the band members in brown, black, white & tan, black & white border band of musical instruments, Ulster, Ireland, 1964, 20 x 31" **$75-150**

Beatles record album, "The Beatles Yesterday And Today," infamous "Butcher Cover" showing the four w/pieces of raw meat & doll parts, pulled from the market, first state, Capitol Records, partially sealed, 1966, 12 1/2" sq. **$4,780**

Beatles Yellow Submarine lunch box, pressed steel, Thermos, 1968 (ILLUS. left with thermos)... **$300-650**

Beatles wallet, pink printed vinyl w/brown photo transfer of the band, Standard Plastic, 1964 .... **$75-160**

Beatles Yellow Submarine toy, diecast model of the submarine, sealed in original box, Corgi, 1968 .... **$350-550**

Beatles Yellow Submarine switch plate cover, color-printed cardboard, DAL Mfg., 1968, in original package, 6 x 10 1/2" **$50-75**

POP CULTURE COLLECTIBLES

Beatles tray, squared metal w/rounded corners, printed in color w/portraits of each band member on a white ground, by Worcester, "Made in Great Britain" sticker on the back, 1964 .... **$35-75**

Bob Dylan lyrics, hand-written in black ballpoint pen on a piece of paper, reading "I'll know your song - well before you more start - singing - And it's a Hard - Rain's a gonna- Fall! - Bob Dylan - '63," 1963, 5 1/2 x 8" **$3,346**

George Harrsigon autographed print, colorful romantic scenes w/black print & lower panel with his autograph **$850-2,500**

Elvis Presley RIAA Gold Record, for album "From Elvis Presley Boulevard Memphis," presented to Taylor Harley- Davidson for the sale of more than 500,000 copies of this album, RCA Records, Inc., matted & framed, 16 x 21" **$777**

Elvis Presley caricature, done by well known artist Al Hirschfeld, Number 147 out of an edition of 150, large 15 x 20" **$1,021**

Elvis Presley record & sleeve, RCA-Victor 45 rpm record of "Never Ending" on A- side & "Such a Night" on B-side, w/original photograph sleeve in red, black & white, the sleeve signed in black ballpoint ink "Thanks from - Elvis Presley," sleeve 7" sq. **$1,195**

Ringo Starr authographed drum head **$350-900**

POP CULTURE COLLECTIBLES

Eric Clapton guitar, blue Fender Stratocaster electric guitar, signed in gold ink by the musician **$2,390**

Fleetwood Mac album, the album "Fleetwood Mac" printed in black & white, the jacket signed by all members of the band in blue or black felt-tip ink, also w/two black & white glamour photos of Stevie Nicks, 12 1/2" sq. **$299**

Rolling Stones concert program, printed in black & white, signed on one page by all members of the band in blue fountain pen, together w/the program cover signed by all members of The Ronettes, who were on the same bill, 1964, 7 x 9 1/2" **$1,793**

Jim Morrison check, written to Morrison on November 6, 1970 in the amount of $100, endorsed by him on the back in blue ballpoint pen, 3 1/2 x 8 1/2" **$1,434**

Frank Sinatra signed menu & sketch, a printed paper Jilly's menu in red, white & black, centered by a quickly rendered Sinatra self-portrait & signed "John - Frank Sinatra," done in blue felt-tip ink, noted in lower left-hand corner in orange by a different hand "Tuesday night 5/9/72," 10 x 12" **$1,195**

Elvis Presley vest, brown polyester & tan suede adorned w/numerous gold-colored studs, worn by Elvis, interior label reads "JC Costume Co. - Hollywood, California," w/1992 letter of authenticity that indicates this was worn as everyday wear by Elvis **$23,900**

Keith Richards guitar, amber-colored Fender Telecaster electric guitar, signed in black felt-tip ink "YCAGWYW - '97 - Keith Richards," meaning "You Can't Always Get What You Want," w/color snapshot of Richards w/this guitar **$2,868**

POSTERS MARKET REPORT

Robert Chisholm of Chisholm Larsson Gallery (www.chisholm-poster.com) in New York City) said that while his walk-in business is down, his Internet business has been steady, due in part to international customers. Chisholm Larsson ships all over the world; in fact, just minutes before being interviewed, Chisholm had sold posters to buyers in Dubai and Spain.

According to Chisholm, "Businesses have been buying posters for their offices instead of fine art, since they can buy five posters for the cost of one painting. Customers in their mid 30s gravitate toward '60s posters. Post World War II movie posters are hot too and go for $200 to $500. Swiss Mid-century posters are popular and run $500 to $1,000. Early 20th century French posters are too old for most people to enjoy. They are also rare and at $1,600 to $5,000 are typically the domain of sophisticated high-end collectors."

Chisholm said fakes aren't all that common and can generally be spotted fairly easily. He does encounter some reproductions printed by Portal Publications of California, which in the '60s and '70s reproduced a large number of classic movie posters such as the *Wizard of Oz* and *Gone with the Wind*. These posters are marked with the Portal Publications name, so they aren't intended to deceive, and often that information is included in eBay listings, but many people don't realize that they aren't originals.

Chisholm cautions buyers to pay close attention to condition when purchasing and to frame posters to protect them from dirt and fingerprints. "It is also important to avoid hanging posters in bright sunlight and to use UV filtered glass or Plexiglas to keep them from fading. In addition, don't hang posters in a bathroom, damp basement or anywhere with high humidity," he said. Check regularly for fading, wrinkling, foxing, and other damage, so steps can be taken early to prevent further damage.

Chisholm further warns collectors "not to dry mount collectible posters, even if a framing or other specialist encourages it. Dry mounting permanently attaches a poster to a background using heat sensitive tissue. Dry mounting is fine for posters that are just used as decoration, but not for valuable posters. Have collectible posters linen mounted instead. This process uses a water soluble paste that can be removed if necessary."

Posters that need to be stored should be stored flat if room permits. However, posters can be rolled, if necessary, as long as they are rolled loosely and not placed in a tight tube.

Chisholm suggests that collectors buy what they like rather than for investment. He also recommends giving gift certificates rather than trying to choose artwork for others, since tastes are very personal and subjective.

Auction Houses
Heritage (www.ha.com)
Doyle New York (www.doylenewyork.com)
Swann (www.swanngalleries.com/index.cgi)
Poster Connection (www.posterconnection.com)
Poster Auctions International (http://www.postersplease.com/)

POSTERS

Book, chromolithograph advertising a French novel, "Une Jeune Marquise-Romand'UneNévrosée -Par Théodore Cahu," scene of a distressed young woman seated beneath a tree, artwork by Jules Cheret, France, late 19th c., creases, some staining, backed w/rag board, matted & framed, 40 1/2 x 54 3/4" **$489**

Masked ball, color lithograph on paper showing costumed late Victorian carnival-goers, printed in red & black "Theatre de L'Opera - Carnaval 1894 - Samedi 6 Janvier - 1er Bal Masque," by Jules Cheret, France, ca. 1894, signed in the plate, 34 x 48" **$3,824**

Safety glass, lithographed in color, a styled figure of a man in black breaking through a shattering window against a dark blue & black ground, green & white wording "La Glace - Securit - se brise sans eclats coupants," by Charles Loupot, France, ca. 1931, signed in the plate, framed, 31 1/2 x 47 1/2" **$4,541**

POSTERS

Tournament of Roses, color lithograph, a bold graphic design w/an action scene of football players at the top framed by an arch of roses all against a light blue ground, printed in yellow & blue "Tournament of Roses - New Years Day 1910 - Midwinter Floral Pageant - Brown University vs State College of Washington - Pasadena California," some foxing & wear, framed, 18 x 26" **$1,300**

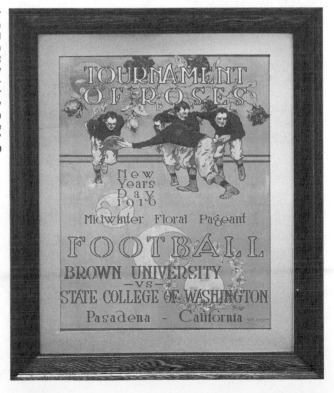

Before the arrival of the Internet, only the largest auction houses had an international following. To get top prices on important items, sellers had to sell through the major houses. Now regional auction houses using the World Wide Web can attract international bidders.

PURSES & BAGS

Novelty Purses

Novelty purses put the "fun" in functional, and in the years following World War II, these whimsies reached their zenith of popularity. One reason for this boom was the result of wartime research that led to the development of new materials and the refinement of old. Such materials were easily adapted to a variety of peacetime uses, including fashion accessories.

Some of the new purse designs were adaptations of earlier styles: the "carryall" or compact purse was a reworking of the more upscale "minaudiere," first introduced by Van Cleef & Arpels. Beaded bags, popular since the 1800s, were now embellished with colorful plastic, wooden and oversized "caviar" beading. Tapestry and needlepoint bags of old were also reborn, often as do-it-yourself kits. Even leathers received a makeover, with hand-tooled designs that relied heavily on Spanish, Mexican, and South American motifs.

New materials and techniques also attracted interest. Bamboo, wicker and straw bags become favorites, often in shapes resembling birdcages and picnic baskets. Actual commercial containers, such as strawberry baskets, egg crates and cheese boxes were also remade as purses.

Plastic proved a newly inexpensive purse material, and, thanks to wartime advances, these bags could now stand up to scuffs, repel water, and be styled in nearly any size, shape or color. Purses fashioned from exotic animal skins also continued to find buyers. Alligator, crocodile and snake had long been fashion favorites, but the goal was now to make them appear as "natural" as possible. Alligator bags, for instance, were offered complete with the actual head and claws.

Some new novelty purse designers specialized in applied art decorating a plain purse with jewels, sequins, felt and other objects to create a three-dimensional illustration. The most famous name in applied purse art was Enid Collins, whose "Collins of Texas" linen, saddle and wood box bags featured whimsical jeweled scenes. Other firms such as Atlas and Souré Bags also had success in this field, but Collins led the way.

Another innovation was the Lucite handbag. Although they held little, were fragile and had garish styling, Lucite purses became a commercial success. Their acrylics could be clear, opaque, tinted or laced with glitter. They also had a wonderful light-transmitting transparency and could be carved, cast or molded. Major manufacturers of Lucite purses included Charles S. Kahn; Dorset-Rex; Florida (Miami) Handbags; Gilli Originals; Gira; Llewellyn Inc. ("Lewsid Jewel"); Majestic; Maxim; Myles Originals; Nelson Originals; Patricia of Miami; Rialto; Toro; Vanity Fashions, and Wilardy Originals.

A comprehensive overview of novelty purses is included in *Popular Purses: It's In The Bag!* by Leslie Pina and Donald-Brian Johnson (Schiffer Publishing Ltd. 2001). Photos for this category are by Dr. Pina with text by Mr. Johnson.

Alligator bag, complete w/alligator head clasp **$200-250**

Bamboo basket bag, composed of sewn split strips **$70-90**

Enid Collins "Glitter Bugs" bag, linen decorated w/jeweled insects, mahogany base **$100-125**

Lucite bag, carpetbag shape, the sides w/an overall gold threaded design w/diamond-patterned end panels **$125-150**

Lucite bag, log-shaped, a toroiseshell base, amber lid, by Rialto **$150-170**

Whiting & Davis

One of the most successful marketing campaigns of the early 20th century was conducted by the Whiting & Davis Company to promote its line of mesh handbags. Prior to the 1909 invention of the automatic mesh-making machine, mesh was hand-linked, a process both time-consuming and costly. With automation, bags could be produced quickly and economically. Whiting & Davis capitalized on this by promoting its product as both an affordable fashion accessory and as a desirable "special occasion" gift. Early film favorites including Joan Crawford appeared in Whiting & Davis ads, and such fashion arbiters as Paul Poiret and Elsa Schiaparelli contributed exclusive designs to the line.

Many Whiting & Davis decorative patterns are reflective of the firm's 1920s and 1930s heyday, featuring Art Deco-influenced geometrics and arresting color combinations. Scenic and figural depictions were also popular, with subjects ranging from modernistic skylines and moonlit beaches to exotic birds, dancing couples, and even movie stars. Over the years, variations on the traditional Whiting & Davis bag have included compact bags, gate-top bags, miniature coin purses, and children's purses. Although other mesh manufacturers emerged,

including Evans, Napier, and Miller Brothers, Whiting & Davis remained the industry leader. The company's most resilient competitor, Mandalian Mfg. Co., specialized in bags with a Middle Eastern flavor, often heavily trimmed with metal fringe and drops. Whiting & Davis acquired Mandalian in the 1940s, soon incorporating the company's techniques and stylings into its own designs.

In the late 1940s and 1950s, Whiting & Davis moved into "solids" - mesh bags all in one color, often gold. In the 1980s and '90s, the company also briefly expanded beyond mesh bags to the manufacture of other mesh accessories: vests, gowns, belts, headbands, and even jewelry. Among the designers whose work has appeared under the Whiting & Davis logo are Anna Sui, Richard Tyler, and Anthony Ferrara. Today, the company name and tradition continue in bags designed by Inge Hendromartono for Inge Christopher.

Complete information on the Whiting & Davis Co. is included in *Whiting & Davis Purses: The Perfect Mesh* by Leslie Pina and Donald-Brian Johnson. (Schiffer Publishing Ltd., 2002). Photos for this category are by Dr. Pina, with text by Mr. Johnson.

Beadlite mesh (armor mesh with the appearance of a beaded bag), Egyptian motif in orange, black & gold **$225-275**

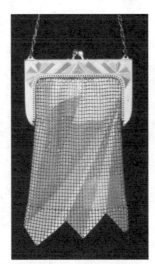

Beadlite mesh, decorated w/blue & orange asymmetrical sunrays, matching enameled frame **$225-275**

Charlie Chaplin bag, 1976 "Star Series" **$1,300-1,500**

Major antique shows often offer one-day seminars for collectors. The fee for attending is usually affordable, often goes to a charitable organization, and sometimes includes admission to the show. They are often conducted by prominent authorities in the trade or by leading dealers who are exhibiting at the show. Most seminars require registering in advance by contacting the show management.

"Dresden mesh" bag, fine ring mesh, pull- bead clasp $300-350

Double compact bag, dot stripes in blues & reds on gold mesh $700-800

Fountain design on gold mesh, blue metal drops at base $350-400

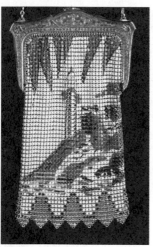

Lighthouse design, in shades of green mesh $350-400

Mandalian Manufacturing, yellow mesh w/central curtain panel, stepped base w/gold teardrops $375-425

Mandalian Mfg. "Peacocks" bag, ... $300- 350

Multicolor Modernistic shapes on mesh, enameled frame $300-350

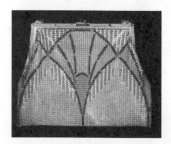

"Poiret Pouch," Egyptian palm fan motif, Paul Poiret design $225-250

RADIO & TELEVISION MEMORABILIA

Not long after the dawning of the radio age in the 1920s, new programs were being aired for the entertainment of the national listening audience. Many of these programs issued premiums and advertising promotional pieces that are highly collectible today.

With the arrival of the TV age in the late 1940s, the tradition of promotional items continued. In addition to advertising materials, many toys and novelty items have been produced that tie in to popular shows.

Below we list alphabetically a wide range of items relating to classic radio and television. Some of the characters originated in the comics or on the radio and then found new and wider exposure through television. We include them here because they are best known to today's collectors because of television exposure.

Charlie's Angels board game, Cheryl Ladd & other stars on the box cover, complete, 1970s **$10**

Battlestar Galactica action figure, "Imperious Leader," molded plastic, on original colorful card, Mattel, 1978 .... **$15-25**

Lost in Space weapons set, includes items showing through cutouts in lid labeled "2 Safe Plastic Roto Missiles," "Launch Cartridge," "Roto Launcher," "Shrieking Space-Tracer" & "Pistol," the red lid top reading "Lost in Space - Roto Jet Gun" in black & "Roto-Sound Weapons Set" in white above white panels w/black & white labeled drawings of weapons, flip side of window display features painting on heavy foil paper of Robinson family fighting off Cyclops monsters w/roto-jet components, in original partially sealed box.... **$7,737**

Charlie's Angels jigsaw puzzle, multiple color images of the original stars, complte w/box, 1977 .... **$8**

Howdy Doody cookie jar, cov., figural head of Howdy, Purinton, 1950s **$863**

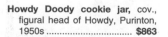

Clarabell's horn, bicycle type, red & black, in original bright yellow & black box without lid reading "ton-air" in bold red lettering & "horn" in black script w/ascender of "h" forming treble clef, Sound Devices, Inc., 1950s........... **$611**

RADIO & TELEVISION

Howdy Doody marionette, composition head w/painted features, hinged lower jaw controlled by string, original clothing, unplayed-with condition in original box, marked "Howdy Doody - ©Bob Smith - Marionette - manufactured by Peter Puppet Playthings, Inc. - Made in U.S.A.," 16" h. **$240**

Orphan Annie book, "Annie Paper Doll Book - Punch-out dolls of Annie & Sandy," Happy House by Random House, 1982, complete & near mint, 8 1/2 x 12" **$12**

M*A*S*H cast photo, black & white glossy photo of cast members in costume, caption at bottom identifying actors, signed in various inks by Larry Linville, Loretta Swit, Alan Alda, McLean Stevenson, Wayne Rogers, Bill Christopher, Gary Burghoff & Jamie Farr, 8 x 10 .... **$902**

Alf doll, plush & felt, Talking Alf, plays tapes, Coledo, 1986, 18" h. **$40-60**

Banana Splits lunch box & thermos, vinyl box w/metal thermos, colorful graphics, King Seeley, 1969, the set. **$350-500**

Lassie toy, stuffed plush model of Lassie w/rubber face, complete w/yellow photo ribbon, Knickerbocker, 1965, 18" l. **$45-75**

RAILROADIANA

At country estates, it is common to find signs of a burn pile, where papers and others items deemed to have no value were burned to clean out the house. Never discard anything old without the advice of someone who is knowledgeable about ephemera. Railroad schedules, stock certificates, and even old hunting licenses are collectible.

Fire grenade, clear tubular glass, embossed "C. & N-W RY," rough sheared & ground lip, smooth base, original dark blue contents, used on the Chicago & Northwestern Railroad, ca. 1880-1900, 17 3/4" h. **$146**

Lantern, "Illinois Central Railroad," tinned metal cage frame & high bail handle, short clear glass globe, early 20 th c., overall 15" h. **$47**

Railroad schedule, painted wood, a long rectangular board w/a double-arch top & the listings divided into two columns, for Interurban railroads, headed "Fostoria RR Bulletin" above the names of other cities & times, orginal worn grey, red & black paint, split in the middle, 19th c., 40" w., 74" h. (ILLUS. of part)............... **$1,955**

Lantern, enameled metal & glass, four bull's-eye lenses w/two in blue & two in amber, black body w/yellow & white shields, wire bail handle, top marked "Dressel Arlington N.J. U.S.A.," some minor rust & chipping, overall 20 1/2" h............................ **$127**

Lithograph, printed in color w/two rectangular scene, the narrow upper panel titled "The Mail Carrier of 100 Years Ago," the lower panel titled "The Flight of the Fast Mail on the Lake Shore and Michigan Southern RY," ca. 1875, framed in tiger maple frame, image 21 x 28" **$4,025**

Locomotive steam whistle, brass & iron, acorn finial atop brass cylinder, long lever side handle, marked "Powell," now on a wood block base, 18" h................... **$92**

ROYCROFT ITEMS

Elbert Hubbard, eccentric entrepreneur of the late 19th century, founded Roycroft Shops and established a craft community in East Aurora, New York in 1895. Individuals were trained in the trades of bookbinding, leather tooling and printing. Craft-style furniture in the manner of Gustav Stickley and known as "Aurora Colonial" furniture was produced. A copper workshop, begun in 1908, turned out numerous items. All of these, along with those pieces of Buffalo Pottery china which were produced exclusively for use at the Roycroft Inn and carry the Roycroft symbol, constitute a special category associated with the Arts and Crafts movement.

Book ends, hand-hammered copper, flat arched side, each half w/a tooled, raised blossom design, original patina, impressed mark, 5 1/2" h., pr. **$600**

Ashtray, floor model, hand-hammered copper, the round bowl-form top w/two cigarette rim rest & an arched handle topped by a bracket to hold a box of matches, raised on a tall slender cylindrical standard on a round foot, orginal patina, small dent at base, signed w/orb mark, early 20th c., 8 1/2" d. 30" h. **$840**

Tray, Arts & Crafts style, hand-hammered copper, round w/a dished center & wide flattened rim decorated w/three small tooled floral designs, original painta, impressed mark, 10" d. **$840**

Vase, hand-hammered copper, footed gently flaring cylindrical body w/a low ruffled rim band, original patina, impressed mark, 5 1/2" h. **$330**

Vase, hand-hammered cylindrical copper w/a closed rim, applied w/a pair of slender nickel bands suspending staggered drops around the sides, original patina, impressed mark, 6 1/4" h. **$1,480**

RUGS, HOOKED

Canada geese, rectangular scene of three Canada geese flying in a row w/a striped blue, pink & grey sky behind them & a tan landscape w/pale green fir trees below, wide black mottled border band w/thin white inner border band, original label from Grenfell Labrador Industries in one corner, Canada, early 20th c., 27 x 40" **$1,955**

Canada geese, rectangular scene of three Canada geese flying in a row w/a striped pale pink sky behind them & a landscape w/light & dark green fir trees below, wide brown border band w/thin tan inner border band, original label from Grenfell Labrador Industries on back corner, Canada, early 20th c., 26 1/4 x 39 1/4" **$4,560**

Dining table setting, long narrow rectangular form, depicting a folky design of a dining room table top set w/plates, cups & saucers, a platter, water pitcher & teapot, in shades of maroon, dark blue, yellow & brown on a tan ground w/maroon end sections, olive green burlap backing, late 19th - early 20th c., 36 x 88" **$2,990**

→

Floral blocks, room-sized, rectangular, the large rectangular center panel composed of fifteen squares each w/a large rounded flower blossom on a leafy stem in shades of deep pink, tan, brown & blue, wide tan border band w/a meandering grapevine in red & green & a red leafy flower in each corner, dark brown scalloped outer border, all-wool, old tag in one corner reads "Great Grandmother Abigail Voter," New Vineyard, Maine, 19th c., few small holes & some fading, overall 58 x 84" **$4,600**

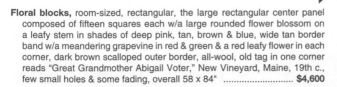

Cottage in a landscape, rectangular, a large oval center panel w/a large quaint multi-cabled pink cottage w/dark brown thatch-like roof & a tall red & black chimney, set back on a green lawn w/meandering flower-lined path, tall leafy trees at each side, a dark gold outer border, ca. 1920s, 27 x 53" **$173**

Dog in landscape, large recumbent animal resembling a Chocolate Labrador in dark brown w/black highlights, on a grassy mound w/a flowering shrub & reeds behind him & a rail fence in the distance, narrow black border band & narrow red inner border w/corner scrolls, burlap backing indicates it is from an E.S. Frost pattern, small section in border missing material, early 20th c., 29 1/2 x 55 1/2" **$1,150**

Geometric, long cotton & wool runner w/a central design of a band of large colorful diamonds framed w/a border of colored stepped pyramidal blocks, dark brown ground, late 19th - early 20th c., 35 3/4 x 77 3/4" **$1,434**

Repairs to an antique rug that have been well executed do not adversely affect the value. Obvious and poorly done repairs, however, will detract from the value. Repairs to valuable rugs should be done by a professional and as soon as possible to prevent further damage.

Florals, long rectangular form w/a central design of large red & dark gold flowers w/green leaves surrounded by black leafy scrolls outlined in red, smaller white, blue & red flowers at the ends, on a shaded tan ground, stabilized w/a burlap backing, late 19th c., small area of fabric loss, 33 1/2 x 66" **$470**

George Washington on horseback, a large colorful central design of Washington in uniform on a white stallion, a banner below reading "Father of His Country," flanked by dark maroon stage curtains, dark tan background, late 19th - early 20th c., 35 x 48" ... **$2,185**

Parrot & date, a life-sized colorful parrot sitting on a branch, the date "1896" to one side, black border w/salmon scrolls, wool on burlap w/additional backing, minor edge loss, mounted, 24 1/2 x 39 1/2" **$374**

Pinwheels, long rectangular form in wool, a large center pinwheel in shades of pink, blue, black, tan & yellow on a dark brown ground flanked by smaller pinwheels & red spots, tan corner blocks enclosing small pinwheels, mounted on wooden stretcher, some edge loss, 26 x 52" **$546**

Robin & dog, wool & cotton, a red-breasted bird perching on leafy maple tree branch filling foreground at one side, a dog looking up at the bird from the lower opposite side, against background of green w/blue sky above, all in primitive scroll border in yellows & reds on black ground, mounted on wood frame, America, 19th c., several small repairs, 25 1/4 x 38 1/2" **$1,293**

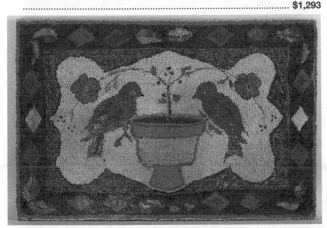

Robins, wool & cotton, brown rectangular central panel containing cream-colored cartouche w/two red-breasted birds perching on either side of flower pot, mounted on wooden frame, several losses & minor repairs, America, 19th c., 23 3/4 x 36" **$1,528**

Pot of flowers, square, the center w/a large cream-colored pot holding a branched plant w/cream & tan flowers on a dark greyish blue ground, large triangular corner blocks composed of numerous small squares in tans, cream & browns, one end fitted for hanging, small loss top top flower, late 19th - early 20th c., 24 x 25" **$805**

Sailing ships at sea, rectangular, seascape showing two-masted schooner in blue water against pink & yellow sunset, two other ships & birds in the distance, mounted on black fabric on stretcher in mottled frame, Grenfell label attached to back, 26 x 39" **$3,450**

Scottie dog, wool on burlap, rectangular, a black & green standing Scottie in the center on a mottled grey & white background, black, red & blue border bands, minor edge wear, small area of repair, 28 x 30" **$115**

Squirrels, two large facing seated brown squirrels on a black band against a grey background, narrow black border, small section of one squirrel missing material, 36" sq. **$900**

Starburst, large circular form composed of radiating bands of multicolored diamond- shaped segments & a central red eight- point star, applied wool braided edge, possibly Shaker, 19th c., some wear, 79" d. **$5,875**

Stripes, long rectangular form composed of narrow multi-colored stripes in shades of brown, blue, green, yellow, orange, red & black all within a thin black border band, burlap backing, late 19th - early 20th c., 33 x 57 1/2" .. **$863**

United States map, colorful design of the continental United States divided into different colored states, part of Canada, Mexico & the oceans seen, blue wave border, stitched penned label on the reverse "Edith Pailes Ipswich, Mass.," early 20th c., 43 1/2 x 69" **$1,093**

Village landscape, long rectangular form, worked in a variety of solid & mottled wool & cotton threads depicting the town of East Machias, Maine, hooked by Catherine Walker, White House Station, New Jersey, 35 1/2 x 65" **$5,378**

Valentine, rectangular, folk art style, the central area w/large flowering vine surrounded by frame of red hearts & blue crosses or Xs, "RWH" at top & "MBH" at bottom of frame, all in border w/corner bow ties, small hearts & arrows, "his Valentine" at top, "Feb 14" in one upper corner & "1941" in the other, "their rug" at bottom, two bites in bottom edge, 40 x 64" **$920**

Village scene, a grouping of simple cottages in a snowy winter landscape, a church steeple in the distance, in shades of brown, yellow, grey, white & blue, 18 x 34" **$546**

Welcome, rectangular, a semicircular panel w/large red flowers in center & flowering vines w/smaller red flowers arching over the word "Welcome" inscribed at bottom, all on natural ground within braided black border, 32 x 44" **$230**

Flatweave textiles have no knots and no pile. Because most flatweaves are reversible, they should be turned over regularly so wear is distributed evenly.

Winter landscape, rectangular, a figure wearing parka & boots walking w/dog through snow-covered hilly landscape w/evergreen trees toward cabin in distance w/smoking chimney, a crescent moon overhead, worked in unraveled burlap in shades of blue, green, red, tan & brown, w/tan line border within wider black border, woven maker's label on reverse, Grenfell Labrador Industries, Newfoundland & Labrador, early 20th c., 24 1/2 x 37 3/4" **$1,645**

Roosters & horse, two large stylized colorful roosters above a large dark brown running horse, all on a mottled tan ground w/areas of pale pink, mounted on new frame backing, 31 1/2 x 32 1/2" **$2,530**

Rectangles, rectangular, decorated w/graduated rectangles in varied geometric designs & colors of dark green, tan, gold, black & red, on a shaded pale green ground, light wear, mounted on a board backing, 21 1/2 x 32 1/2" **$143**

SCALES

Gold scales, iron & brass, includes five penny weight, in original leather-covered case w/a stamped eagle on top, 19th c., case measures 2 1/2 x 5 1/2" **$198**

Jewelry scales, brass, the delicate balance scale w/small pans enclosing in a glazed mahogany case w/a narrow drawer across the bottom, marked "Becker & Sons New York," 19th c., case, 15 x 19" **$230**

Balance scales, painted cast iron w/original pinstriping, left side ceramic platform marked "Fairbanks Standard" w/brass bin on right, base embossed "Fairbanks" & filigree, 13" w., 7" h. **$115**

Balance scales, analytical-type, small brass pans suspended from a pierced metal cross-arm on a central standard, on a rectangular mahogany base, marked "Central Scientific Co.," late 19th - early 20th c., 17 1/2" h. **$182**

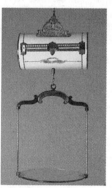

Sidewalk scales, lollipop-style, white porcelain tall case w/an relief-etched brass dial reading "Your Exact Weight," original cast-aluminum plaque reads "Do You Weigh What You Should?," by Mills, early 20th c., some flaking to mirror silvering, a few small porcelain chips, 75" h. **$920**

Store scales, hanging-type, white-painted steel, iron & brass, the cylindrical top scale suspending a round glass tray, made by the U.S. Computing Scale Co., Philadlephia, ca. 1901, restored, 15 1/2" w., 33" h. **$920**

Sidewalk scales, cast metal, Art Deco style w/framed top mirror in red enamel, one-cent coin slot for birth month, read-out in pounds, on a white enameled body w/ chrome decoration, foot plate w/marking of American Scale Manufacturing Co., Washington, D.C., ca. 1938, overall 61" h. (needs calibration).............. **$460**

Store scales, painted cast-iron, spring-action w/glass shelf & beveled glass rear window w/ brass trim, name bar across the top reads "Dayton Moneyweight Scale," patent-dated in 1917, professional restoration, 19 x 20", 31" h. **$805**

Steelyard scale, steel & brass, a slender brass arm w/flattened end suspending a ring, ring & hook & weight, stamped "Wm. B. Preston - Boston," 18 1/4" l. **$94**

SCRIMSHAW

Scrimshaw is a folk art byproduct of the 19th century American whaling industry. Intricately carved and engraved pieces of whalebone, whale's teeth and walrus tusks were produced by whalers during their spare time at sea. In recent years numerous fine grade hard plastic reproductions have appeared on the market, so the novice collector must use caution to distinguish these from the rare originals.

Walrus tusk, engraved on the left end w/a detailed whaling scene inscribed "Seeking The Sperm Whale" & "So. Pacific," engraved on the right end w/three large whales, probably American, 19th c., 17" l. **$4,451**

• Whale bone and teeth were originally used by sailors to make utilitarian shipboard tools. Only later were they used to make decorative objects. The first documented piece of decorative scrimshaw dates to 1817.

• The etched designs in scrimshaw were highlighted against their light background by filling them with dark colored materials such as tobacco juice and soot.

Doll, articulated figure of a lady w/ moveable lower arms, hardwood dress & shoes, inlaid collar & necklace, first half 20th c., 7 1/4" h. **$1,673**

Pie crimper primitive style, a flattened oblong handle w/a long slender curved & pointed tip, mounted w/a crude notched wheel, the handle engraved w/ ornate undulating scrolls, cross-hatching on the wheel, the edge w/some dot-sized decoration & "Grace Sewell," 19th c., 5 3/4" l. **$518**

Whale's tooth, engraved w/a bust portrait of George Washington in an oval reserve, over an American flag & a spread-winged eagle grasping an anchor of Hope & an olive branch in its talons, a banner inscribed "In God We Hope" held in its beak, a three-masted ship sails in the distance, the reverse engraved w/a scene titled "Sperm Whale Fishery," includes a spouting whale w/two scenes below, one of a harbor w/lighthouse, the other a whaling mother ship & three small whale boats w/a whale, scenes faintly trimmed w/red & blue sealing wax, American, 19th c., imperfections, 7 5/8" h. **$27,025**

Whale's tooth, engraved w/an elaborate landscape w/a large factory complex behind a row of trees & a harbor in the distance, inscribed "New England Screw Co. Providence," color-tinted, mid-19th c., 7 1/8" l. **$7,170**

SHEET MUSIC

SHEET MUSIC

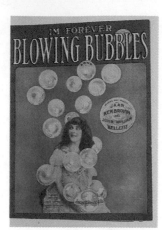

"Alexander's Ragtime Band," by Irving Berlin, ABC Music Corp, Alice Faye version, 1938 ...... **$3**

"Anchors Aweigh," Chas. A. Zimmermann, Navy emblem in red, white & blue on the cover, Robbins Music Corp., 1943 .... **$32**

"I'm Forever Blowing Bubbles," by Helen Carrington, Winter Garden Co., from The Passing Show of 1918 .... **$3**

"Joan of Arc They Are Calling You," by Jack Wells, Alfred Bryan & Willie Weston, World War I era, silhouetted image of Joan of Arc on cover **$5**

"Semper Paratus (Always Ready)," Official Coast Guard Marching Song, by Capt. Francis S. Van Boskerck, photos of large airplane, ship & life saving boat w/Coast Guard emblem on the cover, 1928 .... **$9**

"The Alcoholic Blues (Some Blues)," by Albert Vontilzer & Edward Laska, 1919 .... **$7**

"The Rose of No Man's Land," by James A. Brennan & Jack Caddigan, published by Leo Feiss, Inc., World War I era, dedicated to Red Cross Nurses w/photo of nurse on the cover, 1917 .... **$8**

"When I'm With You," from "The Poor Little Rich Girl" movie starring Shirley Temple, Alice Faye & Jack Haley, photo of Shirley, Alice & Jack on the cover, 1936 .... **$10-20**

SIGNS & SIGNBOARDS

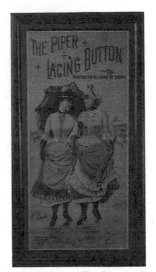

Medicine, "Dr. D. Jaynes's Family Medicines," reverse-painted on glass, wording in silver & gold against a black ground, original gold-painted wooden frame, minor flaw, ca. 1890, 14 1/2 x 26 1/2" **$1,568**

Lacing buttons, "The Piper Lacing Button," colorful lithograph showing to Victorian ladies walking along a beach w/their skirts raised as they step across the wet sand, w/original metal band at the top & bottom, slight restored damage near top metal band, probably late 1880s, framed, 18 x 32 1/2" **$1,323**

Medicine, "Dr. Pierce's Anuric Tablets," colorful lithograph w/a bright blue ground & wording in yellow & red, figure of suffering man at the left, a hand holding a bottle of the product at the center, framed, early 20th c., 8 2/3 x 23" **$805**

Medicine, "Dr. Harshorn's Aromatic Syrup of Rhubarb - A Pleasant Substitue for Every Other Physic," lithographed w/blue & gold wording on a buff coated stock, the package shown at the left, ca. 1884, matted & framed, image 8 x 12" **$420**

Medical remedy, "Munyon's Paw-Paw," relief-molded compostion, upright tall rectangular shape molded w/a tall fruiting tree in green w/yellow fruit above a brown sign w/red lettering, for a homeopahtic remedy, early 20th c., framed, wear to corners, some loss at top, 22 1/2 x 33 1/4" **$575**

After the Pure Food and Drug Act was passed in 1906, requiring ingredients to be disclosed, many manufacturers stopped producing their "medicines."

Saddler's shop, trade-type, carved & painted wood, tin & iron, a large board framing a tall recessed scroll panel w/a pair of overlapping iron horseshoes above a large finely molded tin horse head, 19th c., 18 1/4 x 32 1/2", 44 1/2" h. **$7,800**

SIGNS & SIGNBOARDS

Seeds, "Rice's Seeds," colorful lithographed rectangular paper printed w/a large comical scene of a laughing man bending over to harvest a huge cabbage, advertising in black, white & red reading "Try Rice's Seeds - True Early Winngstadt - Best Cabbage in the World - Grown by Jerome B. Rice," ca. 1890, minor moisture stain, framed, 21 3/4 x 27 1/2" **$1,093**

Shoe blacking, "French Dressing - Satin Polish - Army and Navy - Blacking," very detailed colorful lithographed tin centered by a large vignette of a Victorian family outside under a large tree, crossed American flags above & bottles of the products shown at each side, red, white & blue w/gold lettering on a white ground, ca. 1870s, framed, some light surface rust & blemishes, 17 3/4 x 23 1/2" **$10,063**

Shoes, "Lilly, Young, Pratt & Brackett, Boston, Mass.," albumen photo-type, centered by a grouping of three of their shoes below copies of medals won at the "World's Exposition - Vienna 1873," further advertising across the bottom, in period molded gilt-plaster frame, ca. 1873, near mint, image 11 x 15" **$230**

Soft drink, "Drink Pepsi-Cola," countertop plastic light-up type, self-framed, rectangular panel in dark blue w/a molded glass of Pepsi-Cola & the cap logo below the clear wording lighted by a rotating internal color wheel, ca. 1950s, working, 7 1/2 x 20 1/2", 10" h. **$2,013**

Steamship line, "Cunard Line," self-framed color-printed rectangular w/undulating rope border, a large color scene of the Lusitania under sail, this liner was sunk by a German U-boat during World War I, a few dents in border, scattered light chips & spotting, ca. 1910, 27 1/2 x 38 1/2" **$1,495**

Steamship, "Ericsson Line 20 Knot Day Boat - Between Phila. and Baltimore," self-framed colorful lithographed rectangular w/a large scene of the Lord Baltimore steamship pulling out of harbor, red wording on brown frame, early 20th c., professional paint restoration, 23 x 33" **$2,875**

Theatre, "The Greatest Show of The Plains - A Texas Ranger," colorful lithograph on heavy paper, showing an action scene w/various characters & a cowboy pointing a pistol at an attaching Indian, made by the National Painting & Engraving Company, self-matted, wooden frame, late 19th - early 20th c., 26 x 39" **$476**

Travel agency, "Voyages," neon-type, narrow rectangular frame w/stepped top centered by a white sailing ship below neon tubing & above the word in white outlined in neon, working condition, early 20th c., 8 x 96", 34" h. **$230**

STATUARY

Bronzes and other statuary are increasingly popular with today's collectors. Particularly appealing are works by "Les Animaliers," the 19th-century French school of sculptors who turned to animals for their subject matter. These, together with figures in the Art Deco and Art Nouveau taste, are common in a wide price range.

BRONZE

Bronze

Dalou, Aime Jules, "Moissonneur Affutânt sa Faux," a seated metalworker hammering on a sheet of metal, brown patina, signed "Sasse Freres ed. Paris - Dalou," 5 x 6", 5 1/2" h. **$1,380**

Ghiglieri, Lorenzo E., "First Jump," model of a mare & her colt making its first jump, patinated, on a conforming wood base, signed at base & dated "1999 - 25/135," limited edition, 10 1/4 x 28", 22" h. **$5,750**

Kauba, Carl, Native American Chief w/feathered headdress astride his horse & looking back over his shoulder, naturalistic ground mounted on a thick oblong tan rock slab w/a polished top & rough sides, signed "C Kauba - Geschutzt 6254," late 19th - early 20th c., 11 1/2 x 12 3/4", overall 14 3/4" h. **$2,875**

Mene, Pierre Jules, "The Pointer," realistic model of a hunting dog posed in full- point, on a naturalist base raised on a molded oval plinth base, signed "PJ Mene," good brownish patina, France, late 19th c., 4 x 11", 8" h. **$4,025**

Pierre Jule Mene (1810-1879) was a 19th century French sculptor considered an expert in lost wax modeling and one of the top artists of his time. He is best known for creating small bronze sculptures of domestic animals.

Leduc, Arthur Jacques, "Nessus et Dejanire," gilt-bronze group of a centaur w/a nude female riding on his back, rectangular base on a red marble plinth, France, late 19th c., 9 x 32", 30" h. ... **$5,175**

Mene, Pierre-Jules, "Fauconnier Arabe," equestrian group of an Arab w/a falcon, oblong naturalistic base w/Mene name inscribed, France, ca. 1890, 30 1/2" h. **$7,170**

Potter, Louis McClellan, Eskimo hunter walking holding a rifle & surrounded by four dogs, on a naturalistic base, base signed "Louis Potter 1905 - Copyright 1905 by Gorham Mfg. Co.," 10 x 17", 18" h. **$18,400**

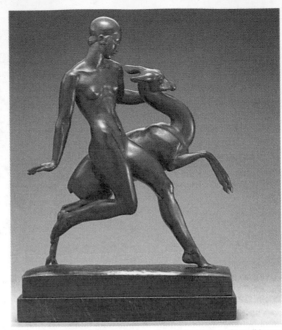

Traverse, Pierre, Art Deco style group of a nude female walking w/ a leaping fawn at her side, rectangular base on a black marble plinth, signed in the maquette & w/the mark of the La Stele Foundry, France, ca. 1925, 11 1/2" l., 16 1/8" h. **$7,765**

Marble

Figure of a nude youth seated examining one foot, titled "The Spinario," after the Antique, probably made in Florence, late 19th c., 24 1/2" h. **$1,725**

Lapini, Cesare, figure of a young girl seated on a chair w/her legs crossed, sewing, squared base inscribed at the front "Vouloir C'est Pouvoir," signed & dated, Florence, Italy, 1888, on a green marble pedestal, figure 27 1/2" h. **$29,875**

Noble, Matthew, bust of "Alexandra, Princess of Wales," signed & dated London, 1867, on a socle base w/some damage, 11 1/2 x 19 1/2", 29 3/4" h. **$5,175**

Other

OTHER

Alabaster, after Auguste Moreau, full- length figure of Aurora, goddess of the dawn, holding behind her a long slender metal crescent, on a domed & paneled base mounted w/a bronze plaque identifying the artist & subject, repaired thumb, late 19th - early 20th c., 31 1/2" h. **$4,485**

Alabaster, figure of a standing young maiden wearing a peasant costume & holding a lute, square marble base, some losses, 19th c., 19" h. **$259**

Terra cotta, stone-painted model of "The Dying Gaul," after the Antique, France, late 19th c., 20" l., 11" h. **$431**

Alabaster, model of a cockatoo w/ ebony- stained features & glass eyes, on a black plinth base, ca. 1970-80, overall 32" h. **$920**

Alabaster, standing figure of the young George Washington standing beside the felled cherry tree w/a small ax in one hand, on a Renaissance-style stained walnut pedestal, unsigned, late 19th c., figure 31" h. **$8,400**

Terra cotta, bust portrait of a young Victorian matron w/a finger-waved coiffure & a shawl across her front, signed "E. Beuilly - 1883," Etienne Beuilly, France, 19th c., 26" h. **$460**

Terra cotta, stylized figures of Native Americans "Nakoma" & "Nakomis," by Frank Lloyd Wright, ca. 1929, ... **$5,975**

STEIFF TOYS & DOLLS

From a felt pincushion in the shape of an elephant, a world-famous toy company emerged. Margarete Steiff (1847-1909), a polio victim as a child and confined to a wheelchair, planned a career as a seamstress and opened a shop in the family home. Her plans were dramatically changed, however, when she made the first stuffed elephant in 1880. By 1886 she was producing stuffed felt monkeys, donkeys, horses and other animal forms. In 1893 an agent sold her toys at the Leipzig Fair. This venture was so successful that a catalog was printed and a salesman hired. Margarete's nephews and nieces became involved in the business, assisting in its management and the design of new items.

Through the years, the Steiff Company has produced a varied line including felt or plush animals, Teddy Bears, gnomes, elves, felt dolls with celluloid heads, Kewpie dolls and even radiator caps with animals or dolls attached as decoration. Descendants of the original family members continue to be active in the management of the company, still adhering to Margarete's motto, "For our children, the best is just good enough."

Lion, airbrushed draylon body w/ brown mohair mane, surface dust, large, 49" l., 32" h. **$58**

Monkey, "60 PB," plush w/velvet hands, feet, ears & face & shoe button eyes, early string jointing w/ horizontal rod between shoulders, bent arms & inoperative voice box, large, some light wear, loose joints, ca. 1903, 32" h. ... **$6,613**

Teddy bear, white mohair, jointed body, swivel head, shoebutton eyes, brown floss nose w/ horizontal stitching, brown floss mouth, nice hump on back, long feet, original metal button in ear, early 20th c., very good condition, 5" **$476**

Teddy bear, beige plush w/glass eyes, felt pads, stitched facial features, hump back, missing button in ear, slight fur loss, moth damage to one paw, 13" h. **$288**

Teddy bear, brown plush, jointed body, shoe button eyes, stitched facial features, felt pads, hump in back, missing button in ear, spots of fur loss, replaced pads, ca. 1910, 16" h. **$3,600**

Teddy bear, white plush, jointed, glass eyes, open mouth, stitched nose & paws, felt pads, wearing leather collar, some fading, minor fur loss, 9" h. **$540**

TEAPOTS

Ceramic

Porcelain - 1750-1850

Arita Ware, squatty bulbous hexagonal form w/a short conforming neck & matching domed cover, paneled upturned spout & squared C-form handle, Imari-style decoration painted in bold colors of cobalt blue & iron-red, mounted w/European gold fittings including a chain connecting the ball finial to the cap on the spout & band on the handle, teapot from Japan, ca. 1700, gold mounts possibly 18th c. Dutch, overall 6 1/4" l. **$5,875**

Porcelain - 1850-1950

English bone china, teapot & undertray, the pot w/four small tab feet supporting the wide squatty molded body w/an overhanging domed cover w/blossom finial, serpentine spout & ornate C-scroll handle, matching round tray, each in white decorated w/green transfer-printed panels of scrolls & blossoms alternating w/small h.p. gold blossom sprigs, second half 19th c., undertray 8" d., teapot 7" h., pr. **$201**

Japanese porcelain, child's size from a snack set, squatty tapering body w/serpentine spout & angled handle, blue lustre body band & cover, h.p. colorful floral sprig, marked "Made in Japan," ca. 1920s-30s, 4 3/4" l., 3" h. ... **$15**

Japanese porcelain, figural Toby-style in the form of the Dickens character Mr. Pickwick, brightly decorated, "made in Japan" mark, ca. 1930s **$35**

Japanese porcelain, spherical body h.p. w/a Dutch windmill landscape scene, serpentine spout, ring handle & small cover w/knob finial, Takito Porcelain, ca. 1930s **$35**

Japanese porcelain, child's size from a tea set, footed bulbous body w/flat shoulder & wide mouth, shaped spout & angled loop handle, domed cover w/knob finial, gold lustre background painted w/large stylized flowers, marked "Japan," ca. 1920s-30s, 3" l., 3 1/8" h. **$15**

CERAMIC

Japanese porcelain, spherical footed body, applied loop handle, short serpentine spout, slightly domed cover w/knob finial, body & lid decorated w/large pink roses & green leaves, handle, spout, finial & rim highlighted in silvery grey, marked "Made in Japan," ca. 1930s, 5 1/2" h. **$35**

Japanese porcelain, Thousand Faces patt., tall ovoid body w/serpentine spout & C-form handle, orange trim, "Made in Japan" mark, ca. 1930s, 6 3/4" l., 6" h. **$65**

Japanese porcelain, Thousand Faces patt., tall waisted body w/serpentine spout & pointed angled handle, black trim, rising sun & "Made in Japan" mark, ca. 1930s, 7 3/4" l., 8 1/8" h. **$75**

Japanese porcelain, wide swelled cylindrical body w/a curved shoulder & flat rim w/inset cover & knob finial, serpentine spout, C-scroll handle, h.p. w/a landscape scene of a cottage next to a lake, early 20th c., Takito Porcelain, Japan **$45**

Japanese porelain, footed tall, gently flaring cylindrical body w/narrow shoulder to a domed cover w/knob finial, long serpentine spout, C-scroll handle, h.p. Japanese landscape design, marked "Futani (?) - Hand Painted Japan," ca. 1930s **$20-30**

Maling (C.T.) & Sons porcelain, upright waisted squared body w/small rim spout, angled handle & low domed cover w/button finial, Blue Willow style decoration, produced for & marked by Ringtons, Limited, Tea Merchants, England, ca. 1930s **$225**

CERAMIC

Occupied Japan porcelain, bulbous tapering body molded w/bright colored stylized flowers, serpentine spout, C-scroll handle & low cover w/ knob finial, 1945-52 .... **$35**

Thermolite Chapus, paneled conical body w/a neck ring & short cylindrical neck w/conical cover & tapering cylindrical knob, paneled angled spout & angled handle, overall scattered floral sprigs, France, ca. 1940s **$125**

Unknown maker, lobed, slightly waisted cylindrical shape w/tapering shoulder & flaring ruffled neck, C-scroll handle, serpentine spout, domed lobed lid w/cut-out finial, the white body w/gold acorn design & green shading, gold highlights on rim, spout, handle & finial, embossing on shoulder & lid, probably Germany, late 19th c., 6" h. **$125**

Porcelain - 1950-2000

Chinese porcelain, Ming Lotus patt., traditional squared upright Chinese teapot form w/large domed cover & overhead bail handle, each side decorated w/ a landscape of flowers & birds, mark of the Toyo China Company, China, 1981 .... **$20**

Zrike porcelain, nearly spherical body w/short cylindrical neck, domed cover w/knob finial, serpentine spout & C-form handle, "In The Garden" h.p. decoration by Michael Sparks, teapot made in China, new **$40**

Zrike is a modern tableware and giftware supplier headquartered in Oakland, New Jersey. It markets designs under various trade names such as Tracy Porter®, Woolrich®, Vintage Kellogg®, Whatever It Takes®, Disney Consumer Products, Coca-Cola®, Campbell's®, and Lynn Chase®.

CERAMIC

Pottery & Earthenware - 1750-1850

Staffordshire creamware, the hexagonal body molded in each panel w/Chinese figures, low domed cover w/pointed knob finial, leaf-molded green spout & handle, the body lead-glazed in mottled dark & light brown, England, ca. 1765, restoration to top rim, slight nick at foot rim, 5" h. **$5,463**

Castleford Pottery, creamy white deep oval paneled body w/ an angled shoulder to the molded chainlink neck, serpentine spout & angled scroll handle, low domed cover w/blossom finial, the body divided into various panels outlined in black & molded w/various designs, the largest side panel featuring the Great Seal of the United States, further black outlining, Castleford, England, late 18th - early 19th c., 11" l. **$1,035**

Pottery & Earthenware - 1850-1950

Alcock, Lindley & Bloore, Ltd., squatty bulbous body w/inset domed cover w/knob finial, angled serpentine spout, C-form handle, dark brown w/pale yellow upper band trimmed w/pale blue stripes, England, ca. 1920-40 .... **$35**

Beswick Ware, figural Sairey Gamp model, designed by Mr. Watkin, introduced in 1939 .... **$300**

Carr China Company, slightly tapering cylindrical body w/flat rim, thick short spout, angled handle, printed band of scrolls & flowers around the rim, Grafton, West Virginia, 1916-1952 .... **$25**

Czechoslovakian pottery, nearly spherical body w/ low domed cover & large knob finial, ring handle & angled spout, Art Deco design w/brightly enameled fruits & leaves on a mottled grey & white background, marked "Made in Czechoslovakia," ca. 1930, 10 1/2" l., 6 1/2" h. **$50**

CERAMIC

Czechoslovakian pottery, spherical body, Carnival patt., overall colorful confetti design, early 1930s **$40**

Ellgreave Pottery Co., footed squatty bulbous body w/a wide flat rim, domed cover w/knob finial, curved spout & C-scroll handle, decorated w/large wild rose blossoms & leaves, England **$40**

Ellgreave Pottery Co., footed wide squatty body tapering sharply to a slightly lobed rim & domed cover w/loop finial, serpentine spout & C-scroll handle, decorated w/an exotic bird in a flowering tree, England **$40**

English earthenware, "Roman Chariot" patt., squatty ovoid body w/almost flat shoulder, short neck, slightly tapered lid w/knob finial, angled handle, serpentine spout, black body decorated w/horizontal bands of dots & geometric designs in beige, red, white & black, marked "K&B England," ca. 1930s, 5" h. **$35**

Fraunfelter China Company, flared base & flaring ovoid body & rounded shoulder tapering to a flat rim, serpentine gold spout & C-form handle, pyramidal cover w/gold button finial, deep green background w/a printed gold band of swags & heart- shaped loops around the shoulder, Model No. 370, marked on the unglazed base, Fraunfelter China Company, Zanesville, Ohio, ca. 1930s, 6 1/2" h. **$145**

Fraunfelter China Company, footed wide cylindrical body w/curved shoulder to the metal rim & hinged domed metal cover, C-scroll handle & serpentine spout, stylized exotic bird & scrolls design in black, red & blue, decorated by the Royal Rochester Company, ca. 1930s **$70-75**

CERAMIC

French China Company, footed wide ribbed baluster-form earthenware body w/ruffled rim, domed cover w/loop finial, serpentine spout & fancy C-scroll handle, printed w/a delicate flower cluster, East Liverpool, Ohio, ca. 1900 .... **$75**

French faience, a tall tapering octagonal body raised on small paw feet, C-scroll handle & tall angular spout, domed octagonal cover w/a figural reclining dog finial, decorated in bright colors of dark blue, rust red, yellow, green & light blue in a Dutch Delft-influenced design of stylized flowers & lattice panels, a central reserve w/a stylized basket of flowers above a ring w/a French fleur-de-lis, unknown maker, 11" h. **$300**

George (W.S.) China Company, squatty bulbous body w/large C-form handle & short spout, disk cover w/disk finial, pale blue glaze, late 1930s - early 1940s **$35-40**

Printed auction catalogs may seem expensive at $20 to $40 but are important tools to help the collector study the items being offered before the sale. They can be used to jot notes to refer to during the sale to verify lot numbers and prevent overbidding. Customers who order an auction catalog are usually sent a list of realized prices after the auction.

George (W.S.) Pottery Co., Bolero patt., footed spherical ribbed body w/conforming cover w/ pointed finial, angled short spout & C-form handle, decorated w/a printed scene of a quaint cottage in trees, ca. 1930 .... **$30**

George (W.S.) Pottery Co., squatty bulbous body w/a short angled shoulder spout, C-form handle & cover w/a wide disk finial, decorated w/a printed scene of a Dutch windmill, East Palestine, Ohio, early 20th c. **$25**

German earthenware, bulbous body w/conical cover & black knob finial, black serpentine spout & C-form handle, the body brightly painted w/large deep red, dark blue & gold flowers & green leaves, Schramberger Majolica Factory, Wurttemberg, Germany, ca. 1920s **$50**

Gibson & Sons, Clifton patt., footed squatty spherical body w/serpentine spout, C- scroll handle, inset cover w/knob finial, decorated w/a delicate lacy white design around the top half, England, early 20th c. **$35**

Grimwades, Ltd., Royal Winton line, footed spherical body w/molded scroll handle & cover w/ molded finial, pink ground printed overall w/white florals, ca. 1930s **$90**

Japanese earthenware, cylindrical body w/angled shoulder to a small domed cover w/knob finial, short spout & squared handle, overall dark mottled green Rockingham-style glaze, marked "NE-NO Heatproof Teapot #2 Japan," made to use on a sterno can **$15**

Homer Laughlin China Co., Shakespeare shape, floral decoration, East Liverpool, Ohio, 1897-1900 .... **$150**

Shady out-of-town auctioneers sometimes conduct sales on the grounds of grand homes, giving the impression the items they're selling came from the wealthy families who lived there. Furnishings sold at these auctions are hauled in and are seldom as described. This deceptive practice is called house packing.

Also be wary of auctions that advertise that they are selling the assets of convicted drug dealers. These auctions are usually a ploy to sell reproductions.

Kingwood Ceramics, squatty bulbous body w/ serpentine spout, C-form handle & flattened cover w/ arched finial, overall Weeping Gold decoration, East Palestine, Ohio, ca. 1939-49 .... **$60**

Knowles China Co. (E.M.), footed wide inverted bell-form body w/an angled shoulder, short spout & fancy loop handle, figure-8 shaped cover finial, floral bouquet decoration, ca. 1922 .... **$40**

Knowles China Co. (E.M.), Roma patt., Newell, West Virginia, ca. 1929 .... **$40**

Knowles, Taylor & Knowles Co., low wide squatty bulbous body w/low domed cover & knob finial, cute animal decoration, East Liverpool, Ohio, ca. 1905 .... **$50**

Leigh China Company, earthenware, footed squatty bulbous body w/flattened cover & lobed finial, squared handle & short serpentine spout, decorated w/bands of stylized blue, red & yellow blossoms on leafy branches, Alliance, Ohio, ca. early 1930s **$65-70**

Because tea leaves float, teapot spouts have traditionally emerged from the base of the teapot to prevent tea leaves from being poured out with the tea. Because coffee grounds sink, coffeepot spouts have traditionally emerge from the top of the coffeepot to prevent the grounds from being poured out with the coffee.

McNichol, Burton & Co., simple baluster- shaped white ironstone body w/serpentine spout, C-form handle & domed cover w/bar finial, East Liverpool, Ohio, 1870-1892 .... **$65**

CERAMIC

Myott, Son & Company, bulbous inverted pear-shaped body, serpentine spout & C- scroll handle, low cover w/scroll loop finial, decorated around the shoulder w/floral sprays & latticework, England, ca. 1930 .... $45

Occupied Japan earthenware, squatty bulbous body w/serpentine spout & angled handle, Hadson Company mark, 1945-52 .... $25

Sebring China Company, individual size, footed tapering hexagonal body w/angled handle & tall spout, paneled domed cover w/pointed finial, white w/a stylized scroll & blossom design in black, pink & gold, thin blue pinstripes, Sebring, Ohio, ca. 1930s $45-50

Sterling China Company, octagonal foot below the wide tapering octagonal body w/flared rim & domed octagonal cover w/button finial, long paneled spout & angular handle, American Limoges earthenware body decorated w/a color transfer scene of Dutch children, Wellsville, Ohio, ca. 1900 .... $65

• If you don't like the risk of selling an item at an auction, consider consigning it to an antique shop or mall. If there is space available and your item is accepted, expect to pay at least 25 percent commission when it sells.

• Noting a point of condition on an item when negotiating a price is acceptable if done in a polite manner. However, berating the merchandise to get a rock-bottom price will only anger the dealer.

Steubenville China, wide low octagonal body w/a wide shoulder sloping to a wide flat rim, flat cover w/flaring finial, short spout & pointed angular handle, Steubenville, Ohio, early 20th c. $35

Thompson Pottery, Glenwood patt., East Liverpool, Ohio, 1916-1938 .... **$30**

Sumida Ware, long half-round flat-bottomed body w/flattened sides & short shoulder spout, the curved cover w/figural child finial, the sides applied w/scene of a child on a red lacquered chair contemplating a large vase w/plant, flowing flambé glaze, black paint on the bottom, applied blue & white signature for artist Ryosai (1845-1905), Japan, ca. 1895, 7" l., 5" h. **$495**

Wade earthenware, squatty bulbous body w/a cream ground h.p. w/large deep red blossoms w/ yellow centers, green leaves & light brown brushstrokes, copper lustre-decorated handle, spout & cover, marked "Wadeheath - England," Wade, Heath & Co., England, ca. 1930s, 9" l., 4 3/4" h. **$65**

A mark alone is never proof that a piece is authentic. In the early 1990s, a Tennessee man discovered that Nelson McCoy Pottery never registered the McCoy trademark. He applied the mark to many pottery reproductions. He wasn't in business long, but his reproductions still cause confusion.

Taylor, Smith & Taylor, earthenware, squatty bulbous lobed & swirled body w/matching lobed cover, C-scroll handle w/embossed blossom & short, wide spout, Paramount shape, decorated w/rust red & orange blossoms & green leaves, Chester, West Virginia, late 1930s - mid-1940s **$30-35**

Taylor, Smith & Taylor, Paramount Ivory, wide squatty octagonal body w/low flaring rim, angled spout, angled loop handle, inset domed cover w/knob finial, printed floral sprigs in each panel, ca. 1928-45 .... **$45**

CERAMIC

Wade, Heath & Co., cylindrical body modeled as a colorful carousel w/pointed cover, Wade, England mark, ca. 1927 .... **$40**

Weil Ware, bulbous body w/a serpentine spout & angled handle, fitted cover w/squared handle, greyish white ground decorated w/yellow bamboo stalks & green leaves, The California Figure Company, Los Angeles, ca. 1930s-40s, 7 1/4" h. **$75**

Wheeling Pottery Co., Moss Rose patt., tapering cylindrical ironstone shaped w/flared rim & domed cover w/bar finial, serpentine spout & C-scroll handle, Wheeling, West Virginia, 1880-86 ... **$65**

Williamson (H.M.) & Sons, tall slightly flaring cylindrical body w/a flattened rim & cover w/ pointed finial, serpentine spout & angled side handle, Gainsborough patt., England, ca. 1908 .... **$120**

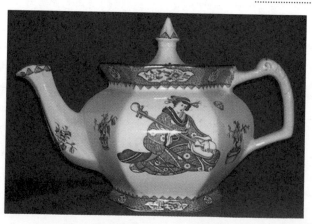

Wood & Sons, Tsing patt., footed squatty bulbous hexagonal body w/flared rim, pointed cover, paneled spout & squared handle, Woods Ware line, England, ca. 1920 .... **$50**

Unknown maker, earthenware square body w/beveled corners & tapering shoulder, oval lid w/ finial, overhead reed bail handle, short serpentine spout, the white ribbed body & lid w/applied maroon flower & log decoration, cobalt blue base, shoulder & end of spout, probably Oriental, early 20th c., 5" sq. **$30**

Unknown maker, earthenware, bulbous wide inverted pear-shaped modernistic body w/tapering spout & down-curved pointed handle, wide flat cover w/swirl finial, stylized brown & green sprig decoration, possibly by the Stetson China Company **$25-30**

"As is" marked on a price tag is the seller's way of noting that the item is damaged and the price relects that damage. Damaged goods may not appreciate in value, and are hard to sell. Therefore, they may be acceptable for utilitarian use, but do not make good investments.

Unknown maker, squatty bulbous tapering body in white decorated w/pink, blue & brown floral sprigs & a blue rim band, short spout, domed cover w/button finial, twisted wire swing bail handle, possibly by the Brock China Company **$50-55**

Pottery & Earthenware - 1950-2000

Canadian pottery, squatty bulbous body w/ serpentine spout, C-form handle & inset domed cover w/arched finial, h.p. w/large stylized blossoms, Royal Canadian Art Pottery, Hamilton, Ontario, 1980s **$25**

Capodimonte earthenware, fancy scroll- footed squatty bulbous body tapering to a domed cover, serpentine ribbed spout & ornate scrolling overhead handle, applied w/large roses & leaves, Naples, Italy, 1990s **$50**

CERAMIC

Capodimonte earthenware, tall tapering bulbous body on scroll feet, high domed cover w/pointed finial, tall ribbed serpentine spout & C-scroll handle, overall molded scroll bands & the side applied w/very large rose blossoms, Naples, Italy, 1990s **$35**

Crownford China, Calico patt., bulbous body w/ serpentine spout, angled handle & domed cover w/knob finial, overall dark blue w/white blossoms, England, 1990s **$35**

Delft pottery, squatty bulbous body w/angled spout & C-form handle, small cover w/button finial, overall h.p. stylized blue florals, Delft, Holland, 1992 .... **$50**

Cauldon Potteries, Ltd., spherical body w/ serpentine spout & C-form handle, domed cover w/knob finial, h.p. w/large flowers, Ceracraft line, England, 1996 .... **$35**

Crespin Pottery, tapering ovoid body w/angled spout, C-form handle & small cover w/knob finial, h.p. w/a stylized rooster, w/matching round trivet, Havelock North, New Zealand, 1992, the set **$20**

Fitz and Floyd, figural Napoleon Bonaparte, Emperor of the French, from the Figures from History series, produced in Taiwan, 1994 ... **$90**

Bid discreetly. Once the auctioneer acknowledges your first bid, he will pay close attention to you until the item is sold. There is no need to whoop or wave your bid card or paddle. Such enthusiastic actions can attract added attention and continued competing bids.

Gibsons, pumpkin-shaped body w/serpentine spout & C-scroll handle, low domed cover w/knob finial, decorated w/scattered roses, made in England mark, ca. 1940s **$35**

Homer Laughlin China Co., Rhythm shape, decorated w/printed scattered rose blossoms, April 1951, Plant #5, double-stamped "Household Institute - Rhythm HLC D51N4," Newell, West Virginia **$40**

Homer Laughlin China Company, Debutante shape, Flame Flower patt., wide low modern streamlined body w/long loop handle & short angled shoulder spout, flattened cover w/scroll finial, designed by Don Schreckengost, Newell, West Virginia, 1950s **$50-55**

Homer Laughlin China Company, Dover shape, Bayberry patt., tapering octagonal body w/ domed cover, long angled handle & serpentine spout, Newell, West Virginia, 1970s **$35-40**

Japanese pottery, footed baluster-form white body w/ruffled rim, domed cover w/C-scroll finial, upright spout & C-scroll handle, the sides molded w/a large turkey below a band of fruits, molded fruits on spout, marked "Napcoware - Japan" **$20**

Kingwood Ceramics Company, Weeping Gold design, squatty bulbous body w/C- form handle & serpentine spout, flattened cover w/arched handle, overall mottled gold glaze, probably made in the late 1970s or early 1980s, East Palestine, Ohio **$45-50**

CERAMIC

Meakin (J. & G.), Classic White design, footed squatty bulbous ribbed body w/flaring ruffled rim, domed cover w/flared finial, ribbed serpentine spout, C-scroll handle, all-white, part of the Wedgwood Group, England, 1962 .... **$50**

Pfalzgraff Pottery, Yorktown line, bulbous body tapering in at shoulder, flaring neck, domed lid w/finial, C-form handle, short serpentine spout, body decorated w/simple floral design in cobalt blue, blue line decoration on rim **$45**

Portuguese earthenware, rounded cylindrical body molded w/spearpoint leaves & sprigs, molded angled spout, C-scroll handle, molded domed cover, Cream Ware II Sparta Group, DECMA Abrigada, Portugal, 1989 .... **$45**

Portuguese pottery, squatty bulbous body w/a short spout & loop handle, small cover w/button finial, h. p. w/a large colorful blossom, marked "Y OAL - Portugal," 1985 .... **$20**

Price & Kensington Potteries, squatty bulbous footed body w/flaring ruffled rim, serpentine spout, fancy C-scroll handle, low domed cover w/knob final, printed w/scattered colorful flowers, England, 1962+ **$40**

Quimper pottery, paneled body w/paneled cover & angled handle, h.p. peasant-style decoration, HB Quimper, France, 1975 .... **$80**

CERAMIC

Sadler (James) & Sons, bold Art Deco- style shape & decoration marked "Inspired by Clarice Cliff's Art Deco Bizarre Ware of the 1930s," England, modern **$50**

Shorter & Son, figural Old King Cole, colorful decoration, Crown Devon group, England, post-1950 .... **$40**

Taylor, Smith & Taylor, LuRay shape w/601 Design, 1950s **$65**

Wedgwood (Enoch), Old Castle patt., baluster-shaped body w/a bold Imari-style decoration, England, after 1965 .... **$130**

Wheeling Decorating Company, squatty bulbous body w/serpentine spout & C- form handle, domed cover w/large knob finial, lightly embossed leaves & blossom design under an overall drippy gold glaze, Wheeling, West Virginia, ca. 1950s .. **$25**

Wood (Arthur) & Son, squatty bulbous body tapering to a short flared & ruffled neck, inset cover, serpentine spout, C- scroll handle, dark rose ground h.p. w/large gold blossoms, England, 1970s **$30**

←

Wood (Arthur) & Son, squatty bulbous body w/a wide flat mouth & inset cover, serpentine spout, C-scroll handle, white upper half, handle & spout, pale blue cover & lower half, decorated w/sprigs of blue & pink flowers & gold trim, England, ca. 1930s **$30**

Sets

Tea Sets - 1750-1850

Rockingham Porcelain: cov. teapot, cov. sugar bowl, creamer, waste bowl & two cups w/one saucer; teapot & serving pieces w/wide squatty bulbous bodies raised on four tab feet, wide angled shoulders & inset domed covers w/blossom finials, leaf-molded short upturned spout on teapot, arched ornate C-scroll handles, each piece decorated about the shoulder or the interior rim w/a wide scrolled cobalt blue border trimmed w/fancy gilt scrolling, gold line trim, No. 252, England, ca. 1830-43, teapot & handles of sugar discolored, teapot 6 1/2" h., the set **$259**

Staffordshire earthenware: two cov. teapots, cov. sugar bowl, creamer, two 7" d. plates & one 9" d. cake plate, nine handleless cups & eleven saucers; h.p. Strawberry patt., the squatty boat- shaped serving pieces w/angled shoulders & inset domed covers, ornate C- scroll handles, all painted w/a design of reddish orange strawberries & green leafy vines, orange banding & some pink lustre trim, England, ca. 1830, teapots 11 1/5" l., the set **$6,325**

Staffordshire earthenware: cov. teapot, cov. sugar bowl & creamer; each piece w/a black-glazed body trimmed w/gilt fruits, leaves & vines, the teapot w/a squatty spherical molded body raised on three mask & paw feet, a crabstock handle & spout, short cylindrical neck w/a low domed cover w/a figural bird finial, matching forms on other pieces, teapot finial missing head, nick on spout rim of creamer, nicks & chips on sugar bowl & bird cover finial repaired, England, 18th c., teapot 4 7/8" h., 3 pcs. (ILLUS. of teapot)... **$1,528**

More tea is consumed worldwide than coffee. Tea also contains more caffeine than coffee by weight in its leaf form, but less tea is used in brewing, so it has less caffeine content per ounce of prepared beverage. The four main types of tea—black, green, white and oolong—can all be produced from the same plant but are processed differently by controlling the stage at which they are fermented by drying and heating.

Tea Sets - 1850-1950

German porcelain: cov. teapot, cov. sugar bowl & creamer; squatty bulbous bodies, D-form handles, domed covers w/knob finials, Cheery Chintz patt., marked "Erphila - Warwick - Germany," early 20th c., the set **$104**

Handel Porcelain: tall tankard-form cov. teapot, squatty bulbous cov. sugar & creamer, small round bowl, larger round bowl w/side handles & oval plate w/end handles; each piece h.p. w/large pink tulip blossoms & green leaves on the white ground, heavy gold rim bands & handles, signed on the base "Handel McMix USA," early 20th c., the set **$1,725**

SETS

Hutschenreuther Porcelain: cov. teapot, creamer, six cups & four saucers; Vienna-style, each piece decorated w/a wide gold body band finely painted w/a continuous scene of festive children in pastel shades, cobalt blue ground w/elaborate gilt scroll trim, the bulbous teapot w/an upright bail handle w/ gilt-bronze figural dolphin supports joined by a porcelain hand grip, artist-signed, impressed monogram & blue beehive marks, Germany, ca. 1900, teapot overall 8" h. **$4,465**

Japanese porcelain: child's size, cov. teapot, cov. sugar bowl & creamer; blue & white Phoenix Bird patt., tapering ovoid bodies & angled handles, marked "Made in Japan," ca. 1930s, teapot 5 1/2" l., 3 3/4" h., the set **$130-150**

Japanese porcelain: child's size, cov. teapot, cov. sugar bowl & creamer; blue & white Phoenix Bird patt., wide cylindrical bodies w/low domed covers & angled handles, very common type, marked w/Morimura Bros. "M" in Wreath mark & "Made in Japan," ca. 1930s, teapot 6 1/2" l., 3 3/4" h., the set **$85-105**

SETS

Japanese porcelain: child's size, cov. teapot, cov. sugar bowl & creamer; blue & white Phoenix Bird patt., wide squatty bulbous bodies w/pointed handles, marked "Made in Japan," ca. 1930s, teapot 5 3/4" l., 3 3/8" h., the set **$135-155**

Japanese porcelain: child's size, cov. teapot, cov. sugar bowl & creamer; blue & white Phoenix Bird patt., wide squatty bulbous bodies w/C-form handles, marked w/a "T" inside a flower above "Japan," ca. 1930s, teapot 6 1/2" l., 3 3/4" h., the set **$125-145**

Japanese porcelain: child's size, cov. teapot, cov. sugar bowl & creamer; Phoenix Bird patt., bulbous ovoid bodies w/pointed loop handles, marked "Made in Japan," ca. 1920s-30s, teapot 5 1/8" l., 4" h., the set **$140-165**

Japanese porcelain: child's size, cov. teapot, cov. sugar bowl & creamer; Phoenix Bird patt., tapering cylindrical shapes, marked "Made in Japan," ca. 1920s-30s, teapot 5 1/2", 3 5/8" h., the set **$110- 135**

Russian porcelain: cov. teapot, open sugar & creamer, four saucers & four egg- shaped covered cups & two open cups; the teapot & sugar of footed squatty bulbous form w/ornate looping handles w/figural horse heads, the footed open sugar of oblong boat shape, footed cups, each piece decorated w/dark red, yellow & black Byzantine-style panels against the white ground, Kornilov Bros. factory, Russia, ca. 1910, teapot 9" h., the set **$2,415**

TEXTILES

Coverlets

Jacquard, double woven, two-piece, the center field w/floral medallions, borders of roses or grapevines, corner block w/label "Manufacd By Jay A. Van Vleck Gallipolis O.," navy blue & natural, good fringe, ca. 1850, 80 x 92" **$403**

Needlework

Statuary dress, silver metallic embroidery, overall design of flowers in blue, pink & green within silver & gold metallic C- scrolls & cartouches, accented w/silver spangles & silver metallic needle lace at the neck & cuffs, on a cream faille ground, the back seam open & dress tacked to padded rectangular backing, Europe, possibly 18th c. **$3,290**

Quilts

Appliqued Mariner's Compass patt., composed of five whole & eight partial blocks w/the compass design in printed red, green, yellow & blue cottom fabrics, set diagonally, red & white sawtooth sashing & oak leaves appliqued in the block corners, sawtooth & swag borders, background fabric w/a fine light blue print on a white background, red binding & the backing matching the background fabric, quilted w/oak leaves, feather & outline stitches, Pennsylvania German or New Jersey, ca. 1845, minor stains, 107" sq. **$14,100**

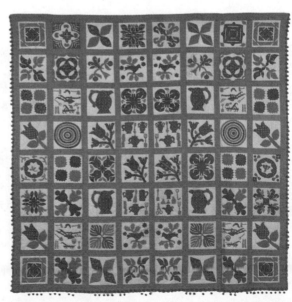

Appliqued Quaker album quilt, composed of 64 blocks of red & green printed calico designs on a white ground, the blocks framed by light blue sashing, outling quilt stitches & diamond quilting on the borders, blue silk binding w/ball fringe tassels applied on three edges, brown glazed cotton backing, made by a member of the Patterson/Regester family, Delaware/ Chester County, Pennsylvania, ca. 1850, minor scattered stains, 85 x 88" **$14,100**

QUILTS

Samplers

Pieced Orange Peel patt., the maind body doen in a orange peel design of diamond- shaped areas w/crazy string piecing using solid & print wool fabrics & a few cottons, each diamond centered w/a folk motif including hearts, flowers, birds, houses, baskets, hands, leaves, etc., red & black zigzag border & a wide black border, red wool binding & black wool backing, feather & crazy quilting over the seam lines, triple cable quilt stitching on out border, Pennsylvania, ca. 1880, minor losses, 78" sq. **$7,638**

Pious verse & building, cotton & silk on linen, a wide meandering red & green floral vine border enclosing a pious verse flanked by large roses at the top above a large three-part brick building flanked by flower sprigs & trees in urns, signed "worked by Maria Taylor in the year 1841," in shades of red, green, pink & black in the Baltimore style, Baltimore, Maryland, some minor flaws, framed, 37 x 37 3/8" **$2,115**

Tapestries

Aubusson-style, wool, decorated w/a landscape scene w/a knight on horseback, a castle in the background & courtly ladies & hounds in the foreground, floral & guilloche borders, tacked to maroon backing, France, 19th c., 78 1/2 x 101 1/2" **$1,528**

Flemish verdure, wool, woven w/a lush wooded landscape in the foreground w/a pavilion & fountain in the background, woven umber & blue borders, tacked on cotton backing, Europe, 17th - 18th c., 95 x 99" **$4,994**

When storing quilts, roll them rather than folding them, as the folded areas can stretch and weaken the fabric and can cause permanent creases. Store the rolled quilts in cloth bags, which will protect them from dust but also allow them to breathe. Plastic bags seal in moisture, which could cause mold or mildew.

TOBACCIANA

Although the smoking of cigarettes, cigars & pipes is controversial today, the artifacts of smoking related items - pipes, cigar & tobacco humidors, and cigar & cigarette lighters - and, of course, the huge range of advertising materials are much sought after. Unusual examples, especially fine Victorian pieces, can bring high prices. Here we list a cross section of Tobacciana pieces.

ADVERTISING ITEMS

Advertising Items

Clock, "Mayo's Tobacco," figure-8 style, Roman numerals, "Mayo's - Tobacco - Smoke - Chew" around clock face, "Smoking - Chewing - Mayo's - Tobacco - is always good" in papier-mâché door of bottom section, along w/"Trade Mark Rec'd. Sept. 1878," Baird Clock Co., Plattsburg, New York, ca. 1893, 18 1/2" w., 30 1/2" h. **$1,898**

Advertisement, "Turkish Trophies Cigarettes," lithograph, three-quarters portrait of young Turkish woman w/Turkish landmarks in the distance, marked "Turkish Trophies Cigarettes" at top, w/ wood frame marked "Turkish Trophies Cigarettes" at bottom, 26 1/2 x 36 1/4" (minor wear to frame)................................ **$495**

Advertisement, "Murray's 'Warrior' Plug Tobacco," cardboard lithograph of a pirate framed in a circle above "Murray - 'Warriors' - Plug - Tobacco," framed, 21 1/2 x 29 1/2" **$220**

Counter display, "Old North State Cigarettes," cardboard, w/color cutout bust illustration of flapper-type woman w/bobbed hair holding cigarette in holder alongside package of "Old North State Superfine Ready Rolled Cigarettes," on black ground, never unfolded for use, 1920s, 10 1/2 x 12" assembled **$72**

Tobacco package, "Plow Boy Chewing and Smoking," color-lithographed paper w/scene of a plow boy, unopened w/contents, early 20th c., 4 1/2" h. **$46**

Mirror, "Old Player's Navy Cut Tobacco," glass reverse-painted w/"Tobacco and Cigarettes," applied paper lifesaver- shaped label w/"Player's Navy Cut" around central bust image of old-time sailor, some silvering loss & light flaking to reverse silvering, 18" w., 22" h. **$460**

Tobacco package, "Red Man - Made From Good Cigar Leaf," paper printed in green, red & white, unopened w/contents, early 20th c., 5" h. **$40**

ASHTRAYS

Ashtrays

Bronze, stand-type, a round openwork saucer foot cast w/grapes, leaves & vines centered by the base of the standard flanked by for small stylized dolphins, the tall slender standard w/central rings & a block supporting the rounded ashtray w/a high arched handle from side to side & fitted w/two rim cigar holders supported by small stylized horses, designed by Oscar Bach w/his applied tag under the base, ashtray insert missing, early 20th c., overall 36" h. **$288**

Bronzed cast iron, silent-butler style, modeled as a griffin-like creature w/the curled tail attached to the hinged shell-form cover, copper liner, late 19th - early 20th c., 11" l. **$374**

Porcelain, advertising-type ashtray-match holder, "Abdulla Pure Virginia Superb Cigarettes," the rectangular ashtray base w/ rounded corners decorated w/printed black border & advertising, opening in top to insert a small box of matches, a box included, early 20th c., 4 x 5", 3" h. **$99**

Glass, model of a clear glass rowboat w/ribbing in the bottom, indentations a the side rims for cigarettes, 1930s................... **$6**

Cans & Containers

Cigar tin, "Possum Cigars," cylindrical red can w/ a color scene on the front of a white possum, complete w/contents & interior label sheet, early 20th c., excellent condition, 5 1/4" d., 5 1/4" h. **$330**

Tobacco store tin, "Polar Bear Tobacco," countertop rectangular container w/a hinged slant top, blue ground w/ white wording, the sides showing a rearing polar bear w/a package, the lower front w/an image of the package, front w/overall staining & wear, late 19th - early 20th c., 14 x 18", 14" h. **$316**

Tobacco store tin, "Sweet Cuba Chewing Tobacco," countertop rectangular container w/a hinged slant top, dark yellow ground printed overall w/ advertising in red & black, good condition, late 19th - early 20th c., 14 x 18", 12" h. **$431**

Tobacco tin, "Dixie Queen Plug Cut," large cylinder w/fitted flat cover, yellow ground printed in orange & black w/a central portrait of a pretty Victorian lady, some rust & scratches, late 19th - early 20th c., 5" d., 6 1/2" h. **$144**

Can, "U.S. Marine Cut Plug Tobacco," tin lunch box-style, bail handle, porthole illustrations of sailor holding package of product, the end panels w/lithos of White Fleet battleships, 4 1/2 x 7 1/2", 5" h. **$210**

Cigar & Cigarette Cases

Cigarette case, silver & cloisonné enamel, flattened rectangular form w/rounded corners, the cover w/an overall ornate scrolling design in blues, red & white w/a central panel of flowered angled bars in blue & white, by Nikolai Zverev, Moscow, Russia, 1898-1914, 3" l. **$460**

19th century Russian silver is prized for its high quality and superb workmanship. Look for marks with the Cyrillic characters of the Russian alphabet.

Cigarette case, Art Deco style, shallow rectangular shape w/rounded corners, in 18k bi-color gold w/enameled reserves depicting abstract black & red flowering branches on a green ground edged by engraved florettes, cabochon emerald thumbpiece, engine-turned sides, ca. 1930s **$1,528**

Cigar case, alligator skin & silver, two-piece model that slides open, the base section w/an ornate scroll & lappet sterling silver band by the Gorham Mfg. Co., ca. 1930s, 4 1/2 x 5 1/2" **$303**

Tobacco tin, "Bagdad Short Cut Pipe Smoking," pocket-type, blue ground w/white wording & color center portrait of a Turkish man wearing a fez, some wear, 3 1/4" w., 3 3/4" h. **$230**

LIGHTERS

Lighters

Cigarette lighter, Ronson "Queen Anne" model table lighter, silver plate, 1950s, 3 1/2" l., 2 1/4" h. **$150**

Cigarette lighter, Ronson "Touch-Tip" table lighter, Art Deco style, black lighter on a long octagonal chrome base, made for Ronson by Art Metal Works, Newark, New Jersey, 1930s, 2 1/2 x 3 1/4", 4" h. **$350**

Part-time dealers often rent a booth at an antique mall. Because these dealers have full-time jobs, they sometimes lack the time, experience, and expertise to properly research and accurately identify all their goods. By visiting these booths often and keeping a sharp lookout, an astute collector can find misidentified and undervalued treasures.

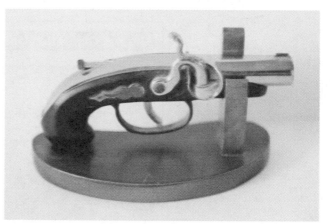

Cigarette lighter, table model, figural, model of a flintlock pistol in Chromium & black plastic on an oval base, marked "Japan," 1960s, 5 3/4" l., 3" h. **$25**

Matchsafes

Match holder-dispenser, cast iron, upright container w/scroll-cast hinged rounded front lid above the word "Matches," dispensing slot & tray at bottom front, late 19th c., 5" h. **$138**

Matchsafe, the rectangular box w/gilt-metal mounts enclosing plaques of banded agate, bloodstone & jasper, 19th c., 5/8 x 2 1/8" **$441**

Tobacco Jars & Humidors

Brass, Arts & Crafts style, the flat hinged rectangular top decorated w/an applied serpentine border band & a central scrolled spearpoint, the flat sides w/corner brackets, latch closure, wood-lined, original patina, impressed mark of Bradley & Hubbard, early 20th c., 9 1/2" l., 3 1/2" h. **$600**

Pottery, cylindrical w/flaring base & stepped domed cover w/pointed finial, the sides transfer-printed in bright colors w/a comical golfing scene, marked "A.G.R. & Company Ltd. - England - Ducal," early 20th c., 7" h. **$472**

Terra cotta, figural jar, modeled as a standing pig waiter wearing a green polka dot shirt, red bow tie & green pants, marked "JM3515," Germany, late 19th - early 20th c., 8 1/4" h. **$776**

Wood, carved presentation-type humidor, carved walnut in the form of a knotty tree stump wrapped in leafy vine w/a rabbit below, the flat inset cover carved w/a wooden branch handle, inscribed on the side "Vive Le Vin Lamour et le Tabac 1871," ("Long Live Wine, Love and Tobacco"), probably French, 7" w., 6 1/2" h. **$316**

Wood, figural box, the squared tall base carved at each corner w/ buttress-style scrolls & blocks, each side panel carved & painted w/a different scene including a house & palm trees, a stag in water, a boy w/dog & fighting animals, the large cover carved as domed rockwork supporting a large carved model of a lion, Spanish cedar wood, tail of lion reattached, late 19th c., 7 x 8", 13" h. **$4,313**

Humidors are designed to keep cigars fresh. They should be kept at 65 to 75 percent relative humidity and at 68 degrees F. or below to avoid mold and prevent tobacco beetles from laying and hatching eggs.

Miscellaneous

Humidor, cov., Arts & Crafts style, brass & leaded glass, a round brass foot supporting the paneled sides composed of a geometric design in green & caramel slag glass centered by a ruby glass jewel, brass rim & low domed cover w/knob finial, ca. 1910, small dents in the cover, rusted bottom, 8 1/4" h. **$58**

Humidor, figural, carved wood model of a standing bear w/his paws raised above his head, shoulder straps support a basket at his waist holding a brass ash holder & match safe, the head hinged for the compartment, inset glass eyes, fine detail, Swiss, ca. 1890, 14 1/4" h. **$3,442**

Smoking stand, carved wood, a paneled domed base carved w/ pointed leaves supporting a ball & the tall draped classical figure w/hands above head supporting a round dished & leaf-carved top receptacle, late 19th c., 28 1/2" h. **$196**

Tobacco cutter - lamp, advertising-type, "Cubanola" brand, cast iron & brass, an oval metal platform cutter w/gold paint, the angled top embossed "Hand Made Cubanola 5¢ Cigar" around a small center cutting hole w/a lever handle to the side, connected to a pedestal-base bulbos embossed brass kerosene font w/a lighter mechanism fitted w/a green glass chimney, late 19th - early 20th c., 5 x 8", 10" h. **$1,150**

Tobacco cutter, advertising-type, "Rocky Ford" brand, cast iron squared platform design w/the hinged top enclosed a color lithograph w/a scene of a crouching Native American, the flanged edges embossed "High - Grade - Havanna - Cigars," late 19th - early 20th c., overall wear, 6 1/2 x 8", 5" h. **$1,093**

Tobacco cutter, cast iron, counter-type, "Brighton" cast into side of base, top of handle cast w/a red elf thumbing his nose, late 19th - early 20th c. **$575**

Tobacco cutter, wooden bellows-shaped base w/ring turned handle & carved tulip, blade is cut-out horse silhouette w/engraved face, bridle, mane & tail, ferule loose, worm holes, 13 1/2" l., 7" h. **$575**

TOOLS MARKET REPORT

Clarence Blanchard, president of Brown Auction Service and *Fine Tool Journal* (www.finetoolj.com) in Pownal, Maine, and author of *Antique Trader Tools Price Guide*, said "the better tools are doing well and the good middle of the road ones are doing okay." One of the hottest segments of the market is unusual patented tools, which are valued for their complexity and ingenuity. Planes still dominate and their plentiful supply helps support the hobby. Handsaws are popular, too, but are more limited in quantity, so they account for a smaller part of the trade. Wrenches are much more popular in the Midwest than on either coast, while the opposite seems true for woodworking tools. Blanchard speculates that the reason is that numerous wrenches were needed for farm equipment in the Midwest, but fewer woodworking tools were needed in that area because it had less wood available. The coasts, on the other hand, had more forests, so woodworking tools were more in demand there.

According to Blanchard, unlike many other categories of antiques and collectibles, "fakes and alterations are really not a problem in the tool collecting hobby because the craftsmen who made them were so highly skilled that to reproduce the tools convincingly would take too much time and effort to be profitable," Blanchard explained.

Tool collecting got its start in the mid- to late-1970s with tradespeople who acquired antique tools just because they loved them. It was common back then for retired shop teachers to be found at shows and flea markets scouting for vintage tools of their trade. While the hobby is aging and a higher percentage of collectors are older, Blanchard does see a number of young professionals buying vintage tools because they value quality workmanship. Blanchard estimates that less than 10 percent of collectors buy strictly for investment, though everyone hopes for an appreciable increase in value over time. Blanchard estimates that a mint tool will typically increase 25 or 30 percent in five years.

Auctions dominate in the tool hobby, with at least 30 percent of low to medium tools and almost all high-end tools sold at auctions. Younger buyers often buy primarily online because they can't afford the time and travel required to attend shows. The show attenders are those who want to personally handle and examine tools before buying them. With the trend toward purchasing online, shows have shrunk some, but most are still in existence.

The high end of the market, incorporating tools that are the rarest and in the best condition, starts at around $500 and extends to thousands and even tens of thousands of dollars. The middle covers the $50 to $400 range and the low end $25 or less, which typically includes worn or damaged tools. Condition is critical, and any tool graded in the top two percent of condition is a tool with the best possibility of achieving a top value or even a record-breaking price.

Blanchard's advice is to "study the field carefully because knowledge is the key to success. He also suggests that collectors buy the best they can afford because the better the quality, the faster the tool will appreciate in value."

Auction Houses
Brown Auction Service (www.finetoolj.com)
Martin J. Donnelly Antique Tools and Books (www.mjdtools.com)
Potomac Antique Tools and Industries Association (www.patinatools.org)

TOOLS

Braces & Bits

Brace, beech & plated metal, marked "Tillotson & Co.," slide chuck as most often found on Ultimatums, good condition, chip on edge of pad **$176**

The brace's crank gives it more torque and power than the gear-driven hand drill. The hand drill, however, is faster and more precise.

Drills

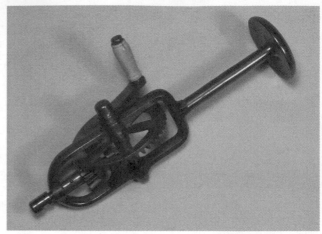

Frame drill, brass & ivory, all-brass except for chuck & ivory handle , open 6-spoke wheel, mushroom pad, very showy, fine condition, 10" l. ... **$193**

Edged Tools

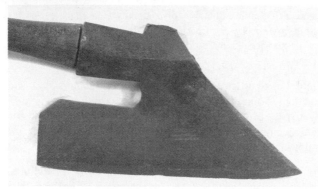

Ax, wrought iron, goosewing-type, marked "G.Sener.," classic American design, old handle, Lancaster, Pennsylvania, very good condition, edge 13 1/2", 8 1/2" l. **$413**

Axe, copper's side-type, hand-wrought iron, stamped "Rubin" w/wheat ears, 19th c., 14" l. **$69**

Champer knives, cooper's, hand-wrought iron w/turned wood handles, 19th c., 14" & 15 1/2" l., pr. **$46**

Axe blade, hand-wrought iron, wide blade tapering sharply to handle mount, stamped "Rotheval," early 19th c., 27 1/2" l. **$345**

Axe, copper's side-type, hand-wrought iron, stamped "Barton," mid-19th c., 16" l. **$46**

Axe, Plumb (Fayette R.), Philadelphia, official Kaw Indian single bit belt style w/embossed logos, original paint, 15" l. **$675**

Axe, Kelly Axe & Tool Works, Charleston, South Carolina, felling axe, emossed "Oil Whetted & Hand Honed," rare, 7" l. **$345**

Levels

Corner level, cast iron w/98% japanning, marked "Millers Falls Co. No. 20," 4" sides w/90 degree corner, can read plumb & level w/ one vial, rare due to limited sales, fine condition **$1,760**

Level, cast iron, marked "Davis & Cook," pinwheel open filigree design, sometimes called pretzel level because of pinwheel shape, needs cleaning, very good condition **$1,045**

Inclinometer, cherry stock w/inset brass fittings, marked "T.F. Deck Gravity Level Co. Patented Dec. 15, 1896. Feb. 14, 1905. Toledo, Ohio," large dial, early type, very clean & working, fine condition, 30" l., 4 1/4" h. **$1,210**

While a level only indicates whether a horizontal surface is out of level or a vertical surface is out of plumb, an inclinometer measures the exact number of degrees of angle in the tilt of a surface.

Planes & Scrapers

Bench plane, cast iron & rosewood, marked "Birdsill Holly Bench," Dwights & French iron, 2" w. cutter, smooth sole, rosewood tote dovetailed to body, Seneca Falls, 1850, rare size, fine condition, 9" l. **$2,860**

The term "bench plane" is general and encompasses a wide range of specific hand planes, but it is generally characterized by having the cutting iron set with the bevel facing up and having a chipbreaker designed to curl and break apart the wood chips as they form.

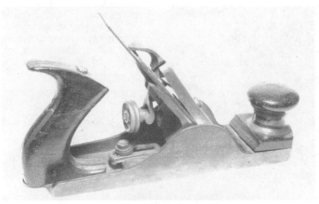

Bench plane, cast iron w/cast-brass cap, marked "H.B. Price Patent June 17, 1879," frog seat w/stair-stepped incline that changes the frog pitch as frog moves up ramp, frog adjustable by sliding the seat, four cutter pitches possible, laminated wood handles, very good condition **$3,960**

Bevel plane, brass framed w/ walnut handle & nob, w/three interchangeable wood bottoms & blades w/varied radius, stamped name of owner, made by James Howarth, first half 20th c., 9 1/2" l., the set **$115**

PLANES & SCRAPERS

Block plane, cabinetmaker's, cast iron w/90% japanning, Stanley No. 9, w/hot dog side handle, finishes fine, ca. 1900, very good condition **$1,430**

Block plane, maple base w/ivory upright front handle & blade wedge, stamped "S&S," probably early 19th c., 9" l. **$173**

Bullnose rebate plane, cast gunmetal w/ebony wedge, no blade, England, 19th c., 1 x 4 1/2" **$69**

Plow plane, beech, marked "Israel White - No. 106," handled three-arm style w/ivory tips & scales, brass & steel fence rollers, ebony slide arms, one of two known, professionally restored, couple of light burn marks, very good condition **$21,450**

Block plane, heavy gunmetal base w/walnut grips & wedges, brass wedge lock, blade stamped w/ illegible trademark, 19th c., 7" l. **$69**

Plow plane, applewood, marked "Chapin Solon Rust Patent Mar. 31, 1868," second model w/screw to hold adjuster arm from side of body & brass fence rods, marked w/Union Factory stamp & patent date on nose, one of only three Rust patent types to surface, good condition, fence replaced **$1,980**

Rabbet plane, steel shouldered rebate w/ebony wedge, mahogany slipcase w/stamped name of owner & also the maker, Spiers Ayr, early 19th c., 6" l. **$144**

Jointer plane, annealed steel w/gunmetal cap, 97% original finish, marked "Norris" blade, postwar model w/adjustment, appears to be an A-1 but isn't dovetailed, fine condition, 22 1/2" l. **$2,970**

Rules & Gauges

Bench gauge, cast iron w/98% japanning & most of gold highlights, marked "Randel & Stickney. Waltham, Mass.," adjustable table & lever action dial indicator, fine condition, 12" h. **$116**

Rule, hinged combination-type, brass- bound boxwood w/level, Stephens #36 model, ca. 1870, 12" l. **$127**

Rule, boxwood, marked "E.A. Sterns & Co. - Makers - Brattleboro, Vt - Warranted Box Wood" and "No. 5," two-fold w/arch joint, slide w/scales & tables, fine condition, 24" l. **$468**

Woodworking gauges, as well as scientific and engineering instruments, are very desirable but should be handled with great care. They are very sensitive and must be in good working order to maintain their value. If storing them, be sure they are kept in areas where humidity and temperature are regulated. If they are to be used, they should first be calibrated to ensure they will give accurate measurements. Also, be aware that foreign-made instruments are likely to be marked in metric or other units of measure.

Saws

Hand saw, steel blade w/ wooden handle, marked "Woodrough & McParlin," ink stamped patent date "Jnr'y 13, 1880" on handle, logo w/panther on blade, handle decorated w/carved panther head on each side, Cincinnati, Ohio, very good condition **$3,300**

Bow saw, steel blade in boxwood frame w/ebony handles & tensioner, marked "Heanshaw Bros. & Nurse - London," England, showy, very good condition **$743**

Special Use & Miscellaneous Tools

Patent model, wood, brass & steel, marked "George A. Royce. Carriage Hinge. Patented Oct. 1st. 1889.," fancy working model w/swing-down & swing-out hinge for carriage, original papers, fine condition **$495**

Machinist's chest, walnut, a rectangular molded hinged top opening to a compartment w/a lock above a case w/four long, shallow drawers w/brass ball pulls, molded base, ca. 1900, 13 1/2 x 22", 14 1/2" h. **$230**

TOYS MARKET REPORT

Tom Miano of Serious Toyz (www.serioustoyz.com) in Croton-on-Hudson, New York, said, "Sales of my low-end toys are slow, but my high-end ones are doing great." At his last auction, a Beatles record player brought $4,000 and its box, $8,500. Only 3,000 of the record players were made, and fewer survived. Far fewer boxes survived, so their greater rarity brings higher prices.

Lunch boxes are doing well too; in February 2008, Joe Soucy of Seaside Toys sold a Superman lunch box for $19,000. Die cast cars, Matchbox, and Hot Wheels remain favorites. Hot Wheels do best when they're still in the original package, but loose ones sell well too.

Early character toys like Disney and Popeye are moving quite well, as are later character toys like He Man, 3-3/4" G.I. Joe, and superheroes, especially Batman. Name recognition is a big factor, as people tend not to buy characters they don't know, like the Yellow Kid. Some battery operated toys are cooling off, but it's hit and miss. "It's hard to predict trends," Miano said. "It used to be easier, but now they change faster, and sales are somewhat circumstantial, so they're not always easily explainable." A number of factors affect sale prices, including condition, demand, era, style, material, aesthetics, and who is participating in an auction when it takes place. In some cases, multiple bidders battle for a piece and drive up the price. In another, a similar piece doesn't have as many interested bidders, so the toy doesn't go quite as high.

As in many antiques and collectibles categories, nostalgia plays a big role, but it's probably an even more significant factor with toys, as they bring back some of the most vivid memories from childhood. "Every generation, when they have good jobs, want their stuff back," said Miano. Collectors buy primarily because they love toys, but they're paying attention to their investment potential as well. "The most important thing to remember about value is condition, condition, condition. Also, it's best to buy one good toy, rather than three lesser ones. But ultimately, it's all about smiling. Buy what you like and makes you happy."

Note: Collectors should be aware that eBay bans toy guns unless they have "clear markings permanently affixed to them (commonly blaze orange markings on the barrel or a blaze orange plug inserted into the barrel)."

Auction Houses
Serious Toyz (www.serioustoyz.com)
Bertoia (www.bertoiaauctions.com)
Hakes (www.hakes.com)
Morphy Auctions (www.morphyauctions.com)
James Julia (www.jamesdjulia.net)
Aumann (www.aumannauctions.com)
Dumouchelle (www.dumouchelle.com)
Noel Barrett (www.noelbarrett.com)
Smith House Toy and Auction Company (www.smithhousetoys.com)

TOYS

Toys

Airplane, cast iron biplane, "Lucky Boy" & red stars cast on the top of the wings, silver body & wings w/red numbers on tail, aluminum propeller, solid metal wheels, Dent, ca. 1930, 12 1/2" wingspan **$8,400**

Airplane, cast iron, "Bremen Junker," green ribbed body & wings w/molded letter & numbers in gold, windows in sides show passengers, two oversized pilots, single propeller, solid metal wheels, early 1930s, 10" wingspan **$6,325**

Airplane, cast iron, "DO-X," red wings mounted by a row of nickel-plated engines above the large blue body w/numerals portholes & door openings, large solid metal wheels, Hubley, two faint hairlines in fuselage, 1930s, 7 1/2" wingspan **$9,200**

Airplane, cast iron, "Bremen Junker," green ribbed body & wings, windows in sides, two oversized pilots, single propeller, solid metal wheels, smaller version, early 1930s, 6 1/2" wingspan **$1,035**

Airplane, cast iron, "TAT," red ribbed body & creamy ribbed tail & wings, windows in sides, nickel-plated triple motors, solid metal wheels, molded "Kilgore" mark, early 1930s, 13 1/2" wingspan **$3,378**

Airplane, cast-iron, orange body w/grey wings molded "Sea Gull" & nickel-plated engine, solid metal wheels, Kilgore, 1930s, fine condition, 8 1/2" wingspan **$1,898**

Battery-operated, tinplate racecar, white & red body w/three tailfins, double plastic domes over two drivers, black rubber tires, moves erratically w/flashing lights, original box in color printed "Cragstan Fire Bird III - Motorized Mystery Action," Japan, 1950s, 11 1/2" l., 3 3/4" h. **$575**

TOYS

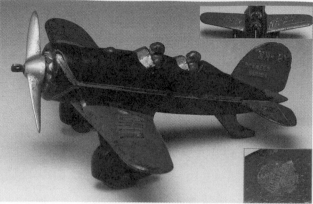

Battery-operated, tinplate, "Cragstan Mystery Action Satellite with Astronaut in Orbit," domed round shape printed in color w/green & red flashing lights, suspends astronaut from top of ship, Japan, 1960s, w/original illustrated box, 5 1/2 x 9" .. **$345**

Airplane, cast iron, "Lockheed Sirius," black body w/red wings embossed "Lindy - NR- 211" & red tail w/molded plane name & matching number, double cockpit w/pilots, nickel-plated propeller, metal wheels, original Hubley decal on tail fin, ca. 1930, 10 1/2" wingspan **$4,600**

Bus, pressed steel long dark green body w/aluminum wheels, untouched & uncleaned, minor fading to decals on side, minor chipping & denting to front fenders, Buddy L, 1930s, 28" h. **$9,200**

Circus animal, gorilla, jointed wood body painted dark brown, snarling open mouth on mask face, Schoenhut & Co., early 20th c., needs restringing, 8 1/4" h. **$3,000**

Before purchasing a cast iron toy, inspect it carefully, as fakes and reproductions abound. If it is joined with phillips head screws, it is either entirely a fake or at least its screws have been replaced. Phillips screws came later than cast iron toys. Also, if the metal is rough or has poorly fitting seams, it is likely a recently made fake.

Cap gun, "Cadet," cast-iron, the trigger hammer slams into the mouth of a black man to explode cap, finely cast, slightly worn nickel-plated finish, early 20th c., 6 1/2" l. **$575**

Fire chief horse-drawn wagon, cast iron, the silver wagon platform raised on four yellow spoked wheels, fire chief in red, drawn by a single prancing horse on a tiny wheel, Ideal, late 19th - early 20th c., 15 1/2" l. ... **$748**

Circus set, "Humpty Dumpty Circus," a large canvas tent w/trapeze & ring, includes a painted-eye dappled horse, a painted-eye brown horse w/saddle, a ringmaster, a clown, a bareback rider, several chairs, barrels, pedestals, etc., w/a rectangular wooden tray base w/worn label on front, Schoenhut & Co., early 20th c., the set **$660**

Clockwork mechanism boy riding velocipede, boy w/papier-mâché head & tin body dressed in cloth jacket & pants steers large velocipede w/cast-iron wheels, Stevens, late 19th c., some wear to clothes, minor flaking on head, 11" l., 7 3/4" h. **$3,450**

Dump truck, cast iron, red open cab & fenders, light blue dump bed, solid metal red & black wheels, w/original driver, original paint w/some wear, Dent, ca. 1920s, wheels old replacements, 10 3/4" l. **$1,150**

Dump truck, pressed steel, "Little Jim" model w/decal on cab roof, green cab, frame & solid metal wheels, red dump compartment, originally sold by J.C. Penney, 1920s, some paint loss & corrosion, 23" l. **$230**

Fire aerial truck, pressed steel red truck w/adjustable ladders & solid metal wheels, Buddy L, untouched condition w/some wear & erosion to front fender, slight fading to decal & dulling to nickel letters, 1930s, 29" l. **$1,265**

TOYS

Fire hook & ladder wagon, tinplate, long narrow platform supporting racks w/wooden ladders, large spoked metal wheels & wagon tongue, w/buckets & bell at the front, possibly by Converse, ca. 1890-1910, missing one support rod, some paint chips & wear, 9 x 24", 14 1/2" h. **$1,840**

Fire horse-drawn hose reel wagon, cast iron, a green wagon frame mounted w/a large red & green hose reel raised on red metal spoked wheels, one fireman driver, pulled by a single white horse, Pratt & Letchworth, late 19th - early 20th c. .. **$1,495**

Fire horse-drawn hose reel wagon, cast iron, black frame mounted w/a double-wheel hose reel, on large red spoked wheels, front & rear firemen, pulled by a single white horse on small wheels, paint wear, mismatched firemen, Carpenter, late 19th - early 20th c, 14 1/2" l. ... **$1,610**

Fire horse-drawn hose tower wagon, cast iron & steel, the long white steel frame supporting the long blue steel tower, on red spoked wheels, single driver, pulled by two black & one white horse on tiny wheels, Dent, late 19th - early 20th c., 30" l. **$805**

Pull toy, goat on wheeled platform, standing goat w/real white fur & carved wood horns, glass eyes, open mouth to voice mechanism that nays as head pulled forward, long narrow shaped wooden base on tiny metal wheels, crack to kid on side of face, Germany, late 19th c., 11 1/2" h. **$690**

Motorcycle & rider, cast iron, overall red paint, rider w/a "5" molded on his back, side of tank reads "Speed," Hubley, 1930s, overall paint chipping & wear, 4 1/4" l. **$518**

Germany was a major toy producer in the 19th and early 20th century. It was well known for high quality dolls, handmade marbles, tinplate and pull toys. Its numerous skilled workers could produce huge volumes at low cost for export.

Racecar, cast iron, boat-tail design w/light blue body & spoked metal wheels w/black rubber tires, complete w/driver, Hubley, 1930s, body repainted, tires w/wear, 10 1/2" l. **$920**

Push-toy, carved & painted wood, folk art style, a flat stylized horse w/dappled paint mounted by a hinged stylized monkey figure w/red jacket & yellow top hat, raised on large wooden six-spoke wheels, a long slender shaped wooden handle at the back, New York, ca. 1860, 9 x 34", 15 1/4" h. **$4,800**

Racecar, gas-powered, "Speed Chief," cast aluminum boat-tail style body w/black tires, w/ Junior Motors engine, body repainted, missing hood, ca. 1950s, 21" l. **$360**

Racecar, tinplate, friction operation, dark grey body w/red trim & yellow lettering "J.T.Y. - Y53," tin driver, black rubber tires w/tin hubs, Japan, ca. 1950s, w/original box w/colorful paper label reading "Jet Racer - with Siren and Fire," near mint, 12" l. **$1,495**

Trolley & horses, tinplate, primitive red trolley w/cut-out windows & black roof, on tiny metal wheels, pulled by two black tin horses, overall paint wear, late 19th c., 9 1/2" l., 3 1/2" h. **$259**

Truck & trailer, pressed steel, "Buddy L Express Line" decal on the side of the green trailer w/rubber-rimmed metal wheels, red open truck cab, trailer w/original roof & tailgate, some paint wear, Buddy L, late 1920s - early 1930s, 24" l. **$201**

Water sprinkler truck, pressed steel, large yellow tank w/black wording & red cap on top, black cab w/yellow striping, yellow running boards, solid metal red & grey wheels, driver dressed in red, front tin bumper missing, minor scuffing, Strauss, 1930s, 10 1/4" l., 5" h. **$403**

TRAYS - SERVING & CHANGE

Both serving and change trays, once used in taverns, cafes and the like and usually bearing advertising for a beverage maker, are now being widely collected.

All trays listed are heavy tin serving trays, unless otherwise noted.

Also see: *Antique Trader Advertising Price Guide.*

Change, "Carnation Chewing Gum," round, metal, yellow & green w/pink carnations & white package in center, red letters reading "Dorne's Carnation Chewing Gum" w/black letters at bottom reading "Chew Dorne's Carnation Gum" & "Taste The Smell" in red letters in the top & bottom border, ca. 1900, 4 1/4" d. **$300- 375**

Change, "City and Suburban Homes Co.," round, metal w/scalloped rim, image of three white horseheads in center, border reads "City and Suburban Homes Co., Ltd. - Real Estate - Loans - Renting Agents - Fire Insurance - 35 and 37 State St., Detroit," litho by H.D. Beach Co., Coshocton, Ohio, ca. 1910, 4 1/4" d. **$125-175**

Change, "DeLaval Cream Separators," round, metal, scene of woman in long red dress & white apron at separator, young child near doorway, gold lettering on border reads "DeLaval Cream Separators - The World's Standard," ca. 1906, 4 1/4" d. **$325-400**

Change, "Frost Wire Fence Co.," round, metal w/scalloped rim, lithographed metal, center w/ three white horseheads, the border marked "Compliments of The Frost Wire Fence Co. - Cleveland, O.," litho by H.D. Beach Co., Coshocton, Ohio, ca. 1910, 4 1/4" d. **$150-200**

Change, "Grain Belt Beer," round, metal, red & yellow logo in center below "A Barley Malt Product" w/"'The Minneapolis Beer'" below, Grain Belt Brewery, Minneapolis, Minnesota, ca. 1920, 4 1/8" d. **$75-125**

Change, "Gypsy Hosiery," round, lithographed tin, center oval w/gypsy girl in red surrounded by scene of tents & horses, top marked "Gypsy Hosiery" & bottom "E.J. Schroeder, Breese, Illinois," Hargadine-McKittrick Co., litho by H.D. Beach Co., Coshocton, Ohio, ca. 1910, 6" d. **$100-150**

Taking written notes during an auction preview is important, especially if the auction has many items that you plan to bid on. It is impossible to remember every detail even if you're interested in only a few items. Many instances of bidders buying the wrong lot are caused by not taking notes.

Change, "King's Pure Malt," oval, center w/black background & image of uniformed maid holding tray w/a glass & bottle, marked in top border "King's" & the bottom w/medals & banner reading "Panama - Pacific - Medal of Award - International Exposition," ca. 1915, 4 1/4 x 6" **$125-200**

Change, "Lehnert's Beer," round, lithographed metal, image of stag w/large antlers, border w/"Drink Lehnert's Beer - Made in Catasauqua, PA," litho by American Art Works, Coshocton, Ohio, ca. 1910, 4 1/4" d. **$150-200**

Change, "Liberty Beer - American Brew. Co. - Rochester, N.Y. - In Bottles Only," round w/central bust portrait of an Indian maiden in a feathered headdress, arrows & peace pipes framing central circle, minor edge scuffs, 4 1/2" d. **$259**

Change, "Lily Beer," rectangular, metal, table set w/ snack food, bottle of beer & full glass below "Lily - A Beverage" flanked by white calla lily, border reading "Pure As It's [sic] Name - In A Class By Itself! - Healthful and Refreshing - Bottled Only By Rock Island Brewing Co. - Rock Island, Illinois," ca. 1915, 4 1/2 x 6 1/2" **$225-300**

Change, "Miller High Life Beer," rectangular, metal, center blue w/stars & Miller girl sitting on crescent moon holding glass, marked "Miller - High Life - The Champagne of Bottle Beer," goldtone border, ca. 1960s, 4 1/2 x 6 1/2" **$50-75**

Change, "Monticello Whiskey," oval, lithographed metal, fox hunt scene w/large building in background, gold border marked "Monticello - It's All Whiskey," litho by Charles Shonk Co., Chicago, Illinois, ca. 1915, 4 3/8 x 6 1/8" **$225- 275**

Change, "White Rock Table Water," round, lithographed metal, scene w/woman kneeling on rock over water, yellow border w/red & black lettering reads "White Rock - The World's Best Table Water," litho by Charles Shonk Co., Chicago, Illinois, ca. 1900, 4 3/8" d. . **$250-300**

Change, "National Cigar Stands Co.," round, metal, center w/ young girl wearing red sleeveless one-shouldered gown, holding daisies & w/a wreath of daisies in her dark upswept hair, the border designed w/various cigar band seals, marked at the top "Our Brands" & at the bottom "National Cigar Stands Co.," ca. 1910, 6" d. **$100-150**

Change, "Resinol Soap and Ointment," round, metal, center bust portrait of beautiful woman w/long brown hair, low cut dress w/red flower decoration, red flowers in hair, black border w/gold lettering reading "Resinol Soap and Ointment - For All Skin Diseases - At All Drug Stores," 4 1/4" d. **$125-150**

Change, "Robert Burns Cigars," metal, round, bust portrait of man in center, border w/"Robert Burns - Cigars," ca. 1910, 4" d. **$100-150**

Change, "Quick Meal Ranges," oval, lithographed metal, scene of young chicks near an empty shell, red border reading "'Quick Meal' Ranges - Made in St. Louis, Mo.," litho by Ohio Art Company, Bryan, Ohio, ca. 1900, 3 1/4 x 4 1/4" **$150-200**

Change, "Sears, Roebuck and Co.," oval, metal, scene of factory w/waist-length image of woman holding scales on right, marked at top "Sears, Roebuck and Co. - Chicago" & at the bottom "Originators of the Guarantee that Stands the Test in the Scales of Justice," ca. 1920, 4 3/8 x 6" **$125-175**

Change, "Stollwerck Chocolate & Cocoa," round, lithographed metal, gold & red, marked "Stollwerck" in center w/"Gold Brand" above & "Chocolate & Cocoa" below, scrolled border, litho by Kaufmann & Strauss Co., New York, ca. 1910, 5" d. **$100-150**
→

Change, "Rockford High-Grade Watches," rectangular w/flared sides & crimped corners, center color scene of seated pretty young maiden w/flowers, near mint, early 20th c., 3 x 4 5/8" **$209**
←

Change, "Swan Vestas - the Smoker's match," glass, square, bright red label pasted on the bottom w/logo & wording in gold, black, white & red, England, 6" sq., 1 3/4" h. **$143**

Change, "The Davenport Company," round, lithographed metal, center w/bust portrait of lady on red background flanked by Art Nouveau floral designs, brown border w/yellow letters reading "Compliments of The Davenport Co.," litho by Meek & Co., ca. 1903, 4 1/4" d. **$100-150**

Change, "The Prefect Havana Cigar," round, central color full-length portrait of man in 17th c. attire, made in Germany, early 20th c., minor scratch & edge scuffs, 4 1/4" d. **$77**

Change, "Welsbach Mantles," round, lithographed tin, center w/shield form, eagle & banner marked "Welsbach Quality" above red scroll, yellow decorated border, litho by Meek & Beech Co., Coshocton, Ohio, ca. 1900, 4 1/4" d. **$125-175**

Serving, "White Rock Beer - Akron Brewing Company," round, large beautiful color center scene of an exotic beauty lounging against the head of a large tiger, 1912, very good condition, 13 1/2" d. **$690**

Serving, "Edelweiss Beer," center color bust portrait of a pretty young red-headed girl wearing a white & red shawl against a black ground, the border band w/edelweiss blossoms, dated 1913, excellent condition, 13" d. **$176**

Serving, "West End Brewing Co.," tin, image of Columbia w/barrel, holding shafts of wheat, near mint condition, some slight chipping at rim edges, 13" d. **$1,380**

Serving, "Hopsburger - the Golden Beer," round, color bust portrait of a lovely young woman wearing an off-the-shoulder gown against a black background, ca. 1910, very light surface wear, 13" d. **$308**

Serving, "John H. Hauser & Co. - Fine Shoes," oval, a large colorful central scene of patriotic allegorical figures among clouds, Liberty standing in the center, early 20th c., spot at bottom left inpainted, few tiny chips, 13 x 16" **$374**

VENDING & GAMBLING DEVICES

Arcade, "Beast - From Which Are You Descended?," electric, upright wood cabinet w/a reverse-painted glass front decorated in color w/various jungle beasts, inserting penny & squeezing handle determines which beast is your ancestor, Exhibit Supply Co., Chicago, copyrighted 1947, good working condition, 10 x 11 1/2", 28" h. **$719**

Arcade, Caille Bros. "Olympic Puncher," cast-iron strength tester, upright pedestal on square base, inserting coin & punching the padded leather disk records the force of the punch on the dial above, red paint on base, nickel-plated cast-iron dial bezel & marquee, oak & cast-iron wall mounting bracket, restored w/ reproduction paper dial face, ca. 1906, 69 1/2" h. **$12,938**

Arcade, "Disposition Register - How Do You Impress People?," upright wooden case w/glass front, inserting penny & squeezing handle indicates how you impress people, Exhibit Supply Co., Chicago, ca. 1934, very good condition, 10 x 11", 23 1/2" h. **$578**

Arcade, "Electric Traveling Crane" digger machine, oak cabinet w/ glass & aluminum front, interior aluminum castings of the Empire State Building flank a background scene of ironworkers erecting steel girders, includes two bags of prizes & capsules, Art Deco graphics, Mutoscope Reel Company, New York, New York, patented 1932, very good condition, 20 x 23", 41 1/2" h. **$2,128**

Arcade, "Electricity Is Life," upright steel cabinet on oak base, one-cent operation, cranking side handles produces mild electric shock, early 20th c., Standard Advertising Company, light restoration, 10 x 16 1/2", 19 1/2" h. **$4,025**

Arcade, "Lift-O-Graph" strength tester, electrified, oak cabinet on a heavy cast-iron base, one-cent operation allowing player to pull up on the large steel handle to measure strength, International Mutoscope Reel Co., early 20th c., 23 x 36", 98" h. **$4,600**

Arcade, "Mill's Autostereoscope," tall upright serpentine-front quarter-sawn oak cabinet w/ raised panel sides & door at the front, raised on cast-iron cabriole legs w/claw & glass ball feet, all-original decorated cast-iron parts including coin feed slot & viewer, top w/upright oak-framed marquee w/original cardboard insert sign reading "The French Doll," w/a photo of a scantily clad woman, appears to be original & untouched, working condition, early 20th c., 16 x 20", 73" h.
.... **$3,450**

Arcade, Model DL mutoscope, early electrified cast-metal "clamshell" style body w/"iron horse" base, upright serpentine marquee frame at top w/cardboard insert card for silent screen star Ted Wells in the Western "Desert Dust," refinished in two-tone blue & white w/gilt trim, ca. 1920s, overall 75" h.
.... **$3,220**

Arcade, "Swami" fortune teller w/ stand, floor-model, cast-aluminum top figure of a turbaned swami peering into a crystal ball, one-cent operation w/handle turning clockwork mechanism, activating internal filmstrip of fortunes & light bulb w/large dry cell battery, fortunes projected up into the crystal ball, Future Products Co., Chicago, Illinois, ca. 1920s, cast-metal crystal ball w/a few cracks, some metal loss to its base, battery dead, good all-original paint, 48" h. **$3,048**

Arcade, "Over The Top" skill game, upright steel case w/aluminum & glass front, the object being to move a coin through the aluminum & glass maze, Boyce Coin Machine Co., Tuckahoe, New York, ca. 1926, 2 x 8 1/2", 20 1/2" h. **$804**

Collar button vendor, "Zeno," upright square glass-sided case w/six interior columns & tin top w/ coin slots, on a square cast-iron base, 10-cent operation, early 20th c., small chip to side of one glass panel, 5 1/2" sq., 10 1/2" h.
.... **$518**

Fortune vendor, Jennings "Duchess Doubl-Jack" fortune telling machine, "bull's-eye" version, cast-aluminum front w/oak case retaining original "Fortune Teller" reel strips, glass viewing window, ca. 1933, 14 x 16", 19" h.
.... **$1,323**

Gambling, Bally "777" tabletop slot machine, electro-mechanical cast metal & plastic case, 10-cent play w/five coin multiplier, late 1960s - early 1970s, few burn marks on top of plastic cabinet, good working condition, 16 x 18 1/2", 33 1/2" h. **$1,080**

Gambling, Buckley "Bones" (dice) tabletop slot machine, cast-metal case w/oak base, coin-op crap game w/25-cent play, ca. 1936, very good original condition w/key & operating instructions, 11 1/2 x 16", 12 1/2" h. **$1,825**

Gambling, Caille "Roulette" counter-top slot machine, wood-finished metal & cast aluminum & nickel, roulette wheel on the top, slot panel across the top front, working, 13" sq., 16" h. **$33,350**

Gambling, Clawson "Automatic Dice Machine," floor-model, Gorsky reproduction of the ca. 1890s dice machine, 5-cent play, machine picking up dice, shaking & tossing them via a clockwork mechanism, professionally restored, w/key, 9 3/4 x 10", case 26 1/2" h., stand 30" h. **$3,680**

> Old slot machines or "one armed bandits" could be rigged relatively easily. The operator only had to block one of the holes in the spinning wheel to prevent a metal spring-loaded finger from poking through to release a payout. Modern slot machines are controlled by computer chips and are monitored by state gaming commissions to prevent game fixing. Still, the odds are against the player, as casinos have carefully calculated odds in their favor.

Gambling, Mills "Bell-O-Matic" tabletop slot machine, cast-metal classic "hightop" triple-7 machine w/Art Deco styling, ca. 1949, some light paint wear, replaced coin view window, w/key not working, 15 x 16", 26 1/2" h. **$1,323**

Gambling, Mills "Brown Front Bell" tabletop slot machine, cast-aluminum front & original stenciled oak case, front w/variant of "Bursting Cherry" design, 10-cent play, ca. 1938, cracked glass coin window, original working condition w/keys, 15 x 16", 26" h. **$1,725**

Gambling, Mills "Q.T." slot machine on stand, cast-aluminum case w/Art Deco designs, introduced in 1934 w/a one-cent play, this later version w/5-cent play, on original sheet metal Q.T. customer stand, front repainted, replacement jackpot card, good working order w/original front & rear locks w/ key, slot machine 12 1/2 x 13", 18" h. **$1,610**

Gambling, Mills "Liberty Bell Gum-Fruit" tabletop slot machine, early cast-iron footed case w/three reels showing playing card symbols, 5-cent play, original marquee showing various playing card pay-outs in trade, unique horizontal coin mechanism & side panel castings w/the Statue of Liberty & the New York skyline, ca. 1914, appears all-original, original worn paint, rear door w/small vertical crack, working condition, no key, 13 x 13", 20 1/2" h. **$8,050**

Gambling, Mills "Operator Bell" slot machine on oak stand, cast-aluminum front w/oak record cabinet base, w/classic Mills owl designs, 25-cent play, hinged door in base opens to two pull-out drawers, slot w/replacement rear door, lock, coin drawer, coin chute & payout card, original reels, working condition w/key, ca. 1921, slot machine 15 x 16", 24" h., cabinet 18" sq., 35" h. **$1,668**

Gambling, Mills "War Eagle" tabletop slot machine, cast-aluminum front w/eagle motif on oak case, 25-cent play, original excellent decals, front casting repainted w/new jackpot card, working condition w/keys, ca. 1930s, 15 x 16", 26" h. .. **$1,955**

Gambling, Mills "Pilot" counter-type trade stimulator, cast-iron case molded w/a large sailing ship, one reel machine w/playing card symbols, unrestored, ca. 1906, 11 1/2 x 12", 14 3/4" h. .. **$7,475**

Gambling, Caille's "Spinx" slot machine, 5-cent play, Egyptian decoration w/Sphinx at bottom left & right, ca. 1930s, Caille Bros., Detroit, Michigan.... **$1,850**

Gambling, roulette wheel on base, colorfully painted wooden wheel on a cross-form base, good patina & paint, ca. 1900, wheel 25" d., overall 34" h. **$978**

Gambling, Jennings "Little Duke" countertop slot machine, cast-metal front w/red, yellow & black enamel trim, wood sides & back, 1-cent play, some overall wear, no key, nail added in back, ca. 1930s, 11 x 16", 22" h. **$1,650**

VENDING & GAMBLING DEVICES

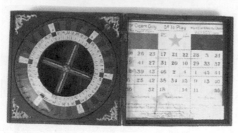

Gambling, Mills roulette wheel, portable miniature version in a wooden case, featuring a paper numbers face on a wooden wheel fastened to a cast-iron bearing assembly, interior box lid showing the gaming number layout for placing nickel bets w/cigar payoffs, stamped-brass decorative cartouches applied inside & outside, early 20th c., overall paint wear to box, moisture staining on paper, some chips to inside of paper roulette wheel face, 13" sq., 4 1/2" h. **$900**

Gambling, roulette wheel, Evans reverse-painted glass type, wheel w/nickel-plated pins & framework, reverse decoration on glass appears to represent dice, center reverse-painted star, signed "Arthur Popper, New York" inside the hub, original cast-iron tripod base & wood post & indicator, slight damages, flaps replaced or repaired, some rust on foot, some bent pins, early 20th c., wheel 53" d., overall 7' h. **$1,725**

Gambling, roulette wheel, wooden board mounted w/colorful six-panel lithographed paper wheel illustrating various animals in each panel, made in France, early 20th c., 9 1/2" d. **$150**

Gambling, wheel of fortune, a two-sided spinning wooden wheel painted white w/black Arabic numerals, raised on a tall square post on a double-rung cross-form base, early 20th c., 67" h. **$345**

Gambling, Caille "Quintette" floor model poker machine, five-player, oak w/cast-iron fittings & pedestal base, replated castings, new finish on base, early 20th c., 6' h. **$29,900**

Gambling, Caille "Wasp" tabletop slot machine, nickel-play, nickel-plated case & swivel base, original untouched condition, early 20th c., 14" h. **$14,950**

Gambling, roulette wheel, wooden wheel decorated w/elaborate nickel-plated ornaments, on its original cast-iron tripod base, by the H.C. Evans Co., Chicago, Illinois, ca. 1900, working condition, wheel 33" d., overall 47" h. **$1,955**

Gambling, Watling "Rol-A-Top" tabletop slot machine, classic cast-metal front w/cornucopia & gold coins, twin jackpot model w/5-cent play, ca. 1930s, professionally repainted, cracked wired glass jackpot window, working condition w/keys, 15 x 16", 26 1/2" h. **$2,645**

Gambling, wheel of fortune, large narrow wooden wheel painted dark yellow w/blocks painted w/card suit signs & four panels w/a racing horse, eight baluster- and ring-turned red-painted spokes around a small red & black wheels w/knob finials, late 19th - early 20th c., 42" d. **$834**

Gum machine, Mansfield's "Automatic Clerk," tall vertical glass sides w/white enamel slot panel at top reading "Winter Green - Blood Orange - 5¢," glass front etched "Automatic Clerk - Manfield's Choice Pepsin Gum," patented in 1902, missing marquee, 7" w., 12" h. ... **$1,150**

Gum vendor, "Adams' Pepsin Tutti-Frutti Gum," upright wood cabinet w/white porcelain front & side porcelain panels, two- column style, one-cent operation, ca. 1898, old red wood finish, some wood loss on rear panel, small chip on one side panel, 5 x 11 1/2", 29 1/2" h. **$6,038**

Gum vendor, "Pulver Chewing Gum," upright red porcelain case w/glass front showing rare cop & robber characters inside, one-cent operation, a few paint chips, w/key, ca. 1930s, 4 1/2 x 0", 20 1/2" h. **$1,553**

Gumball vendor, "Topper," stepped metal top on the squared glass jar above the cast-metal base, Victor Vending Corp., some paint loss & corrosion to base, w/key, ca. 1960s, 16" h. **$90**

Gumball vendor, Pierce Tool & Mfg. Co. "Gypsy Fortune Teller," 1-cent play, spinning roulette-style wheel w/gypsy designs, replaced rear door, ca. 1934, 6 x 14 1/2", 15" h. **$330**

Lighter fluid vendor, "Van-Lite," cast-metal figural countertop gas pump for refilling pocket lighters, by Arthur Kauf, Lockport, New York, ca. 1933, good condition, 19" h. ... **$540**

Peanut vendor, Northwestern Model 33, red porcelain lid on the cylindrical glass container on a red metal base, one-cent operation, concealed chip to glass globe rim, w/key, ca. 1930s, 15 1/2" h. ... **$345**

Popcorn vendor, tall square glass-enclosed top w/a metal lid, the lower cast metal case marked "Hot Popcorn - 10¢," raised on a tall trestle base, electrified, Electro-Serve Inc., Peoria, Illinois, ca. 1940s, 60" h. .. **$360**

Trade stimulator, Rock-Ola "Five Jacks" tabletop coin drop machine, cast-aluminum front panel on a dovetailed quarter-sawn oak case w/5-cent play mechanism, orange & green enameled trim, player inserts nickel & launches it w/finger, Rock-Ola Mfg. Co., Chicago, Illinois, ca. 1930, working condition w/key, 10 x 17 3/4", 20" h. **$1,035**

Trade stimulator, Rock-Ola "Five Jacks" tabletop coin drop machine, cast-aluminum front panel on a dovetailed quarter-sawn oak case w/5-cent play mechanism, pink & green repainted enameled trim, player inserts nickel & launches it w/finger, Rock-Ola Mfg. Co., Chicago, Illinois, ca. 1930, working condition w/key, 10 x 17 3/4", 20" h. **$1,560**

Trade stimulators became popular in saloons in the 1880s as an alternative to gambling machines. They were deemed legal because they paid out in products like cigars, chewing gum, and stamps, rather than cash. The machines became popular in stores and restaurants as well, and although they were supposed to pay out only in products, some clerks awarded their customers in cash, a powerful enticement for increased patronage.

WATCHES

WATCHES MARKET REPORT

According to Girard Sensoli, of Pinckney, Michigan, who runs Girard's (www.girards.com) and World Wide Traders Shows (www.wwtshows.com), vintage watches are still increasing in value. While his sales volume has been down during the recession, prices have been holding steady. His sales are strongest in the $100 to $500 price range.

He has seen a significant increase in the number of people buying at shows versus online. He attributes this to people wanting to see and hold timepieces before buying rather than just purchasing from a photo and description. People have been burned buying on eBay because too many sellers don't guarantee their watches or offer a return policy. Also, extremely convincing fakes and reproductions are prolific, so buyers are turning to trusted dealers who will guarantee their goods. "The best way to buy is from a reputable dealer who has been in business for many years and has earned the trust of his customers," he said. The same is true with auctions. If you buy at an auction, rather than from a dealer, make sure the auction house guarantees authenticity.

Sensoli has seen growing sales from Japanese customers. While the Japanese produce huge numbers of high-tech watches, they are also fond of antique watches and have disposable income. The Chinese are an up-and-coming market as well. The Germans and Italians, however, are not buying like they used to five to eight years ago, as prices have climbed past the point they are willing to pay.

Pocket watch sales have increased in the last few years and now comprise 10 to 15 percent of Girard's sales. He estimates that 40 percent of his customers purchase watches for everyday use, 10 percent are serious collectors, and 50 percent are speculators who are investing for profit later.

Sensoli believes the future is bright for watches because they are status symbols. He recommends buying quality watches, and in particular, Omega, Longines, and pre-1960s Hamilton watches—those that were made in the United States before the company was sold and moved to Switzerland.

He advises novice collectors to specialize in a particular area, studying it carefully by consulting experts, researching prices, and reading books to learn about its characteristics, movements, and other essential information, such as whether parts are available. He cautions collectors to be wary of fads. For example, a number of years ago, the prices of Swatch watches became inflated, creating an unsustainable boom that eventually collapsed, making them hard to sell now.

Auction Houses
Antiquorum (www.antiquorum.com)
Doyle New York (www.doylenewyork.com)
Leslie Hindman (www.lesliehindman.com)
Weschler's (www.weschlers.com)
Heritage (www.ha.com)

WATCHES

Pocket Watches & Pendants

Hunting case, man's, National Watch Co., 14k gold case w/ fine scroll engraving, late 19th c., w/original box, not working, 1 3/4" d. **$403**

Lady's hunting case watch, Elgin, delicately engraved gold-filled Dueber case, keywind mechanism, late 19th c., 1 3/4" d. **$173**

Lady's hunting case watch, pendant-style, 18k gold case polished & set w/a diamond, sapphire & ruby accent, the white enameled dial w/Arabic numerals, jeweled & adjusted damascened lever escapement movement, late 19th - early 20th c. **$264**

> The earliest pocket watches were made by German locksmith Peter Henlein in the the early 1500s. Pocket watches remained in style until after World War I, when wristwatches came in vogue.

Lady's hunting case watch, the round case decorated in green guilloche enamel centered by a rose-cut diamond starburst & bordered by tiny diamonds, suspended from a double old European- and rose-cut diamond-mounted chain & bail joined to an enameled baton & seed pearl necklace, the silvertone dial w/ Arabic numerals, platinum & 18k gold mount, some enamel loss, Edwardian, England, early 20th c. **$3,878**

Lady's hunting case watch, Vacheron & Constantin, 18k gold case w/three bands of rose-cut diamonds ending in cabochon garnets, the white enamel dial w/ Arabic numerals, a jeweled nickel movement, suspended from a scrolling openwork gold pink trimmed w/cabochon garnets & tiny diamonds, triple signed, fitted box, early 20th c. **$2,585**

Lady's open face watch, pendant-type, enamel, platinum & diamond, the back of the platinum-topped 18k gold case in marine blue guilloché enamel centerd by a square set w/rose-cut diamonds & bordered by a narrow white enamel Greek key band, the goldtone dial w/Arabic numerals, suspended from a platinum, enamel baton & rose-cut diamond fancy link chain, Edwardian, England, early 20th c., overall 22" l. **$2,468**

Lady's pendant watch, Art Deco style, the round silvertone engine-turned dial w/Arabic numerals, a jeweled damascene nickel movement, platinum matte polished hunting case bow-set w/rose-cut diamonds & sapphires w/a cabochon sapphire in the center, w/a 14k white gold & sapphire bar pin, case interior inscribed "Paris," ca. 1920s **$2,115**

Lady's pendant watch, hunting case, Art Deco style, a flattened teardrop form set w/baguette and single-cut diamonds highlighted by buff-top calibré-cut rubies & channel-set calibré-cut only floral designs, accented w/cabochon emerald, ruby & onyx pieces, millegrain accents, scrolling foliage engraved on the sides & back, crystal, two onyx & two diamonds missing **$4,700**

Lady's verge watch, L'Epine, Paris, France, designed in the shape of a mandolin w/multicolored enamel decoration on the 18k gold ground, opens to revealed a signed gilt movement, suspended from a trace link chain, late 19th - early 20th c. **$4,700**

Man's hunting case watch, E. Howard Watch Co., seventeen jewel movement, 14k yellow gold case w/central shield on engine-turned ground, case marked "Keystone," ca. 1903 .... **$805**

Man's open-face watch, Patek Philippe, 18k yellow gold, the silvertone dial w/Arabic numerals enclosing an 18-jewel eight adjustment damascened nickel movement, the reverse w/worn monogram, 20th c., triple-signed, boxed **$1,880**

Man's hunting case watch, Illinois, lever- set movement, finely engraved 14k yellow gold case, slight case wear, minor hairlines in dial, ca. 1880 .... **$1,035**

Man's hunting case watch, Elgin, lever-set movement, in a finely engraved 14k gold case applied w/an elk head, w/original Elgin mahogany case, late 19th c., w/short watch chain .... **$460** →

POCKET WATCHES & PENDANTS

Man's hunting case watch, Waltham, 14k tri-color gold case engraved w/foral & leaf designs among interlocking circles, the white enamel dial w/Roman numerals & subsidiary seconds dial, jeweled adjusted nickel movement, late 19th - early 20th c. **$646**

Man's open-face watch, Art Deco-style, 14k gold, goldtone metal dial w/Arabic numerals & subsidiary seconds dial, stepped bezel, enclosing a 17-jewel nickel lever escapement movement, w/rectangular trace link fob chain, w/Dreicer & Co. box, ca. 1930s (ILLUS of watch) **$323**

Man's open-face watch, E. Howard Watch Co., open-faced w/marked dial w/Arabic numerals, small seconds dial, seventeen jewel movement, 14k yellow gold case marked "KW.C.C.O.," minor hairline in dial, tiny fleck at numeral 4, ca. 1900 .... **$403**

Man's open-face watch, Tiffany & Co., 18k yellow gold & platinum, Art Nouveau design, gold case w/applied platinum wire in a looped clover-style design against a chased & répoussé ground w/a small bird, the gilt dial w/applied free-form Arabic numerals, curved & scrolling bi-color hands, subsidiary seconds dial, jeweled & damscened nickel lver escapement movement, ca. 1890s, triple-signed (ILLUS. of back) **$35,250**

Man's open-face watch, Vacheron, 18k gold, the white enamel dial w/ Roman numerals & a subsidiary seconds dial, enclosing a jeweled lever escapement movement, early 20th c. **$646**

Pocket watch, open-face, man's, Elgin, octagonal white gold-filled case marked "Sparton 0781559," works marked by Elgin, white enameled dial w/Arabic numerals & a subsidiary seconds dial, minor hairline cracks in face, ca. 1903 .... **$207**

As their name suggests, hunting-case pocket watches were made with a lid to protect them from the elements during outdoor use. Other pocket watches, mainly used indoors, were left open faced for aesthetic reasons. Railroad pocket watches, which had to meet stringent requirements to ensure rail safety, were required to be open-faced so their dials would be visiible at all times.

Wrist Watches

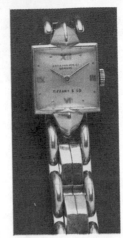

Cartier, lady's Art Deco style, the diamond- shaped silvered dial w/Roman numerals framed by rose-cut diamonds & onyx tablets framed by more diamonds, rose-cut diamond winding stem, completed by a later strap, the platinum-topped 18k gold case enclosing a 19-jewel movement, eight-adjustment, signed by Cartier, Paris, ca. 1920 .... **$15,275**

Patek Philippe, man's Retro style 14k gold, the square silvertone dial w/Roman & abstract numerals under a domed crystal, on a shaped end lugs attached to a pyramidal arched bracelet, an 18-jewel damascened movement, Tiffany & Co., mid- 20th c., 6 1/2" l. **$1,880**

Wrist watch, lady's, Lucien Piccard, 14k rose gold, citrine & diamond, the rosetone metal dial w/Arabic & dot numerals, an unadjusted 17-jewel Swiss movement, the wide bezel set w/a ring of fancy-cut citrines flanked by a row of three more citrines on the triple-link chain strap, four diamond accents, signed, crystal detached, 6 1/4" l. **$1,410**

Wrist watch, lady's, Patek Philippe & E. Gubelin, 18k gold, the square silver tone metal dial w/Roman & baton numerals, a jeweled nickel movement, on a flexible gold bracelet of shaped & rectangular links, dial, case, movement & band signed, 6 3/4" l. **$1,998**

Wrist watch, lady's, Hublot, stainless steel, white gold, diamond & mother-of-pearl, the mother-of-pearl round diamond w/date aperture, full-cut diamond bezel, a quartz movement, completed by a rubber band w/ deployant clasp **$3,290**

• Thieves sometimes target estate auctions that will be conducted in an unoccupied home. They find the address in advertisements and stake out the site. Precautions should be taken, including having the dwelling occupied or guarded in the days leading up to the auction.

• Valuable watches should be cleaned at least every five years to minimize wear and ensure that they keep time correctly. Even a well-sealed watch case will gradually accumulate moisture and dust inside that will cause excess friction and wear to moving parts. A professional watch repair and cleaning firm can clean all internal parts of a watch ultrasonically to keep it in good working order.

WRIST WATCHES

Wrist watch, lady's, Waltham, Art Deco style, platinum, emerald & diamond, the long rectangular silver tone dial w/Arabic numerals framed by bead- and bezel-set marquise, full- & single-cut diamonds, channel-set emerald highlights, engraved case joined to a bracelet of box- set old European- and transitional-cut diamonds, millegrain accents, diamonds weighing about 3.07 cts., missing two emeralds, 6 1/4" l. **$3,819**

Wrist watch, lady's, platinum & diamond, Art Deco style, oval case w/the bezel bead-set w/ rose-cut diamonds joining arched lugs further set w/rose- and old European-cut diamonds, round ivory tone dial w/Arabic numerals, jeweled movement, white gold snake chain bracelet, by Agassiz, 5 1/2" l. **$1,763**

Wrist watch, man's, gold (14k) & diamond, square case w/ black enamel bezel edged w/68 diamonds, square goldtone dial w/no numerals, on a black alligator strap w/an 18k gold & diamond clasp, by Concord, 9" l. **$705**

Wrist watch, man's, gold (14k), square case & round silver tone dial w/stick numerals & cushion-shape bezel, automatic movement, w/a brown leather band, closure not original, retailed by Tiffany & Co. **$470**

Wrist watch, lady's, Rolex, 14k gold, the rounded dial w/fancy Arabic numerals on the yellow gold case fitted w/a 15 jewel movement, new lizard skin band, vintage **$717**

Wrist watch, man's, Hermès, "Arceau" model, the white metal dial w/Arabic numerals, enclosing a quartz movement, gilt- metal case joined to a textured leather strap, 18k gold closure **$823**

Wrist watch, lady's, Longines, Art Deco style, platinum & diamond, the silver tone metal dial w/Arabic numbers, enclosing a Longines 18-jewel five-adjustment move- ment, case & lugs bead-set w/single- and full-cut diamonds weighing about 1.16 cts., joining a 14k white gold woven mesh band, 6 3/8" l. **$881**

Wrist watch, lady's, Whiteside & Blank, Art Deco style, platinum & diamond, a white metal dial w/Arabic numerals, signed Cressarow Swiss 18-jewel adjusted movement, octagonal case w/openwork bezel bead-set w/single-cut diamonds, completed by a grosgrain strap, company mark, closure replaced....... **$823**

Jewels are used in watches in order to reduce friction. They are effective because they resist wear and can be polished very smooth.

WEATHERVANES

Cod fish, carved wood & gilt metal, large wood body w/six gilt-metal fins & a large gilt-metal tail, open mouth w/large nail as barbel, retains 50-70% of gilding, great finish, from Kennebunkport, Maine, 19th c., piece missing from end of tail & upper slice off body, some bullet holes in metal, 49" l., 16" h. **$7,475**

Cow, molded copper, old yellow paint, standing animal w/applied horns & tail, on a modern base, possibly Cushing & White, Waltham, Massachusetts, late 19th c., 32" l., 18 3/4" h. **$8,365**

Eagle, gilt copper, full-bodied flying eagle by Fiske, balanced on a ball w/an arrow below, some wear & minor dents & splits, late 19th c., on modern base, 34" l., 27" h. **$3,163**

Eagle, copper, hollow-bodied spread-winged bird perched on a ball above a long arrow, mid-20th c., 22" w., 19" h. **$518**

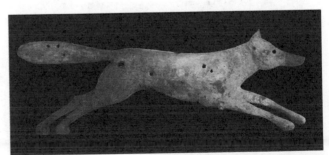

Fox, leaping, cast & molded copper, hollow-cut eyes & ear & cut tail, old holes, attributed to A. Jewel & Co., Waltham, Massachusetts, mid-19th c., 42 1/2" l., 15 1/2" h. **$20,315**

WEATHERVANES

Horse & jockey, the horse composed of molded sheet copper w/cast-iron head, the jockey having zinc head w/copper visor on his hat, verdigris patina w/traces of gilt, includes black metal stand, America, 19th c., dents, minor seam separations, 34" l., 19 1/4" h. **$8,813**

Gamecock, molded copper w/a flattened full-body w/sheet copper tail & embossed detailings, gilt finish, mounted on an arrow w/iron point & corrugated sheet copper tail, weathered surface, no stand, American, second half 19th c., 25 3/4" w., 21 1/2" h. **$11,750**

Horse & rider, molded copper & zinc, the male riding holding the reins, rust on his head & shoulders, attributed to J.W. Fiske & Company, New York, New York, late 19th c., 37 1/2" l., 18 1/2" h. **$15,535**

Horse, cast & sheet iron, prancing pose w/cast mane & sheet metal tail, Rochester Iron Works, Rochester, New Hampshire, 1850-75, 25" l., 19 1/4" h. **$19,200**

Horse, copper, prancing stance, full body mounted on original rod support, verdigris patina over areas of gilt, America, 19th c., 25" l., 22" h. **$10,350**

Horse, gilt copper & cast metal, horse w/copper body, flame-style mane, stamped tail & cast-metal head jumping through iron hoop, set in custom wood stand w/metal rod, A.L. Jewell & Co., America, one old tiny split to front hoof, 30" l., 15 1/4" h. from top of hoop to bottom of hoop **$16,100**

Lady equestrian, gilt molded copper & cast zinc, a fashionable lady rider wearing a top had sitting side-saddle on a prancing horse, A. L. Jewell, Waltham, Massachusetts, late 19th c., 28" w., 27" h. **$36,000**

Horse, molded copper & cast zinc, "Patchen," racing pose w/flying mane & tail, cast zinc head, late 19th c., 42" l., 19" h. **$3,600**

Horse, running, molded copper, swell-bodied model w/flowing tail mounted on a rod, fine verdigris, New England, last quarter 19th c., minor imperfections, traces of gilting, 30" l., 15 1/2" h., ... **$2,530**

Rooster, tin, narrow full body w/ sheet cutout tail, a round hollow rod at center of body extending through leg, painted red, crimped & soldered edge, 19th c., rusted hole to bottom edge, some repair to beak & some loss to comb & tail tip, 28 3/4" h. **$2,300**

Locomotive, steel, flat cut-out design of a primitive locomotive on four wheels, open back compartment & two looped slats to hold bar, rustry, 23 1/4" l., 13" h. **$288**

Quill, gilt molded & sheet copper, long feather quill on a rod w/a ball & spearpoint finial, late 19th c., 49" l., 30" h. **$8,400**

WEATHERVANES

Ram, molded copper, full-bodied form w/articulated mouth, eyes, hairs & curled horns, New England, 19th c., on rod support w/modern base, 35" w., 28 1/2" h. **$13,145**

Rooster, copper, molded hollow body, standing pose w/green patina, one bullet hole in one side, probably early 20th c., one foot loose at solder joint, 18 1/2"w., 22" h. **$1,495**

Rooster, gilded sheet copper, stylized bird w/low serrated comb & crest feather, high around & deeply cut-out tail, weathered gilded surface w/verdigris, w/ weighted three-dimensional head & breast, w/a black metal stand, 19th c., 23 1/2" l., 23" h. **$7,638**

Rooster, gilt molded copper, standing bird w/head raised high, finely detailed feathers & head, late 19th c., 16" w., 26 1/2" h. **$8,400**

Rooster, molded copper, Hamburg rooster w/flattened full body, verdigris patina w/traces of gilt, attributed to L.W. Cushing & Sons, Waltham, Massachusetts, late 19th c., repairs, bullet holes, dents, 29" l., 28" h. **$25,850**

Rooster, painted wood & iron, a stylized long serpentine body w/a high & wide arched pierced tail, mounted w/a conforming narrow iron bar for support, remnants of old paint, late 19th c., 26" l., 27" h. **$24,000**

Centaur, molded copper & cast lead, the flattened full-body figure drawing a bow & arrow w/molded sheet copper tail, the surface w/vestiges of yellow sizing, gilt, verdigris & black paint, attributed to A.L. Jewell & Co., Waltham, Massachusetts, 1852-67, repairs, 39 1/4" l., 32 1/4" h........ **$51,700**

Sailboat, molded copper, fully rigged w/rippling metal sheet sails, American, late 19th - early 20th c., 37" l., 36 3/4" h. **$7,768**

Goddess Liberty, gilt molded copper & painted sheet iron, woman wearing a flowing dress, shoulder banner & Liberty cap, one arm pointing forward, the other holding up a large American flag, together w/original iron, copper & wood post, ball directionals & a period photo of the vane in situ, William Henis, Philadelphia, mid-19th c., 29" w., 30" h.............. **$1,080,000**

WESTERN CHARACTER COLLECTIBLES

Since the closing of the Western frontier in the late 19th century, the myth of the American cowboy has loomed large in popular fiction. With the growth of the motion picture industry early in this century, cowboy heroes became a mainstay of the entertainment industry. By the 1920s major Western heroes were a big draw at the box office, this popularity continuing with the dawning of the TV age in the 1950s. We list here a variety of collectibles relating to all American Western personalities popular this century.

Annie Oakley holster set, "Annie Oakley Daisy Holster Set," genuine black leather, no pistols included in the set, based on the TV show, ca. 1954-56, near mint in original box **$700**

Buffalo Bill booklet, color-printed paper, "Buffalo Bill's - Wild West," includes 11 full-color illustrations of the show, stamp on last page inscribed "Original Pictures - Buffalo Bill's Wild-West - Cy. 1891," light soiling, 5 x 7" (ILLUS. of two views) **$461**

Buffalo Bill mug, china, figural, designed as a bust of Buffalo Bill w/a figural buffalo handle, bronze-colored paint finish, early 20th c., 5 3/4" w., 4 3/4" h. (ILLUS. of two views) **$152**

Buffalo Bill paperweight, oblong flattened thick clear glass w/an early black & white photo of Buffalo Bill applied to the bottom, made by the Abrams Paperweight Company, Pittsburgh, patent dated November 29, 1892, 2 1/2 x 4" **$230**

Buffalo Bill program, for "Niblo's Garden - Scouts of the Prairie," which included Buffalo Bill Cody, Texas Jack, Ned Buntline & 25 Indian warriors, 1873, 8 1/2 x 11" **$1,188**

Gene Autry cap gun, nickel-plated cast- iron pistol w/red plastic grips, Autry name raised above trigger, by Kenton Hardware, ca. 1940, one grip damaged, 8 3/8" l. **$81**

Gene Autry lunchbox, metal w/ thermos, marked "Universal Landers, Frary & Clark, New Britain, Conn.," 1954, scratches, 8 1/2" w., 3 1/2" deep, 7" h. **$275**

Buffalo Bill photograph, large sepia-toned image of the complete Wild West cast in London, titled across the bottom "Buffalo Bill's West West Company's Presentation to their Chief on his Birthday at Olympia, London, February 26, 1903," blindstamp of James E. Hunt, London, England, minor wear along top right corner of images, matted & framed, 9 1/2 x 11 1/2" **$575**

Lone Ranger cap gun, cast-iron pistol w/ivory-colored plastic grips, Lone Ranger name stamped above grips, by Kilgore, ca. 1938, 8 1/2" l. **$104**

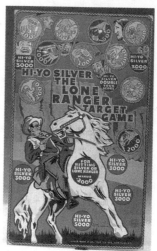

Lone Ranger target game, large color- lithographed tin target featuring a large image of the Lone Ranger & Silver below various rope-enclosed circle targets w/various point values, by Louis Marx, ca. 1938, 16 x 27" **$127**

Rex Allen comic book, Dell Publishing, color cover photo of Rex & his horse, 1940s . **$10-40**

Rin Tin Tin comic book, Dell #11, color photo of Rin Tin Tin carrying a holster in his mouth, 1950s, depending on condition **$20-75**

The original Rin Tin Tin was just a puppy when an American soldier, Lee Duncan, found him in a partially destroyed dog kennel in France during World War I. Duncan brought the dog back to the United States, where he began demonstrating his talents. Rin Tin Tin's film career began after producer Charles Jones discovered him performing at a dog show. When "Rinty" died in 1932 at 14, he was returned to France and buried in a pet cemetery near Paris. A number of his descendents carried on his movie and television role for decades after he passed from the scene.

Rin Tin Tin comic book, Dell #12, color photo of Rin Tin Tin holding lit sticks of dynamite in his mouth, 1950s, depending on condition **$20-75**

WESTERN CHARACTER COLLECTIBLES

Rin Tin Tin comic book, Dell #16, color photo of Rin Tin Tin resting on a saddle, 1950s, depending on condition **$20-75**

Roy Rogers comic book, Dell #25, color cover photo of Roy & his dog, Bullet, 1950, depending on condition **$20-75**

Roy Rogers guitar, toy-type, cardboard & wood, printed w/image of Roy & Trigger, Range Rhythm Toys, 1950s, depending on condition .. **$75-175**

Tom Mix poster, rectangular, full color oval bust portrait of white-hatted Mix under "TOM MIX CIRCUS" in dark bold letters, oval at bottom containing facsimile Tom Mix signature over "Entertainment Insurance - Plus Courtesy, Honesty - and Appreciation," all on textured gold/orange ground, 28 x 42" ... **$605**

Tom Mix booklets, a set of card-sized eight-page paper booklets w/two-color cover featuring a sketched scene w/Tom Mix, issued by National Chicle, 1934, excellent to near mint, set of 48 ....**$3,687**

Tom Mix Big Little Book, Terror Trail, No. 762, 1934, The Big Little Book series (binding damaged & taped) **$30-40**

Tom Mix secet manual & decoder badge, original Ralston premium set also including booklet titled "The Life of Tom Mix," mint & unused in original mailing envelope, the set................. **$66**

Tom Mix secret writing kit, included manual w/code information, cardboard decoder, two glass vials of ink, developer material, Ralston Purina promotion, 1940 .... **$425**

Tom Mix photograph, sepia-toned bust portrait of Mix w/one hand at the brim of his hat, inscribed "Best luck - To my friend Fred Warrell - Tom Mix," Warrell being the assistant manager of the Sells- Floto Circus where Mix was a star, w/clippings & biographical information on Warrell, 8 x 10" **$338**

WOOD SCULPTURES

WOOD SCULPTURES

American folk sculpture is an important part of the American art scene today. Skilled wood carvers turned out ships' figureheads, cigar store figures, plaques and carousel animals of stylized beauty and great appeal. The wooden shipbuilding industry, which had originally nourished this folk art, declined after the Civil War, and the talented carvers then turned to producing figures for tobacconists' shops, carousel animals and show figures for circuses. These figures and other early ornamental carvings that have survived the elements and years are eagerly sought.

Angel, one-piece pine plank naively carved w/the face of an angel w/a cheerful expression & outstretched wings w/radiating layered feathers, traces of original polychrome paint, light weathering w/greyish patina, possibly Pennsylvania, 19th c., 41" w., 9" h. **$863**

Cat, pine, minimalist style carving of feline lying in relaxed crouch position, carved in full relief, mounted on pine board, vestiges of white paint, America, 19th c., 15 x 31 5/8", 10 3/8" h. including base **$10,575**

Coconut creature, the original oblong nut shell ornately pierce-carved w/entwining costumed figures leaping over crowned lions, couples dancing, a man riding a bull & various other figures & animals, one end carved as the face of an anthropomorphic creature w/a gaping mouth, Europe, early 19th c., 3 1/2" d., 6" l. **$690**

Cigar store Indian Chief, carved & painted, half-sized figure standing & holding a pipe close to his chest, wearing moccasins & a red robe, a feathered headdress & long black hair around his gold face, the natural-colored base carved w/a bundle of cigars & a rock, small hole at front of chest possibly to hold a flag, paint appears original, back w/some nails & loop hardware probably for affixing the figure, metal plaque on the back reading "Bought of H.H. Robertson - National Stockyards, IL," 42 1/2" h. **$5,750**

Cigar store Indian Princess, standing wearing a tall feathered headdress, a fringed & feathered skirt & a sash cinched at her waist, one foot resting on a plinth, one hand holding aloft a bunch of tobacco leaves, the other holding a cigar box, green-painted platform base, old repaint, wear, abrasions, second half 19th c., base 28 1/2 x 34", overall 79" h. **$28,200**

Dog umbrella stand, seated animal holding a twisted carved wood pretzel-form umbrella frame, metal drip pan below, inset glass eyes, Switzerland, ca. 1900, 21 1/4" h. **$5,405**

Eagle with banner, pine, carved bird w/head pointed to side, sharply hooked beak w/red tongue, red eye, spread wings w/paint-enhanced feathers & red & blue line decoration at tail, attached to pole w/red-bordered banner reading "Don't Give Up The Ship!" in blue & red on white, a carved white five-pointed star on blue at one end, by John H. Bellamy, Kittery Point, Maine, repaired break where banner meets pole, 26" l. **$24,150**

Eagle, double-headed eagle w/ spread wings, carved in the style of John H. Bellamy, w/heads pointed to either side, sharply hooked beaks w/red tongues, deeply carved eyes, feathers & talons, front view w/triangle shape in breast, probably Masonic symbol, 30" w., 30 1/2" h. **$5,750**

Figure of Evangeline, a standing woman w/her hands clasped in front, wearing a robe covering her head & continuing down & wrapping around her lower body, a flower-decorated inner robe, on a round gadrooned platform on a round foot, old polychrome paint & inset glass eyes, 25" h. **$575**

Eagle, carved & painted, folk art bird w/original bright yellow body trimmed in black, red & green, carved by Wilhelm Schimmel (1817-1890), Cumberland County, Pennsylvania, edge damage to tail, 8" h. **$6,325**

Eagle, carved giltwood, ship pilot house- type, in the form of an eagle w/spread wings as if about to take flight, perched on carved rockery, America, ca. 1875, old regilding, minor wear, 26 x 31", 25" h. **$2,468**

If you wish to make a gift "in kind,"—an object rather than money—to a museum, you must have it appraised. The IRS no longer permits museum personnel to appraise donations. The temptation to overvalue items is considered too great.

Eagle, long spreadwinged narrow gold eagle w/a square beak holding a long slender red, white & blue banner reading "Don't Give Up the Ship," attributed to John Bellamy, Kitterh/Portsmouth, Maine, minor damage, 19th c., 45 1/2" l. **$25,300**

WOOD SCULPTURES

Figure of St. Anthony of Padua, carved & painted, carved in the full round, long brown robe & flesh-colored hands & head set w/glass eyes, scattered losses, Spain, 18th c., 24" h. **$1,840**

Figure of St. Mary, tall standing woman w/a simple long dress, removable joined arms, the hairless head set w/glass eyes, atop a beveled square base, thin old paint, 19th c., 40" h. **$1,840**

Figures of seated couple, carved figures in traditional costume seated on bench, the woman wearing red skirt w/white apron & fringed shawl w/pink rose, green brimmed hat, the man wearing shorts w/suspenders w/design resembling embroidery, knee socks & green Alpine hat, holding a lute in one hand, his other arm around the shoulders of the woman, life- size, original paint worn in many places, 36" w., about 53" h. **$3,450**

Male saint, carved, painted & gilded, standing figure of a young man, apparently a warrior king-saint, w/long blond hair, wearing a long golden cloak over his gilt upper armor above a dark blue underskirt above armored leggings, one hand holding an open book, the other hand probably held a scepter, probably South German, probably 16th c., 34" h. **$2,990**

Man & woman, gessoed polychrome paint, large seated couple wearing native German costume, both w/green hats & black shoes, seated on a curved trestle-base bench, wear, some age cracks, lute man holds not shown, 26 x 39", 52 1/2" h. **$1,553**

Man & woman, painted pine, standing figures dressed in Napoleonic era clothing, she w/a long white gown trimmed in gold at the hem & w/crossed red ribbons at the bosom, long yellow gloves & slippers, he wearing a dark brown short coat w/tails, white cravat, gold vest & dark green kneebreeches over blue stockings & brown shoes, each on a square wood base, pieced repairs & some damage, 19th c., 36" & 36 1/2" h., pr. **$2,300**

Owl, folk art-style carving of bird on perch, off-white w/faint black feather highlights, inset carved eyes painted gold & black, sculpted beak, feet, ears & tail feathers, mounted on dowel w/ brass fitting, one ear repaired, minor chips to tail feathers, 16" h. **$4,025**

Panther head, a large realistically-carved trophy-style head w/open mouth w/fangs & tongue, mounted on a crossed-branch bracket w/tall brass leafy branches projecting from the top, probably Europe, late 19th c., 13" w., 17" h. **$2,703**

Whirligig, folk art Hessian-style soldier wearing blue pants, red coat & white shirt, red, black & blue hat, the coat w/tuxedo-type tail made of separate piece of wood screwed onto rear, eyes & mouth indicated by minimal carving, the protruding nose nailed to face, arms extending to 8" shaped metal knife blades, 7 3/4" w. at shoulders, 17 3/4" h. **$5,750**

Panther, carved walnut, long stylized model of a crouching panther, mounted on a pine base, a WPA School project, inscribed "J.S. Iowa City 1933," 20" l. **$288**

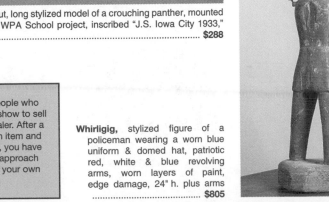

Pay attention to people who attend an antique show to sell something to a dealer. After a dealer examines an item and decides not to buy, you have the opportunity to approach the seller and start your own negotiations.

Whirligig, stylized figure of a policeman wearing a worn blue uniform & domed hat, patriotic red, white & blue revolving arms, worn layers of paint, edge damage, 24" h. plus arms **$805**

WOODENWARES

The patina and mellow coloring, along with the lightness and smoothness that come only with age and wear, attract collectors to old woodenwares. The earliest forms were the simplest, and the shapes of items whittled out in the late 19th century varied little in form from those turned out in the American colonies two centuries earlier. A burl is a growth, or wart, on some trees in which the grain of the wood is twisted and turned in a manner that strengthens the fibers and causes a beautiful pattern to be formed.

Treenware is simply a term for utilitarian items made from "treen," another word for wood. While maple was the primary wood used for these items, they are also abundant in pine, ash, oak, walnut and other woods. "Lignum Vitae" is a species of wood from the West Indies that can always be identified by the contrasting colors of dark heartwood and light sapwood and by its heavy weight, which caused it to sink in water.

Basket, carved burl, one-piece type w/large natural arched handle above the shallow oblong basket, resembles bird's-eye maple, 19th c., 9 x 10", 8" h. **$690**

Dough bowl, maple, long shallow carved oval shape w/some figure, 13 3/4 x 22 3/4", 5 4/8" h. **$144**

Flax hatchel, oak & wrought iron, the thick rectangular plank top w/rectangular top handle incised w/a band of hearts & rosettes above the row of long iron comb teeth, early 19th c., 2 3/4" thick, 23" l. **$173**

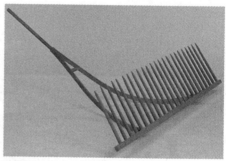

Hay rake, the curved forked handle ending in a long thin crossbar fitted w/numerous long pointed teeth, 19th c., 73" w., 67" l. **$1,195**

Trencher, hand-hewn, rectangular w/ very widely flaring shallow sides, original slate blue exterior paint w/wear, 19th c., 12 1/2 x 22", 5 1/4" h. **$460**

Jar, cov., painted poplar, wide round slightly swelled cylindrical base w/ ringed base & rim, fitted low domed cover w/button finial, original red over dark mustard yellow vinegar decoration in the form of stylized leaves or feathers, first half 19th c., 6 3/4" d., 6 1/4" h. **$2,645**

WOODENWARES

Spoon rack, carved & painted pine, the top crest carved w/ears & a center hanging hole, incurved sides mounted w/two spoon racks above an open box base, mustard-colored paint, American, 18th c., w/10 old pewter spoons, loss, repair, 5 1/4 x 15", 18" h. **$3,408**

Pipe box, hanging-type, cherry, the high rounded back w/a pierced hanging hole above the long open box w/scroll-cut top edges, a thumb-molded front panel above a single small bottom drawer w/a brass pull, includes five clay pipes, Connecticut or Rhode Island, late 18th - early 19th c., imperfections, 5 1/4 x 5 3/4", 22" h. **$4,818**

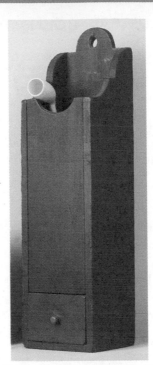

Pipe box, stained poplar, tall slender square from w/stepped, cut-out sides & arched crest w/hanging hole, small dovetailed drawer at the bottom w/original small brass knob, old red stain, minor wear, early, 4 1/2" w., 17 1/2" h. **$1,840**

Watch hutch, carved tiger stripe maple, miniature model of a tall case clock, arched bonnet top carved on the sides w/large pinwheels, center front w/red wax inlaid overlapping hearts, additional leaves & stringing, early 19th c., cracks, losses, 8 3/4" h. **$1,998**

Pipe box, pine, hanging-type, arched tall backboard w/shaped sides & pierced hanging hole, deep box above a small dovetailed drawer w/turned wood knobs, applied molding at the base, late 18th - early 19th c., refinished, 4 1/4 x 6 3/8", 17 1/8" h. ... **$999**

Wall box, the crestboard w/ scalloped sides & flat top centered by a large heart-shaped cut-out hanging hole, a wide slanted hinged lid above the slant-sided box w/raised molding around the sides & the narrow bottom drawer w/a brass knob, dovetailed construction, green old dark green ground trimmed w/light green, some paint wear, one side molding missing, 19th c., 8 x 11 1/2", 12 1/2" h. **$1,438**

In an auction that is not catalogued, the auctioneer will usually announce the order of the sale beforehand while discussing terms and conditions. The order may change depending on how the sale progresses. Don't miss an item by going to lunch at the wrong moment.

WORLD'S FAIR COLLECTIBLES

There has been great interest in collecting items produced for the great fairs and expositions held through the years. During the 1970s, there was particular interest in items produced for the 1876 Centennial Exhibition and more interest is focusing on those items associated with the 1893 Columbian Exposition. Listed below is a random sampling of prices asked for items produced for the various fairs.

1876 Philadelphia Centennial

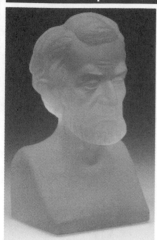

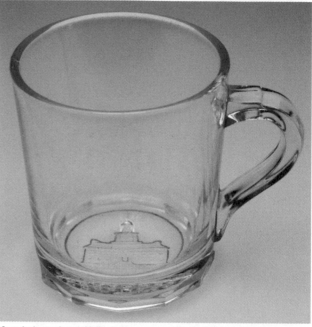

Bust of Abraham Lincoln, clear frosted pressed glass, embossed on the front bottom "A. Lincoln," embossed on the back "Centennial Exhibition - Gillinder & Sons," in-the-making chip under base, 6" h. **$187**

Kerchief, fabric, unhemmed design in blue on orange, a large scene of the Memorial Hall Art Gallery in the center w/round vignettes in each corner w/varied scenes at the fair, a large spread-winged American eagle & shield at top center w/a banner in its beak above swags w/"Centennial International" & "Exhibition - Fairmount Park - Philadelphia - 1776-1876" at the bottom center, folded, four tiny tack holes, 26" sq. **$184**

Mug, Independence Hall, clear pressed glass, cylindrical w/plain sides, the Philadelphia Indendence Hall building embossed under the base w/the title & date of 1876, 3 1/4" h. **$77**

Statuette, Drummer Boy , clear frosted pressed glass, boy w/ drum & his dog, embossed on the bottom "Gillinder & Sons - Centennial Exhibition 1876," flake to back hat brim, 4 1/2" h. .. **$99**

1876 PHILADELHIA

Paperweight, Lion, frosted clear recumbent lion on an oval base, ribbed base sides, embossed under the base "Gillinder & Sons - Centennial Exhibition," minute edge flakes, 2 3/4 x 5 1/2" .. **$99**

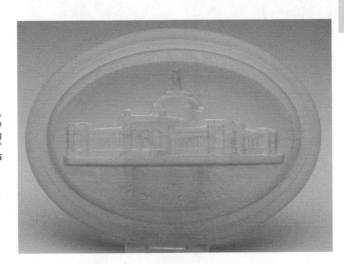

Paperweight, Memorial Hall, clear frosted pressed glass, the Philadelphia Centennial building in the center, 3 7/8 x 5 1/4" **$55**

• If you are buying more than one or two items at an auction, it is a good idea to write down your purchases and prices paid. The information will be helpful at the end of the sale if there is a discrepancy with the cashier's total. Also, keeping a running total will help prevent you from spending more money than you had planned. Don't forget to calculate the buyer's premium for each sale.

• Occasionally an auctioneer misses a bid and hammers down a lot to another bidder. To prevent this from happening, make sure you don't wait unitl the last second to make a bid and be sure your bid can be seen or heard.

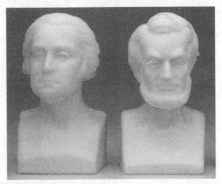

Bust of Abraham Lincoln, pressed milk glass w/satin finish, embossed at front base "A. Lincoln," marked on back of base "Centennial Exhibition - Gillinder & Sons," minute base flake, long shallow chip on back edge, 6" h. (ILLUS. right) **$303**
Bust of George Washington, pressed milk glass w/satin finish, embossed at front base "Washington," marked on back of base "Centennial Exhibition - Gillinder & Sons," 6" h. (ILLUS. left) **$505**

1893 COLUMBIAN

1893 Columbian Exposition

Advertising display piece, made for the American Thread Co. of Holyoke, Massachusetts, a unique spool display an elaborate sphere composed of thread & spools enclosed in a large clear blown blass footed sphere w/a turned wood finial & raised on a turned wood pedestal base, paper label on the base, some spools broken, 35" h. **$1,495**

Clock, novelty-type, cast-metal w/bronzed finish, cast as a ship under sail w/Columbus standing near the stern while natives grovel in the foreground, a world globe & eagle at the bow, the sail inset w/the clock dial w/Arabic numerals, key-wound mechanism not working, 12 3/4" h. **$316**

Lamp, kerosene table model, the openwork cast brass base & stem supporting a bulbous milk glass font printed on one side w/a colorful scene of the Landing of Columbus above the dates 1492 - 1892, the back w/a color transfer of a ship, w/a period burner & Big Bulge glass chimney decorated w/eagles, 8 1/4" h. **$66**

Plate, 7" d., clear pressed glass, a diamond cut-like border band around the embossed words "The World's Fair Game," centered by a small round bust of Columbus framed by "Columbus - 1493 - Chicago - 1893," also marked w/a patent dated of July 22, 1890, shallow rim flake **$440**

The first World's Fair was held in 1851 in London, England, at The Crystal Palace in Hyde Park. Called "The Great Exhibition," it showcased the products of the Industrial Revolution and set the precedent for the following World Fairs. Although small compared to those that followed, it established a tradition that has lasted for more than 150 years.

1901 Pan American Exposition

Mug, Bristol-glazed stoneware, footed cylindrical body w/a molded band above the foot, one side molded in relief & trimmed in cobalt blue w/a tavern scene, the other side impressed & trimmed in cobalt blue w/a map of North & South America w/the wording "Pan-American Exposition - 1901 Buffalo - NY U.S.A.," bottom impressed "Whites Pottery - Utica, N.Y.," 5" h. **$176**

1904 St. Louis World's Fair

Clock, cast-metal case w/painted gold finish, an upright domed case w/fancy cast scallops & scrolls w/four flaring front legs, a bust portrait of Jefferson below crossed American flags at the front below the round dial w/Arabic numerals, not working, 8 1/2" h. **$411**

Ribbon, woven silk, political-type, white ground woven at the top "Souvenir - St. Louis - 1904" above a banner reading "Republican Candidates" w/the names & portraits of Theodore Roosevelt & his running mate, Charles Fairbanks, a large American flag below, portraits woven w/a brown or bronzed thread, excellent condition, 3 x 7 1/4" **$274**

Match safe, brass, souvenir-type, rectangular, depicts The Electricity Building at St. Louis World's Fair in 1904, 1 1/2 x 2 5/8" **$75-150**

Medal, 1904, St. Louis, Summer, award medal, goldplated AE, of Louisiana Purchase Exposition, this is the first of the gold medals seen goldplated, light wear on high points, approx. 2 3/4" **$275**

Plate, cast spelter w/gilt finish, cast w/scroll-enclosed vignettes of various fair buildings w/fair name in bottom banner, 7" d. **$49**

1939-40 New York World's Fair

Broadside, printed paper, advertising "Billy Rose's Aquacade," w/ illustrated endorsement for Arco skates, 1940, 8 x 11"............ **$12**

Nut set: master dish & four side dishes; lithographed metal, advertising Planters Peanuts w/Mr. Peanut logo & Trylon & Perisphere in center of each, the set **$98**

Tumblers, glass, juice, w/various scenes, including Administration Building, Theme Center & Transportation Building & two others, 5 oz., set of 5......... **$125**

Poster, color-printed paper, vertical comic-style scene of a family racing to the fair, the man on a highwheel bicycle, the girl on a scooter, a boy on a bicycle & a lady pushing a baby in a carriage, in color on a dark blue & white ground, reads "Go by all means - World's Fair in New York - 1940 - Admission Fifty Cents," artwork by S. Ekman, good condition, 20 x 30" **$132**

Program, from opening day - April 30, 1939, in orange & blue colors of the fair, with the Trylon & Perisphere.......................... **$200**

Salt & pepper shakers, Bakelite, in the shape of the Trylon & Perisphere, two sets, one in orange w/blue base & one in blue w/orange base, each............. **$30**

Tapestry, in full color, featuring the Trylon & Perisphere, Federal Building, Administration Building, Constitution Mall & Lagoon of Nations, made in Belgium, Lic. #839............. **$350**

Teapot, cov., white pottery, Trylon & Perisphere embossed on side & tinted in blue, green & tan **$100**

WRITING ACCESSORIES

Early writing accessories are popular collectibles and offer a wide variety to select from. A collection may be formed around any one segment — pens, letter openers, lap desks, inkwells, etc.—or the collection may revolve around choice specimens of all types.

Material, design and age usually determine the value. Pen collectors like the large fountain pens developed in the 1920s but also look for pens and mechanical pencils that are solid gold or gold-plated. Also see: BOTTLES & FLASKS

Inkwells & Stands

Bronze stand, Zodiac patt., rectangular box w/ pen trays on each side flanking the paneled tapering well w/domed cap & original well insert, green, red & brown patina, stamped mark "Tiffany Studios - New York - 1073," some damage to original well insert, 9 3/4 x 10 1/2" **$2,070**

Bronze well, figural, molded as a large crab w/a hinged shell, the large front claws framing the round well w/a shell-topped cover, chocolate brown patina, signed "Tiffany Studios New York 21149" w/Tiffany Glass and Decorating logo, inkwell section appears to be a modern replacement w/a broken hinge & minor dents to insert, early 20th c., 7 x 8" **$6,325**

Bronze well, wide flattened round base cast w/a lappet rim band around a ring of wavy leafy vines centered by the raised well platform w/a flattened florette-cast cap, missing insert, hinge loose, signed "Tiffany Studios New York 1039," 6 1/2" d., 2" h. **$840**

Copper well, Art Nouveau style, a wide flat- bottomed stepped down w/a narrow neck fitted w/a silver rim & stepped, domed cover, the body wrapped w/undulating bands of sterling silver, base marked "Tiffany & Co. 15025 Makers - 4564 Sterling Silver 925-1000 T & other Metals," early 20th c., 8 1/4" d., 6" h. **$748**

Bronzed cast-metal stand, figural, the thick oblong base w/a cast zigzag border design mounted by the model of a seated winged griffin, the high curved wings supporting two coiled snake pen rests joined by a rod, a large square cut crystal well w/original metal cover in front, verdigris patina, embossed mark, "N. Muller - N.Y. #611," ca. 1900, 6" h. **$575**

Bronze is an alloy of copper and tin, and sometimes aluminum, silicon, manganese or phosphorus. Bronze has been used in sculpture since ancient times because it casts well and shows fine detail.

Gilt-bronze stand, Louis XV-style, an ornate oblong scroll-cast stand fitted at one end w/a covered cylindrical holder for a blown glass inkwell, underside touchmarked "EG" in block letters, w/a later rose gold-mounted & inlaid carved ivory nib pen, France, late 19th c., stand 4 x 7 1/4", 3 1/4" h. **$460**

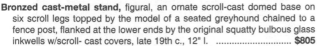

Bronzed cast-metal stand, figural, an ornate scroll-cast domed base on six scroll legs topped by the model of a seated greyhound chained to a fence post, flanked at the lower ends by the original squatty bulbous glass inkwells w/scroll- cast covers, late 19th c., 12" l. **$805**

Copper well, Arts & Crafts style, a rectangular metal case w/sloping sides & outswept scroll feet, the hinged flattened rectangular cover opening to original double inserts, decorated w/stylized flowers in red, green & blue, stamped mark of the Buffalo Art Craft Shop, Buffalo, New York, early 20th c., original dark patina, 3 x 7 1/2" **$403**

Enameled bronze well, figural, designed as a whimsical large toad stool w/a hinged cover flanked by two small seated gnomes, blown glass ink cup, worn original polychrome enamel, Austria, late 19th c., unmarked, 4 1/2" l. **$518**

Gilt-bronze stand, Rococo-style, the rectangular base w/small dolphin feet supporting incurved sides cast w/long scrolls & grotesque masks, the top w/a low raised gadrooned edge, the high arched & pierced backplate centered by a lion mask framed by scrolls & small pineapple corner finials, the top inset w/two inkwells w/domed ringed covers w/small pineapple finials, France, late 19th c., 14" l. **$460**

Red marble & bronze stand, First Empire taste, the rectangular red marble base fitted w/patinated bronze covered center ink vase flanked by a pens vase & short vase, trimmed in gilt-bronze & on gilt- bronze feet, France, late 19th c., 6 x 13 1/4", 7 1/2" h. **$690**

Rockingham ware stand, waisted octagonal form w/flatted top w/large central hole surrounded by four small holes, overall mottled streaky brown glaze, possibly Bennington, Vermont, ca. 1850, 3" w., 2" h. **$198**

> It is possible to sense high quality and a good value even though you can't immediately identify the manufacturer, craftsman, or artist. If the price is right, savvy buyers will take a chance on an unknown item.

Silver plate well, Arts & Crafts style, a thin rectangular base plate supporting four slender squared legs w/riveted curved feet supporting a rectangular box frame w/a pierced design on the front, the wide flat overhanging cover centered by a large Ruskin cabochon, stamped initials, mark of Duchess Sutherland Cripples Guild, England, late 19th - early 20th c., 3 3/4 x 5 1/4", 5" h. **$805**

Lap Desks & Writing Boxes

Inlaid lacquer, rectangular w/a narrow rectangular top above a hinged slant lid decorated w/a mother-of-pearl landscape centered by a large three-storied house w/front columns & surrounded by trees w/water & a church in the background, lid opens to a fitted interior w/two crystal & silver inkwells, a pen tray & a long-lidded compartment, the lower case inlaid & h.p. w/flowers, narrow molded gilt-trimmed base band raised on flatted square feet, overall decoration of inlaid & h.p. florals, mid-19th c., 11 1/2 x 15", 5 1/4" h. **$633**

Inlaid & veneered mixed woods, hand- crafted rectangular form, the flat hinged top inlaid in the center w/a large spread- winged American eagle & flag, each corner inlaid w/floral sprigs, the widge-form cover opening to a slanted felt-lined writing surface & small compartments, the sides inset w/hand-cut round brass recessed swivel handles, the lower portion w/a hidden compartment, America, Civil War era, ca. 1860-65, made for a Field Officer, 11 x 22", 8" h. **$2,760**

INDEX

Easy Antiques Identification

Warman's® Depression Glass Identification and Value Guide
by Ellen T. Schroy

The process of identifying Depression glass is as easy as 1, 2, 3 when you have this all-encompassing book in hand.

In addition to thumbnail pattern illustrations and color photos throughout, in this guide you'll also find:

- Timeline of colors of glass released
- Complete catalog of patterns and shapes
- Background details about each pattern

Hardcover • 8-1/4 x 10-7/8 • 304 pages
650 color photos
Item# Z3745 • $27.99

Answers to Questions About Old Jewelry
by C. Jeanenne Bell G.G.

Authoritative details, such as maker's marks, outlined in this guide help you to identify, date and assess everything from brooches and pins to pendants, rings and lockets from the mid-1800s through the 1950s. Packed with 1,000 exquisite color photos and organized in a category and period format, this new edition of the best selling guide to antique jewelry will inspire you and enlighten you.

Softcover • 8-1/4 x 10-7/8 • 448 pages
1,000 color photos
Item# Z2343 • $29.99

Warman's® Fakes & Reproductions
By Mark Moran

This DVD gives you the tips, tricks and expert insight to spot reproductions before you make them part of your collection, or identify those you may already own. Authoritative appraisers Mark F. Moran and Mary Manion walk you through authenticating antiques, where to look for maker marks, and how to use color and shape to help you with accurate identification of true pieces.

Format: DVD
Item# Z5684 • $9.99

200 Years of Dolls Identification and Price Guide
by Dawn Herlocher

You will easily and effectively locate, identify and assess the value of your dolls using the 5,000 listings and 500 color photos in this expanded edition of the ultimate book to collectible dolls. A bonus CD contains makers' marks to help you confirm identity and production year for dolls of all shapes, styles, influences and genres.

Softcover • 8-1/4 x 10-7/8
400 pages
500 color photos
Item# Z3043• $32.99

Visit **shop.collect.com** for references about what you collect

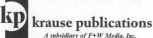

kp krause publications
A subsidiary of F+W Media, Inc.

700 East State Street • Iola, WI 54990-0001
715-445-2214 • 888-457-2873
www.krausebooks.com

Call **800-258-0929** 8 a.m. - 5 p.m. to order direct from the publisher, or visit booksellers nationwide or antiques and hobby shops.

Please reference **offer ACB9** with all direct-to-publisher orders.